The Secret War Diaries of

Abraham Lincoln

Including His Recurring Dreams

Volume Two of Four Volumes

January 1, 1862 to January 1, 1863

By Paul R. Dunn

Cover Design by Charles Kendall

Cover Photos: The Abraham Lincoln Presidential Library & Museum, Springfield, Illinois.

ISBN: 978-0-9991567-2-8

First U.S. edition 2018.

Dedication

To Shelby Dade Foote, Jr.

November 17, 1916 to June 27, 2005

An inspired and inspiring historian
whose 1990 appearance on Ken Burns' PBS documentary
The Civil War introduced a generation of Americans
to the brutal war, which he called "central to all our lives."
His three-volume work, *The Civil War: A Narrative*,
set the standard for capturing the spirit of that
tragic period in American history.

3

Introduction to Volume II

The Secret War Diaries of Abraham Lincoln
Including His Recurring Dreams

This book is the second volume of a four-volume work. It begins on New Year's Day, 1862, and continues to December 31, 1862. It provides fictional diary entries; President Abraham Lincoln never kept a diary. Each entry, usually written by Lincoln at night, is based upon historic chronological records. Author's notes inform the reader of events and people referred to on that date's entry.

The dreams of Lincoln that are described are fictional, but are based upon actual happenings in his life. There are some days in which no entries are made due to the exigencies of the period. During bitter times of grief following the death of his son, William Wallace Lincoln, and the mental collapse of his wife, there are times when no entries are made, or those that are made are shorter than usual.

The purpose of the diaries is to give the reader insights into the inner workings of the president's mind. They present the day by day doings of Lincoln, and endeavor to show how the 16th president might have reacted to the people and challenging events swirling around him during the Civil War.

Volume II reveals a harried Lincoln changing from a leader, who in the beginning of the war relied greatly upon his generals and Cabinet members for advice and results. Now we see him as a more involved war president, who is forced to take a much more commanding role in the war's execution. The man of almost infinite patience comes to realize that what he hoped might be a short war has become a desperate struggle with no easy victories. He realizes that he has few generals who are willing to fight the war with the intense vigor he demands. He concludes that General George B. McClellan cannot be relied upon to deliver promised victories, and discovers that General Ulysses Grant will be the general who does so. Lincoln finds that the new role that he must assume is that of a far more involved commander-in-chief, with all that the title implies.

Paul R. Dunn

The White House – Wednesday, January 1, 1862

Mother and I held a New Year's reception from 11 A.M. to 2 P.M. I find these social affairs tedious in the extreme, because they take me from my more important duties, but Mother must be obeyed! She relishes these events and is a marvelous hostess. Members of the Cabinet entered first, followed by the diplomatic corps, the justices of the Supreme Court, and officers of the Army and Navy. At noon, the gates were opened to the public. Later in the day I sent messages to Generals Buell at Louisville and Halleck in St. Louis, advising them that McClellan is at home and is seriously ill. I said that they should be in communication and act in concert with each other.
I sent a note to McClellan, telling him not to worry about a Congressional Investigating Committee. I informed him that the committee is made up of sensible men and that he should not fear them. I doubt that he believed me; he is suspicious by nature.

Author's notes:

Throughout early January, General McClellan was seriously ill from typhoid fever. During this period, Lincoln warned the general that Congress' Joint Committee, established to investigate military incompetence, was agitating that he be fired. The investigation had begun following Union defeats at Bull Run in July and Ball's Bluff in October. Senator Benjamin Wade of Ohio was the most outspoken to call for McClellan's removal. Lincoln refused, but realized that when McClellan returned to duty, there had to be aggressive movement against the enemy or the war could not be won.

The White House – Thursday, January 2, 1862

Today Hay and Nicolay brought me good news in a detailed report of a battle fought at Mt. Zion Church in Boone County, Kentucky, on the 27th and 28th of December. The 3rd Missouri Cavalry and Birge's Western Sharpshooters under the command of Brigadier General Benjamin M. Prentiss defeated troops of the Missouri State Guard who were commanded by Colonel Caleb Dorsey. Although outnumbered more than two to one, our men overwhelmed the secessionist Missouri guardsmen. The rebels were mostly local green troops who lacked military weapons and ran out of ammunition, causing them to be overrun. We took 150 prisoners.

Author's notes:

This small but decisive battle ended Confederate recruiting in the region. It resulted in conventional Confederate forces leaving the state until the desperate 1864 invasion by General Sterling Price and his Missouri State Guard.

Today the church and associated cemetery are listed on the National Register of Historic Places. The cemetery contains the remains of the yhree Union and 25 Confederate soldiers who perished in Mt. Zion. There is a memorial marker for the Missouri State Guard

The White House – Saturday, January 4, 1862

Last evening, I attended the 5th lecture given by Horace Greeley, the editor of the Tribune which he gave at the Smithsonian Institute. Every seat was filled. Congressman George Julian kindly invited me to sit next to him on the platform. Horace declared forcefully that slavery's abolition is the "sole purpose of the war." I told Congressman Julian that I admired the lecture and felt it was full of good thoughts. Greeley kindly gave me a copy of his address and I plan to read it tomorrow. I asked Homer Byington, the Tribune's Washington correspondent, "What in the world is wrong with Uncle Horace? Why can't he restrain himself and wait a little while?" I want Greeley to restrain himself on the issue of slavery, but I know that he will never change his very strong abolitionist views. I intend to write to Greeley one day soon.

Author's notes:

Two months later, on March 16, Lincoln wrote to Greeley in part about emancipation, "If I were to suggest anything, it would be that the North is already for the measure, but we should urge it persuasively, and not menacingly, upon the South. I would like the bill to have the three main features: gradual implementation, federal compensation to slave owners, and a vote by the people. I do not talk to members of Congress on the subject, except when they ask me. I am not prepared to make any suggestion about confiscation."

*In August 19, 1862's edition of the Tribune, Greeley published an open letter to President Lincoln titled, "The Prayer of Twenty Millions."
It urged immediate emancipation.*

The White House – Sunday, January 5, 1862

Yesterday forenoon Tad and Willie joined Mother and me for a review of the impressive 6th U.S. Cavalry, as it trotted past the sidewalk in front of the White House. It was organized just five months ago and is now an important part of the Army of the Potomac. The men gave the boys a blue and yellow regimental flag which shows an erect horse with the slogan, "Ducit Amor Patriae," which means, "Led by love of country."

Postmaster General Montgomery Blair came by after dinner to give me his thoughts on foreign affairs. Blair is undoubtedly the most politically savvy member of my Cabinet. I rely upon him to keep me informed on matters in his border state of Maryland. He has often recounted talks he overheard as a young boy between his father, Francis Preston Blair, and President Andrew Jackson, who was a close family friend. As a graduate of West Point, Montgomery has excellent insights into military matters, and I trust his counsel highly.

Author's notes:

The 6th U.S. Cavalry saw action in 16 major and minor campaigns, including the Peninsula Campaign, Antietam, Fredericksburg, Winchester, Fairfield, Chancellorsville, The Wilderness, Petersburg, Shenandoah Valley, Richmond, Trevilian Station, Spotsylvania Court House, Cold Harbor and Appomattox.

Montgomery Blair served Lincoln from 1861 to 1864. He was a highly effective Postmaster General. He established free city delivery, the adoption of the money order system, and the use of railway cars. After the war, Blair differed from the Republican Party on Reconstruction policy and adhered to the Democratic Party, along with his brother, Francis Preston Blair, Jr., who was the Democratic vice-presidential candidate in 1868 on the losing ticket with Horatio Seymour.

The White House – Tuesday, January 7, 1862

Yesterday I visited General McClellan at his home. He is still weak from typhoid fever but seems to be strengthening. I discussed the military situation in East Tennessee after sharing a telegram with him from General Buell. At 7:30 P.M. the Cabinet met here at the request of the Committee on Conduct of the War. I objected to its call for the removal of McClellan. Tomorrow I will request Halleck and Buell to name the day they can move southward in concert to protect East Tennessee.

We held a levee from 8:30 to 10:30 P.M. for an overflow crowd. Seward read a memorial sent to us from English Friends, which contained generous suggestions in the interests of "Peace and Humanity."

Late evening, I spent considerable time in the telegraph office with Captain Anson Stager who is in charge of operations there. Service to and from Louisville, Kentucky, has been erratic. I find myself spending more and more hours there. I now fully believe that the telegraph is an invention that will help shorten the war. When hostilities began, the practice was for the telegraphers to share messages only with McClellan, and not provide simultaneous messages to the White House. Secretary of War Cameron had ceded control of military telegraphic messages to the Army to the exclusion of the elected government. I have advised Cameron that this is unacceptable.

Author's notes:

Congress soon passed legislation allowing the government to assume control of the telegraph lines, as deemed necessary for military requirements. The networks would still be owned by private companies and continue to carry civilian messages. Control would be under the Secretary of War and managed by the newly created U.S. Military Telegraph Corps. Henceforth, the secretary of war's department and not McClellan's headquarters would be the hub of all telegraphic traffic related to the war effort. For the rest of the conflict, Lincoln would travel from the White House to the telegraph office, often staying for hours to await important news. Upon arrival, Lincoln would open the telegraph clerk's desk drawer and read all the dispatches received since his last visit. Lincoln's messages, written in longhand, still exist.

The White House – Wednesday, January 8, 1862

Mother and I visited cavalry troops stationed at Tennallytown, D.C. Later we met here with General James Shields, who once challenged me to a duel back in Missouri in the fall of 1842. It was all over a dumb letter I had written to the Sangamon Journal critical of Shields. Had the affair been consummated, I might not be here writing about it. As the challenged party, I had the right to pick the weapons. I feared pistols would get me shot. With longer arms I felt swords might give me an advantage. I had proposed that the weapon be cavalry broadswords of the largest size. That plank 10 feet long, and from 9 to 12 inches broad be firmly fixed on the edge on the ground as a line between us, which neither is to pass his foot over upon forfeit of life. Next a line drawn on the ground on either side of the plank and parallel with it, each at the distance of the whole length of the sword and three additional from the plank; the passing of such line by either party during the fight shall be deemed a surrender of the contest. When we finally met on the dueling ground in Alton wiser heads prevailed; we shook hands and the duel never took place. Since then Shields and I have become good friends. He is brave, having distinguished himself in the Mexican War, where he was wounded three times. He is highly regarded by the troops he commands.

Author's notes:

James Shields is the only man to have served as a United States senator from three states: Illinois, Minnesota and Missouri. During the Valley Campaign in the Civil War, he was wounded at the Battle of Kernstown, on March 22, 1862. There his troops inflicted the only tactical defeat for General Thomas J. "Stonewall" Jackson during the war. The day after, Shields was promoted to major general.

The White House – Thursday, January 9, 1862

Hay brought me the copy of General Halleck's 1846 book, "Elements of Military Art & Science," which I had requested from the Library of Congress. I doubt if war is as much a science as it is a very unrefined form of art. Science favors certainty and precision. War is random and more often than not the results are totally unpredictable, as I've learned all too often.

Before he left, General Scott told me that Halleck, or "Old Brains," as he called him, is perhaps the most intelligent of all our serving West Point graduates. He was third in his class. As a lawyer, I admire his financial success in California, where his law firm, Halleck, Peachy and Billings, is one of the most prestigious in the state. Hay tells me that Halleck was sent by Scott to France to study European fortifications, and that a subsequent series of lectures he gave in Boston became the basis for his book, which was published 16 years ago. Later he translated Jomini's "Vie Politique et Militaire de Napoleon" into English. I shall ask Mother to read it, as it is in her favorite foreign language. She is more impressed by the fact that Halleck's wife, Elizabeth, is the granddaughter of Alexander Hamilton than by his impressive military credentials.

I sent a note to McClellan suggesting that he meet with the Congressional Committee at the earliest moment his health will allow. I also informed him that neither General Buell nor Halleck meets my request to name a date, when they can be ready to move against the enemy.

Author's notes:

During the Mexican-American War, Halleck saw action during the battle to capture the Port of Mazatlán in 1847. Lieutenant Halleck served as lieutenant governor of the occupied city. He was later transferred north and was soon appointed military secretary of state of the California Territory. At the 1849 convention in Monterey he helped draft the state's constitution and became secretary of state for the newly annexed California.

After his resignation from the Army as a captain in 1854, Halleck devoted himself full time to building a lucrative legal practice in San Francisco. Halleck added to his personal fortune through land speculation and during his stint as president of the Atlantic & Pacific Railroad. Before the Civil War erupted, he was a major general in the California militia.

The White House – Friday, January 10, 1862

I told Nicolay this evening that this should be called "Black Friday," because everything seems to have gone wrong that could possibly go wrong! I told General Meigs that with McClellan bed-ridden, Buell and Halleck unable or unwilling to move, and with Chase pleading he cannot raise more money, that "the bottom is out of the tub!"

I called a special Council of War at 8 P.M., which was attended by Generals McDowell and Franklin, who were soon joined by Secretaries Seward, Chase and Assistant Secretary of War Thomas A. Scott. I informed everyone that plans must be quickly formulated for a concerted drive against the rebels in which we exercise our considerable might. I am impressed by Scott, who joined the administration from the Pennsylvania Railroad Company, where he was its first vice president. The railroad is the largest corporation in America. Scott started as a station agent and worked his way up. He is an American success story. Now the question is whether he can prove to be a successful War Department executive.

Author's notes:

Within a day of this meeting, Lincoln would remove Secretary of War Simon Cameron and replace him with Edwin Stanton, who would be well-served by Thomas Scott. Cameron had helped Lincoln gain the Republican nomination and the president had long hesitated to fire him, but realized that Cameron was "incapable of either organizing details or conceiving and advising general plans."

The White House – Saturday, January 11, 1862

Today I informed Secretary of War Simon Cameron that I was sending his name to the Senate for him to be confirmed as our Minister to Russia. Before doing so I asked to receive his resignation as secretary of war. It was a difficult meeting. We go back a long way and I owe Simon much.

Simon admitted that he had erred when he included a sentence in his department's Annual Report, which read: "It is clearly a right of the government to arm slaves when it may become necessary; it is to take gunpowder from the enemy." To make matters worse, he had sent copies of the report to important newspapers. I had to recall the report. Our policy is not to arm slaves who are loyal to the Union.

I pointed out to Simon that with Britain and France always vulnerable to appeals from the Confederacy to grant it recognition, it was of paramount importance to our foreign relations that we do all we can to maintain especially close relations with the Tsar's government. I stressed that he could render a very valuable contribution to the war effort by taking this post. He was crushed, but took it like a gentleman, promising to leave for Russia as soon as practical.

Author's notes:

Simon Cameron replaced Cassius Clay Marcellus as minister to Russia. Cameron was confirmed as Minister to Russia on January 17, 1862 and presented at the Russian court on June 25, 1862. He resigned on September 18, 1862.

Simon Cameron was a U.S. senator from Pennsylvania from 1845 to 1849, and from 1857 to 1860. His brother, Colonel James Cameron, was killed at the Battle of Bull Run. After the Civil War, he was senator from 1866 to 1877. His son, James Donald Cameron, was named secretary of war by President Ulysses S. Grant in 1876.

The White House – Sunday, January 12, 1862

Reports of an impressive Union victory two days ago in eastern Kentucky in Floyd County at Middle Creek were reviewed favorably with my Council of War, which was attended by General McClellan, who is still weakened, but gradually recovering. Each side at Middle Creek had about 2,500 troops engaged. It was fought in dreadfully cold and rainy weather and resulted in General Buell's forces, commanded by Colonel James Garfield, driving the Confederates from the field.

My close friend Senator Orville Browning came by after dinner. I told him in confidence that I had been seriously thinking of taking to the field myself. The senator predicted that rebel sharpshooters would have a field day aiming just below the brim of my top hat.

Author's notes:

In recognition of his success, Garfield was promoted to brigadier general at age 30. Following a skirmish at Pound Gap, the last Confederate forces were outflanked and ordered to march back to Virginia on January 24th. This engagement and the Battle of Mill Springs nine days later assured Union control of Eastern Kentucky until Confederate General Braxton Bragg returned later in 1862. In 1992, the battlefield was designated a National Historic Landmark by the National Park Service.

The White House – Monday, January 13, 1862

At our 11 A.M. Cabinet meeting I named Edwin M. Stanton as secretary of war. His name was immediately sent to the Senate for confirmation, as was Simon Cameron's to be minister to Russia.

So there can be no confusion as to my thinking about war strategy, I explained to the Cabinet and General McClellan these general principles: We have greater numbers, and the enemy has the greater facility of concentrating forces upon points of collision; we must fail, unless we can find some way of making our advantage an over-match; this can only be done by menacing him with our superior forces at different points at the same time. I wrote out this strategy and sent it to Buell and Halleck today. To my mind, timing will be everything. Changes in leadership will have to occur if the commanders cannot move in tandem against the enemy. The fact that General McClellan was unwilling to reveal details of his plans has not raised his stock with the Cabinet. He is living on borrowed time.

Last night I dreamed of the early families of New Salem, Illinois, and of the Rutledges. Anne was a beautiful girl. She was sadly taken from this world long before her time. I often think of what might have been.

Author's notes:

In Herndon's "Life of Lincoln," the author recounts that Isaac Cogsdale, a New Salem pionee was told by Lincoln at the time he was leaving for Washington that, "I have loved the name of the Rutledges to this day. I have kept my mind on their movements ever since." Cogsdale said, "Of Anne, Lincoln spoke with some feeling, saying I loved her dearly. She was a handsome girl, would have made a good, loving wife; she was natural, and quite intellectual, though not highly educated. I did honestly and truly love the girl, and think often of her now."

The White House – Tuesday, January 14, 1862

Today I arranged for a demonstration of Greek Fire artillery shells, which were invented by Levi Short of Connecticut. They are filled with sulfur and "other suffocating matter" as described by the inventor. The ordnance experts, who observed the exercise, doubt that the shells can be safely fired from our cannons without a high risk of premature explosion, which would put the gunners at risk. My sense is that they should be carefully investigated and if need be, the government should consider spending money to help further develop the shells. We seem to rely on the weapons of old rather than developing new and better weapons for tomorrow. Mr. Short gave me a short history of Greek fire, and I have asked Hay to see if the Library of Congress can provide me with more information about this strange weapon. Short told me that Constantine IV's fleet used Greek Fire to destroy the Saracens' ships. Short uses naphtha mixed with sulfur as his combustible agents, and has also tested various solutions of phosphorus in bisulfide of carbon, and also turpentine. He believes they can not only help us on land, but also on sea. I have asked Stanton to keep me advised on how this potential new weapon may be used in a way that does more harm to our enemies than to our own gunners.

Earlier this evening Molly and I hosted a public reception at the White House attended by several hundred people. Mother looked particularly beautiful in a new light blue gown. Yours truly shook more hands than usual. As usual several guests were job seekers.

Author's notes:

Edward C. Boynton, an American artillery officer and chemistry professor reported that Levi Short died in the summer of 1863. Boynton concluded that "5 out of every 6 of the Greek Fire shells loaded with his preparation, either from attrition of particles in the rotary motion of the shell, or from some other cause, burst in the gun, or just in front of it; and it is a matter of extreme doubt whether a single shell thus charged ever reached the city of Charleston during its bombardment." Lincoln often called Mary Lincoln Molly.

The White House – Wednesday, January 15, 1862

The Senate confirmed Stanton's nomination as secretary of war. I penned a note to Stanton asking that he find a clerkship for Richard Goodwin. I also wrote to General Halleck suggesting that he receive Governor Gustave P. Koerner of Illinois, who is a personal friend of mine and whose judgment I trust implicitly. I gave Koerner a sealed letter for him to give to Halleck. Koerner was instrumental in establishing the 43rd Illinois Volunteer Infantry Company.

Author's notes:

Koerner had been imprisoned as a young lawyer in Germany, and was forced to flee the country when warrants were issued for his arrest for revolutionary activities. He was a close friend of Mary and Abraham Lincoln, who appointed him brigadier general. He was appointed U.S. minister to Spain on April 11, 1862, replacing Carl Schurz, and served until July 20, 1864. When Lincoln was assassinated, Koerner was named one of his 12 pallbearers.

The White House – Saturday, January 18, 1862

The boys brought up the name of John Brown again this evening. They are particularly fascinated by Brown. Our dinner guests were Senator Orville Browning and his wife, Eliza. We discussed Brown's ill-fated raid on Harper's Ferry, which occurred in October of 1859. John Brown is often incorrectly described by some as a "noble martyr." I disputed that false claim carefully when I gave my speech at Cooper Union, which happened just four months after Brown's raid. Browning told the boys that it is his strong belief that had I not spoken at Cooper Union I would not have received the Republican nomination for president in May of 1860. There I made the point that John Brown was surely no Republican and that his desperate raid on the arsenal was exceedingly peculiar. I argued that it was not a slave insurrection, but a mad attempt by a small number of white men to get up a revolt among slaves, in which the slaves refused to participate. In fact, it was so absurd that the slaves with all their ignorance saw plainly enough that it could not succeed. Fortunately for me, the newspapers that covered my Cooper Union talk reported it word for word, and the wide circulation of my views surely helped the public understand my thoughts on the dangers of reckless abolitionism.

Author's notes:

Orville Hickman Browning was a close personal friend of the Lincoln family for over 30 years. He was appointed to fill the Senate seat of Stephen A. Douglas after Douglas' untimely death. He served from June 26, 1861, to January 12, 1863. A Whig delegate to the Anti-Nebraska Convention held in Bloomington, Illinois, in May of 1856, he helped lay the groundwork for the Republican Party. A prominent lawyer, he successfully defended five men who had been accused of the murder of Joseph Smith, founder of the Latter-Day Saint movement. Browning was named secretary of the interior by President Andrew Johnson.

The White House – Monday, January 20, 1862

Late this evening I received telegraph reports of an important Union victory yesterday in Kentucky at Mill Springs. Our forces under the command of Brigadier General George Thomas successfully engaged troops under Confederate Major General George Crittenden. In the early dawn on the 19th, Thomas sought to drive the enemy across the Cumberland River. The rebels achieved early successes, but with the death of Rebel General Felix Zollicoffer, our men repulsed a second Confederate assault, forcing them from the field into a general retreat. General Thomas communicated that he believes his forces were outnumbered by an estimated 1,500 troops. We lost 39 killed, 207 wounded. Thomas reports enemy losses are probably double ours. He reports that Zollicoffer mistakenly rode into Union 4th Kentucky Infantry believing they were Confederates firing on their own men. He was killed by Union Colonel Speed Fry. The enemy abandoned 12 artillery pieces, 150 wagons, over 1,000 horses and all their dead and wounded.

Author's notes:

The rebel forces retreated all the way to Chestnut Mound, Tennessee, which is about 50 miles due east of Nashville. At one point in the battle the lines were so close together that Colonel Robert McCook, commanding Thomas' Third Brigade, wrote, "The lines were so close that the enemy and the Second Minnesota were poking their guns through the same fence."

The Mill Springs Battlefield, a historic landmark, is in Pulaski County, near Nancy, Kentucky. The Confederate dead are buried here. The Union dead are buried in the National Cemetery in Nancy. Commemorative ceremonies are held at the battlefield each year, including candlelight tours, living history presentations and battle reenactments.

Soon after the battle, Currier and Ives released the Battle of Mill Springs, a popular hand-colored print.

The White House – Tuesday, January 21, 1862

This evening we hosted another reception here. A good-sized crowd but well-behaved, with many Army and Navy officers in attendance. I made a note to myself to speak to Stanton tomorrow about Lorenzo Thomas, our adjutant general. His official responsibility is to attend me wherever I go in public. This is not to my liking, and is an uncompensated encumbrance both to him and me. I think it is a waste of his valuable time. I respect his military judgment and prefer to have his counsel only when needed.

Earlier in the day a delegation from California presented an oil portrait of the late Colonel Edward Dickinson Baker as a gift from William B. Farewell of San Francisco. It is striking in appearance and brings back many fond memories of my close friend, Senator Baker, who gave his life for the Union at the Battle of Ball's Bluff in October.

Tomorrow there will be another exhibition of Greek Fire on the grounds south of the White House. I am certain the boys will love it. I am afraid the generals and high naval officers invited will continue to be negative about the implementation of the shells before a great deal more testing has been done. The wheels of government turn slowly!

The White House – Wednesday, January 22, 1862

I dreamed last evening of that day, when as a very young boy, I joined my father, Thomas, as we sowed pumpkin seeds on our small Kentucky farm. My father taught me to walk with him as he plowed the soil. Then he instructed me to drop two pumpkin seeds in every second hill, in every second row later made by his hoe. At the end of the day I was proud of my accomplishments. Then on the following day, the Sabbath, a great cloudburst burst upon the hills above where we had planted the seeds. I remember vividly that the water flowed down from higher ground, washing away corn kernels, pumpkin seeds and precious topsoil. It was a difficult and cruel lesson for a mere boy. I cried when the next day I saw the ruin the terrible storm had caused. My father informed me that the fruit of our labor was all gone, and that we must replant. I think that is the earliest memory I have of feeling deep pain. I have frequently said in speeches that I believe, "No men living are worthier to be trusted than those who toil on the land and rise up from poverty." When I spoke those words, I had my father and me in my mind, going way back to that sad day when we lost all we had sown.

Author's notes:

Lincoln signed into law an Act of Congress establishing "At the seat of government of the United States a Department of Agriculture" on May 15, 1862. Two and a half years later, in his last message to Congress, Lincoln said, "The Agriculture Department, under the supervision of its present energetic and faithful head, is rapidly commending itself to the great and vital interest it was created to advance. It is precisely the people's Department, in which they feel more directly concerned than in any other. I commend it to the continued care of Congress." Lincoln appointed Isaac Newton to head the department. He was a farmer who had served as chief of the Agricultural Section of the Patent Office since August 1861.

The Homestead Act, approved by Lincoln on May 20, 1862, provided for giving 160 acres of the public domain to any American or prospective citizen who was the head of a family or over 21 years of age. Title to the land was issued after the settler had resided on it for five years and made improvements on it.

The Morrill Land Grant College Act, donating public land to the states for colleges of agriculture and the mechanical arts, became law on July 2, 1862. Every state accepted the terms of the act and established one or more such institutions.

The White House – Thursday, January 23, 1862

Last evening, Mother read poems to the boys and me from several pages of poetry from the 1860 edition of Walt Whitman's "Leaves of Grass." Mother tells me that Ralph Waldo Emerson has recommended Whitman positively to those who hold poetry in high esteem. I find his words inspirational, although they do not rhyme in the ordinary sense, but flow freely as his mind guides his pen. The boys prefer less sophisticated fare. I have often regretted that the few attempts I have made at creating a poem have not been met with success. Plutarch in 'De Gloria Atheniensium III' wisely observed, "Painting is silent poetry, and poetry painting that speaks."

The morning began with a productive meeting with Navy Lieutenant Henry Wise of the Bureau of Ordnance regarding the manufacture of mortars in Pittsburgh. It is of paramount importance that our production of this type of siege weapon be significantly increased. They have the advantage of firing high over enemy entrenchments and walls, and can destroy structures inside a fortification, including barracks, magazines and bombproof shelters. Wise advises that the weight of four types of mortars now being produced range from 164 pounds to 17,120 pounds. The latter is a 13-inch seacoast mortar, which can shoot 4,300 yards with great accuracy.

Author's notes:

Whitman came to Washington in December 1862 following the Battle of Fredericksburg to check on his brother, George, who had been wounded. He began aiding the many seriously wounded men who were transported to Washington and continued to work with the wounded, Southern or Northern, for the remainder of the war. He remained in Washington until 1873, working as a clerk in the Army Paymaster's Department, the Bureau of Indian Affairs and the Attorney General's office. Lincoln and Whitman never met, although the president told his assistants that he recognized Whitman, who had been frequently pointed out to him, on the streets of the city.

The White House – Friday, January 24, 1862

Last night, Mother and I attended a performance of Verdi's "Il Trovatore" at Washington Theatre. There was not an empty seat in the house. Senator and Mrs. Orville Browning were our guests. The opera's story is absurd and illogical, yet it held the attention of those in attendance from start to finish. The audience was particularly enthusiastic and gave the cast a rousing ovation at the end of the performance. I wonder if foreign operas will ever be sung in English. I believe that most opera fans fail to comprehend exactly what is going on. I can only assume that the translations would not sound quite as beautiful.

For one hour, starting at 2 o'clock, I met with E. Delafield Smith, U.S. district attorney for New York, who recommended that I not interfere in the case of Captain Nathaniel Gordon, who was sentenced to be hanged for slave trading. Gordon's ship, Erie, loaded 897 slaves aboard at Sharks Point, Congo River, West Africa. Most were children. He preferred to carry children because they could not rise up to avenge his cruelties. The U.S.S. Mohican captured the ship 50 miles from Sharks Point on August 8, 1860, and took the slaves to Liberia and freedom. At his first trial Gordon had a hung jury. At the second trial, he was found guilty in the Circuit Court in Manhattan and sentenced to death on February 7, 1862. I have been asked by his family and supporters to pardon the captain. I can find no reason to do so.

Author's notes:

Lincoln issued a stay of execution, setting the new date for February 21, 1862, giving Gordon two weeks to make his final preparations, "For the awful change which awaits him." Lincoln refused to meet with Gordon's supporters. Lincoln wrote, "I believe I am kindly enough in nature, and can be moved to pity and to pardon the perpetrator of almost the worst crime that the mind of man can conceive or the arm of man can execute; any man, whom, for paltry gain and stimulated only by avarice, can rob Africa of her children to sell into interminable bondage, I never will pardon."

The White House – Saturday, January 25, 1862

William Herndon came by and gave to me a small book in which one of my favorite poems, "The Last Leaf," is included. I have recited it for years to anyone willing to listen to me. Mary and the boys do not particularly like it, but Herndon cannot seem to get enough of it. The author is Oliver Wendell Holmes, Sr., of Boston.

The Holmes poem that the boys like best is "Old Ironsides," which he wrote to call public attention to the fact that America's most ancient warship, which was named U.S.S. Constitution by George Washington, deserves to be carefully preserved. Last year we moved it north from where it was berthed at Annapolis, Maryland, because the Navy Department believed that Confederate sympathizers might do the ship harm while in port.

Author's notes:

In 1867, Herndon, Lincoln's law partner, wrote of "The Last Leaf," "I have heard Lincoln recite it, praise it, laud it, and swear by it." Henry C. Whitney wrote to Herndon from Lawrence, Kansas, in December of 1866, "Dr. Oliver Wendell Holmes, Sr., is quite anxious that it should be incorporated into your Life of Lincoln, the high estimation Lincoln had for his poem 'The Last Leaf.' Governor Andrew of Massachusetts says that in the darkest days of our history, while being in consultation with Lincoln, that the latter repeated to him the entire poem."

The U.S.S. Constitution was ordered north from the Naval Academy in Annapolis in April 1861. Several companies of Massachusetts volunteer soldiers were stationed aboard for her protection. She was towed to New York City, where she arrived on April 29, 1861, and later relocated, along with the Naval Academy, to Fort Adams, near Newport, Rhode Island, for the duration of the Civil War. Her sister ship, the U.S.S. United States, was abandoned by the Union and then captured by Confederate forces at the Gosport Shipyard in Norfolk, Virginia.

As this is written the U.S.S. Constitution is in dry dock in Boston undergoing repairs. The adjacent U.S.S. Constitution Museum is open to visitors.

The White House – Sunday, January 26, 1861

Today Mother and I were joined by Noah and Sarah Swayne for dinner. On the 24th of January Noah was confirmed by the Senate as a justice of the Supreme Court. He is my first such appointment and will be sworn in tomorrow. Noah takes the place of the late Justice John McLean, who died in the fall. I admired McLean, who had properly dissented in the vile Dred Scott v. Sanford decision along with Justice Curtis. The Swaynes are devout Quakers and as such are strong Abolitionists. I believe Noah may do much to improve the legal rights of Negroes in our nation, North and South. His son, Wager, is now serving with the 43rd Ohio Volunteer Infantry Regiment.

Author's notes:

Justice Swayne (1804 – 1884) attended the Jacob Mendenhall Academy in Waterford, Virginia, where he studied Latin, Greek and mathematics. His schoolmate was Robert E. Lee, with whom he spent many pleasant hours. They remained lifelong friends. Swayne originally studied medicine and later switched to law. He is the only Quaker to ever serve on the Supreme Court. Swayne sought the presidency in 1860, losing the nomination to Lincoln. His most famous court decision was in Springer vs. U.S. 1882, upholding the U.S. income tax, imposed by the Revenue Act of 1864. His son Wager lost a leg in the war, rose to the rank of major general and was awarded the Medal of Honor. Swayne served 18 years on the bench. I had lunch with William Swayne, Noah's great-grandson, who kindly gave me a copy of a venerable document, describing his distinguished ancestor, dated May 1, 1881, which modestly begins, "The sons of Mr. Justice Swayne have deemed it not improper to print what follows for distribution to the members of the family and a few friends."

The White House – Monday, January 27, 1862

Yesterday I spent all morning at the War Department. The generals and their staff provided numerous reports, which I had requested and which I carefully reviewed. I also studied large maps covering the land our troops will be required to traverse when orders are issued to move upon the enemy. My decision has been made to formally take personal command by issuing Executive War Orders. For too long I have deferred to the generals expecting initiative and aggressive action, which has not ensued. I have almost lost all trust in our army to be used in the best manner to assure victory. I see no reason to accept further excuses for not attacking on several fronts simultaneously. We are the stronger and larger force. My sense is the enemy cannot prevail, if pressured at many key points at the same time. At 5 P.M. War Order No. 1 was written and released to all concerned.

Author's notes:

Lincoln's War Order No. 1 read: Executive Order – General War Order No. 1, January 27, 1862.

Ordered, that the 22nd of February 1862 be the day for a general movement of the United States against insurgent forces; that especially the army at and about Fortress Monroe, The Army of the Potomac, The Army of Western Virginia, the army near Munfordville, Ky., the army and flotilla at Cairo, and a naval force in the Gulf of Mexico be ready to move on that day.

That all other forces, both land and naval, with their respective commanders, obey existing orders for the time and be ready to obey additional orders when duly given.

That the heads of departments, and especially the Secretaries of War and of the Navy, with all their subordinates, and the General in Chief, with all other commanders and subordinates of land and naval forces, will severally be held to their strict and full responsibilities for prompt execution of this order. ABRAHAM LINCOLN

The White House – Tuesday, January 28, 1862

I met with Secretary Stanton to stress my wishes that War Order No. 1 be followed without exception. The forces to be involved must move forward with vigor and enthusiasm and inspired leadership.

Mother has been ill and not able to receive public visitors who came to see us. She was not running a fever but felt weak and shaky. This house is drafty and poorly heated, as my assistants will attest. There is never enough heat where they work. Some days they wear gloves when writing. Part of the problem flows from the fact that the front door is never closed; visitors flow in and out all-day long. There are lots of shortages in wartime ,but never is there a shortage of job seekers. They are an inexhaustible force! The boys have suggested that I charge an admission fee. Not a bad idea!

Thomas Hicks, a newspaperman, asked me about my earliest days. I told him that I was born February 12, 1809, in Hardin County, Kentucky, at a point within the now recently formed County of Larue, a mile or a mile and a half from where Hodgenville now is. My parents being dead and my own memory serving, I know no means of identifying the precise locality. It was on Nolin Creek. My father, Thomas, possessed 348½ acres of land when I was born. In 1811 Thomas Lincoln moved the family from our Nolin River farm to a better property of 230 acres, located 10 miles north and six miles east of Hodgenville. It was on Knob Creek. In December 1816, we moved from Kentucky to the new state of Indiana in Spencer County. The trip of 91 miles in bad weather took us five miserable days. In 1818 my dear mother, Nancy Hanks Lincoln, died of milk sickness and was buried near Thomas and Elizabeth Hanks Sparrow. In 1819 my father married Sarah Bush Johnston in Elizabethtown. The family Bible records that Reverend George L. Rogers of the Methodist church performed the ceremony.

Author's notes:

Lincoln described Indiana at this time as, "A wild region with many bears and other wild animals in the woods." Thomas settled in an unbroken forest, and the clearing away of surplus wood was the great task ahead for him and his son. Though very young, Abraham Lincoln was large for his age and had an ax put in his hands at once and tells that from that young age until he was "within his 23rd year, he was almost constantly handling that most useful instrument – less of course, in plowing and harvesting seasons."

The White House – Wednesday, January 29, 1862

I had a productive meeting with Assistant Secretary of the Navy Gustavus Fox. I explained to him my deep frustration that our production of mortars cannot seem to get into full swing. Fox has over 18 years of naval service; it is my sense that he knows how to get things accomplished. More mortars mean more explosive shells that can fall upon the enemy, particularly those who are located behind high walls, which defy traditional artillery shells. I have asked that he take a personal interest in this problem and that he report to me weekly on production results.

This evening I shook hands for over two hours at a levee in the Blue Room. Mother was in improved health and helped me greatly with the hospitalities. She has a far better memory for names of guests than her husband. When in doubt as to the name of someone, approaching me in the line, I will give her a nudge, and she will, when she can do so, address the guest in line by name so I know to whom I am speaking. Mary is a far better politician than her husband.

Author's notes:

Gustavus Fox served in his post throughout the Civil War and was consulted by Lincoln on matters related to both military and naval affairs. The mortars were used by both branches of the services.

The White House – Thursday, January 30, 1862

Yesterday I met with Dr. Henry Whitney Bellows, president of the U.S. Sanitary Commission, and George T. Strong, a commission member. It was created in June and is beginning to show positive results. They assure me that this private relief agency should be able to generate sufficient funds from voluntary donations to do the job needed to help our wounded troops. Since it was established, Sanitary Inspectors have visited over 400 regimental camps, which were inspected for sanitation methods. Standards are being set to improve the health of our men. A central office has been set up inside the nearby Treasury Building under the direction of Frederick Law Olmsted. Bellows advises that there have been thousands of volunteers offering to assist our wounded men. Strong tells me that the organization is being modeled after the British Sanitary Commission, established during the Crimean War and after the Indian Rebellion of 1857.

Author's notes:

Other commission members included Dr. William Van Buren, Dr. Hayes Agnew and Dr. Oliver Wolcott Gibbs. During the war, the U.S. Sanitary Commission operated 30 soldiers' homes, lodges or rests for Union soldiers. The Women's Central Relief Association of New York collected donations, made uniforms, worked as nurses, ran kitchens in army camps and administered hospital ships, soldiers' homes and rests for traveling or disabled soldiers. They organized sanitary fairs in numerous cities to support the Union Army with funds and supplies and funds for the work of the USSC. Women often worked in harsh conditions. They included Louisa May Alcott, Almira Fales, Eliza Emily Chappell Porter, and many other patriotic women.

The White House – Friday, January 31, 1862

I feel that February will prove to be a month of troop movement and success at arms. My patience has been sorely tried. The more I read books on military strategy, the more convinced I have become that the Union will only win when it can time its attacks in such a way that we overwhelm the enemy, through valor and strength of numbers. I am reminded that while we plan, so does the enemy and it is wily and determined. I was forced to resort to the mechanism of an executive order, because General McClellan has refused to share his plans with the Cabinet or with me. If he cannot use the troops we have provided to him, I may have to borrow them myself!

Details of the Trent affair have been sent to the Congress. The information I have received from Secretary Seward suggests that both Great Britain and France are at least for now presently unwilling to recognize the Confederacy. Maintaining their neutrality must continue to be our principle foreign policy objective.

I greatly admire Mother's understanding. I spend less and less time with her and the boys, as the demands of the war continue to consume all of my time. War is a seven-day-a-week concern that must be met.

Author's notes:

According to Hay and Nicolay, Lincoln worked seven days a week with never a day off. He came to work early and usually stayed late. During America's next major war, World War I, President Woodrow Wilson is estimated to have played 1,000 rounds of golf. President Dwight Eisenhower, who took office while the Korean conflict was still being waged, is believed to have played 800 rounds of golf. Ike was a proud member of Augusta National Golf Club and paid 45 visits to it while president, each typically lasting a week.

The White House – Saturday, February 1, 1862

I wrote a letter to Queen Victoria, expressing our sympathy for the death of her husband, Prince Albert. I have been told that the prince was instrumental in recommending to the prime minister that the matter of the Trent Affair be settled amicably. America owes a great deal to him for his intercession in a matter that came close to leading to war. One day I would enjoy visiting Great Britain. I am particularly interested in seeing London. My ancestors came from England, but I am not familiar with when and where our ancients lived in Britain, or when they left for America. In 1848, I was contacted by Solomon Lincoln of Hingham, Massachusetts, who wrote to advise me that he believed that it was possible that I was related to the Lincolns who lived in Hingham, Massachusetts. Perhaps one day Robert may have time to research our genealogy.

Author's notes:

During his lifetime, Lincoln was never able to ascertain his family's genealogy. He wrote to various cousins in Kentucky and Massachusetts, seeking information of possible family ties, but apparently never met with them or followed up with them with correspondence on the subject. Historians believe that Thomas Lincoln, Abraham's father, had two cousins in Boston, Amos and Jedidiah, who married Paul Revere's daughters and served in the American Revolution. Going back to its origins in England, the Lincoln family tree looks like this:

Samuel Lincoln (born in Norwich, England. Immigrated to America in 1637).
His son, Mordecai Lincoln (born in Hingham, Massachusetts, 1657).
His son, Mordecai Lincoln (born in Hingham, Massachusetts, 1686 and later moved to New Jersey and Pennsylvania).
His son, John Lincoln (born in New Jersey, 1711).
His son, Abraham Lincoln (born in Virginia, 1744).
His son, Thomas Lincoln (born in Virginia, 1778).
His son, Abraham Lincoln (born in Kentucky, 1809).

The White House – Sunday, February 2, 1862

Congressman Alfred Ely of the 29th District of New York visited me with Secretary Seward. I wanted their advice on the advisability of placing Confederate privateers, who have been detained in New York and Philadelphia harbors, on the same legal footing as prisoners of war. International law has determined they should be treated as pirates and hung for their predatory practices. Ely has had direct experience with Confederate prison practices because he was captured by the rebels while observing the Battle of Bull Run. For almost six months he was held in Richmond's Libby Prison until he was exchanged for Charles J. Faulkner. Ely recommends that we treat all privateers as prisoners of war. I tend to agree with his thinking.

Author's notes:

Charles J. Faulkner was elected to Congress from Virginia's 10th District as a Whig and Democrat serving from 1851 to 1859. He was appointed by President James Buchanan as minister to France in 1860, serving until he was arrested in August of 1861 on charges of negotiating sales of arms for the Confederacy while in Paris. He was imprisoned at Fort Warren in Boston and ultimately released in December of 1861 after negotiating his own release for Alfred Ely. During the Civil War, Faulkner enlisted in the Confederate Army and was assistant adjutant general on the staff of General Thomas J. "Stonewall" Jackson. After the war, he was a member of the West Virginia Constitutional Convention and was elected to the House of Representatives as a Democrat from West Virginia, serving from 1874 to 1877.

The first federal trial for piracy was of 13 men, including Captain Thomas Harris Baker, who were captured aboard the Confederate privateer Savannah. The trial was held in the U.S. Circuit Court for the Southern District of New York beginning October 23, 1861. The trial ended in a deadlock. The Confederacy had advised Lincoln that it would retaliate by killing 13 Union prisoners, if the Savannah prisoners were hung. The Savannah prisoners were ultimately exchanged for Union prisoners of war. In time, the Confederacy ceased operating privateers, relying instead upon regularly commissioned Confederate Navy ships.

The White House – Monday, February 3, 1862

Yesterday Senator Sumner introduced me to Ralph Waldo Emerson. Mother and I are great admirers of his poetry. I heard him lecture at the Smithsonian on the 31st of January. He reiterated his strong views about slavery and spoke to me about John Brown, who had visited Emerson's home in Concord, Massachusetts, several years ago. I did not realize that Brown had fathered 20 children. Emerson considered Brown to be an idealist, who put his passionate and dangerous ideas into action. He told me that he had been shocked and distressed when he learned that Brown had invaded the federal arsenal at Harper's Ferry with just a handful of men. Emerson, along with Amos Bronson Alcott and Henry Thoreau, helped raised funds for Brown's family after Brown was hung. Emerson urged me to take whatever action I could to free the slaves; I explained to him how difficult it is for me to do so at this time. He mentioned that he gave his first speech on the subject of slavery in 1837 and has lectured and spoken on the subject ever since.

Author's notes:

Emerson was disappointed in Lincoln's early presidency because the president had not taken prompt action to free the slaves. After meeting the president, Emerson's feelings about Lincoln began to soften. In 1865, he spoke at a memorial service held for the president in Concord, and said, "Old as history is and manifold as are its tragedies, I doubt if any death has caused so much pain, as this has caused, or will have caused, on its announcement."

The White House – Tuesday, February 4, 1862

Willie has been feeling ill, and Mother and I are very concerned that he seems to be weakening from whatever is ailing him. He is pale but has no high fever. Tad is looking a bit peaked about the face. Mother sent out invitations to 600 people to attend a ball to be held in the newly redecorated East Room tomorrow evening and now regrets the timing, since our boys are ill and deserve all of our attention.

Author's notes:

Willie and Tad Lincoln are believed to have contracted typhoid fever or malaria. Willie fought his terminal illness for two weeks. The most likely cause of the disease may have been from putrid water, which was pumped into the White House from a canal located south of the executive mansion.

The White House – Thursday, February 6, 1862

Today Tad's facial appearance is no longer pallid and he seems a bit stronger, but his brother continues to be weak and listless. Dr. Stone has recommended that they both be given beef tea for added nutrition and strength.

Last night's ball, followed by a midnight supper, was attended by hundreds of well-dressed Washingtonians, with a great many of them in uniform. The consensus is that it was a social success, but emotionally it was very difficult for Mother and me; all of our thoughts are upon our two ill boys.

I signed a letter today thanking the King of Siam for the gift of a sword, an autographed photograph of him and two large elephant tusks. In the letter, I declined his kind offer of two elephants. I doubt I shall ever be offered such an unusual gift again. The presidency is indeed an odd job, with the whole world involved, and often in very strange ways.

I provided General McClellan with a letter asking that he further clarify for me his rationale for proposed movements of the Army of the Potomac that are in ways contrary to those that I have proposed.

Author's notes:

The Washington Star reported that the ball and following dinner were "The most superb affair of its kind ever seen here."

The White House – Friday, February 7, 1862

Yesterday I approved the new federal policy that Southern sympathizers are not to continue receiving pension payments. Hay brought me the 1860 edition of Emerson's "Representative Men," which he borrowed from the Library of Congress. The book includes seven of Emerson's lectures that were given in 1850. In the collection Emerson describes the roles of six "great men" in past societies whom he deems to be great: Plato, Swedenborg, Montaigne, Shakespeare, Napoleon and Goethe. I will be particularly interested in reading what he has to say about Napoleon. I wonder if from the lectures I may gain new insights into McClellan, who is often referred to as the "Young Napoleon." Hay and Nicolay reminded me that photographs of the general usuaily show him with his right hand placed inside his military coat jacket, the exact manner of Emperor Napoleon Bonaparte.

Most of this day was spent with Mother and Willie, who at times seems to rally, and then to slip back into a fitful sleep. This afternoon he had a low fever. He is kept cool with damp cloths placed on his forehead. Tad appears to grow stronger, as Willie gets weaker. Mother has cancelled the usual Tuesday reception for next week.

Author's notes:

Typhoid fever is usually caused by salmonellae typhi bacteria and is contracted by the ingestion of contaminated food or water. Symptoms are poor appetite, headaches, generalized ache and pains, fever and lethargy. The bacteria are deposited through fecal contamination in water or food by a human carrier and are spread to other people in the area. In modern times, it is rare in industrialized countries, but continues to be a significant public health issue in developing nations. Approximately 5,700 cases are reported annually in the United States. Worldwide the disease affects more than 21 million people annually, with over 200,000 patients dying of the disease. Travelers to endemic areas should receive vaccination for typhoid fever.

The White House – Saturday, February 8, 1862, to Tuesday, February 25, 1862

Author's notes:

From February 8, 1862, until February 25, 1862, President Lincoln did not make diary entries due to the pressures caused by the illness of his two sons and the deteriorating mental condition of Mary Lincoln.

Willie Lincoln died at 5 p.m. on February 20. His body was embalmed using a new process by Dr. Charles D. Brown on February 22, 1862. Lincoln visited the Green Room, where Willie's body lay in state on that date. On February 23, Willie's body was viewed by many friends of the family. On February 24 at 2 P.M., Dr. Phineas D. Gurley conducted a simple funeral service in the East Room, while the body remained in the adjoining Green parlor. A large crowd, including Cabinet officials, foreign ministers, members of Congress and the public, attended.

President Lincoln was accompanied by his oldest son, Robert Lincoln and Senators Browning and Trumbull of Illinois to Oak Hill Cemetery Road and Washington Streets, where Willie's body was placed in W.T. Carroll's vault. Tad Lincoln's health improved considerably. Mary Lincoln had been inconsolable since her son's death and did not attend the funeral.

Carl Sandburg wrote that "His body was later sent to Illinois for burial. And the mother clutched at his memory and if his name was mentioned, her voice shook and the tears came. She could not bear to look upon his picture, said Mrs. Keckley. And after his death she never crossed the threshold of the Guest's Room in which he died, or the Green Room, where he was embalmed."

Sandburg reported that Mrs. Keckley said, "He was his father's favorite. They were intimates, often seen hand in hand. And there sat the man, bent now with the load at both heart and brain, staggering under the blow of taking from him his child. His men of power sat around him: McClellan, with a moist eye when he bowed to the prayer, as I could see from where I stood."

The White House – Wednesday, February 26, 1862

Mother is almost beyond consolation. When surrounded by war deaths every hour of every day as I am, one should become numb to its touch, but when it strikes a helpless young one, who is so dearly beloved, it is almost impossible to cope. I must be doubly strong, so that Mary can survive her terrible grief. Xenohon wrote, "I knew my son was mortal." And alas, I sadly found that my favorite one was too. May a kind God bless you, dearest Willie, and may He continue to bring wellness to Tad!

Author's notes:

On February 13, 1862, Lincoln, who found solace in poetry, borrowed a translation of Johann Wolfgang von Goethe, Goethe's Werke (Borrower's Ledger, page 114), Library of Congress. He copied these words from the poem, "Wandrers Nachtlied" (Wanderer's Night Song):

> *O'er all the hilltops*
> *Is quiet now,*
> *In all the treetops*
> *Hearest thou*
> *Hardly a breath;*
> *The birds are asleep in the trees*
> *Wait; soon like these*
> *Thou too shalt rest.*

During the period when he made no diary entries, the president attended to official business without interruption. He continued to meet with his Cabinet, signed treaties, appeared before the House Judiciary Committee, met with his generals, issued executive orders related to political prisoners, and kept apprised of General Grant's campaign to take Fort Donelson in Tennessee. He also met with the Committee on the Conduct of the War and made appointments to various overseas posts.

The White House – Thursday, February 27, 1862

Today I appointed a commission to review cases of state prisoners remaining in military custody. I was informed that General Scott, because of his ill health, has declined my invitation to become envoy extraordinary and minister plenipotentiary to Mexico. Scott continues to be a very valuable source of knowledge on military matters. No one has his breadth of experience, or knows our top Army officers better than Scott.

While matters in the East continue to proceed without military satisfaction, affairs in the West are proceeding far better than I ever anticipated. The fall of Fort Henry and Fort Donelson in Tennessee have thrilled the nation. The surrender of Ft. Henry opens the Tennessee River south to the Alabama border. General Grant and Flag Officer Foote combined to achieve this win. They are splendid leaders.

Since Fort Donelson fell on February 16, the Tennessee and Cumberland Rivers, two major water routes in the Confederate West, will now become Union waterways for the movement of troops and material against the rebels in the months to come.

Author's notes:

While Lincoln found comfort in the progress made by his successful armies and naval forces in the West, his unhappiness with General McClellan continued. On February 27th, after meeting with General Randolph G. Marcy, McClellan's father-in-law, Lincoln said to his aide John Nicolay, "The general impression is daily gaining that the General (McClellan) does not intend to do anything."

The White House – Friday, February 28, 1862

The latest summary received from General U.S. Grant's headquarters indicates that just over 11,000 Confederate prisoners surrendered at Fort Donelson. His reply to General Simon Bolivar Buckner's request for terms of surrender, "Unconditional and immediate," were to the point and have been widely acclaimed by the nation. Newspapers are now writing of "Unconditional Surrender Grant," in their reports about the successful general. Too bad Grant's mother didn't have twins, for I could use another Grant along the Potomac!

Grant ordered General William "Bull" Nelson to advance on Nashville with his division and take the city. Mayor Richard Cheatham surrendered to Union forces of General Don Carlos Buell on the 24th of February after Confederate troops had fled the city. The next morning Nelson arrived on the gunboat Conestoga, and later in the day Buell accepted the formal surrender of Nashville, the first Confederate capital to fall into Union hands. Grant wrote to me that after the surrender he called upon Sarah Polk, the widow of President James Polk, to assure her safety. I have appointed Grant major general of volunteers despite charges against him that he drinks more than he should. I like a man who fights and wins.

Author's notes:

The loss of Nashville was an incredibly serious blow to the Confederacy. It was the second largest city in Tennessee, second to Memphis, and the eighth largest in the Confederacy. It was an industrial center and home to the Nashville Armory, a private company (College Hill Arsenal) that had manufactured arms for the rebels. Nashville possessed one of the few facilities in the South capable of casting artillery.

By seizing the city, the federals now controlled the hub of four important railroad lines, which had carried raw materials in and manufactured goods out. The railroad lines were The Louisville and Nashville, The Tennessee and Alabama, The Nashville and Chattanooga, and Nashville and N.W.

The White House – Saturday, March 1, 1862

Secretary of the Navy Gideon Wells and several Navy and Army officers visited here today to present a summary of amphibious activities in North Carolina waters beginning on February 7, during which Army forces under the command of Brigadier General Ambrose E. Burnside and naval units under Flag Officer Louis Goldsborough attacked and captured four rebel forts. This was a well-coordinated attack by a flotilla of Union Navy gunboats supported by gunboats under Army control. Army troops managed to capture Roanoke Island after our ship's guns pounded the forts and defeated a fleet of small enemy ships. On land, we outnumbered the enemy 10,000 to 3,000. We lost 264 killed, the enemy, 2,643 killed. On February 8 Confederate Colonel Henry Shaw surrendered and we took 2,000 prisoners.

Author's notes:

Roanoke Island remained under Union control throughout the rest of the Civil War. Soon after the Battle of Roanoke Island, federal gunboats destroyed the remainder of the Confederate ships at the Battle of Elizabeth City. Operations by Burnside's forces ended in July, when the general was called to take part in the campaign to take Richmond. In time Union forces assaulted New Bern and Fort Macon, North Carolina, taking their capture.

The White House – Sunday, March 2, 1862

Yesterday, at Secretary of War Stanton's urging, I agreed to appoint Dr. Isaac Hayes, surgeon of volunteers with initial responsibility for the patients at Saterlee Hospital outside of Philadelphia. It currently treats several thousand sick or wounded Union soldiers. Dr. Hayes is a Quaker who spent 15 months (July 1860 to October 1861) in the Arctic seeking a passage to the North Pole. When he left our shores, America was at peace, and when he returned he found his homeland engaged in a deadly civil war. Stanton recommends him highly. That is good enough for me.

Stanton was authorized to appoint nine major generals and nine brigadier generals. I approved his list without exception.

Assistant Secretary of the Navy Fox advises me that the U.S.S. Monitor is seaworthy, and that it is being sent post haste to Hampton Roads. This is a very controversial vessel. I will be severely criticized if it fails, because its radical design is so foreign to established naval construction traditions, and because I am the one who fought strongest for its building and launch. They say that haste makes waste. The ship was created in record-breaking time because of wartime needs. She may soon be in harm's way. May the Almighty protect her brave crew.

Author's notes:

The steam-powered U.S.S. Monitor was ordered by the Navy Department on October 4, 1861, its keel laid down October 25 and commissioned February 25, 1862. Displacement: 987 tons, length 179 feet, beam 41 feet, draft 10 feet 6 inches, speed 6 knots.

At the Battle of Hampton Roads on March 9, 1862, she fought the casement ironclad C.S.S. Virginia, formerly the steam frigate U.S.S. Merrimack, to a standstill. When Confederate forces abandoned Norfolk on May 11, 1862, they were forced to destroy the Virginia.

The Monitor's distinctive revolving turret was designed by Theodore Timby. The remainder of the ship was designed by John Ericsson and built in 101 days. Cost: $275,000. Built at the Continental Iron Works, Greenpoint, Brooklyn. She was lost at sea on December 31, 1862. Her wreck was discovered August 27, 1973, and has been partly salvaged.

The White House – Monday, March 3, 1862

I had tea with Mary's sister, Elizabeth Todd Edwards, today. Her constantly being with Mary has been a Godsend. Mother has been as near to madness as is humanly possible. Elizabeth has been worth her weight in gold, because no one else has been able to reach Mother in her grief. Tad continues to improve in appearance and health. We hope that the worst will soon be over for our brave little boy.

Tomorrow I will appear before the Committee on the Conduct of the War to discuss various matters in Kansas, among other issues. General David Hunter, who has served there, will accompany me. Assistant Secretary Fox confirmed that the Monitor has sailed for Hampton Roads to join our fleet there. The Navy fears it could founder when in the ocean in rough seas; its deck is built very low to the water. I am anxious to learn when it arrives safely at its destination.

Author's notes:

General Hunter was a highly controversial officer whose political connections to the president predated his election. When stationed in Fort Leavenworth, Kansas, in 1860, he began correspondence with Lincoln in which he stressed his strong anti-slavery views. He accompanied Lincoln from Springfield to Washington in February of 1861, and after the firing on Fort Sumter, he was appointed the fourth-ranking brigadier general of volunteers. He was wounded at the Battle of Bull Run and in the winter of 1861 was transferred to command the Department of Kansas and in March of 1862 to command the Department of the South and the X Corps.

The White House – Tuesday, March 4, 1862

Today the Senate approved the appointment of Senator Andrew Johnson of Tennessee to become military governor of his state. I can relate to Johnson in the sense that we both are products of extreme poverty in our youth. He became a successful tailor and represented Tennessee in the U.S. Congress for five terms. He served as governor of his state from 1853 to 1857 and was the only sitting Southern senator willing to stand by the Union upon secession; he did not resign his seat. Since then he has received opprobrium from his fellow citizens in return.

Author's notes:

The Republican Party named Johnson, a War Democrat and Southern Unionist, as the vice-presidential running mate to Abraham Lincoln in the 1864 campaign. He took office as president on April 15, 1865, upon the assassination of Abraham Lincoln. In 1868 Johnson was impeached by the House of Representatives, and narrowly missed conviction in the Senate. After leaving office in 1869, he returned to Tennessee. He was elected to the U.S. Senate March 4, 1875 and died in office July 31, 1875. He was the only former president to serve in the Senate. Although some admire his strict constitutionalism, his strong opposition to federally guaranteed rights for African-Americans is widely criticized. He is regarded by many historians as one of the worst American presidents.

The White House – Wednesday, March 5, 1862

We had a tedious cabinet meeting that began at 7 P.M. and lasted until 10:30. The subject: compensated emancipation. At the end, I asked Senator Sumner to join me for breakfast tomorrow to continue our talk on the same controversial subject. The concept is founded upon the principle that the federal government would make money available to the border slave states that have been loyal to the Union. I have calculated the plan would cost an estimated $173 million to compensate the owners for the loss of their slaves. That amount is predicated upon the loss of 432,622 slaves now estimated to be held in those states, at a payment to the owners of $400 per slave. My principle argument has been that this sum of money represents what the national government is currently spending to fund the war every 87 days. My theory is that compensated emancipation will shorten the war by far more than 87 days. Sumner likes my plan, but no Cabinet member shares his enthusiasm.

Author's notes:

Lincoln submitted his plan for compensated compensation to Congress, but no border state ever accepted the proposal or requested the money offered.

The White House – Thursday, March 6, 1862

I attended a funeral service at the home of Secretary Chase for General Frederick Lander, who died of pneumonia in Paw Paw, Virginia, on March 2nd. Lander was a remarkable leader. A graduate of Norwich Military Academy, he was a brilliant engineer and explorer who made five successful transcontinental surveys for the government before the war.

I sent Colonel Lander on a secret mission to meet with Sam Houston, the former U.S. senator who was then serving as the governor of Texas. Houston did not want Texas to leave the Union. I offered Houston 50,000 Union troops to help prevent Texas' secession from the United States. Lander notified me that Houston had graciously declined the offer, saying, "Allow me to most respectfully decline any such assistance of the United States government." Lander mailed me a newspaper article reporting an impromptu speech Houston made after being evicted from his office of governor on March 16, 1861. He was prescient; he warned his fellow Texans that the Confederacy must ultimately be overwhelmed by the more powerful North.

Lander was also a gifted poet. He mailed several of his poems to me, which I admired and shared with Mother. The boys particularly enjoyed it when I read to them his patriotic poem "The Battle of Ball's Bluff," the fight in which Lander had been seriously wounded.

Author's notes:

After leaving the governor's mansion, Houston traveled to Galveston. People along the way demanded an explanation for his refusal to support the Confederacy. On April 19, 1861, from a hotel window, he told a large crowd, "Let me tell you what is coming. After the sacrifice of countless millions of treasure and hundreds of thousands of lives you may win Southern independence if God is not against you, but I doubt it. I tell you that, while I believe with you in the doctrine of states' rights, the North is determined to preserve this Union. They are not a fiery, impulsive people as you are, for they live in colder climates. But when they begin to move in each direction, they move with the steady momentum and perseverance of a mighty avalanche; and what I fear is, they will overwhelm the South."

Frederick William Lander was born December 17, 1821, in Salem, Massachusetts. In 1859, he completed the difficult construction of the Lander Road, which ran from the Wyoming Territory to the Oregon Territory. He was appointed to the rank of brigadier general in May of 1861. He was badly wounded in his last fight, while leading a successful charge at Edwards Ferry during the Battle of Bloomery Gap.

The White House – Friday, March 7, 1862

Today I met with James F.B. Marshall of Massachusetts to discuss the appointment of a U.S. commissioner for Honolulu. He is an experienced businessman who has spent considerable time in the Hawaiian Islands. Because of its appealing climate and friendly citizens, I seem to receive more appeals for this appointment than any other. I have advised Secretary Seward to take Marshall's case in hand, and come back to me with a final recommendation for the post. I have had several especially friendly letters from King Kamehameha IV expressing his support for our war effort. Although his kingdom is "officially" neutral, he tells me that some of his citizens have come to America to fight on the side of the Union, for which I am grateful.

One day perhaps Mother and I may sail to these inviting shores. I have given Tad a book with pictures in it of Honolulu. I know he would be willing to visit the islands tomorrow!

Author's notes:

King Kamehameha IV ruled from January 11, 1855, to November 30, 1863. Upon his death, King Kamehameha V assumed the throne. The monarchy lasted until 1893, when Queen Liluokalani was deposed by a United States government-led coup. On November 23, 1993, the U.S. Congress passed Public Law 103-150, an apology resolution, which was signed by President Bill Clinton on that date.

The White House – Saturday, March 8, 1862

Yesterday I sent to the Senate for its approval treaties that were signed at Paola, Kansas with the united tribes of the Kaskaskia, Peoria, Piankashaw and Wea Indian nations. Whenever I am involved in Indian affairs I cannot help but think back to my own family's unfortunate dealings with Native Americans. My paternal grandfather, Abraham Lincoln, was a pioneer from Virginia who was killed by Indians two years after he settled in Kentucky. He was murdered while laboring to clear forest land for a farm. Abraham had three sons. My father, Thomas, was only 6 years old when his father was slaughtered. His older brother, Mordecai, shot the Indian who had killed his father. Their brother Josiah ran to a nearby fort, and brought armed neighbors who could drive other Indians away, leaving behind one of them dead and one wounded. Thomas kept in touch with Mordecai and Josiah all their lives. My father told me that Mordecai died in Hancock County, Illinois, around 1830, and Josiah in Harrison County, Indiana, in 1835 or 1836. He said that Mordecai died rich and Josiah died poor. My father died January 17, 1851, in Coles County, Illinois.

Author's notes:

On this date, the president summoned General McClellan to the White House to express serious concerns that the capital and government might be at risk if his plans to attack the enemy failed to provide sufficient forces to defend Washington.

The White House – Sunday, March 9, 1862

The press has been particularly critical of me of late. McClellan's lack of initiative does not help matters. Dickens observed back in 1842 that "You no longer set up an idol firmly than you are sure to pull it down and dash it into fragments." He noted that "Any man who attains a high place among you, from the President downward, may date his downfall from that moment." How very true that observation is about American presidents, and very astute, coming from an Englishman, at that! Hay read to me a quotation from Polk, which was written in 1846. "The idea seems to prevail with many persons that the President is from his position compelled to contribute to every loafer who applies." I told Hay that the tug of the hand is much easier to bear than that upon the heartstrings for all manner of favors beyond my power to grant. I get letters daily from every corner of the nation from which our post office still delivers, relating to every possible subject. Many citizens greatly enlarge the powers of the president in their minds, and invoke his interference and protection in all their troubles. It is my policy that every letter deserves an answer.

Yesterday the Confederate ship Merrimac sank the frigate Cumberland, burned the Congress, and made the Minnesota run aground. Earlier the Cabinet had discussed our options should the Merrimac enter Chesapeake Bay and approach Washington via the Potomac. Today, a 4 P.M. dispatch reached the telegraph office, describing the battle fought between the Merrimac and the Monitor, which took place this morning between 8 A.M. and noon in Hampton Roads. The report confirms that the Merrimac withdrew when faced with the Monitor's powerful 11-inch smooth bore Dahlgren cannons. Even more powerful 13-inch guns had been ordered for the ship, but were not ready at the time of launch.

Author's notes:

In the confrontation between the Monitor and Merrimac, neither ship could destroy the other. This was the first battle waged between two armored warships. It marked the turning point in naval warfare. Navies of the world were soon building armored ships to replace their more vulnerable wooden ones. After the Confederates were forced to destroy the Merrimac in early May, Monitor sailed up the James River with four other Union ships to support the Union Army during the Peninsula Campaign. It participated in the Battle of Fort Darling on Drewry's Bluff on May 15. Confederate forces, with the help of a battery salvaged from the guns of the Merrimac, repulsed the Union ships just seven miles from the Confederate capital at Richmond.

The White House – Monday, March 10, 1862

I received at the Telegraph Office details of the March 7 to March 8 battles fought at Pea Ridge in northwest Arkansas. The Union Army of the Southwest under General Samuel Curtis was victorious over the Confederate forces led by General Earl Van Dorn. Estimates are that our forces, numbering over 10,000 men, beat a far larger force, perhaps numbering 16,000 or 17,000 in total. Curtis reports 1,300 casualties and estimates 2,000 or more rebel losses. Our men were primarily soldiers from Iowa, Indiana, Ohio and Illinois with about half of our troops German-Americans, serving under General Franz Sigel. According to Curtis, the Confederates lost many senior officers, which contributed greatly to confusion and loss of control at critical moments in the battle. The battle was waged in bitterly cold weather.

William Vandever's 700-man brigade marched 42 miles in 16 hours from Huntsville to Little Sugar Creek, an amazing achievement considering weather conditions. Vandever was a Republican member of Congress when the war began, serving Iowa's 2nd Congressional District. He was a member of the Peace Conference held in Washington in 1861. He tried to prevent the war and is now doing all he can to end it.

Author's notes:

Historians credit this victory for securing most of Missouri and northern Arkansas for the Union. The Pea Ridge National Military Park was established in 1956. It includes a 2.5-mile section of the Trail of Tears, and is one of the best preserved Civil War battlefields.

Today prints of The Battle of Pea Ridge, Arkansas, by Kurz and Allison, are highly valued by collectors.

After the war, William Vandever resumed the practice of law and was appointed U.S. Indian inspector by President Ulysses Grant in 1873, serving until 1877. He moved to San Buenaventura, California, in 1884 and was elected to represent California's 6th Congressional District in the 50th and 51st Congresses. At the time, the district represented more than half of the area of the state, extending from San Diego County to Mono County. He died in 1893.

The White House – Tuesday, March 11, 1862

Yesterday evening I met with Lieutenant John Lorimer Worden, commander of the USS Monitor, who was almost blinded by a shell during a fierce four-hour naval engagement with the Merrimac in Hampton Roads. He is an incredibly brave officer who not only risked his life in battle, but also took incredible risks just by sailing aboard this highly controversial and experimental ship.

Author's notes:

During his 52-year Navy career, Worden was assigned to the Naval Observatory in Washington, D.C., several times. After the war, he was promoted to commodore and in 1869 began a five-year tour as superintendent of the U.S. Naval Academy. In the 1870s, he commanded the European squadron.

After the battle of the Monitor and Merrimac (called the C.S.S. Virginia by the South), he was presented with a custom-made 37-inch gold and silver inlaid sword made by Tiffany & Company. The handle was emblazoned with the Roman god of the sea, Neptune. In 1912 his family donated it to the Naval Academy, from which it was stolen in 1931. In 1998 the FBI found the weapon, which had been sold illegally to a collector. It was confiscated and was returned to the Naval Academy. Four Navy ships have been named for Worden.

The White House – Wednesday, March 12, 1862

Last night I had a remarkable dream. It is the second time that I have been visited in my sleep by the five presidents who immediately preceded me: Buchanan, Pierce, Fillmore, Taylor and Polk. I may have dreamed of Polk because earlier in the day Nicolay had shown me a quotation from him in which he had said, "No president who performs his duties faithfully can have any leisure." I told Nico that I could not agree more with that sentiment!

In my dream, the five presidents were sitting around the Cabinet table. Each was giving me advice on how I should deal with General McClellan. Old Rough and Ready Taylor was a former general, and as such he was the most outspoken of the assembled former presidents. He agreed that I was right yesterday when I removed McClellan from all commands, except that of the Army of the Potomac. Taylor had said of our government that it was "the most stable and permanent on earth." Ironically, his fellow Virginians are now perhaps the most disloyal of all the Confederates. Pierce (also a former general) told me that McClellan should be fired from the Army for his repeated failures and lack of elan. Polk and Buchanan, who know McClellan, had little to offer in the way of advice.

There are portraits of each of these former commanders-in-chief in the White House. I look at them often. They all had strong fears that a civil war might break out. Not one of them fully realized just how fevered the passions might become on both sides, so as to finally cause the fatal breach. I mentioned the dream to Mother this morning. She takes dreams seriously but had little to say about this one. Her views of McClellan have long been negative.

Author's notes:

On March 11th Lincoln had finally had enough and removed McClellan from command of all Union armies in the field other than the ARMY of the Potomac. He issued War Order No. 3. Effective immediately, Lincoln himself assumed command of all theaters of operation. General Halleck was given command of the Department of the Mississippi and General Fremont command of the Mountain Department.

The White House – Thursday, March 13, 1862

Mother is now on the sick list. She has no fever, but says she feels weak. Tad is now almost feeling like his usual self after his very difficult illness. I handed him a check at breakfast this morning for $5.00; he brightened as he put it in his pocket. He has spoken of wanting to buy a pocket watch, and now he has the money needed to do so. Tad was with me when I gave a short acceptance speech to a delegate from Massachusetts, who kindly presented me with a handsome buggy whip. The one I had brought from Springfield was in pretty bad shape.

I composed a letter for Secretary Stanton to send to McClellan: 1st, leave such force at Manassas Junction, as shall make it entirely certain that the enemy shall not repossess himself of that position.... 2nd Leave Washington secure. 3rd Move remainder of force down the Potomac, choosing a new base at Fortress Monroe... Or at all events, move such remainder of the Army at once in pursuit of the enemy....

Stanton tells me this campaign has every chance of succeeding. I hear what he says, but I remember too many disappointments in the past from General McClellan's promises to believe my ears!

Author's notes:

Lincoln's check was written, "Pay to Tad (when he is well enough to present) or bearer Five Dollars $5.00."

The White House – Friday, March 14, 1862

Mother has warned me that I should not go near any senators tomorrow – for it is the Ides of March. She reminded me of what happened to Julius Caesar on that momentous date when he met with his traitorous Senate. Mother was born superstitious! From the day that we left Springfield she has been fearful of an assassination attempt being made upon me. I've told her repeatedly that although Jefferson Davis is the enemy, he is a man of honor and would never order an assassination as a matter of resolving the differences between us. Davis wants a negotiated peace and has made that abundantly clear in personal messages sent and in public statements made. Mother pointed out to me that in Julius Caesar, Act III, ii that Shakespeare wrote ironically, "For Brutus is an honorable man; so are they all, all honorable men." I'm afraid that Mother will always worry! My dear mother shares the same fear that her son will be murdered while in office.

Author's note:

Abraham Lincoln was an avid reader of Shakespeare. His personal copy of Shakespeare's plays was well-worn, with certain passages marked with messages written in ink. He often quoted his favorite passages. His friend and law partner, William Herndon, wrote that "When young he read the Bible, and when of age he read Shakespeare; but though he often quoted from both, he never read either one through. He read less and thought more than any man of his standing in America."

The White House – March 15, 1862, The Ides of March

Today the subject to be considered was the Capitol's new dome and the costs associated with its construction. Architect Thomas Walter showed me the plans for the work now underway. Senator Foot of Vermont joined us. He is an expert on the subject and kindly filled me in on the dome's history. Many have written to me suggesting that in a time of war, with the high costs associated with the dome's completion, that the work on it should be suspended for the duration of the struggle. I have advised them and the Congress that it is my strong belief that to suspend the work would send the wrong signal to the nation and the world. I advised the Congress today that if people see the Capitol going on, it is a sign we intend the Union shall go on. When inaugurated I looked at the uncompleted dome as I made my remarks and said to myself, if I am re-elected I trust that on the date of my second inauguration that the dome will be completed. Walter expects that the statue, which is planned for the top of the dome, should be in place by December of next year.

Author's notes:

Beginning in 2013, the architect of the Capitol began an enormous restoration of the dome of the U.S. Capitol Building in Washington, D.C. In October of 2016, the restoration was completed, at a cost of $59.5 million. More than a thousand cracks were repaired, interior and exterior decorations scraped, cleaned, restored, and 1,215 gallons of paint used to repaint the exterior.

In the Rotunda visitors will find the marble sculpture of Lincoln by Vinnie Ream, who sketched Lincoln during the last five months of his life. It was dedicated in 1871, while President Grant and other dignitaries looked on. David Davis, Lincoln's lifetime friend, had the honor of officially unveiling it. There is a bust of Lincoln in the Capitol crypt sculpted by Gutzon Borglum of Mt. Rushmore fame. A bronze replica of the bust stands in front of the Lincoln tomb in Springfield, Illinois, where it has greeted millions of visitors.

The White House – Monday, March 17, 1862

Today began with an especially pleasant visit from a delegation of officers and men from the Irish Brigade, led by its commanding officer, Brigadier General Thomas Meagher. He informed me that there are no more loyal men serving in the Union Army than the Irish soldiers. He gave me a brief history of the Irish in America, many of whom are directly related to those who fled Ireland during the horrible potato famine of 1845 to 1849, when over a million of their countrymen perished. Today, March 17th is officially Saint Patrick's Day in Washington. He told me that it was first officially celebrated in New York City in 1766 and in Boston in 1775. The Brigade proudly presented Tad with The Fighting 69th's very colorful flag, which features a large golden harp on a field of green filled with bright green shamrocks.

Later I met with General Frémont to discuss various details of his new Mountain Command, which will include parts of Virginia, Tennessee and Kentucky. I reminded him that I vividly remembered that he was the one who last year recognized in General Grant an iron will, when Grant was under his immediate command at Cairo, Illinois. Grant hasn't disappointed me since.

At the end of the day Secretary Seward came by with railroad builder Cornelius Vanderbilt, who has generously presented his private yacht to the Navy Department to use in coastal services.

Author's notes:

Meagher was born in Waterford, Ireland, in 1823. He was an Irish revolutionary who was a leader of the Young Irelanders in the Revolution of 1848. Convicted of sedition by Great Britain, he was an escapee from Tasmania, became an influential speaker in America and a Union general in the Civil War. The Irish Brigade fought bravely in the First Battle of Bull Run, Antietam, Fredericksburg, Gettysburg and Spotsylvania, with significant casualties in every conflict. After the war Meagher was appointed acting governor of the Territory of Montana. On July 1, 1867, Thomas Francis Meagher mysteriously fell, jumped or was pushed off a steamboat on the Missouri River and was presumed dead. His body was never recovered.

The White House – Tuesday, March 18, 1862

Today I met with Wendell Phillips at the suggestion of Secretary Seward, who has known him for years, as has Senator Sumner, who joined us for an hour discussion. Phillips is an attorney and a Harvard Law School graduate. He is perhaps the most prominent Abolitionist in the nation, and has been an active member of the Anti-Slavery Society since it was founded. He befriended John Brown, and before hostilities broke out he had favored disunion for decades. He proposed to me that if I were to free the slaves by executive proclamation that I should simultaneously call for an amendment to the Constitution, which would guarantee voting rights to the freedmen. His argument is that without the right to vote, freedmen will inevitably be ground into powder by white Southerners, who will very likely again be in power in all the states of the Confederacy after this war is won. I thanked him for the clarity of his reasoning and asked that he correspond with me from time to time about reconstruction and the rights of freedmen.

Author's notes:

Under President Grant, the 15th Amendment was ratified on March 30, 1870. It reads, Section I. "The right of citizens of the United States to vote shall not be denied or abridged by the United States or by any State on account of race, color, or previous condition of servitude."

Section II. "The Congress shall have power to enforce article by appropriate legislation."

The White House – Wednesday, March 19, 1862

Several reports have been received today of an important Union victory, which was achieved on March 14th near the small city of New Bern, North Carolina. A captured Confederate officer informed General Ambrose Burnside that only six regiments of troops had been assigned to defend the entire coast of the state, with most of North Carolina's troops assigned to the defense of Richmond, Virginia. Many of the troops our forces were engaged with were poorly armed with shotguns and hunting rifles. In this operation, The Coast Division of the North Atlantic Blocking Squadron provided 14 gunboats to support over 11,000 Union troops. Their cannon fire discouraged the rebel forces, who were soon in retreat. New Bern will soon be under our complete control. The city is small but important because the Atlantic and North Carolina Railroad stationed there connects this coastal city to the interior of the state. Holding New Bern helps deny the enemy access from the sea of military material.

Author's notes:

New Bern remained under the control of the Union Army throughout the Civil War. After this victory, Burnside concentrated his forces on gaining control of the ports of Beaufort and Morehead City, North Carolina, which were defended by Fort Macon. The casemated masonry fort surrendered to Union troops after bombardment following a siege that lasted from March 23 to April 26, 1862. The Confederates did not defend Morehead City, which was soon occupied by Union forces

The White House – Thursday, March 20, 1862

Mother provided me with her translation of a poem by Pierre de Ronsard, who lived from 1524 to 1585. She reads Ronsard in the original French and then kindly writes out the poetry for me to read in English. Her depressed state of late has been slowly easing, and I believe the poems of Ronsard have given her a certain comfort. These are the touching lines that she gave me at breakfast this morning:

> "…and when the evening darkens mortal eyes
> Seeking what's to come, I scan the skies
> Where God inscribes, in letters plain to see,
> Of all who live, the changing destiny.
> For He, discerning humankind astray,
> Sometimes moved by pity, shows the way:
> By Heaven's stars, which are His alphabet,
> Foretells what good may rise, what evil set:
> But men, by death and earthly error gripped,
> Disdain the message and ignore the script."

Author's notes:

Pierre de Ronsard was educated at the Collège de Navarre in Paris. He served as a page to the Duke of Orléans and to James V, the King of Scotland. After nearly losing all of his hearing in 1541, he studied Greek at the Collège de Coqueret with the renowned scholar Daurat. He became the official poet of King Charles IX's court and led a generation of poets known first as the Brigade, and later as Le Pléiade, who endeavored to bring the values of humanism to French verse. He used a variety of forms and meters to explore themes of romantic love and portraits of royal life. His collections of poetry include Odes (1550), Les Amours (1552), Le Bocage (15544) and La Franciade (1572).

Mary Lincoln attended Shelby Female Academy (also called Wards), where she was a model student who was fluent in French. She entered the school in 1827 and graduated in 1832 at the age of 14. Tuition was $44 a year. French was an additional $8. When the family moved into an elegant 14-room house, Mary entered Madame Mentelle's School for Young Women to continue her education. Tuition increased to $120 a year. She boarded during the week and came home weekends. The school was run by Madame Mentelle, a 62-year-old, well-traveled French woman, and her husband. She thrived at the school and acted in French plays. It was here that she was introduced to the poetry of Ronsard.

The White House – Friday, March 21, 1862

Mother, who has been confined to her room since Willie's death, is almost back to her usual self. Today she was well enough to receive a visit by General Irvin McDowell's wife, Helen. This is a first for Mother and a very good sign. She tells me that she would like to enjoy the company of more friends in the weeks to come. Hallelujah! I spent several hours in conversation with General McDowell while Mary and Helen were together. A seasoned West Point graduate, the general comes highly recommended by Secretary Chase.

At 3 o'clock I visited the Navy Yard with Commander Dahlgren, where we departed by ship to visit General McClellan at his headquarters in Alexandria. Upon my return, I met at the White House with Secretaries Stanton, Welles and Assistant Navy Secretary Gustavus Fox to discuss planned movements of Army of the Potomac forces.

Author's notes:

When Presidential War Order No. 2 was issued on March 8, the reorganization of the Army of the Potomac under General McClellan included the creation of four Army corps under Generals Irvin McDowell, Samuel P. Heintzelman, Erasmus D. Keyes and Edwin V. Sumner. On March 14 McDowell was named major general of U.S. volunteers.

63

The White House – Sunday, March 23, 1862

Today I had an informative meeting with Carl Schurz, our minister to Spain, who asked me to accept his resignation. No one in our government has his command of events now taking place overseas. He gave me excellent insights into America's standing in the various courts of Europe. I accepted his resignation while thanking him for having successfully encouraged the Spanish court to remain neutral, and to not recognize the Confederacy. Schurz wishes to serve his country in the war effort as a military officer and no longer continue in the diplomatic corps. I will bring to the Senate his immediate nomination to serve as a brigadier general.

Author's Notes:

Schurz had been a revolutionary in Germany before coming to America. He fought in the Civil War with distinction, and after hostilities was elected U.S. senator from Missouri in 1868, becoming the first German-American to be elected to that body. He is famous for the saying "My country right or wrong." His wife, Margarethe, established the first kindergarten system in the United States. Schurz was appointed secretary of the interior by President Rutherford Hayes in 1891.

The White House – Monday, March 24, 1862

Representative Schuyler Colfax, Jr., of Indiana told me today that Horace Greeley will support gradual, compensated emancipation in his newspaper. I wrote to the famous editor that I am grateful for the generous sentiments expressed by him in his newspaper, but cautioned that I am uneasy about abolishing slavery in the District of Columbia, as to the time and manner of doing so. I prefer a bill from the Congress, which would have three main features: gradual, compensated and by the vote of the people.

I reminded Colfax that I had introduced emancipation legislation into the second session of the 30th Congress. It called for the freeing of slaves in D.C. It was an amendment to a resolution instructing the Committee on the District of Columbia to report a bill abolishing slavery there. That was January 10, 1849! It found a lodgment "on the table" and was carefully laid to rest by a vote of the House.

Author's notes:

Schuyler Colfax, Jr., was a journalist, businessman and politician who was a founder of the Republican Party. He served in the House of Representatives from 1855 to 1869. He was speaker of the House from 1863 to 1869. He served as President Ulysses S. Grant's vice president from 1869 to 1873. To date he is one of only two Americans (John Nance Garner is the other) to have been both house speaker and vice president.

The White House – Tuesday, March 25, 1862

At the telegraph office last evening, I read several messages announcing a Union victory in Kernstown, Virginia, which took place on the 23rd. Our forces defeated troops under the command of Confederate General Jackson, whose soldiers call him "Stonewall." I am told by General McClellan that Jackson is considered by General Lee to be his most trusted and accomplished lieutenant. According to General Kimball, we suffered about 500 casualties. Kimball estimates that his forces outnumbered those of Jackson by two to one.

At lunch today, Vice-President Hamlin asked me to appoint his nephew to a captaincy, which I gladly acceded to. He has two sons who are already serving as generals in the army. Hannibal has been very loyal and helpful to me in many ways. He is not a member of the Cabinet but is a seasoned politician who gives me excellent and unvarnished advice when I ask for it. He strongly favors an Emancipation Proclamation and believes strongly that if I issue one it will shorten the war. He also favors the enlistment of Negro soldiers.

I sent to Secretary Stanton an order to suspend the death sentence for breach of parole that an Army court martial passed upon Colonel Ebenezer Magoffin. The Confederate officer was found to have violated the terms of his parole while on duty in Missouri, and to have killed a Union soldier. Magoffin is the brother of the governor of Kentucky, Beria Magoffin, who last May affirmed his state's neutrality. For myriad reasons, I believe shooting Colonel Magoffin may be militarily correct, but politically unwise. We need states like Kentucky to stay in the Union.

Author's notes:

Lincoln considered Vice President Hamlin a member of the legislative branch due to his constitutional role as presiding officer of the Senate, and therefore did not include him in his Cabinet meetings. Hamlin was said to have regarded himself as the "fifth wheel" on a wagon. He had a remarkable political career spanning more than three decades. He was a member of the House of Representatives from 1843 to 1847, U.S. senator from 1848 to 1857, governor of Maine from January 8 to February 25, 1857, vice president from 1861 to 1865, collector of customs for Boston 1865 to 1866, senator from Maine 1869 to 1881, U.S. minister to Spain 1881 to 1882. He retired to his home in Bangor, Maine. The Hannibal Hamlin House was posted on the National Register of Historic Places in 1979.

The White House – Wednesday, March 26, 1862

I happened to mention to Commander Dahlgren that I have been keeping a diary. I told him that one reason I do so, aside from memorializing my thoughts and decisions, is that I find it easier to act decisively once I put something down on paper. Many times I have found that the rationale that governed my reasoning was often less compelling when I reread my notes. As a practicing lawyer, I found that I was far better in court after I'd made extensive notes than when I went before the judge and jury with little to refer to before I opened my mouth. Dahlgren confessed that he too has been keeping a diary. Unlike me, he began the practice several years before the war began. He said he does so now, in part, for him to have an accurate record of his thinking on the most important decisions that he makes related to naval matters.

We also discussed plans now being developed for the taking of New Orleans this April by our naval and military forces working in close coordination. I told Dahlgren that my aversion to slavery has been with me most of my life. It was reinforced by a trip to that city in March of 1828 with Allen Gentry. We took a boat owned by his father, James, who had entrusted us with a cargo of grain and meat. My pay was eight dollars a month and board. There I saw for the first time the slave markets and their vile and inhuman treatment of enslaved men, women and children. Three years later I made the same trip with my first cousin, John Hanks,,, in the employ of Denton Offutt. We were on a less substantial flatboat, moving past Alton, St. Louis, Cairo, Memphis, Vicksburg and Natchez before reaching New Orleans in May, where we spent a month in the city. It was there that I again observed the true horrors of slavery.

Author's notes:

William Herndon, in the "Life of Lincoln," wrote, "He saw negroes in chains – whipped and scourged. Against this inhumanity his sense of right and justice rebelled, and his mind and conscience were awakened to a realization of what he had often heard and read. One of his companions has said, 'Slavery ran the iron into him then and there.'" The whole scene was so revolting that Lincoln moved away with a deep feeling of unconquerable hate. Bidding his companions follow him, he said, 'By God, boys, let's get away from this. If I ever get a chance to hit that thing (meaning slavery) I'll hit it hard.' This incident had been furnished to me in 1865 by John Hanks, and I have also heard Lincoln refer to it himself."

The White House – Friday, March 28, 1862

Yesterday I pardoned two British subjects who had already served three years of a seven-year sentence in the D.C. jail for resisting the master of an American vessel in Florida waters. I did so, in part, because I felt their sentences were unusually harsh since no one had been injured in the incident that caused their arrests. I also did so because I am anxious to maintain the best relations possible with Great Britain. Lord Russell, England's very competent minister to the United States, has raised this matter with Seward and with me on several occasions. At this critical time in the war we need to do all we can to keep Britain neutral. We cannot afford to have it recognize the Confederacy. Freeing two English sailors is a small price to pay for improving our relations with Great Britain.

Author's notes:

During his time in office, President Lincoln pardoned 343 individuals, including 264 of 303 Dakota Indians who were charged with attacking settlers during the Great Sioux Uprising at the end of 1862. Two-term Ohio Congressman Clement Vallandigham was the most famous person that he pardoned. After the notorious Vallandigham was convicted of disloyalty and opposition to the war in 1863 by a military court martial, his sentence was commuted by Lincoln, and he was deported to the Confederacy.

President Andrew Johnson granted full and unconditional pardons and amnesty to over 6,50l former Confederates on December 25, 1868. He pardoned Jefferson Davis, former president of the Confederates State of America, and Dr. Samuel Mudd, who had been charged with conspiring to murder President Lincoln. Mudd was released from federal prison in 1869.

President Ulysses Grant pardoned 1,332 people, and all but 500 of the top Confederate leaders as part of the Amnesty Act of 1872.

The White House – Saturday, March 29, 1862

Friday afternoon our new minister to Russia Simon Cameron, stopped by for a farewell chat with me and Secretary Seward. I offered to place a Navy frigate at his disposal for the long trip to the court at St. Petersburg, but he prefers to go by commercial ship, and to do so without fuss. Cameron was not a successful secretary of war, but he may still be of service to his nation in his new role of diplomat. I have received several letters from Tsar Alexander II. He has been sympathetic to our efforts to preserve the Union, and has shown no interest in recognizing the Confederacy. Alexander has a very competent gentleman, Eduard de Stoecki, representing him in America. Two years ago, during the Buchanan administration, Stoecki met with American officials and raised the possibility of the sale of the Russian colony in North America. Congressmen from California and Oregon have long felt that the United States should acquire Alaska. According to Stoecki, Alexander understands that once our war is over, the question of future U.S. acquisition of Alaska should again be considered. I will be pleased to hear more on this subject once Cameron is firmly established at the Russian court.

Author's notes:

Five years later, on March 30, 1867, the United States Senate ratified a treaty signed by President Andrew Johnson to acquire Alaska. The agreement added 586,412 square miles to the U.S. Some called the deal "Seward's Folly." Originally organized as the Department of Alaska (1867 – 1884), the area was renamed the District of Alaska (1884 – 1912), and the Territory of Alaska (1912 – 1959), before becoming the modern state of Alaska in 1959. The purchase price was $7.2 million.

The White House – Sunday, March 30, 1862

Saturday, I wrote a short note to Secretary Stanton, reminding him that I want Jesse W. Fell to be named a paymaster of the regular Army as early as July 1, 1862. This is the second time I've brought this matter to Stanton's attention. I added to my note the postscript, "I want nothing to interfere with this." Maybe that may get the secretary's attention. Stanton is efficient, and I am certain I will not need to write him a third time on the subject.

Early this evening, General McClellan stopped by to visit preparatory to his sailing down the Potomac to begin the Army's campaign to take Richmond.

Author's notes:

Jesse W. Fell (1808 – 1887), one of the founders of the Republican Party in Illinois, is the person who suggested to Lincoln that he challenge Stephen A. Douglas to debate in 1854. Lincoln maintained that Judge Douglas would not cooperate in such a scheme. Fell persisted in their having a joint debate and continued to agitate for it until four years later, when it occurred in the contest for U.S. senator from Illinois. Fell had met Lincoln in 1834 while Fell was still engaged in the practice of law. He was a remarkable man whose career included law, business, journalism, real estate, planter, trader, university founder (Illinois State Normal University) and developer with railroad connections. He was strongly anti-slavery.

The White House – Monday, March 31, 1862

We have learned that between March 26 to March 28, Union forces in New Mexico Territory fought a battle with Confederate troops at a place called Glorieta Pass. The rebels were under the command of Brigadier General Henry Sibley, who had captured Sante Fe and Albuquerque before this event took place. Sibley's men were met by Colorado infantry and U.S. Cavalry forces posted in Apache Canyon. The report indicates that when a detachment of our infantry burned their supply train, the enemy were forced to retreat.

Later in the day I transmitted to the Senate a treaty of commerce and navigation with the Ottoman Empire.

I wrote to McClellan advising him that I felt constrained to transfer Blenker's Division to Frémont. I noted that I did so with great pain, understanding that he would wish it otherwise.

Author's notes:

Glorieta Pass is commonly referred to as the "Gettysburg of the West." It was here that federal forces were finally able to turn back the Confederate invasion of New Mexico Territory. 2,640 soldiers were engaged (Union 1,300, Confederate 1,340). Casualties: 147 Union, 222 Confederate. The Glorieta Pass Battlefield is managed by the Pecos National Historical Park. Of roughly 10,500 actions of the Civil War, 384 were identified by the Civil War Advisory Commission in 1993 as principal battles and rated according to their significance and threat of loss. The Battle of Glorieta Pass received the highest rating, Priority I (Class A). It was placed on the same level as battles such as Gettysburg and Antietam, but also as one of the most highly endangered battlefields on the nation. Only 10 other battlefields received Priority I (Class A) rating. It is designated as a National Historic Landmark and recommended for preservation.

The White House – Tuesday, April 1, 1862

When I visited the telegraph office this evening, the men handed me a wire from Richmond, Virginia, dated April 1. It read, "Because the Confederate States of America cannot resist the overwhelming arms of the Union forces approaching Richmond, I hereby agree to enter into an agreement to surrender all of our forces unconditionally. Jefferson Davis. President, CSA." After I read it they all broke into unconstrained laughter at their joke. They had remembered, and I had forgotten, that today is the First of April or All Fools Day, which they felt obligated to acknowledge with their startling message. Oh but that it might have been true. One day for certain such a message must be received, and the South must sooner or later realize its fate is sealed.

Later in the day Commander Dahlgren, Ninian Edwards and Tad joined me in a sail to Alexandria to see General McClellan, who plans to leave tomorrow for Old Point Comfort at the Peninsula to join his troops. Tomorrow I intend to return by boat to Mount Vernon with Mother and Tad.

Author's notes:

Ninian Edwards was married to Elizabeth Todd Edwards, Mary Lincoln's older sister. Edwards was the son of Illinois' first governor. He was a prominent attorney who served as a state representative, senator and superintendent of Education. Lincoln and Edwards served in the legislature together. Abraham Lincoln and Mary Todd were married at the Edward's mansion in Springfield, Illinois, on November 4, 1842. They had originally planned to wed on January 1, 1841, but Lincoln failed to show up. William Herndon wrote of the January event, "The wedding supper was untouched, the guests quietly and wondering withdrew and darkness settled over all for the night. What the feelings of a lady as sensitive, passionate, and proud as Miss Todd were, we can only imagine – no one can ever describe them."

During the Civil War, Edwards frequently asked Lincoln for a patronage appointment, which became controversial when the propriety of some of Edwards' financial dealings as a commissary of subsistence was questioned.

Elizabeth Edwards rescued Mary Lincoln from an insane asylum in 1875, and gave her a home in Springfield, Illinoi,s where Mary died on July 16, 1882.

The White House – Wednesday, April 2, 1862

I just penned a thank you letter to Mr. Michael Crock of Philadelphia, who kindly sent Tad a present of several beautiful white rabbits. They arrived just in time for his birthday, which will be celebrated on Friday of this week. Tad will be 9 years old. Every day he seems to get stronger and stronger, which is a blessing to his mother, who is constantly worrying.

Assistant Secretary Fox introduced me to John Ericsson, the engineer who designed and helped build the U.S.S. Monitor. This Swedish-American genius is regarded as the world's foremost naval engineer and inventor. Before the Monitor, Ericsson worked on the U.S.S. Princeton, the Navy's first screw-propelled steam frigate. Without the Monitor, our obsolete wooden naval vessels would have been destroyed by the once-formidable Confederate ironclad vessel, the C.S.S. Virginia, or as commonly called, the C.S.S. Merrimack.

Author's notes:

John Ericsson designed other naval vessels and weapons, including a torpedo, and destroyer, a torpedo boat that could fire cannon from an underwater port. He designed "sun engines," which collected solar heat for hot air engines. He is regarded as the finest naval engineer in America in the 19th century. The John Ericsson National Memorial is on the Mall in Washington, D.C. The U.S.S. Ericsson is named for him. A 1926 U.S. postage stamp was issued in his honor, and his statue is in Battery Park, New York.

The White House – Friday, April 4, 1862

Orders were issued to Secretary Stanton by me yesterday directing that either the troops of General McDowell or those of General Sumner are to be stationed in front of Washington in the absence of the Army of the Potomac. They are to remain until further notice. General McClellan is therefore required to move forward from his present base against the foe without their numbers.

Today I spent considerable time with the Commission on the Conduct of the War, which is made up of Senators Wade of Ohio, Zachariah Chandler of Michigan, Andrew Johnson of Tennessee and Joseph A. Wright of Indiana. The Senate members were all appointed by Vice-President Hannibal Hamlin. House members George Julian of Indiana, John Covode of Pennsylvania, Daniel Gooch of Massachusetts and Moses Odell of New York were appointed by Speaker of the House Galusha Grow. The Commission is authorized to take testimony from witnesses, mostly Union officers. My fear is that it may act like a board of inquiry when defeats occur, as they surely will. Wade is their chairman.

Author's notes:

The Commission was active for over a year before it issued its first report in 1863. The committees are considered by historians to be among the harshest congressional investigating committees in U.S. history. They conducted inquiries until May 1865. Senator Harry S. Truman cited their style as an example he did not wish to follow in leading the Truman Committee, which investigated military appropriations during World War II. Truman refused to second guess war strategy. His committee succeeded in finding government waste and inefficiency in order to aid the war effort. His reputation for even-handed treatment of those called to testify influenced his being named President Roosevelt's running mate in 1943.

The White House – Saturday, April 5, 1862

Today I informed Senators Browning and Sumner that I am willing to sign a bill abolishing slavery within the District of Columbia. I have long favored this move. In January of 1849, while serving in the House of Representatives, I introduced a measure to achieve that end. Unfortunately, the timing was not propitious, and the bill went nowhere. My early legislation provided for compensation from the federal treasury to be paid to the slave owner for the slave's freedom.

Author's notes:

The District of Columbia Compensated Emancipation Act, or the Compensated Emancipation Act, ended slavery within the District of Columbia by paying slave owners for releasing their slaves. Lincoln signed it on April 16, 1862, and in the city it is officially known as Emancipation Day. The bill passed the Senate by a vote of 29 to 14. Following passage of the act, Lincoln proposed several changes to it, which were approved by the legislature. The act, which provided $1,000,000, gave Union slave owners up to $300 for each freed slave. An additional $100,000 was allocated to pay for each freed slave if he or she chose to leave the United States and colonize in such places as Haiti or Liberia. Beginning April 16, 2005, Emancipation Day was celebrated as an official holiday in Washington, D.C. This act was the only compensated emancipation plan enacted in the United States. 3,185 slaves were freed by the act.

The White House – Sunday, April 6, 1862

After discussing the Army of the Potomac's slow progress to date, I sent a telegram to General McClellan which reads, "I think you better break the enemy's line from Yorktown to Warwick River, at once." Reports from the area, given to me by Commander Dahlgren and Secretary Stanton, are not encouraging. It was on this very spot that Washington, aided by the French, achieved final victory over the British during the Revolution. It is my view that the Union can only win this war if it conducts aggressive action on more than one front at a time. Now that our forces in the west are pressing enemy forces at Pittsburg Landing, it is doubly important that our Eastern armies do likewise. McClellan never seems to get the message, or if he does, it must go in one ear and out the other rather quickly!

Author's notes:

On this date in Tennessee, the Battle of Pittsburg Landing, or Shiloh, began when Grant, with reinforcements from Buell, repulsed the forces of Generals Albert Sidney Johnson and P.G.T. Beauregard. The victory would go to the Union, but the North lost more men than the South.

The Siege of Yorktown by McClellan continued from April 5 to May 4. It was an inconclusive engagement, but most military historians generally consider it a Union win. McClellan had landed over 121,000 troops who were transported by 389 vessels. Fifteen batteries of over 70 heavy guns could fire 7,000 pounds of ordnance into enemy positions with each volley. When the Confederates finally deserted their positions and retreated toward Richmond, McClellan learned that he had outnumbered his enemy by more than two to one.

The White House – Wednesday, April 9, 1862

A major battle has been fought and won at Shiloh Church, located near Pittsburg Landing, which is located near the border of Mississippi, Alabama and southwestern Tennessee. Our Western troops under Generals Grant and Buell triumphed over those of General Albert Sidney Johnston and P.G.T. Beauregard. Johnston, who was highly regarded by General Scott both personally and professionally, was killed in the fray. I am told that he will be a major loss to the Confederacy. When the final count is tallied, I've been informed that our side had casualties more than 13,000 and the South 10,000.

Author's notes:

Northern forces at Pittsburg Landing were better armed and outnumbered their enemy 63,000 to 40,335. The Battle of Shiloh was the bloodiest in American history up to that time. It was exceeded in September of 1862 by the Battle of Antietam, then the following year by the Battle of Chancellorsville and later at Gettysburg, which would turn out to be the bloodiest of all battles in the war.

Mary Todd Lincoln was informed on April 10th that her half-brother, Samuel B. Todd, was mortally wounded in heavy fighting while serving with Confederate troops at Shiloh during what was a ferocious struggle on both sides.

The White House – Thursday, April 10, 1862

Again, the vexing matter of Confederate Colonel Magoffin presents itself to me. He is being held in Alton and reports are that he is very ill. I have directed General Halleck that if the rigor of confinement threatens his life, it is to be mitigated and at once. I want the man to live so that our already strained relations with Kentucky are not further damaged.

Today was spent in bed. I have been feeling poorly and felt a day's rest was not an unreasonable idea. Mother fed me beef tea, which seems to be the best medicine in the world. Senator Browning and I discussed the treaty with Britain, which I am transmitting to the Senate tomorrow. It will continue to suppress the slave trade, and more importantly it will improve our relations with England. There is strong sympathy in England for the Southern cause due to its production of cotton, but few in England can abide the slavery that grows it.

I also signed a Proclamation of Thanksgiving for recent victories by our land and sea forces. In Missouri, we have learned that General Pope has achieved a decisive victory at the battle for Island No. 10 on the Mississippi, which began on February 28. This win and the triumph of our arms at Shiloh have reassured the nation that we are finally moving in the right direction. If only our Army of the Potomac could emulate its western cousins in this regard.

Author's notes:

The Battle or Siege of Island Number 10 involved 23,000 Union troops, six gunboats and eleven mortar rafts. The Confederate forces numbered 7,000 troops, who surrendered. Brigadier John Pope commanded the Army of the Mississippi forces, and Flag Officer Andrew H. Foote commanded the Western Gunboat Flotilla. Rebel forces were led by Major General John P. McCown, who was replaced by Brigadier General William W. Mackall on March 31. The battle began on February 28 and the siege started on March 15. The battle ended on April 8.

The White House – Friday, April 11, 1862

Reports now confirm the magnitude of the fierce battle fought at Pittsburg Landing, or Shiloh, on April 6 and April 7. We were surprised by the enemy on the first day, and it was indeed a very close call for our side. Then on the second day, troops of General Grant, reinforced by those of General Buell required the Confederates to retreat as our superiority in numbers decided the issue. Grant has telegraphed estimates of approximately 65,000 men on our side to 45,000 on the enemy's. Our casualties totaled about 13,000 to an estimated 10,000 for the Confederates, with both sides losing over 1,700 killed. The newspapers will bring strong public disapproval once the number of dead and wounded is reported.

Ironically, I was told by Hay that the word Shiloh in Hebrew means "Place of Peace."

Hay brought me 10 court martial rulings, each one calling for the death penalty. I reviewed each one quickly, and in every case, wrote in red ink, "Not to be shot until further orders." Last month after doing this, a father of a sentenced soldier from Ohio wrote to me asking if it wasn't possible that his boy "Might still be ordered to be shot." I informed the concerned father that "If your son never looks on death until further orders come from me to shoot him, he will live to be a great deal older than Methuselah." Sadly, too many officers are quick to order a man shot. My wish is to grant clemency except in unusual circumstances, like rape or deserting and going over to the enemy. Those accused of sleeping on watch I always pardon. That is because I remember when I once did that myself. It was 30 years ago during my brief service in the Black Hawk War. It is easy for a man who is dog-tired from marching all day, or fighting, to fall asleep when he should be wide awake.

Author's notes:

On this day, as on the previous day, Lincoln spent much of his time in bed. He was still feeling out of sorts. But despite his desire to rest, he forced himself to meet with Assistant Secretary Fox, Postmaster Blair and Lieutenant Wise for two hours starting at 7 P.M. to discuss matters related to the lack of progress of the Army of the Potomac.

Lincoln received many letters calling for the removal of Grant following the Battle of Shiloh. Grant was accused of being drunk during the battle, a charge that had long followed him during his military career. To those who wrote to him or spoke to him urging Grant's removal, Lincoln rejected the criticism of the general, and usually replied, "I cannot spare this man; he fights."

The White House – Sunday, April 13, 1862

Twelve delegates from the Freedman's Association spent a fruitful hour with me and Secretary Stanton. They described the important need for federal relief for Negro slaves who are living on abandoned rice plantations in the Port Royal area of South Carolina. These people are the descendants of slaves who were brought to America from the west coast of Africa. Their ancestors had grown rice in Africa, and their children and grandchildren have been growing rice here for generations. The slaves' masters deserted their plantations when Union forces recently occupied the Beaufort Sea Islands area. Some of them have asked to join the Union Army. I have asked Stanton to see that these people are helped in this hour of need. The Freedman's Society members say that Quaker missionaries from Pennsylvania plan to provide schooling for these industrious people, who have never been to a school one day in their entire lives.

Author's notes:

The African-American slaves in the Beaufort area and others residing in the Low Country of South Carolina and Georgia are called the Gullah. They have preserved more of their African linguistic and cultural heritage than any other former slave community in the United States. They speak an English-based Creole language containing many African loanwords and significant influences from African languages in grammar and sentence structure. Gullah storytelling, cuisine, music, folk and religious beliefs, crafts and farming techniques all show strong influences from West African cultures. Most of their ancestors were brought to the ports of Charleston and Savannah as slaves. Half of all slaves brought to America came through Charleston. At the time of the Civil War, South Carolina and Georgia were covered by thousands of acres of rice fields. When federal troops occupied the Beaufort area, they found the Gullah people eager for freedom, and willing to defend it. Many Gullahs served with distinction in the Union Army's First South Carolina Volunteers. This was the first place in the South where slaves were freed. Penn Center on St. Helena Island began as the first school for freed slaves.

The White House – Monday, April 14, 1862

My longtime friend Representative Dan Voorhees of Indiana stopped by for a friendly chat. A Democrat who believes in the importance of maintaining an agrarian society, Dan is the most generous person I guess I've ever known. We were discussing Shiloh and the dreadful butcher's bill for that horrific conflict. Many from his state fell in the battle. I asked him if he didn't think it queer that I, who couldn't cut the head off a chicken, and who is always sick at the sight of blood, should be cast into the middle of a great war, with blood flowing all about me? One thing I admire about Dan, he never takes advantage of our friendship and thus never asks for an appointment for a friend or constituent, or has an Indiana colonel in mind who ought to be named a brigadier general. That is a sign of true friendship.

Author's notes:

The Cabinet held a special meeting to consider establishing military government over islands along the South Carolina coast. Later Lincoln interviewed two paroled Confederate prisoners.

The White House – Tuesday, April 15, 1862

The telegraph ticked out marvelous news this morning of a significant Union victory at a battle fought at Fort Pulaski, located on Cockspur Island off Savannah, Georgia. It occurred on the 10th and 11th of this month. I'm told that the siege of Fort Pulaski had been conducted by our forces for 112 days. Stanton tells me that this fort was worked on by Robert E. Lee when he was a young engineering officer. Apparently, the fort was most recently within his current area of command responsibility. Our naval units were under Flag Officer Samuel DuPont, with the Army acting under Gen. David Hunter. DuPont had 15 warships on-site and 36 transports to move over 10,000 Union troops. According to the Navy Department, a 30-hour bombardment of the fort by our ships' Parrott Rifle cannons, armed with percussion shells, destroyed the 7 1/2 –foot brick walls of a fort previously believed to be impervious to naval gunfire. Our new and more powerful weapons are making Confederate Southern coastal forts obsolete. This operation has effectively closed Savannah as a port for receiving important war materiel from overseas.

Author's notes:

Mary Boykin Chestnut kept a diary during the Civil War. Her husband served as a Confederate general in the struggle. Her entry for April 14, 1862, reads, "The enemy has flanked Beauregard at Nashville. There is grief enough for Albert Sidney Johnston now: we begin to see what we have lost. We were pushing them into the River when General Johnston was mortally wounded. Beauregard was lying in his tent, at the rear, in a green sickness – melancholy – but no matter what the name of the malady. He was too slow to move, and lost all advantage gained by our dead hero. Without him there is no head to our Western army. Pulaski has fallen. What more is to fall?"

The White House – Wednesday, April 16, 1862

Today I visited a recently opened Army field hospital in Washington. I make it a point to always speak to and shake the hands of hospitalized Confederate soldiers. My view is that they are young American boys who have found themselves in a situation way beyond their control. My hope is that when the fighting finally ends that these young men will return to the Union and again submit to our laws. I will want no one punished, but only wish to see them treated liberally all around, with friendship that eventually leads to trust. Once they surrender, if we treat them with respect and decency, then when they reach their homes and farms, they should have no reason to ever again take up arms.

In the evening, I met with Assistant Secretary of the Navy Fox to again go over the Navy's plans for the capture of New Orleans, the South's largest city and a vital hub of commerce. It is also the site of the few important shipyards available to the Confederacy.

Author's notes:

On this date, the president signed "an act for the release of certain persons held to service, or labor in the District of Columbia," and for the appointment of a board of commissioners to appraise slaves of loyal citizens and allow payment not exceeding an average of $300. Lincoln named J.G. Berret, former mayor of Washington, former Congressman Samuel F. Vinton (Ohio), and Daniel R. Goodloe, formerly of North Carolina, as commissioners to act for the abolition of slavery in the District of Columbia.

The White House – Thursday, April 17, 1862

This was Foreign Relations Day for me. First, I recognized C.F. Adac as Consul of Saxe-Altenburg to be stationed in Cincinnati. I then sent to the Senate for passage a resolution extending time for the ratification of an extradition treaty with Mexico. Later Hay gave me a document to sign transmitting to the Senate a treaty with Nicaragua as approved June 1860, with amendments included as proposed by the Congress of Nicaragua. Most American citizens are unaware of the fact that, although we have a civil war to fight, there are numerous and important duties of state that we are required to perform dealing with the rest of the world. In every instance, our obligation is to keep our relationships with foreign countries as amicable as possible. This is particularly important when treating with Great Britain and France, two nations that are thankfully well-represented in this country by reliable ministers.

Tad asked me about my salary at dinner. I told him that an honest laborer digs coal at about 70 cents a day, while the president digs abstractions at about $70 a day. Coal is clearly worth far more than the abstractions, and yet what a monstrous inequality in the wages. I had given him a check for $5 on his birthday, the 4th of April. He showed me a very fine little knife that he purchased with his money. He said that because he has been a very good boy that perhaps he is entitled to a raise. I told him I would take it under advisement. It is what I tell my Cabinet members every day!

Author's notes:

On this date, the president used his March salary warrant of $ 2,083.33 to purchase 1861 treasury notes. Two days earlier the president had sent to the Senate a treaty with the Sac and Fox Tribes of the Missouri, and the Iowa Tribes of Indians.

The White House – Friday, April 18, 1862

The ancient adage is that April showers bring May flowers. The downpours have been particularly heavy of late and worrying to me. Heavy rains are never good for an Army on the move, particularly an army strongly committed to the use of heavy cannons and mortars for possible siege operations. Men and horses suffer alike when roads are turned into mud. The plight of Napoleon's army in Russia teaches that generals must heed weather warnings or proceed at their own peril. For Napoleon it was snow; for McClellan it could be rain. I hope not. All he needs is another excuse for inaction.

Author's notes:

Throughout April, McClellan complained to Lincoln that, rain, mud and heavy roads bogged down his army. Lincoln remarked to Hay that McClellan "seemed to think, in defiance of Scripture, that Heaven sent its rains only on the just and not on the unjust." Soon, when seriously wounded Confederate General Joseph E. Johnston was replaced by Robert E. Lee, Lincoln began to fear that Lee would outsmart the slow-moving McClellan. Throughout the Peninsula Campaign, Lincoln complained to Stanton, Seward and several members of Congress that McClellan's "got the slows."

The White House – Saturday, April 19, 1862

A busier than usual day. I announced the ratification of a treaty with the Potawatomi Indians of Kansas after breakfast. At 2:30, I was joined by Stanton, Chase, Dahlgren and D. Dudley Field, a prominent New York City merchant, at the Navy Yard, where we departed for a trip down the Potomac on the revenue cutter, "Miami." We were supposed to meet General McDowell at Aquia Creek, who failed to arrive. We spent the night aboard ship.

Author's notes:

The U.S.S. Miami was purchased in 1862 and commissioned on January 28. It was one of the first propeller-driven vessels in the revenue cutter service. She was built in Scotland in 1853 as the Lady Le Marchant, and the federal government paid $25,000 for the commercial steamer. She measured 115 feet in length with a schooner sail rig and a two-cylinder oscillating steam engine. On the morning of April 20, 1862, Lincoln conferred with General McDowell before returning to Washington on the Miami.

In early May, Lincoln became the first U.S. president to direct troops and assets in the field. After meeting with his flag officers at Fortress Monroe, he reconnoitered possible troop landing beaches near Norfolk, Virginia, and ordered the shelling of Confederate fortifications at Sewell's Point, near the landing area. Lincoln boarded a shallow-draft tugboat to sound water depth along the intended landing beaches and ordered the Miami in advance of troop transports to cover the landings.

Before dawn on May 11, Union troop transports carrying 6,000 men and 100 cavalry horses appeared at present-day Ocean View Beach, where the Miami waited at anchor. Union troops landed and marched on Norfolk with little opposition. When Union forces arrived at Norfolk, the mayor and City Council surrendered the city.

The White House – Sunday, April 20, 1862

Today, General McDowell joined us. We left Aquia Creek, Virginia, to return to Washington. We landed at 2:30 in the afternoon and later dined at Commander Dahlgren's residence. The drive from the Navy Yard did not lack for excitement because the team of horses pulling our carriage was spooked along the way, and we had to change carriages and horses for the rest of the trip. After dinner, I spent time with Senator Browning. We discussed current events in Yorktown, Virginia, and impending matters at Corinth in northeast Mississippi. Browning is a close friend. His wife has been a strong comfort to Mother at her time of great sadness.

General Grant has notified the War Department that the Southern troops now occupying Corinth are under the command of General Albert Sidney Johnson. Our Army leaders agree that Corinth is as important to the Confederacy as Richmond is. That is because two major railroads, the Memphis and Charleston, running east and west, and the Mobile and Ohio R.R., running north and south, cross in its downtown area. Corinth has become an important hub for the rebels who ship troops, arms, food and ordnance all over the Confederacy through this key location. Its warehouses store vital war materials.

Author's notes:

The Battle of Shiloh on April 6 – April 7, in which the Confederates surprised Union forces at nearby Pittsburg Landing, Tennessee, to defend Corinth, was fought over possession of the city's vital railroads. Union forces laid siege to Corinth in May of 1862.

The White House – Tuesday, April 22, 1962

Tad reminded me that I had not sent a letter to my law partner, William Herndon, thanking him for this fine leather-bound diary in which I have been entering my thoughts since the first of the year. It had slipped my mind completely, and I was embarrassed by the oversight. Herndon is a man of great energy, and I imagine that no man knows me better than he does. When this dreadful war is over, I look forward to returning to our humble law office and tending to legal matters, just as we did for so many years. That is my fervent hope.

I met with Margarethe Schurz for almost an hour. She is a remarkable young woman who came to our country from Germany and established the first Kindergarten classes for young children in America. It is her hope that when this war is ended that more of the nation's energies will be directed to education. She also hopes that when slaves are ultimately freed that they will for the first time be taught to read and write. Her husband, Carl Schurz, was appointed Minister to Spain but asked to be relieved and transferred to the Army, where he is now a serving general. His troops are mainly German-Americans.

Author's notes:

Carl Schurz fought for reforms in the Revolutions in Germany of 1848 and 1849, where he came to know Franz Sigel, Alexander Schimmelfennig, Fritz Anneke, Friedrich Beust, Ludwig Blenker and others, many of whom he would meet again in the Union Army during the U.S. Civil War. Like many "Forty-Eighters," he emigrated to America. He settled in Wisconsin and established a legal practice in Milwaukee. He was anti-slavery and joined the Republican Party, unsuccessfully running for governor of Wisconsin. After briefly representing the United States as minister to Spain in 1861, he served as a general in the Civil War, fighting at the Battle of Gettysburg and other major engagements. After the war, he was elected U.S. senator from Missouri from 1869 to 1875. Rutherford B. Hayes named him secretary of the interior (1877 – 1881). He later became editor of the New York Evening Post, The Nation, and an editorial writer for Harper's Weekly.

The White House – Thursday, April 24, 1862

Yesterday, I made no diary entries due to an especially long late meeting with Secretary Stanton, who ordered General McClellan not to cross the Rappahannock. Today I met with General James W. Ripley, an officer who has put in 48 years of service, beginning back in 1814! Ripley has great knowledge about armaments and is now chief of ordnance of the Army. It was Ripley who has quickly converted many old smooth bore cannons into Parrott guns, which are now more powerful and accurate. Ripley has been skeptical of acquiring breech-loading repeating rifles, but promises to give them a fair hearing and more testing. He dislikes the fact that they tend to waste ammunition. He also points out that having more than one size bullet means our supply teams may run out of one or the other in a crisis. My sense of this matter is that troops, which are armed with weapons that can fire the most bullets in the shortest period, should be able to strike the greatest number of enemy soldiers.

Author's notes:

Ripley was never sanguine about breech-loading rifles and was replaced as head of the Ordnance Department in September of 1863 for his failure to purchase them. He was then appointed inspector of New England fortifications.

The White House – Friday, April 25, 1862

3,000 soldiers under Brigadier General Jesse Reno were disembarked from transports from Roanoke Island on April 18th. The next day an engagement took place in South Mills, a town located about four miles below Elizabeth City, North Carolina. Our troops were unsuccessful in dislodging determined Southern forces blocking the highway that our men were using to reach the locks of a canal in the Dismal Swamp. The enemy set fire to wood from buildings and fences on each side of the highway, thus preventing outflanking measures. It had been General Burnside's plan to blow up the locks, thereby preventing small ironclad rebel boats from entering Albemarle Sound, and doing damage to our naval forces in the region. Although outnumbering the Confederates, our men could not overcome the fire and strong resistance the enemy soldiers put up. We were forced to retreat. We lost 13 killed and over 100 wounded in the fighting.

Author's notes:

Confederate Colonel Ambrose R. Wright stationed five companies of men and three cannons in a ditch crossing the road Reno's troops were advancing upon. Reno's men arrived late in the morning and deployed for attack. Wright's men held the Union forces off for four hours before running out of ammunition. Wright's 900 men then fell back, assuming another defensive position, but Reno's men were ordered to retreat, returning to their ships below Elizabeth City. Reno was troubled by inaccurate rumors of massive Confederate reinforcements and decided his prospects for success were too limited to continue the attack.

The White House – Saturday, April 26, 1862

Navy Secretary Wells rushed here yesterday with a copy of a Richmond newspaper that had been smuggled into Washington. It announces that our forces under Flag Officer David G. Farragut, U.S.N. have taken New Orleans. We have no official confirmation of this victory, but if the report is accurate, it means that the most important Confederate port will be permanently closed to the rebels. This is significant news for our side.

Hay borrowed for me from the Library of Congress a copy of Samuel Butler's "His Hudibras and Other Works," published in London in 1846. It is marvelous. Later in the evening I spent 90 minutes with Senator Browning reading poetry. I particularly like the lines from Canto I,

> "When civil fury first grew high,
> And men fell out they knew not why."

It could have been written to describe how things are today in America. Browning read me this line and then reread it for emphasis,

> "As the ancients
> Say Wisely, have a care o' th' main chance,
> And look before ere you leap;
> For as you sow, ye are like to reap."

Author's notes:

On this date, President Lincoln was joined by Secretary Seward and Commander Dahlgren aboard a Navy cutter. They sailed from the Navy Yard and boarded the French frigate "Gassendi" lying at anchor in the Potomac River. Lincoln became the first American president to board a French warship and receive a 21- gun salute.

The White House – Sunday, April 27, 1862

I wrote a letter to a sweet young lady named Lulu Waldron, who is the daughter of Judge George Waldron of Yankton, Dakota Territory. She kindly sent me elegant studs made of pipestone. Mother admires them, and I will try and remember to wear them often. The first time I saw pipestone was during the Black Hawk War, when one of our soldiers showed me a ceremonial pipe that he had bought from a Black Hawk Indian that was made of pipestone. That was reddish brown in color. The studs are made of a more yellowish pipestone.

The Cabinet met today to discuss the urgent need for more cannons for our army. Stanton remarked that Napoleon said that "God fights on the side with the best artillery," and that Frederick the Great claimed that "A battery of field artillery was worth a thousand muskets." When war broke out I was told that our Army possessed only 60 batteries containing 163 serviceable pieces of artillery. Included in that sad total were weapons of at least seven different calibers and capabilities. Most were bronze 6-pounders or 12-pounders with smooth bores. Most of the cannons now being used by the Confederates were seized when they occupied federal arsenals within their territory. The Army recommends that we manufacture and purchase Napoleons, the 12-pound field gun developed originally in France about 15 years ago. Our side has been making this weapon since 1857. It can fire solid shot and exploding cannon balls.

Author's Notes:

During the Civil War, the Tredgar Iron Works in Richmond produced about 1,100 cannons. Union forces purchased more than 4,000 light artillery pieces, and 3,800 specialized, large-bore weapons. For daily use both sides preferred light artillery pieces with muzzles ranging from 3 inches to 4.6 inches wide. They were light enough to be towed by a team of six horses and capable of accurately firing shells weighing from 6 to 12 pounds at targets from a few hundred yards to 2,100 yards away. Perhaps as many as 1,000 cannons were captured by the Confederates from Union forces.

The White House – Tuesday, April 29, 1862

Tomorrow Nicolay will be back from his stay in Illinois, where he visited his family. I am anxious to get his thinking on recent events, and to learn how the people of the state feel about our prosecution of the war. Nicolay has grown to be a very perceptive observer. I am proud that this orphan, who at one point was a printer's devil, has grown into such an accomplished young man. His suggestion that I hire Hay has proven to be one of his best. Both are top-notch. They put in long hours and yet seem tireless. I am particularly interested in what Nicolay's friends may have told him about General Grant. I get more complaints about Grant than any of our generals.

I have decided not to provide information to the Congress on our recent evacuation of Jacksonville, Florida.

Author's notes:

On this date, Lincoln withheld from the House of Representatives his reasons for the April evacuation of Jacksonville, Florida. During the war Union forces occupied Jacksonville on several occasions. Union naval forces maintained a blockade of Jacksonville, Cedar Key, Key West and Pensacola. Federal ships had difficulty intercepting blockade runners because there were 8,436 miles of coastline and over 11,000 miles of rivers and waterways to patrol.

Florida was a major supplier of beef cattle and pork to the Confederacy, and raised over 15,00 troops, including 12 regiments of infantry, two of cavalry and several artillery batteries and supporting units. Most were sent to aid the Army of Northern Virginia under General Edward A. Perry and Colonel David Lang. The famed "Florida Brigade" distinguished itself under General Robert E. Lee's leadership by twice charging Cemetery Ridge during the Battle of Gettysburg, including the ill-fated Pickett's Charge. Tallahassee became the second-last Confederate state capital to fall to the Union Army. State governor John Milton shot himself, rather than submit to Union occupation.

The White House – Thursday, May 1, 1862

Tad's health is greatly improved, while Mother's mental state is still extremely fragile. Willie's death and the loss of her half-brother, Samuel B. Todd, from fatal wounds received at the Battle of Shiloh on April 10th have been too much grief for dear Mary to endure. Sam was a favorite of Mary. Today she spoke of him at breakfast, talking of his life before the war. Unfortunately, she has several close family members serving in the Confederate Army and naturally worries constantly about their well-being.

Later in the day Mother was cheered when I told her that we had received confirmation that our naval forces were successful in taking New Orleans from the enemy. Earlier reports from Southern newspapers reported our victory, but it was only today that we had official word of Flag Officer Farragut's important achievement. This news means much here in America, and it will strengthen our position overseas, when Europe gets the news. The Confederates had been hoping to be recognized by Britain and France. This news will put a damper on their hopes.

Author's notes:

Fort Jackson and Fort St. Phillip defended the downriver approaches to New Orleans. After a powerful Union naval attack, in which the forts endured for 96 hours over 13,000 shells, the garrisons mutinied, spiked the guns and forced their officers to surrender. General Ben Butler's force of 18,000 men then ascended 75 miles upriver unopposed and entered the city of New Orleans, which had been abandoned by Confederate forces.

Later, Baton Rouge would soon fall as New Orleans had, once the powerful guns of the fleet were trained on the city.

The White House – Friday, May 2, 1862

Stanton showed me a request from General McClellan that arrived yesterday, asking for Parrot guns, which I found to be another absurd request from our Little Napoleon. I telegraphed him at once, and wrote that I found no justification for Parrots, and considered the request to be another disappointing sign of indefinite procrastination. I ended the telegram with these words, "Is anything to be done!"

Later, Nicolay provided me with an auditor's report, which shows monies spent for goods advanced by the citizens of Oregon and Washington during Indian uprisings in 1855 and 1856. It confirms just how slowly the wheels of government turn. That was six and seven years ago. Later this evening Senator Browning came by. We spent time together in the family room discussing McClellan before I retired. I don't sleep soundly when I have Mac on my mind!

Tomorrow I will visit the Navy Yard to watch a demonstration of a new cannon manufactured by James Holenshade of Cincinnati.

Author's notes:

Lincoln could not resist an opportunity to view demonstrations of new weapons. On this occasion Mary Lincoln and Tad joined the president in an examination of Holenshade's breech-loading cannons. They watched the firing of the cannons for over an hour before returning to the Executive Mansion.

The White House – Monday, May 12, 1862

I have been away from Washington since May 5th. My initial time was well-spent on the revenue cutter U.S.S. Miami, which took our party, which included Stanton, Chase and others to Fortress Monroe, located approximately 15 miles below Alexandria, Virginia. After conferring with General John Ellis Wool, the commanding officer at the fortress, I visited the flagship of Flag Officer Louis Goldsborough, commander of the North Atlantic Blockading Squadron. On the 7th we breakfasted aboard the yacht Vanderbilt. I then saw the ruins of Hampton, Virginia, which had been burned by the rebels. Later I reviewed our soldiers who are stationed at Camp Hamilton, Virginia. On the 8th I consulted with Goldsborough and Wool who agreed to land troops on Sewell's Point under cover of naval gunfire. Later we watched from a Navy tug the shelling of Sewell's Point and Craney Island. It was a powerful display of our formidable naval power. On May 9th I ordered Army forces to land and occupy Norfolk. During the day I read Shakespeare to Colonel Cannon. On May 10th Stanton, Chase and I accompanied General Wool, to a landing place at Willoughby Point, and watched troops marching toward Norfolk. At 11 P.M. Wool arrived and announced our possession of Norfolk. On May 11th our party returned to Washington aboard the U.S.S. Baltimore, but not before we sailed up the Elizabeth River to visit Norfolk for an hour. We later learned that the rebels blew up the once-dreaded Merrimac rather than let it fall into Union hands.

Author's notes:

General John Wool was the oldest general serving on either side during the Civil War. He was two years older than General Winfield Scott. Unlike Scott, who suffered from obesity, gout and other ailments, Wool was fit and could mount a horse. In August of 1861 he was named by Lincoln to command the U.S. Army Department of Virginia. He held that post until June of 1862. Lincoln rewarded Wool for his aggressive actions at Norfolk by promoting him to full major general in the regular army, thereby becoming only the 23rd man to hold this rank since its creation in 1791. After the Battle of Gettysburg, Wool led his troops to regain control of New York City during and after the draft riots of that year. At age 79, he retired after 51 years of service.

The White House – Tuesday, May 13, 1862

It was a marvelous experience to be with our highly motivated and competent soldiers and seamen these past few days. I greatly enjoyed seeing them in action against the enemy. I enjoy talking to men of all ranks. One learns greatly by listening to their complaints. The naval blockade proclaimed on April 19, 1861, will be raised on the Southern ports of Beaufort, S.C., Port Royal, S.C., and New Orleans as of June 1, 1862, pursuant to Treasury regulations, except for contraband of war. Last evening, I visited Seward, who is home confined to his bed for injuries sustained when thrown from his carriage. His spirit is strong. He deeply regrets not having been fit enough to join our Norfolk adventure.

At 11 A.M. I welcomed a committee of the General Synod of Evangelical Lutheran Churches, who offered prayers for my health and for the safety of our servicemen. They informed me about the activities of chaplains of their faith serving with our armed forces.

Members of the 12th Indiana Regiment visited today. They presented Tad with a large regimental flag. I reminded them that I was a Hoosier before I moved to Illinois. I told them that my father came to Indiana from Kentucky in 1816, and purchased land under the "two dollars an acre law." It was located on the banks of Pigeon Creek, about 16 miles back from the river that he had come down on in a handmade raft. Thomas and Betsy Sparrow and Dennis Hanks joined us there. We initially built a crude temporary structure about 14 feet square of small unhewn logs. People called such places a "half-faced camp." It had neither floor, doors or windows. Soon my father, Thomas Lincoln moved into a typical log cabin with walls on four sides. For many years I helped my father clear the forest and construct the home. From that time, until I was age 23, I was expected to wield an ax unless I was plowing in harvesting seasons.

Author's notes:

Lincoln as president would often hold an ax away from his body at arm's length for several minutes. He would challenge anyone to hold it similarly. Most young soldiers so challenged never matched his strength. Even in his fifties his physical powers were remarkable.

The White House – Wednesday, May 14, 1862

I was very pleased to sign a recommendation which was sent to the Senate and House today. It states that Flag Officer D.G. Farragut receives a vote of thanks from Congress for his splendid services, as well as the naval officers who commanded vessels engaged in the recent brilliant operations of his squadron that captured New Orleans. There is no doubt in my mind that this action will help greatly to shorten the war. By this one act we have cut off Confederate access to the lower Mississippi and the Gulf of Mexico.

Author's notes:

Farragut's mortar flotilla had opened fire on New Orleans' protecting forts on April 18. Throwing caution to the wind, Farragut then sailed past the defending forts and destroyed the Confederate fleet, which included two ironclads and 13 gunboats. He took formal possession of the city on April 27, 1862.

Mary Chestnut, wife of Confederate General James Chestnut Jr., wrote in her diary on April 27th "New Orleans gone and with it the Confederacy. That Mississippi ruins us if lost. The Confederacy has been done to death by the politicians. What wonder. We are lost."

The White House – Thursday, May 15, 1862

It is now clear that the so-called "brilliant victory" that General McClellan declared had been won at Williamsburg on the 5th of this month was, upon analysis by the War Department, less than brilliant. It may have not been a victory at all. It seems to me that it was at best a draw. My sense is that we failed to win because our forces were divided at a critical time when they should have been united. McClellan was surprised when General Joseph E. Johnston unexpectedly withdrew his forces from the Warwick Line at the siege of Yorktown on the night of May 3. McClellan failed to mount an immediate pursuit. On the 4th of May he ordered cavalry under Brigadier General George Stoneman to pursue Johnson's rear guard. He also ordered Brigadier General William Franklin's division to board transport ships on the York River and to move upstream, to cut off Johnson's retreat. That ambitious plan failed because it took two days to board the men on the ships. Franklin's division would instead be later engaged at Eltham's Landing on the 7th of May. Meanwhile, Stoneham was skirmishing with cavalry under Confederate general J.E.B. Stuart, Johnston's rear guard. This delaying action allowed Johnston's forces to get free and to make its stand at Fort Magruder, an earthen fortification, which straddles the Williamsburg Road. It is located four miles southeast of Williamsburg. After battle reports indicate that we fielded 40,000 troops at Fort Magruder; the rebels an estimated 32,000. Our casualties were over 2,000. Rebel casualties are estimated to be about the same as ours. The result was that the bulk of a large Confederate Army was not destroyed but continued its withdrawal toward Richmond.

Author's notes:

The Battle of Eltham's Landing was little more than a heavy skirmish. Franklin missed a golden opportunity to intercept the Confederate retreat from Williamsburg, allowing it to pass unmolested. Confederate General Johnston had ordered General John Bell Hood of Texas to "feel the enemy gently and fall back." After the battle, he humorously asked Hood, "What would your Texans have done, sir, if I had ordered them to charge and drive back the enemy?" Hood replied, "I suppose General, they would have driven them into the river, and tried to swim out and capture the gunboats."

The White House – Friday, May 16, 1862

Yesterday, I approved the establishment of the Department of Agriculture. It will not have Cabinet status, but I believe that it soon may have such standing in our government. Most of our citizens are engaged in agriculture and as such they deserve to receive whatever help we can extend to them in terms of crop improvement, better roads and railroads to facilitate the movement of farm products to market. I will be interviewing Isaac Newton to head up the department. He is a respected farmer. He has served as chief of the agricultural section of the Patent Office since August 1861. Research should be undertaken to improve crop yields, the development of new farming implements and methods. I remember as a boy living on a 30-acre farm of which only 14 could be cultivated. In 1816, when we moved to Southern Indiana we farmed 160 acres of very marshy land. It was a difficult struggle. After seven years of hard work, my father finally had only 10 acres in corn, five in wheat and two in oats. The last farm I worked on was our family farm on land along the Sangamon River in Illinois.

Author's notes:

The year before he was elected president, Lincoln addressed the Wisconsin Agricultural Society's Annual Fair. He praised substituting horse-drawn machines for hand power, and predicted steam-powered plows. He endorsed education and said that free labor would achieve its greatest potential if farm workers were educated. When he ran for president he favored homestead legislation and the construction of a railroad to the Pacific Ocean. The Homestead Act, passed May 20, 1862, provided giving 160 acres of the public domain to citizens or prospective citizens over 21 years of age. The settler had to reside on the land for six months and pay $1.25 an acre. An act granting Western land and making payments for the Union Pacific-Central Pacific was signed into law on July 1, 1862. The railroad would be completed on May 10, 1869, when two sections were joined at Promontory Summit, Utah. The Morrill Land Grant College Act, donating public land to states for colleges of agriculture and mechanical arts, became law on July 2, 1862. Every state accepted the terms of the act and established one or more such institutions.

Isaac Newton served as commissioner of the Agricultural Department for nearly five years. It collected useful information on plants and animals; answered farmers' inquiries; tested farm implements; conducted chemical analyses of soils, grains, fruits, plants, vegetables and manures; established a professorship of botany and entomology; and created an agricultural library and museum.

The White House – Saturday, May 17, 1862

On April 30, General McClellan relieved General Charles Smith Hamilton, who had command of the 3rd Division, III Corps during the Siege of Yorktown, for insubordination. When I questioned this decision, McClellan wrote that I could not do anything better calculated to injure my army than to restore General Hamilton to his division. I interviewed Hamilton yesterday. I attempted to understand his side of the story. Smith is a West Pointer, who served with distinction in the Mexican War. He was wounded at the Battle of Molino del Rey and served in the Army from 1843 to 1853. After war broke out he enlisted in May of 1861 and was appointed colonel of the 3rd Wisconsin Infantry. Hamilton has powerful friends in the Senate, who were alarmed to learn that he had been relieved by McClellan. Several have written to me about Hamilton's situation, and the way he was treated by McClellan. I believe he is an excellent officer who should continue to be useful to our cause. Accordingly, I have ordered Stanton to find a suitable slot for him in the Western Theater.

Author's notes:

Hamilton would command the 3rd Division of the Army of the Mississippi at the Battles of Iuka and Corinth, which were both Union victories, in September and October of 1862. Following the Corinth victory, he was promoted to major general. When Grant ordered him to Vicksburg to serve under General John Alexander McClernand, Hamilton offered his resignation from the Army on April 13, 1863. Grant was pleased to see him go and gladly accepted his resignation, forwarding many pages of documentation to Washington to support his case in the matter. After his service, Hamilton became a U.S. marshal and a paper manufacturer. He died in Milwaukee, Wisconsin, in 1891.

The White House – Monday, May 19, 1862

Mother was in a much better mood yesterday. Tad's improvement in health has had a continuing salutary effect on his mother. We visited our wounded men in the Army Hospital at Columbia College in the afternoon. Senator Browning joined us. Sundays are a good day for me to find the time needed to see our troops. When they see Mary, they are particularly pleased. She reminds them of their own mothers. They are often prone to cheer us when we first arrive. Harewood Hospital, which will open this year, will be located on the commute between our summer retreat at the Soldier's Home and the White House. It will be the most convenient hospital for us to attend. I know that I cannot bring them relief from pain, but I believe it helps them if I can just say, "I can't stay, boys, but I hope you are comfortable and getting along nicely here." I try to shake hands with every soldier in turn. When I leave a ward, I am sometimes near to tears, particularly when I have just left men who have lost a limb or sight. This terrible war has required incredible sacrifices. The least we can do for our soldiers and sailors is to provide the best medical care possible.

Author's notes:

The president and Mrs. Lincoln visited thousands of wounded troops during the war. Between 1861 and 1865, General Army Hospitals treated over one million soldiers, with a mortality rate of only 8 percent. Washington's 16 General Hospitals comprised nearly 30,000 beds.

The White House – Tuesday, May 20, 1862

Ten days ago, General David Hunter, who commands forces in the Department of the South, issued General Order No. 10, freeing slaves in South Carolina, Georgia and Florida without informing either Secretary Stanton or yours truly. Last evening, I declared that order to be unauthorized and that Hunter, or any other commander or person has not been authorized to make proclamations declaring the slaves of any state free. I informed Stanton that Hunter's resignation, if offered, is not to be accepted.

After lunch today, I approved legislation securing homesteads to actual settlers on public domain, another act providing primary schools for public instruction in the District of Columbia outside Washington and Georgetown, and legislation prescribing qualification for electors in cities of Washington and Georgetown, including an oath of allegiance.

On the 18th, Navy Assistant Secretary Fox informed me that five Union gunboats, which were moving up the James River toward Richmond, were repulsed on the morning of May 15th at a rebel fort located eight miles from Richmond. Fox says it is located on a high point at a bend of the river. For 3 hours and 20 minutes heavy cannon fire from the fort and a riverside battery forced our ships to retreat. The Galena was hit 18 times. I telegraphed McClellan to advise me as soon as possible about the Confederate batteries located there, which are impeding our progress.

Author's notes:

The officer in charge of the earthworks at Drewry's Bluff was General Lee's son, General G.W.C. Lee. Fort Darling was sited 80 to 100 feet above the James River. Its garrison was joined by the crew of the C.S.S. Virginia, who had scuttled their ship with the fall of Norfolk on May 9th. On May 15th, the U.S.S. Monitor, U.S.S. Galena, Port Royal, Aroostook and Naugatuck attacked Fort Darling at 7:45 A.M. The three wooden ships (Galena, Port Royal and Aroostook) were unable to advance as the cannon fire from Fort Darling, high on the bluff, was too heavy. The Monitor's guns could not be elevated to hit the fort. Only the Galena engaged the fort, but after 18 hits pierced her armor and caused fires, the attack was called off. For two years Fort Darling saw no more action. The site became the training ground for the Confederate Naval Academy and the Confederate Marine Corps Camp of Instruction. On May 8, 1864 Fort Darling was attacked by Union forces under General Benjamin F. Butler. Upon the arrival of 18,000 rebel infantry under General P.G.T. Beauregard, the Union forces were routed on May 16, 1864. After the Battle of Appomattox Court House on April 9, 1865, the troops stationed at Fort Darling joined the movement westward and surrendered. When Abraham Lincoln visited Richmond after Lee's surrender, the obstacles on the James River were removed. He observed the deserted fort on his way to Richmond.

The White House – Wednesday, May 21, 1862

Nicolay extracted from today's mail pile a letter from Sarah Sophia Fane, Lady Villiers, who requested my autograph. I was told by Lord Lyons, the British ambassador, that Her Ladyship is a prominent society hostess in London, as well as the senior partner in Child & Company. Her eldest son, George, is married to Julia, Sir Robert Peel's daughter. She has not only been engaged in her bank's management, but has set up schools for tenants on the family's vast estates in Oxfordshire. Lyons tells me that she has taken a strong interest in the living conditions of those who work on her lands. I was very pleased to comply by writing to her, "I beg that her ladyship will accept the assurance of my sincere gratification at this opportunity of subscribing myself." I signed it, Very truly, Her Ladyship's obedient servant.

Author's notes:

Sarah Sophia Fane was born in 1785. She was the daughter of John Fane, 10th Earl of Westmoreland, and Sarah Anne Child. In 1793 her mother and grandmother died. In 1806 Sarah inherited an annual income of around 60,000 pounds, as well as her grandfather's estate at Osterley Park, Middlesex. Sarah became the senior partner of Child & Company, the family bank, although she was unable to act in her own right until her 21st birthday. She was an active member of the bank throughout her life.

Child & Company, a formerly private independent bank, is now owned by The Royal Bank of Scotland Group, which incorporates Child & Co., bankers based at 1 Fleet Street, London. It can trace its roots to Sir Francis Child, who established his business as a goldsmith in 1664, when he entered into a partnership with Robert Blanchard. Child married Blanchard's stepdaughter and inherited the whole business on Blanchard's death. Renamed Child and Co., the business thrived, and was appointed "Jeweler in ordinary" to King William III. Child's grandson Robert Child was senior partner in the firm. When he died in 1782 without any sons to inherit the business, he did not want to leave it to his only daughter, Sarah Anne Child, because he was furious over her elopement with John Fane, earlier in the year. To prevent the Earl of Westmoreland from ever acquiring his wealth, he left it in trust to his daughter's second surviving daughter, Lady Sarah Sophia Fane, who married George Child-Villiers, 5th Earl of Jersey, in 1804.

The White House – Saturday, May 24, 1862

It is good to be back after spending two days and nights in Fredericksburg, Virginia, accompanied by Stanton and Dahlgren. The troops we inspected were in fine shape and in a strong fighting spirit. When I spoke to Lieutenant Colonel Hicks, he expressed negative views of the secretary of war, while at the same time he sought elevation in rank. This offended me greatly, and I have advised Stanton that he is not to be promoted under any circumstances. Yesterday, I rode on the north side of the Rappahannock in an open railroad car to McDowell's headquarters. I reviewed several divisions of troops along the way. I waved my tired old top hat to the men, and they responded with loud cheers. Colonel Herman Haupt, aide-de-camp to McDowell and chief of construction and transportation on military railroads explained to me the role railroads are now playing and the need for more railroad cars. Whenever I meet a military expert, he can always make a good case for "more." Got back to the White House at 5 A.M. I have asked Stanton to consider the military possession and operation of all railroads in the country.

Author's notes:

On May 25, 1862, President Lincoln issued an Executive Order – Taking Military Possession of Railroads. It read:

Ordered: By virtue of the authority vested by act of Congress, the President takes military possession of all the railroads in the United States from and after this date until further order, and directs that respective railroad companies, their officers and servants, shall hold themselves in readiness for the transportation of such troops and munitions of war as may be ordered by the military authorities, in the exclusion of all other businesses. By order of the Secretary of War: M.C. Meigs, Quartermaster-General.

The White House – Sunday, May 25, 1862

I telegraphed General McClellan, "I think the time is near when you must either attack Richmond or give up the job and come to the defense of Washington." To General Halleck at Corinth, Mississippi, who asks for more troops, I wired him that, "We do the best we can," and reminded him that each of our commanders along our line from Richmond to Corinth supposes himself to be confronted by numbers of men that are far superior to his own. I can only imagine that if Hannibal had possessed a telegraph, he would probably have been wiring Carthage to send more elephants as soon as humanly possible. If the rebels had as many soldiers as our generals typically assume, they would have won the war long ago.

Senator Browning spent several hours here this evening. He is not only a good friend, but an excellent sounding board for yours truly. I trust him and admire his candor.

Author's notes:

During the month of May 1862, Union forces fought battles in Virginia at Williamsport, Etham's Landing, McDowell, Drewry's Point, Princeton Court House (later West Virginia), Front Royal, Winchester, Hanover Court House and Seven Pines. All were either inconclusive or Confederate victories. Following the battle of Seven Pines, where General Joseph E. Johnston was seriously wounded, General Robert E. Lee was given command of Confederate forces. Losses were high on both sides at Seven Pines, and McClellan never got closer to Richmond during the Peninsula campaign.

The White House – Monday, May 26, 1862

Nicolay and Hay helped me prepare a suitable document for the Congress related to its resolution of censure of former Secretary of War Simon Cameron for questionable War Department purchases. I personally deem Cameron to be an honorable man, if not a particularly effective administrator. Sadly, he lost his brother, Colonel James C. Cameron, at the Battle of Bull Run. He and his family have given much to help us achieve victory.

In the response to the Congress, I stressed the important fact that "not only the president, but all the other heads of departments were equally responsible with Cameron for whatever error, wrong or fault was committed in his premises." I trust this will put an end to the matter. I owe much to Simon. I still consider his counsel in political matters valuable, particularly as they relate to Pennsylvania. I trust this will put an end to congressional disquiet over Simon. Meanwhile, I will trust him to represent America effectively at the Court of St. Petersburg.

Author's notes:

Simon Cameron had made a fortune in railroads, canals and banking. Initially, Cameron was a conservative on the issue of slavery, but once in Lincoln's Cabinet he began to accept the Abolitionists' viewpoint that the central purpose of the war was to bring the institution of slavery to an end. His annual report for 1861 contended that the government was right to arm slaves, "when it may become necessary as it is to use gunpowder or guns taken from the enemy." Lincoln rejected this premature emancipation (which had been authored by Edwin Stanton) and ordered copies of it recalled. In January of 1862 Cameron resigned, and was later named minister to Russia. In 1866 he returned to the U.S. Senate from Pennsylvania. He had served in the Senate from 1845 to 1849, from 1857 to 1861, and from 1867 to 1877. His son, Donald Cameron, succeeded him in the Senate.

The White House – Tuesday, May 27, 1862

Twelve schoolteachers from the city of Washington came to see me this morning. I confessed to them that their president was a poorly educated man, who had gone to school only rarely during his entire lifetime. My school was perhaps best called the School of Hard Knocks. In those backwoods days, there were no special qualifications required of a teacher, beyond readin', writin', and cipherin'! If a straggler who supposed to actually understand Latin happened to sojourn in the neighborhood, he was looked upon as a wizard. In my early years I always misspelled that word. My way was to always write it "wizzard." When I came of age I did not know much. I could read, write and cipher to the Rule of Three; but that was about it. My formal schooling did not exceed one year in total. Thank God for my mother, who encouraged me to borrow books. I sometimes would walk as far as five miles to get one from a neighbor. Like all my classmates, I made my own arithmetic textbooks. I showed one of them to Tad recently, for I have kept it all these years as a reminder of how we learned in the so-called Good Old Days. I showed the teachers my textbook and they were stunned. Today, their pupils are provided with excellent texts covering all subjects taught. I confessed that the only book my parents owned was the Holy Bible. I showed them my copy, which is kept right on my desk. I often refer to it. I love the language of the Saint James version. I also told the teachers that I believe that one book, Weem's "The Life of Washington," may have been the most influential book I read as a young boy. It taught me the meaning of democracy. I remember the accounts in it of the battlefields and the struggles for the liberties of our country. It taught me that there was something more than common that those brave men struggled for. I told the teachers that those same feelings of patriotism are now being shown by our brave men in uniform.

Author's notes:

As a boy, Lincoln borrowed "Robinson Crusoe," "Pilgrim's Progress" "Aesop's Fables," several histories of the United States and school books from neighbors and friends. While president, he borrowed hundreds of books from the Library of Congress and purchased many books. On May 27, 1862 he ordered these books from W.F. Richstein: "East Lynne," $.50, "Castle Wafer," $.50, "Earl Herr," $.50, "Chemmings," $.50, "Heir to Ashley," $.50," Life Secret," $.50, and several novels by Mrs. Ellen Price Wood, including "The Plain Gold Ring" and "The Earl's Heirs, A Tale of Domestic Life." Many, or all of these books, may have been ordered for Mary Lincoln.

The White House – Wednesday, May 28, 1862

I appeared this morning before the Committee on the Conduct of the War. I reviewed with it the construction of a 480-foot-long railroad bridge thrown up over Potomac Creek, located a few miles north of Frederick. It was built under the direction of Colonel Herman Haupt. He achieved this in just nine rainy days using mostly unskilled infantry troops to get it built. I told the committee that he had performed this miracle using just cornstalks and beanpoles. Stanton believes that Haupt may prove to be one of the most valuable men in the Army. It is his responsibility to keep our military railroads operating as effectively as possible.

Most of my day and night was spent at the telegraph office trying unsuccessfully to get our senior generals, McClellan, Fremont and McDowell, to coordinate their efforts against the foxy General Jackson. I am learning the hard way the difference between being a country lawyer and a wartime president. A lawyer can win a case, get a ruling from the judge, and in almost every instance that order will be promptly carried out. As president, I can order generals to do things, but experience has taught me that they lack either the will or ability to make things happen with speed. In war, speed is a vital element if victory is ever to be achieved.

Author's notes:

By the end of the war, the U.S. Military Railroads, an agency operated by the War Department, operated 2,105 miles of railroad, with a combined rolling stock of 419 engines and 6,330 cars, 642 miles of track, and 26 miles of bridges built or rebuilt, at a cost of nearly 30 million dollars. The agency's Construction Corps grew from 300 men in 1863 to nearly 10,000 men by the war's end. On April 27, 1862, Herman Haupt, former chief engineer of the Pennsylvania Railroad, was given the rank of colonel and appointed aide-de-camp to Major General Irvin McDowell, then in command of the defenses of Washington, D.C. Haupt organized career railroaders, soldiers, laborers, and even former slaves to do the monumental jobs required to build, repair and operate railroads under the worst conditions. Some of the lines were destroyed and rebuilt as many as five time during the conflict.

The White House – Thursday, May 29, 1862

May has been one of the most difficult and depressing months of the war. Battle after battle fought has been either inconclusive or resulted in a Confederate victory. We should be winning, yet we are so often losing. Tonight, I expect to again spend long hours at the War Department reviewing telegraph messages from the fields of conflict. Messages back and forth between the department and Generals Fremont, Banks, McClellan, McDowell and Marcy during the day have kept me informed, but surely not enthused.

A long letter from Dr. Anson G. Henry, my longtime friend and doctor, helped cheer me up a bit. I have known and trusted Anson since 1832, when we first met in Springfield. He has often been our guest at the White House whenever he is in the city. He was instrumental in getting the capital of Illinois moved from Vandalia to Spring-field. He was named commissioner of the Capital Building Construction, the venue where I gave my "House Divided" speech." Anson is a very creative man with an inquiring mind. His thoughtful letters keep me well-informed on many war issues, and for that I am grateful.

Author's notes:

After Lincoln's re-election, Dr. Anson Henry stayed at the White House for two months. At the war's end in April of 1865, Lincoln dispatched him to Richmond as liaison between the Army and the White House. While in Richmond, Lincoln was assassinated. Henry returned to the White House to console the family and accompanied them to Springfield, where he helped Mary and Robert select a burial spot in Oak Ridge Cemetery. New President Andrew Johnson named him governor of the Washington Territory. Heading home to assume his new position, the ship on which he was a passenger, The Brother Jonathan, struck a reef off California and sank. His body was never recovered.

The White House – Saturday, May 31, 1862

Yesterday there was no time for diary entries. I was at the telegraph office throughout the day and I again stayed late into the evening. Most of the messages were to and from General Fremont, who has made a mess of matters within his area of operation. When speed has been called for he has repeatedly failed to deliver. Nicolay showed me a quotation from an ancient Chinese military strategist, which states, "He whose ranks are united in purpose will be victorious." How true. My attempts to coordinate matters with our forces have not been successful in creating unity over the past few weeks. Coordination of action has completely eluded our forces. I fear that as soon as current military matters are brought to a satisfactory resolution, I will be obligated to remove Freemont. He is personally popular, but does not possess a "military mind." To him orders are not to be automatically obeyed, but to be "interpreted." I have directed a special military commission to meet in July to resolve matters involving editors who have apparently violated restrictions on publishing news. Freedom of the press is vitally important, but careless reporting of military matters can often hurt more than it helps.

Author's notes:

The Battle of Seven Pines or Fair Oaks was fought on May 31 to June 1, 1862. The Union Army had reached a point within 6 miles of Richmond, Virginia. On the second day of the battle, Confederate General Joseph E. Johnston was seriously wounded by an artillery shell. The battle was tactically inconclusive, but it stopped McClellan's advance on the rebel capital. Johnston was replaced by General Robert E. Lee, who would lead the Army of Northern Virginia for the rest of the war. Lee would succeed in driving McClellan from the Peninsula during the Seven Days Battles of late June. After recovering from his wounds, Johnston would be appointed by Jefferson Davis commander of the Department of the West in November of 1862. This gave him control of the Army of Tennessee and the Trans-Mississippi Department.

The White House – June 1, 1862

Assistant Navy Secretary Gustavus Fox spent all morning with me at the War Department awaiting news of battles now being waged on the Peninsula. The news has not been favorable. Fox is one of the brightest men I've met in the naval forces. He spent 28 years on duty and saw action during the Mexican War. Mother invited Virginia Fox to join us for lunch and presented her with a bouquet of roses. Mrs. Fox is one of Mary's closest friends. Mary continues to deal with her grief over son Willie's sudden death, and the presence of a genuine friend like Virginia Fox is a great blessing.

Author's notes:

In 1866, Secretary Fox was sent on a mission to Russia by President Andrew Johnson, where he conveyed Johnson's congratulations to Tsar Alexander II upon his escape from assassination. His trip was made on the U.S.S. Miantonomoh, accompanied by the U.S.S. Augusta. In 1882 Fox published a paper suggesting that Samana Cay in the Bahamas was Guanahani, or San Salvador, the first island that Christopher Columbus reached in his discovery of the Americas. Little attention was paid to his findings until 1986, when the National Geographic Society also concluded that Samana Cay was San Salvador.

The White House – Monday, June 2, 1862

At 3 P.M., I walked the grounds with Joseph C.G. Kennedy, the superintendent of the U.S. Census. Kennedy was first appointed as secretary of the U.S. Census Board in 1849. At that time its board consisted of the secretary of state, the attorney general and the postmaster general. When responsibility for the census was transferred to the newly created Department of the Interior, he was appointed its superintending clerk. He told me that when he visited Europe in 1851, he met with public officials and studied their methods of census taking. He then urged the adoption of a uniform classification system for America. He was superintendent of the census until 1853, when James DeBow was appointed to the post by President Franklin Pierce. DeBow left in 1857 and now supports the Confederacy. Kennedy returned in 1858 to prepare a digest of statistics from the 1850 census, and has been the superintending clerk of the eighth census since 1860. A very smart man.

Author's notes:

When completed, the 1860 census reported:
31,443,321 U.S. population
3.953,761 slave population - 12.6 percent
10.6 persons per square mile
Percent increase of population since 1850 - 35.6 percent
Official enumeration date: June 1, 1860
Number of states: 33
Cost per capita: $ .06
Total cost: $1,969,000
Total pages published: 3,189
Number of enumerators: 4,417
Number of office staff: 184
Number of questions asked: 14

10 largest urban places and population:
New York City, NY – 813,000   Philadelphia, PA – 565,529   Brooklyn, NY – 266,661
Baltimore – MD – 212,418   Boston, MA – 177,840   New Orleans, LA – 168, 675
Cincinnati, OH – 161,044   St. Louis, MO – 160,773   Chicago, IL – 112,172
Buffalo, NY – 81,129

King Christian IX of Denmark awarded Kennedy a gold medal in recognition of his work in the field of statistics.

The White House – Tuesday, June 3, 1862

I watched a demonstration of explosive musket shells, which are the invention of Samuel Gardiner, Jr. They were brought to my attention by John Tucker, assistant secretary of war. It was impressive to watch, and this new weapon may hold a great deal of promise for our soldiers. Little has been done to improve the power of our shells for decades. Weapon research is an area of weakness in our military establishment. I've written to General James Ripley, who is chief of the Ordnance Bureau. I want to see if this explosive musket shell may be tested quickly to determine if we should be using it in action. Right now, our musket shells and those of the enemy are of equal power. Why not introduce some that have far greater power?

Author's notes:

General James W. Ripley would report in June of 1862 that the Gardiner musket shell had, "no value as a service projectile." He did this every time they were requested. Ultimately the Army would order 20,000 shells and cartridges for trial by the 11th Corps. Several hundred were used and the rest remained unused during the war. Whenever a request was made for their manufacture, General Ripley would always refuse to order them.

The White House – Wednesday, June 4, 1862

I directed the attorney general to draw up the papers so that I may pardon General Herman Franks of New Orleans, at the request of a large Kentucky delegation led by Joshua Speed, my old and truest friend from the Blue Grass State. They made their case for Franks this morning in a meeting that lasted less than an hour. Franks had been indicted for treason. I have known Joshua since before I was licensed to practice law in March of 1837. He has done much to support our cause in Kentucky. I was pleased that I could accommodate Speed's wishes, and those of his associates.

A congratulatory telegraph message was sent to General Halleck after reading his wire, sent to Stanton, reporting that 10,000 prisoners had been captured at Corinth and its environs during the campaign there. I asked for more news on military matters in Memphis and other nearby areas of Mississippi River.

Author's notes:

During his time in office, Lincoln pardoned 343 people, including 264 Dakota Indians who had attacked white settlers in the Great Sioux Uprising of 1862. He also commuted the sentence of Congressman Clement Vallandigham, a Copperhead who was then deported to the Confederacy. Many pardoned were various men who had joined the Army underage, gone absent without leave or were bounty jumpers.

After the federal victory at Corinth, the railroads linking Memphis with the eastern areas of the Confederacy reduced the strategic importance of the city. In early June, Memphis and nearby forts were abandoned by the rebel forces.

The White House – Thursday, June 5, 1862

I signed State Department documents, prepared for the Senate, which describe the settlement of claims against Paraguay for damages to the U.S.S. Water Witch. This matter has been simmering since 1855, when the Water Witch was fired upon by troops in Fort Itapirū. The warship, then commanded by Lieutenant Thomas J. Page, was exploring the Paraná River. One seaman was killed in the incident and several injured. Return gunfire from the Water Witch killed several Paraguayan troops. We have received an apology from Paraguay and a payment of a $10,000 indemnity to pay the seaman's family.

Author's notes:

The third U.S.S. Water Witch was a wooden-hulled, sidewheel naval gunboat. It was launched in Washington in 1851. Its complement included 64 officers and enlisted men. During the Civil War the ship served in the Gulf Blockading Squadron off Pensacola, Florida, and later in the area around the mouth of the Mississippi River. On June 3, 1864, a Confederate Marine boat force boarded and captured the ship when it was stationed in Ossabaw Sound 15 miles south of Savannah, Georgia. The prize was taken into the Confederate Navy under the same name, Water Witch. On December 19, 1864 Confederates burned her to prevent recapture. The National Civil War Naval Museum constructed a full-scale reproduction of the ship using original plan drawings at their facilities in Columbus, Georgia. The museum displays the ship's original bell, one of her flags, and an original Bible taken from the ship.

The White House – Friday, June 6, 1862

The bill providing commissioners to Liberia and Haiti was signed by me this morning. These are the first negro governments to be recognized by the United States government. For years I have favored the successful development of these nations, and the populating of them by American negroes. So far, I have yet to discover negroes who share my enthusiasm for this idea.

The Cabinet received Colonel John R. Kenly of the First Maryland Regiment. He is a genuine hero of the Battle of Front Royal, Virginia. He was accompanied by Governor Bradford of his state. Kenly is an attorney who volunteered for the Mexican War, where he rose to the rank of major. On May 23 he was badly wounded at Front Royal on the Shenandoah and taken prisoner. His brave stand is credited with saving General Bank's division at Winchester.

Later in the day I met with Vincent Colyer, a dedicated educator from North Carolina. We discussed Military Governor Stanly's closing of Colyer's school for loyal negroes, which was done to foster good relations with the people of North Carolina. I want to see his schools continue operating and have asked Stanton to get personally involved. The black race will only prosper in our nation if their children are properly educated. This is an area where the slave owners have done great damage. Their historic reluctance to teach slaves to read and write has been unconscionable.

Author's notes:

John Reese Kenly joined the Army of the Potomac after the Battle of Gettysburg and was assigned to I Corps during the Bristoe Campaign. Later he commanded the Third Division of the Corps. Afterward he was assigned to the Middle Department, commanding the Third Brigade in 1864. He served to the end of the war, rising to the rank of brevet major general.

The White House – Saturday, June 7, 1862

A wire was sent to McClellan advising him that Halleck has confirmed the taking of Memphis, Fort Pillow and Randolph. I spent time with the Cabinet as Seward explains matters in Mexico. Since December 8, 1861, British, French and Spanish fleets have arrived in Veracruz. The stated purpose was to settle their debts with Mexico. However, since then European forces have advanced to Orizaba, Cordoba and Tehuácan. The city of Campeche surrendered to the French fleet on February 27 and a French army arrived on March 5. Seward believes that when the Spanish and British realized that French ambitions are to conquer all of Mexico, they withdrew their supporting forces on April 9, leaving Mexico on April 24. Last month the French man-of-war Bayonnaise blockaded Mazatlán for a few days. All this activity is a clear violation of the Monroe Doctrine by France, and Seward has informed all the European parties involved that their recent behavior has offended the United States. On May 5, Mexican forces under general Zaragoza defeated a French army in the Battle of Puebla. With a civil war to fight, I dare not intrude into these matters, but the United States has assured Mexico that it will continue to maintain proper relations with its legitimate government.

Author's notes:

The Battle of Puebla on May 5, 1862, is commemorated in Mexico as the very popular Cinco de Mayo holiday. On May 31, 1863, President Juárez fled Mexico City with his Cabinet, retreating northward to Paso del Norte and later to Chihuahua. His government-in-exile remained there until 1867. In 1863 French forces under General Bazaine defeated the Mexican Army and entered Mexico City on June 7, 1863.

The White House – Sunday, June 8, 1862

Seward brought me a copy of the Treaty with Great Britain for the Suppression of the Slave Trade yesterday. This diplomatic arrangement was skillfully negotiated by U.S. Secretary of State Seward and British Ambassador to the U.S. First Viscount Lyons. It was unanimously ratified by the Senate on April 25, 1862, and the agreement was exchanged in London on May 25th. It was my good fortune to be able to formally proclaim it yesterday. It sets forth aggressive measures to end the odious Atlantic slave trade. Both nations agree to use their navies to seize merchant vessels carrying captured Africans, including any vessel bearing indications of being a slave trading ship, such as grated hatches instead of closed hatches, stores of food and water far exceeding the needs of a normal crew, and shackles or chains. Seward, by his skillful negotiating of the Trent Affair, which preceded the treaty discussions, virtually committed Great Britain to accept the U.S. government's attitude toward the slave trade. The Treaty does not refer to slavery in the United States. However, my plans are to hopefully emancipate American slaves in any state that does not end its rebellion against the Union by January 1, 1863.

At mother's request I have ordered the Marine Band to discontinue performing summer concerts on the White House lawn or at Lafayette Park as previously done. Mary is still in deep mourning and fears the music will cause her unrest and more suffering.

Author's notes:

Slavery was of vital importance to the Confederate's war economy. The Suppression of the Slave Trade Treaty, and the imposition of a U.S. naval blockade of Southern ports, resulted in a severe reduction in the number of slaves able to enter the South for the remainder of the war.

The White House – Monday, June 9, 1861

Tad and I met with Captain Commander Jan Schonheyden and Lieutenant Steen Bitlee of the Royal Danish Navy. They were brought to the White House by Navy Secretary Wells. They presented Tad with a beautifully made model of the Dronning Juliane Marie, a Danish warship that was built in 1746. Tad is ecstatic. The officers told me that the Danish Navy is about to rebuild its fleet, which now operates few steam vessels. They informed us that news of the victory of the Monitor over the Merrimac has stimulated plans in Denmark to no longer rely on wooden hulls and sail, but to now operate only steam-powered warships that are armor-plated with steel.

Author's notes:

In 1814, Denmark and Norway were separated peacefully, after more than 300 years together. At that time, the Common Fleet was split into the Royal Danish Navy and the Royal Norwegian Navy. By the outbreak of World War I (1914), the Danish Navy was a very modern fleet, mainly equipped with armored steam ships and only a few sailing ships still in its fleet.

The White House – Wednesday, June 11, 1861

Mother sent fresh strawberries and cut flowers from our garden to her close friend, Mrs. G.V. Fox. Picking flowers and arranging them gives her a feeling of happiness at this unhappy time in her life. Her favorite flowers are roses. Even in mourning she will place a rose or several rose blossoms on her dress. She tells me the aroma of the roses lifts her spirits.

I conferred with General Ambrose Burnside. He will leave tomorrow for Fort Monroe in Virginia. He told me that he is the fourth of nine children. His great-great-great-grandfather came from Scotland and settled in South Carolina. His father freed his slaves and moved the family to Indiana. He is a Military Academy man who graduated 18th in the class of 1847. We talked a bit about Braxton Bragg, under whom he served in the 3rd U.S. Artillery before the war. Burnside says that Bragg has a strong tendency to be impatient and disregards the feelings and opinions of subordinates. As such, he believes Bragg may not prove to be a successful opponent of the Union. He showed me the scar on his neck from being shot by an arrow of an Apache brave in 1849. What I particularly like about Burnside is the fact that when he left the Army he remained in Rhode Island's militia and used his business talents to start a company that manufactured the Burnside carbine. I admire a man with an inventive mind. I also like his carbine.

Author's notes:

Burnside conducted successful campaigns in North Carolina and East Tennessee, as well as countering the raids of Confederate General John Hunt Morgan, but suffered disastrous defeats at the Battle of Fredericksburg and the Battle of the Crater. After the war he succeeded Nelson W. Aldrich as the 30th governor of Rhode Island and served as U.S. senator from Rhode Island from 1875 to 1881.

The White House – Thursday, June 12, 1862

An angry delegation from Kentucky visited me today to protest the prisoner exchange of Confederate General Simon B. Buckner for General Benjamin M. Prentiss. Mother spent a good part of the day visiting two military hospitals. She tells me that the men perk up when she speaks to them. Often when she returns home from such visits she breaks into tears. She remains in a very fragile state of mind after the loss of our dear boy.

Author's notes:

General Buckner graduated from the U.S. Military Academy. After the Mexican War, Buckner had paid for then-Captain Grant's lodgings in New York when Grant was destitute. When the Civil War broke out Buckner returned to Kentucky, and when its neutrality was breached he accepted a commission in the Confederate Army. In 1862, he accepted Ulysses S. Grant's demand for "unconditional surrender" at Fort Donelson. The surrender was a humiliation for Buckner and a strategic defeat for the Confederacy. It lost over 12,000 men and control of the Cumberland River, which led to the evacuation of Nashville. Grant offered to loan Buckner money to see him through his impending imprisonment, but Buckner declined. Buckner then spent five months as a prisoner of war. General Buckner was exchanged for Brigadier General George A. McCall, and the next day was promoted to major general and ordered to Chattanooga, Tennessee, to join Bragg's Army of Mississippi. Later, he participated in Braxton Bragg's failed invasion of Kentucky. After the war he served as governor of Kentucky. Buckner acted as a pallbearer for his friend Grant and helped pay for his funeral. He also provided Grant's widow a monthly payment, so she could live out her years in peace.

General Prentis fought at the Battle of Shiloh and was captured at the infamous Hornet's Corner. After being released in October 1862 as part of a prisoner exchange, Prentiss was promoted to major general. He won the Battle of Helena on July 4, 1863, and soon resigned to attend to his family.

The White House – Friday, June 13, 1862

Seward and I met with Lord Lyons on the day before his departure for Europe and a well-deserved vacation. I admire his intelligence and wit. He is genuinely a true friend of the Union. He agrees with me that nothing must disturb the historic goodwill between our peoples. I will forever be indebted to this fine public servant, who helped Britain and the United States avoid war over the nasty matter of the Trent affair. Later Mary, Tad and I with several servants moved into the Soldiers' Home, which will be our residence for the summer. Since I will be writing diary entries from there and from the White House, I intend to continue to head my entries with only the familiar White House address.

This morning officers and men from two Illinois regiments came by to pay their respects. They were standing near a wall downstairs where two heavy fire axes were hanging crossed. I mentioned to them that I sometimes do an exercise in which I will hold an ax out at arm's length from my body, continuing to hold it for a few minutes. I asked if any of the men thought they could do that. Three tried and failed. I showed them how I do it, and they were surprised by Old Abe's strength at his age. I confessed that I had first done this exercise at age 18, and have continued to do so all my life.

Author's notes:

Carl Sandburg, in The War Years, Volume II provided these comments by General Egbert L. Viele, who commanded at the taking of Norfolk. Viele wrote of a trip on the Revenue Cutter Miami: "Few were aware of the physical strength of Mr. Lincoln. In muscular power he was one in a thousand. One morning while we were sitting on deck, he saw an ax in a socket on the bulwarks, and taking it up, held it at arm's length at the extremity of the helve with his thumb and forefinger ... continuing to hold it there for several minutes. The most powerful sailors on board tried in vain to imitate him."

The White House – Saturday, June 14, 1862

I wired General Frémont informing him that General "Stonewall" Jackson's "game" is to keep our troops away from Richmond, and that "our game" is to not allow this. I would gladly trade 12 of my best generals for just one "Stonewall" Jackson. For every mile our well-equipped troops march, his soldiers are usually able to travel twice as far. Reports from recent conflicts indicate that his men are usually poorly shod, often going barefoot.

Later in the day, Mother and I listened to Tad read to us from a marvelous book that was written 10 years ago by Harriet Beecher Stowe. The 268-page book is titled "A Key to Uncle Tom's Cabin." Nicolay discovered it at the Library of Congress and borrowed it for our family. He is always thinking of ways to be helpful. Mother has just recently finished another Stowe book, titled "Pearls of Ord Island."

Author's notes:

Within almost 11 months of this date, Lieutenant-General Thomas Jonathan "Stonewall" Jackson would be dead. He died at Guinea Station, Virginia, on May 10, 1863, of wounds received from shots fired by Confederate soldiers. He was also called "Old Jack," "Old Blue Light" and "Tom Fool" by his men. He was the most famous Southern general after Robert E. Lee. He played a prominent role in nearly all military engagements in the Eastern Theater of the war until his death, and won many important battles.

"A Key to Uncle Tom's Cabin" was written by Harriet Beecher Stowe in 1853, and published by Jewett, Proctor & Worthington following the 1852 printing of her famed novel. The book was subtitled "Presenting the Original Facts and Documents upon Which the Story is Founded, Together with Corroborative Statements Verifying the Truth of the Work."

It was an immediate best-seller when it first came out, selling over 90,000 copies within just a few months. It drew negative reviews from Southern editors. One critic, William Simms, accused Stowe of using faulty argumentation by gathering facts to prove her assumptions, instead of forming opinions based upon facts. George Holmes questioned whether "scenes of license and impurity and ideas of loathsome depravity and habitual prostitution are to be made the cherished topics of the female pen." "Uncle Tom's Cabin" became the nation's best-selling novel of the 19th century, and the best-selling book of that century, except for The Holy Bible. During the Civil War, millions of copies were sold in the United States and over a million more in Great Britain, where it fostered strong pro-Union sympathy.

The White House – Monday, June 16, 1862

I discussed with the Cabinet my decision to convert General Robert E. Lee's home at Arlington Heights into a hospital for our troops. By joining the rebellion, I believe that the general has forfeited all rights to the property. Let some of those brave men shot by guns in the hands of Lee's troops now begin to receive medical care on his estate. It seems only just to me. It is poetic justice.

However, the attorney general wonders if the government may have legal problems after the war by seizing Lee's property. Edward Bates is a very cautious and careful lawyer. I have asked him to study the matter fully before we move on the property. Bates has an excellent legal mind. He rarely offers a legal opinion unless asked. Postmaster and Bates raised an interesting point; is the land Lee's, or does it possibly belong to his wife?

They wonder if the land might be legally owned by Mary Anna (Custis) Lee, who may have inherited it. If it belongs to Lee's wife, and not to the general, Bates wonders if we may not be able to seize the land. Mrs. Lee, as the great-granddaughter of President George Washington may have legally inherited the property. Many in the country, North and South, would not want to see an heir of George Washington and/or wife offended by their government through a wrongful taking of the Lee estate.

Author's notes:

After the Civil War, Robert E. Lee settled with his family in Lexington, Virginia, having decided not to reclaim Arlington House and his property, which was seized by the federal government. Years later, Lee's son, George Washington Custis Lee, sued the U.S. government for illegally seizing the property. The Supreme Court ruled in his favor. Lee sold the property back to the government for $150,000. Arlington National Cemetery was officially established on May 13, 1864. It is owned and operated by the U.S. Department of the Army. It covers 624 acres and contains over 400,000 graves. Its website is: www.ArlingtonCemetery.mil

The White House – Tuesday, June 17, 1862

Nicolay and Hay helped me finalize a message to the House of Representative related to recommendations for the necessary reorganization of the Army Medical Bureau. Its practices to date have been scandalous, resulting in the mistreatment of our troops. The breakout of the war found the Bureau totally understaffed, underfunded, and ill-equipped to handle the heavy demands placed upon it. Less than two months ago, following the removal of surgeon general Clement Finley, I appointed Dr. William Alexander Hammond, a physician and neurologist, to be our 11th Surgeon General. His rank: Brigadier General. Stanton didn't like the appointment, but I interviewed the man and believe he is competent. Furthermore, he has military experience, having served in the peacetime Army from 1849 to 1860, where he was involved in the Sioux Wars. He has also been to Europe and observed how military hospitals are managed there.

Author's notes:

In 1860, Hammond resigned the chair of Anatomy and Physiology at the University of Maryland School of Medicine in Baltimore to rejoin the Army, and in less than a year was named Surgeon General. He quickly launched many needed reforms; raised requirements for admission into the Army Medical Corps; increased the number of hospitals; and created the Satterlee Hospital in West Philadelphia, which provided over 4,500 beds in hundreds of tents. It treated Union and Confederate patients with a low mortality rate. He founded the National Museum of Health and Medicine, then called the Army Medical Museum. He designed new ambulance wagons; proposed a permanent Medical Corps; centralized issuance of medications; and transferred responsibility for sanitary trains from private companies to the Army. Mortality decreased significantly

Despite his Herculean achievements, Secretary of War Stanton removed Hammond from his post in May of 1863 and appointed his own personal doctor to replace him. After a court martial trial, which found Hammond guilty of "irregularities in the purchase of medical equipment" (Stanton used false data), he was dismissed on August 18, 1864. In 1874 he founded, with others the American Neurological Association. In 1878 he was restored to the Army with the rank of brigadier general, without pay or allowances. Hammond was a vocal critic of Spiritualism and attributed the practice to suggestion and sleight of hand. He argued that it was itself a form of mental illness.

The White House – Thursday, June 19, 1862

Yesterday I recognized the appointment of Baron von der Osten-Sacken as counsel general of Russia at New York. In the evening Vice-President Hamlin and I rode to the Soldiers' Home for dinner. Later I read him my draft copy of the planned Emancipation Proclamation. Hamlin is supportive of the measure, agreeing that the timing for its issuance must be preceded by a major victory. I sent a strong message to McClellan advising that if the enemy has sent 10,000 troops to the Shenandoah Valley, that is as good as a reinforcement to him of an equal force. My sense is that he will fail to move on Richmond with dispatch. He is more of a drill sergeant than a general. He looks the part but fails to act the part.

Author's notes:

Lincoln's wire to McClellan read, "If large reinforcements are going from Richmond to Jackson, it proves one of two things, either they are very strong in Richmond, or do not mean to defend the place desperately."

The White House – Friday, June 20, 1862

I wrote to Counsel General William Sydney Thayer of Egypt, at the suggestion of Secretary Seward, advising him of my concerns for the safety of Christian missionaries in Egypt. He is to communicate to the Ottoman authorities that the United States expects that country to exert pressure upon local officials to see that American missionaries are protected as they practice their religious faith there.

Author's notes:

William Sydney Thayer served in Egypt from July 1, 1861, until April 10, 1864, when he died at his post. When a Syrian Christian, Faris el Hakin, an agent employed by American missionaries, had been abused by a mob of angry Egyptians, Lincoln's administration issued a White Paper titled, "Religious Toleration in Egypt." Sa'id Pasha, the wali of Egypt for the Ottoman, assured that those responsible would be punished. He also agreed that any Confederate presence in Ottoman waters would not be tolerated. British Christians supported Lincoln's White Paper, and the Crown ultimately did not support the Confederacy.

When the Union naval blockade of Southern ports went into effect, cotton exports from the Confederacy fell from 13 million tons to six million tons in one year. The Egyptian economy received its "manna" from heaven in the form of exploding exports to the European continent. Egyptian cotton exports to Britain rose from 60 million pounds in 1861 to 274 million pounds in 1865. This new source of wealth helped Europeanize Egypt and laid the foundation for the construction of the Suez Canal.

The White House – Saturday, June 21, 1862

After an early breakfast with Nicolay and Hay, I nominated 255 generals, of whom 19 are to serve as major generals. I wonder which ones will prove to be winners and which ones will become losers. It is clearly impossible to predict. Who would have imagined that the much-slandered General U.S. Grant would prove to be such a dependable winner? They keep telling me he drinks too much whiskey. Whatever he is imbibing it seems to be of an especially high grade!

Late yesterday afternoon a delegation of Progressive Friends (Quakers), who were joined by Senators Wilmot of Pennsylvania and Wilson of Massachusetts presented me with a memorial against slavery. I told these gentle people that I sometimes thought that perhaps I might be an instrument of accomplishing a great work in relation to slavery. I did not refer to the Emancipation document, which I keep in my desk drawer. I am anxious to release it and yet fear the uproar it will undoubtedly cause, particularly in the border states. In the Confederacy it will be anathema.

Author's notes:

Since Lincoln was a very young, boy he was taught by his mother, and later by his stepmother that slavery was an abomination. His enlightened views on the subject were crystalized during the Lincoln-Douglas Debates and on February 27, 1860, by his speech given at Cooper Union in New York City. Millions read his words as newspapers across the nation carried the message.

The White House – Sunday, June 22, 1862

D.O. Macomber of the firm of Ferriss & Macomber was interviewed by Stanton and me. He and his business partner are designing large cannons, which they believe will be able to fire projectiles distances of 8 to 10 miles at high velocity with unprecedented accuracy. I've instructed Stanton to arrange a demonstration as soon as practical.

I signed a postal convention with Mexico and sent to the Senate two treaties providing for a loan to Mexico. I also returned to the Senate an act regarding the circulation of bank notes with objections.

Tomorrow I leave for West Point to visit General Scott, whose advice I look forward to receiving. At noon on the 24th I will review the cadets after a tour of the Military Academy, which is scheduled from noon to 3. After dinner we will travel to Parrott's Cold Spring Foundry, which is located 3 miles away, to see rifled cannons in production. I regret that Scott is no longer at my side in Washington. He knows the men in the army better than anyone I've met to date. His judgment is always safe to rely upon.

Author's notes:

The Parrott Rifle was a muzzle-loading rifled artillery weapon used by both sides in the Civil War. Ten and 20-pounders were invented by Captain Robert Parker Parrott, a West Point graduate, who resigned from the Army in 1836 to become superintendent of the West Point Foundry in Cold Spring, New York. He created the first Parrott rifle in 1860 and patented it in 1861. The cannons were made of a combination of cast and wrought iron. Naval versions of Parrott guns in 20-30-60-and 100-pound versions were used by the Union Navy. The gun had a poor record for safety, and it was shunned by many artillerists.

The White House – Friday, June 27, 1862

After being away for a week, it is good to be back in Washington again. But from time to time it is important for me to get away from all of this. Spending time with General Scott makes me believe that I can now make some very significant decisions to improve the overall management of the war. I believe they will be the right decisions. It is helpful to be able to discuss matters of strategy and personnel in complete confidence with such a knowledgeable man. Based upon my talks with Scott, I issued orders yesterday combining the forces of Frémont, Banks and McDowell into the new Army of Virginia, under the single command of General John Pope.

A treaty negotiated with the Kansas Indians was sent to the Senate for ratification.

Author's notes:

On June 25,1862, The Seven Days Battle began. General McClellan's army was attacked by General Lee at Oak Grove, Virginia. Battles were then fought at Beaver Dam Creek or Mechanicsville, Gaines' Mill or Chickahominy River, Garnett's and Golding's Farm, Savage's Station, Glendale, White Oak Swamp, ending at Malvern Hill on July 1, 1862. McClellan defeated Lee but withdrew after the battle. He moved westward toward the James River.

General Pope would soon fail. Frémont would be relieved of command and his resignation accepted on June 27th.

The White House – Saturday, June 28, 1862

Much of today was spent composing a letter, which Secretary Seward may quote if he feels it might be helpful. He will be at a conference of Union governors who are meeting in New York City. Seward is to urge them to issue new calls for troops. I wrote that I expect to maintain this contest until successful or till I die, or am conquered, or my term expires, or Congress or the country forsakes me. Seward is a good man on his feet, and I expect he will be successful in his endeavors to enlist more soldiers.

Telegrams have been sent to McClellan notifying him that we will send him reinforcements as soon as we possibly can. Fearful battles have been raging in Virginia as I put pen to paper. Tomorrow I will meet with Charles C. Fulton, editor of the Baltimore American. He has just returned from the battlefields near Richmond. I am anxious to hear his views on the fighting that is still raging there.

Author's notes:

On this day, Lincoln found time to write a letter to cadet Quintin Campbell, who was unhappy at the U.S. Military Academy. He wrote, "Take the advice of a friend, who though he never saw you, deeply sympathizes with you, and stick to your purpose." He signed it "Sincerely your friend." Lincoln wanted Campbell to stay at the Academy and graduate.

When casualties were finally counted for the Seven Days struggle, (June 25 to July 1), Confederate losses for Lee's Army of Northern Virginia, which did the attacking, repeatedly and ferociously, totaled 20,000 men. The Union forces under McClellan lost 16,000, of whom 6,000 were captured. McClellan destroyed his supply base and retreated south. He reported to Stanton, "I have lost this battle because my force was too small. The government must not and cannot hold me responsible for the results." The fact was that the Union forces outnumbered the Confederates by over 50,000 troops.

The White House – Sunday, June 29, 1862

Breakfasted with Assistant Secretary of War Peter Watson and the Baltimore American's editor, Charles Fulton, at the Stanton residence. We were all enlightened about our Peninsula Campaign by Fulton, who observed much of the action there while he was with McClellan's Army. He confirmed for us that the carnage was horrific. After seeing all that bloodshed, the editor is convinced that although our men are brave, our military leaders seem to lack the necessary élan required to gain their objectives. He stressed that the average soldier still has a high regard for McClellan.

Later in the day we received eight elderly women at the White House who had travelled here by rail from Philadelphia, Pennsylvania to present Mother with a beautiful blanket that they had quilted. They had also quilted a smaller one for Tad. The larger one is in a log cabin pattern, with rails around the border. They said the design was to represent my young days as a rail-splitter. Tad's quilt had many stars on it representing every state in the Union, including those that are in rebellion. They had sewn the message "The Union Forever" in red, white and blue thread. The ladies said that women in their area are now holding craft bazaars to raise money for Union hospitals, with most of the items sold being hand-made quilts. I have been told that Southern women have been making "Gunboat Quilts," with funds from the sales of these items going to pay for three ironclad gunboats.

Author's notes:

Northern women were accustomed to meeting together and sewing for a cause. Church and abolition groups simply changed their focus when war came to helping soldiers. Many thousands of Soldiers' Aid Societies were formed. Once the Sanitation Commission was established to prevent the death of soldiers from disease, an urgent need for bedding became apparent. The Commission included the collection and distribution of donated quilts to their activities. At first family quilts were donated. Then women began to produce quilts specifically for the war effort. An estimated 25,000 quilts and comforters were made for Union soldiers. Few quilts made for the soldiers survived. Many had been worn out by rough use, and soldiers were frequently buried in their quilts.

Southern women did not have a tradition of quilting for causes. Wealthier women were accustomed to having their slaves do the everyday sewing. The South could not get sewing materials through their blockaded ports, and had no real textile manufacturing base of its own. Calico cost as much as $25 a yard at the end of the war. Old clothes were cut up and mattresses were torn apart for quilting material. Southern women raised enough money from fairs and auctions of quilts to buy three ironclad gunboats.

The White House – Monday, June 30, 1862

William Whiting, a well-known Boston abolitionist, and one of the leading attorneys in New England, mailed me an autographed copy of his just-published pamphlet, "The War Powers of the President, and the Legislative Powers of Congress in Relation to Rebellion, Treason and Slavery." I must write him a thank-you letter. It is a very thoughtful treatise. It reviews the legalities of the most important subject upon my own mind – Emancipation. I am very grateful for his gift. He has given me new insights into my war powers, and the limits placed upon them under the Constitution. I've had many doubts about my legal authority to issue an Emancipation Proclamation. Lawyers whom I have spoken to about it all offer me mixed advice. But then again, lawyers are trained to take either side of any issue presented to them. Whiting holds that the laws of war give the president "full belligerent rights as Commander-in-Chief to seize enemy property, (slaves) being used to wage war against the United States." He argues that slaves once seized by the government would never be allowed to be re-enslaved. I concur.

Author's notes:

William Whiting (March 3, 1813 – June 29, 1873) attended Concord Academy and graduated from Harvard Law School in 1833. His pamphlet had a large sale in the United States and abroad. Lincoln appointed him solicitor of the War Department (1862 to 1865). In 1868 he was a presidential elector. In 1872 he was elected to the 43rd Congress and served until his death in 1873. Colby gave him the degree of Doctor of Law in 1872. He left a scholarship to Harvard University. He was for five years president of the New England Historic Genealogical Society.

The White House – Tuesday, July 1, 1862

There are few men that I have met since taking office who impress me as much as Captain Andrew H. Foote. He is the consummate naval officer: brave, inspiring and best of all, a winner. At the recommendation of Navy Secretary Gideon Wells, I have recommended to Congress that Foote receive a second vote of confidence for his recent achievements in the West. This time he is to be honored for his remarkable achievements at Fort Henry, Fort Donelson and Island Ten. He and General Grant make a great pair. They work in tandem and the results are there for all to see.

Author's notes:

In 1837 Foote circumnavigated the globe. Before the Civil War he became an abolitionist, and in 1854 he authored a 390-page book, "Africa and the American Flag." It described the geography of the African continent, the customs of its people, the establishment of U.S. colonies in Africa and the evils of slavery. In 1856 Commander Foote was assigned the mission of observing British operations against Canton, China, during the Second Opium War.

Late in 1862, Foote was promoted to rear admiral. In 1863, on his way to assume command of the South Atlantic Squadron, he suddenly died. His untimely death shocked the nation. Three United States naval vessels have been named after him.

The White House – Tuesday, July 2, 1862

My approval was given to an Internal Revenue tax of 3 percent on incomes in excess of $600 and less than $10,000. The income produced by this tax is to pay for support of the government and to make payments on the public debt. After much discussion within the Cabinet, and with congressional leaders, I have asked the governors of 17 states and the military board of Kentucky to furnish our armed forces with 300,000 volunteers.

We also discussed the matter of polygamy in Utah. Marriage can be a difficult arrangement in normal times, but it is particularly demanding in wartime. I must get 300 to 400 letters a day, and most of them are from women, including widows. Some are left in dire straits when the man of the house is called to war or worse, when he is wounded or killed. Imagine how a Mormon man must feel if he has two, three or more wives to worry about. I have found that one wife is just the right number!

The Morrill Anti-Bigamy Act was introduced on April 9, 1862, by Congressman Justin Smith Morrill of Vermont and passed by the House on April 28. I plan to sign the bill next week. I have written to General Patrick Connor, commanding officer of the Fort Douglas garrison in Utah, ordering him not to confront the Mormons over this matter, or any other issue.

Author's notes:

During the Civil War, Mormon men did not join either the Union or Confederate Armies. Lincoln chose not to enforce the Morrill Act. He entered into an agreement with Brigham Young, the Mormon leader, not to allocate funds to enforce the law, in exchange for Young agreeing not to become involved in the war. In 1890, the Church of Latter Day Saints discontinued the practice of polygamy and "no longer encouraged or gave countenance to any manner of practices in violation of law, or contrary to good morals or public policy."

The White House – Thursday, July 3, 1862

Tomorrow will be the Fourth of July. Tad will be expecting to watch some fireworks in the evening on the lawn of the Soldiers Home. Nicolay and Hay have been instructed to make all the arrangements. I gave them $50 for the purchase of firecrackers, rockets and Roman candles. To my mind The Declaration of Independence, which was agreed upon by the Continental Congress and presented to John Hancock to sign on that day in 1776, is the single most significant document in the history of our country. My job, just 86 years later, is to ensure that what those brave and wise men signed shall continue to inspire all of our people, North and South. The words should be taught in our schools. Let America's young children learn to recite them.

At 3 P.M. I signed a Treaty of Commerce with the Ottoman Empire. Later Stanton and I discussed the treatment of fugitive slaves, who grow in number as the war expands into new territories covered by our forces. My decision is that negroes who flee to our side cannot be forced back to their masters. They cannot be allowed to starve and should be given food, work to do and paid reasonable wages for their efforts.

Author's notes:

On the Fourth of July, soldiers of the War of 1812 assembled in the Post Office Department at 11 A.M. and marched to the White House to pay their respects to the president. Lincoln replied to remarks made by Colonel William W. Seaton, president of the Association of Surviving Soldiers of the War of 1812 and editor of the Washington Intelligencer.

The White House – Friday, July 4, 1862

Early in the morning I met a long train of 25 or more ambulances on the road that leads from the Soldiers Home to the capital. The passengers were casualties from recent fighting during the Peninsula campaign. I talked to about 20 of the men, who though they were wounded or sick, were still able to stand. It was a sorry sight. These men were pleased to shake my hand, and I was proud to shake theirs. When I left them, they gave me a loud holler of a cheer. It made my heart pound to be among such brave and heroic boys.

At the White House I signed the Pacific Railroad Act. As I did so my thoughts were of my hero, Henry Clay, who favored "internal improvements," as he called them. How proud Henry would be to learn that by this law, the United States government will promote construction of a transcontinental railroad through the issuance of bonds and grants of land to railroad companies. It is ironic that the person who was authorized by the Congress in 1853 to conduct surveys of five different potential routes for a transcontinental railroad was then-Secretary of War Jefferson Davis.

Author's notes:

The 30-year federal government bonds authorized by the act would provide the capital raised to the railroad companies upon completion of sections in return for a lien on that section. From 1850 to 1871, the railroads received more than 175 million acres of public land. Railroad expansion provided new avenues of migration into the American interior. Railroads sold portions of land to arriving settlers at handsome profits. The act established the official gauge of the Pacific Railroad and its branches. It was standardized at 4 feet and 8.5 inches. This was the same exact gauge that had been previously used by George Stevenson for the Liverpool and Manchester Railroad in 1830. It was already popular in the Northeastern states. Today this is known as Standard Gauge. Lincoln never lived to see the railroad completed, which occurred on May 10, 1869, when the western and eastern railroads met at Promontory Summit, Utah.

The White House – Sunday, July 6, 1862

Saturday evening, I retired early. I was too exhausted to keep several appointments. Earlier in the day I transmitted to the Senate the recently concluded treaty with the Sac and Fox Indian tribes on the Mississippi. These Indians have many grievances against the federal government, and against other branches of their own tribe. They feel they are being cheated and I tend to agree with them. Once this war is over it will be one of my goals to review all our government's many agreements with native Americans. Too often I fear we have broken promises made with impunity. I have made a note to myself to do so. One of these days I am going to buy a notebook, and in it make a "To Do" list of all my future plans.

Mother is concerned about my sleeping habits. Lately I have not been sleeping well. Too much on my mind, I guess. I did find time to send a telegram to McClellan. It quoted a copy of the Richmond Examiner, which came into my hands today. Its editor censured the Confederate generals severely for "failing to capture General McClellan and his army." It pronounces, "McClellan's whole movement a masterpiece of strategy." I do not share the editor's viewpoint; it was not a masterpiece of strategy! My plans for the next four days are to travel to Fortress Monroe and Harrison's Landing in Virginia to carefully inspect the condition of the Army of the Potomac, including its senior officers.

Author's notes:

Lincoln had a longtime habit of penning his thoughts on small pieces of paper, which he then often saved in drawers, and boxes, and even in his top hat. After the war his assistants, Hay and Nicolay, found many of his jottings and saved them. Lincoln did not date his notes. They were not signed or titled, but they were in his distinctive handwriting. Iowa Congressman James F. Wilson told Lincoln that he admired the president's ability to sit down and write eloquent public letters. Lincoln disagreed, saying, "I had it nearly all in there," pointing to an open desk drawer in his White House office. He told Wilson that he often referred to disconnected thoughts, which he had written down on separate scraps of paper, even on the back of envelopes. He said that many of these notes had been saved for years. He called them his "best thoughts" and "best ideas" on many important subjects.

The White House – Friday, July 11, 1862

We returned yesterday from a visit to our troops aboard the U.S.S. Ariel. While gone I had Nicolay send son Robert $280. Robert would like to serve in the war, but Mother is adamant that he remains at Harvard, where he has been getting respectable grades.

The three-day trip to Virginia allowed me to spend time with senior military and naval officers, as well as with the common soldiers. I dined with General Burnside aboard the steamer, Alice Price on the 9th of July. Our ship ran aground on Kettle Shoals, and the delay of several hours in getting off allowed us time to take a pleasant swim in the Potomac. Burnside is a modest man in speech, who impresses me as a thoughtful man of caution. He was born in Indiana, the descendant of slave-owning Scots who had settled in South Carolina. He told me that his parents sold their slaves before moving north. His mother died when he was a lad, and he was apprenticed to a local tailor, eventually becoming a partner in the business. He then managed to gain an appointment to West Point, graduating 18th in a class of 47. He ran for Congress as a Democrat in 1858. He told me that he lost in a landslide.

Author's notes:

Unlike his father, who had little formal education, Robert Todd Lincoln entered Phillips Exeter Academy in 1859 before attending Harvard. He graduated from Harvard in 1864 and received an Army commission as captain and assistant to General Ulysses S. Grant in 1865. He witnessed Lee's surrender at Appomattox Court House and six days later watched his father die of gunshot wounds. He studied law at the University of Chicago and passed the Illinois bar examination in 1867. He inherited $36,991.54 from his father's estate. In 1868 he married Mary Eunice Harlan in Washington, D.C. In 1875 he committed his mother, Mary Todd Lincoln, to a mental institution, after a public trial declared her insane. He became secretary of war under President James Garfield in 1881 and witnessed Garfield being shot. He inherited $84,035 from his mother's estate in 1884. In 1889 President Benjamin Harrison named him minister to England, where he was presented to Queen Victoria at Windsor Castle. He became president of the Pullman Car Company in 1897. He moved to Hildene, his country estate in Manchester, Vermont in 1905. He retired from the Pullman Company on January 14, 1922. May 30, 1922, he attended the dedication of the Lincoln Memorial. He died July 26, 1926, in Vermont. His last known descendant, Robert Todd Lincoln Beckwith, died in 1985 at age 81 in Saluda, Virginia.

The White House – Saturday, July 12, 1862

Last evening General Halleck was ordered to take command of all the land forces of the Union Army as general-in-chief. I expect that he will bring about much better coordination among our forces. I took this action in keeping with the recommendation of General Scott two weeks ago, who attests to Halleck's wisdom. The question remains; do I need more wisdom in a general, or more audacity and willingness to destroy our enemies?

Another reason why I did this is because McClellan made a disastrous mistake during the Battle of Malvern Hill, when Lee made a frontal attack on our lines in the face of over 240 Union cannons. Lee's Army was seriously damaged, yet McClellan, instead of attacking him, retreated from the field, claiming he was badly outnumbered. Several who I talked to on my trip contended that, had McClellan exploited Lee's serious losses, we might have taken Richmond and captured much of Lee's Army.

I also made this significant change because in a letter presented to me by McClellan, he stated that the forcible abolition of slavery should not be contemplated by our administration. He also asked that I appoint a new Commander-in-Chief, forgetting I guess, that I hold that title; it is not one to be delegated to anyone else. The issue of slavery and the abolition of it is a purely political matter, not one of military concern to our generals.

Author's notes:

On this date Lincoln signed a bill creating a national award for valor, known as the Congressional Medal of Honor. He also invited senators and representatives of border states to the White House and appealed to them to support compensated emancipation.

Only one U.S. president has been awarded the Congressional Medal of Honor. It was awarded to President Theodore Roosevelt posthumously.

The White House – Sunday, July 13, 1862

After attending church services early this morning with Mother and Tad, I spent quite a bit of time calculating and recalculating the number of troops and he enemy forces had engaged in the Peninsula campaign. The records that General McClellan provided to me during my recent visit to his headquarters showed a total of 160,000 men involved in the campaign against Richmond. The War Department figures show 23,500 killed, wounded and missing. My sense of the matter is that McClellan has again overestimated the strength of the enemy.

Mother says that I am beginning to look weary, careworn and troubled. I told her that, based upon the past few weeks of worrying about our soldiers, I surely should have a troubled look about me.

Author's notes:

Later estimates showed that Lee's Army of Northern Virginia suffered heavy casualties (3,494 killed, 15,758 wounded and 952 captured or missing) out of 90,000 soldiers engaged. McClellan had casualties of about 16,000 (1,734 killed, 8,062 wounded and 6,053 captured) out of a total of 105,445 engaged. Northern morale suffered because of McClellan's withdrawal. Confederate morale skyrocketed, and Lee was emboldened to continue his aggressive strategy through Second Bull Run and the Maryland campaign.

The White House – Monday, July 14, 1862

Tad and I were visited this morning by Major Thelonius Sledge. He is the son of a former neighbor from New Salem, Illinois. His father, Thomas Sledge, was a gifted attorney, I knew for many years in Springfield. I asked Thelonius to stand behind me so that I could compare his height with mine. I stand 6 feet 4 inches. He had me beat by an inch. Sledge was in several of the battles leading up to the recent fighting at Malvern Hill. In that fight, his artillery company suffered FIVE men killed. Sledge was slightly wounded in the arm and expects to be back with his unit within another week or so. He mentioned the family names of some of his comrades who are from Springfield, but I did not recognize any of them from the past. Tad found his first name very interesting and asked if it comes from the Latin language. Thelonius told Tad that in Latin the name means "one who plows the earth." If my father had known that, he might have called me Thelonius, instead of Abraham, for I surely plowed a lot of earth.

When I read for the law, New Salem was a very small community. I moved to Springfield when New Salem's population fell. In April of 1837 I rode to Springfield carrying all my worldly possessions in my saddlebags. I became a partner in the law firm of Stuart and Lincoln. It was then that I became acquainted with Thomas Sledge, who remains a strong abolitionist. I asked Thelonius to give my best regards to his father, who is no longer practicing law. It was pleasant remembering far happier days in Illinois.

Author's notes:

Lincoln gave this sage advice to a law student "If you are resolutely determined to make a lawyer of yourself, the thing is more than half done already. It is but a small matter whether you read with anybody or not. I did not read with anyone. Get the books and read and study them until you understand them in all their principal features; and that is the main thing. It is of no consequence to be in a large town while you are reading. I read in New Salem, which never had 300 people living in it. The books, and your capacity for understanding them, are just the same in all places. Always bear in mind that your own resolution to succeed is more important than any other one thing."

The White House – Tuesday, July 15, 1862

Today, I worked for several hours researching the legal basis for the Emancipation Proclamation, which I plan to share with the Cabinet in a week from now. I have kept useful notes about slavery for over about 20 years. Many date back to my earliest days as a young attorney who spent his days traveling the legal circuit. Tad and I discussed the Emancipation Proclamation with Mother, who is fully supportive of the liberating ideas in the document. My main concern is that when it is finally issued the nation will realize that its goal is to shorten the war by treating slaves as material of war who aid our enemy. By our liberating its millions of slaves, the Confederacy must ultimately grow increasingly weaker, as it loses valuable labor on its farms and plantations. If slavery is the key underpinning of the Confederacy, then it follows that this act must over time greatly diminish the South's economic and military strength.

Author's notes:

Lincoln calculated that the circuit he traveled as a lawyer included 15 counties in Illinois and roughly 8,000 square miles. He tried his first case in the Circuit Court in Sangamon County. Within two years of his admission to the bar he was practicing in federal courts, and a year later before the State Supreme Court. Many cases were handled before justices of the peace. Lincoln traveled the circuit for six months each year. He loved his life as a traveling lawyer. His travels made him well known throughout Illinois.

The White House – Thursday, July 17, 1862

I notified Congress that Commodore Cornelius Vanderbilt has presented his steamer, "Vanderbilt," as a gift to the country. It shall be used for Coast Guard duty. Vanderbilt is a remarkable self-made man. His generosity is greatly appreciated.

Author's notes:

The Vanderbilt cost $1,000,000, and at 355 feet in length was the world's largest personal yacht. It had dual smoke stacks and gigantic side paddle wheels. Vanderbilt refused to take money for the ship and paid for its armaments, including a steel ram. After the war, Vanderbilt bailed Jefferson Davis out of a federal prison. He married a cousin and a Southern woman who had the unusual name of, Frank Armstrong Crawford. She had been loyal to the Confederacy. In 1873, at age 79, he donated $1,000,000 to found Vanderbilt University, located in Nashville, Tennessee, his only major philanthropy. Congress awarded him a gold medal to honor his contribution of the Vanderbilt to the war effort.

The White House – Friday, July 18, 1862

Senators Lyman Trumbull of Illinois and James Doolittle of Wisconsin joined me for breakfast to discuss important political and military appointments. I trust the sound judgment of both men. James Doolittle is a no-nonsense gent; whose political insights are of high value to me. We also reviewed the military picture, including A Union victory at Cotton Plant in Arkansas on the 7th of the month, and our defeat at Murfreesboro, which occurred in Tennessee five days ago.

Author's notes:

During the First Battle of Murfreesboro, in Rutherford County, Tennessee, Confederate cavalry troops under Nathan Bedford Forrest outnumbered Union forces 1,400 to 900. Forrest had left Chattanooga on July 9 with two cavalry regiments to strike Murfreesboro, a key Union supply center on the Nashville & Chattanooga Railroad. Forrest's men surprised Union pickets and quickly overran a federal hospital and the camp of the 9th Pennsylvania Cavalry. Confederate troops attacked other Union positions, including at the jail and courthouse. By late afternoon all Union forces had surrendered to Forrest. Union supplies and railroad tracks were destroyed.

A second battle would be fought at this site from December 31, 1862, to January 2, 1863, resulting in a Union win. Confederate General Braxton Bragg would be forced to withdraw, after a loss of 1,739 men.

The White House – Saturday, July 19, 1862

I received 12 committee members of the Synod of the Reformed Presbyterian Church this morning, who kindly presented me with a resolution on the evils of slavery. It calls for the federal government to free all the slaves now held in America. These good people are passionate abolitionists who believe, as I do, that no man may own another man or woman in slavery. Most members of this conservative sect are descendants of Scottish protestant believers, who accept the scriptures of the Old and New Testaments to be the word of God, and the only infallible rule for faith and life. They are among the very strictest Bible believers. No members may own slaves. They represented members from Rhode Island, New Jersey and Pennsylvania congregations. They promised to pray for me. I asked that they also pray for the nation in this time of turmoil.

Author's notes:

The Reformed branch of the Presbyterian Church had 7,076 members in 75 North American congregations in 2016, along with 238 more members in four congregations in Japan. Most church members live in Kansas, central Indiana and western Pennsylvania. The denomination sponsors Geneva College in Beaver Falls, Pennsylvania, and operates the Reformed Presbyterian Theological Seminary in Pittsburgh, Pennsylvania. A denominational magazine, the Reformed Presbyterian Witness, is published monthly.

The White House – Monday, July 21, 1862

At a very long Cabinet meeting, we discussed proposed military actions and the vexing issue of slavery in the loyal border states. Secretary Wells brought up the subject of Assistant Professor William R. Hopkins, who was recently dismissed by the Naval Academy. After hearing the charges leveled against Hopkins, I asked that he be restored to his teaching place, if he is found to be loyal to the Union. Letters I have received from several serving naval officers strongly support Hopkins. They write that he is a fine officer and a great teacher. Their opinions carry a great deal of weight with me. I've agreed to Welles' suggestion that Vanderbilt's schooner, America, which we've taken for naval use, be permanently assigned to the Naval Academy to serve as a training ship. We still use "Old Ironsides," the U.S.S. Constitution, which was commissioned by George Washington.

Author's notes:

By the Civil War's end, 400 graduates of the United States Naval Academy served in the Union Navy and 95 in the Confederate Navy; 23 were killed in action. On August 9, 1865 the Academy returned to Annapolis after four years at Newport, Rhode Island. They sailed aboard the U.S.S. Constitution, the oldest commissioned ship in the U.S. Navy, and one of the world's oldest warships. She was retired from active duty in 1881. In 1931 she toured the United States in a 90-port tour and sailed again in 1997 on her 200th birthday. Every Fourth of July she sails into Boston Harbor to turn the ship around so that it gets equal exposure to the elements when docked. During this annual sail she salutes Fort Independence with her cannons during each round trip from her location at Charlestown Navy Yard. The U.S.S. Constitution is open for guided tours throughout the year.

The White House – Tuesday, July 22, 1862

Last night I tried, without great success, to teach Tad the words to "Old Ironsides," one of my favorite poems. It was written by Oliver Wendell Holmes, whose son is now serving in the Army. If his father had not written the poem, the U.S.S. Constitution would probably have been allowed to rot, and that great ship would no longer be serving the nation.

I explained to Tad that it was one of the original six frigates of our Navy, which were commissioned way back in 1794 by George Washington. Holmes wrote the poem after he had read that the ship, which had defeated H.M.S. Guerriere, was about to be dismantled and scrapped. The poem was reprinted in newspapers across the nation and public opinion led to the ship's preservation. I particularly like these lines:

> "Aye tear her tattered ensign down
>   Long has it waved on high,
> And many an eye has danced to see
>   That banner in the sky;
> Beneath it rung the battle shout,
>   And burst the cannon's roar:
> The meteor of the ocean air
>   Shall sweep the clouds no more."

Author's notes:

Oliver Wendell Holmes, Jr., son of the poet, enlisted in the Union Army in 1861 while attending Harvard University. He fought for three years as a Captain in the 20th Massachusetts Volunteer Infantry, a unit that was nicknamed "Harvard's Army." He was wounded three times. In 1864 he began attending Harvard Law School, and later taught there as a professor. In 1902 President Theodore Roosevelt appointed him to the U.S. Supreme Court. He retired in 1931, at the age of 91.

The White House – Wednesday, July 23, 1862

Yesterday, I read to the full Cabinet my latest draft of an Emancipation Proclamation. As written it will become effective January 1,1963. After much back and forth, Seward recommended that we delay the public announcement until the Union Armies have achieved a significant victory. I think that's a wise suggestion and will take it.

Once again, much time was given to the question of keeping or firing of General McClellan. Secretary Chase strongly recommends that he be removed from command of the Army of the Potomac. Secretary Stanton was granted liberty to take all necessary steps to enroll militia of the several states to draft men to fill old regiments that have been depleted in strength from recent military actions.

Author's notes:

Seward told Lincoln that he should postpone the announcement "until you can give it to the country supported by military success." Otherwise the world might view it as an incitement to slave insurrections, "as the last measure of an exhausted government, a cry for help...our last shriek, on the retreat." Lincoln later said that this advice "struck me with very great force." So he placed the Proclamation in his desk drawer and held it for what proved to be a longer wait than he had anticipated.

The White House – Thursday, July 24, 1862

When I returned to the Executive Office, after attending an educational program at the Smithsonian Institution, where I handed student awards, I received a telegraphic message advising me that former President Martin Van Buren died at 2 A.M. this morning at his home in Kinderhook, New York. He is the only president to have been alive during both the Revolutionary War and the Civil War. In the last election he supported my friend Stephen A. Douglas for president, and helped create a fusion ticket in New York of Democratic electors pledged to Douglas and Breckinridge. I, however, carried New York and every Northern state except New Jersey. Once Fort Sumter was attacked, Van Buren made public his strong support for the Union cause. He was very helpful in trying for many years to keep the Southern states from succeeding. He was 79 years of age when he died.

I issued an order that, as a mark of respect, the Executive Mansion and all government offices except War and Navy be placed in mourning, and that all business be suspended tomorrow, July 25. I admired Van Buren and appreciated his welcomed support when war broke out. He had a remarkable career in public service. Few Americans have held so many important posts during their political careers. Raised speaking Dutch, for him English was a second language.

Author's notes:

Van Buren's home in Kinderhook, New York, which he called Lindenwald, is now the Martin Van Buren National Historic Site. Counties are named for him in Michigan, Iowa, Arkansas and Tennessee. He was the eighth president of the United States, eight vice-president, minister to the United Kingdom, tenth U.S. secretary of state, ninth governor of New York, attorney general of New York, U.S. senator and surrogate of Columbia County, New York.

The White House – Saturday, July 26, 1862

Brigadier General George Foster Shepley met with Seward, Stanton and me to discuss the military occupation of New Orleans. Shepley attended Dartmouth College and studied law at Harvard. He has been a lawyer in Maine since his admission to the bar in 1839. He was U.S. attorney for the District of Maine before he enlisted as a colonel of the 12th Maine Volunteer Infantry Regiment. He has been acting as military mayor of New Orleans since May 20 of this year. When he returns he will assume the post of military governor of all the occupied parishes of Louisiana. It is vitally important that we have a man in this post who will be highly regarded and respected by the citizens of this key state. Our strategy, now that we possess New Orleans, will be to move our forces ever northward up the Mississippi. The goal: total control of the river from its northern source to the Delta. I think under Shepley the city will be in good hands.

Author's notes:

After the war Shepley returned to private law practice in Portland, Maine, where he served as a member of the Maine House of Representatives from 1866 to 1867. President Ulysses Grant nominated him to a new seat on the U.S. Circuit Court in 1869, and he continued to serve on that court until his death in 1878.

The White House – Sunday, July 27, 1862

Secretary Seward suggested that I consider appointing Thomas Dow Jones as consular to Italy. Jones is a very interesting man, who I first met in Springfield in early 1860. He had been commissioned by the leading Republicans of Cincinnati to sculpt a portrait bust of me, to be finished before my inauguration. He arrived on Christmas Day with letters of recommendation from Salmon Chase, and Thomas Ewing, Sherman's father-in-law. I agreed to sit for Jones and gave him permission to sculpt my likeness at the St. Nicholas Hotel in Springfield. He was to work on the bust until I had to leave for my trip to Washington. He told me that he came from humble beginnings, starting out as an apprentice stonecutter and mason, who worked alongside his father in Ohio. Before doing statues and busts he made a living sculpting grave monuments. He eventually opened a studio on Broadway in Manhattan. His works have been exhibited in New York and throughout the Midwest. Mother was very pleased with his finished work of me. It is the first bust made of me with a beard. I have written to George Marsh, our ambassador to Italy seeking his opinion on our adding another person to his staff,

Author's notes:

A white painted copy of the plaster cast of Lincoln by Jones may be seen in the Indiana State House. It measures 33 inches by 25 inches by 18 inches. It is a copy of an 1861 clay bust. Jones' bust of Lincoln is also in the permanent collection of the Smithsonian National Portrait Gallery in Washington, D.C. The figure is draped in a cape, wearing a suit and tie. The bust is inscribed, Patented June 3, 1862, on the bust's posterior center. It is found on a white, wooden base in the northeast exterior niche of the Indiana Statehouse rotunda. A gold plaque reads: Abraham Lincoln, Born Feb. 12, 1809 – Died Apr. 15, 1865. Came to Indiana 1816. Served in the Black Hawk War, 1832. Illinois House of Representatives, 1834 – 1841. Congressman from Illinois, 1847 – 1849. U.S. President, Mar. 4, 1861 until his death Apr. 15, 1865.

Thomas Dow Jones was commissioned to create portrait busts of Chief Justice Salmon P. Chase, Henry Clay and General Winfield Scott. He was a member of the National Academy of Design, where he exhibited his work from 1853 to 1856. This author has found no evidence that Jones ever received a presidential consular appointment to Italy or any other country.

The White House – Monday, July 28, 1862

Mother had two spiritualists visiting her this weekend. She believes they possess the ability to contact the dead. I do not hold with the practice of séances. After Willie left us, Mother was told that Jane Pierce was successful in doing this after she was contacted by the Fox sisters, Leah, Margaret and Kate, who held several séances in the White House. Jane's life was filled with tragedies, from the deaths of her children to the tragic alcoholism of her husband.

Since Willie died, Mary has been contacted by several spiritualists, including Cranston Laurie, Nettie Colburn Maynard and William Shockle. She has also written to Arthur Colchester of Georgetown. When Mary attends a spiritual meeting, it is always held in the Red Room. I attended once. It was more than enough for me. Cranston Laurie has made Mary doubt the loyalty of Secretary Chase, and I find this intrusion into the personalities of Cabinet members disturbing. Mary has agreed not to invite him back. Mary's sister, Emilie, told me that Mary believes Willie sometimes comes to her at night and stands at the foot of her bed with the same sweet adorable smile he has always had; and he does not always come alone. Little Eddie is sometimes with him. If Mary can get comfort from her seances, I will do nothing but support her participation in them. But I fear that she is hanging on to a very thin thread. The last time we spoke on the subject, she told me that "a very slight veil separates us from the beloved and the lost, and though unseen they are very near."

Author's notes:

President Franklin Pierce and his wife, Jane, had three children, all of whom died young: Franklin Pierce, Jr. (February 2 – 4, 1836), Franklin "Frank" Robert Pierce (1839 – 1843) – died age 4 from typhus, and Benjamin "Bennie" Pierce (April 1841 to 1853) – two months before Franklin Pierce's inauguration as president. A tragedy occurred as the family traveled by train from Andover, Massachusetts, to Concord, New Hampshire, to attend a family friend's funeral. Minutes after departure, their passenger car broke loose from the train and rolled down an embankment. The only fatality was Benjamin Pierce. Jane Pierce took this as a sign that God was displeased with her husband's political ambitions. She became consumed by melancholy after losing every one of her young children. She never recovered from the shocking death of Benjamin. For nearly two years she remained upstairs in the living quarters of the White House, spending her days writing letters to her dead son. She died of tuberculosis in Andover, Massachusetts, on December 2, 1863. President Pierce died October 8, 1869.

The White House – Tuesday, July 29, 1862

I hear repeated complaints about General Benjamin Butler, probably more often than against any other general in the Army. He is an odd duck, but a smart duck. He is undoubtedly a man of initiative and creative thinking. However, he tends to want to hang men for offenses most would not consider hanging offenses. His doing so to William B. Mumford of New Orleans for tearing down an American flag was unwise and unjustified. I have instructed him that any future death penalties in New Orleans must be approved by me before being carried out. We have been receiving complaints about Butler from foreign governments including France, Britain and Holland. I've asked Seward to send Reverdy Johnson down to New Orleans in investigate these foreign complaints about some of Butler's policies. We don't benefit from any policies that offend nations we wish to keep neutral, particularly England and France. My sense of the matter is that the general may have outlived his usefulness in his present post, but that he may be of far greater service to the Union in a new assignment I have in mind.

Author's notes:

The hanging of Mumford outraged the South. Confederate President Jefferson Davis, who knew Butler very well before the war, condemned Butler in General Order 111 as a felon deserving of capital punishment, who if captured should be reserved for execution. After the war, Butler payed off the mortgage of Mumford's widow and helped her to find government employment.

The White House – Wednesday, July 30, 1862

It has been three months since the Confederacy initiated military conscription. From a Richmond newspaper report we learn that their new law drafts healthy, white males 18 to 35 for three-year terms and extends terms of those serving under one-year enlistments for another two years. The act also allows those drafted to find substitutes to serve in their place, and it exempts men serving in vital occupations. It also provides exemptions for men who own or oversee 20 or more slaves. This act shows that in terms of manpower the South is weaker than we initially thought. The truth is that the Union may soon find itself in the same position that the South does now. Our volunteer well may run dry.

Yesterday, I met with a New York committee to discuss recruiting for old regiments. I instructed Seward to advise Thurlow Weed of New York that I am opposed to forced conscription at this time, but that I am also aware that we should plan for it, if our calls for volunteers fail to meet our assigned manpower quotas to the governors.

I personally admire Weed. He and I share similar life stories. He was born dirt poor in upstate New York. As a boy he worked as a cabin boy on boats that sailed the Hudson River. He told me that in his first political campaign he was for John Quincy Adams. He began the Albany Evening Journal in 1830. He told me he was editor, reporter, proofreader and political exert. I believe him. He and I have spoken several times about Henry Clay, my political hero and his. Since my election, he has served as an unofficial envoy to Britain and France. I've discussed my Emancipation document with him and he cautions releasing it at this time. He considers it too radical and prefers a more "gradual emancipation." I've told him that is like recommending that a woman be just a little bit pregnant. To my mind, Emancipation must ultimately be full or not at all.

Author's notes:

Thurlow Weed was instrumental in the presidential nominations of William Henry Harrison, Zachary Taylor, Winfield Scott and John Frémont. He led the New York effort to nominate William Seward at the 1860 Republican Convention, but the convention nominated Abraham Lincoln instead. After the Civil War, Weed and Seward allied with President Andrew Johnson and supported Johnson's approach to Reconstruction. Weed retired from public life in 1867 and died in 1882, at age 85.

The White House – Thursday, July 31, 1862

I composed a letter and mailed it to New York financier August Belmont. He had written that "I must take a decisive course as to restoration of Union." I referred Mr. Belmont to my Inaugural Address, to two regular messages to Congress and to many more documents issued by me since the inauguration. I stressed to Belmont that those in the rebellious states must understand that they cannot experiment for 10 years trying to destroy the government of the U.S., and if they fail, still come back into the Union unhurt. My view is that if they expect ever to have the Union as it was, that now is the time for them to act. Unfortunately, I learned over many years as a country lawyer that few, if any divorces, ever lead to an "amicable reunion." Just the opposite is the case. Belmont was a strong backer of Stephen Douglas for president. Douglas always spoke highly to me of Belmont, calling him a man of high character.

Author's notes:

Belmont was born in the Grand Duchy of Hesse, in Germany, in 1813. He clerked for the Rothschild banking firm in Frankfurt, Germany. In 1837, he formed the firm of August Belmont & Company in New York. In 1844, he was named consul-general of the Austrian Empire in New York City. In 1853, President Franklin Pierce named Belmont chargé d'affaires to The Hague of the Kingdom of the Netherlands. He served as minister resident there until 1857. While in the Netherlands he urged American annexation of Cuba as a new slave state in what became known as the Ostend Manifesto. In 1860 Stephen Douglas nominated Belmont as chairman of the Democratic National Committee. He supported the Union cause during the Civil War as a "War Democrat." He helped Representative Francis P. Blair of Missouri raise and equip the Union Army's first predominantly German-American regiment. He influenced European business and political leaders to support the Union cause in the Civil War and helped persuade the Rothschilds and French bankers from lending funds or giving credit for military purchases to the Confederacy. He met with Lord Palmerston, the British prime minister and Emperor Napoleon III's government in Paris.

The White House – Friday, August 1, 1862

Colonel Henry Denning of Connecticut came by with Stanton today. He presented me with two enemy officers' swords with scabbards, which were sent to me by General Butler from New Orleans. Butler is the only general in the war to do so. He is a rara avis. I shall show them to Tad this evening. I'm sure he'll want to keep one. They will both be sent to the Smithsonian.

In compliance with a recent act of Congress, I pardoned 90 imprisoned soldiers for various crimes. My sense of military justice is that a man who has gotten in minor trouble is better off when put back in the line, rather than become a burden to the Army as a prisoner, particularly in times like these, when we are asking governors to send us more men. A good man who has done a bad or dumb thing is still after all a good man. At least in my eyes. He cannot shoot many Confederates from his jail cell.

I signed a letter today, with an attached Joint Resolution of Congress. It is to be delivered to Rear Admiral Andrew H. Foote. It thanked him for his eminent services and gallantry at Fort Henry, Fort Donelson and Island Number 10, while in command of our victorious naval forces there. Foote is now stationed at New Haven, Connecticut.

Author's notes:

On this day Lincoln telegraphed Sydney H. Gay, editor of the Tribune, inviting him to come to the White House to discuss a letter Gay had received from a reader questioning the national government's recent actions in the Peninsula Campaign. The letter writer accused the Army of the Potomac of "hiding away under the protection of gunboats and cannot or dare not move. The president with full power to act...hangs back, hesitates and leaves the country to drift. Does the president with full power to act not care what becomes of the country? Does this mean that he does not care what becomes of the country? Is he ready to play conservative to the ruin of the nation?" Later that day, Gay advised Lincoln that "a death in the family alone prevents my answering your call instantly. It shall be done as soon as possible."

The White House – Sunday, August 3, 1862

Mother was more than a little angry that yours truly scheduled Cabinet meetings for both Saturday and Sunday this week. As a concession to her I made certain that the Sunday meeting was limited to just two hours. Both meetings concentrated on matters related to emancipation. Chase stressed three points repeatedly: 1. That freedom granted to negroes in seceded states be only upon condition of loyalty. 2. That we organize the best of them into military companies. 3. That we provide for the cultivation of plantations by the remaining ones who are experienced farm workers. My sense of the matter is that we plan to initially use these men as laborers rather than as soldiers. The Cabinet is divided on how negroes are best employed. Experience will soon show us the way. There is no doubt in my mind that a black man who labors for us, rather than for his former master, will be doing much to shorten the war.

Stanton showed me a copy of Atlantic Monthly, which includes in it the sheet music for "Glory Hallelujah," as written by Julia Ward Howe last year. The Atlantic editor titles the piece "The Battle Hymn of the Republic." Stanton has agreed that it will soon be played here and be sung by a military band. I am anxious to hear it performed.

Author's notes:

Julia Howe submitted the lyrics she wrote to the Atlantic Monthly, and it was published in the February 1862 issue of the magazine. This author has sung the song in church choirs and particularly likes the words to the fifth stanza:

"In the beauty of the lilies Christ was born across the sea,
With a glory in His bosom that transfigures you and me.
As He died to make men holy, let us die to make me free,
While God is marching on."

Many modern versions of the ballad use the lyric "As He died to make men holy, let us live to make men free," as opposed to the lyric Howe originally wrote. It was played at the state funerals of Richard Nixon and Ronald Reagan. It was one of Sir Winston Churchill's favorite songs and was played at his funeral in St. Paul's Cathedral in 1965. The Marine Corps Band performed it on April 16, 2008 for Pope Benedict XVI and President George W. Bush on the South Lawn of the White House

The White House – Monday, August 4, 1862

A delegation of some of the leading men from Indiana, including their representatives in Congress, called upon me to offer two negro regiments from their state. I thanked them courteously but informed them that I preferred at this time to limit negro services to labor only. I am not ready to make them soldiers although I believe that they would make good ones.

I asked Stanton to see Judge Edmund Davis, formerly at the U.S. District Court in Austin, Texas, and John L. Haynes, both formerly of Texas. They have asked if we could send 3,000 rifles on a vessel to the vicinity of the Rio Grande to re-inaugurate the national authority on the Rio Grande first, and then on the Nueces River. I suggested that Stanton get the opinion of General Halleck on this proposal.

Author's notes:

A reporter for the New York Tribune reported on August 5, 1862, that the Indiana deputation came away satisfied that it is the determination of the Government not to arm negroes unless some new and more pressing emergency arises. The president argued that "the nation could not afford to lose Kentucky at this crisis and gave it as his opinion that to arm the negroes would turn 50,000 bayonets from the loyal Border States against us there were for us."

The War Committee of the Citizens of New York, headed by John A. Stevens, Jr. and including John Haynes, Andrew J. Hamilton and Edward L. Plumb (formerly minister to Mexico), would make a similar proposal on October 9, 1862. Stanton and Lincoln did not find the proposal practicable at the time.

The White House – Tuesday, August 5, 1862

Tad came to me this morning and asked if he might have an allowance each week. He suggested 50 cents as a fair amount. He pointed out to me that he provided his mother with many helpful services for which he was not being paid. I told Tad that as a young man, just starting out as a surveyor back in 1834, my fee for surveying was $3.00 for a long day's labor as a surveyor, and that I charged my clients 50 cents for making the map of the land surveyed. For a job that took three days and often longer, I would typically be paid $9.50 in total. I asked Tad if 50 cents were not quite a large sum for the modest services that he was rendering for his mother. Tad reflected, and then said that perhaps 25 cents might be the proper amount. I thanked him for his modesty and told him that I felt a dollar seemed to me a suitable amount. We shook hands and I gave him a greenback for last week's services. Tad was very pleased.

Author's notes:

The Cabinet on this date agreed to Lincoln's proposal that the states be asked to draft 300,000 militia men to serve for nine months.

On this day, Lincoln sent a reply to a letter from a Swiss liberal author, Agéner-Etienne de Gasparin, who asked the president if the Union will be able to press on with the war after it had not succeeded in its Peninsula Campaign. Lincoln wrote the author, who had strongly supported the Union cause in the war, "I can only say that I have acted upon my best convictions without selfishness or malice, and that by the help of God, I shall continue to do so." Theodore Fay, former U.S. ambassador to Switzerland, told Lincoln that the Union cause was suffering "on account of a poorly defined policy."

The White House – Thursday, August 7, 1862

At 5 P.M. last evening, I said a few words to an enthusiastic audience, which met in front of the Capitol Building. Because there has been press speculation about the relationship of McClellan and Stanton, I felt obligated to say a few words on the subject. Before I said my say, Edward Jordan, solicitor of the Treasury, George Boutwell, commissioner of Internal Revenue, and Lucius Chittenden, register of the Treasury, spoke to the crowd about Stanton's order for the draft of 300,000 militia, issued this week. They called for supportive measures which will bear with the most crushing weight upon those in rebellion. The audience cheered heartily upon hearing their words. I defended the actions of McClellan and Stanton. I pointed out that McClellan frequently asks for things that Stanton cannot give him. I said that Stanton is not to blame because he has never withheld something when he had none to give. I took it upon myself, as justice requires me to do, to say that the secretary of war has withheld no one thing at any time in my power to give McClellan. I told the crowd that I know that both men are brave and able.

Author's notes:

Earlier in the day, Lincoln, Seward, Stanton and Captain John A. Dahlgren and others spent two hours at the Navy Yard observing experiments with the "Rafael" repeater cannon. The gun was the invention of James Richard Haskell and Azels Lyman. A multi-charge gun, it was designed to increase muzzle velocity by detonating additional propellant charges behind the projectile or shell as it moved up the gun's barrel. In 1862, with a French inventor named George Raphael, a supplier of revolvers and swords to the Union Army, Haskell built a rapid-fire machine gun, which was named the Rafael Repeater. It was mounted on a light artillery carriage and fired standard rifle bullets. Lincoln observed the gun in action at the Navy Yard. He discovered the gun's range and accuracy were remarkable. At a range of 1,800 yards nearly all of 16 shots fired at a target at 600 yards were hits. The gun fired 40 shots in 20 seconds. Tested in 1863 at 6th Corps headquarters in Virginia, it was praised by a board composed of two brigadier generals and one colonel. Lincoln asked the secretary of war to refer the gun to the Bureau of Ordnance, which did not order a single gun.

The White House – Friday, August 8, 1862

Nicolay finished writing a presidential order directing the secretary of war to arrest persons engaged in discouraging enlistments. There is always the matter of First Amendment rights to be considered in such matters, but it is my thinking that when a nation is at war, and a civil war at that, that those few citizens who act in a clearly subversive manner have to be curbed in their actions, which can seriously harm the war effort. Enlistments have been coming in as requested, but that could be seriously disrupted if badly motivated people act to curtail them.

I signed a letter to Queen Victoria offering sincere congratulations upon the marriage of her daughter Princess Alice Maud Mary to Prince Lewis Charles William Lewis of Hesse. I recommended to the royal family the protection of the Almighty. The queen has been kind to me and particularly kind to Mary at this very difficult time in our lives. We both regretted learning of the death of her devoted husband, Prince Albert. I will never forget his support during the Trent matter. I have been reliably informed that it was Prince Albert who cautioned diplomatic language and restraint by the British government at a time when passions were running high in England against the United States.

I directed General Halleck to investigate claims by General Silas Casey that he is being treated unfairly by McClellan following his troop's actions at the Battle of Seven Pines.

Author's notes:

Silas Casey attended the U.S. Military Academy at West Point, graduating in 1826 (39th out of 41 cadets). He served in the Army from 1826 until 1868, retiring as a brevet major general. During the Battle of Seven Pines, Casey's Division was attacked by D.H. Hill's Confederate forces and driven from the field. General McClellan blamed them for the disaster. Casey was removed from Division command and replaced by Brigadier General John J. Peck. On July 17, 1862, Casey was promoted to Major General of Volunteers in a general promotion of all the army's corps and division commanders. On August 12, Casey was assigned to receiving and encamping new troops as they arrived in Washington. In December 1862 he was appointed to the board that convicted Major General Fitz John Porter of disobedience and cowardice for his actions at the Second Battle of Bull Run. His three-volume "System of Infantry Tactics" was published by the Army in 1862, and "Infantry Tactics for Colored Troops" was published in 1863.

The White House – Saturday, August 9, 1862

Yesterday I received, via Adams Express, a gift sent to me by my good friend, John M. Clay. It contained a snuff box that belonged to his distinguished father. I will donate it to the Smithsonian Institution for public display. Clay wrote me of his father, "whose avowed sentiment that he owed a higher allegiance to the Constitution and Government of the United States than to the Constitution and Government of any State is mine, and whose noblest sentiment that he would rather be right than be President, I hope may ever be yours." I answered him by writing that I recognize his father's voice, speaking as it ever spoke, for the Union, the Constitution and the freedom of mankind. Henry Clay, in my opinion, was one of America's greatest patriots.

Author's notes:

Lincoln wrote to John Clay: "Thanks for this memento of your great and patriotic father. Thanks also for the assurance that, in these days of dereliction, you remain true to his principles. In the concurrent sentiment of your venerable mother, so long the partner of his bosom and his honors, and lingering now, where he was, but for the all to rejoin him where he is, I recognize his voice, speaking as it ever spoke, for the Union, the Constitution, and the freedom of mankind."

The White House – Sunday, August 10, 1862

Mrs. Lincoln is an avid reader who cannot seem to find enough good books to keep her mind occupied. Today she showed me a list of 23 books she is ordering from T.J. Crowen, Publisher, Book Seller and Stationer, 699 Broadway, New York City. I am to pay $61.00 for 14 of the books listed and the remainder of $52.00 is to be paid for from our annual appropriation of $250.00 for books for the White House. This fund is administered by Commissioner Benjamin Brown French. French is called "Major French" because he held that rank in the militia of New Hampshire when he was a young man. Major French and Mother get along very well. She tells me that French has served the government since he arrived here in 1845. Because he has held so many federal posts, including Clerk of the House from 1845 to 1847, he can be relied upon to get things done efficiently.

Author's notes:

Benjamin Brown French lived in Washington for nearly 40 years. His home was near the White House. From 1847 to 1850 he was president of the Magnetic Telegraph Company. In 1853 he was appointed Commissioner of Public Buildings under President Franklin Pierce and was the chief marshal of the 1861 inaugural parade of Abraham Lincoln, who appointed him commissioner of Public Works. He was responsible for all federal buildings in Washington, D.C., including the U.S. Capitol.

French was a tireless chronicler. He maintained an 11-volume journal, which is the centerpiece of the Benjamin B. French Family Papers, now in the Manuscript Division of the Library of Congress. His papers include remarkable observations and commentaries beginning in 1828 and continuing until his death in 1870.

The White House – Monday, August 11, 1862

We had a longer than expected Cabinet meeting this afternoon and covered quite a bit of ground. Seward, Stanton and Blair brought up the exemplary conduct of General John S. Phelps in Louisiana. Phelps is an attorney who enlisted in the Army with the rank of private in the Missouri Infantry when the war began. He was soon promoted to lieutenant colonel and then in December 1861 to full colonel. He represented Missouri in the Congress for 18 years as a Democrat, starting in 1845. In the 35th Congress he campaigned for bounties for soldiers, aid to railroads and inexpensive postage. Blair also told me that in 1857 Missourians named a county after Phelps. In March of this year he led Phelps' regiment in the fierce fighting at Pea Ridge in Arkansas. He was mustered out of the Army with the rank of brigadier general on May 13, 1862. Last month he was appointed military governor of Arkansas. The latest dispatch from him reports that he is not in good health and that he therefore advises me that he must resign his post. I regret losing him. He has been a strong supporter of the Union cause.

Author's notes:

John S. Phelps left his home in Washington in 1864 to resume his law practice in Springfield, Missouri. He was an unsuccessful candidate for governor of Missouri in 1868, but in 1876 was elected the state's 23rd governor with support from Northern and Southern factions in the state. He strongly supported public education and retired in 1881, praised as one of Missouri's best governors. He died in 1886, aged 71, in St. Louis, Missouri.

The White House – Tuesday, August 12, 1862

I had a long talk with Judge David Noggle of Wisconsin, including lunch, following a thankfully short morning Cabinet meeting. No major matters came up during the cabinet session. The judge is the father of Lieutenant Charles L. Noggle. I've known the judge for many years and admire him for the progressive stands he has taken in favor of homestead exemptions, an elective judiciary and the rights of married women. Today, he told me that his son and another officer, Lieutenant George A. Rowley, have been cashiered out of the Army by court martial for misconduct at the Battle of June 27th at Gaines Mill, Virginia. I've read the records of both cases. I note that in this matter that John F. Lee, the judge advocate, suggests that the men deserve to be reinstated to duty without prejudice. Based upon my understanding of this matter I've written to General McClellan recommending that the lives of these men not be ruined for so slight causes. I've also asked Judge Noggle to keep me informed as to the future of his son, whom I have never met but believe is most likely a chip off the old Noggle block.

Author's notes:

The cases were ultimately referred to Major General F.J. Porter, who forwarded the matters to Brigadier General George Sykes. After due deliberation by the Army, including General Henry W. Halleck, Lincoln reappointed Second Lieutenants Rowley and Noggle of the 14th Infantry to active duty on January 31, 1863.

The White House – Wednesday, August 13, 1862

Today I interviewed Sydney H. Gay, the editor of the New York Tribune. When he asked me about General Banks I informed Gay that I consider Nathaniel Banks to be one of the best men in the Army, and that he gives me no trouble. I also advised General Cassius Clay that I shall be quite willing, and even gratified, to again send him to Russia if our present minister, Simon Cameron, resigns with full notice of my intention. Cameron is wily as a fox, but a man to whom I owe much. I would probably not have been elected without his political help in Pennsylvania.

Author's notes:

Born in 1816, Nathaniel Banks had a rag to riches life story. A poor millworker in Massachusetts, he was called "The Bobbin Boy." He became famous as a local debater, and his oratorical skills were soon noted by the Democratic Party. However, his abolitionist views fitted him better for the nascent Republican Party in the 1850s. He became speaker of the U.S. House of Representatives and the 24th governor of Massachusetts. When the Civil War began, President Lincoln appointed him one of the first "Political Major Generals." Banks replaced Benjamin Butler at New Orleans as commander of the Department of the Gulf, charged with the administration of Louisiana and the gaining of control of the Mississippi River. Banks was instrumental in early reconstruction efforts in Louisiana, which were intended by Lincoln to serve as a model for later such activities. After the war, Banks served in the U.S. Congress, where he supported Manifest Destiny, influenced the Alaska Purchase legislation and supported women's suffrage. He died in 1894.

The White House – Thursday, August 14, 1862

Edward M. Thomas, president of the Anglo-African Institute for the Encouragement of Industry and Art and four of his members came at my invitation to the White House today. I gave them my candid views upon the worthiness of making it possible for negro freemen and their families to leave the United States voluntarily for purposes of colonizing overseas. They were introduced to me by the Reverend J. Mitchell, commissioner of emigration. I explained to them that a sum of money has been appropriated by Congress and placed at my disposition for aiding the colonization in some country of people of African descent. I asked them if they favored people of their race being colonized, and if so, where? My view has long been that separation for their race is beneficial to them and the nation. I told them that I expected that many of them would oppose going to a foreign country, preferring to remain here. We discussed Liberia, where less than 12,000 negroes have been sent from this country. I told them that I favored a Central American country, admitting that the political situation in that country is not quite as satisfactory as I would wish. I asked them if they thought that 50 or 100 tolerably intelligent men, with their wives and children, might be interested in making a commencement, provided I can present evidence of local encouragement and protection. The chairman of the delegation said that they would hold a consultation and in a short time give me their opinion on the subject.

Author's notes:

Edward Thomas wrote to Lincoln on August 16 that it would be necessary to consult with leading colored men in Philadelphia, New York and Boston "upon the movement of emigration to the point recommended to your address." Ultimately negroes in the District of Columbia became almost entirely hostile to Lincoln's proposal of emigration. Plans were made to send 500 able-bodied negroes to the first colony to be settled on a site on the Isthmus of Chiriquí, located in Western Panama on the border with Costa Rica. The project was abandoned when first Honduras and later Nicaragua and Costa Rica protested the scheme and hinted that force might be used to prevent the settlement. Frederick Douglas, and many prominent negro leaders opposed migration. In the end Lincoln lost interest in having the government sponsor African-American emigration to Haiti, South or Central America or Africa.

The White House – Friday, August 15, 1862

Secretary Wells was here in particularly good humor. We talked for an hour or so about various naval appointments. He is a wise Cabinet member and steady as a rock. He says that initial reports indicate that our combined Navy and Army forces have been victorious at Baton Rouge, Louisiana. Sadly, Brigadier General Thomas Williams was killed during this action. Colonel Thomas Cahill took over and his men routed the Confederate forces that had entered the city. Cahill was successful because his men had the protection of Union gunboats on the Mississippi River. The rebel ship Arkansas arrived in time for the battle, but her engines failed, and she was set on fire by her captain and sunk. Without sufficient naval support, the Confederate forces under Major General John Breckenridge withdrew. This victory, coupled with news of a Union win at Kirksville in Missouri, is great news for the nation.

Author's notes:

John Breckenridge served as the 14th vice-president of the United States under President James Buchanan. During the Civil War he commanded Confederate troops in several theaters of war before being named Confederate secretary of war by Jefferson Davis in 1865. At the war's end he fled the United States for Cuba, later moving to Great Britain and Canada. He returned to the United States after President Andrew Johnson granted amnesty in 1868 to former Confederate officers and officials. He died at age 54 in Kentucky.

The White House – Saturday, August 16, 1862

At the recommendation of Secretary Seward, I am sending Richard M. Blatchford, who has served as a member of a committee of three to superintend the disbursement of public funds appropriated to raise troops for the Union, to Rome to be our new minister to the State of the Church of Rome. He will soon be meeting with Pope Pius IX. Seward and Blatchford were college classmates at Union College back in 1815. They practiced law together in Manhattan and Auburn, New York. His specialty has been corporate, railroad and banking law. He also served in the New York legislature and was a longtime friend of Daniel Webster, whom I have always held in the highest regard. Seward tells me that Blatchford is now one of the wealthiest men in New York state. I am counting upon him to keep the pope from recognizing the Confederate states as a legitimate nation.

Author's notes:

In 1859, Richard M. Blatchford was appointed to the commission which oversaw the creation and operation of New York City's Central Park. Originally a Whig, he became a Republican in the mid-1850s when the party was founded. At the start of the Civil War, Lincoln named John Adams Dix, George Opdyke and Blatchford commissioners of the Union Defense Committee. They were responsible to expend federal funds on the initial raising and equipping of troops for the Union Army.

The law firm that Richard Blatchford and William Seward founded is now known as Cravath, Swaine and Moore. 2018 was its 200th year of operation. It is one of the world's premier law firms. Blatchford's son, Samuel Blatchford, served as an associate justice of the U.S. Supreme Court. Appointed by President Chester Arthur, he served from 1882 until his death in 1893.

Blatchford served as U.S. minister to the Vatican from August 9, 1862, to October 7, 1863. He was succeeded in the post by Rufus King. He was born on April 23, 1798, and died in Newport, Rhode Island, on September 4, 1875.

The White House – Monday, August 18, 1862

Yesterday was spent at church and then all day with the family – no Cabinet meetings and no staff meetings. It was either that or my going to war with Mother, and for me one war at a time was the rule for Sunday. We took a leisurely carriage ride to Georgetown escorted by two cavalry officers. Marshall Ward Lamon had told Mary that he thought that we would be safer with guards along for the ride. The new carriage has superior springs and the ride was as smooth as silk. Mother and Tad waved frequently to people we saw walking the streets when we were recognized by them. It was a beautiful day to be out and about. I can't remember the last time I was not cooped up in my office on a Sunday.

I asked Hiram Barney to buy $200 worth of lemons and $100 worth of oranges for Mrs. Lincoln to distribute to the wounded in military hospitals. Barney, like William Seward, is another Union College man. He came from New York to Springfield and made suggestions to me of several men for the secretary posts of Interior and War in my Cabinet in 1861. I did not follow his advice but appreciated it. As a young man he had been the president of the Young Men's Anti-Slavery Society of New York City. A close friend of Secretary Chase, he now serves as collector for the Port of New York.

Author's notes:

Hiram Barney was collector for the Port of New York during the first three years of the Lincoln administration. He was accused of improprieties in office and resigned. He refused an appointment to a foreign mission and returned to the practice of law in New York City.

The White House – Tuesday, August 19, 1862

At first light this morning, I visited the camps of two regiments of recently arrived Pennsylvania volunteers. The men looked fit and their spirits were high. At 2 P.M., Secretary Wells and I approved a list of men for appointment to the Naval Academy.

The Washington Star confirmed today the death of Mother's half-brother Captain Alexander Humphreys Todd of wounds he received during the Battle of Baton Rouge on August 5th. These are scars of war that Mother finds terribly difficult to bear. On April 7th her half-brother Colonel Samuel Briggs Todd was mortally wounded, reportedly by friendly fire near Baton Rouge. How tragic is the loss of a close relative, and how even greater is the loss when the death is caused by friendly fire?

Author's notes:

The following year, Confederate Brigadier General Benjamin Helm, the husband of Mary Lincoln's half-sister Emilie Helm, was killed in action at the Battle of Chickamauga on September 24, 1863. He was leading the First Kentucky Brigade, known as the "Orphan's Brigade," which was part of General Braxton Bragg's attempt to counter General William Rosecrans' offensive against Chattanooga, Tennessee. President Lincoln had offered his brother-in-law Benjamin Helm a commission as Army paymaster in the Union Army at the start of hostilities, which Helm declined.

Helm was a Kentucky politician and a successful practicing attorney before the war. He was also the son of Kentucky Governor John L. Helm. He attended the Kentucky Military Institute and then West Point Military Academy, studied at the University of Louisville and Harvard University. He ranked ninth in his class of 42 cadets at West Point in the Class of 1851. He resigned his commission after a year, when diagnosed with inflammatory rheumatism. He served as a Kentucky state legislator, state attorney general, and as assistant inspector-general of the Kentucky State Guard.

The White House – Wednesday, August 20, 1862

Mary and I had a long and exceedingly pleasant lunch today with our very close friends, Gustav Koerner and his wife, Sophia. Afterward, Gustav and I discussed his duties as our new ambassador to Spain. It is my confident hope that he will be able to prevent Spain from entering the Civil War on the side of the Confederacy. He is a remarkable man, an immigrant from Germany who became an attorney, judge and lieutenant governor of Illinois. When the war began he was instrumental in raising the 43rd Illinois Volunteer Infantry Regiment and served as colonel of volunteers under General Fremont. Upon Fremont's removal, he has most recently been serving on the staff of General Halleck as a brigadier general.

Author's notes:

Koerner was not content in Spain and asked Lincoln several times to be replaced. An important reason for his request was that the modest stipend for his ambassadorship was not sufficient to cover the huge financial obligations expected of him at the Spanish court. In 1864 he resigned and returned to the United States. After Lincoln's assassination, Koerner was named one of the pallbearers who carried the coffin in the state funeral. Other men who joined him were Jesse Dubois, Stephen Logan, James Lamb, Samuel Hubbel Treat, Jr., John Williams, Erastus White, J.M. Brown, Jacob Bunn, Charles Matheny, Elisha Iles and John T. Stuart.

In 1874, Koerner's wife, Sophia, and Henry Raab established, with others, one of the first kindergartens in America. She became the first president of the Belleview Kindergarten Association.

The White House – Thursday, August 21, 1862

Halleck and Stanton provided some disturbing information about the Union victory at the battle fought at Kirksville in northeastern Missouri on the 6th, 7th and 8th of August, where our soldiers captured the town. Fifteen Confederate prisoners, who had broken parole agreements not to take up arms until exchanged, were ordered shot by Colonel John McNeil of the 2nd Missouri Cavalry Regiment, following a court-martial proceeding. He also ordered the execution of Confederate Lieutenant Colonel Frisby McCullough, who was shot as a bushwhacker, even though he was wearing a Confederate officer's uniform when captured. He also had papers on him authorizing him to recruit troops. I've asked Halleck to get me more information on the killing of the captured rebels as soon as possible. As a lawyer, I believe a crime was very possibly committed by McNeil by his very questionable behavior.

Author's notes:

Colonel John McNeil was soon involved in another questionable shooting incident. It took place in Palmyra, Missouri, on October 18, 1862. It became known as the Palmyra Massacre. Ten Confederate soldiers were executed in reprisal for the abduction of a local Union supporter, Andrew Alsman. The officer who ordered the execution was Colonel McNeil. He would later be called the "Butcher of Palmyra." McNeil left the Army in 1865, after receiving the honorary promotion of rank of major general of volunteers in recognition of his faithful service to the Union. The Confederate soldiers who were shot had no connection with the abduction of Alsman. They were shot by a firing squad from the Second Missouri State Militia on October 18, 1862. After the war, McNeil would go on to serve two terms as sheriff of St. Louis County, dying June 7, 1891.

The White House – Friday, August 22, 1862

Archbishop John Hughes of New York payed a morning visit to the White House accompanied by his close friend William Seward. He and Thurlow Weed have just returned from an eight-month visit to Paris, Rome and Dublin, where Hughes used his extensive clerical and diplomatic connections to promote the cause of the Union in Europe. He saw French Emperor Napoleon and the Pope on our behalf. He stressed to Empress Eugenie, who is Spanish by birth, that an independent Confederacy would probably seize Cuba from Spain. The United States government contributed $5,200 toward the trip's expenses. I plan to write to the pope to thank him for Hughes' help on behalf of our nation. I will suggest in the letter that I would be gratified in any honor which the pope might have it in his power to confer upon the Archbishop.

Author's notes:

The archbishop was never named a cardinal of the Church of Rome. After John Hughes died on January 3, 1864, Lincoln wrote to William Starr, administrator of the Diocese of New York, to pay tribute to the work done by the archbishop for the Union cause. Lincoln recognized Hughes' role in building many churches and schools, his founding of Fordham University, and the building of a new St. Patrick's Cathedral on Fifth Avenue in New York City, located between 50th Street and 51st Street. Hughes laid the cornerstone for it on August 15, 1858. During the draft riots of July 1863, John Hughes spoke forcefully to his largely Irish immigrant flock, urging them to remain peaceful. Hughes was succeeded by Bishop John McCloskey, who was named the first American-born cardinal by Pope Leo XIII in 1878. Hughes' body was interred in the new cathedral.

The White House – Saturday, August 23, 1862

After reading an intemperate editorial in the New York Tribune of August 19th titled, "The Prayer of Twenty Millions," I replied to Horace Greeley yesterday. I reiterated my purposes and informed him that my personal wish is that all men everywhere be free.

Author's note:

Lincoln's letter to Greeley was reprinted in the New York Tribune on August 25, 1862. It read, in part: "My paramount object in this struggle is to save the Union and is not either to save or to destroy slavery. If I could save the Union without freeing any slave I would do it, and if I could save it by freeing all the slaves I would do it; and if I could save it by freeing some and leaving others alone I would also do that. What I do about slavery, and the colored race, I do because I believe it helps to save the Union; and what I forbear, I forbear because I do not believe it would help save the Union."

After reading Greeley's editorial, Thurlow Weed a New York publisher and Republican politician wrote to Lincoln, "It clears the atmosphere, and gives ground to stand on."

The White House – Sunday, August 24, 1862

I was visited today by Orestes Brownson, editor of Brownson's Review. I have read many of the articles that he has written about slavery, emancipation and colonization over the years. Brownson is a heavy thinker. He told me that after having been a Transcendentalist for decades, he has become a practicing Roman Catholic. After lunch I met with Senator Samuel Pomeroy of Kansas, who has agreed to serve as commissioner of African Colonization.

Author's notes:

On August 28th ministers of several Central American governments protested American plans to establish colonies of negro freedmen on the Isthmus of Chiriquí. After several false starts, Lincoln's plans for colonization would never come to fruition, and by 1863, various attempts by the federal government to create colonies here were discontinued.

The White House – Monday, August 25, 1862

By my personally becoming more active in daily military matters, I fear that I may run the risk of misdirecting our armies in the field. By being passive, I believe that our military leadership will fail to show the initiatives so badly needed, and not take the risks needed to win battles. It is a quandary I find myself in, a predicament that is frustrating. Stanton recently told me that there is an ancient Chinese saying that may be particularly timely: "To put a rein on an able general while at the same time asking him to suppress a cunning enemy is like tying up the Black Hound of Han and then ordering him to catch elusive hares." Is the elusive hare in the present-day situation Confederate General Thomas J. Jackson? I wonder.

Author's notes:

On the evening of August 26th, after passing around Union Major General John Pope's right flank, via Thoroughfare Gap, General Jackson's Army struck the Orange and Alexandria Railroad at Bristoe Station, and on August 27th marched to capture a massive Union supply depot at Manassas Junction. The move forced Pope's Army of Virginia to retreat from his defensive line along the Rappahannock River. On the 27th, Jackson routed a Union brigade near Bull Run Bridge, mortally wounding Union General George W. Taylor. General Richard Ewell's Confederate division fought a rear-guard action against Union General Joseph Hooker's division at Kettle Run. That night Jackson marched his divisions north to the First Battle of Bull Run battlefield, where he took position behind an unfinished railroad grade.

After the Second Battle of Manassas or Bull Run, General Jackson became popularly known as "Stonewall Jackson."

The White House – Friday, August 29, 1862

This has been the worst week of the war. McClellan has failed to support Pope at Bull Run, as he was ordered to do by Halleck. It is almost incomprehensible that our Army, which suffered an early defeat at Bull Run, is now doing the same thing. My fear is that the losses will be horrific. Halleck broke down when all was going badly. He seems to act more like a frightened clerk than a commanding general. My sense of the matter is that McClellan wants Pope to fail. He has done nothing within his power to support Pope in his and the nation's hour of need. He has an excuse for everything. Mrs. Lincoln has visited soldiers in Odd Fellows Hall Hospital this morning. She reports that there are very crowded conditions there, and that the men are not only suffering from their wounds, but from the terrible heat.

Author's notes:

The Second Battle of Bull Run, like the first (July 21, 1861,) was a momentous tactical victory for the Confederates, this time under General Robert E. Lee. Union casualties were about 14,000 killed and wounded out of 62,000 engaged; the Confederates lost about 1,000 killed and 7,000 wounded out of 50,000. Lee sent Jackson on a flanking march to interpose his Army between Pope and Washington. Pope countered the move and the two forces clashed at the Battle of Chantilly or Ox Hill on September 1st. Union Generals Isaac Stevens and Philip Kearny were killed in this inconclusive battle. On September 3rd, Lee crossed the Potomac River, marching toward a fateful encounter with the Army of the Potomac in Maryland at the Battle of Antietam. Pope would be relieved of command on September 12, 1862, and his Army merged into the Army of the Potomac as it marched into Maryland under McClellan. Pope spent the rest of the war in the Department of the Northwest in Minnesota, dealing with the Dakota War.

The White House – Saturday, August 30, 1862

I was unenthusiastically required to dismiss 11 officers of the 71st Ohio Regiment who had advised Colonel Rodney Mason to surrender his forces in Clarkesville, Tennessee, on August 18th without putting up a fight. I do not recall any similar situation since hostilities began. From the best reports provided to me by Stanton, our soldiers were ordered to surrender by Colonel Mason because their officers felt that, without adequate artillery, they were no match for the enemy facing them. Mason claimed that he was faced by forces at least four or five times as large as his, and that it would be a useless bloodbath to resist the enemy. Mason and the 10 officers who made the decision not to fight have been severed from the Army.

At the Cabinet meeting I was presented with an indictment signed by Chase, Smith and Bates calling for the removal of McClellan. I told Hay in confidence that I believe that McClellan disobeyed orders from Halleck to relieve Pope, and that as far as I can figure, McClellan wanted to see Pope defeated. Reports continue to flow in from Bull Run and the picture is grim.

The past few days I have spent countless suspenseful hours in the telegraph office. Colonel Herman Haupt has been incredibly helpful to me by reporting from the field reliable information about the status of the military situation at the front. The first time we met he told me that he was appointed to the U.S. Military Academy when only 14 years of age by President Andrew Jackson. His background as an engineer and railroad expert makes him an invaluable officer. As an inventor myself, I was impressed to learn that Haupt patented two bridge construction techniques known as the Haupt Truss in 1839. Two of his truss bridges now stand in Altoona and Ardmore, Pennsylvania.

Author's notes:

On September 6, 1862, President Lincoln wrote to Secretary of War Edwin M. Stanton, "The indiscriminate dismissal of all the officers of Col. Mason's regiment, who surrendered Clarksville Tennessee may be wrong. Will the Sec. of War please see and hear Capt. Houck?

Lincoln's endorsement was written on an envelope containing a letter from Samuel S. Cox to Lincoln from Columbus, Ohio, dated August 30, 1862, on behalf of Captain Solomon J. Houck, 71st Ohio Volunteers, cashiered along with 11 fellow officers for having published a card stating that they had advised Colonel Rodney Mason to surrender Clarksville, Tennessee, on August 18, 1862. Lincoln's endorsement on Cox's letter reads "Submitted to the Sec. of War," and is dated September 6. Stanton referred the case to Halleck, who on September 17 endorsed it as follows: "It being shown that Captain S.J. Houck did not advise the surrender of Clarksville and that he signed the card justifying the surrender under a misapprehension of its contents, I respectfully recommend that the order of his dismissal be revoked." On September 18, 1862, Adjutant General Order 120 revoked "so much of General Orders, No. 120 as cashiered Houck."

The White House – Monday, September 1, 1862

My father told me when I was a young boy that bad things usually happen by twos. I guess my father was right. After all our losses at Bull Run this past week, we are now learning of a dreadful Union defeat in Kentucky, at Richmond. Halleck brought me a telegram last evening that he had just received from General Horatio G. Wright from his headquarters in Cincinnati, Ohio. It reads: "Nelson has been badly beaten, I fear, in an encounter with the enemy near Richmond, Kentucky; his force being, as he says, hopelessly broken and scattered. He is in Lexington, wounded. I leave for that place in a couple of hours to see what can be done. He gives me no particulars. My orders were to make the Kentucky River the line of defense, and his orders in pursuance seem to have been disregarded. At any rate his force has been routed." I've telegraphed General Jeremiah T. Boyle for more details.

Author's notes:

The Battle of Richmond, Kentucky, was fought August 29 and August 30, 1862. It was the first major battle fought in Kentucky, and a stunning Confederate victory by Major General Edmund Kirby Smith against Union General William "Bull" Nelson's forces, defending Richmond. Each army fielded about 6,500 troops. Union casualties totaled 5,353 (206 killed and 4,303 captured). Confederate casualties totaled 78 killed (and 372 wounded and 1 missing). Civil War historian Shelby Foote said that "Smith accomplished in Kentucky the nearest thing to Cannae ever scored by any general, North or South, during the entire war."

Two discontinuous areas totaling 214 acres, including four buildings, were listed on the National Register of Historic Places as the Battle of Richmond Historic Areas in 1996. The Mount Zion Church, which served as a hospital during the battle, still has cannonballs embedded in its brick walls.

The White House – Tuesday, September 2, 1862

Over the weekend, Mother, Tad and I discussed the question of Divine Will as it relates to all wars, and the Civil War in particular. Does the will of God prevail and if so, does it favor Union or Confederate arms? The fact that our Army has had so many reverses caused Mary to bring up the subject. I read them an ancient Latin quote given to me by Seward. It is taken from Lucan, who lived from 39 to 68 A.D. Lucan wrote, "If the victor had the gods on his side, the vanquished had Cato." (Victrix causa deis placuit, sed victa Catoni.)

Author's notes:

Lincoln wrote a Meditation on the Divine Will in September. The date is uncertain. His aides Nicolay and Hay, who found it after his death, wrote, "The fragment was written in September of 1862, while his mind was burdened with the weightiest question of his life." They left the actual date blank. They noted that it was not written to be seen by men. Some historians credit the writing to a time around the Battle of Bull Run when Lincoln seems to have plumbed his lowest depths. Attorney General Bates then wrote, "He seemed wrung by the bitterest anguish – said he felt almost ready to hang himself." Others understood it to refer to the issuing of the Emancipation Proclamation later in the month.

Lincoln's Meditation:

The will of God prevails. In great contests each party claims to act in accordance with the will of God. Both may be, and one must be wrong. God cannot be for and against the same thing at the same time. In the present civil war, it is quite possible that God's purpose is something different from the purpose of either party – and yet the human instrumentalities, working just as they do, are of the best adaptation to affect His purpose. I am almost ready to say this is probably true – that God wills this contest, and wills that it shall not end yet. By his mere quiet power, on the minds of the now contestants, He could have either saved or destroyed the Union without a human contest. Yet the contest began. And having begun He could give the final victory to either side any day. Yet the contest proceeds.

The White House – Wednesday, September 3, 1862

Halleck and I called upon General McClellan yesterday morning and directed him to take immediate command of all troops falling back upon Washington after our defeat at Bull Run. He is to have charge of the fortifications of the city, and of all troops required for the defense of the capital. Later, at noon, when I presented this information to the Cabinet, my decision was met not with defiance, but with total lack of enthusiasm. Chase believes he should not be kept but should be shot! McClellan has no friends in the Cabinet. I have regretted his reappointment, but I also realize that he is the best general for the specific task at hand. The Army has faith in him, and I need the Army to follow where he leads.

Seward came to the Soldiers Homes after spending time in New York City. We conferred until midnight. Seward also has lost faith in McClellan.

Author's notes:

On September 4, 1862, Lee's Army of Northern Virginia started over the Potomac River into Maryland seeking another fight. On September 13, McClellan was given a copy of Lee's order No. 191, which had been lost by a careless rebel courier. It called for more than half of Lee's army under General Stonewall Jackson to attack the Union garrison at Harper's Ferry.

The White House – Thursday, September 4, 1862

A dispirited General Pope came to the White House and read to Secretary Wells and me his official report of the recent campaign in Virginia. Later we met with Stanton at the War Department. I have strong feelings for Pope. He was failed by McClellan in his greatest hour of need. But as my father often said, "There's no use in crying over spilt milk!" Later in the day the full Cabinet met with me to discuss McClellan and future war plans. There is incredibly strong pessimism in the Cabinet, and in the Congress about the general. The Cabinet's consensus is that Pope is being wrongly punished, and McClellan unjustly rewarded. Sadly, I must admit that they are right, but I have no choice but to place my wager on McClellan. Mother believes the Cabinet is right, and her husband is dead wrong. Only Tad supports his father!

Author's notes:

The next morning, Lincoln found a military guard had been stationed at the Old Soldiers Home as a protective measure by General McClellan. The men assigned belonged to Companies D and K of the 150th Pennsylvania Rifles. Soon Company D was reassigned, and the men from Company K remained on security detail for the remainder of Lincoln's presidency.

The White House – Friday, September 5, 1862

I sent Stanton a note agreeing with his views and those of General Halleck that General Ivan Turchin be given a brigade and sent where active duty is now required in Kentucky. Turchin was court martialed for the pillage of Athens, Alabama, in May of 1862. I promoted him to brigadier general before the trial was concluded at the recommendation of Halleck, Stanton and Governor Richard Yates of Illinois. They concluded that the misbehavior of his troops happened when he was away and therefore beyond his control.

Turchin, also known as John Basil Turchin, is very popular in Chicago. In Russia, he served on the staff of the Imperial Guards in St. Petersburg and fought in Hungary to help the Austrian Empire suppress the Hungarian Revolution in 1848. He also served in the Crimean War. He immigrated to the United States and worked for the Illinois Central Railroad before the Civil War. He enlisted in the Union Army at the outbreak of the war and became a colonel of the 19th Illinois Volunteer Infantry Regiment.

Author's notes:

Turchin, a Don Cossack of Ukrainian ancestry, graduated from the Imperial Military School in St. Petersburg in 1852 and served as a colonel of staff in the Russia Guards. During the American Civil War he distinguished himself during the battles of Chickamauga, Chattanooga and the Atlanta campaign. His wife, Nadezhda Lvov Turchin, always joined her husband on his campaigns and accompanied him on the field, witnessing the battles. She wrote the only woman's diary of the military campaigns he was in.

The White House – Saturday, September 6, 1862

Major General Cassius Marcellus Clay, our former minister to Russia, was given my enthusiastic consent to return to Russia upon the return of Ambassador Simon Cameron, who is expected to resign his post there. Clay was a far better minister than Cameron, who has never found Russia or the Russians to his liking. Last year when he was at the Court of St. Petersburg, Clay witnessed the Tsar's Emancipation Edict, freeing Russia's serfs. Clay is a remarkable man. An abolitionist, he owned a great many slaves that he inherited from his land-rich father. He freed his own slaves in 1844 and paid them wages from then on. Before the war he granted 10 acres of his expansive estate to John Fee, also an abolitionist, who founded Berea College there. Fee opened it up to people of all races, men and women alike. Clay was also the founder of the Republican Party in Kentucky. He has urged me to sign and release the Emancipation Proclamation, which I am anxious to do.

Author's notes:

Clay resigned his military commission in 1863 and returned to Russia, where he served as ambassador until 1869. He was influential in negotiations to purchase Alaska. Clay died at his home, White Hall in 1903. White Hall is maintained by the Commonwealth of Kentucky as a historic shrine.

The White House – Monday, September 8, 1862

Major General Samuel Heintzelman visited with me yesterday at McClellan's headquarters. He is still suffering from a nasty wound received last month at the Battle of Glendale in the Seven Days struggle. Popular with his men, he is held in the highest regard by the Army. He is known to be the kind of officer who can always be counted upon when the going gets the hardest. Because of his age, he is being transferred to command Washington's defenses.

Sometimes when I am down a bit, I find it helpful to get away from the office and visit with the men at the Navy Department, which is a refreshing short walk to its location at 17th Street and Pennsylvania Avenue. There early this morning, we discussed the current naval situation in the Savannah River area. It is a difficult place to operate in. It is where occasionally ships successfully break through our blockade, usually at night to deliver arms to the rebels. Increases in our naval forces there lead the Navy to believe that fewer ships are getting through than was the situation six months ago.

The great mystery seems to be, where is General Braxton Bragg? We continue to receive conflicting reports about his whereabouts, most of which seem to be unreliable.

Author's notes:

On September 7, 1862 Lincoln telegraphed Brigadier General Jeremiah T. Boyle. He asked, "Where is General Bragg? What do you know on the subject?" He also wired Major General Don Carlos Buell, and asked him, "What degree of certainty have you that Bragg, with his command, is now in the valley of the Shenandoah, Virginia?" Later in the day he messaged Major General John E. Wool and asked him, "What about Harper's Ferry? Do you know anything about it? How certain is your information about Bragg being in the valley of the Shenandoah?" Later he wired Brigadier General Horatio G. Wright, "Do you know of any certainty, where General Bragg is? May he not be in Virginia?" Wright replied at 5:30 P.M., "Nothing reliable about Bragg. All rumors agree that he has crossed the river above Chattanooga and a gentleman late from Nashville reported his advance at Sparta, Tenn. All intelligence coming to me from Nashville from the southward is very unreliable."

The White House – Tuesday, September 9, 1862

Hay has scheduled a meeting with John Ross, also known as Koo-wi-s-gu-wi, for Friday of this week. Ross is the principal chief of the Cherokee Nation. Hay tells me that he is known as the Moses of his people. He has acted to keep his nation either neutral or allied to the Union during this war. Unfortunately, his tribe is divided in its loyalties, with many Indians who own slaves favoring ties to the Confederacy. Ross is one-eighth Indian and seven-eighths Scottish descent, and fluent in English and Cherokee. As a young man he was a successful tobacco farmer, operating a tobacco warehouse and trading post on the Tennessee River. A ferry that he ran carried passengers from the south side of the river (Cherokee Nation) to the north side (U.S.A.). It was called Ross's Landing and is now called Chattanooga. Since his tribe was forced west of the Mississippi he has been considered the Cherokee's premiere chief. The tribe has many legal issues with the United States, which I know he will wish to discuss with me when we meet. They involve complicated issues of national boundaries, land ownership and white encroachment. He has been coming to Washington since 1816, always seeking justice for his Indian nation.

A group of concerned Baltimore citizens came by to ask that the Army provide greater resources to defend the city from possible rebel attacks. Similar entreaties have also been received from citizens of Philadelphia. Recent failures of the Army under Pope's command have caused public fears of Confederate advances. I told the Baltimoreans that in my opinion the government's defense of their city is adequate. Later when visiting Halleck's office, I informed him that a recent count shows that McClellan presently has 95,000 men in his command.

Author's notes:

General Robert E. Lee's decision to cross the Potomac River and enter Maryland was in part motivated by the strong belief held by President Jefferson Davis that a major Southern victory would lead to European recognition for the Confederacy.

The White House – Wednesday, September 10, 1862

Three members of New York City's National War Committee, also representing New England governors, visited with me this morning. They brought with them demands that I remove Secretary Seward and Postmaster General Blair. Last week, I had letters from other governors suggesting that I fire Chase and Stanton. In every instance, I advise those who make suggestions for changes in my cabinet that I am presently pleased by the advice and counsel that I have been receiving from my team. To my mind, the Cabinet is made up of loyal, hard-working and honest men. I encourage them to always tell me the truth and to speak without fear that I may be offended. Differences of opinion are the lifeblood of sound decision-making. When mistakes are made, it is their president who is to be blamed, not those who endeavor to guide him along the path. Most of our decisions are unanimously arrived at. But from time to time, when there are strong differences among us, it falls to me to make the final choice. When I want to see who is to blame when things go wrong, I only have to look in the mirror to find the answer.

Author's notes:

On this date, Lincoln advised General Halleck that by his reckoning, General McClellan had 95,000 men within his command.

The White House – Thursday, September 11, 1862

Today I spent time discussing the character of Robert E. Lee with General Halleck. Lee is the man that General Winfield Scott had proposed to be our leading field general when I first arrived in Washington. Scott told me at that time that Lee's strength as a leader is that he is always willing to take risks that many men in his place would not take. Scott said that Lee is not reckless but bold. He also has certain advantages. He has lived most of his life in the areas where he is now commanding troops. He knows the lay of the land far better than I do. His weaknesses are also significant. He has fewer resources. Less population to draw upon for added troops when needed. Less manufacturing base for the needs of war. And a significant percentage of his nation's population is enslaved. Men who could be fighting against us are instead either engaged in farming or doing manual labor. Because he led many of his present-day officers in the Mexican War and is acquainted with those who attended West Point with him, and when he commanded there, he has an excellent understanding of the leadership traits of Confederate and Union officers. Unlike McClellan, Lee obviously does not need to be spurred into action.

Author's notes:

Lincoln after the Second Battle of Bull Run expected Lee to rest after his victory, but Lee persisted, crossing the Potomac and invading Maryland. Demands in the press called for a complete reorganization of the administration. The changing of Eastern Army command from McClelland to Pope and then from Pope back to McClelland caused the Lincoln Cabinet to protest McClelland's reappointment bitterly. To Chicago Christians who petitioned him to issue a proclamation of emancipation, Lincoln answered by writing on September 13, "It is my earnest desire to know the will of providence in this matter. And if I can learn what it is I will do it!" He later told his Cabinet that he made a vow, a covenant that if God gave us the victory in the approaching battle, he would consider it an indication of Divine Will, and that it was his duty to move forward in the cause of emancipation."

The White House – Friday, September 12, 1862

I shared with Stanton a letter I received from August Belmont. In its pages he recommends that Halleck be made secretary of war, thus replacing Stanton, and that McClellan be appointed commander-in-chief of all Eastern military forces. In that scenario, Stanton would lose his job and so would I because the commander-in-chief role in our government is exclusively that of the president. Stanton had a good laugh over the letter. Whenever we suffer defeats, the number of unsolicited suggestions for changes that should be made soars. Belmont is a good man all the same.

Chief John Ross conferred with me about Cherokee Nation matters. He informed me that his tribesmen needed protection in Kansas, where other Indian tribes were being stirred up by Confederate agents. Caleb Smith, in charge of the Interior Department, has only good things to say about Ross. Smith's department is responsible for Indian Affairs. Many Indians who visit with me come in Indian costume, but Ross always comes dressed as a well-to-do white businessman. I admitted to Ross that although I am a lawyer, I am woefully unfamiliar with our treaty obligations with his and the other tribes. I told him that I believed that the red man was far more likely to fight and kill members of his race than are white men. He laughed loudly and said that he could read in the newspapers just how well the white race was doing these days.

Author's notes:

On December 26, 1862, 37 Sioux men were executed for crimes committed in Minnesota during an Indian uprising. A military commission appointed by General Pope had recommended that 303 Sioux be executed. Lincoln reviewed each Indian's record and limited executions to those he deemed to be guiltier or more influential among those convicted by the Army. Lincoln considered rape and the murder of white farmers the most serious offenses. This was the largest public execution in American history. In Minnesota, public opinion favored more, not fewer, hangings. In 1864, Republicans lost strength in Minnesota. Senator (formerly governor) Ramsey told Lincoln that if he had hanged more Indians he would have had a larger majority. Lincoln replied, "I could not afford to hang men for votes."

The White House – Saturday, September 13, 1862

While riding here this morning from the Soldiers' Home I sprained my left wrist while checking my runaway horse. I don't know what spooked him, but I believe it may have been two passing carriages. Fortunately, I am right-handed, so my injury will not affect my diary writing. Mother has recommended that I soak it in warm water several times today. I did it once and it gave me some relief, so I'll do it again after lunch. For the next few days I'll use the carriage and let Hay or Nicolay do the driving.

I replied to a delegation of Chicago Christians who presented me with a memorial written in favor of national emancipation. It was adopted at a large public meeting of Christian men and women at Bryan Hall in their city on September 7. They also gave me a similar memorial written in German and signed by German citizens of Chicago. I explained to them that I have spent many hours over the past months considering the matter of the freeing of slaves. I told them that I am being given the most opposite advice on the subject, often by men of the cloth. Some tell me that their thoughts represent Divine Will. I have told many of them that if it is possible that God would reveal his will to others that it might be supposed he would reveal it directly to me; for unless I am more deceived in myself than I often am, it is my earnest desire to know the will of Providence in this matter. And if I can learn what it is, I will do it! But these are not the days of miracles, and I do not expect a direct revelation. Good men do not agree on this issue, religious and non-religious. I told them that I respected their views and that in the final decision I make I trust will be found God's will.

Author's notes:

From Washington to Trump, only eight presidents have been left-handed. They are: James A. Garfield, Herbert Hoover, Harry S. Truman, Gerald Ford, Ronald Reagan, George H.W. Bush, Bill Clinton and Barack Obama.

The White House – Sunday, September 14, 1862

Major General Cassius Clay came to the White House at 3 P.M. He brought with him orders to go to New Orleans. I issued a counter order and told him that he need not go there until he hears from me again. My plans are to send him to Russia once Simon Cameron is back in the United States from his service there. We discussed my most recent draft of an Emancipation Proclamation. I confided in him that it is my fervent hope to promulgate it once our military forces win a significant military victory. He concurs. I know that he will make a splendid representative of our nation once he reaches St. Petersburg.

Author's notes:

J. Wilson Shaffer, a personal acquaintance of President Lincoln, wrote on September 14, "You know Mr. Lincoln that whatever good qualities General Clay may possess he has not the elements of a prudent and skillful general. General Butler listens much to those around him (who have had experience on proper military education) on military matters and I earnestly hope for the success of the department that none but military officers of known ability will be sent to him, he can then trust his army in the field to them and he take charge of the rebels and the Negroes. Did I not feel deeply the importance to the country and to you of what I yesterday said to you and what I now write I would not trouble you with this letter. Your friend and Obt. Servt. J. Wilson Shaffer." Lincoln sent Shaffer's letter to Edwin Stanton with this note: "The writer of this is a personal acquaintance of mine who has been on duty at New Orleans as a Quarter Master. I have thought it not improper that the Sec. of War should see his suggestion. A. Lincoln."

The White House – Monday, September 15, 1862

I told Hay today that sometimes I feel that the ghost of President Andrew Jackson is in this room, which had been used by him as an office. General Jackson is frequently abused by writers of history. I believe that he was an exceptional American. He foresaw the Civil War and did all he could to prevent one from happening. The Hero of New Orleans wanted to keep the Union whole. A few months ago, I had an old oil portrait of Old Hickory hung on the wall in this room. Now I often look him in the eyes and ask, "What would you do, General?" when I have serious doubts, which I now have more often than ever. Postmaster Montgomery Bair told me the other day that his father, Frank Blair, who lived across the street from the White House, once milked his cow, so Jackson could have the milk.

Author's notes:

In 1864, a friend of Lincoln sent him a copy of a letter that Andrew Jackson had written warning that the Southern states might secede over the pretext of slavery. In the letter, Jackson had written that "ambitious men who would involve their country in civil wars should be sent to Haman's gallows."

The White House – Tuesday, September 16, 1862

I declined to accept three Negro regiments raised in Rhode Island and Massachusetts. I appreciated the kind offer, but believe it is premature. Reports shown me at the War Department are disturbing. Lee has apparently divided his forces that are now known to be in Maryland, with columns under the command of Stonewall Jackson aimed at Harpers Ferry, while his other forces are directed at Hagerstown. Halleck has warned that Harpers Ferry is a difficult place to defend in as much as it lies in a natural saucer, surrounded by commanding steep hills on three sides, which make it susceptible to devastating bombardment from above.

Author's notes:

For three days Jackson's troops placed artillery on the heights overlooking Harpers Ferry. On the morning of September 15th, he ordered an artillery barrage that bombarded the small but strategic town, which was followed by an infantry assault by Major General A.P. Hill's forces at 8 A.M. Union Colonel Dixon S. Miles, convinced the situation was hopeless, decided to surrender the garrison and its more than 12,000 troops. Miles was killed by an artillery shell during the battle. Jackson took possession of Harpers Ferry before joining Lee's Army at Sharpsburg. Hill's troops processed the parole of over 12,000 Union prisoners. The Union had 14,000 men involved. The Confederate forces totaled 30,000 troops.

The White House – Thursday, September 18, 1862

Preliminary reports received at the War Department indicate that a fierce battle was fought near Sharpsburg Maryland yesterday.

Author's notes:

This battle would become known as the Battle of Antietam. The Battle of Antietam was over by 5:30 P.M. on the 17th. On the morning of the 18th, Lee's Army prepared to defend against a federal assault that never came. After an improvised truce, both sides recovered bodies and exchanged their wounded. Lee's forces began to withdraw across the Potomac River that evening to return to Virginia. The Union had 12,410 casualties with 2,108 dead. Confederates suffered 10,316 with 1,546 dead.

Lincoln was disappointed in McClellan's performance. He believed that he was overly cautious, and poorly coordinated actions in the field had forced the battle to a draw rather than a crippling Southern defeat. Lincoln was astonished that from September 17 to October 26, despite repeated War Department entreaties, McClellan declined to pursue Lee across the Potomac. He cited shortages of equipment and the fear of overextending his forces. Halleck wrote in his official report, "The long inactivity of so large an army in the face of a defeated foe, and during the most favorable season for rapid movements and a vigorous campaign, was a matter of great disappointment and regret." Lincoln relieved McClellan of his command of the Army of the Potomac on November 5, 1862 effectively ending his military career. He was replaced by General Ambrose Burnside.

After the war, Lieutenant James Longstreet, C.S.A., wrote, "The great mistake of the Maryland campaign was the division of Lee's Army. If General Lee had kept his forces together, he could not have suffered defeat. At Sharpsburg he had hardly 37,000 men, who were in poor condition for battle, while McClellan had about 87,000, who were fresh and strong."

The White House – Friday, September 19, 1862

I think I lost more sleep this week than in any week of the war. It has been a cliff hanger situation, awaiting word of results in the field. The expression – The fog of war – is apt. I am informed that McClellan received prior intelligence of where Lee's Army was headed several days in advance of the battle fought at Sharpsburg. This rarely happens. General Halleck pointed out to me that the information we received about Lee's intended movements could have been reliable, or it could have been a clever ruse. Fortunately, the information turned out to be accurate.

Author's notes:

On Saturday, September 13th, a young enlisted man in the 27th Indiana Infantry fortuitously found three cigars wrapped in papers. The papers were the official orders from Lee to his forces outlining his Maryland campaign plans. The orders indicated that Lee was splitting his forces. The cigars were found in an area where the Hoosiers were bivouacking. It had been occupied by the rebels just the day before. Although he moved slowly, McClellan did act upon the information, giving him a significant edge in the battle to come. He believed the documents were genuine and was rewarded for his belief.

The White House – Saturday, September 20, 1862

I took mother and Tad for a very pleasant and relaxing carriage ride. The brisk fall air cleared the brain a bit. Tad now wears an Army uniform that the soldiers on guard duty at the Old Soldiers Home gave to him. He is my proud little Lieutenant. I spent most of this afternoon working on a draft of the Emancipation Document. It is my firm belief that our victory of arms this week is the sign I have been waiting for that it should now be issued. I plan to present it to the Cabinet on Monday. I promised God that if our forces drove Lee's Army from Maryland I would consider that act of victory as His sign that the emancipation of slaves should become our national war policy.

Several Jewish citizens from Philadelphia came to Washington by train to thank me for appointing Jacob Frankel as an Army chaplain. Frankel will be the first American rabbi to hold such a position.

Author's notes:

6,500 Jews fought in the Union Army during the Civil War. In the beginning of the war there were no Jewish chaplains to administer to Jewish soldiers. When several rabbis asked to enlist, they were refused on the grounds that only Christians could serve as clergy or chaplains. The YMCA and other Christian organizations lobbied Congress to exclude rabbis from the armed forces. In December of 1861, Lincoln met with Isaac Mayer Wise and Isaac Leeser from the Board of Delegates of the American Israelites and other prominent Jewish leaders. He told them that he believed the exclusion of Jewish chaplains was unintentional on the part of Congress and agreed that something should be done to allow rabbis to serve as chaplains. A bill eliminating the requirements that chaplains be only Christian ministers was passed on July 17, 1862. President Lincoln commissioned three rabbis to serve as Army chaplains during the Civil War: Jacob Frankel of Philadelphia, Berhard Gotthelf of Louisville, and Ferdinand Sarner of Rochester.

The White House – Sunday, September 21, 1862

Today with the help of Nicolay and Hay, I put the finishing touches on the Emancipation Proclamation document. Mother, Tad and I went to the New York Avenue Presbyterian Church for the early service. I spoke to the Reverend Phineas Gurley, the minister as we were leaving and asked him to pray for me. Tad is in the church's Sabbath School. The pastor tells me that Tad has a healthy curiosity about the stories in the Old Testament. I must remember to ask Mary to invite the Gurley's to dinner at the White House one evening soon. We all enjoyed attending the wedding of their lovely daughter, Mary Frances last year.

Author's notes:

When Willie Lincoln died, the Rev. Phineas Gurley preached the funeral sermon in the White House East Room. As Willie lay dying, he bequeathed his savings to the Sunday School, and at the next month's congregational meeting Dr. Gurley reported Willie's $5.00 gift. When the president was assassinated, the family sent for Dr. Gurley, and he spent six hours at Lincoln's bedside, most of it spent trying to console a distraught and hysterical Mary Lincoln. When death came, he escorted Mary back to the White House where he announced the tragic news to young Tad Lincoln. He delivered the sermon at the White House state funeral on April 19. He escorted Lincoln's body on the long trip to Springfield, Illinois, where he closed the burial services with a prayer and a hymn he composed enroute.

In 1970, Commodore and Mrs. Herbert C. Ruckmick donated a stained-glass window to the church. It is located along the north side of the church at the balcony level. It shows President Lincoln standing beside his pew during pastoral prayer, as was his custom. The window's central theme is Lincoln's dependence on divine help during the Civil War. The American flags and eagle at the top center unite the opposing armies at the sides. A fragment from Lincoln's second inaugural address appears above all: "With malice toward none, with charity for all, with firmness in the right as God gives us to see the right." At the bottom right, the president is shown helping to free the slaves. The New York Avenue Presbyterian Church is located at 1313 New York Avenue NW, Washington, D.C. The pew that Lincoln rented for $50 a year is in the same place that it was in the 1860s. Visitors are allowed to sit in it.

The White House – Monday, September 22, 1862

Today I put my signature and caused the seal of the United States to be affixed to the Emancipation Proclamation. It is now the law of the land. How will people react to it? Will it bring the war to a faster conclusion? Will it cause trouble in the border states? The nation has the time between now and January 1,1863, when it goes into effect, to consider what has just been ordered. I deem it to be a decision based upon military necessity.

The paramount section in the document reads: "That all slaves of persons who shall hereafter be engaged in rebellion against the government of the United States, or who shall in any way give aid and comfort thereto, escaping from such persons and taking refuge within the lines of the army; and all slaves captured from such persons or deserted by them and coming under the control of the government of the United States; and all slaves of such persons found on (or) being within any place occupied by rebel forces and afterwards occupied by the forces of the United States, shall be deemed captives of war, and shall be forever free of their servitude and not again held as slaves."

Author's notes:

The final proclamation of January 1,1863, differed from the September 22, 1862, initial version in several ways. It specifically listed the states considered to be in rebellion and allowed ex-slaves to be received into the armed forces of the United States. Specifically, slaves were allowed to serve in "garrison forts, positions, stations and other places, and to man vessels of all sorts in said service." Lincoln added this phrase, "And upon this act, sincerely believed to be an act of justice, warranted by the Constitution, upon military necessity, I invoke the considerate judgment of mankind, and the gracious favor of Almighty God."

Within two years of enactment the Union enlisted 200,000 black soldiers and sailors who played a significant role in ending the rebellion. A massive pro-Union reaction occurred throughout Europe – particularly in Great Britain. Henry Adams wrote from London, "It has done more for us here than all our former victories and all our diplomacy. It is creating an almost convulsive reaction in our favor." The American ambassador to the Netherlands wrote, "Everyone can understand the significance of a war where emancipation is written on one banner and slavery on the other."

The White House – Wednesday, September 24, 1862

Early in the evening, a large military band from Michigan and over 300 or more citizens, including many soldiers, came to the White House lawn. Speeches were made and songs were sung to celebrate the news of the Emancipation Proclamation. A men's choir of young soldiers serenaded the crowd with a beautiful rendition of the Battle Hymn of the Republic. Mother and I were particularly moved by the words, "In the beauty of the lilies Christ was born across the sea, with a glory in his bosom that transfigures you and me. As He died to make men holy, let us die to make men free, While God is marching on." When the men sang, she and I joined in the singing. When the men then loudly sang, "Glory, glory, hallelujah!" three times followed by "While God is marching on," we saw people young and old crying with joy. What a night this has been for us here in Washington and for the nation.

Author's notes:

Lincoln spoke to the crowd. He said, "I can only trust in God I have made no mistake. I shall make no attempt on this occasion to sustain what I have done or said by any comment. It is now for the country and the world to pass judgment on it, and, maybe, take action upon it. I will say no more on the subject. In my position I am environed with difficulties. Yet they are scarcely so great as the difficulties of those who upon the battlefield are endeavoring to purchase with their blood and lives the future happiness and prosperity of this country. Let us never forget them. I only ask you, at the conclusion of these few remarks, to give three hearty cheers to all good and brave officers and men who fought in recent successful battles." After Lincoln spoke, the crowd paraded to the residence of Secretary Chase, where they heard speeches from Chase and Cassius M. Clay, and thence to the residence of Attorney General Bates, who also made a speech.

The White House – Thursday, September 25, 1862

Edward Everett was my guest at the White House today. I was honored to be with him. Few men have done so much for our country as Everett. During his lifetime he has been a politician, pastor, educator, Harvard College president, diplomat and famed orator. He has served in the House of Representatives and Senate, was secretary of state and governor of Massachusetts. He was ambassador to the United Kingdom. When he ran for vice president of the United States on the Constitutional Party ticket in 1860, he and John Bell received 39 electoral votes, all from Southern states. Throughout his entire life he has been a close friend of Daniel Webster and did all he could for decades to keep the South from leaving the Union. Since hostilities began, he has been outspoken in favor of the Union war effort.

Everett asked me to write a letter of introduction for him to use while in Europe. I wrote, "Hon. Edward Everett goes to Europe shortly. His reputation and the present condition of our country are such that his visit there is sure to attract notice and may be misconstrued. I therefore think fit to say that he bears no mission from this government, and yet no gentleman is better able to correct misunderstandings in the minds of foreigners in regard to American affairs. While I commend him to the consideration of those whom he may meet, I am quite conscious that he could better introduce me than I him, in Europe."

When we shook hands as he was leaving, he told me that he believes the emancipation document will do much to influence thinking in Europe in favor of the Union cause. I trust he is right.

Author's notes:

In 1863, when Lincoln spoke at the dedication ceremony of the Gettysburg National Cemetery, he was preceded by the featured orator, Edward Everett, who spoke for two hours. Lincoln spoke for just two minutes.

The White House – Friday, September 26, 1862

I sent a letter of congratulations to Emperor Alexander II of Russia on the birth of his nephew, Viatcheslaw, the son of his brother, the Grand Duke Constantin Nicolaewitsch. I admire the tsar for his freeing of the serfs in his country and other progressive reforms, including reorganizing the judicial system, setting up elected local judges, abolishing capital punishment, promoting local self-government and imposing universal military service. If the United States had enacted universal military service before the Civil War, perhaps Southern secessionists might have thought twice before firing on Fort Sumter. Such a program should be considered for the future. I discussed this issue with General Scott and he believes that a nation is much stronger when it has a citizenry that has been trained in military and naval matters. Too many of the young men we take into the Army have never fired a gun, not even to shoot a squirrel!

Author's notes:

In 1867, Tsar Alexander II sold Alaska to the United States. Like Lincoln, the tsar was assassinated. He was killed on March 13, 1881. He ruled from March 2, 1855, to March 13, 1881. He was also king of Poland and the grand duke of Finland.

The White House – Saturday, September 27, 1862

Yesterday, I was informed that Major John J. Key on General Halleck's staff is reported to have said to Major Levi Turner after the Battle of Antietam, when asked why was not the rebel Army bagged immediately after the battle? "The object is that neither army shall get much advantage of the other; that both shall be kept in the field until they are exhausted, when we will make a compromise and save slavery." I gave Major Key 24 hours to prove he did not make the answer as reported. After meeting with Key and Judge Advocate Major Levi Turner at 11 A.M. today, I decided to dismiss Key at once from military service. I informed him that his views are unacceptable and contrary to our war aims.

Before removing Key, I discussed the matter with Postmaster Blair, who agrees that an example must be made of officers like Key. Blair noted that Key's brother serves on McClellan's staff.

Author's notes:

Major John J. Key was an acting judge advocate on General Halleck's staff. His brother was an aide to General George C. McClellan. There was fear that Key's comments represented a broader feeling among the officer corps. Two years after the event, Lincoln said to John Hay, "I dismissed Major Key for his silly treasonable talk because I feared it was staff talk and I wanted an example."

When Key appealed his removal in November of 1862, Lincoln wrote him, "I cannot find sufficient ground to change the conclusion therein arrived at. I dismissed you as an example and a warning...I bear you no ill will; and I regret that I could not have the example without wounding you personally. I really feel sorry for the pain the case gives you, but I do not see how, consistently with duty, I can change it. Yours, A. Lincoln."

The White House – Sunday, September 28, 1862

Today was spent at the Soldiers' Home. We will soon be back living in the White House. Mother is anxious to attend to various decorating details. She has made a long "to do" list. It is her opinion that the People's House should be much more welcoming to guests, particularly foreign dignitaries. She believes (and I agree) that the place has been badly neglected for decades. My own sense is that the more time she spends thinking about the White House, the less time she'll have to think upon recent tragedies in her life.

I received a very positive letter from Vice-President Hamlin. He is still up in Bangor, Maine. He writes of the reaction to the preliminary Emancipation Proclamation among those he has spoken to in his home state. Hamlin believes that it will stand as the "great act of the age." I seriously wonder about that. It is too early to see how it will be received in states where slaves are currently held. The South fears it will trigger slave revolts. I do not believe that it will.

The initial response to the proclamation has been rather muted, with a few press exceptions.

When Hamlin returns to Washington, I look forward to discussing with him my views on negro colonization. As far as I can judge, there is little to no support for the idea among the leaders of the black community. Without their enthusiastic support it cannot possibly succeed. My discussions with black leaders have not borne fruit. But on the issue of the emancipation, word from the black community has been overwhelmingly encouraging.

Author's notes:

On this date Lincoln wrote to the surgeon general asking him to allow Dr. S.W. Forsha to treat wounded soldiers with his "Healing Balm." On February 13, 1863, Surgeon General William Hammond, reported to Lincoln, "I have met with Dr. Forsha before, and am satisfied that he is an ignorant quack."

The White House – Monday, September 29, 1862

I met with Brigadier General Edward Stanly today, wishing him well as he returns to North Carolina as our military governor of the state. I asked that he do all he can to ensure that congressional elections will again be held in North Carolina starting next year. Stanley served as a representative in the U.S. Congress from 1837 to 1843 and from 1849 to 1853. He then moved to California, where he was the Republican candidate for governor in 1857. He practiced law in San Francisco. Before the war Stanly was an outspoken Southerner who always strongly emphasized the Union cause over state's rights.

Later in the day I reviewed the 145th New York Regiment. Tad joined me and fully enjoyed the experience, particularly when the troops enthusiastically cheered yours truly. It was refreshing to hear their loud voices shouting out their hurrahs. Senate President J.W. Forney joined us, and we had a brief discussion on the probable effects of the Emancipation Proclamation and the recent suspension of writs of habeas corpus.

Author's notes:

Edward Stanly was born in New Bern, North Carolina. He graduated from the American Literary, Scientific and Military Academy, Norwich University, in 1829. He then studied law and was admitted to the North Carolina bar in 1832. He was known as one of North Carolina's greatest orators and served as speaker of the State House from 1844 to 1846. From 1847 to 1848 he was attorney general of North Carolina. Lincoln appointed Stanly military governor of North Carolina on May 26, 1862. He resigned the office on March 2, 1863, in a dispute with President Lincoln over the Emancipation Proclamation.

The White House – Thursday October 2, 1862

Little was accomplished in Tuesday's Cabinet meeting. We mostly talked about cotton purchases and various trade regulations. No important decisions were reached. I suggested that a watchman be hired to protect the White House and proposed that Thomas Stackpole be employed. I know him to be a competent individual.

Wednesday morning, I left by special train to visit the headquarters of the Army of the Potomac and the bloody battlefields near Antietam. The party consisted of General McClernand, Captain Wright Rives, Marshall Lamon, Ozias Hatch and John Garrett, President of the B & O Railroad. We arrived at noon. With General McClellan I reviewed troops at Bolivar Heights and then spent the night at Harpers Ferry. The Second Cavalry Band serenaded our party.

Today, I reviewed troops with General Sumner and O.M. Hatch at Loudain Heights and Maryland Heights. I have tremendous respect for Hatch because it was Hatch, as secretary of state of Illinois, who recommended that U.S. Grant, then an unknown colonel, command one of Illinois' newly formed regiments. I hate to think where we would be without General Grant.

The White House – Saturday, October 4, 1862

Friday at sunrise O.M. Hatch and I surveyed the headquarters camp of the Army. I told Hatch that what he was looking at was "General McClellan's bodyguard." Later in the morning I reviewed General Burnside's corps. At midday McClellan and I rode ambulances to Bakersville, Maryland, to review cavalry and troops of General Fitz John Porter and General Franklin's corps.

Today McClellan and I visited wounded soldiers near headquarters. We spent time with General Dick Richardson, who was in a farmhouse dying of fatal wounds incurred at Sharpsburg. Richardson's poise was remarkable for a man about to leave this mortal coil. At noon we visited the battlefield at South Mountain. The land was covered with the debris of war and evidence all about, the signs of the fierceness of the struggle. Later I visited the home of Mrs. Mary Ramsey to see Brigadier General George Hartsuff, who is recovering from wounds received at Antietam. He was in remarkably good spirits for a man who has suffered so greatly. Our party returned by fast train to Washington.

Author's notes:

Before leaving the railway station in Frederick, Maryland, Lincoln spoke to a crowd that had gathered to see him off. He said, "I return thanks to our soldiers for the good service they have rendered, for the energies they have shown, the hardships they have endured, and the blood they have so nobly shed for this dear union of ours; and I also return thanks to the good citizens of Maryland, and to all the good men and women of this land, for their devotion to our glorious cause. I say this with no malice to those who have done otherwise.

In the president's absence, Mary Lincoln sent 1,000 pounds of grapes to military hospitals.

The White House – Monday, October 6, 1862

Governor Morton of Indiana and Secretary Chase came by to discuss my giving furloughs to Indiana soldiers, so they may go home to vote. No governor in any state has been more supportive of the Union cause than Morton. I remember the first time I cast my ballot. I regret that every citizen who is entitled to vote does not do so. It harms our democracy. Everyone who can legally vote should always learn all he can about the candidates and vote.

I instructed General Halleck to telegraph General McClellan to "cross the Potomac and give battle to the enemy or drive him south."

Author's notes:

The president received his salary warrant, for $2,022.33, which is $61 under the previous warrant because of a 3 percent income tax deduction.

215

The White House – Tuesday, October 7, 1862

At the noon Cabinet meeting we discussed General McClellan's recent actions and General Halleck's order sent yesterday directing that he move his Army forward with dispatch. We spent a long time reviewing the Army's recent performance at Antietam and considered McClellan's failure to pursue Lee when he had the opportunity to do so. From what I can figure, September 17 at Antietam had to have been the bloodiest day of the war for our side. Halleck has estimated that our casualties totaled 12,401 killed, wounded and captured. We have no numbers for the rebels, but Halleck believes their losses were almost as high as ours.

Author's notes:

Rutherford B. Hayes and William McKinley fought at Antietam. Harvard graduate Hayes was a colonel in command of the 23rd Ohio Volunteer Infantry. At the Battle of South Mountain, he was wounded in the arm and put out of action for several months. 19-year-old William McKinley was a commissary sergeant in Hayes' 23rd unit. He was cited for bravery when he drove his commissary wagon through enemy gunfire to deliver badly needed food and coffee to his regiment's battle line. Both men were elected president of the United States. McKinley was the last Civil War veteran to be elected president.

The Maryland State Monument located on the battlefield is the only monument dedicated there to the men who fought on both sides of the battle.

The White House – Wednesday, October 8, 1862

I telegraphed General Grant today congratulating him and all concerned on their recent battles and victories. I inquired as to the condition of General Oglesby, who is a close friend of mine from Illinois. I also sent my sympathies for the death in battle of Brigadier General Pleasant Adams Hackleman on October 3rd at Corinth. I informed the Cabinet today that Hackleman's final words were, "I am dying, but I die for my country." He was shot through the neck as he was rallying his brigade at a critical point in the battle.

Author's notes:

Pleasant Hackleman was from Franklin County, Indiana, and was the only Indiana general to be killed during the Civil War. He was a lawyer, probate judge and was elected to the Indiana Legislature. He had been the editor of the Rushville Republican newspaper and was a delegate to the National Republican Convention in Chicago that nominated Abraham Lincoln as the Republican presidential candidate. During the Battle of Corinth, Hackleman was attached to command the First Brigade in the 2nd Division of the Army of Tennessee. On October 3, the Confederate Army attacked Rosencrans' Army of the Mississippi. When the Union line began to fall back, Hackleman bravely attempted to rally his men and was shot through the neck. He soon died from his wound.

Richard Oglesby was appointed colonel of the 8th Illinois Volunteer Infantry Regiment on April 25, 1861. He had served in the U.S. Army during the Mexican-American War. He was given command of troops under General Grant at the Battles of Fort Henry and Fort Donelson and promoted to brigadier general on March 21, 1862. At the Siege of Corinth, he commanded the 2nd Brigade, 2nd Division, Army of Tennessee. In October of 1862, he was wounded in the chest and back at Corinth. Oglesby was promoted to major general on November 29, 1862, and after a period of recovery, commanded the left wing of the XVI Corps, Army of the Tennessee, from April to July 1863. He resigned his commission to successfully run for governor of Illinois on the Republican ticket. He was present in the room at the Petersen House when President Lincoln died on April 15, 1865. He served three terms as governor and as U.S. senator from Illinois from 1873 to 1879.

The White House – Friday, October 10, 1862

General Jeremiah T. Boyle telegraphed Halleck today at 2 P.M. today notifying us that "Men from Tennessee report John C. Breckenridge moving northward. Some believe his purpose is to attack Nashville; others believe he is coming up to reinforce Bragg." He advises that there was terrible slaughter yesterday near Perryville. Buell drove Bragg eight miles with great slaughter on both sides.

Author's notes:

On the 12th of October Boyle advised, "Battle was fought on Wednesday, October 8, by two divisions of McCook's corps, and most of rebel force under William J. Hardee and Leonidas Polk, Braxton Bragg commanding the whole. We lost Generals James S. Jackson, William R. Terrill, Colonel George Webster, Lieutenant Colonel George P. Jouett, Major William P. Campbell. Our estimated loss at 1,500 to 2,000 killed. The enemy's loss as great and believed to be greater. Buell is pressing the enemy. Heavy fighting reported at Harrodsburg."

During the Battle of Perryville or the Battle of Chaplin Hills, 55,000 Union and 16,000 Confederate forces were engaged from October 7 to October 9. By that time, Union reinforcements were threatening the Confederate left. Bragg, short of men and supplies, withdrew during the night toward the Cumberland Gap. The battle was a Confederate tactical victory, though the heavy bloodshed forced Bragg to retreat into Tennessee. His Army would never return to Kentucky.

There were 7,621 casualties: 4,220 Union and 3,401 Confederate.

The White House – Sunday, October 12, 1862

Telegraphed messages were sent to General Boyle today and yesterday seeking news of the fate of General Buell and his Army. Nothing has been learned of our forces or the whereabouts of General Bragg. We must find ways to improve our communication methods. A commander cannot command with confidence when he is kept in the dark. I fear that Buell may turn out to be no more aggressive than McClellan. I've been told that Napoleon's men subsisted on half the rations provided to our men, and that he used half as many wagons and horses as we do. It seems the rebels are faster than we are in retreat than we are in pursuit in large part because they are not encumbered with so much extraneous equipment.

I found comfort this evening in reading Shakespeare's "Henry VI." Mother cannot abide Henry. I like to quote from this play more than any of his others. I recently paraphrased Shakespeare when I wrote to a supporter in Philadelphia that, "This war has carried mourning to almost every home, until it can almost be said that the heavens are hung in black." Whenever "Hamlet" or "Henry VI" are played in Washington, I move heaven and earth to attend the performances. In Henry's time the Houses of York and Lancaster waged brutal civil war. How sad that history always finds a way to repeat itself.

Author's notes:

Lincoln often misquoted the lines of the Duke of Beford, from Henry VI, Act I, Scene I:

Hung be the heavens with black, yield day to night!
Comets, importing change of times and states,
Brandish your crystal tresses in the sky,
And with them scourge the bad revolting stars
That have consented unto Henry's death!
King Henry the Fifth, too famous to live long!
England ne're lost a king of so much worth.

The White House – Monday, October 13, 1862

After a relatively quiet day I spent several hours at the Soldiers' Home discussing military issues and my displeasure with both generals McClellan and Buell with Vice-President Hamlin. It seemed that we talked all night. He is a very patient listener and a man of quiet wisdom. He is also a very good sounding board. He brings to the discussion the benefits of his having spoken to many private citizens about the war, and how news of the Emancipation Proclamation has affected their thinking. He says that in his part of the country the proclamation has been well-received by those that he has spoken to. I hope that is generally the case. I have received few letters about it since it was issued.

Author's notes:

On this date Lincoln sent a detailed two-page letter to General McClellan again urging him to take positive action against the Confederate forces. He criticized McClellan for his "over-cautiousness." He wrote, "Are you not overcautious when you assume that you cannot do what the enemy is constantly doing? Should you not claim to be at least his equal in prowess, and act upon the claim?

On October 16, McClellan replied, "I promise you that I will give to your views my fullest and most unprejudiced consideration, and that it is my intention to advance the moment my men are shod, and my cavalry are sufficiently renovated to be available."

The White House – Tuesday, October 14, 1862

Positive word has reached us that our Navy was victorious at Galveston, Texas, on October 4th. The Union Navy under Commander William B. Renshaw, of our Western Gulf Blockading Squadron, successfully entered Galveston Harbor and disabled Fort Point. The U.S Navy had been blockading Galveston since July of 1861. A representative of Colonel Joseph J. Cook of the Confederate forces then agreed to a four-day truce to evacuate women and children from the city. Reports indicate that the rebel forces then evacuated, taking guns, ammunition and supplies. The port is now closed to commerce, thus denying the Confederates access to goods from overseas. Renshaw was on the cutter, U.S.S. Harriet Lane during the hostilities and was joined by four Union steamers with a mortar boat in tow. Our Navy disabled guns at Fort Point and at Fort Bankhead. The negotiations for the evacuation of civilians were conducted aboard the U.S.S. Westfield. Renshaw's threat to bombard the city convinced the enemy to withdraw without further bloodshed.

Author's notes:

The fall of Galveston meant that one more Southern port was closed to commerce and the importation of goods of military value.

Not long after Renshaw's seizing of Galveston, the Second Battle of Galveston on January 1, 1863, resulted in a victory by Confederate forces under Major General John B. Magruder and Commander Leon Smith of the Texas Marine Department. Two Confederate cotton-clad river boats, C.S. Bayou City and C.S. Neptune, under Smith engaged the Union fleet in Galveston Harbor, which consisted of the U.S.S. Clifton, U.S.S. Harriet Lane, U.S.S. Westfield, U.S.S. Owasco, U.S.S. Corypheus and U.S.S. Sachem. The Neptune was sunk. After the loss of cutter Harriet Lane, Union fleet Commander Renshaw was killed when trying to blow up the stranded USS Westfield to save it from falling into enemy hands. Union troops on shore mistakenly thought the fleet was surrendering and laid down their arms. Four hundred Union troops were taken prisoner. The remaining U.S. ships succeeded in retreating to Union-controlled New Orleans. Galveston remained in southern hands for the rest of the war.

The White House – Wednesday, October 15, 1862

Tad was ecstatic this morning. Captain John Dahlgren came by and presented the boy with a small brass cannon. It looks deadly but cannot harm him in any way. Dahlgren is a great friend of the family. The gun was made for Tad by sailors who are stationed at the Navy Yard.

I've asked Attorney General Edward Bates to advise me if I can legally appoint David Davis to the Supreme Court while the Senate is in recess. I've known Davis most of my professional life as a lawyer and consider him among the finest men to sit on the bench. He has distinguished himself on the Eighth Circuit from 1848 until today. It is where we both practiced law. He is owed a great debt of gratitude from me for having served as my campaign manager during the recent election.

Author's notes:

On October 15, 1862, Bates wrote to Lincoln, "I have examined the matter which you mentioned yesterday, touching your power to fill a vacancy on the bench of the Supreme Court now, in recess of the Senate...I give it as my opinion that you have the lawful power, now, in recess of the Senate to fill up a vacancy...which...existed during the last session of the Senate, by granting a commission which shall expire at the end of their next session."

On October 17, 1862, Lincoln wrote to Attorney General Edward Bates, "Please make out and send me a commission for David Davis of Illinois, as an Associate Justice of the Supreme Court of the United States, for the eighth judicial circuit."

Davis was appointed on October 17th and confirmed by the Senate on December 8, 1862. When Lincoln died, Davis was appointed executor of his estate.

The White House – Thursday, October 16, 1862

General Benjamin Prentiss and two of his officers visited me early this morning. They were captured at the Battle of Shiloh and were only recently exchanged. During the fight at Shiloh, Prentiss and his troops were the first to be attacked by the rebels and suffered heavy casualties. He had to surrender his division after a long and bloody struggle at a place they aptly called the Hornet's Nest, where the Confederates made unrelenting repeated attacks. He described the fierce fighting there and told me that he didn't think that any of his men would get out alive. I thanked them profusely for their remarkable service to the cause.

Author's notes:

During the Mexican War, Prentiss served as a captain in the First Illinois Infantry and fought at the Battle of Buena Vista. After the war he returned to Illinois and practiced law. He continued to serve in the militia and reached the rank of colonel. In 1860 he ran unsuccessfully for Congress as a Republican. When war broke out he led Union troops in Missouri operating against the Missouri State Guard. General Grant assigned him to lead a division at Shiloh, where it bore the brunt of the Confederate assault. He served on the court-martial board that convicted General Fitz John Porter. He voted for Porter's acquittal. In 1863 Prentiss was sent to Arkansas, where he led Union forces to victory at the Battle of Helena on July 4th. Later he resigned to attend to family matters. After the war he became a lawyer and served as postmaster of Bethany, Missouri. He was a delegate to the 1880 and 1884 Republican National Conventions, but never ran for public office again.

General Fitz John Porter was found guilty of disobeying a lawful order at the Second Battle of Bull Run and misconduct in front of the enemy. He was removed from command. The court-martial was later found to be unjust and overturned. Porter was ultimately reinstated into the U.S. Army.

The White House – Friday, October 17, 1862

Mary and Tad were enchanted earlier today when P.T. Barnum, the famous American showman, came to the White House at my invitation and presented Commodore Nutt, a dwarf he advertises as "Pigmy." Nutt arrived wearing the uniform of a commodore in the Union Navy. He is 14 years old and measures just 29 inches tall. Nutt asked Secretary of the Treasury Chase if he was the man who was "spending so much of Uncle Sam's money." Secretary Stanton interrupted to say that he was the "big spender," to which Nutt replied, "It is in a good cause, anyhow, and I guess it will come out all right." As Barnum and Nutt were leaving, Mary and Tad shook Nutt's hand. I said to him that as commodore he should "wade ashore" if his "fleet" was ever in danger. He looked up and down my long legs and said, "I guess, Mr. President, you could do that better than I could." Barnum has arranged for the commodore to visit the Navy Yard and entertain the sailors stationed there.

Author's notes:

Commodore Nutt's real name was George Washington Morrison Nutt. He was born April 1, 1848 and died May 25, 1881. He toured the world between 1869 and 1872 appearing before royalty with Tom Thumb and his wife, Lavinia Warren Thumb, and Minnie Warren, Lavinia's sister. In 1879 he married Lilan Elston of Redwood City, California.

When Nutt appeared for Barnum at his American Museum in New York City, he traveled around town in a miniature carriage in the shape of an English walnut. The top of the vehicle was hinged and when it was lifted the little commodore could be seen sitting inside. It was pulled by Shetland ponies and driven around Manhattan by Rodnia Nutt, Jr., the Commodore's 21-year old, 49-inch brother dressed in the uniform of a coachman. Barnum believed that these little trips around the city were the best form of advertising. Nutt's carriage is now exhibited in the Barnum Museum in Bridgeport, Connecticut.

In 1862, "The Commodore Nutt Polka," written by Thomas Baker, was a popular-selling sheet music song of the day.

The White House – Saturday, October 18, 1862

A committee of distinguished gentlemen from Baltimore complained to me that many soldiers who are half-sick are being denied hospitalization there. This concerns me greatly. I can understand how it is possible that men who are wounded in combat may find care inadequate during and after battle. But I fail to comprehend how it is possible that men who have arrived for treatment at a hospital are not being well-treated. Perhaps the large number of wounded is overwhelming the hospital system. The casualty numbers of late are particularly worrisome. They claim that in the city of Baltimore citizens are seeing straggling soldiers walking about who are half-sick and uncared for. Some of these sick men claim to have been turned away from hospitals without knowing where to go next.

I have instructed Surgeon General Hammond to investigate the matter at once and get back to me.

Author's notes:

Hammond replied the same day that, "I am sure there is no blame attached to the military authorities in Baltimore." On October 22, 1862, Surgeon Josiah Smith reported to Lincoln, "I would state that the allegation made by the Committee of Baltimore Citizens is entirely without foundation."

The White House – Sunday, October 19, 1862

I discussed with Halleck and Stanton the increasing value of the telegraph to the war effort. I pointed out to them that while speed is priceless, accuracy is even more so. There have been instances when some messages did not reach me because the military may have preferred that I be kept in the dark. I believe that problem has now been solved. My experience with messages wired to me from General Grant are that they are always to be trusted, and that those sent to him are followed by him as ordered. He is often accused of drinking, but my belief is that Grant is alert, perceptive and dogged in his efforts. His messages do not waste words. He is logical and direct. An honest man. I wish we had more generals like him: He gets results. Lately I have been spending more and more time in the telegraph office. Its relatively secluded space gives me the solitude I like to gather my thoughts. It was there that much of my thinking and writing related to the Emancipation document took place.

Author's notes:

During the Civil War, Abraham Lincoln sent almost 1,000 telegrams. After 13 months Lincoln began to use the telegraph office as his Situation Room, where he reviewed the incoming flow of telegraph messages but also carried on communications with the field. During the Second Battle of Manassas he did not return to the White House for sleep but slept on a cot in the telegraph office. In time, Lincoln developed a routine in which he would come into the telegraph office and open the telegraph clerk's desk draw and read all the dispatches that had been received since his last visit.

The White House – Monday, October 20, 1862

Today I was pleased to establish a provisional court of record for Louisiana and appoint Judge Charles A. Peabody of New York to be its judge. This had to be done because the insurrection has temporarily swept away the civil institutions of the state. Ever since we occupied New Orleans foreign governments have made claims to the secretary of state for the protection of the rights of their citizens living there.

Thus, it has been necessary to hold the state in military occupation, which requires that there shall be some judicial tribunal existing there capable of administering justice. Judge Peabody is a distinguished jurist who I am confident will prove capable of doing so in this jurisdiction. Judge Peabody may hear cases in law, equity, revenue and admiralty, his judgment to be final and conclusive. He may also establish such rules and regulations as may be necessary and appoint a prosecuting attorney, marshal and clerk of the court.

Author's notes:

In 1863, Peabody was later appointed by Lincoln to be chief-justice of the Supreme Court of Louisiana – the Appellate Court of last resort. In 1865 he returned to the practice of law in New York City.

The White House – Tuesday, October 21, 1862

I authorized General John A. McClernand to raise troops in the states of Indiana, Illinois and Iowa for a campaign against Vicksburg and to clear the Mississippi River to New Orleans. John and I go back a long way. He is a compelling advocate for our cause, and I expect that he will do well raising troops for this good purpose.

I issued a notification that draftees who may claim exemption because of alienage should apply to the State Department or through their nations' ministers or consuls. A great many Irishmen in New York have found themselves wearing blue uniforms when they are not subject to our laws. This should clarify the matter once and for all. Only American citizens may be subject to our draft laws.

Author's notes:

John Alexander McClernand served in the Illinois House of Representatives from 1840 to 1843 and as a member of the U.S. House of Representatives from Illinois' 2nd District in 1843 to 1851, and from Illinois' 6th District from 1859 to 1861. McClernand was a prominent Democratic politician and lawyer. He was firmly dedicated to the principles of Jacksonian Democracy and supported the Compromise of 1850. He served as a subordinate of General U.S. Grant in the Western Theater, fighting in the Battles of Belmont, Fort Donelson and Shiloh in 1861 and 1862.
During the Siege of Vicksburg, Grant relieved McClernand of his command by citing his intemperate and unauthorized communications with the press. He left the Army in 1864 and served as a judge and politician in the postbellum era.

The White House – Wednesday, October 22, 1862

I greatly enjoyed being aboard the steamer Mount Washington today as we sailed pleasantly to reach the camp of General Sickles' division located near a contraband camp. I find that my traveling on a ship allows me to relax and clear my brain. To get away from Washington is good for my well-being. We arrived at 2:30 P.M. and did not get back here until dusk. Upon my return I signed an order to General Grant and Governor Andrew Johnson of Tennessee advising them that Thomas R. Smith should be assisted in seeing to it that the upcoming elections in that vital state are held in a fair and honest way. I would like to see as large a voter turnout as possible as Tennesseans go to the polls to elect local officials, congressmen and a U.S. senator.

General Halleck and I conferred about General McClellan's impending plans and his persistent inactivity. Sickles' men were in high spirits and gave me a loud cheer as we departed. It was greatly appreciated.

Author's notes:

Daniel Edgar Sickles (1819 – 1914) was born to a wealthy New York City family. He was elected to the New York State Assembly in 1847 and to the New York Senate in 1856. He was a member of the U.S. House of Representatives, New York 3rd District, from March of 1857 to March of 1861. He represented New York's 10th Congressional District from March 1893 to March 1895. He served as ambassador to Spain from May 1869 to January 1874. In 1859 he killed his wife's lover, Francis Scott Key's son, Philip Barton Key II, who was the district attorney of Washington. Sickles was acquitted after using temporary insanity as a legal defense for the first time in U.S. history.

Sickles fought in the Peninsula Campaign, Seven Days Battles, Fredericksburg and Gettysburg, where he was wounded by cannon fire and had to have his leg amputated. He reached the rank of major general and eventually received the Medal of Honor.

The White House – Thursday, October 23, 1862

Today I received an especially warm letter from William "Billy" Herndon, my law
partner and loyal friend. He also sent me a new book of poems by Emerson and
reminded me of the time in 1855 or 1856, when he brought into our law office a copy
of Walt Whitman's "Leaves of Grass." At the time Whitman was highly controversial.
Mother was then very much shocked by Whitman's writings. She felt he was
outrageous then and remains so to this very day. She reminded me that Charles Eliot
Norton had said that the poet's words should be "banished from polite society."
I told her that Edward Everett Hale believes Whitman to be our "foremost poet of the
day." Herndon told me that Fanny Fern, a prominent newspaper columnist, referred
to Whitman in the New York Ledger as "this glorious Native American." Herndon
recited these lines by Whitman from his copy of "Leaves of Grass," which I have
never forgotten:

"I am the hounded slave I wince at the bite of dogs.
Hell and despair are upon me, crack and again crack the marksmen,
I clutch the rails of the fence, my gore dribs, thinned with the ooze of my skin..."

Author's notes:

Whitman saw Lincoln at the Astor House when he visited New York for the first time and later saw him in Washington, where Whitman worked as a clerk in the Paymaster's office during the Civil War and attended to wounded soldiers hospitalized in the city.

After the assassination, Whitman composed his famous poem, "O Captain! My Captain!" Its first stanza reads:

O Captain! my captain! our fearful trip is done;
The ship has weather'd every rack, the prize we sought is won;
The port is near, the bells I hear, the people all exulting,
While follow eyes the steady keel, the vessel grim and daring;
But O heart! heart! heart!
Leave you not the little spot,
Where on the deck my captain lies,
Fallen cold and dead.

In later editions he changed the sixth line to read:" O the bleeding drops of red."
On the 25th anniversary of Lincoln's death, Whitman delivered a lecture on Lincoln and read his poetry at a sold-out Madison Square Garden in Manhattan. His final words were, "Dear to the muse – thrice dear to humanity – to the whole human race – precious to this Union – precious to Democracy – unspeakably and forever precious – their great Martyr Chief." The applause from the audience went on and on after those words were spoken. Someone called for Whitman to recite, "O Captain! My Captain!" He started again and recited it to the hushed and rapt audience. As the poet spoke softly, he wept, and tears flowed down his whiskered cheeks.

The White House – Friday, October 24, 1862

Late this evening I received word in the telegraph office of a victory for our side in a battle fought on October 22 in Delaware County in Eastern Oklahoma at Beatties Prairie near Old Fort Wayne by forces under Brigadier General James Blunt and his Kansas Infantry and Cavalry, Indian Home Guard, and Indiana Light Artillery. Prior to this win there had been skirmishes going on for three days near Newtonia. The enemy was significantly outnumbered by our forces and beat a retreat back into Indian Territory. We captured artillery and other equipment. Our side had 14 casualties and the enemy perhaps 10 times as many. General Blunt estimates that his division may have been faced by as few as a rebel brigade, including Indians from the Choctaw, Chickasaw and Lower Creek tribes.

Author's notes:

The Confederate forces retreated nearly 70 miles to Fort Gibson, Oklahoma. The Union Army gained undisputed possession of the Indian Territory north of the Arkansas River. For his decisive victory, Blunt was appointed major general of volunteers.

On this date, Lincoln telegraphed General McClellan, "I have just read your dispatch about sore tongued and fatigued horses. Will you pardon me for asking what the horses of your army have done since the battle of Antietam that fatigue anything?" The next day McClellan reported that his six regiments of his cavalry had made reconnaissance, scouting trips and picketing trips of 200 miles, marching 55 miles in one day, while endeavoring to reach Stuart's cavalry, while also scouting 150 miles of river front ever since the battle of Antietam. He wrote, "If any instance can be found where overworked cavalry has performed more labor than mine since the battle of Antietam, I am not conscious of it."

The White House – Saturday, October 25, 1862

General Scott and Archbishop Hughes paid a courtesy visit. It was good to have time to spend with both men. I admire each of them and always benefit from the sound advice Scott renders when it comes to senior serving officers on both sides of the struggle. I had occasion to discuss the matter of General Jefferson Columbus Davis with him. Davis is in the hottest possible water because he shot and killed General William Nelson, an unarmed senior officer, after being reprimanded by him. Normally such a matter would be resolved by an official court-martial. However, such affairs take time and require the testimony of witnesses who might better spend their time waging war. Scott knows both officers and recommends that Davis be allowed to continue serving without a trial because he is badly needed right now. There are few experienced officers in his area available to assume the important post he now holds. The Cabinet reluctantly agreed that we should not try Davis but allow him to continue with his service in the field. He has a distinguished record. Before the shooting he was granted home leave after the Siege of Corinth because of exhaustion. Had he been well and rested it is most likely the altercation and shooting would never have occurred. War fatigue affects some men differently than others. We feel Davis deserves another chance to prove himself.

Author's notes:

General Davis would go on to serve as a corps commander under General William Tecumseh Sherman during his March to the Sea in 1864. Davis was appointed the first commander of the Department of Alaska from 1867 to 1870 and assumed field command during the Medoc War of 1872-1873.

The White House – Sunday, October 26, 1862.

Soldiers Jose Maria Rivas, Sely Lewis and Conrad Zachringer have a good reason to thank me for what I have done today. Each man received a mitigation of his sentence of death. Rivas and Lewis were both going to be hung as spies. I concluded that they were not spies. Rivas will remain a prisoner of war. Zachringer will serve only six months imprisonment for smuggling. He was scheduled to be shot for attacking two officers. He pleaded that he was drunk and knew nothing of the offenses. I believe time in jail without access to alcohol and its dire effects upon this soldier should serve the cause of justice in this matter.

Mrs. Lincoln returned from her visit to New York City yesterday. She informed me that she was serenaded from the balcony of the Metropolitan Hotel by a hundred enthusiastic Manhattanites. Among the songs they sang, she enjoyed their spirited rendition of Julia War Howe's "Battle Hymn of the Republic." She told me that when she hears her favorite verse sung she always bursts into tears. It is the beautiful stanza that reads,

"In the beauty of the lilies Christ was born across the sea,
      With a glory in his bosom that transfigures you and me;
As he died to make men holy, let us die to make men free,
      While God is marching on."

She felt great friendship flowing toward her from those who sang to her. Mother needs all the love and kind attention she can receive. Her sense of grief is still almost overwhelming. Getting away to New York to shop in its stores is good medicine for the lady.

Author's notes:

Mrs. Eliza P. Gurney, wife of Joseph J. Gurney, an English Quaker, held a prayer meeting in the president's office on this day. He told his Quaker visitors, "If I had my way this war would never have been commenced...but we find it still continues; and we must believe that He permits it for some wise purpose of his own, mysterious and unknown to us."

The White House – Monday, October 27, 1862

I often dream of my formative years and not one dream does not contain vivid images of my dear stepmother, Sarah Bush Johnson Lincoln. What a remarkable mother she was to me. Without her love and encouragement, I might now be slaving away on some small farm somewhere in Kentucky or Indiana. Sarah had what might be called steely blue-gray eyes. They were warm and beautiful. They still are. The first words she spoke to me when my father brought her to our miserable abode were, "Howdy, Abe Lincoln, I reckon we will be good friends." We have been until this very day. She possessed great wisdom. She was never idle. She wove homespun shirts, which had been dyed from roots and plants found on our property. She made me deerskin breeches and moccasins because my parents often had no money with which to buy factory-made shoes. She encouraged me to walk about 18 miles or so to borrow books from a lawyer named Pitcher, who lived at Rockport. Few in our area owned even one book. To this day, I read as many books as I can fit into my busy schedule. It is a lifelong habit acquired with the inspiration of Sarah Lincoln. Whenever I open my mail and find a letter written to me by her, my day is a much brighter one than it would have been without kind words from her. I wish I could kiss her cheek right this minute.

Author's notes:

Sarah Bush Johnson Lincoln lived four years after Lincoln's death. She died December 10, 1869. Her homesite has been made into The Lincoln Log Cabin State Historic Site in Lerna, Illinois. It includes a reproduction of the two-room cabin that Abe and his father, Thomas Lincoln, built. It stands on 86 acres of land owned by the state of Illinois. A working, living history farm has been developed around the cabin. The cabin was constructed in 1933 and 1934 during the Great Depression with labor provided by the Civilian Conservation Corps, the CCC.

The White House – Tuesday, October 28, 1862

I took Tad to Stuntz Fancy Store on New York Avenue this morning, where Tad picked out some spinning toy tops, which he will be giving as gifts to his friends on Halloween. Mother and the servants have begun planning to set up spooky decorations in the White House for a Halloween party to be held here on Friday afternoon. Tad is happily assisting as her busy assistant in making things to help set the mood. Cornstalks and pumpkins will be in array in the dining room, and for the big day children of family friends have been invited to enjoy cider, nuts and doughnuts, while playing games found in Robert Burns' odd poem, "Halloween." Children have been asked to wear costumes appropriate for the occasion. Tad has asked me if he may wear my tallest top hat, to be accompanied with a long black cape. Mother has hired a Gypsy fortune teller to give young and old guests a good time. I am very pleased to see her busy with this diversion, which is taking her mind off her recent grief. General Halleck has promised to send a men's choir from one of New York's Irish regiments to sing a medley of songs from the "Auld Sod" for Tad and his friends. It should be a grand event.

Author's notes:

During the 18th and 19th centuries, Scottish and Irish immigrant entered the United States by the thousands and brought their Halloween folk customs with them. The Germans brought an exceptionally vivid witchcraft lore to celebrate All Hallows Eve. The English and Dutch favored a dramatic flair for masquerade. Superstitions about ghosts and black cats were commonplace. In general, Halloween was the night when the spirits of the dead were thought to be out – it was a time of anarchy and mischief. The eve of All Hallows was traditionally a time of plenty. It marked the end of the farmer's year. Larders were full, and flocks sheltered. This was a traditional time for pleasure and food enough to share. Masking, tricks, performances and processions were enacted in exchange for treats or money. All Hallows had kicked off the season in Europe for centuries, and then in America as well. In New York City Halloween could mean parades and firecrackers; in the Ozarks barn dances; in Philadelphia tavern-hosted costume parties; and in Massachusetts, going out souling and other festivities.

The White House – Thursday, October 30, 1862

Secretary Steward came by to discuss General McClellan again. He is pleased to learn that the general has finally begun to move, but questions whether we can trust him to proceed with dispatch and achieve military success.

He asked me to sign a letter of congratulations to Charles Frederick, the grand duke of Baden, upon the marriage of his granddaughter, Leopoldine of Baden. I was pleased to do so. I understand that diplomacy requires such actions if we are to keep our European friends sanguine and neutral during these difficult days. She was married in Karlsruhem in September to Prince Hermann of Hohenlohe-Langenburg, the second son of Prince Ernst I of Hohenlohe-Langenburg and Princess Deodora of Leiningen. I will never fully appreciate the concept of royalty, and the idea that only a chosen few may rule based upon heritage rather than upon political skill and popularity among the governed. My reading of history tells me that the Founding Fathers toyed briefly with the idea of making Washington our first king. They wisely concluded that royalty would be uncongenial to Americans.

Author's notes:

Lincoln's presidency coincided with Count Otto von Bismarck's nation-building efforts among the German states. Once Germany became united (1870 to 1871), Lincoln the nation-builder became firmly entrenched in German public awareness. Lincoln the American unifier was admired by German politicians and writers. Prussia and the German states had overwhelmingly supported the Union during the Civil War. Karl Marx had sent a letter to Lincoln congratulating him upon his re-election in 1864. He believed that Lincoln symbolized a successful class struggle that had ended slavery and the dominance of the "planter class." Admiration for Lincoln continued into the 20th century in Germany as seen in the case of Willy Brandt. Between 1850 and 1860, close to a million Germans emigrated to the United States, and then again in the second half of the 19th century approximately 4 million Germans came to the U.S. – the tie between the two nations was very close. At the eve of the First World War 20 percent of the American population had been born in Germany, including the author's great grandparents.

The White House – Friday, October 31, 1862

Wednesday, Hay and Nicolay helped me prepare a report required by law for the allotment of Supreme Court justices to the circuits now existing by law. This was needed because two associate justices have been appointed since the last adjournment of the court. Samuel F. Miller of Iowa was appointed by me on July 16, 1862, and David Davis of Illinois on October 17, 1862. We released the allotment today.

I received an odd letter from David Nelson, who was captured six months ago and imprisoned by the rebels. He is the son of T.A.R. Nelson, a former member of Congress from Tennessee, who joined the secession, much to the shame of his loyal son. David commanded a militia company when he was captured. He now asks to be reinstated into the Union Army. I've written to Governor Andrew Johnson about young Davis and trust we may again have him in the ranks fighting loyally on our side, even if his father is to be found on the other.

Author's notes:

The allotment:

First Circuit – Nathan Clifford
Second Circuit – Samuel Nelson
Third Circuit – Robert C. Grier
Fourth Circuit – Roger B. Taney, chief justice
Fifth Circuit – James M. Wayne
Sixth Circuit – John Catron
Seventh Circuit – Noah H. Swayne
Eighth Circuit – David Davis
Ninth Circuit – Samuel F. Miller.

The White House – Sunday, November 2, 1862

Today at church, the preacher had occasion to reference Matthew's account of the deliverance of Jesus to Pilate and of his cruel treatment and trial. There are references to Jesus' trial in verses: Matt. 26 and 27; Mark 14 and 15; Luke 22 and 23, and John 18 and 19. As I've noted before, as a lawyer I wonder what I could have done to save Christ had I represented him before Jewish and Roman tribunals. Much that was done clearly violated Roman and Jewish laws and customs, yet Christ was crucified. After this war is over I would like to discuss his trial with prominent Christian and Jewish lawyers to get their legal opinions on the matter. To my mind, a powerful case could have been made in his defense. Of course, as Christians we are taught that God's will in the matter was that Christ was fated to die for our sins. Therefore, had an attorney stepped in, he would have probably been killed as well. Perhaps I should have written the date above as, "In the year of our Lord eighteen hundred and sixty-two."

Today word was received of a Union victory in Labadieville in Lafourche Parish, Louisiana. General Butler, commanding the Department of the Gulf, initiated action here to eliminate the Confederate threat to the area and to make sure that sugar and cotton crops would come into Union hands. Brigadier General Godfrey Weitzel commanded troops from New Hampshire, New York and Connecticut who defeated significantly the outnumbered rebel forces from Louisiana. This was a successful joint operation of Army and Navy, which contributed transports and gunboats.

Author's notes:

On this date, Mary Lincoln was in Manhattan, New York, accompanied by her son, Tad and General and Mrs. Robert Anderson. They called upon retired General Winfield Scott. She next visited Boston, Massachusetts, where she stayed at the Parker House Hotel. While in Boston she received Governor and Mrs. John Andrews, Senator Charles Sumner, author and reformer Julia Ward Howe, Harvard professor of natural history, Jean L. Agassiz, and others. She left Boston for Washington on November 12, 1862.

The White House – Monday, November 3, 1862

Mother's dressmaker and companion Elizabeth Keckley is a great comfort to her. Keckley purchased her freedom in 1855, and since then has made a living sewing for prominent women, including Varina Davis, the wife of Jefferson Davis, and Mary Anna Custis Lee, the wife of Robert E. Lee. Recently she has been active in raising funds from prominent negroes, which are used to aid former slaves now residing in Washington. Mother has given her $200 and introduced her to important people who find the idea of assisting former slaves a worthy goal. In August, Mrs. Keckley formed a charitable organization called the Contraband Relief Association. I admire her intelligence and her initiative. I trust that she'll be able to raise enough money to be helpful to colored people now living in needy conditions. Many former slaves come to Washington with little or no money and few if any friends. Mrs. Keckley deserves praise for her efforts to help these poor people.

Author's notes:

Mary Lincoln introduced Elizabeth Keckley to many philanthropists in New York, Boston and Washington. President and Mrs. Lincoln made many contributions to the Contraband Relief Association. After the president's assassination, Mrs. Keckley's memoir, "Behind the Scenes," was published in 1868. The book included revelations about Mary Lincoln's private life, and feeling betrayed, the former first lady shunned Mrs. Keckley. Her dressmaking business declined, and she died in poverty in 1907 at the Home for Destitute Women and Children in Washington, one of the institutions she had helped to found.

The White House – Wednesday, November 5, 1862

I directed General Halleck to order General McClellan removed from command of the Army of the Potomac today, with General Ambrose Burnside to be placed in immediate command. Chase, Stanton, Smith and Bates signed off on the decision. Blair and Welles declined to sign with Welles stating that he had no confidence in McClellan. There was the Cabinet's consensus before today that McClellan had to go, but there was also our concern that to act before Election Day might cause harm to the Republican cause at the polls. McClellan had many good qualities and was held in high regard by his soldiers. What he lacked was backbone and a willingness to take risks. He was never anxious to attack, which is a fatal flaw in a general. The public may be offended by my actions in this matter, but a war cannot be won when armies are led by over-cautious men. Our goal is not to take land but to destroy Confederate Armies.

Author's notes:

Burnside was a graduate of West Point, Class of 1847. He graduated 18th in a class of 47. Burnside decided to attempt a rapid approach to Richmond upon taking command. It led to the costly defeat of the Union Army at the Battle of Fredericksburg, during which Union forces suffered 13,000 casualties. He was soon relieved of command, replaced by General Joseph Hooker. In March of 1863, Burnside was given command of the Department of the Ohio. In Autumn of 1863 he successfully defended Knoxville, Tennessee, until troops under General William T. Sherman arrived and forced General Longstreet's forces to retreat. He fought in the battles of the Wilderness, Spotsylvania Court House, North Anna and Cold Harbor. After his failure to exploit the results of the Battle of the Crater, he resigned his commission on April 15, 1865. He served briefly as senator from Rhode Island.

The White House – Thursday, November 6, 1862

Results from the Congressional elections are not positive. Even in my home district of Springfield, Illinois, results reported by telegraph show that John T. Stuart, a Democrat and one of my former law partners, defeated the Republican incumbent. All reporting is not in and counted, but it is clear that the Republican Party did poorly in Pennsylvania, Ohio, Indiana and New York. Democrats have hailed their victories as a repudiation of the Emancipation Proclamation. The Cincinnati Gazette wrote that the voters "are depressed by the interminable nature of this war, as so far conducted, and by the rapid exhaustion of the national resources without progress." I think that is a fair assessment of affairs.

Author's notes:

Speaker of the House of Representatives Galusha A. Grow was defeated in the November 1862 election. Grow was first elected to Congress as a Democrat in 1850. He switched parties in the wake of President Pierce's signing of the Kansas-Nebraska Act. He ran as a Republican in 1856 and remained a member of that party for the rest of his political career. In the 37th Congress he was voted speaker of the House. Under Grow's leadership the Morrill Land-Grant College Act and the Pacific Railway Act authorizing land grants to encourage the construction of the transcontinental railroad, and the Homestead Act, which over a century resulted in the establishment of 1.6 million homesteads, were enacted. Grow was a delegate to the Republican National Convention in 1864 and 1868. He was elected representative at large from Pennsylvania and served from 1894 to 1903.

The White House – Friday, November 7, 1862

The Cabinet discussed the subject of Ellet's rams, now operating on the Mississippi with Union forces, and whether or not they should be under Army or Navy command. Assistant Secretary Fox convinced me that this should be a Navy operation. Secretary Welles, Stanton and General Halleck are all in accord.

I requested that the Army forward to my personal attention copies of the Picayune and True Delta newspapers from New Orleans whenever it is possible. I want to be able to take the political temperature from time to time.

Author's notes:

The United States Ram Fleet was established in March 1862 by the Union Army to operate on the Western rivers. Civil engineer Charles Ellet converted powerful river towboats, heavily reinforcing their hulls for ramming. The ships had light protection for their boilers; engines and upper works were protected with wood and cotton. The sidewheel ships included the U.S.S. Lioness, Mingo, Samson, Fulton, T.D. Horner, Lancaster, Monarch, Queen of the West and Switzerland. After Ellet's death at the Battle of Memphis, command was given to Colonel Charles R. Ellet, son of Charles Ellet Jr. The rams were engaged in battles near Vicksburg, Mississippi, into 1863. The ram fleet was disestablished in August 1864 and the surviving ships assigned to other duties.

The White House – Saturday, November 8, 1862

This week I seem to have had more citizens visiting me than usual. I like to meet as many as I can within reason. I spoke to Stanton and General Halleck about the case of a young soldier who is the son of Green Berry Walters, who was wounded at Donelson and discharged for disability. James W. Walters has been accused of desertion. I believe this charge is unreasonable and request that he be returned to his unit with his military record unsullied by these charges. Technically James may have deserted, but I believe he was merely absent without leave, a far lesser offense. I have known Green Berry Walters for most of my adult life, and know him to be an honorable man and a patriot loyal to the Union. Let his son not be punished but allowed to serve in the ranks with an unblemished record of service.

Author's notes:

The next day General Ambrose Burnside assumed command of the Army of the Potomac as ordered by the president.

The White House – Sunday, November 9, 1862

Today I telegraphed Mary at the Parker House in Boston asking if Mrs. Cuthbert and Aunt Mary the nurse should move to the White House. They are complaining that the Soldiers' Home has become uncomfortably cold. Mother plans to return to Washington on the morning of the 11th. The sooner the better. No church for me today. Instead, I was busy with planned appointments of district judges. A telegraphic message arrived late this evening advising that a battle was fought on November 7th in Douglas County, Missouri. Apparently, a small Union force under Captain Hiram Barstow was forced to surrender to a rebel unit 10 times its strength after a five-hour struggle. Our men were part of the 10th Illinois Cavalry and the Missouri State Militia.

Author's notes:

Mary Ann Cuthbert was a seamstress, and later a stewardess at the White House. "Aunt Mary" Dines was an African-American nurse employed by the Lincolns.

The White House – Monday, November 10, 1862

Federal Circuit Judge Elisha Mills Huntington died on October 26th. Governor Oliver Morton of Indiana asked that I defer appointment of a successor until I receive an expression from the state. However, I have decided that the judgeship for the Federal District of Indiana should go to Caleb Blood Smith, who currently serves as secretary of the interior. Caleb has been a very fine secretary but is not in the best of health. He prefers to return to his home state of Indiana and serve there, rather than remain in Washington. I will therefore send his nomination to the Senate for prompt confirmation. Caleb is a very interesting man. He has been an attorney, state legislator, congressman and successful editor and publisher of the Sentinel newspaper. He initially opposed the Emancipation Proclamation but, in the end, strongly supported it. He has suggested that I appoint his assistant, John Palmer Usher, to fill the secretary job and I will follow his advice in the matter.

Author's notes:

Caleb Blood Smith was a member of the U.S. House of Representatives from 1843 to 1849. Judge Smith served on the federal bench until he died on January 7, 1864. President Lincoln ordered that government buildings be draped in black for two weeks in a sign of mourning for Smith's death. In the famed painting of the First Reading of the Emancipation Proclamation by artist Francis Bicknell Carpenter, Caleb Smith is seen standing to the far right.

The White House – Tuesday, November 11, 1862

I had a lengthy discussion with Secretary Stanton and Andrew Carnegie, who oversees our telegraphic system, which is now called the U.S. Military Telegraph Corps. Carnegie reports that he anticipates that by year end we will have trained 1,200 operators, strung 4,000 miles of wire and may have sent over 1,000,000 messages to and from the battlefields. He notes that we have a significant advantage over the Confederate states because they lack the manufacturing resources needed to make wire and machines.

Author's notes:

During the war the Union strung 15,389 miles of field, land and submarine telegraphic lines. The first line built connected the War Department with the Navy Yard.

The White House – Wednesday, November 12, 1862

I asked Rear Admiral David Farragut to cooperate closely with Major General Nathaniel Banks and provide him and his land forces operating in the south every assistance possible. It is hard to realize that Farragut began his career in the United States Navy as a midshipman at the age of 9! He fought in the War of 1812 at the age of 12. He is the first naval officer to be elevated to the rank of rear admiral, which happened after his victory at New Orleans. He is an inspiration to his men and the nation.

Author's notes:

Before the Civil War broke out, Farragut lived in Norfolk, Virginia. The navy had some doubts about his loyalty to the Union because of his southern birth and that of his wife. He made it clear to all who knew him that he considered secession to be treason and offered his services to the Union Navy. On February 3, 1862, he was appointed to command the Gulf Blockading Squadron, sailing from Hampton Roads on the U.S.S. Hartford, bearing 25 guns, which he made his flagship of 17 ships. He reached the mouth of the Mississippi River, near the banks of the river, with a combined armament of more than 100 heavy guns and 700 men. On April 18, Farragut ordered mortar boats to bombard two forts guarding the mouth of the river. After heavy bombardment he ran past Forts Jackson and St. Philip to take the city and port of New Orleans on April 29, 1862, a decisive event of the war. On August 5, 1864, Farragut won a great victory in the Battle of Mobile Bay, Mobile, Alabama. His words, "Damn the torpedoes. Four bells, Captain Drayton, go ahead Jouett, full speed" made him a national hero. On December 21, 1864, Lincoln promoted him to vice admiral.On July 25, 1866, he was promoted to full admiral, the first U.S. Naval officer to hold that rank.

The White House – Thursday, November 13, 1862

This week I've had several discussions about my personal safety and how it can best be secured. As General Heintzelman has stressed, it is now possible for an assassin, armed with a rifle with a mounted telescope, to fire accurately from a substantial distance and hit his target. As I am tall and easily identified, Heintzelman has concluded that I could make an easy target and that I should exercise more care as to my well-being. I informed him that I have complete confidence in Captain David Derickson and Company K of the 150th Pennsylvania Volunteers, who have been serving as the presidential guard. The general believes they will provide good protection, but that they may not be able to save me from a sharpshooter firing from a great distance.

To stress his point as to my vulnerability, Heintzelman set up a firing station at the Navy Yard and asked a sharpshooter to demonstrate a Whitworth rifle for me. It is a single-shot muzzle-loaded weapon that has been manufactured in England since 1854. It costs four times as much as a standard Enfield rifle, but it outperforms the Enfield 3-to-1 in trials for accuracy and distance shooting. The gun has been purchased by the French Army and is now being bought by the Confederate Army. Its charm is that the shooter can hit a target at 2,000 yards. The Enfield is only good at 1,400 years. A representative of the Whitworth Company told me that Queen Victoria fired the rifle two years ago at Wimbledon and hit the bull's eye at 400 yards. The gun I watched being fired used a four-power telescopic sight, as well as a standard sight with an adjustment for windage. It rarely misses!

Author's notes:

The Union Army did not adopt the Whitworth rifle, but the Confederate Army did. The rifled musket fired a .451 caliber bullet and had a rate of fire of two to three rounds a minute. It weighed 9 pounds. It was typically used to fire 800 to 1,000 yards but enjoyed a maximum firing range of 1,500 yards. The Confederates used models fitted with classic iron sights, and a small number were fitted with telescopic sights. Sharpshooters usually rested the gun against a tree or log when shooting to increase accuracy. Some sharpshooters carried their own forked rests for the rifle. Sharpshooters used the weapon to eliminate Union artillery gun crews or mounted officers. At the Battle of Chickamauga, a sharpshooter killed Union General William Lytle, who was leading a charge at the time. A surviving example of a Confederate Whitworth was auctioned in 2017 for $161,000.

The White House – Friday, November 14, 1862

Mary and Tad joined me today as I walked over to the War Department to watch a demonstration by James M. Swaim of new flag codes, which were being tested by the Army's telegraph operators on White House grounds. It is vitally important that messages sent and responded to are done with the highest level of accuracy and speed. The officers gave Tad a set of flags that he and his friends are going to use.

Yesterday a delegation from New York City came by to urge me to enforce better observance of the Sabbath by the Army. I told them that I would issue an order for Sabbath observance by officers and men. It will inform our Christian soldiers and sailors that there are sacred rights which require weekly rest, including that Sunday labor in the military and naval forces be reduced to the measure of strict necessity.

Author's notes:

The Union Army did not accept Swaim's flag code system, which was based upon a number code, with each letter in the alphabet given a two-digit identification number.

In Lincoln's order for Sabbath Observance, issued November 15, 1862, he noted that General George Washington's First General Order issued to the Army addressed the issue of Sabbath Day observance. Washington wrote in 1776, "Men may find enough to do in the service of God and their country without abandoning themselves to vice and immorality." He also wrote, "The General hopes and trusts that every officer and man will endeavor to live, and act as becomes a Christian soldier defending the dearest rights and liberties of his country."

The White House – Saturday, November 15, 1862

We had a narrow escape today. When Seward, Chase and I met Captain Dahlgren at the Navy Yard early this morning to observe a trial test of the Hyde rocket, a defective missile exploded sending pieces of metal in our direction. Fortunately, no one was injured. Dahlgren was apologetic – he explained that the day before there had been several tests with no misfires. I explained to him that one must expect the bad with the good sometimes. The rocket when fired properly was impressive to observe.

Later in the day I met with Gideon Welles to discuss the U.S.S. Vanderbilt and the possibility of commissioning more heavy steamers to be used in intercepting Confederate ships raiding on our commerce. Perhaps we might benefit by having two or three more ships like the Vanderbilt in the Navy.

Author's notes:

The U.S.S. Vanderbilt was a heavy (3,360-ton) passenger steamship obtained by the Union Navy in 1862 and utilized as a cruiser. It had a high speed of 14 knots and was outfitted with a large battery of heavy guns. She searched the seas for the Confederate commerce raider C.S.S. Alabama but never located the enemy ship. She did capture the British blockade runner Gertrude and the British bark Saxon. Later she was deployed with the Union Navy blockade off Wilmington and participated in the unsuccessful first amphibious assault on Fort Fisher in the Cape Fear River of North Carolina. In 1865 it served as a training vessel at the Portsmouth Navy Yard during the summer of 1865.

251

The White House – Sunday, November 16, 1862

Newly named Associate Justice and longtime friend David Davis joined me for lunch here today to discuss, among other things, General Grant and developing plans to send a massive Union military force down the Mississippi. Davis seems right at home in his new judicial role and is in high spirits generally. He holds Grant in the highest esteem. He is very enthusiastic about the emancipation document and believes strongly that it will help shorten the war. I hope he is right about that. Mother remains in New York, staying at the Metropolitan Hotel after a pleasant stay in Boston. These trips away from here definitely cheer her up, and that is very encouraging. Getting her mind off recent unhappiness here is vitally important to her well-being. Later Hiram Barney, the collector for the Port of New York, joined me after Davis left to discuss political matters and appointments.

Author's notes:

Judge Davis was Abraham Lincoln's campaign manager in 1860. He served on the U.S. Supreme Court until 1877. He wrote the majority opinion in the Ex Parte Milligan case, limiting the government's power to try citizens in military courts. He served as a U.S. senator from Illinois from 1881 to 1883. He retired from public life in 1883.

The White House – Monday, November 17, 1862

The War Department estimates that there have been 150,000 casualties or more by the two sides to this struggle during the past 11 months, and still there is no sign of an honorable end in sight. Meanwhile, in Europe our diplomats tell Seward that there is political pressure mounting in St. Petersburg, Paris and London for their leaders to step in and offer mediation. The rulers of Europe are motivated by humanitarian concerns as well as by the so-called "cotton famine," which has plagued mill owners and workers in England and France. In Britain alone perhaps as many as 700,000 workers are currently living off charity, with typhoid on the rise. Our minister, Charles Francis Adams sends only discouraging messages to Seward. He fears that the emperor of France may finally convince Prime Minister Palmerston and the tsar of Russia to intervene in our affairs. The British mill owners favor the slave-owning South, the workers favor the North, which now offers freedom to the slaves. Adams writes that some British leaders fear that by intervening they might ultimately risk war with the U.S. and lose Canada and their Caribbean possessions. In my view mediation is the equivalent of recognition of the Confederacy as a legitimate nation, and therefore contrary to our national interests.

Author's notes:

During the Civil War, Lord Palmerston's sympathies were with the Confederacy. It was recognized as a belligerent but never recognized as a sovereign state. Britain depended more upon Union corn than Confederate cotton. Although a professed opponent of the slave trade, Palmerston held a lifelong hostility toward the United States. He believed a dissolution of the Union would weaken America, thereby enhancing British power, yet Britain maintained a policy of neutrality throughout the war.

The White House – Tuesday, November 18, 1862

Today the Cabinet discussed future military and civil matters in the state of Arkansas. It is our strong hope that one day soon the loyal citizens of that state, which has joined the Confederacy, may again enjoy the liberties and freedoms found there before secession. We would like to see the vote restored and elections held for members of the House and Senate. I have written to General Frederick Steele, General John S. Phelps and others that the men elected should be "gentlemen of character, willing to swear support to the Constitution, as of old, and known to be above treasonable suspicion of duplicity."

It is remembered that when the citizens of Arkansas were offered a vote before Fort Sumter was fired upon, they voted to remain in the Union. Since it seceded from the Union it has raised a great many infantry regiments, artillery and cavalry units for the Confederate Army. But at the same time the citizens of Arkansas have also raised four infantry regiments, four cavalry regiments and one artillery battery for the Union Army.

Author's notes:

Arkansas joined the Confederacy on May 18, 1861. During the Civil War, Arkansas provided 73,901 Confederate soldiers, 9,236 Union white soldiers and 5,526 Union colored troops. The state capital at Little Rock was captured by Union forces in 1863. Arkansas was officially readmitted to the Union in 1868.

In 1862, General John Phelps led his regiment in fierce fighting at Pea Ridge in Arkansas. He was appointed military governor of Arkansas in July of 1862 but soon resigned because of poor health. He served as governor of Missouri from 1877 to 1881. During his tenure he supported public education and is regarded as one of Missouri's finest governors.

Major General Frederick Steele was a friend and classmate of Ulysses S. Grant. He graduated West Point in 1843, served in the Mexican War and then in various posts until the Civil War, when he commanded forces in Alabama, Florida and Louisiana. He died of a stroke on January 12, 1868, while in command of the Department of the Columbia (Pacific Northwest).

The White House – Wednesday, November 19, 1862

I sent William M. McPherson of St. Louis to Arkansas to hopefully persuade the good people of that state, who want peace, to elect members of Congress and perhaps a legislature, state officers and even United States senators. My sense is that it may now be far too early in the game to be successful on the political side when so much needs to be achieved in Arkansas on the military side. But I look forward to learning what McPherson finds out from his discussions with leaders in this rebel enclave. My belief is that the Emancipation Proclamation may seriously complicate McPherson's efforts because the slave population is so large there.

Author's notes:

The U.S. Census of 1860 revealed a total population of Arkansas of 435,450, with 324,35 free and 111,115 slaves.

255

The White House – Thursday, November 20, 1862

Two letters were sent by me today to Brigadier General George Foster Shepley, the military governor of several Union-occupied parishes of Louisiana. Shepley is a Maine man with a strong educational background – Harvard for law and then to Dartmouth for his college degree. Most men do it the other way around. I informed Shepley that I was annoyed to learn that congressional elections had not been held as requested by me on October 14th. I stressed that I want the elections as a movement of the people of the districts and not a movement of our military and quasi-military authorities there. The military is to only protect the people who vote from secession interference. I ordered Shepley to order an election day in all the districts that he controls, and to have it in as many places as possible. I explained that what I want is conclusive evidence that respectable citizens of Louisiana are willing to be members of Congress and to swear support for the Constitution; and that other respectable citizens there are willing to vote for them and send them.

I have had apprehension that federal officers, not citizens of Louisiana, might be set up as candidates. There could be no possible object in such an election. To send a parcel of Northern men here, as representatives, elected as would be understood (and perhaps really so,) at the point of the bayonet would be disgusting and outrageous, and were I a member of congress here I would vote against admitting any such man to a seat.

Author's notes:

After practicing law in Bangor and Portland, Maine, George Shepley became the U.S. attorney for the District of Maine from 1848 to 1849 and from 1853 to 1861.

Shepley replied to Lincoln's letters, "In accordance with the views expressed by you, I have issued a proclamation for an election in the First and Second Congressional Districts. I have no doubt these elections will result in the choice of two representatives of unquestioned loyalty to the Government". The election took place on December 3, 1862, and resulted in the election of Benjamin F. Flanders in the First District and Michael Hahn in the Second District.

The White House – Friday, November 21, 1862

I met today with Senator Henry M. Rice. Before entering the Senate, Henry was a delegate to the House of Representatives from Minnesota Territory's At-Large Congressional District. Henry is originally from Vermont. We have in common the fact that we were both surveyors. He at age 18 surveyed the canal route around the rapids of Sault Ste. Marie between Lake Superior and Lake Huron. My work was far more modest and paid considerably less. Henry was also a fur trader with the Ho-Chunk and Chippewa (Ojibwe) Indians. In 1847 he negotiated a treaty with the Ojibwe Indians in which they ceded extensive lands. It was Henry who lobbied for years for a territory and then statehood for Minnesota, which passed in 1857. Today he handed me a memorial signed by 18 Episcopal bishops related to Indian affairs. In order to ensure future peace with the nation's Indian tribes, we will need men of Henry's caliber to earn and hold their trust. Too often they have been cheated by unscrupulous men who have represented the United States government.

Author's notes:

H.M. Rice participated in official or unofficial capacities in several Indian treaties. He died in 1894. In 1916, the state of Minnesota donated a marble statue of Rice to the National Statuary Hall Collection at the United States Capitol. Rice County in Minnesota is named for him. He was a direct descendant of Edmund Rice, an early immigrant to Massachusetts Bay Colony, as follows:

Son of Edmund Rice, 1784 to 1829
Son of Jedidiah Rice, born 1755
Son of Ashur Rice, 1694 to 1773
Son of Thomas Rice, 1654 to 1747
Son of Thomas Rice, 1626 to 1682
Son of Edmund Rice, 1594 to 1663

The White House – Saturday, November 22, 1862

Attended a conference at the home of Secretary Seward. The subject came up of Confederate scrip. I had received a letter from W.L. Vance of Woodford County, Virginia, who advised me that he has $270,000 of Confederate scrip in his possession. He claimed that it had been forced upon Union men of Kentucky by the rebels during a recent raid in exchange for supplies taken by the enemy. He asks permission to use the money to purchase cotton in the cotton states and to then bring the cotton out. I advised Mr. Vance that the U.S. government could not condone citizens using Confederate scrip for commercial purposes. I told Vance that I regretted learning that Union citizens had been forced to take it in exchange for merchandise. I also mentioned that most citizens who have merchandise taken from them have received no payments from the rebels. If the government condoned the scrip's use, then citizens would give it currency value. Our policy is that the Confederacy is not a legitimate government and therefore its currency is just like counterfeit money and should be worth just as much: in other words, nothing.

An order prohibiting the export of arms and munitions was issued by me yesterday. This was done after learning that American citizens were sending war materiel to Canada. This materiel could then have been transshipped from Canada to the Confederacy. I authorized that the goods headed for Canadian buyers found at Rouse's Point be held by the secretary of war until it can be determined if they may be exported to Canada for purchase by legitimate buyers. We have asked the Canadian government for its advice as to the legitimacy of the buyers of the armaments.

Author's notes:

There is an active market for Confederate money. Some of it being sold today is counterfeit. Let the buyer beware: caveat emptor.

The White House – Monday, November 24, 1862

Sunday, I spent time reading several recent newspaper editorials written by Reverend Henry Ward Beecher. I still remember visiting the Plymouth Church, where he was the pastor, the day before I delivered the Cooper Union speech on February 27, 1860. It seems like it was just yesterday. How time flies. Beecher has a flaming demonstrative nature, and, when he delivers a sermon it is incredibly moving. Two weeks before I met him, he had auctioned off a slave girl named Pinky in his church. She had been brought from Virginia to Brooklyn specifically, so she could be sold off into freedom. I believe he raised $900 to pay for her freedom and another $1100 for the education of that little girl, whose name is now Rose Ward Hart. I enjoyed hearing him preach very much. I had known of him long before I met him because my law partner, William Herndon, often gave me copies of his speeches and those of other abolitionist preachers to read. The man has an incredibly productive mind. Secretary Chase told me that Beecher always has "one foot in heaven and one foot in politics." I agree with Chase on that score. His sister is a piece of work too. Today Beecher is undoubtedly the most famous preacher in the country. Beloved as he is in the North, he is hated in the South for his powerful abolitionist views.

Today I wrote to former Captain John J. Key, whose son was recently killed at the Battle of Perryville in Kentucky. I informed him that I regretted the death of his brave and noble son, and told him that his dismissal from the service was done as a warning to a class of officers. I personally bear him no ill will and regret that I was not able to have the example made without wounding him personally. I never charged him with disloyalty but had to dismiss him as an example and a warning to other officers. I cannot therefore restore him to service.

Author's notes:

Henry Ward Beecher's preaching and newspaper editorials throughout the war were often pro Lincoln and frequently anti-Lincoln, but on balance more favorable to the president and the war effort than negative. Many felt that he did almost as much for the cause of abolition as his sister, Harriet Beecher Stowe, the author of "Uncle Tom's Cabin."

The White House – Tuesday, November 25, 1862

Mother has informed me that she will be back in Washington on the 27th from her travels to New York and Boston. I inquired of General Burnside if it will be convenient for us to meet in a boat off Aquia Creek at dark tomorrow evening. I want to pass an hour or two with him discussing impending military movements. He has agreed to our meeting. I have not informed Halleck or Stanton of my planned meeting. Mother will not be happy that I will be away when she returns.

Samuel Ruggles came by to discuss various subjects related to New York City. His friend Seward told me that Ruggles graduated from Yale at the age of 14. He then read for the law and had to wait a number of years to be admitted to the bar because he was under the legal age of 21 when he completed his studies. He has become a large landowner in Manhattan and has donated the land for Gramercy Park and Union Square to the city. His daughter, Ellen, is married to George Templeton Strong, who has funded a New York Army regiment. Strong helped found the U.S. Sanitary Commission and is a strong Republican, as well as a trustee of Columbia College.

Author's notes:

Ruggles served as a member of the New York State Assembly and was a canal commissioner from 1839 to 1842. Of parks and squares he said, "Come what will open squares will remain forever imperishable. Buildings, towers, palaces, may molder and crumble beneath the touch of time, but-space free, glorious, open space – will remain to bless the City forever."

George Templeton Strong was a famous diarist. Strong's 2,250-page diary, now in the collection of the New York Historical Society, whose first entry was recorded on October 5, 1835, was discovered in the 1930s. Starting at age 15, he wrote almost every day of his life. He died on July 21, 1875. Excerpts from his diary are featured in Ken Burns' 1990 documentary "The Civil War." Extensive selections were published in four volumes in 1952 and remain of interest to historians. Strong served as president of the New York Philharmonic Society for many years.

The White House – Thursday, November 27, 1862

On Wednesday, I visited Belle Plain and Aquia Creek, Virginia, and conferred with General Burnside on board the steamer Baltimore to discuss his plans for the impending attack on Fredericksburg. He and his staff did not think that my suggestion that three forces move simultaneously, one from Port Royal directly up the south side of the Rappahannock, one from the north side of Pamunkey, while another force attempts to cross at Fredericksburg, would prove successful. They fear that it may be too complicated to execute. I must defer to the judgment of my generals, but I also believe that one must not fear to take certain risks in war. I returned to Washington before noon on the 27th. Mother greeted me upon my return and presented me with a pair of fine dark brown leather gloves, which she purchased in New York. Mother surely owns more gloves than any woman in America.

Upon my return I huddled with legal counsel to discuss the strange and unfortunate case of Congressman Edson Baldwin Olds of Ohio. He served in the 31st to 33rd Congress. On August last, he was arrested for treasonable acts, including the discouraging of Army enlistments. He was imprisoned but had never had a trial and apparently has spent four months and 22 days in solitary confinement. While confined he won election to the Ohio House of Representative. The voters obviously like the man! He is a popular Copperhead, of that there is no doubt. But to discourage enlistments is to harm the war effort. I believe that he is not a traitor as charged, but is sincere and badly misinformed.

Author's notes:

When released from prison on December 12, 1862, Olds returned to Ohio. In 1863 he filed a warrant for Governor Tod's arrest for kidnapping and filed a civil suit for $100,000 against the governor. That case was transferred to federal court, and Olds ultimately dropped his complaint. Olds went on to serve in the Ohio House from 1862 to 1866.

In the 1860s, the Copperheads were a vocal faction of Democrats in the Northern United States of the Union who opposed the American Civil War and wanted an immediate peace settlement with the Confederates. Republicans started calling the anti-war Democrats "Copperheads," likening them to venomous snakes. They thought the war was unjustified and being waged in an unconstitutional manner.

The White House – Friday, November 28, 1862

I went for an early morning walk by myself in the cool fall weather. I probably walked 15 blocks. Very few people were about. Marshal of the District Ward Lamon warns that walking about unescorted is to risk assassination. My sense of the matter of assassination is that it may happen, but if it does it could come from anyone, anywhere and at any time. It is not possible to protect fully against it. Mary disagrees and believes I should have a Praetorian Guard as in the days of Rome. I trust the American people. I also do not believe that Jefferson Davis, as a matter of policy, would ever condone assassination ordered by the Confederate government. I believe him to be a gentleman and an honorable man who would never stoop so low as to homicide.

I assume he realizes that if there's ever to be a peace agreement it will take two men to negotiate it, and he knows that I will be one of those men, God willing.

Author's notes:

After the assassination, Lincoln's aides found over 100 threatening letters in his desk drawer that he had saved since taking office.

The White House – Saturday, November 29, 1862

I have known Kentucky State Court of Appeals Judge George Robertson since the 1840s and consider him to be a smart and serious student of the Constitution. He has written to me complaining that Union soldiers are forcibly detaining slaves of Union Kentuckians, including himself. It seems that one of his slaves fled into the camp of the 22nd Wisconsin Regiment stationed in Kentucky. Colonel William Utley has refused to return the young boy slave to Robertson and has banned the judge from the camp. Utley now finds himself being sued by Robertson, who has had Utley indicted in federal district court for harboring a slave. Utley now appeals to me to protect him from the court actions of Robertson. I telegraphed Robertson advising him that "if he conveys the slave to Colonel Utley so that he can make him free I will pay him $500 for the slave's freedom. Robertson has refused my offer. I will therefore ask the attorney general to handle this legal issue. My sense is that Utley cannot be punished for obeying the orders of his commander-in-chief.

Author's notes:

Robertson refused Lincoln's offer of $500. He claimed that he neither intended nor desired to seek any money and that the issue was far from mercenary – it was solely to try the question of whether the civil or military power was constitutionally supreme in Kentucky. Robertson pressed his suit in the U.S. Circuit Court for the Eastern District of Wisconsin in the amount of $908.06 plus costs of $26.40. On October 6, 1871, Robertson received a $935 judgment against Utley. Two years later, the U.S. Treasury paid the bill for the relief of Utley. Thus, six years after the Civil War, the federal government reimbursed Robertson for his lost slave. Robertson died in 1874.

The White House – Sunday, November 30, 1862

This evening at the telegraph office, we received good news announcing a victory two days ago at Cane Hill in Washington County Arkansas. Our soldiers under the command of Brigadier General James Blunt defeated a smaller cavalry force led by John Marmaduke in a battle that raged over nine hours. Casualties were light on both sides of the conflict.

This morning, Mary, Tad and I attended services at the New York Avenue Presbyterian Church. The church choir sang the "Battle Hymn of the Republic" joined by the congregation. It was very moving, and mother cried copiously. When we returned home, Noah Brooks came by and joined us for lunch. Noah is an old and trusted friend who hails from Castine, Maine. He is now a journalist writing for the Sacramento Daily Union newspaper. He often comes by to chew the fat, and what he writes based upon our discussions often appears in reports in the Sacramento newspaper he serves.

Author's notes:

Brooks' 258 dispatches for the Sacramento Daily Union were published under the name "Castine." In 1895 he published his biography of Lincoln, "Washington in Lincoln's Time," based upon the Castine articles, as well as personal observations and interviews. Brooks was able to maintain a close relationship with Lincoln and Mrs. Lincoln. When Brooks was detailed to cover the 1864 Republican Convention in Chicago, Lincoln asked him to also report back in detail by private letter.

The White House – Monday, December 1, 1862

It is difficult to realize that the rebel attacks on Fort Sumter took place over 19 months ago. Since that terrible event, the actual number of lives lost or shattered to preserve the Union, and the number wasted to destroy the Union, is far beyond comprehension. The number of widows and fatherless children created by this horrific event cannot be imagined. The mournful count increases every hour of every day. What will 1863 soon bring? I fear to think about the costs in lives and treasure still to come.

My annual message to Congress was delivered today to the Senate and the House of Representatives. I began by noting that, "It has not pleased the Almighty to bless us with a return of peace, we can but press on, guided by the best light He gives us, trusting that in His own good time, and wise way, all will yet be well." Included in the message is correspondence touching foreign affairs. It is important for the Congress to comprehend the vital importance of keeping our European friends neutral in this conflict. I referenced that the treaty with Great Britain for the suppression of the slave trade was put into effect with a good prospect of complete success. I included references to our favoring the connecting of the United States to Europe via an Atlantic cable and for a Pacific cable to extend across the Russian Empire. Reports are included from the various Cabinet secretaries. Importantly, our finances are in good order. The message includes proposals for new Articles to be added to the Constitution. I trust the Congress will receive the message with thoughtful consideration.

Author's notes:

As part of the annual message, President Lincoln include an analysis of the nation's population from 1790 (3,929,827) to 1860 (31,443,790), to a projected population in 1900 of 103,208,415, and in 1930 of 251,680,914. Lincoln notes that the proposed emancipation will "shorten the war, perpetuate peace, ensure the increase of population, and proportionately the wealth of the country."

The White House – Tuesday, December 2, 1862

Hay and Nicolay helped me prepare a message for the House and Senate related to the matter of the collision of the U.S. war steamer San Jacinto and the French brig Jules et Marie. The event took place exactly one year ago tomorrow off the coast of Cuba. Our warship was not badly damaged, but the French ship received serious injuries. In order to determine responsibility, a commission of American and French naval officers met in New York to assess fault in the matter. A naval officer from Italy served as arbiter. They determined that the San Jacinto failed to reverse engines in time to avoid the Jules et Marie. Once it was established that the United States was at fault, our counsel in Havana conferred in Havana with the French counsel to determine damages. This has been done and the amount agreed upon is $9,500. I find this to be a fair settlement and have recommended to Congress that this sum be paid to the owners of the Jules et Marie. This is a small matter in terms of money, but a large matter in terms of our relations with France. I want to maintain close and friendly relations with the French at a time when keeping their neutrality is of vital interest to our war efforts.

Author's notes:

For several months there had been discussions among the leaders of Russia, France and Great Britain concerning a possible mediation effort to end the Civil War. In the end the parties decided not to intervene in the matter. News of the Emancipation Proclamation significantly increased European support among national leaders and the public for the Union, and seriously weakened support for the slave-owning Confederacy.

The White House – Wednesday, December 3, 1862

Mother sent an array of flowers to Mrs. Fox. She does this quite often, and it gives her great pleasure. The ladies are close friends, and at this time in her life Mary needs all the true friends she can have in her troubled life. She and Tad brought to my office a small painting that was given to me during the presidential campaign by Abraham Kohn. He is an immigrant from Bavaria who began his career in Chicago as a peddler and is now a prominent merchant of the city. Kohn painted a replica of the American flag and on the white stripes inscribed these words in Hebrew from the book of Joshua: "Be strong and of good courage; be not afraid or dismayed; for the Lord your God will be with thee whithersoever thou goest." The flag is now framed and hanging on the wall where I can see it every day. Its inspired message will give me hope, particularly on bad days.

Author's notes:

A photograph of the American flag drawn by Abraham Kohn with its inscription in pencil and ink is in the possession of the Spertus Institute of Jewish Learning and Leadership in Chicago, Illinois.

The White House – Thursday, December 4, 1862

I received a resolution of the Senate asking that we furnish it with "all information in our possession touching the late Indian barbarities in the state of Minnesota." I've asked, Secretary of Interior Caleb Smith to have the commissioner of Indian Affairs send me a detailed report as to matters in this regard. I also asked Stanton to find a suitable position for John W. True, whom I personally know and admire. True is currently serving with the 54th Regiment of Illinois Volunteers around Union City guarding the Mobile and Ohio Railroad. He would like to secure a paymaster's position if possible. True speaks his mind. In his letter he admits in confidence that he "does not admire some of our field officers." I also share that opinion from time to time.

Author's notes:

John True had been serving as adjutant for the past year in his Illinois unit. Lincoln's endorsement of True appears in a letter True had written to William Dole of Union City, Tennessee. Lincoln wrote Stanton, "I personally know the writer of this to be a good man." During the war, Lincoln's practice was to write short messages to responsible officials on letters and envelopes he received. Fortunately for historians, many hundreds of these penciled and penned notes have been saved.

The White House – Friday, December 5, 1862

Seward informed me today that a communication from Anson Burlingame, our minister to China, describes a civil war in that ancient kingdom that dwarfs ours in size and in the number of casualties suffered by soldiers and civilians. Burlingame writes of the poverty and starvation being endured by millions of Chinese citizens. He refers to it as the Taiping Rebellion. The Imperial forces are opposed by the Taiping Heavenly Kingdom's forces. The conflict has been going on for over 11 years. Millions have died from battle and starvation, famine and pestilence. Burlingame estimates that the number killed may be 30 times as great as have died in the United States during our present struggle. He predicts that the Qing dynasty of the Manchus may ultimately fall.

Author's notes:

Anson Burlingame was a popular foreign representative at the Chinese court. In 1868 China and the United States concluded the Burlingame-Seward Treaty, which expanded upon the Treaty of Tianjin of 1858. It aimed to ease immigration restrictions and represented a Chinese effort to limit American influence in internal Chinese affairs. The treaty protected commerce conducted in Chinese ports and cities, and established the right of China to appoint consuls to American port cities. It promoted measures that promised the Chinese the right to free immigration and travel within the United States and allowed for the protection of Chinese citizens in the United States in accordance with the most-favored-nation principle. It gave the citizens of the two nations reciprocal access to education and schooling when living in the other country. The treaty reinforced the principle of equality between the two nations.

The White House – Saturday, December 6, 1862

I had a nasty duty to perform today. I was required to order the execution on December 19th of 39 Dakota Indians who were sentenced to be hanged by the Military Commission sitting in Minnesota. The crimes were barbarities committed in Minnesota. I reviewed each case carefully before signing off on the executions; 265 other condemned Indians being held by the authorities are to be held subject to further orders. I will be criticized in the press for not executing all the Indians in this case, but I believe justice will be done. I also am not pleased by the fact that none of the Indians tried had the services of an attorney to defend them in the military court. As requested, the Senate has been sent a full report describing the recent Indian attacks in the state of Minnesota. It is my belief that the U.S. government must become far wiser in its dealings with its Indian populations. Promises made to the Indians have not been kept. Attacks on settlers can only happen again unless we are far more enlightened in our approach to the tribes.

Author's notes:

The 265 Dakota Indians whose lives Lincoln spared were either fully pardoned or died in prison. Lincoln and the Congress subsequently removed the Sioux and Winnebago, who had nothing to do with the uprising in Minnesota, from their lands in Minnesota. In the city of Mankato, where the executions were carried out, a new historical marker has been erected at the site of the scaffold, at a place now called Reconciliation Park. The marker displays the names of the Dakota who were executed.

The White House – Monday, December 8, 1862

Yesterday we had a relaxed and pleasant Sunday dinner with Senators Ira Harris of New York and Orville Browning of Illinois as our guests. John Nicolay, William Stoddard and John Hay joined us. The conversation was devoid of references to the war. Mother was an inspired hostess. She told many stories of her recent visit to Boston and New York. We discussed the books that we read. I confessed that I had never completed reading a novel. I mentioned "Ivanhoe," which I had started, but never finished it. Browning and Harris are my two most frequent evening visitors at home. I value their judgments very much. Harris is always asking me for an appointment or two. I once told him that before I go to bed at night I always look under my bed to see if he is there, seeking another patronage appointment. Whenever Secretary Seward comes under attack from the Congress or the press (which is often), Harris can always be counted upon to defend Seward. Harris had been a law professor and served for 13 years on the State Supreme Court in Albany. The 5th New York Cavalry has been named by its men The Ira Harris Guard and has seen lots of action in the war.

Author's notes:

Senator Harris was close to Secretary Seward, to whose political machine Harris owed his election to the U.S. Senate. Because Harris was so frequently with Lincoln, it made him privy to Lincoln's patronage. Harris encouraged Lincoln to keep Seward in his cabinet when many Senators were urging his removal. Harris argued that Seward's departure from the Cabinet would injure the Republican Party. Lincoln stood by Seward. Harris served only one term in the Senate.

The White House – Tuesday, December 9, 1862

General Henry Sibley was telegraphed and ordered not to hang an innocent Indian because of confusing similar names.

A Union victory was claimed in a wire received late this evening at Prairie Grove, Arkansas, on December 7th. Federal forces suffered 1,251 casualties and report that the rebels had losses of the same size. Our men remained in possession of the battlefield. The Confederates withdrew in the direction of Van Buren, Arkansas. There was severe hand-to-hand fighting but, in the end, we prevailed. Our officers believe the enemy is so significantly demoralized that future Union efforts may be able to drive them from Northern Arkansas permanently.

At the same time, in Northern Tennessee, at a place called Hartsville, Units of XIV Corps under Union Colonel Absalom Moore were beaten by rebels who took our men by complete surprise early in the early morning of the 7th. By 8:30 A.M. our soldiers were surrounded and surrendered. The rebels took over 2,000 men prisoner. By the time a much larger unit of Union troops, who were stationed eight miles away, arrived, they found dead soldiers from both side lying in the snow. The rebels had stripped the bodies of clothing and shoes.

Author's notes:

On February 13, 1863, General Halleck recommended that Colonel Absalom B. Moore be dismissed for neglect of duty. Moore was not dismissed, however, but resigned because of disability. His resignation took effect on September 9, 1863.

The White House – Wednesday, December 10, 1862.

While most of my daily war thoughts and worries concern the Army, I am very pleased to learn from Secretary Welles that our fleet is doing exceptionally good works. He confirms that our force now includes 427 vessels that have a combined armament of 1,577 guns with 28,00 officers and sailors, plus over 12,000 mechanics and laborers employed at Navy yards and stations. Our ships continue to capture vessels bringing materials of war to rebel ports. Assistant Secretary Fox has estimated that within two years our Navy will be the most powerful naval force in the entire world, and that includes Great Britain and France.

Author's notes:

Welles reported to Lincoln that the embargo of the Confederates, the capture of New Orleans and the Union Navy's blockade combined to curtail greatly the export of the South's major product, cotton. The North's control of the seas threatened only by a few Confederate commerce raiders granted the Union access to the world markets for the importation of war materials and exportation of produce such as wheat and corn, which was a major factor deterring European powers from recognizing the Confederacy.

The White House – Thursday, December 11, 1862

This was a day for diplomacy. I recognized Ludwig von Baumbach as consul of Grand Duchy of Hesse-Darmstadt for the states of Wisconsin and Minnesota, and B.B. Haagsma as consul of the Netherlands for Missouri, Iowa and Illinois. Later I took Mrs. Lincoln and Tad for a carriage ride. Tad is having troubles with arithmetic. I can sympathize with him, as it gave me trouble too when I was his age. Later in life, I conquered the geometry of Euclid, and have ever since felt a sense of achievement in so doing.

At 3 o'clock Secretary Seward brought Richard Lyons, 1st Viscount Lyons, to the White House to discuss the implementation of the Treaty for the Suppression of the Slave Trade, which was proclaimed in the United States on May 25th of this year. Lyons is an excellent representative of his nation. It is the hope of each country that this treaty's strict enforcement will greatly reduce and ultimately end the ability of slavers to send their captives to countries still willing to accept them. We also discussed the rebellion in India against British rule, which took place in 1857, and its effects upon British policy in India. The queen of England is now the empress of India. Lyons informed me that British rule is secured by treaties with over 500 Indian princes that assure a new constitutional relationship. Under the arrangement, Victoria is queen of India as well as of Great Britain, and India's governor general has become her viceroy as well as the British government's chief executive in India. We discussed America's future once our Civil War is successfully concluded. Victoria had 500 princes she had to please, whereas I will have the entire population of the seceded states to deal with. My goal must be one of reconstruction, justice and unity. The freedom of the large Southern slave population will present formidable challenges.

Author's notes:

President Lincoln shared a distaste for the practice of slavery with Queen Victoria's husband and royal consort, Prince Albert, who was outspoken in his condemnation of slavery. The prince advocated the adoption of governmental policies that would lead to the suppression of slavery. Prince Albert died on December 14, 1861.

The Treaty for the Suppression of the Slave Trade is also known as the Lyons-Seward Treaty. It was concluded in Washington, D.C., on April 7, 1862, and unanimously ratified by the United States Senate on April 25, 1862. Ratifications were exchanged in London on May 25, 1862. It was proclaimed by President Lincoln on June 7, 1862. It set forth aggressive measures to end the Atlantic slave trade, including an agreement that the respective countries would use their navies to seize merchant vessels carrying captured Africans, including any vessel bearing indications of being a slave trading vessel, and led to searches and seizures in African and Cuban waters.

The White House – Friday, December 12, 1862

A long meeting at the War Department was held to learn as much as possible about the status of the Army of the Potomac, which is now near or at Fredericksburg, Virginia. I later ordered John Nicolay to hand-deliver a letter to Genera; Burnside seeking clarity on several questions I have about our troop locations. Later, Secretary Welles and I discussed the matter of Commander George H. Preble, U.S.N. We decided that he shall be dismissed for failure to do his duty in permitting the Confederate ship, Florida to run the naval blockade at Mobile, Alabama.

Hay was dispatched to Congress to present three Confederate swords that were captured by our troops during hostilities at New Orleans. They were kindly sent to me by General Butler.

Author's notes:

Later it was determined that the Florida had entered Mobile Bay flying the ensign of the British Navy. Preble had shots fired at the ship to stop it, but the Florida then raised the rebel flag and continued into the Southern port. It was later determined that the iron boilers on Preble's ship, the Oneida, had been shut down for repairs and only one was in operation. With only one boiler working, the Oneida was unable to keep pace with the Florida, which escaped into the bay. Preble kept up fire on the enemy ship for 29 minutes until it was safely under the protection of Fort Morgan's guns. Preble was reinstated and later commanded the sailing sloop St. Louis, only to have the Florida escape him again, off Madeira Island, Portugal. Preble continued to serve in the Navy, retiring as a rear admiral in 1878.

The three swords had belonged to Confederate General David E. Twiggs, the hero of Monterey in the Mexican War. One had been presented to him by Congress before the Civil War. The other swords had been given to Twiggs by the state of Georgia and the city of Augusta. After the Civil War the swords were given to Twiggs' daughter by the Treasury Department.

The White House – Sunday, December 14, 1862

Generals Heintzelman, McDowell and former Secretary of War Cameron joined me at the White House to discuss the future of the Army of the Potomac. We later repaired to the War Department, where we met with Generals Haupt and Halleck. We learned that the Union has suffered large losses at Fredericksburg. I know that the Army of the Potomac and the public, when it hears the news, will be demoralized. Burnside has accepted full responsibility for the loss, unlike McClellan, who always had 10 excuses for failure. I have issued a congratulatory proclamation to the men who fought at Fredericksburg. It tells them that although they were not successful the effort was not made in error. I wrote that, "The courage with which you, in an open field maintained the contest against an entrenched foe, shows that you possess all the qualities of a great army, which will yet give victory to the cause of the country."

Author's notes:

Burnside's Army numbered over 120,000 officers and men. He expected to quickly move to Fredericksburg, where pontoon bridges would enable it to cross the Rappahannock River before Lee arrived. Once across the river, Burnside would try to get between Lee and the Confederate capital, Richmond. The pontoons were delayed, and when they finally arrived, Lee had reached the hills behind Fredericksburg and deployed his smaller Army for battle. The main battle took place on December 13. Casualties totaled 12,653 federals and only 5,309 rebels. It turned out to be Lee's most lopsided victory of the Civil War.

The White House – Monday, December 15, 1862

Senator Wilson of Massachusetts brought the war correspondent Henry Villard to visit me here last evening. Villard had been at the battlefield and revealed to me what he had observed at Fredericksburg. It is not a pretty story. The advance of the Union men up Marye's Heights, where the rebels lay in waiting for them, resulted in an unbelieveable slaughter of our brave soldiers. Villard believes that as many as one in 10 of Burnside's men was a casualty, dead, wounded or missing.

Author's notes:

Twenty years after the battle, General James Longstreet, lieutenant-general, C.S.A. wrote of Marye's Hill, "A fifth time the Federals formed and charged and were repulsed. A sixth time they charged and were driven back, when night came to end the dreadful carnage, and the Federals withdrew, leaving the battle-field literally heaped with the bodies of their dead. Before the well-directed fire of Cobb's brigade, the Federals had fallen like the steady dripping of rain from the eaves of a house. Our musketry alone killed and wounded at least 5,000; and these, with the slaughter of artillery, left over 7,000 killed and wounded before the foot of Marye's Hill. The dead were piled sometimes three-deep, and when morning broke, the spectacle that we saw upon the battle-field was one of he most distressing I ever witnessed. The charges had been desperate and bloody, but utterly hopeless. I thought, as I saw the Federals come again and again to their death, that they deserved success if courage and daring could entitle soldiers to victory."

The White House – Tuesday, December 16, 1862

Mother is busy making plans for Christmas. We expect Robert to be home from Harvard. She asked me what I thought Tad and Robert would like to receive as gifts. I must give that some thought. I was thinking that a compass might please Tad. I have no idea what Robert might like to get. Perhaps Hay or Nicolay may have some ideas on the matter.

I had to make changes in the government's plans for the execution on the 19th of the month of the condemned Dakota Indians in Minnesota. The final date agreed upon was decided to be December 25th. But soon after the telegraphic message was sent setting that date, I was reminded by Mother that the 25th is Christmas Day. I cannot imagine any of our soldiers wishing to carry out such an obnoxious order on the holiest day of the year, so I must now send out another message changing that order to a later date.

I ordered Major General Curtis, stationed in St. Louis, to restore N.W. Watkins (Henry Clay's half-brother) to his home. Apparently, Colonel Albert Jackson drove the old man away from his residence, giving him but three hours' notice. I am friendly to the Clay family and want this done as soon as humanly possible. I asked Curtis to please give Mr. Watkins my sincere apology for what has happened to him and his family.

Author's notes:

Nathaniel Watkins, a prominent old Whig, had led a force of Missouri State Guards (Confederates) in the early months of the war. On November 30th, he wrote Lincoln advising him that he was now a loyal citizen and that he took no part in the rebellion. He asked Lincoln to restore his rights as an American citizen.

The White House – Wednesday, December 17, 1862

I spent some time this afternoon with Assistant Secretary Fox. We discussed my idea that we attempt to retake Fort Sumter, and that we man it with negro troops. Fox was not encouraging. He believes that such a venture would cost far too much in ships lost and sailors and soldiers killed. I found his arguments persuasive.

At 10 P.M. Senator King came by and delivered to me letters of resignation from Secretary Seward and his son, Frederick, who serves as assistant secretary of State. This follows upon the actions of the Republican senatorial caucus. I told King that I would like to meet with the full caucus tomorrow at 10 A.M. to discuss the Seward matter, and the possible need to reconstruct the Cabinet.

The final execution date for the Dakota Indians was again delayed.

Author's notes:

On December 27th General Henry H. Sibley advised Lincoln that the executions of the condemned Dakota Indians finally took place at Mankato at 10 A.M. on Dec. 26, 1862. He advised, "Everything went off quietly, and the other prisoners are well secured." One prisoner, Chaska-don or Chaska-etay, alias Robert Hopkins, was not executed, but was pardoned.

The White House – Thursday, December 18, 1862

A committee of Congressmen, including Crittenden of Kentucky, Crisfield of Maryland and Hall of Missouri, met with me at 10 A.M. to discuss the views of people in the border states. In those states the issuing of the Emancipation Proclamation has caused concerns by loyal slave-owning families.

At 7 P.M. I conferred for several hours with nine members of the Republican senatorial caucus to discuss their suggestion that Secretary Seward resign. I wish to keep my Cabinet in place. My understanding from the caucus members is that they believe we are not very well-organized and that Seward pretty much runs the show. I know, particularly after the sad events at Fredericksburg, that the press is looking for a scapegoat and the senators would like Seward to be that man. I do not agree. I admire him and benefit from his wise counsel. I asked the senators to return tomorrow to continue the dialogue.

When they left I met with Senator Browning, who was joined by D.W. Wise of Boston, who has suggested that I deserve to have my biography written. I thanked him for the flattering suggestion but advised him that I have neither interest nor time for such a book to be written. Perhaps after the war we might again discuss the matter.

Author's notes:

The move to remove Seward was greatly instigated by the ambitions of Secretary Chase. Chase felt that Seward dominated the Cabinet and often caused the president to make poor decisions. Lincoln heard the senators out and asked them to return the next day to continue the discussion.

The White House – Friday, December 19, 1862

At a morning meeting of the Cabinet we considered a report from the Senate Caucus Committee, which would like to see me fire Secretary Seward and reconstruct my Cabinet. At 7:30 this evening I met again with the Cabinet, with Seward absent at my request. I had all the members of the Senate caucus join us. The meeting went on and on until midnight. The caucus members were surprised that I had included the Cabinet members in the meeting, and that I had earlier read to them the report of the caucus, which criticized me and the Cabinet for not being as well-organized as they felt we should be. I told them the caucus members that I was not aware of any divisions or disunity in the Cabinet. I then asked each Cabinet member if they felt differently on the subject. No Cabinet member spoke of a lack of unity. I believe that the senators were embarrassed for bringing the subject up. After the senators left, Postmaster Blair offered to resign. I asked him to stay, as I am not displeased with his services.

Author's notes:

Secretary Seward had submitted his resignation to Lincoln as soon as he heard from Senator Preston King that the Caucus of Republican Senators were seeking a "no vote of confidence" in him on December 16th. Lincoln held on to his resignation letter. On December 20th Secretary Chase met with Lincoln and told the president that he had prepared a resignation letter. Lincoln asked Chase for it. At that moment, Lincoln was also offered Stanton's resignation, which Lincoln declined.

Later that day, Lincoln wrote to Seward and Chase:

"Gentlemen: You have respectively tendered me your resignations, as Secretary of State and Secretary of the Treasury of the United States. I am apprised of the circumstances which may render this course personally desirable to each of you; but, after most anxious consideration, my deliberate judgment is, that the public interest does not admit of it. I therefore have to request that you will resume the duties of your Departments respectively. Your Obt. Servt. A. Lincoln."

The White House – Saturday, December 20, 1862

This evening General Burnside arrived for a private meeting to discuss his many serious concerns following the defeat of our forces at Fredericksburg. My sense is that the man has lost much of his self-confidence, and it is easy to understand why. I have asked Burnside to join me with General Halleck and Secretary Stanton the day after tomorrow, so we can begin to plan our next moves.

Earlier in the day, Hay handed me a copy of Thomas Paine's "The American Crisis." He pointed out familiar lines that I have found reassuring since becoming president. They are, "It is not a field of a few acres of ground, but a cause, that we are defending, and whether we defeat the enemy in one battle, or by degrees, the consequences will be the same." When Paine wrote those lines during the American Revolution, our cause was faltering. Washington faced incredible difficulties and France had yet to enter the war on our side. I shared Paine's sentiment with Burnside. I reminded the general that one may not look back, but only forward when at war.

Author's notes:

Secretary Welles meets with Secretary Seward and then reported to Lincoln that Seward had agreed to withdraw his resignation. The Cabinet remained undisturbed and fully constituted with men Lincoln needed and relied upon. Thus, the Cabinet crisis officially ended.

The White House – Sunday, December 21, 1862

Mother is staying at the Continental Hotel in Philadelphia today and will be back in Washington tomorrow, when she plans to visit a nearby military hospital where wounded boys from the recent fighting at Fredericksburg are now being treated and recuperating. Her presence with the soldiers helps raise their spirits. She will be bringing several friends with her who will write letters for the men to be sent to their worrying families.

Senator Browning and I discussed possible Cabinet changes this evening. He fears that the Cabinet cannot be improved without my making some changes, but my belief is that the nation wants to see stability in our leadership, not changes made simply for the sake of change. The recent discussions with the Republican Senate caucus and the resignations that were produced have cleared the air. I am content to continue with the Cabinet members I started with in the belief that they will improve with age.

Author's notes:

With the formal issuance of the Emancipation Proclamation soon to take place, Lincoln wished to present to the press and the public an image of unity in his Cabinet. On December 21, 1862, Seward wrote to Lincoln, "I have cheerfully resumed the functions of this department, in obedience to your command." Chase replied to Lincoln on December 22, 1862, concluding, "I shall resume, therefore, my post as Secretary of the Treasury; ready, however, at any moment, to resign it, if in your judgment, the success of your administration may be, in the slightest degree, promoted."

The White House – Monday, December 22, 1862

Captain Dahlgren joined me and other naval officers to observe the testing of a new gunpowder. Later, Senator Browning and I discussed the bill to create the new State of West Virginia, which is to be made up of 48 counties from the Northwestern part of present-day Virginia. When I asked the Cabinet to give me its opinion on the constitutionality of the bill I got a 3-3 split decision. Therefore, it is up to me now to agree to the measure or reject it. In my opinion the bill is constitutional, and I will sign it into law on December 31st.

John Weiss Forney stopped by to discuss the status of the Cabinet. I explained to him that there will be no immediate changes. Forney has spent his adult life in the newspaper business, starting out as a printer in Lancaster, Pennsylvania. In the 1850s he became clerk of the House of Representatives. Most recently he has served as secretary of the U.S. Senate. He also publishes The Sunday Morning Chronicle, which recently became a daily newspaper. I am told that the public considers his publication to be the official organ of the Lincoln administration. Simon Cameron introduced us soon after I came to Washington. I have always found him trustworthy. He usually prints what I wish to see in his papers, and therefore I can always speak to him in complete confidence.

Author's notes:

In 1868 Forney disposed of his interest in the Chronicle and returned to Philadelphia, where in 1871 he was made collector of the port by President Ulysses S. Grant. He held the office for one year, when he developed the system of direct transportation of imports in bond without appraisement and examination at the port of original entry. He was an earnest promoter of the Philadelphia Centennial Exposition of 1876 and traveled to Europe in its interest. The Forney Publishing Company continued to publish a weekly newspaper, the Progress, after his death in 1881.

The White House – Tuesday, December 23, 1862

Mary read to me this evening from Sir Walter Scott's "Poetical Works," which she borrowed from the Library of Congress this morning. I love to read his words and I appreciate hearing his words spoken by a man with a Scottish accent. Tad read me this line, which is a country truth from" The Legend of Montrose": "There is a Southern proverb – fine words butter no parsnips." He also read me this bit of truth: "Spur not an unbroken horse; put not your plowshare too deep into new land." It is from "The Monastery." Mother recited a bit from "Woodstock." We agreed to the wisdom found in Scott's verse, "If you keep a thing for seven years, you are sure to find a use for it."

Colonel William McCullough of the 4th Illinois Cavalry was killed near Corinth, Mississippi, in a night battle on December 5th. Today, I wrote a letter of sympathy to his daughter, Fanny. I knew Bill McCullough before the war, when he served as clerk of the McLean County Court at Bloomington. He was a mighty fine gentleman and a brave one. I only wish it was possible to write a personal note to every young daughter and son of a man lost in this dreadful war.

Author's notes:

Lincoln wrote, in part to Miss Fanny McCullough, "You are sure to be happy again. To know this, which is certainly true, will make you some less miserable now. I have had experience enough to know what I say; and you need only to believe it, to feel better at once. The memory of your dear father, instead of an agony, will yet be a sad sweet feeling in your heart, of a purer, and holier sort than you have known before. Please present my kind regards to your afflicted mother.
Your sincere friend. A. Lincoln. "

The White House – Wednesday, December 24, 1862

Mother and I were discussing dreams at breakfast today. The subject came up because I have certain recurring dreams, one of which I described to her. It came to me again last night after I had read a historic report of the meeting of Napoleon I and Alexander I at Tilsit on July 7, 1807, where they met on a raft floating in the Neman River. I like to study Napoleon because I admire his ability to inspire his marshals to achieve great military deeds. In the dream I meet with Jefferson Davis. He is accompanied by Lee and Jackson; I am accompanied by Grant and Halleck. We meet in a large tent, which is surrounded by thousands of soldiers – Confederate and Union. The meeting is polite and cordial. I explain to Davis that there is no possible way for the South to win the war, and that an honorable peace is only possible if he will end the rebellion. As in past dreams, when I take his hand to shake it, I discover it is ice cold. I then I awaken from my slumber. It is vivid and quite stunning. I must discuss this sometime with Henri Mercier, the current minister to the United States from France. I would also like to hear his views on the military genius of Napoleon.

Mother is planning to bring Christmas meals to wounded soldiers in military hospitals. We will visit several of them tomorrow on Christmas Day.

Author's notes:

On this day, John Pitcher, a boyhood friend of Lincoln, visited him in the White House. They discussed Pitcher's son, who was recuperating from wounds received at the Battle of Cedar Mountain. The battle took place on August 9, 1862 in Culpepper, Virginia. Union forces were outnumbered 16,868 to 8,030. After that fierce battle, Sara Barton appeared at a field hospital at midnight with a wagonload of supplies drawn by a four-mule team. The surgeon on duty later wrote, "I thought that night if heaven ever sent out an angel she must be one – her assistance was so timely." Throughout the war, Barton and her supply wagons traveled with the Union Army, giving aid to Union casualties and Confederate prisoners. At the Second Battle of Bull Run, Chantilly, Harpers Ferry and South Mountain, transportation was provided by the Army quartermaster, but most of the supplies were purchased from donations solicited by Barton or by her own funds. After Antietam she wrote, "I always tried to succor the wounded until medical aid and supplies could come up. I could run the risk; it made no difference to anyone if I were shot or taken prisoner."

The White House – Thursday, December 25, 1862

Senator Sumner spent much of last evening with me discussing the Emancipation Proclamation. He has long argued for it and is fully supportive of its language. He believes we do not have the right general in command of the Army of the Potomac and recommends that Burnside be removed. Everyone is always suggesting who should be fired, but few ever recommend who the replacement should be.

Mother, Tad and I, joined by members of the White House staff, brought food to wounded soldiers late in the afternoon. Tad was particularly helpful in the effort. The soldiers all love him. His good-natured spirit is contagious and brings smiles to the men who are often in pain. He proudly showed the soldiers his new compass. It was made in England and is of a very high quality. I think for his 10th birthday, which will be celebrated on April 4th, we should find a high-quality telescope or binoculars for him. I'll ask Stanton to find out what the Army is now buying. I am told that the best optical equipment is now made in France.

I returned to the office to sign a letter congratulating Emperor Francis Joseph of Austria on the forthcoming marriage of his brother.

Author's notes:

Mary Lincoln borrowed from the Library of Congress on the 24th of December "The Wagoner of the Alleghenies," by Thomas Buchanan Reed, Philadelphia, 1862.

The president considered a plan of General Haupt's to form a military council of seven to plan campaigns and determine policies.

The White House – Friday, December 26, 1862

The photographs of the Antietam battlefield taken by Mathew Brady, which are now being shown to the public at his studio in New York City, have caused much consternation there according to letters I've received and newspaper comments. Between the casualty reports and grim pictures of men on both sides of the struggle lying in the fields, morale in the city has been seriously impacted.

Our visit to the men in hospitals yesterday was a very moving experience. They are so patient and uncomplaining. It is always heartbreaking to experience. The volunteers who go daily to assist the men are the war's true heroes.

The Cabinet came by for a two-hour meeting this afternoon. The main subject was the new state of West Virginia and how it is to be received into the Union and its citizens protected by our government. Forty-eight counties of Virginia will make up the new state of West Virginia. When I sign the bill accepting the state, I will explain that the division of any state is a dreaded precedent, but a measure made expedient by this war and should not be considered a precedent for times of peace. It is strictly a practical measure that recognizes the reality in Virginia, which seceded from the Union and is at war with our nation. This procedure is not secession against the Constitution, but it is secession in favor of the Constitution. The people of West Virginia will soon vote to ratify a revised state constitution allowing the gradual emancipation of slaves within its territory.

Author's notes:

William Tecumseh Sherman (1820 – 1891) said, "War is at best barbarism... Its glory is all moonshine. It is only those who have neither fired a shot nor heard the shrieks and groans of the wounded who cry aloud for blood, more vengeance, more desolation. War is hell." (Attributed to a graduation address at Michigan Military Academy, June 19, 1879)

The White House – Saturday, December 27, 1862

Stanton and Halleck joined several Army and Navy officers at the War Department early this morning to present a comprehensive report of recent activities within the state of North Carolina. Two weeks ago, a battle was waged at Kinston, where troops under Brigadier General John G. Foster defeated rebel forces under Brigadier General Nathan Evans. In the engagement our men were successful, and the Confederates withdrew north of the Neuse River in the direction of Goldsboro. Halleck estimates that the rebels had 4,000 troops in the field to our 10,000. On the 16th of December, a significantly larger Union force engaged rebels in Wayne County at White Hall. In this two-day battle, an estimated 30,000 Union troops were employed. The 3rd New York Cavalry and the 23rd New York Artillery joined Foster's forces. On the 17th our men reached the Goldsboro railroad bridge near Everetteville and burned it. They then returned to base at New Bern on December 20th.

Author's notes:

Between December 12 and December 16, a naval force including the U.S.S. Delaware, Shawsheen, Lockwood and Seymour, with armed transports entered the Neuse River to support an Army expedition to destroy the Wilmington and Weldon Railroad bridge and track near Goldsboro, North Carolina; low water prevented the gunboats from advancing more than about 15 miles up the river. Total Army casualties for the campaign were Union 577 and Confederate 738.

The White House – Sunday, December 28, 1862

Attorney General Bates brought Reverend Samuel B. McPheeters, pastor of the Pine Street Presbyterian Church in St. Louis to meet with me yesterday afternoon. It seems that the pastor has been ordered to leave Missouri with his family by Provost Marshall Franklin Dick for reasons that suggest the minister is in sympathy with the rebellion and not to be trusted. I found the pastor to be a sincere man who has sympathies with rebels, some of whom are relatives. But I do not believe he is a security risk. I therefore telegraphed General Samuel Curtis to let the order in regard to Dr. McPheeters and family be suspended until he hears from me again. I discussed this case with Mother, who sympathizes strongly with McPheeters and his family because she too has many relatives who favor the Southern cause. My concern is not one of sympathy for rebels, but fear that our military authorities will begin to interfere in church matters, which should be none of their business.

Author's notes:

Dr. McPheeters was expelled from his church by a vote of the congregation, but he was not forced by the military to leave the state. Lincoln wrote General Curtis on January 2, 1863, that "The U.S. government must not, as by this order, undertake to run the churches. When an individual, in a church or out of it, becomes dangerous to the public interest, he must be checked; but let the churches, as such take care of themselves. It will not do for the U.S. to appoint Trustees, Supervisors, or other agents for the churches. A. Lincoln"

The White House – Monday, December 29, 1862

I read to the full Cabinet my most recent draft language of the soon-to-be issued Emancipation Proclamation. I asked each Cabinet member to provide to me no later than tomorrow any suggestions for making changes in the language before final issuance on January 1, 1863. In the present iteration the names of the states in rebellion are now specifically named.

We also spent more time discussing West Virginia's act of joining the Union. Later, I met privately with Generals John Newton and John Cochrane, who are presently serving on General Burnside's staff. Their comments and genuine concerns are disturbing. Neither man has confidence in his superior officer, General Burnside. They came to me because they fear that Burnside may take precipitous actions that could harm the Army of the Potomac.

Senator Browning and Judge James Hughes called upon me late at night on behalf of Major John Key. I explained to them that as far as I am concerned, the matter of Key is settled, and he is not going to be reinstated into the Army.

Author's notes:

The next day Lincoln advised General Burnside not to make a "general movement of the Army without letting me know." Burnside replied, "Your dispatch is received. I have rescinded some orders that had already been given. I am summoned to give evidence in a court martial tomorrow at Washington and will see you."

The White House – Tuesday, December 30, 1862

I wrote General Butler asking him to arrange to meet me in Washington at his earliest convenience. He is a particularly effective general, albeit his methods are often controversial. But I remember that when the war began how effective he was in getting troops raised when no one else was able to do so. I would like to see him assume broader duties in New Orleans during the New Year.

Mother wishes to go to see the latest opera. Hay, who has seen it, raves about it.

Author's notes:

Lincoln wrote to Butler, "I believe you have a family, and I dislike depriving you of an early visit to them. But I really wish to see you at the earliest moment. I am contemplating a peculiar and important service for you, which I think and hope you will think, is as honorable, as it is important. I wish to confer with you upon it. Please come immediately upon your arrival at New York. A. Lincoln."

Lincoln suggested to Secretary of War Stanton that Butler be returned to New Orleans again. On January 23, 186,3 Lincoln informed Stanton that Butler would be unwilling to go unless he was restored to command of the department. Lincoln realized this might wound the feelings of General Banks, who wished to go to Texas with a substantial force. Butler never got to return to New Orleans but was assigned to command the 18th Army Corps and the Departments of Virginia and North Carolina on October 28, 1863.

The White House – Wednesday, December 31, 1862

We began our Cabinet meeting at 10 A.M. and worked on final language refinements in the emancipation document for several hours.

Stanton proposed language, which I have accepted, which reads, "And upon this act, sincerely believed to be an act of justice, warranted by the Constitution, upon military necessity, I invoke the considerate judgment of mankind, and the gracious favor of Almighty God." The document is dated January 1, 1863, the 87th year of the independence of the United States of America.

Later, I met with General Burnside on many military matters. He wishes to resign his command because of strong difference of opinion with his senior officers. Halleck also wishes to resign, according to Stanton. If I might make a New Year's resolution it should be that all my generals will suddenly find a way to cooperate fully and happily with one another.

Finally, it will soon be New Year's Eve! Mother prays the year 1963 will prove to be the last year of this dreadful war. I fully concur!

Author's notes:

Lincoln approved the act admitting the state of West Virginia into the Union. Lincoln, who had the weight of the world on his shoulders, always tried to make time for those citizens who came to him with personal problems. On this day he wrote to Secretary Stanton, "Yesterday a piteous appeal was made to me by an old lady of genteel appearance, saying she had, with what she thought sufficient assurance that she would not be disturbed by the government, fitted up two South Divisions of the old Duff Green building in order to take boarders, and has boarders already in it, and that now is she is ordered to be out of it by Saturday the 3rd Inst; and that, independently of the ruin it brings on her, by her lost out-lay, she neither has, nor can find shelter for her own head. I know nothing about it myself but promised to bring it to your notice. Yours truly. A. Lincoln." (The Duff Green Building presumably referred to the former residence of Duff Green, which was located on the north side of E Street, a short distance east of 10th Street in Washington, D.C.)

Epilogue

Volume III of The Secret War Diaries of Abraham Lincoln –
Including His Recurring Dreams will be the next book to be published in this
four-book series. It will cover the period from January 1,1863, to December 31, 1863.

Volume I and Volume II are now available at Amazon.com and on Kindle.
Autographed copies may be ordered from The Country Bookshop, 140 N.W. Broad
Street, Southern Pines, NC, 28387
Phone: (910) 692-3211

Paul R. Dunn, Author
125 Lake Shore Drive
Pinehurst, North Carolina 28374

Paulandbj@nc.rr.com
(910) 235 0397

46907   8/18

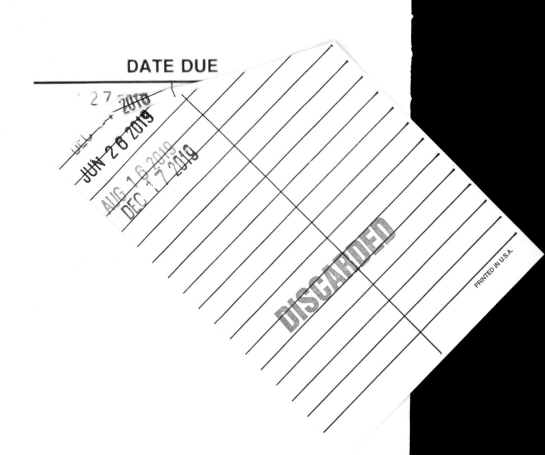

DATE DUE

27 2018

JUN 2 0 2019

AUG 1 6 2019

DEC 1 7 2019

DISCARDED

PRINTED IN U.S.A.

Programming in Go

Programming in Go

Creating Applications for the 21st Century

Mark Summerfield

✦✦Addison-Wesley

Upper Saddle River, NJ · Boston · Indianapolis · San Francisco
New York · Toronto · Montreal · London · Munich · Paris · Madrid
Capetown · Sydney · Tokyo · Singapore · Mexico City

Library of Congress Cataloging-in-Publication Data

Summerfield, Mark.
    Programming in Go : creating applications for the 21st century / Mark Summerfield.
        p. cm.
    Includes bibliographical references and index.
    ISBN 978-0-321-77463-7 (pbk. : alk. paper)
1. Go (Computer program language) 2. Computer programming 3. Application software—Development I. Title.

    QA76.73.G63S86 2012
    005.13′3—dc23

                                                                        2012001914

ISBN-13: 978-0-321-77463-7
ISBN-10:   0-321-77463-9

Text printed in the United States on recycled paper at RR Donnelley in Crawfordsville, Indiana.
First printing, April 2012

This book is dedicated to
Jasmin Blanchette and Trenton Schulz

Contents at a Glance

www.qtrac.eu/gobook.html

Contents

Tables

Introduction

The purpose of this book is to teach solid idiomatic Go programming using all the features the language provides, as well as the most commonly used Go packages from Go's standard library. The book is also designed to serve as a useful reference once the language is learned. To meet both of these goals the book is quite comprehensive and tries to cover every topic in just one place—and with forward and backward cross-references throughout.

Go is quite C-like in spirit, being a small and efficient language with convenient low-level facilities such as pointers. Yet Go also offers many features associated with high- or very high-level languages, such as Unicode strings, powerful built-in data structures, duck typing, garbage collection, and high-level concurrency support that uses communication rather than shared data and locks. Go also has a large and wide-ranging standard library.

The reader is assumed to have programming experience in a mainstream programming language such as C, C++, Java, Python, or similar, although all of Go's unique features and idioms are illustrated with complete runnable examples that are fully explained in the text.

To successfully learn any programming language it is necessary to write programs in that language. To this end the book's approach is wholly practical, and readers are encouraged to experiment with the examples, try the exercises, and write their own programs to get hands-on experience. As with all my previous books, the quoted code snippets are of "live code"; that is, the code was automatically extracted from .go source files and directly embedded in the PDF that went to the publisher—so there are no cut and paste errors, and the code works. Wherever possible, small but complete programs and packages are used as examples to provide realistic use cases. The examples, exercises, and solutions are available online at www.qtrac.eu/gobook.html.

The book's key aim is to teach the Go *language,* and although many of the standard Go packages are used, not all of them are. This is not a problem, since reading the book will provide enough Go knowledge for readers to be able to make use of any of the standard packages, or any third-party Go package, and of course, be able to create their own packages.

Why Go?

The Go programming language began as an internal Google project in 2007. The original design was by Robert Griesemer and Unix luminaries Rob Pike and Ken Thompson. On November 10, 2009, Go was publicly unveiled under a liberal open source license. Go is being developed by a team at Google which includes the original designers plus Russ Cox, Andrew Gerrand, Ian Lance Taylor, and many others. Go has an open development model and many developers from around the world contribute to it, with some so trusted and respected that they have the same commit privileges as the Googlers. In addition, many third-party Go packages are available from the Go Dashboard (godashboard.appspot.com/project).

Go is the most exciting new mainstream language to appear in at least 15 years and is the first such language that is aimed squarely at 21st century computers—and their programmers.

Go is designed to scale efficiently so that it can be used to build very big applications—and to compile even a large program in mere seconds on a single computer. The lightning-fast compilation speed is made possible to a small extent because the language is easy to parse, but mostly because of its dependency management. If file *app.go* depends on file *pkg1.go*, which in turn depends on *pkg2.go*, in a conventional compiled language *app.go* would need both *pkg1.go*'s and *pkg2.go*'s object files. But in Go, everything that *pkg2.go* exports is cached in *pkg1.go*'s object file, so *pkg1.go*'s object file alone is sufficient to build *app.go*. For just three files this hardly matters, but it results in huge speedups for large applications with lots of dependencies.

Since Go programs are so fast to build, it is practical to use them in situations where scripting languages are normally used (see the sidebar "Go Shebang Scripts", ➤ 10). Furthermore, Go can be used to build web applications using Google's App Engine.

Go uses a very clean and easy-to-understand syntax that avoids the complexity and verbosity of older languages like C++ (first released in 1983) or Java (first released in 1995). And Go is a strongly statically typed language, something which many programmers regard as essential for writing large programs. Yet Go's typing is not burdensome due to Go's short "declare and initialize" variable declaration syntax (where the compiler deduces the type so it doesn't have to be written explicitly), and because Go supports a powerful and convenient version of duck typing.

Languages like C and C++ require programmers to do a vast amount of bookkeeping when it comes to memory management—bookkeeping that could be done by the computer itself, especially for concurrent programs where keeping track can be fiendishly complicated. In recent years C++ has greatly improved in this area with various "smart" pointers, but is only just catching up with Java with regard to its threading library. Java relieves the programmer from the burden of memory management by using a garbage collector. C has only third-party threading libraries, although C++ now has a standard threading library. However, writing concurrent programs in C, C++, or Java requires considerable bookkeeping by programmers to make sure they lock and unlock resources at the right times.

The Go compiler and runtime system takes care of the tedious bookkeeping. For memory management Go has a garbage collector, so there's no need for smart pointers or for manually freeing memory. And for concurrency, Go provides a form of CSP (Communicating Sequential Processes) based on the ideas of computer scientist C. A. R. Hoare, that means that many concurrent Go programs don't need to do any locking at all. Furthermore, Go uses *goroutines*—very lightweight processes which can be created in vast numbers that are automatically load-balanced across the available processors and cores—to provide much more fine-grained concurrency than older languages' thread-based approaches. In fact, Go's concurrency support is so simple and natural to use that when porting single-threaded programs to Go it often happens that opportunities for using concurrency arise that lead to improved runtimes and better utilization of machine resources.

Go is a pragmatic language that favors efficiency and programmer convenience over purity. For example, Go's built-in types and user-defined types are not the same, since the former can be highly optimized in ways the latter can't be. Go also provides two fundamental built-in collection types: *slices* (for all practical purposes these are references to variable-length arrays) and *maps* (*key–value* dictionaries or hashes). These collection types are highly efficient and serve most purposes extremely well. However, Go supports pointers (it is a fully compiled language—there's no virtual machine getting in the way of performance), so it is possible to create sophisticated custom types, such as balanced binary trees, with ease.

While C supports only procedural programming and Java forces programmers to program everything in an object-oriented way, Go allows programmers to use the paradigm best suited to the problem. Go can be used as a purely procedural language, but also has excellent support for object-oriented programming. As we will see, though, Go's approach to object orientation is radically different from, say, C++, Java, or Python—and is easier to use and much more flexible than earlier forms.

Like C, Go lacks generics (templates in C++-speak); however, in practice the other facilities that Go provides in many cases obviate the need for generics. Go does not use a preprocessor or include files (which is another reason why it compiles so fast), so there is no need to duplicate function signatures as there is in C and C++. And with no preprocessor, a program's semantics cannot change behind a Go programmer's back as it can with careless #*define*s in C and C++.

Arguably, C++, Objective-C, and Java have all attempted to be better Cs (the latter indirectly as a better C++). Go can also be seen as an attempt to be a better C, even though Go's clean, light syntax is reminiscent of Python—and Go's slices and maps are very similar to Python's lists and dicts. However, Go is closer in spirit to C than to any other language, and can be seen as an attempt to avoid C's drawbacks while providing all that's best in C, as well as adding many powerful and useful features that are unique to Go.

Originally Go was conceived as a systems programming language for developing large-scale programs with fast compilation that could take advantage of distributed systems and multicore networked computers. Go's reach has already gone far beyond the original conception and it is now being used as a highly productive general-purpose programming language that's a pleasure to use and maintain.

The Structure of the Book

Chapter 1 begins by explaining how to build and run Go programs. The chapter then provides a brief overview of Go's syntax and features, as well as introducing some of its standard library. This is done by presenting and explaining a series of five very short examples, each illustrating a variety of Go features. This chapter is designed to provide just a flavor of the language and to give readers a feel for the scope of what is required to learn Go. (How to obtain and install Go is also explained in this chapter.)

Chapters 2 to 7 cover the Go language in depth. Three chapters are devoted to built-in data types: Chapter 2 covers identifiers, Booleans, and numbers; Chapter 3 covers strings; and Chapter 4 covers Go's collection types.

Chapter 5 describes and illustrates Go's statements and control structures. It also explains how to create and use custom functions, and completes the chapters that show how to create procedural nonconcurrent programs in Go.

Chapter 6 shows how to do object-oriented programming in Go. This chapter includes coverage of Go structs used for aggregating and embedding (delegating) values, and Go interfaces for specifying abstract types, as well as how to produce an inheritance-like effect in some situations. The chapter presents several complete fully explained examples to help ensure understanding, since Go's approach to object orientation may well be different from most readers' experience.

Chapter 7 covers Go's concurrency features and has even more examples than the chapter on object orientation, again to ensure a thorough understanding of these novel aspects of the Go language.

Chapter 8 shows how to read and write custom binary, Go binary, text, JSON, and XML files. (Reading and writing text files is very briefly covered in Chapter 1 and several subsequent chapters since this makes it easier to have useful examples and exercises.)

The book's final chapter is Chapter 9. This chapter begins by showing how to import and use standard library packages, custom packages, and third-party packages. It also shows how to document, unit test, and benchmark custom packages. The chapter's last sections provide brief overviews of the tools provided with the *gc* compiler, and of Go's standard library.

Although Go is quite a small language, it is a very rich and expressive language (as measured in syntactic constructs, concepts, and idioms), so there is a surprising amount to learn. This book shows examples in good idiomatic Go style right from the start.* This approach, of course, means that some things are shown before being fully explained. We ask the reader to take it on trust that everything will be explained over the course of the book (and, of course, cross-references are provided for everything that is not explained on the spot).

Go is a fascinating language, and one that is really nice to use. It isn't hard to learn Go's syntax and idioms, but it does introduce some novel concepts that may be unfamiliar to many readers. This book tries to give readers the conceptual breakthroughs—especially in object-oriented Go programming and in concurrent Go programming—that might take weeks or even months for those whose only guide is the good but rather terse documentation.

Acknowledgments

Every technical book I have ever written has benefited from the help and advice of others, and this one is no different in this regard.

I want to give particular thanks to two friends who are programmers with no prior Go experience: Jasmin Blanchette and Trenton Schulz. Both have contributed to my books for many years, and in this case their feedback has helped to ensure that this book will meet the needs of other programmers new to Go.

The book was also greatly enhanced by the feedback I received from core Go developer Nigel Tao. I didn't always take his advice, but his feedback was always illuminating and resulted in great improvements both to the code and to the text.

I had additional help from others, including David Boddie, a programmer new to Go, who gave some valuable feedback. And Go developers Ian Lance Taylor, and especially Russ Cox, between them solved many problems both of code and concepts, and provided clear and precise explanations that contributed greatly to the book's accuracy.

During the writing of the book I asked many questions on the `golang-nuts` mailing list and always received thoughtful and useful replies from many different

---

* The one exception is that in the early chapters we always declare channels to be bidirectional, even when they are used only unidirectionally. Channels are declared to have a particular direction wherever this makes sense, starting from Chapter 7.

posters. I also received feedback from readers of the Safari "rough cut" preview edition that led to some important clarifications.

The Italian software company www.develer.com, in the person of Giovanni Bajo, was kind enough to provide me with free Mercurial repository hosting to aid my peace of mind over the long process of writing this book. Thanks to Lorenzo Mancini for setting it all up and looking after it for me. I'm also very grateful to Anton Bowers and Ben Thompson who have been hosting my web site, www.qtrac.eu, on their web server since early 2011.

Thanks to Russel Winder for his coverage of software patents in his blog, www.russel.org.uk. Appendix B borrows a number of his ideas.

And as always, thanks to Jeff Kingston, creator of the *lout* typesetting system that I have used for all my books and many other writing projects over many years.

Particular thanks to my commissioning editor, Debra Williams Cauley, who so successfully made the case for this book with the publisher, and who provided support and practical help as the work progressed.

Thanks also to production manager Anna Popick, who once again managed the production process so well, and to the proofreader, Audrey Doyle, who did such excellent work.

As ever, I want to thank my wife, Andrea, for her love and support.

1 An Overview in Five Examples

This chapter provides a series of five explained examples. Although the examples are tiny, each of them (apart from "Hello Who?") does something useful, and between them they provide a rapid overview of Go's key features and some of its key packages. (What other languages often call "modules" or "libraries" are called *packages* in Go terminology, and all the packages supplied with Go as standard are collectively known as the *Go standard library*.) The chapter's purpose is to provide a flavor of Go and to give a feel for the scope of what needs to be learned to program successfully in Go. Don't worry if some of the syntax or idioms are not immediately understandable; everything shown in this chapter is covered thoroughly in subsequent chapters.

Learning to program Go the Go way will take a certain amount of time and practice. For those wanting to port substantial C, C++, Java, Python, and other programs to Go, taking the time to learn Go—and in particular how its object-orientation and concurrency features work—will save time and effort in the long run. And for those wanting to create Go applications from scratch it is best to do so making the most of all that Go offers, so again the upfront investment in learning time is important—and will pay back later.

1.1. Getting Going

Go programs are compiled rather than interpreted so as to have the best possible performance. Compilation is very fast—dramatically faster than can be the case with some other languages, most notably compared with C and C++.

The Go Documentation

Go's official web site is golang.org which hosts the most up-to-date Go documentation. The "Packages" link provides access to the documentation on all the Go standard library's packages—and to their source code, which can be very helpful when the documentation itself is sparse. The "Commands" link leads to the documentation for the programs distributed with Go (e.g., the compilers, build tools, etc.). The "Specification" link leads to an accessible, informal, and quite thorough Go language specification. And the "Effective Go" link leads to a document that explains many best practices.

The web site also features a sandbox in which small (somewhat limited) Go programs can be written, compiled, and run, all online. This is useful for beginners for checking odd bits of syntax and for learning the Go fmt package's sophisticated text formatting facilities or the regexp package's regular expression engine. The Go web site's search box searches only the Go documentation; to search for Go resources generally, visit go-lang.cat-v.org/go-search.

The Go documentation can also be viewed locally, for example, in a web browser. To do this, run Go's godoc tool with a command-line argument that tells it to operate as a web server. Here's how to do this in a Unix console (xterm, gnome-terminal, konsole, Terminal.app, or similar):

```
$ godoc -http=:8000
```

Or in a Windows console (i.e., a Command Prompt or MS-DOS Prompt window):

```
C:\>godoc -http=:8000
```

The port number used here is arbitrary—simply use a different one if it conflicts with an existing server. This assumes that godoc is in your PATH.

To view the served documentation, open a web browser and give it a location of http://localhost:8000. This will present a page that looks very similar to the golang.org web site's front page. The "Packages" link will show the documentation for Go's standard library, plus any third-party packages that have been installed under GOROOT. If GOPATH is defined (e.g., for local programs and packages), a link will appear beside the "Packages" link through which the relevant documentation can be accessed. (The GOROOT and GOPATH environment variables are discussed later in this chapter and in Chapter 9.)

It is also possible to view the documentation for a whole package or a single item in a package in the console using godoc on the command line. For example, executing **godoc image NewRGBA** will output the documentation for the image.NewRGBA() function, and executing **godoc image/png** will output the documentation for the entire image/png package.

The standard Go compiler is called *gc* and its toolchain includes programs such as 5g, 6g, and 8g for compiling, 5l, 6l, and 8l for linking, and godoc for viewing the Go documentation. (These are 5g.exe, 6l.exe, etc., on Windows.) The strange names follow the Plan 9 operating system's compiler naming conventions where the digit identifies the processor architecture (e.g., "5" for ARM, "6" for AMD-64—including Intel 64-bit processors—and "8" for Intel 386.) Fortunately, we don't need to concern ourselves with these tools, since Go provides the high-level go build tool that handles the compiling and linking for us.

All the examples in this book—available from www.qtrac.eu/gobook.html—have been tested using *gc* on Linux, Mac OS X, and Windows using Go 1. The Go developers intend to make all subsequent Go 1.*x* versions backward compatible with Go 1, so the book's text and examples should be valid for the entire 1.*x* series. (If incompatible changes occur, the book's examples will be updated to the latest Go release, so as time goes by, they may differ from the code shown in the book.)

To download and install Go, visit golang.org/doc/install.html which provides instructions and download links. At the time of this writing, Go 1 is available in source and binary form for FreeBSD 7+, Linux 2.6+, Mac OS X (Snow Leopard and Lion), and Windows 2000+, in all cases for Intel 32-bit and AMD 64-bit processor architectures. There is also support for Linux on ARM processors. Go prebuilt packages are available for the Ubuntu Linux distribution, and may be available for other Linuxes by the time you read this. For learning to program in Go it is easier to install a binary version than to build Go from scratch.

Programs built with *gc* use a particular calling convention. This means that programs compiled with *gc* can be linked only to external libraries that use the same calling convention—unless a suitable tool is used to bridge the difference. Go comes with support for using external C code from Go programs in the form of the cgo tool (golang.org/cmd/cgo), and at least on Linux and BSD systems, both C and C++ code can be used in Go programs using the SWIG tool (www.swig.org).

In addition to *gc* there is also the gccgo compiler. This is a Go-specific front end to gcc (the GNU Compiler Collection) available for gcc from version 4.6. Like *gc*, gccgo may be available prebuilt for some Linux distributions. Instructions for building and installing gccgo are given at golang.org/doc/gccgo_install.html.

1.2. Editing, Compiling, and Running

Go programs are written as plain text Unicode using the UTF-8 encoding.* Most modern text editors can handle this automatically, and some of the most popular may even have support for Go color syntax highlighting and automatic

---

* Some Windows editors (e.g., Notepad) go against the Unicode standard's recommendation and insert the bytes 0xEF, 0xBB, 0xBF, at the start of UTF-8 files. This book's examples assume that UTF-8 files do not have these bytes.

Go Shebang Scripts

One side effect of Go's fast compilation is that it makes it realistic to write Go programs that can be treated as shebang #! scripts on Unix-like systems. This requires a one-off step of installing a suitable tool. At the time of this writing, two rival tools provide the necessary functionality: gonow (github.com/kless/gonow), and gorun (wiki.ubuntu.com/gorun).

Once gonow or gorun is available, we can make any Go program into a shebang script. This is done with two simple steps. First, add either #!/usr/bin/env gonow or #!/usr/bin/env gorun, as the very first line of the .go file that contains the main() function (in package main). Second, make the file executable (e.g., with chmod +x). Such files can only be compiled by gonow or gorun rather than in the normal way since the #! line is not legal in Go.

When gonow or gorun executes a .go file for the first time, it will compile the file (extremely fast, of course), and then run it. On subsequent uses, the program will only be recompiled if the .go source file has been modified since the previous compilation. This makes it possible to use Go to quickly and conveniently create various small utility programs, for example, for system administration tasks.

indentation. If your editor doesn't have Go support, try entering the editor's name in the Go search engine to see if there are suitable add-ons. For editing convenience, all of Go's keywords and operators use ASCII characters; however, Go identifiers can start with any Unicode letter followed by any Unicode letters or digits, so Go programmers can freely use their native language.

To get a feel for how we edit, compile, and run a Go program we'll start with the classic "Hello World" program—although we'll make it a tiny bit more sophisticated than usual. First we will discuss compiling and running, then in the next section we will go through the source code—in file hello/hello.go—in detail, since it incorporates some basic Go ideas and features.

All of the book's examples are available from www.qtrac.eu/gobook.html and unpack to directory goeg. So file hello.go's full path (assuming the examples were unpacked in the home directory—although anywhere will do) is $HOME/goeg/src/hello/hello.go. When referring to files the book always assumes the first three components of the path, which is why in this case the path is given only as hello/hello.go. (Windows users must, of course, read "/"s as "\"s and use the directory they unpacked the examples into, such as C:\goeg or %HOME-PATH%\goeg.)

If you have installed Go from a binary package or built it from source and installed it as root or Administrator, you should have at least one environment variable, GOROOT, which contains the path to the Go installation, and your PATH should now include $GOROOT/bin or %GOROOT%\bin. To check that Go is installed correctly, enter the following in a console (xterm, gnome-terminal, konsole, Terminal.app, or similar):

```
$ go version
```

Or on Windows in an MS-DOS Prompt or Command Prompt window:

```
C:\>go version
```

If you get a "command not found" or "'go' is not recognized..." error message then it means that Go isn't in the PATH. The easiest way to solve this on Unix-like systems (including Mac OS X) is to set the environment variables in .bashrc (or the equivalent file for other shells). For example, the author's .bashrc file contains these lines:

```
export GOROOT=$HOME/opt/go
export PATH=$PATH:$GOROOT/bin
```

(handwritten) me — export GOROOT = /usr/local/go — export PATH = $PATH; $GOROOT/bin ✳✳

Naturally, you must adjust the values to match your own system. (And, of course, this is only necessary if the go version command fails.)

On Windows, one solution is to create a batch file that sets up the environment for Go, and to execute this every time you start a console for Go programming. However, it is much more convenient to set the environment variables once and for all through the Control Panel. To do this, click Start (the Windows logo), then Control Panel, then System and Security, then System, then Advanced system settings, and in the System Properties dialog click the Environment Variables button, then the New... button, and add a variable with the name GOROOT and a suitable value, such as C:\Go. In the same dialog, edit the PATH environment variable by adding the text ;C:\Go\bin at the end—the leading semicolon is vital! In both cases replace the C:\Go path component with the actual path where Go is installed if it isn't C:\Go. (Again, this is only necessary if the go version command failed.)

From now on we will assume that Go is installed and the Go bin directory containing all the Go tools is in the PATH. (It may be necessary—once only—to open a new console window for the new settings to take effect.)

Two steps are required to build Go programs: compiling and linking.* Both of these steps are handled by the go tool which can not only build local programs and packages, but can also fetch, build, and install third-party programs and packages.

---

* Since the book assumes the use of the *gc* compiler, readers using gccgo will need to follow the compile and link process described in golang.org/doc/gccgo_install.html. Similarly, readers using other compilers will need to compile and link as per their compiler's instructions.

For the go tool to be able to build local programs and packages, there are three requirements. First, the Go bin directory ($GOROOT/bin or %GOROOT%\bin) must be in the path. Second, there must be a directory tree that has an src directory and under which the source code for the local programs and packages resides. For example, the book's examples unpack to goeg/src/hello, goeg/src/bigdigits, and so on. Third, the directory *above* the src directory must be in the GOPATH environment variable. For example, to build the book's hello example using the go tool, we must do this:

```
$ export GOPATH=$HOME/goeg
$ cd $GOPATH/src/hello
$ go build
```

We can do almost exactly the same on Windows:

```
C:\>set GOPATH=C:\goeg
C:\>cd %gopath%\src\hello
C:\goeg\src\hello>go build
```

In both cases we assume that the PATH includes $GOROOT/bin or %GOROOT%\bin. Once the go tool has built the program we can run it. By default the executable is given the same name as the directory it is in (e.g., hello on Unix-like systems and hello.exe on Windows). Once built, we can run the program in the usual way.

```
$ ./hello
Hello World!
```

Or:

```
$ ./hello Go Programmers!
Hello Go Programmers!
```

On Windows it is very similar:

```
C:\goeg\src\hello>hello Windows Go Programmers!
Hello Windows Go Programmers!
```

We have shown what must be typed in **bold** and the console's text in roman. We have also assumed a $ prompt, but it doesn't matter what it is (e.g., C:\>).

Note that we do *not* need to compile—or even explicitly link—any other packages (even though as we will see, hello.go uses three standard library packages). This is another reason why Go programs build so quickly.

If we have several Go programs, it would be convenient if all their executables could be in a single directory that we could add to our PATH. Fortunately, the go tool supports this as follows:

```
$ export GOPATH=$HOME/goeg
$ cd $GOPATH/src/hello
$ go install
```

Again, we can do the same on Windows:

```
C:\>set GOPATH=C:\goeg
C:\>cd %gopath%\src\hello
C:\goeg\src\hello>go install
```

The go install command does the same as go build only it puts the executable in a standard location ($GOPATH/bin or %GOPATH%\bin). This means that by adding a single path ($GOPATH/bin or %GOPATH%\bin) to our PATH, *all* the Go programs that we install will conveniently be in the PATH.

In addition to the book's examples, we are likely to want to develop our own Go programs and packages in our own directory. This can easily be accommodated by setting the GOPATH environment variable to two (or more) colon-separated paths (semicolon-separated on Windows); for example, export GOPATH=$HOME/app/go:$HOME/goeg or SET GOPATH=C:\app\go;C:\goeg.* In this case we must put all our program and package's source code in $HOME/app/go/src or C:\app\go\src. So, if we develop a program called myapp, its .go source files would go in $HOME/app/go/src/myapp or C:\app\go\src\myapp. And if we use go install to build a program in a GOPATH directory where the GOPATH has two or more directories, the executable will be put in the corresponding directory's bin directory.

Naturally, it would be tedious to export or set the GOPATH every time we wanted to build a Go program, so it is best to set this environment variable permanently. This can be done by setting GOPATH in the .bashrc file (or similar) on Unix-like systems (see the book's example's gopath.sh file). On Windows it can be done either by writing a batch file (see the book's example's gopath.bat file), or by adding it to the system's environment variables: Click Start (the Windows logo), then Control Panel, then System and Security, then System, then Advanced system settings, and in the System Properties dialog click the Environment Variables button, then the New... button, and add a variable with the name GOPATH and a suitable value, such as C:\goeg or C:\app\go;C:\goeg.

Although Go uses the go tool as its standard build tool, it is perfectly possible to use make or some of the modern build tools, or to use alternative Go-specific build

---

* From now on we will almost always show Unix-style command lines only, and assume that Windows programmers can mentally translate.

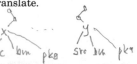

tools, or add-ons for popular IDEs (Integrated Development Environments) such as Eclipse and Visual Studio.

1.3. Hello Who?

Now that we have seen how to build the hello program we will look at its source code. Don't worry about understanding all the details—everything shown in this chapter (and much more!) is covered thoroughly in the subsequent chapters. Here is the complete hello program (in file hello/hello.go):

```
// hello.go
(1)  package main

     import (  ❶
         "fmt"
         "os"
         "strings"
     )

(2)  func main() {
         who := "World!"  ❷
         if len(os.Args) > 1 { /* os.Args[0] is "hello" or "hello.exe" */  ❸
             who = strings.Join(os.Args[1:], " ")  ❹  // replace "World!"
         }
         fmt.Println("Hello", who)  ❺
     }
```

Go uses C++-style comments: // for single-line comments that finish at the end of the line and /* ... */ for comments that can span multiple lines. It is conventional in Go to mostly use single-line comments, with spanning comments often used for commenting out chunks of code during development.★

Every piece of Go code exists inside a package, and every Go program must have a main package with a main() function which serves as the program's entry point, that is, the function that is executed first. In fact, Go packages may also have init() functions that are executed before main(), as we will see (§1.7, ➤ 40); full details are given later (§5.6.2, ➤ 224). Notice that there is no conflict between the name of the package and the name of the function.

Go operates in terms of packages rather than files. This means that we can split a package across as many files as we like, and from Go's point of view if they all have the same package declaration, they are all part of the same package and no different than if all their contents were in a single file. Naturally, we can also

---

★ We use some simple syntax highlighting and sometimes highlight lines or annotate them with numbers (❶, ❷, ...), for ease of reference in the text. None of this is part of the Go language.

break our applications' functionality into as many local packages as we like, to keep everything neatly modularized, something we will see in Chapter 9.

The import statement (14 ◄, ❶) imports three packages from the standard library. The fmt package provides functions for formatting text and for reading formatted text (§3.5, ➤ 93), the os package provides platform-independent operating-system variables and functions, and the strings package provides functions for manipulating strings (§3.6.1, ➤ 107).

Go's fundamental types support the usual operators (e.g., + for numeric addition and for string concatenation), and the Go standard library supplements these by providing packages of functions for working with the fundamental types, such as the strings package imported here. It is also possible to create our own custom types based on the fundamental types and to provide our own methods—that is, custom type-specific functions—for them. (We will get a taste of this in §1.5, ➤ 21, with full coverage in Chapter 6.)

The reader may have noticed that the program has no semicolons, that the imports are not comma-separated, and that the if statement's condition does not require parentheses. In Go, blocks, including function bodies and control structure bodies (e.g., for if statements and for for loops), are delimited using braces. Indentation is used purely to improve human readability. Technically, Go statements are separated by semicolons, but these are put in by the compiler, so we don't have to use them ourselves unless we want to put multiple statements on the same line. No semicolons and fewer commas and parentheses give Go programs a lighter look and require less typing.

Go functions and methods are defined using the func keyword. The main package's main() function always has the same signature—it takes no arguments and returns nothing. When main.main() finishes the program will terminate and return 0 to the operating system. Naturally, we can exit whenever we like and return our own choice of value, as we will see (§1.4, ➤ 16).

The first statement in the main() function (14 ◄, ❷; using the := operator) is called a *short variable declaration* in Go terminology. Such a statement both declares and initializes a variable at the same time. Furthermore, we don't need to specify the variable's type because Go can deduce that from the initializing value. So in this case we have declared a variable called who of type string, and thanks to Go's strong typing we may only assign strings to who.

As with most languages the if statement tests a condition—in this case, how many strings were entered on the command-line—which if satisfied executes the corresponding brace-delimited block. We will see a more sophisticated if statement syntax later in this chapter (§1.6, ➤ 29), and further on (§5.2.1, ➤ 192).

The os.Args variable is a *slice* of strings (14 ◄, ❸). Arrays, slices, and other collection data types are covered in Chapter 4 (§4.2, ➤ 148). For now it is sufficient to know that a slice's length can be determined using the built-in len() function and its elements can be accessed using the [] index operator using a subset of the Python syntax. In particular, slice[n] returns the slice's *n*th element (counting from zero), and slice[n:] returns another slice which has the elements from the *n*th element to the last element. In the collections chapter we will see the full generality of Go's syntax in this area. In the case of os.Args, the slice should always have at least one string (the program's name), at index position 0. (All Go indexing is 0-based.)

If the user has entered one or more command line arguments the if condition is satisfied and we set the who string to contain all the arguments joined up as a single string (14 ◄, ❹). In this case we use the assignment operator (=), since if we used the short variable declaration operator (:=) we would end up declaring and initializing a *new* who variable whose scope was limited to the if statement's block. The strings.Join() function takes a slice of strings and a separator (which could be empty, i.e., ""), and returns a single string consisting of all the slice's strings with the separator between each one. Here we have joined them using a single space between each.

Finally, in the last statement (14 ◄, ❺), we print Hello, a space, the string held in the who variable, and a newline. The fmt package has many different print variants, some like fmt.Println() which will neatly print whatever they are given, and others like fmt.Printf() that use placeholders to provide very fine control over formatting. The print functions are covered in Chapter 3 (§3.5, ➤ 93).

The hello program presented here has shown far more of the language's features than such programs conventionally do. The subsequent examples continue in this vein, covering more advanced features while keeping the examples as short as possible. The idea here is to simply acquire some basic familiarity with the language and to get to grips with building, running, and experimenting with simple Go programs, while at the same time getting a flavor of Go's powerful and novel features. And, of course, everything presented in this chapter is explained in detail in the subsequent chapters.

1.4. Big Digits—Two-Dimensional Slices

The bigdigits program (in file bigdigits/bigdigits.go) reads a number entered on the command line (as a string), and outputs the same number onto the console using "big" digits. Back in the twentieth century, at sites where lots of users shared a high-speed line printer, it used to be common practice for each user's print job to be preceded by a cover page that showed some identifying details such as their username and the name of the file being printed, using this kind of technique.

We will review the code in three parts: first the imports, then the static data, and then the processing. But right now, let's look at a sample run to get a feel for how it works:

```
$ ./bigdigits 290175493
  222    9999    000       1   77777  55555       4    9999   333
2   2   9   9   0   0   11        7   5          44   9   9   3   3
    2   9   9   0       0   1        7   5         4 4   9   9       3
    2   9999   0       0   1        7     555   4 4    9999      33
2       9   0       0   1   7             5   444444       9       3
2       9   0   0       1   7         5   5       4       9   3   3
22222       9    000   111   7           555       4       9  333
```

Each digit is represented by a slice of strings, with all the digits together represented by a slice of slices of strings. Before looking at the data, here is how we could declare and initialize single-dimensional slices of strings and numbers:

```
longWeekend := []string{"Friday", "Saturday", "Sunday", "Monday"}
var lowPrimes = []int{2, 3, 5, 7, 11, 13, 17, 19}
```

Slices have the form []*Type*, and if we want to initialize them we can immediately follow with a brace-delimited comma-separated list of elements of the corresponding type. We could have used the same variable declaration syntax for both, but have used a longer form for the lowPrimes slice to show the syntactic difference and for a reason that will be explained in a moment. Since a slice's *Type* can itself be a slice type we can easily create multidimensional collections (slices of slices, etc.).

The bigdigits program needs to import only four packages.

```
import (
    "fmt"
    "log"
    "os"
    "path/filepath"
)
```

The fmt package provides functions for formatting text and for reading formatted text (§3.5, ➤ 93). The log package provides logging functions. The os package provides platform-independent operating-system variables and functions including the os.Args variable of type []string (slice of strings) that holds the command-line arguments. And the path package's filepath package provides functions for manipulating filenames and paths that work across platforms. Note that for packages that are logically inside other packages, we only specify the last component of their name (in this case filepath) when accessing them in our code.

For the `bigdigits` program we need two-dimensional data (a slice of slices of strings). Here is how we have created it, with the strings for digit 0 laid out to illustrate how a digit's strings correspond to rows in the output, and with the strings for digits 3 to 8 elided.

```
var bigDigits = [][]string{          // slice of slices
    {"  000  ",         ← slice
     " 0   0 ",         ← slice
     "0     0",
     "0     0",
     "0     0",
     " 0   0 ",
     "  000  "},
    {"  1  ", " 11  ", "  1  ", "  1  ", "  1  ", "  1  ", "111"},
    {"  222  ", "2    2", "    2  ", "   2   ", "  2    ", "2      ", "22222"},
    // ... 3 to 8 ...
    {" 9999", "9   9", "9   9", " 9999", "    9", "    9", "    9"},
}
```
(handwritten left margin: "0th member slice", "1st →", "9th →")

Variables declared outside of any function or method may not use the `:=` operator, but we can get the same effect using the long declaration form (with keyword `var`) and the assignment operator (`=`) as we have done here for the `bigDigits` variable (and did earlier for the `lowPrimes` variable). We still don't need to specify `bigDigits`' type since Go can deduce that from the assignment.

We leave the bean counting to the Go compiler, so there is no need to specify the dimensions of the slice of slices. One of Go's many conveniences is its excellent support for composite literals using braces, so we don't have to declare a data variable in one place and populate it with data in another—unless we want to, of course.

The `main()` function that reads the command line and uses the data to produce the output is only 20 lines.

```
func main() {
    if len(os.Args) == 1 {  ❶
        fmt.Printf("usage: %s <whole-number>\n", filepath.Base(os.Args[0]))
        os.Exit(1)
    }
    stringOfDigits := os.Args[1]        // eg "290175493"
    for row := range bigDigits[0] {  ❷  // all digits have same row count
        line := ""
        for column := range stringOfDigits {  ❸  // count of digits input
            digit := stringOfDigits[column] - '0'  ❹  // convert 'd' → d
            if 0 <= digit && digit <= 9 {  ❺
```

```
                line += bigDigits[digit][row] + "  "   ❻
            } else {
                log.Fatal("invalid whole number")
            }
        }
        fmt.Println(line)
    }
}
```

The program begins by checking to see if it was invoked with any command-line arguments. If it wasn't, `len(os.Args)` will be 1 (recall that `os.Args[0]` holds the program's name, so the slice's length is normally at least 1), and the first if statement (18 ◄, ❶) will be satisfied. In this case we output a suitable usage message using the `fmt.Printf()` function that accepts % placeholders similar to those supported by the C/C++ *printf()* function or by Python's % operator. (See §3.5, ➤ 93 for full details.)

The `path/filepath` package provides path manipulation functions—for example, the `filepath.Base()` function returns the basename (i.e., the filename) of the given path. After outputting the message the program terminates using the `os.Exit()` function and returns 1 to the operating system. On Unix-like systems a return value of 0 is used to indicate success, with nonzero values indicating a usage error or a failure.

The use of the `filepath.Base()` function illustrates a nice feature of Go: When a package is imported, no matter whether it is top-level or logically inside another package (e.g., `path/filepath`), we always refer to it using only the last component of its name (e.g., `filepath`). It is also possible to give packages local names to avoid name collisions; Chapter 9 provides the details.

If at least one command-line argument was given, we copy the first one into the `stringOfDigits` variable (of type `string`). To convert the number that the user entered into big digits we must iterate over each row in the `bigDigits` slice to produce each line of output, that is, the first (top) string for each digit, then the second, and so on. We assume that all the `bigDigits`' slices have the same number of rows and so take the row count from the first one. Go's for loop has various syntaxes for different purposes; here (18 ◄, ❷ and 18 ◄, ❸) we have used for ... range loops that return the index positions of each item in the slices they are given.

The row and column loops part of the code could have been written like this:

```
for row := 0; row < len(bigDigits[0]); row++ {
    line := ""
    for column := 0; column < len(stringOfDigits); column++ {
        ...
```

This is a form familiar to C, C++, and Java programmers and is perfectly valid in Go.* However, the for ... range syntax is shorter and more convenient. (Go's for loops are covered in §5.3, ➤ 203.)

At each row iteration we set that row's line to be an empty string. Then we iterate over the columns (i.e., the characters) in the stringOfDigits string we received from the user. Go strings hold UTF-8 bytes, so potentially a character might be represented by two or more bytes. This isn't an issue here because we are only concerned with the digits 0, 1, ..., 9 each of which is represented by a single byte in UTF-8 and with the same byte value as in 7-bit ASCII. (We will see how to iterate over a string character by character—regardless of whether the characters are single- or multibyte—in Chapter 3.)

When we index a particular position in a string we get the *byte* value at that position. (In Go the byte type is a synonym for the uint8 type.) So we retrieve the byte value of the command-line string at the given column and subtract the byte value of digit 0 from it to get the number it represents (18 ◄, ❹). In UTF-8 (and 7-bit ASCII) the character '0' is code point (character) 48 decimal, the character '1' is code point 49, and so on. So if, for example, we have the character '3' (code point 51), we can get its integer value by doing the subtraction '3' - '0' (i.e., 51 - 48) which results in an integer (of type byte) of value 3.

Go uses single quotes for character literals, and a character literal is an integer that's compatible with any of Go's integer types. Go's strong typing means we cannot add, say, an int32 to an int16 without explicit conversion, but Go's numeric constants and literals adapt to their context, so in this context '0' is considered to be a byte.

If the digit (of type byte) is in range (18 ◄, ❺) we can add the appropriate string to the line. (In the if statement the constants 0 and 9 are considered to be bytes because that's digit's type, but if digit was of a different type, say, int, they would be treated as that type instead.) Although Go strings are immutable (i.e., they cannot be changed), the += append operator is supported to provide a nice easy-to-use syntax. (It works by replacing the original string under the hood.) There is also support for the + concatenate operator which returns a new string that is the concatenation of its left and right string operands. (The string type is covered fully in Chapter 3.)

To retrieve the appropriate string (19 ◄, ❻) we access the bigDigits's slice that corresponds to the digit, and then within that to the row (string) we need.

If the digit is out of range (e.g., due to the stringOfDigits containing a nondigit), we call the log.Fatal() function with an error message. This function logs the

---

* Unlike C, C++, and Java, in Go the ++ and -- operators may only be used as statements, not expressions. Furthermore, they may only be used as postfix operators, not prefix operators. This means that certain order of evaluation problems cannot occur in Go—so thankfully, expressions like *f(i++)* and *a[i] = b[++i]* cannot be written in Go.

date, time, and error message—to os.Stderr if no other log destination is explicitly specified—and calls os.Exit(1) to terminate the program. There is also a log.Fatalf() function that does the same thing and which accepts % placeholders. We didn't use log.Fatal() in the first if statement (18 ◀, ❶) because we want to print the program's usage message without the date and time that the log.Fatal() function normally outputs.

Once all the number's strings for the given row have been accumulated the complete line is printed. In this example, seven lines are printed because each digit in the bigDigits slice of strings is represented by seven strings.

One final point is that the order of declarations and definitions doesn't generally matter. So in the bigdigits/bigdigits.go file we could declare the bigDigits variable before or after the main() function. In this case we have put main() first since for the book's examples we usually prefer to order things top-down.

The first two examples have covered a fair amount of ground, but both of them show material that is familiar from other mainstream languages even though the syntax is slightly different. The following three examples take us beyond the comfort zone to illustrate Go-specific features such as custom Go types, Go file handling (including error handling) and functions as values, and concurrent programming using goroutines and communication channels.

1.5. Stack—Custom Types with Methods

Although Go supports object-oriented programming it provides neither classes nor inheritance (*is-a* relationships). Go does support the creation of custom types, and Go makes aggregation (*has-a* relationships) extremely easy. Go also allows for the complete separation of a type's data from its behavior, and supports *duck typing*. Duck typing is a powerful abstraction mechanism that means that values can be handled (e.g., passed to functions), based on the methods they provide, regardless of their actual types. The terminology is derived from the phrase, "If it walks like a duck, and quacks like a duck, it *is* a duck". All of this produces a more flexible and powerful alternative to the classes and inheritance approach—but does require those of us used to the more traditional approach to make some significant conceptual adjustments to really benefit from Go's object orientation.

Go represents data using the fundamental built-in types such as keyword!!struct ⸮ bool, int, and string, or by aggregations of types using structs.* Go's custom types are based on the fundamental types, or on structs, or on other custom types. (We will see some simple examples later in this chapter; §1.7, ➤ 40.)

---

* Unlike C++, Go's structs are *not* classes in disguise. For example, Go's structs support aggregation and delegation, but not inheritance.

Go supports both named and unnamed custom types. Unnamed types with the same structure can be used interchangeably; however, they cannot have any methods. (We will discuss this more fully in §6.4, ➤ 275.) Any *named* custom type can have methods and these methods together constitute the type's interface. Named custom types—even with the same structure—are not interchangeable. (Throughout the book any reference to a "custom type" means a *named* custom type, unless stated otherwise.)

An interface is a type that can be formally defined by specifying a particular set of methods. Interfaces are abstract and cannot be instantiated. A concrete (i.e., noninterface) type that has the methods specified by an interface fulfills the interface, that is, values of such a concrete type can be used as values of the interface's type as well as of their own actual type. Yet no formal *connection* need be established between an interface and a concrete type that provides the methods specified by the interface. It is sufficient for a custom type to have the interface's methods for it to satisfy that interface. And, of course, a type can satisfy more than one interface simply by providing all the methods for all the interfaces we want it to satisfy.

The empty interface (i.e., the interface that has no methods) is specified as interface{}.* Since the empty interface makes no demands at all (because it doesn't require any methods), it can stand for any value (in effect like a pointer to any value), whether the value is of a built-in type or is of a custom type. (Go's pointers and references are explained later; §4.1, ➤ 140.) Incidentally, in Go terminology we talk about types and values rather than classes and objects or instances (since Go has no classes).

Function and method parameters can be of any built-in or custom type—or of any interface type. In the latter case this means that a function can have a parameter that says, for example, "pass a value that can read data", regardless of what that value's type actually is. (We will see this in practice shortly; §1.6, ➤ 29.)

Chapter 6 covers all of these matters in detail and presents many examples to ensure that the ideas are understood. For now, let's just look at a very simple custom type—a stack—starting with how values are created and used, and then looking at the implementation of the custom type itself.

We will start with the output produced by a simple test program:

```
$ ./stacker
81.52
[pin clip needle]
-15
hay
```

---

* Go's empty interface can serve the same role as a reference to a Java *Object* or as C/C++'s *void*∗.

Each item was popped from the custom stack and printed on its own line.

The simple test program that produced this output is `stacker/stacker.go`. Here are the imports it uses:

```
import (
    "fmt"
    "stacker/stack"         24 ff
)
```

The `fmt` package is part of Go's standard library, but the `stack` package is a local package specific to the `stacker` application. A Go program or package's imports are first searched for under the `GOPATH` path or paths, and then under `GOROOT`. In this particular case the program's source code is in `$HOME/goeg/src/stacker/stacker.go` and the `stack` package is in `$HOME/goeg/src/stacker/stack/stack.go`. The `go` tool will build both of them so long as the `GOPATH` is (or includes) the path `$HOME/goeg/`.

Import paths are specified using Unix-style "/"s, even on Windows. Every local package should be stored in a directory with the same name as the package. Local packages can have their own packages (e.g., like `path/filepath`), in exactly the same way as the standard library. (Creating and using custom packages is covered in Chapter 9.)

Here's the simple test program's `main()` function that produced the output:

```
func main() {
    var haystack stack.Stack
    haystack.Push("hay")
    haystack.Push(-15)
    haystack.Push([]string{"pin", "clip", "needle"})
    haystack.Push(81.52)
    for {
        item, err := haystack.Pop()
        if err != nil {
            break
        }
        fmt.Println(item)
    }
}
```

The function begins by declaring the `haystack` variable of type `stack.Stack`. It is conventional in Go to always refer to types, functions, variables, and other items in packages using the syntax *pkg.item*, where *pkg* is the last (or only) component of the package's name. This helps prevent name collisions. We then push some items onto the stack and then pop them off and print each one until there are no more left.

One amazingly convenient aspect of our custom stack is that despite Go's strong typing, we are not limited to storing homogeneous items (items all of the same type), but can freely mix heterogeneous items (items of various types). This is because the stack.Stack type simply stores interface{} items (i.e., values of *any* type) and doesn't care what their types actually are. Of course, when those items are *used,* then their type does matter. Here, though, we only use the fmt.Println() function and this uses Go's introspection facilities (from the reflect package) to discover the types of the items it is asked to print. (Reflection is covered in a later chapter; §9.4.9, ➤ 427.)

Another nice Go feature illustrated by the code is the for loop with no conditions. This is an infinite loop, so in most situations we will need to provide a means of breaking out of the loop—for example, using a break statement as here, or a return statement. We will see an additional for syntax in the next example (§1.6, ➤ 29); the complete range of for syntaxes is covered in Chapter 5.

Go functions and methods can return a single value or multiple values. It is conventional in Go to report errors by returning an error value (of type error) as the last (or only) value returned by a function or method. The custom stack. Stack type respects this convention.

Now that we have seen the custom stack.Stack type in use we are ready to review its implementation (in file stacker/stack/stack.go).

```
package stack

import "errors"

type Stack []interface{}     // Create a new type w. underlying a slice
                             // This represents a slice of "anything"
```

The file starts conventionally by specifying its package name. Then it imports other packages that it needs—in this case just one, errors.

When we define a named custom type in Go what we are doing is binding an identifier (the type's name) to a new type that has the same underlying representation as an existing (built-in or custom) type—and which is treated by Go as different from the underlying representation. Here, the Stack type is a new name for a slice (i.e., a reference to a variable-length array) of interface{} values—and is considered to be different from a plain []interface{}.

Because all Go types satisfy the empty interface, values of any type can be stored in a Stack.

The built-in collection types (maps and slices), communication channels (which can be buffered), and strings, can all return their length (or buffer size) using the built-in len() function. Similarly, slices and channels can also report their capacity (which may be greater than the length being used) using the built-in cap() function. (All of Go's built-in functions are listed in Table 5.1, ➤ 187, with cross-references to where they are covered; slices are covered in Chapter 4; §4.2,

➤ 148.) It is conventional for custom collection types—our own, and those in the Go standard library—to support corresponding Len() and Cap() methods when these make sense.

Since the Stack type uses a slice for its underlying representation it makes sense to provide Stack.Len() and Stack.Cap() methods for it.

```go
func (stack Stack) Len() int {
    return len(stack)
}
```

Both functions and methods are defined using the func keyword. However, in the case of methods the type of value to which the method applies is written after the func keyword and before the method's name, enclosed in parentheses. After the function or method's name comes a—possibly empty—parenthesized list of comma-separated parameters (each written in the form *variableName type*). After the parameters comes the function or method's opening brace (if it has no return value), or a single return value (e.g., as a type name such as the int returned by the Stack.Len() method shown here), or a parenthesized list of return values, followed by an opening brace.

In most cases a variable name for the value on which the method is called is also given—as here where we have used the name stack (and with no conflict with the package's name). The value on which the method is called is known in Go terminology as the *receiver*.★

In this example the type of the receiver is Stack, so the receiver is passed by value. This means that any changes made to the receiver would be made on a copy of the original value and in effect lost. This is no problem for methods that don't modify the receiver, such as the Stack.Len() method shown here.

The Stack.Cap() method is almost identical to the Stack.Len() method (and so is not shown). The only difference is that the Stack.Cap() method returns the cap() rather than the len() of the receiver stack. The source code also includes a Stack.IsEmpty() method, but this is so similar to Stack.Len()—it just returns a bool indicating whether the stack's len() equals 0—that again it isn't shown.

```go
func (stack *Stack) Push(x interface{}) {
    *stack = append(*stack, x)
}
```

The Stack.Push() method is called on a pointer to a Stack (explained in a moment), and is passed a value (x) of any type. The built-in append() function takes a slice and one or more values and returns a (possibly new) slice which has the

---

★ In other languages the receiver is typically called *this* or *self*; using such names works fine in Go, but is not considered to be good Go style.

original slice's contents, plus the given value or values as its last element or elements. (See §4.2.3, ➤ 156.)

If the stack has previously had items popped from it (➤ 28), the underlying slice's capacity is likely to be greater than its length, so the push could be very cheap: simply a matter of putting the x item into the len(stack) position and increasing the stack's length by one.

The Stack.Push() method always works (unless the computer runs out of memory), so we don't need to return an error value to indicate success or failure.

If we want to modify a value we must make its receiver a pointer.[*] A *pointer* is a variable that holds the memory address of another value. One reason that pointers are used is for efficiency—for example, if we have a value of a large type it is much cheaper to pass a pointer to the value as a parameter than to pass the value itself. Another use is to make a value modifiable. For example, when a variable is passed into a function the function gets a *copy* of the value (e.g., the stack passed into the stack.Len() function; 25 ◄). This means that if we make any changes to the variable inside the function, they will have no effect on the original value. If we need to modify the original value—as here where we want to append to the stack—we must pass a pointer to the original value, and then inside the function we can modify the value that the pointer points to.

A pointer is declared by preceding the type name with a star (i.e., an asterisk, *). So here, in the Stack.Push() method, the stack variable is of type *Stack, that is, the stack variable holds a pointer to a Stack value and not an actual Stack value. We can access the actual Stack value that the pointer points to by *dereferencing* the pointer—this simply means that we access the value the pointer points to. Dereferencing is done by preceding the variable name with a star. So here, when we write stack we are referring to a pointer to a Stack (i.e., to a *Stack), and when we write *stack we are dereferencing the pointer, that is, referring to the actual Stack that the pointer points to.

So, in Go (and C and C++ for that matter), the star is overloaded to mean multiplication (when between a pair of numbers or variables, e.g., x * y), pointer declaration (when preceding a type name, e.g., z *MyType), and pointer dereference (when preceding a pointer variable's name, e.g., *z). Don't worry too much about these matters for now: Go's pointers are fully explained in Chapter 4.

Note that Go's channels, maps, and slices are all created using the make() function, and make() always returns a *reference* to the value it created. References behave very much like pointers in that when they are passed to functions any changes made to them inside the function affect the original channel, map, or slice. However, references don't need to be dereferenced, so in most cases there's no need to use stars with them. But if we want to modify a slice inside a func-

---

[*] Go pointers are essentially the same as in C and C++ except that pointer arithmetic isn't supported —or necessary; see §4.1, ➤ 140.

tion or method using append() (as opposed to simply changing one of its existing items), then we must either pass the slice by pointer, or return the slice (and set the original slice to the function or method's return value), since append() sometimes returns a different slice reference than the one it was passed.

The Stack type uses a slice for its representation and therefore Stack values can be used with functions that operate on a slice, such as append() and len(). Nonetheless, Stack values are values in their own right, distinct from their representation, so they must be passed by pointer if we want to modify them.

```
func (stack Stack) Top() (interface{}, error) {
    if len(stack) == 0 {
        return nil, errors.New("can't Top() an empty stack")
    }
    return stack[len(stack)-1], nil
}
```

The Stack.Top() method returns the item at the top of the stack (the item that was added last) and a nil error value; or a nil item and a non-nil error value, if the stack is empty. The stack receiver is passed by value since the stack isn't modified.

The error type is an interface type (§6.3, ➤ 265) which specifies a single method, Error() string. In general, Go's library functions return an error as their last (or only) return value to indicate success (where error is nil) or failure. Here, we have made our Stack type work like a standard library type by creating a new error value using the errors package's errors.New() function.

Go uses nil for zero pointers (and for zero references); that is, for pointers that point to nothing and for references that refer to nothing.* Such pointers should be used only in conditions or assignments; methods should not normally be called on them.

Constructors are never called implicitly in Go. Instead Go guarantees that when a value is created it is always initialized to its zero value. For example, numbers are initialized to 0, strings to the empty string, pointers to nil, and the fields inside structs are similarly initialized. So there is no uninitialized data in Go, thus eliminating a major source of errors that afflicts many other programming languages. If the zero value isn't suitable we can write a construction function—and call it explicitly—as we do here to create a new error. It is also possible to prevent values of a type being created without using a constructor function, as we will see in Chapter 6.

---

* Go's nil is in effect the same as *NULL* or *0* in C and C++, *null* in Java, and *nil* in Objective-C.

If the stack is nonempty we return its topmost value and a `nil` error value. Since Go uses 0-based indexing the first element in a slice or array is at position 0 and the last element is at position `len(sliceOrArray) - 1`.

There is no formality when returning more than one value from a function or method; we simply list the types we are returning after the function or method's name and ensure that we have at least one `return` statement that has a corresponding list of values.

```
func (stack *Stack) Pop() (interface{}, error) {
    theStack := *stack
    if len(theStack) == 0 {
        return nil, errors.New("can't Pop() an empty stack")
    }
    x := theStack[len(theStack)-1]    ❶
    *stack = theStack[:len(theStack)-1]    ❷
    return x, nil
}
```

The `Stack.Pop()` method is used to remove and return the top (last added) item from the stack. Like the `Stack.Top()` method it returns the item and a `nil` error, or if the stack is empty, a `nil` item and a non-`nil` error.

The method must have a receiver that is a pointer since it modifies the stack by removing the returned item. For syntactic convenience, rather than referring to `*stack` (the actual stack that the `stack` variable points to) throughout the method, we assign the actual stack to a local variable (`theStack`), and work with that variable instead. This is quite cheap, because `*stack` is pointing to a `Stack`, which uses a slice for its representation, so we are really assigning little more than a reference to a slice.

If the stack is empty we return a suitable error. Otherwise we retrieve the stack's top (last) item and store it in a local variable (x). Then we take a slice of the stack (which itself is a slice). The new slice has one less element than the original and is immediately set to be the value that the `stack` pointer points to. And at the end, we return the retrieved value and a `nil` error. We can reasonably expect any decent Go compiler to reuse the slice, simply reducing the slice's length by one, while leaving its capacity unchanged, rather than copying all the data to a new slice.

The item to return is retrieved using the [] index operator with a single index (❶); in this case the index of the slice's last element.

The new slice is obtained by using the [] slice operator with an index range (❷). An index range has the form *first:end*. If *first* is omitted—as here—0 is assumed, and if *end* is omitted, the `len()` of the slice is assumed. The slice thus obtained has elements with indexes from and including the *first* up to and *excluding* the *end*. So in this case, by specifying the last index as one less than the length, we slice up to the last but one element, effectively removing the last element from the slice. (Slice indexing is covered in Chapter 4, §4.2.1, ➤ 153.)

In this example we used Stack receivers rather than pointers (i.e., of type *Stack) for those methods that don't modify the Stack. For custom types with lightweight representations (say, a few ints or strings), this is perfectly reasonable. But for heavyweight custom types it is usually best to always use pointer receivers since a pointer is much cheaper to pass (typically a simple 32- or 64-bit value), than a large value, even for methods where the value isn't modified.

A subtle point to note regarding pointers and methods is that if we call a method on a value, and the method requires a pointer to the value it is called on, Go is smart enough to pass the value's address rather than a copy of the value (providing the value is addressable; §6.2.1, ➤ 258). Correspondingly, if we call a method on a pointer to a value, and the method requires a value, Go is smart enough to dereference the pointer and give the method the pointed-to value.*

As this example illustrates, creating custom types in Go is generally straightforward, and doesn't involve the cumbersome formalities that many other languages demand. Go's object-oriented features are covered fully in Chapter 6.

1.6. Americanise—Files, Maps, and Closures

To have any practical use a programming language must provide some means of reading and writing external data. In previous sections we had a glimpse of Go's versatile and powerful print functions from its fmt package; in this section we will look at Go's basic file handling facilities. We will also look at some more advanced features such as Go's treatment of functions and methods as first-class values which makes it possible to pass them as parameters. And in addition we will make use of Go's map type (also known as a data dictionary or hash).

This section provides enough of the basics so that programs that read and write text files can be written—thus making the examples and exercises more interesting. Chapter 8 provides much more coverage of Go's file handling facilities.

By about the middle of the twentieth century, American English surpassed British English as the most widely used form of English. In this section's example we will review a program that reads a text file and writes out a copy of the file into a new file with any words using British spellings replaced with their U.S. counterparts. (This doesn't help with differences in semantics or idioms, of course.) The program is in the file americanise/americanise.go, and we will review it top-down, starting with its imports, then its main() function, then the functions that main() calls, and so on.

---

* This is why Go does not have or need the -> indirection operator used by C and C++.

americanise.go

```go
import (
    "bufio"
    "fmt"
    "io"
    "io/ioutil"
    "log"
    "os"
    "path/filepath"
    "regexp"
    "strings"
)
```

All the `americanise` program's imports are from Go's standard library. Packages can be nested inside one another without formality, as the `io` package's `ioutil` package and the `path` package's `filepath` package illustrate.

The `bufio` package provides functions for buffered I/O, including ones for reading and writing strings from and to UTF-8 encoded text files. The `io` package provides low-level I/O functions—and the `io.Reader` and `io.Writer` interfaces we need for the `americanise()` program. The `io/ioutil` package provides high-level file handling functions. The `regexp` package provides powerful regular expression support. The other packages (`fmt`, `log`, `filepath`, and `strings`) have been mentioned in earlier sections.

```go
func main() {
    inFilename, outFilename, err := filenamesFromCommandLine()  ❶
    if err != nil {                                          33
        fmt.Println(err)  ❷
        os.Exit(1)
    }
    inFile, outFile := os.Stdin, os.Stdout  ❸    // defaults
    if inFilename != "" {
        if inFile, err = os.Open(inFilename); err != nil {
            log.Fatal(err)          returns a ptr to an os.File, ie, *os.File
        }
        defer inFile.Close()  ❹    // When main() returns, inFile.close() is called
    }                                returns a *os.File (creating it if necess.,
    if outFilename != "" {                                 else truncating an existing
        if outFile, err = os.Create(outFilename); err != nil {
            log.Fatal(err)
        }
        defer outFile.Close()  ❺
    }                     35
    if err = americanise(inFile, outFile); err != nil {
        log.Fatal(err)
```

```
        }
    }
}
```

The main() function gets the input and output filenames from the command line, creates corresponding file values, and then passes the files to the americanise() function to do the work.

The function begins by retrieving the names of the files to read and write and an error value. If there was a problem parsing the command line we print the error (which contains the program's usage message), and terminate the program. Some of Go's print functions use reflection (introspection) to print a value using the value's Error() string method if it has one, or its String() string method if it has one, or as best they can otherwise. If we provide our own custom types with one of these methods, Go's print functions will automatically be able to print values of our custom types, as we will see in Chapter 6.

If err is nil, we have inFilename and outFilename strings (which may be empty), and we can continue. Files in Go are represented by pointers to values of type os.File, and so we create two such variables initialized to the standard input and output streams (which are both of type *os.File). Since Go functions and methods can return multiple values it follows that Go supports multiple assignments such as the ones we have used here (30 ◀, ❶, ❸).

Each filename is handled in essentially the same way. If the filename is empty the file has already been correctly set to os.Stdin or os.Stdout (both of which are of type *os.File, i.e., a pointer to an os.File value representing the file); but if the filename is nonempty we create a new *os.File to read from or write to the file as appropriate.

The os.Open() function takes a filename and returns an *os.File value that can be used for reading the file. Correspondingly, the os.Create() function takes a filename and returns an *os.File value that can be used for reading or writing the file, creating the file if it doesn't exist and truncating it to zero length if it does exist. (Go also provides the os.OpenFile() function that can be used to exercise complete control over the mode and permissions used to open a file.)

In fact, the os.Open(), os.Create(), and os.OpenFile() functions return two values: an *os.File and nil if the file was opened successfully, or nil and an error if an error occurred.

If err is nil we know that the file was successfully opened so we immediately execute a defer statement to close the file. Any function that is the subject of a defer statement (§5.5, ➤ 212) must be called—hence the parentheses after the functions' names (30 ◀, ❹, ❺)—but the calls only actually occur when the function in which the defer statements are written returns. So the defer statement "captures" the function call and sets it aside for later. This means that the defer statement itself takes almost no time at all and control immediately passes to the following statement. Thus, the deferred os.File.Close() method won't

actually be called until the enclosing function—in this case, main()—returns
(whether normally or due to a *panic,* discussed in a moment), so the file is open
to be worked on and yet guaranteed to be closed when we are finished with it, or
if a panic occurs.

If we fail to open the file we call log.Fatal() with the error. As we noted in a
previous section, this function logs the date, time, and error (to os.Stderr unless another log destination is specified), and calls os.Exit() to terminate the
program. When os.Exit() is called (directly, or by log.Fatal()), the program is
terminated immediately—and any pending deferred statements are lost. This
is not a problem, though, since Go's runtime system will close any open files, the
garbage collector will release the program's memory, and any decent database
or network that the application might have been talking to will detect the application's demise and respond gracefully. Just the same as with the bigdigits
example, we don't use log.Fatal() in the first if statement (30 ◄, ❷), because the
err contains the program's usage message and we want to print this without the
date and time that the log.Fatal() function normally outputs.

In Go a *panic* is a runtime error (rather like an exception in other languages).
We can cause panics ourselves using the built-in panic() function, and can stop
a panic in its tracks using the recover() function (§5.5, ➤ 212). In theory, Go's
panic/recover functionality can be used to provide a general-purpose exception
handling mechanism—but doing so is considered to be poor Go practice. The
Go way to handle errors is for functions and methods to return an error value
as their sole or last return value—or nil if no error occurred—and for callers to
always check the error they receive. The purpose of panic/recover is to deal with
genuinely exceptional (i.e., unexpected) problems and *not* with normal errors.★

With both files successfully opened (the os.Stdin, os.Stdout, and os.Stderr files
are automatically opened by the Go runtime sytem), we call the americanise()
function to do the processing, passing it the files on which to work. If ameri-
canise() returns nil the main() function terminates normally and any deferred
statements—in this case, ones that close the inFile and outFile if they are not
os.Stdin and os.Stdout—are executed. And if err is not nil, the error is printed,
the program is exited, and Go's runtime system closes any open files.

The americanise() function accepts an io.Reader and an io.Writer, not *os.Files,
but this doesn't matter since the os.File type supports the io.ReadWriter interface (which simply aggregates the io.Reader and io.Writer interfaces) and can
therefore be used wherever an io.Reader or an io.Writer is required. This is
an example of duck typing in action—the americanise() function's parameters
are interfaces, so the function will accept any values—no matter what their
types—that satisfy the interfaces, that is, any values that have the methods the

---

★ Go's approach is very different from C++, Java, and Python, where exception handling is often used
for both errors and exceptions. The discussion and rationale for Go's panic/recover mechanism is at
https://groups.google.com/group/golang-nuts/browse_thread/thread/1ce5cd050bb973e4?pli=1.

interfaces specify. The `americanise()` function returns `nil`, or an `error` if an error occurred.

return triplet

```
func filenamesFromCommandLine() (inFilename, outFilename string,
    err error) {
    if len(os.Args) > 1 && (os.Args[1] == "-h" || os.Args[1] == "--help") {
        err = fmt.Errorf("usage: %s [<]infile.txt [>]outfile.txt",
            filepath.Base(os.Args[0]))          // like Printf
        return "", "", err
    }
    if len(os.Args) > 1 {
        inFilename = os.Args[1]
        if len(os.Args) > 2 {
            outFilename = os.Args[2]
        }
    }
    if inFilename != "" && inFilename == outFilename {
        log.Fatal("won't overwrite the infile")
    }
    return inFilename, outFilename, nil
}
```

The `filenamesFromCommandLine()` function returns two strings and an `error` value—and unlike the functions we have seen so far, here the return values are given variable names, not just types. Return variables are set to their zero values (empty strings and `nil` for `err` in this case) when the function is entered, and keep their zero values unless explicitly assigned to in the body of the function. (We will say a bit more on this topic when we discuss the `americanise()` function, next.)

The function begins by seeing if the user has asked for usage help.* If they have, we create a new `error` value using the `fmt.Errorf()` function with a suitable usage string, and return immediately. As usual with Go code, the caller is expected to check the returned `error` and behave accordingly (and this is exactly what `main()` does). The `fmt.Errorf()` function is like the `fmt.Printf()` function we saw earlier, except that it returns an `error` value containing a string using the given format string and arguments rather than writing a string to `os.Stdout`. (The `errors.New()` function is used to create an `error` given a literal string.)

If the user did not request usage information we check to see if they entered any command-line arguments, and if they did we set the `inFilename` return variable to their first command-line argument and the `outFilename` return variable

---

* The Go standard library includes a `flag` package for handling command-line arguments. Third-party packages for GNU-compatible command-line handling are available from `godashboard.appspot.com/project`. (Using third-party packages is covered in Chapter 9.)

to their second command-line argument. Of course, they may have given no command-line arguments, in which case both inFilename and outFilename remain empty strings; or they may have entered just one, in which case inFilename will have a filename and outFilename will be empty.

At the end we do a simple sanity check to make sure that the user doesn't overwrite the input file with the output file, exiting if necessary—but if all is well, we return.* Functions or methods that return one or more values *must* have at least one return statement. It can be useful for clarity, and for godoc-generated documentation, to give variable names for return types, as we have done in this function. If a function or method has variable names as well as types listed for its return values, then a bare return is legal (i.e., a return statement that does not specify any variables). In such cases, the listed variables' values are returned. We do not use bare returns in this book because they are considered to be poor Go style.

Go takes a consistent approach to reading and writing data that allows us to read and write to files, to buffers (e.g., to slices of bytes or to strings), and to the standard input, output, and error streams—or to our own custom types—so long as they provide the methods necessary to satisfy the reading and writing interfaces.

For a value to be readable it must satisfy the io.Reader interface. This interface specifies a single method with signature, Read([]byte) (int, error). The Read() method reads data from the value it is called on and puts the data read into the given byte slice. It returns the number of bytes read and an error value which will be nil if no error occurred, or io.EOF ("end of file") if no error occurred and the end of the input was reached, or some other non-nil value if an error occurred. Similarly, for a value to be writable it must satisfy the io.Writer interface. This interface specifies a single method with signature, Write([]byte) (int, error). The Write() method writes data from the given byte slice into the value the method was called on, and returns the number of bytes written and an error value (which will be nil if no error occurred).

The io package provides readers and writers but these are unbuffered and operate in terms of raw bytes. The bufio package provides buffered input/output where the input will work on any value that satisfies the io.Reader interface (i.e., provides a suitable Read() method), and the output will work on any value that satisfies the io.Writer interface (i.e., provides a suitable Write() method). The bufio package's readers and writers provide buffering and can work in terms of bytes or strings, and so are ideal for reading and writing UTF-8 encoded text files.

---

* In fact, the user could still overwrite the input file by using redirection—for example,
$ ./americanise infile > infile—but at least we have prevented an obvious accident.

```
var britishAmerican = "british-american.txt"
func americanise(inFile io.Reader, outFile io.Writer) (err error) {
    reader := bufio.NewReader(inFile)
    writer := bufio.NewWriter(outFile)
    defer func() {
        if err == nil {
            err = writer.Flush()
        }
    }()
    var replacer func(string) string               ❶
    if replacer, err = makeReplacerFunction(britishAmerican); err != nil {
        return err
    }
    wordRx := regexp.MustCompile("[A-Za-z]+")
    eof := false
    for !eof {
        var line string                            ❷
        line, err = reader.ReadString('\n')
        if err == io.EOF {
            err = nil   // io.EOF isn't really an error
            eof = true  // this will end the loop at the next iteration
        } else if err != nil {
            return err  // finish immediately for real errors
        }
        line = wordRx.ReplaceAllStringFunc(line, replacer)
        if _, err = writer.WriteString(line); err != nil {    ❸
            return err
        }
    }
    return nil
}
```

Handwritten annotations: these are if's; named return value; @ 46; // anonymous deferred function; name of file w/ lines: orig-word u replacement; 38; // loop to read lines from a file; // up to and including '\n'; 37; @ 37; the compiled re; func that takes a string and returns a string.

The americanise() function buffers the inFile reader and the outFile writer. Then it reads lines from the buffered reader and writes each line to the buffered writer, having replaced any British English words with their U.S. equivalents.

The function begins by creating a buffered reader and a buffered writer through which their contents can be accessed as bytes—or more conveniently in this case, as strings. The bufio.NewReader() construction function takes as argument any value that satisfies the io.Reader interface (i.e., any value that has a suitable Read() method) and returns a new buffered io.Reader that reads from the given reader. The bufio.NewWriter() function is synonymous. Notice that the americanise() function doesn't know or care what it is reading from or writing to—the reader and writer could be compressed files, network connections, byte slices

([]byte), or anything else that supports the io.Reader and io.Writer interfaces. This way of working with interfaces is very flexible and makes it easy to compose functionality in Go.

Next we create an anonymous deferred function that will flush the writer's buffer before the americanise() function returns control to its caller. The anonymous function will be called when americanise() returns normally—or abnormally due to a panic. If no error has occurred and the writer's buffer contains unwritten bytes, the bytes will be written before americanise() returns. Since it is possible that the flush will fail we set the err return value to the result of the writer.Flush() call. A less defensive approach would be to have a much simpler defer statement of defer writer.Flush() to ensure that the writer is flushed before the function returns and ignoring any error that might have occurred before the flush—or that occurs during the flush.

Go allows the use of named return values, and we have taken advantage of this facility here (err error), just as we did previously in the filenamesFromCommand-Line() function. Be aware, however, that there is a subtle scoping issue we must consider when using named return values. For example, if we have a named return value of *value*, we can assign to it anywhere in the function using the assignment operator (=) as we'd expect. However, if we have a statement such as if *value* := ..., because the if statement starts a new block, the *value* in the if statement will be a new variable, so the if statement's *value* variable will shadow the return *value* variable. In the americanise() function, err is a named return value, so we have made sure that we never assign to it using the short variable declaration operator (:=) to avoid the risk of accidentally creating a shadow variable. One consequence of this is that we must declare the other variables we want to assign to at the same time, such as the replacer function (35 ◄, ❶) and the line we read in (35 ◄, ❷). An alternative approach is to avoid named return values and return the required value or values explicitly, as we have done elsewhere.

One other small point to note is that we have used the *blank identifier,* _ (35 ◄, ❸). The blank identifier serves as a placeholder for where a variable is expected in an assignment, and discards any value it is given. The blank identifier is not considered to be a new variable, so if used with :=, at least one other (new) variable must be assigned to.

The Go standard library contains a powerful regular expression package called regexp (§3.6.5, ➤ 120). This package can be used to create pointers to regexp.Regexp values (i.e., of type *regexp.Regexp). These values provide many methods for searching and replacing. Here we have chosen to use the regexp.Regexp.ReplaceAllStringFunc() method which given a string and a "replacer" function with signature func(string) string, calls the replacer function for every match, passing in the matched text, and replacing the matched text with the text the replacer function returns.

If we had a very small replacer function, say, one that simply uppercased the words it matched, we could have created it as an anonymous function when we called the replacement function. For example:

```
line = wordRx.ReplaceAllStringFunc(line,
    func(word string) string { return strings.ToUpper(word) })
```

However, the americanise program's replacer function, although only a few lines long, requires some preparation, so we have created another function, makeRe-placerFunction(), that given the name of a file that contains lines of original and replacement words, returns a replacer function that will perform the appropriate replacements.

If the makeReplacerFunction() returns a non-nil error, we return and the caller is expected to check the returned error and respond appropriately (as it does).

Regular expressions can be compiled using the regexp.Compile() function which returns a *regexp.Regexp and nil, or nil and error if the regular expression is invalid. This is ideal for when the regular expression is read from an external source such as a file or received from the user. Here, though, we have used the regexp.MustCompile() function—this simply returns a *regexp.Regexp, or panics if the regular expression, or "regexp", is invalid. The regular expression used in the example matches the longest possible sequence of one or more English alphabetic characters.

With the replacer function and the regular expression in place we start an infinite loop that begins by reading a line from the reader. The bufio.Reader.Read-String() method reads (or, strictly speaking, *decodes*) the underlying reader's raw bytes as UTF-8 encoded text (which also works for 7-bit ASCII) up to and including the specified byte (or up to the end of the file). The function conveniently returns the text as a string, along with an error (or nil).

If the error returned by the call to the bufio.Reader.ReadString() method is not nil, either we have reached the end of the input or we have hit a problem. At the end of the input err will be io.EOF which is perfectly okay, so in this case we set err to nil (since there isn't really an error), and set eof to true to ensure that the loop finishes at the next iteration, so we won't attempt to read beyond the end of the file. We don't return immediately when we get io.EOF, since it is possible that the file's last line doesn't end with a newline, in which case we will have received a line to be processed, in addition to the io.EOF error.

For each line we call the regexp.Regexp.ReplaceAllStringFunc() method, giving it the line and the replacer function. We then try to write the (possibly modified) line to the writer using the bufio.Writer.WriteString() method—this method accepts a string and writes it out as a sequence of UTF-8 encoded bytes, returning the number of bytes written and an error (which will be nil if no error occurred). We don't care how many bytes are written so we assign the number to the blank identifier, _. If err is not nil we return immediately, and the caller will receive the error.

Using bufio's reader and writer as we have done here means that we can work with convenient high level string values, completely insulated from the raw bytes which represent the text on disk. And, of course, thanks to our deferred anonymous function, we know that any buffered bytes are written to the writer when the americanise() function returns, providing that no error has occurred.

← name of file   *return pair*

```go
func makeReplacerFunction(file string) (func(string) string, error) {
    rawBytes, err := ioutil.ReadFile(file)
    if err != nil {
        return nil, err     // caller: 35
    }
    text := string(rawBytes)    // convert rawBytes (form: [] byte) to string

    usForBritish := make(map[string]string)
    lines := strings.Split(text, "\n")   // 109: lines is [] string
    for _, line := range lines {
        fields := strings.Fields(line)   // 108: fields is [] string
        if len(fields) == 2 {
            usForBritish[fields[0]] = fields[1]
        }
    }

    return func(word string) string {
        if usWord, found := usForBritish[word]; found {
            return usWord   // boolean: if true head usForBritish[word] == usWord
        }
        return word
    }, nil
}
```

The makeReplacerFunction() takes the name of a file containing original and replacement strings and returns a function that given an original string returns its replacement, along with an error value. It expects the file to be a UTF-8 encoded text file with one whitespace-separated original and replacement word per line.

In addition to the bufio package's readers and writers, Go's io/ioutil package provides some high level convenience functions including the ioutil.ReadFile() function used here. This function reads and returns the entire file's contents as raw bytes (in a []byte) and an error. As usual, if the error is not nil we immediately return it to the caller—along with a nil replacer function. If we read the bytes okay, we convert them to a string using a Go conversion of form *type(variable)*. Converting UTF-8 bytes to a string is very cheap since Go's strings use the UTF-8 encoding internally. (Go's string conversions are covered in Chapter 3.)

The replacer function we want to create must accept a string and return a corresponding string, so what we need is a function that uses some kind of lookup table. Go's built-in map collection data type is ideal for this purpose (§4.3, ➤ 164). A map holds *key–value* pairs with very fast lookup by *key*. So here we will store British words as keys and their U.S. counterparts as values.

Go's map, slice, and channel types are created using the built-in make() function. This creates a value of the specified type and returns a reference to it. The reference can be passed around (e.g., to other functions) and any changes made to the referred-to value are visible to all the code that accesses it. Here we have created an empty map called usForBritish, with string keys and string values.

With the map in place we then split the file's text (which is in the form of a single long string) into lines, using the strings.Split() function. This function takes a string to split and a separator string to split on and does as many splits as possible. (If we want to limit the number of splits we can use the strings.SplitN() function.)

The iteration over the lines uses a for loop syntax that we haven't seen before, this time using a range clause. This form can be conveniently used to iterate over a map's keys and values, over a communication channel's elements, or—as here—over a slice's (or array's) elements. When used on a slice (or array), the slice index and the element at that index are returned on each iteration, starting at index 0 (if the slice is nonempty). In this example we use the loop to iterate over all the lines, but since we don't care about the index of each line we assign it to the blank identifier (_) which discards it.

We need to split each line into two: the original string and the replacement string. We could use the strings.Split() function but that would require us to specify an exact separator string, say, " ", which might fail on a hand-edited file where sometimes users accidentally put in more than one space, or sometimes use tabs. Fortunately, Go provides the strings.Fields() function which splits the string it is given on whitespace and is therefore much more forgiving of human-edited text.

If the fields variable (of type []string) has exactly two elements we insert the corresponding *key–value* pair into the map. Once the map is populated we are ready to create the replacer function that we will return to the caller.

We create the replacer function as an anonymous function given as an argument to the return statement—along with a nil error value. (Of course, we could have been less succinct and assigned the anonymous function to a variable and returned the variable.) The function has the exact signature required by the regexp.Regexp.ReplaceAllStringFunc() method that it will be passed to.

Inside the anonymous replacer function all we do is look up the given word. If we access a map element with one variable on the left-hand side, that variable is set to the corresponding value—or to the value type's zero value if the given key isn't in the map. If the map value type's zero value is a legitimate value, then how can we tell if a given key is in the map? Go provides a syntax for this case—and that is generally useful if we simply want to know whether a particular key is in the map—which is to put two variables on the left-hand side, the first to accept the value and the second to accept a bool indicating if the key was found. In this example we use this second form inside an if statement that has a simple statement (a short variable declaration), and a condition (the found Boolean). So we retrieve the usWord (which will be an empty string if the given word isn't a key in the map), and a found flag of type bool. If the British word was found we return the U.S. equivalent; otherwise we simply return the original word unchanged.

There is a subtlety in the makeReplacerFunction() function that may not be immediately apparent. In the anonymous function created inside it we access the usForBritish map, yet this map was created outside the anonymous function. This works because Go supports *closures* (§5.6.3, ➤ 225). A closure is a function that "captures" some external state—for example, the state of the function it is created inside, or at least any part of that state that the closure accesses. So here, the anonymous function that is created inside the makeReplacerFunction() is a closure that has captured the usForBritish map.

Another subtlety is that the usForBritish map is a local variable and yet we will be accessing it outside the function in which it is declared. It is perfectly fine to return local variables in Go. Even if they are references or pointers, Go won't delete them while they are in use and will garbage-collect them when they are finished with (i.e., when every variable that holds, refers, or points to them has gone out of scope).

This section has shown some basic low-level and high-level file handling functionality using os.Open(), os.Create(), and ioutil.ReadFile(). In Chapter 8 there is much more file handling coverage, including the writing and reading of text, binary, JSON, and XML files. Go's built-in collection types—slices and maps—largely obviate the need for custom collection types while providing extremely good performance and great convenience. Go's collection types are covered in Chapter 4. Go's treatment of functions as first-class values in their own right and its suppport for closures makes it possible to use some advanced and very useful programming idioms. And Go's defer statement makes it straightforward to avoid resource leakage.

1.7. Polar to Cartesian—Concurrency

One key aspect of the Go language is its ability to take advantage of modern computers with multiple processors and multiple cores, and to do so without burdening programmers with lots of bookkeeping. Many concurrent Go programs can be written without any explicit locking at all (although Go does have locking primitives for when they're needed in lower-level code, as we will see in Chapter 7).

Two features make concurrent programming in Go a pleasure. First, *goroutines* ✗ (in effect very lightweight threads/coroutines) can easily be created at will without the need to subclass some "thread" class (which isn't possible in Go anyway). Second, *channels* provide type-safe one-way or two-way communication with goroutines and which can be used to synchronize goroutines.

The Go way to do concurrency is to *communicate data, not to share data*. This makes it much easier to write concurrent programs than using the traditional threads and locks approach, since with no shared data we can't get race conditions (such as deadlocks), and we don't have to remember to lock or unlock since there is no shared data to protect.

In this section we will look at the fifth and last of the chapter's "overview" examples. This section's example program uses two communication channels and does its processing in a separate Go routine. For such a small program this is complete overkill, but the point is to illustrate a basic use of these Go features in as clear and short a way as possible. More realistic concurrency examples that show many of the different techniques that can be used with Go's channels and goroutines are presented in Chapter 7.

The program we will review is called polar2cartesian; it is an interactive console program that prompts the user to enter two whitespace-separated numbers—a radius and an angle—which the program then uses to compute the equivalent cartesian coordinates. In addition to illustrating one particular approach to concurrency, it also shows some simple structs and how to determine if the program is running on a Unix-like system or on Windows for when the difference matters. Here is an example of the program running in a Linux console:

```
$ ./polar2cartesian
Enter a radius and an angle (in degrees), e.g., 12.5 90, or Ctrl+D to quit.
Radius and angle: 5 30.5
Polar radius=5.00 θ=30.50° → Cartesian x=4.31 y=2.54
Radius and angle: 5 -30.25
Polar radius=5.00 θ=-30.25° → Cartesian x=4.32 y=-2.52
Radius and angle: 1.0 90
Polar radius=1.00 θ=90.00° → Cartesian x=-0.00 y=1.00
Radius and angle: ^D
$
```

The program is in file polar2cartesian/polar2cartesian.go, and we will review it top-down, starting with the imports, then the structs it uses, then its init() function, then its main() function, and then the functions called by main(), and so on.

```
import (
    "bufio"
    "fmt"
    "math"
    "os"
    "runtime"
)
```

The polar2cartesian program imports several packages, some of which have been mentioned in earlier sections, so we will only mention the new ones here. The math package provides mathematical functions for operating on floating-point numbers (§2.3.2, ➤ 64) and the runtime package provides functions that access the program's runtime properties, such as which platform the program is running on.

```
type polar struct {
    radius float64
    θ        float64
}

type cartesian struct {
    x    float64
    y    float64
}
```

In Go a struct is a type that holds (aggregates or embeds) one or more data fields. These fields can be built-in types as here (float64), or structs, or interfaces, or any combination of these. (An interface data field is in effect a pointer to an item—of any kind—that satisfies the interface, i.e., that has the methods the interface specifies.)

It seems natural to use the Greek lowercase letter theta (θ) to represent the polar coordinate's angle, and thanks to Go's use of UTF-8 we are free to do so. This is because Go allows us to use any Unicode letters in our identifiers, not just English letters.

Although the two structs happen to have the same data field types they are distinct types and no automatic conversion between them is possible. This supports defensive programming; after all, it wouldn't make sense to simply substitute a cartesian's positional coordinates for polar coordinates. In some cases such conversions do make sense, in which case we can easily create a conversion method (i.e., a method of one type that returned a value of another type) that made use of Go's composite literal syntax to create a value of the target type populated by the fields from the source type. (Numeric data type conversions are covered in Chapter 2; string conversions are covered in Chapter 3.)

```
var prompt = "Enter a radius and an angle (in degrees), e.g., 12.5 90, " +
    "or %s to quit."
func init() {
    if runtime.GOOS == "windows" {
        prompt = fmt.Sprintf(prompt, "Ctrl+Z, Enter")
    } else { // Unix-like
        prompt = fmt.Sprintf(prompt, "Ctrl+D")
    }
}
```

If a package has one or more init() functions they are automatically executed
before the main package's main() function is called. (In fact, init() functions must
never be called explicitly.) So when our polar2cartesian program is invoked
this init() function is the first function that is called. We use init() to set the
prompt to account for platform differences in how end of file is signified—for
example, on Windows end of file is given by pressing Ctrl+Z then Enter. Go's runtime package provides the GOOS (Go Operating System) constant which is a string
identifying the operating system the program is running on. Typical values are
darwin (Mac OS X), freebsd, linux, and windows.

Before diving into the main() function and the rest of the program we will
briefly discuss channels and show some toy examples before seeing them in
proper use.

Channels are modeled on Unix pipes and provide two-way (or at our option,
one-way) communication of data items. Channels behave like FIFO (first in,
first out) queues, hence they preserve the order of the items that are sent into
them. Items cannot be dropped from a channel, but we are free to ignore any or
all of the items we receive. Let's look at a very simple example. First we will
make a channel:

```
messages := make(chan string, 10)
```

Channels are created with the make() function (Chapter 7) and are declared using the syntax, chan *Type*. Here we have created the messages channel to send and
receive strings. The second argument to make() is the buffer size (which defaults
to 0); here we have made it big enough to accept ten strings. If a channel's buffer
is filled it blocks until at least one item is received from it. This means that any
number of items can pass through a channel, providing the items are retrieved
to make room for subsequent items. A channel with a buffer size of 0 can only
send an item if the other end is waiting for an item. (It is also possible to get
the effect of nonblocking channels using Go's select statement, as we will see in
Chapter 7.)

Now we will send a couple of strings into the channel:

```
LHOp              RHOp          binary
messages <- "Leader"
messages <- "Follower"
```

＊ When the <- communication operator is used as a binary operator its left-hand
operand must be a channel and its right-hand operand must be a value to send
to the channel of the type the channel was declared with. Here, we first send the
string Leader to the messages channel, and then we send the string Follower.

```
         RHOp         unary
message1 := <-messages
message2 := <-messages
```

＊ When the <- communication operator is used as a unary operator with just a
right-hand operand (which must be a channel), it acts as a receiver, blocking
until it has a value to return. Here, we retrieve two messages from the messages
channel. The message1 variable is assigned the string Leader and the message2
variable is assigned the string Follower; both variables are of type string.

＊ Normally channels are created to provide communication between goroutines.
Channel sends and receives don't need locks, and the channel blocking behavior
can be used to achieve synchronization.

Now that we have seen some channel basics, let's see channels—and goroutines
—in practical use.

```
func main() {
                              type
    questions := make(chan polar)    // default: buffer size ∅
    defer close(questions)
    answers := createSolver(questions)   // 45  returns a channel
    defer close(answers)
    interact(questions, answers)
}
```

Once any init() functions have returned, Go's runtime system then calls the
main package's main() function.

Here, the main() function begins by creating a channel (of type chan polar) for
passing polar structs, and assigns it to the questions variable. Once the channel
has been created we use a defer statement to call the built-in close() function
＊ (▶ 187) to ensure that it is closed when it is no longer needed. Next we call the
createSolver() function, passing it the questions channel and receiving from it
an answers channel (of type chan cartesian). We use another defer statement to
ensure that the answers channel is closed when it is finished with. And finally,
we call the interact() function with the two channels, and in which the user
interaction takes place.

```
func createSolver(questions chan polar) chan cartesian {
    answers := make(chan cartesian)
    go func() {        // anon func
        for {               - polar struct
            polarCoord := <-questions    ❶    // retrieve polar struct from questions channel
            θ := polarCoord.θ * math.Pi / 180.0 // degrees to radians
            x := polarCoord.radius * math.Cos(θ)    // create cartesian struct and...
            y := polarCoord.radius * math.Sin(θ)
            answers <- cartesian{x, y}    ❷    // ... put it into the answers channel
        }
    }()        // anon. function is defined then invoked
    return answers
}
```

The createSolver() function begins by creating an answers channel to which it will send the answers (i.e., cartesian coordinates) to the questions (i.e., polar coordinates) that it receives from the questions channel.

After creating the channel, the function then has a go statement. A go statement is given a function call (syntactically just like a defer statement), which is executed in a separate asynchronous goroutine. This means that the flow of control in the current function (i.e., in the main goroutine) continues immediately from the following statement. In this case the go statement is followed by a return statement that returns the answers channel to the caller. As we noted earlier, it is perfectly safe and good practice in Go to return local variables, since Go handles the chore of memory management for us.

In this case we have (created and) called an anonymous function in the go statement. The function has an infinite loop that waits (blocking its own goroutine, but not any other goroutines, and not the function in which the goroutine was started), until it receives a question—in this case a polar struct on the questions channel. When a polar coordinate arrives the anonymous function computes the corresponding cartesian coordinate using some simple math (and using the standard library's math package), and then sends the answer as a cartesian struct (created using Go's composite literal syntax), to the answers channel.

In ❶ the <- operator is used as a unary operator, retrieving a polar coordinate from the questions channel. And in ❷ the <- operator is used as a binary operator; its left-hand operand being the answers channel to send to, and its right-hand operand being the cartesian to send.

Once the call to createSolver() returns we have reached the point where we have two communication channels set up and where a separate goroutine is waiting for polar coordinates to be sent on the questions channel—and without any other goroutine, including the one executing main(), being blocked.

$$1 = \frac{\pi \ rad}{180°}$$

$$y \ rad = x° * \frac{\pi \ rad}{180°}$$

```
const result = "Polar radius=%.02f θ=%.02f° → Cartesian x=%.02f y=%.02f\n"
func interact(questions chan polar, answers chan cartesian) {
    reader := bufio.NewReader(os.Stdin)
    fmt.Println(prompt)    // 43
    for {
        fmt.Printf("Radius and angle: ")
        line, err := reader.ReadString('\n')
        if err != nil {
            break
        }
        var radius, θ float64
        if _, err := fmt.Sscanf(line, "%f %f", &radius, &θ); err != nil {
            fmt.Fprintln(os.Stderr, "invalid input")
            continue
        }
        questions <- polar{radius, θ}    // composite literal rep of a polar val
        coord := <-answers
        fmt.Printf(result, radius, θ, coord.x, coord.y)
    }
    fmt.Println()
}
```

This function is called with both channels passed as parameters. It begins by creating a buffered reader for os.Stdin since we want to interact with the user in the console. It then prints the prompt that tells the user what to enter and how to quit. We could have made the program terminate if the user simply pressed Enter (i.e., didn't type in any numbers), rather than asking them to enter end of file. However, by requiring the use of end of file we have made polar2cartesian more flexible, since it is also able to read its input from an arbitrary external file using file redirection (providing only that the file has two whitespace-separated numbers per line).

The function then starts an infinite loop which begins by prompting the user to enter a polar coordinate (a radius and an angle). After asking for the user's input the function waits for the user to type some text and press Enter, or to press Ctrl+D (or Ctrl+Z, Enter on Windows) to signify that they have finished. We don't bother checking the error value; if it isn't nil we break out of the loop and return to the caller (main()), which in turn will return (and call its deferred statements to close the communication channels).

We create two float64s to hold the numbers the user has entered and then use Go's fmt.Sscanf() function to parse the line. This function takes a string to parse, a format—in this case two whitespace-separated floating-point numbers—and one or more pointers to variables to populate. (The & address of operator is used to get a pointer to a value; see §4.1, ➤ 140.) The function returns the number of items it successfully parsed and an error (or nil). In the case of an error, we print an error message to os.Stderr—this is to make the error message visible on the console even if the program's os.Stdout is redirected to a file. Go's powerful and flexible scan functions are shown in use in Chapter 8 (§8.1.3.2, ➤ 380), and listed in Table 8.2 (➤ 383).

If valid numbers were input and sent to the questions channel (in a polar struct), we block the main goroutine waiting for a response on the answers channel. The additional goroutine created in the createSolver() function is itself blocked waiting for a polar on the questions channel, so when we send the polar, the additional goroutine performs the computation, sends the resultant cartesian to the answers channel, and then waits (blocking only itself) for another question to arrive. Once the cartesian answer is received in the interact() function on the answers channel, interact() is no longer blocked. At this point we print the result string using the fmt.Printf() function, and passing the polar and cartesian values as the arguments that the result string's % placeholders are expecting. The relationship between the goroutines and the channels is illustrated in Figure 1.1.

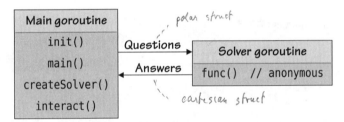

Figure 1.1 *Two communicating goroutines*

The interact() function's for loop is an infinite loop, so as soon as a result is printed the user is once again asked to enter a radius and angle, with the loop being broken out of only if the reader reads end of file—either interactively from the user or because the end of a redirected input file has been reached.

The calculations in polar2cartesian are very lightweight, so there was no real need to do them in a separate goroutine. However, a similar program that needed to do multiple independent heavyweight calculations as the result of each input might well benefit from using the approach shown here, for example, with one goroutine per calculation. We will see more realistic use cases for channels and goroutines in Chapter 7. 315

We have now completed our overview of the Go language as illustrated by the five example programs reviewed in this chapter. Naturally, Go has much more to offer than there has been space to show here, as we will see in the subsequent chapters, each of which focuses on a specific aspect of the language and any relevant packages from the standard library. This chapter concludes with a small exercise, which despite its size, requires some thought and care.

1.8. Exercise

Copy the `bigdigits` directory to, say, `my_bigdigits`, and modify `my_bigdigits/bigdigits.go` to produce a version of the `bigdigits` program (§1.4, 16 ◀) that can optionally output the number with an overbar and underbar of "*"s, and with improved command-line argument handling.

The original program output its usage message if no number was given; change this so that the usage message is also output if the user gives an argument of -h or --help. For example:

```
$ ./bigdigits --help
usage: bigdigits [-b|--bar] <whole-number>
-b --bar  draw an underbar and an overbar
```

If the --bar (or -b) option is *not* present the program should have the same behavior as before. Here is an example of the expected output if the option *is* present:

```
$ ./bigdigits --bar 8467243
****************************************************
 888     4     666   77777  222     4     333
8   8    44   6          7  2   2    44   3   3
8   8   4 4   6          7      2   4 4       3
 888    4 4   6666       7      2   4 4      33
8   8  444444 6   6  7      2       444444    3
8   8    4    6   6  7      2           4   3   3
 888     4     666  7        22222     4     333
****************************************************
```

The solution requires more elaborate command-line processing than the version shown in the text, although the code producing the output only needs a small change to output the overbar before the first row and the underbar after the last row. Overall, the solution needs about 20 extra lines of code—the solution's `main()` function is twice as long as the original (~40 vs. ~20 lines), mostly due to the code needed to handle the command line. A solution is provided in the file `bigdigits_ans/bigdigits.go`.

Hints: The solution also has a subtle difference in the way it builds up each row's line to prevent the bars extending too far. Also, the solution imports the `strings` package and uses the `strings.Repeat(string, int)` function. This function returns a string that contains the `string` it is given as its first argument repeated by the number of times of the `int` given as its second argument. Why not look this function up either locally (see the sidebar "The Go Documentation", 8 ◀), or at `golang.org/pkg/strings`, and start to become familiar with the Go standard library's documentation.

It would be much easier to handle command-line arguments using a package designed for the purpose. Go's standard library includes a rather basic command line parsing package, flag, that supports X11-style options (e.g., -option). In addition, several option parsers that support GNU-style short and long options (e.g., -o and --option) are available from godashboard.appspot.com/project.

2 Booleans and Numbers

This is the first of four chapters on procedural programming that lay down the foundations for Go programming—whether procedural, object-oriented, concurrent, or any combination of these approaches.

This chapter covers Go's built-in Boolean type and all of Go's built-in numeric types, and briefly introduces two of the numeric types from Go's standard library. Apart from the need to explicitly convert between different types of numbers and the convenience of having a built-in complex type, programmers coming from C, C++, and Java should find few surprises in this chapter.

This chapter's first section covers some of the language's basics, such as how comments are written, Go's keywords and operators, what constitutes a valid identifier, and so on. Once these preliminaries have been covered, there are sections on Booleans, integers, and floating-point numbers, the latter including coverage of complex numbers.

2.1. Preliminaries

Go supports two kinds of comments, both adopted from C++. Line comments begin with // and end at the newline; these are treated simply as a newline. General comments begin with /* and end with */ and may span multiple lines. When a general comment is all on one line (e.g., /* inline comment */), it is treated as a space, and when a general comment spans one or more lines it it treated as a newline. (Newlines are significant in Go, as we will see in Chapter 5.)

A Go identifier is a nonempty sequence of letters and digits where the first character must be a letter, and which is not the name of a keyword. A letter is the underscore, _, or any character that is in the Unicode categories, "Lu" (letter, uppercase), "Ll" (letter, lowercase), "Lt" (letter, titlecase), "Lm" (letter, modifier), or "Lo" (letter, other); this includes all the English alphabetic characters (A–Z and a–z). A digit is any character in the Unicode category "Nd" (number, decimal digit); this includes the Arabic digits (0–9). The compiler will prevent the use of an identifier that has the same name as a keyword; see Table 2.1.

Table 2.1 *Go's Keywords*

break	default	func	interface	select
case	defer	go	map	struct
chan	else	goto	package	switch
const	fallthrough	if	range	type
continue	for	import	return	var

Go has many predefined identifiers; it is possible—but rarely wise—to create an identifier with the same name as a predefined identifier; see Table 2.2.

Table 2.2 *Go's Predefined Identifiers*

append 156	copy	int8	nil	true
bool	delete	int16	panic	uint
byte	error	int32	print	uint8
cap	false	int64	println	uint16
close	float32	iota 54	real	uint32
complex	float64	len	recover	uint64
complex64	imag	make	rune	uintptr
complex128	int	new	string	

Identifiers are case-sensitive, so for example, LINECOUNT, Linecount, LineCount, lineCount, and linecount are five different identifiers. Identifiers that begin with a capital letter, that is, with a character in Unicode category "Lu" (including A–Z), are considered to be public—*exported* in Go terminology—while all others are considered to be private—*unexported* in Go terminology. (This rule does not apply to package names which are conventionally all lowercase.) We will see this distinction in action when we discuss object-oriented programming in Chapter 6, and packages in Chapter 9.

The blank identifier, _, serves as a placeholder for where a variable is expected in an assignment, and discards any value it is given. The blank identifier is not considered to be a new variable, so if it is used with the := operator, at least one other (new) variable must be assigned to. It is legitimate to discard some or all of a function's return values by assigning them to the blank identifier. However, if no return values are wanted it is more conventional to simply ignore them. Here are some examples:

```
count, err = fmt.Println(x)    // get number of bytes printed and error
count, _ = fmt.Println(x)      // get number of bytes printed; discard error
_, err = fmt.Println(x)        // discard number of bytes printed; get error
fmt.Println(x)                 // ignore return values
```

It is not uncommon to ignore the return values when printing to the console, but the error value should always be checked when printing to files, network connections, and so on—for example, using fmt.Fprint() and similar functions. (Go's print functions are fully covered later; §3.5, ➤ 93.)

2.1.1. Constants and Variables

Constants are declared using the const keyword; variables can be declared using the var keyword, or using the short variable declaration syntax. Go can infer the type of the declared type, although it is legal to specify it if we wish to or need to—for example, to specify a type that is different from the type Go would normally infer. Here are some example declarations:

```
const limit = 512          // constant; type-compatible with any number
const top uint16 = 1421    // constant; type: uint16
start := -19               // variable; inferred type: int
end := int64(9876543210)   // variable; type: int64        val : 9876543210
var i int                  // variable; value 0; type: int
var debug = false          // variable; inferred type: bool
checkResults := true       // variable; inferred type: bool
stepSize := 1.5            // variable; inferred type: float64
acronym := "FOSS"          // variable; inferred type: string
```

For integer literals Go infers type int, for floating-point literals Go infers type float64, and for complex literals Go infers type complex128 (the numbers in their names refer to how many bits they occupy). The normal practice is to leave types unspecified unless we want to use a specific type that Go won't infer; we will discuss this further in §2.3, ➤ 57. Typed numeric constants (e.g., top) can only be used in expressions with other numbers of the same type (unless converted). Untyped numeric constants can be used in expressions with numbers of any built-in type, (e.g., limit can be used in an expression with integers or in one with floating-point numbers).

The variable i was not given any explicit value. This is perfectly safe in Go since Go *always* assigns variables their type's zero value if no other value is specified.

This means that every numeric variable is guaranteed to be zero and every string to be empty—unless we specify otherwise. This ensures that Go programs don't suffer from the problems of uninitialized garbage values that afflict some other languages.

2.1.1.1. Enumerations

Rather than repeat the const keyword when we want to set multiple constants, we can group together several constant declarations using the const keyword just once. (We used the same grouping syntax when importing packages in Chapter 1; the syntax can also be used to group variables declared with var.) For those cases where we just want constants to have distinct values and don't really care what those values are, we can use Go's somewhat bare-bones enumeration support.

```
const Cyan = 0        const (              const (
const Magenta = 1       Cyan    = 0          Cyan     = iota // 0
const Yellow = 2        Magenta = 1          Magenta          // 1
                        Yellow  = 2          Yellow           // 2
                      )                    )
```

These three code snippets all achieve exactly the same thing. The way a group of consts works is that the first one is set to its zero value unless explicitly set (either to a value or to iota), and the second and subsequent ones are set to their predecessor's value—or to iota if their predecessor's value is iota. And each subsequent iota value is one more than the previous one.

More formally, the iota predefined identifier represents *successive* untyped integer constants. Its value is reset to zero whenever the keyword const occurs (so every time a new const group is defined), and increments by one for each constant declaration. So in the right-hand code snippet *all* the constants are set to iota (implicitly for the Magenta and Yellow ones). And since Cyan immediately follows a const, iota is reset to 0 which become's Cyan's value; Magenta's value is also iota but at this point iota's value is 1. Similarly, Yellow's value is iota whose value is now 2. And if we added Black at the end (but within the const group) it would be implicitly set to iota whose value at that point would be 3.

On the other hand, if the right-hand code snippet *didn't* have iota, Cyan would be set to 0 and Magenta would be set to Cyan's value and Yellow would be set to Magenta's value—so they would all end up being set to 0. Similarly, if Cyan was set to 9, then they would all be set to 9; or if Magenta was set to 5, Cyan would be set to 0 (first in the group and not assigned an explicit value or iota), Magenta would be 5 (explicitly set), and Yellow would be 5 (the previous constant's value).

It is also possible to use iota with floating-point numbers, simple expressions, and custom types.

```
type BitFlag int
const (
    Active  BitFlag = 1 << iota      // 1 << 0 == 1     iota is 0
    Send    // Implicitly BitFlag = 1 << iota    // 1 << 1 == 2   iota is 1
    Receive // Implicitly BitFlag = 1 << iota    // 1 << 2 == 4   iota is 2
)
flag := Active | Send          // flag is a BitFlag
```

In this snippet we have created three bit flags of custom type `BitFlag` and then
set variable `flag` (of type `BitFlag`) to the bitwise OR of two of them (so `flag` has
value 3; Go's bitwise flags are shown in Table 2.6, ➤ 60). We could have omitted
the custom type in which case Go would have made the constants untyped
integers and inferred `flag`'s type as `int`. Variables of type `BitFlag` can have any
`int` value; nonetheless `BitFlag` is a distinct type so can only be used in operations
with `int`s if converted to an `int` (or if the `int`s are converted to `BitFlag`s).

The `BitFlag` type is useful as it stands, but it isn't very convenient for debugging.
If we were to print `flag` we would just get 3 with no indication of what that
means. Go makes it really easy to control how values of custom types are printed, because the `fmt` package's print functions will use a type's `String()` method   ✳
if it has one. So to make our `BitFlag` type print in a more informative way, we
can simply add a suitable `String()` method to it. (Custom types and methods are
covered fully in Chapter 6.)

```
func (flag BitFlag) String() string {        // method on BitFlag
    var flags []string
    if flag&Active == Active {
        flags = append(flags, "Active")
    }
    if flag&Send == Send {
        flags = append(flags, "Send")
    }
    if flag&Receive == Receive {
        flags = append(flags, "Receive")
    }
    if len(flags) > 0 { // int(flag) is vital to avoid infinite recursion!    S
        return fmt.Sprintf("%d(%s)", int(flag), strings.Join(flags, "|"))
    }
    return "0()"        // when no BitFlag is set
}
```

This method builds up a (possibly empty) slice of strings for those bit fields that
are set and then prints the bit field's value as a decimal `int` and with the strings
to indicate its value. (We could easily have printed the value as a binary number
by replacing the `%d` format specifier with `%b`.) As the comment notes, it is essen-

tial that we convert the flag (of type BitFlag) to its underlying int type when passing it to the fmt.Sprintf() function, otherwise the BitFlag.String() method will be called recursively on the flag which will take us into an infinite recursion. (The built-in append() function is covered in §4.2.3, ➤ 156; the fmt.Sprintf() and strings.Join() functions are covered in Chapter 3.)

```
Println(BitFlag(0), Active, Send, flag, Receive, flag|Receive)
0() 1(Active) 2(Send) 3(Active|Send) 4(Receive) 7(Active|Send|Receive)
```

This snippet shows how BitFlags with the String() method in place look when printed—clearly, this is much more useful for debugging than bare integers.

It is, of course, possible to create a custom type that represents a restricted range of integers, and to create a more elaborate custom enumeration type; we cover custom types more fully in Chapter 6. Go's minimalist approach to enumerations is typical of the Go philosophy: Go aims to provide everything that programmers need—including many powerful and convenient features—while keeping the language as small, consistent, and fast (to build and run) as possible.

2.2. Boolean Values and Expressions

Go provides two built-in Boolean values, true and false, both of type bool. Go supports the standard logical and comparison operators, all of which produce a bool result; they are shown in Table 2.3.

Boolean values and expressions are used in if statements (§5.2.1, ➤ 192), in the conditions of for statements (§5.3, ➤ 203), and sometimes in the conditions of switch statements' case clauses (§5.2.2, ➤ 195), as we will see in Chapter 5.

The binary logical operators (|| and &&) use short-circuit logic. This means that if we have *b1* || *b2* and expression *b1* evaluates to true, the result must be true no matter what *b2* is, so true is returned and *b2* is not evaluated. Similarly, if we have *b1* && *b2* and expression *b1* evaluates to false, the result must be false, so false is returned and *b2* is not evaluated.

Go is strict about the values that can be compared using the comparison operators (<, <=, ==, !=, >=, >). The two values must be of the same type, or—if they are interfaces—they must implement the same interface type. If one value is a constant then it must be of a type that is compatible with the other's type. This means that an untyped numeric constant can be compared with another value of *any* numeric type, but numbers of different types—and that are not constants—cannot be compared unless one of them is explicitly converted to be of the same type as the other. (Numeric conversions are discussed in §2.3, ➤ 57.)

Table 2.3 *Boolean and Comparison Operators*

Syntax	Description/result
`!b`	Logical NOT operator; `false` if Boolean expression *b* is `true`
`a || b`	Short-circuit logical OR operator; `true` if either Boolean expression *a* or *b* is `true`
`a && b`	Short-circuit logical AND operator; `true` if both Boolean expressions *a* and *b* are `true`
`x < y`	`true` if expression *x* is less than expression *y*
`x <= y`	`true` if expression *x* is less than or equal to expression *y*
`x == y`	`true` if expression *x* is equal to expression *y*
`x != y`	`true` if expression *x* is not equal to expression *y*
`x >= y`	`true` if expression *x* is greater than or equal to expression *y*
`x > y`	`true` if expression *x* is greater than expression *y*

The `==` and `!=` operators can be applied to operands of any comparable types, including arrays and `struct`s whose items or fields are comparable using `==` and `!=`. These operators cannot be used to compare slices, although such a comparison can be done using the Go standard library's `reflect.DeepEqual()` function. The `==` and `!=` operators can be used to compare two pointers or two interfaces—or to compare a pointer or interface or reference (e.g., to a channel, map, or slice) with `nil`. The other comparison operators (`<`, `<=`, `>=`, `>`) may be applied only to numbers and strings. (Since Go—like C and Java—doesn't support operator overloading, for our own custom types we can implement our own comparison methods or functions if needed, such as `Less()` or `Equal()`, as we will see in Chapter 6.)

2.3. Numeric Types

Go provides a wide range of built-in numeric types, and the standard library adds integers of type `big.Int` and rationals of type `big.Rat` which are of unbounded size (i.e., limited only by the machine's memory). Every numeric type is distinct: This means that we cannot use binary arithmetic operations or comparisons (e.g., + or <) on numeric values of different types (e.g., of type `int32` and type `int`). Untyped numeric constants are compatible with any (built-in) typed number they are in an expression with, so we can add or compare an untyped numeric constant with another number, no matter what the other number's (built-in) type.

If we need to perform arithmetic or comparisons on typed numbers of different types we must perform conversions—usually to the biggest type to avoid loss of accuracy. Conversions take the form *type*(*value*) and where valid (e.g., from one type of number to another) they always succeed—even if this results in data loss. Here are some examples:

```
const factor = 3 // factor is compatible with any numeric type
i := 20000       // i is of type int by inference
i *= factor
j := int16(20)   // j is of type int16; same as: var j int16 = 20
i += int(j)      // Types must match so conversion is required
k := uint8(0)    // Same as: var k uint8
k = uint8(i)     // Succeeds, but k's value is truncated to 8 bits ✗
fmt.Println(i, j, k) // Prints: 60020 20 116
```

If we want to perform safe downsizing conversions we can always create suitable functions. For example:

```
func Uint8FromInt(x int) (uint8, error) {
    if 0 <= x && x <= math.MaxUint8 {
        return uint8(x), nil
    }
    return 0, fmt.Errorf("%d is out of the uint8 range", x)
}
```

This function accepts an int argument and returns a uint8 and nil if the int is in range, or 0 and an error otherwise. The math.MaxUint8 constant is from the math package which also has similar constants for Go's other built-in numeric types. (Of course, there are no minimum constants for the unsigned types since they all share a minimum of 0.) The fmt.Errorf() function returns an error based on the format string and value or values it is given. (String formatting is covered in §3.5, ➤ 93.)

Numbers of the same type can be compared using the comparison operators (see Table 2.3, 57 ◀). Similarly, Go's arithmetic operators can be applied to numbers; these are shown in Table 2.4 (➤ 59) applicable to all built-in numbers, and in Table 2.6 (➤ 60) applicable only to integers.

Constant expressions are evaluated at compile time; they may use any of the arithmetic, Boolean, and comparison operators. For example:

```
const (
    efri     int64 = 10000000000                     // type: int64
    hlutföllum     = 16.0 / 9.0                       // type: float64
    mælikvarða     = complex(-2, 3.5) * hlutföllum    // type: complex128
    erGjaldgengur = 0.0 <= hlutföllum && hlutföllum < 2.0 // type: bool
)
```

The example uses Icelandic identifiers as a reminder that Go fully supports native language identifiers. (We will discuss complex() shortly; §2.3.2.1, ➤ 70.)

Table 2.4 *Arithmetic Operators Applicable to All Built-In Numbers*

Syntax	Description/result
+*x*	*x*
−*x*	The negation of *x*
x++	Increments *x* by the untyped constant 1
x−−	Decrements *x* by the untyped constant 1
x += *y*	Increments *x* by *y*
x −= *y*	Decrements *x* by *y*
x *= *y*	Sets *x* to *x* multiplied by *y*
x /= *y*	Sets *x* to *x* divided by *y*; if the numbers are integers any remainder is discarded; division by zero causes a runtime panic[*]
x + *y*	The sum of *x* and *y*
x − *y*	The result of subtracting *y* from *x*
x * *y*	The result of multiplying *x* by *y*
x / *y*	The result of dividing *x* by *y*; if the numbers are integers any remainder is discarded; division by zero causes a runtime panic[*]

Although Go has sensible rules of precedence (unlike, say, C and C++), we recommend using parentheses to make intentions clear. Using parentheses is particularly recommended for programmers who use multiple languages so as to avoid subtle mistakes.

2.3.1. Integer Types

Go provides 11 separate integer types, five signed and five unsigned, plus an integer type for storing pointers—their names and values are shown in Table 2.5 (➤ 60). In addition, Go allows the use of byte as a synonym for the unsigned uint8 type, and encourages the use of rune as a synonym for the int32 type when working with individual characters (i.e., Unicode code points). For most processing purposes the only integer type that we need is int. This is suitable for loop counters, array and slice indexes, and all general-purpose integer arithmetic; it is also normally the integer type that offers the fastest processing speeds. At the time of this writing, the int type is represented by a signed 32-bit integer (even on 64-bit platforms), but is expected to change to 64-bit in a future Go version.

The other integer types that Go provides are needed when it comes to reading and writing integers outside the program—for example, from and to files or network connections. In such cases it is essential to know exactly how many bits must be read or written so that integers can be handled without corruption.

---

[*] A *panic* is an exception; see Chapter 1 (32 ◄) and §5.5, ➤ 212.

Table 2.5 *Go's Integer Types and Ranges*

Type	Range
byte	Synonym for uint8
int	The int32 or int64 range depending on the implementation
int8	[−128, 127] *{ math . MaxInt8 / MinInt8*
int16	[−32 768, 32 767] *{ math.MaxInt16 / MinInt16*
int32 *or int*	[−2 147 483 648, 2 147 483 647]
int64	[−9 223 372 036 854 775 808, 9 223 372 036 854 775 807]
rune	Synonym for int32
uint	The uint32 or uint64 range depending on the implementation
uint8	[0, 255] *math . Max Uint8*
uint16	[0, 65 535]
uint32	[0, 4 294 967 295]
uint64	[0, 18 446 744 073 709 551 615]
uintptr	An unsigned integer capable of storing a pointer value *(advanced)*

Table 2.6 *Arithmetic Operators Applicable Only to Built-In Integer Types*

Syntax	Description/result
^x	The bitwise complement of x
x %= y	Sets x to be the remainder of dividing x by y; division by zero causes a runtime panic
x &= y	Sets x to the bitwise AND of x and y
x |= y	Sets x to the bitwise OR of x and y
x ^= y	Sets x to the bitwise XOR of x and y
x &^= y	Sets x to the bitwise clear (AND NOT) of x and y
x >>= u	Sets x to the result of right-shifting itself by unsigned int u shifts
x <<= u	Sets x to the result of left-shifting itself by unsigned int u shifts
x % y	The remainder of dividing x by y; division by zero causes a runtime panic
x & y	The bitwise AND of x and y
x | y	The bitwise OR of x and y
x ^ y	The bitwise XOR of x and y
x &^ y	The bitwise clear (AND NOT) of x and y
x << u	The result of left-shifting x by unsigned int u shifts
x >> u	The result of right-shifting x by unsigned int u shifts

A common practice is to store integers in memory using the int type, and to convert to or from one of the explicitly signed and sized integer types when writing or reading integers. The byte (uint8) type is used for reading and writing raw bytes—for example, when handling UTF-8 encoded text. We saw the basics of reading and writing UTF-8 encoded text in the previous chapter's americanise example (29 ◄), and will see how to read and write built-in and custom data in Chapter 8.

Go integers support all the arithmetic operations listed in Table 2.4 (59 ◄), and in addition they support all the arithmetic and bitwise operations listed in Table 2.6 (60 ◄). All of these operations have the expected standard behaviors, so they are not discussed further, especially since we will see plenty of examples throughout the book.

It is always safe to convert an integer of a smaller type to one of a larger type (e.g., from an int16 to an int32); but downsizing an integer that is too big for the target type or converting a negative integer to an unsigned integer will silently result in a truncated or otherwise unexpected value. In such cases it is best to use a custom downsizing function such as the one shown earlier (58 ◄). Of course, when attempting to downsize a literal (e.g., int8(200)), the compiler will detect the problem and report an overflow error. Integers can also be converted to floating-point numbers using the standard Go syntax (e.g., float64(*integer*)).

Go's support for 64-bit integers makes it realistically possible to use scaled integers for precise calculations in some contexts. For example, computing the finances for a business using int64s to represent millionths of a cent allows for calculations in the range of billions of dollars with sufficient accuracy for most purposes—especially if we are careful about divisions. And if we need to do financial calculations with perfect accuracy and avoid rounding errors we can use the big.Rat type.

2.3.1.1. Big Integers

In some situations we need to perform perfectly accurate computations with whole numbers whose range exceeds even that of int64s and uint64s. In such cases we cannot use floating-point numbers because they are represented by approximations. Fortunately, Go's standard library provides two unlimited accuracy integer types: big.Int for integers and big.Rat for rationals (i.e., for numbers than can be represented as fractions such as $\frac{2}{3}$ and 1.1496, but not irrationals like e or π). These integer types can hold an arbitrary number of digits—providing only that the machine has sufficient memory—but are potentially a lot slower to process than built-in integers.

Since Go—like C and Java—does not support operator overloading, the methods provided for big.Ints and big.Rats have names—for example, Add() and Mul(). In most cases the methods modify their receiver (i.e., the big integer they are called on), and also return their receiver as their result to support the chaining of operations. We won't list all the functions and methods provided by the math/big package since they can easily be looked up in the documentation and may have been added to since this was written; however, we will look at a representative example to get a flavor of how big.Ints are used.

✳ Using Go's float64 type allows us to accurately compute to about 15 decimal digits—which is more than enough for most situations. However, if we want to compute to a large number of decimal places, say, tens or hundreds of places, as we might want to when computing π, no built-in type is sufficient.

In 1706 John Machin developed a formula for calculating π to an arbitrary number of decimal places, and we can adapt this formula in conjunction with the Go standard library's big.Ints to compute π to any number of decimal places. The pure formula, and the *arccot()* function it relies on, are shown in Figure 2.1. (No understanding of Machin's formula is required to understand the use of the big.Int package introduced here.) Our implementation of the *arccot()* function accepts an additional argument to limit the precision of the calculation so that we don't go beyond the number of digits required.

$$\pi = 4 \times (4 \times arccot(5) - arccot(239)) \qquad arccot(x) = \frac{1}{x} - \frac{1}{3x^3} + \frac{1}{5x^5} - \frac{1}{7x^7} + \cdots$$

Figure 2.1 *Machin's formula*

The entire program is less than 80 lines and is in the file pi_by_digits/pi_by_digits.go; here is its main() function.✳

```
func main() {
    places := handleCommandLine(1000)
    scaledPi := fmt.Sprint(π(places))
    fmt.Printf("3.%s\n", scaledPi[1:])
}
```

The program assumes a default value of 1 000 decimal places, although the user can choose any number they like by entering a value on the command line. The handleCommandLine() function (not shown) returns the value it is passed or the number the user entered on the command line (if any, and if it is valid). The π() function returns π as a big.Int of value 314159...; we print this to a string, and then print the string on the console properly formatted so that the output appears as, say, 3.14159265358979323846264338327950288419716939937510 (here we have used a mere 50 digits).

```
func π(places int) *big.Int {
    digits := big.NewInt(int64(places))
    unity := big.NewInt(0)
    ten := big.NewInt(10)
    exponent := big.NewInt(0)
    unity.Exp(ten, exponent.Add(digits, ten), nil)  ❶
    pi := big.NewInt(4)
    left := arccot(big.NewInt(5), unity)
    left.Mul(left, big.NewInt(4))  ❷
    right := arccot(big.NewInt(239), unity)
    left.Sub(left, right)
    pi.Mul(pi, left)  ❸
    return pi.Div(pi, big.NewInt(0).Exp(ten, ten, nil))  ❹
}
```
big.∅ overwritten by big 10^{10}

The π() function begins by computing a value for the unity variable ($10^{digits+10}$) which we use as a scale factor so that we can do all our calculations using integers. The +10 adds an extra ten digits to those given by the user, to avoid rounding errors. We then use Machin's formula with our modified arccot() function (not shown) that takes the unity variable as its second argument. Finally, we return the result divided by 10^{10} to reverse the effects of the unity scale factor.

To get the unity variable to hold the correct value we begin by creating four variables, all of type *big.Int (i.e., pointer to big.Int; see §4.1, ➤ 140). The unity and exponent variables are initialized to 0, the ten variable to 10, and the digits variable to the number of digits requested by the user. The unity computation is performed in a single line (❶). The big.Int.Add() method adds 10 to the number of digits. Then the big.Int.Exp() method is used to raise 10 to the power of its second argument ($digits + 10$). When used with a nil third argument—as here—big.Int.Exp(x, y, nil) performs the computation x^y; with three non-nil arguments, big.Int.Exp(x, y, z) computes x^ymod z. Notice that we did not need to assign to unity; this is because most big.Int methods modify their receiver as well as return it, so here, unity is modified to have the resultant value.

The rest of the computation follows a similar pattern. We set an initial value of pi to 4 and then compute the inner left-hand part of Machin's formula. We don't need to assign to left after creating it (❷), since the big.Int.Mul() method stores the result in its receiver (i.e., in this case in variable left) as well as returning the result (which we can safely ignore). Next we compute the inner right-hand part of the formula and subtract the right from the left (leaving the result in left). Now we multiply pi (of value 4) by left (which holds the result of Machin's formula). This produces the result but scaled by unity. So in the final line (❹) we reverse the scaling by dividing the result (in pi) by 10^{10}.

Using the big.Int type takes some care since most methods modify their receiver (this is done for efficiency to save creating lots of temporary big.Ints). Compare the line where we perform the computation pi × left with the result being stored in pi (63 ◄, ❸) to the line where we compute pi ÷ 10^{10} and return the result (63 ◄, ❹)—not caring that the value of pi has been overwritten by the result.

Wherever possible it is best to use plain ints, falling back to int64s if the int range isn't sufficient, or using float32s or float64s if the fact that they are approximations is not a concern. However, if computations of perfect accuracy are required and we are prepared to pay the price in memory use and processing overhead, then we can use big.Ints or big.Rats—the latter particularly useful for financial calculations—scaling if necessary as we did here, when floating-point computations are required.

2.3.2. Floating-Point Types

Go provides two types of floating-point numbers and two types of complex numbers—their names and ranges are shown in Table 2.7. Floating-point numbers in Go are held in the widely used IEEE-754 format (http://en.wiki-pedia.org/wiki/IEEE_754-2008). This format is also the native format used by many microprocessors and floating-point units, so in most cases Go is able to take direct advantage of the hardware's floating-point support.

Table 2.7 *Go's Floating-Point Types*

Type	Range
float32	±3.402 823 466 385 288 598 117 041 834 845 169 254 40 × 10^{38} The mantissa is reliably accurate to about 7 decimal places.
float64	±1.797 693 134 862 315 708 145 274 237 317 043 567 981 × 10^{308} The mantissa is reliably accurate to about 15 decimal places.
complex64	The real and imaginary parts are both of type float32.
complex128	The real and imaginary parts are both of type float64.

Go floating-point numbers support all the arithmetic operations listed in Table 2.4 (59 ◄). Most of the math package's constants and all of its functions are listed in Tables 2.8 to 2.10 (➤ 65–67).

Floating-point numbers are written with a decimal point, or using exponential notation, for example, 0.0, 3., 8.2, –7.4, –6e4, .1, 5.9E–3. Computers commonly represent floating-point numbers internally using base 2—this means that some decimals can be represented exactly (such as 0.5), but others only approximately (such as 0.1 and 0.2). Furthermore, the representation uses a fixed number of bits, so there is a limit to the number of digits that can be held. This is not a Go-specific problem, but one that afflicts floating-point numbers in all mainstream programming languages. However, the imprecision isn't always apparent, because Go uses a smart algorithm for outputting floating-point numbers that uses the fewest possible digits consistent with maintaining accuracy.

Table 2.8 *The Math Package's Constants and Functions #1*

All the math *package's functions accept and return* float64s *unless specified otherwise. All the constants are shown truncated to 15 decimal digits to fit neatly into the tables.*

Syntax	Description/result
math.Abs(x)	$|x|$, i.e., the absolute value of x
math.Acos(x)	The arc cosine of x in radians
math.Acosh(x)	The arc hyperbolic cosine of x in radians
math.Asin(x)	The arc sine of x in radians
math.Asinh(x)	The arc hyperbolic sine of x in radians
math.Atan(x)	The arc tangent of x in radians
math.Atan2(y, x)	The arc tangent of $\frac{y}{x}$ in radians
math.Atanh(x)	The arc hyperbolic tangent of x in radians
math.Cbrt(x)	$\sqrt[3]{x}$, the cube root of x
math.Ceil(x)	$\lceil x \rceil$, i.e., the smallest integer greater than or equal to x; e.g., math.Ceil(5.4) == 6.0
math.Copysign(x, y)	A value with x's magnitude and y's sign
math.Cos(x)	The cosine of x in radians
math.Cosh(x)	The hyperbolic cosine of x in radians
math.Dim(x, y)	In effect, math.Max(x - y, 0.0)
math.E	The constant e; approximately $2.718\,281\,828\,459\,045$
math.Erf(x)	$erf(x)$; x's Gauss error function
math.Erfc(x)	$erfc(x)$; x's complementary Gauss error function
math.Exp(x)	e^x
math.Exp2(x)	2^x
math.Expm1(x)	$e^x - 1$; this is more accurate than using math.Exp(x) - 1 when x is close to 0
math.Float32bits(f)	The IEEE-754 binary representation of f (of type float32) as a uint32
math.Float32frombits(u)	The float32 represented by the IEEE-754 bits in u (of type uint32)
math.Float64bits(x)	The IEEE-754 binary representation of x (of type float64) as a uint64
math.Float64frombits(u)	The float64 represented by the IEEE-754 bits in u (of type uint64)

Table 2.9 *The Math Package's Constants and Functions #2*

Syntax	Description/result
math.Floor(*x*)	$\lfloor x \rfloor$, i.e., the largest integer less than or equal to x; e.g., math.Floor(5.4) == 5.0
math.Frexp(*x*)	*frac* of type float64 and *exp* of type int such that $x = frac \times 2^{exp}$; the inverse function is math.Ldexp()
math.Gamma(*x*)	$\Gamma(x)$, i.e., $(x - 1)!$
math.Hypot(*x*, *y*)	math.Sqrt(*x* * *x*, *y* * *y*)
math.Ilogb(*x*)	The binary exponent of *x* as an int; see also math.Logb()
math.Inf(*n*)	A float64 of value $+\infty$ if *n* of type int is ≥ 0; otherwise $-\infty$
math.IsInf(*x*, *n*)	true if *x* of type float64 is $+\infty$ and *n* of type int is > 0, or if *x* is $-\infty$ and *n* is < 0, or if *x* is either infinity and *n* is 0; otherwise false
math.IsNaN(*x*)	true if *x* has the IEEE-754 "not a number" value
math.J0(*x*)	$J_0(x)$, the Bessel function of the first kind
math.J1(*x*)	$J_1(x)$, the Bessel function of the first kind
math.Jn(*n*, *x*)	$J_n(x)$, the order-*n* (where *n* is of type int) Bessel function of the first kind
math.Ldexp(*x*, *n*)	$x \times 2^n$ where *x* is of type float64 and *n* is of type int; the inverse function is math.Frexp()
math.Lgamma(*x*)	$\log_e(\Gamma(x))$ as a float64 and the sign of $\Gamma(x)$ as an int (–1 or +1)
math.Ln2	$\log_e(2)$; approximately 0.693 147 180 559 945
math.Ln10	$\log_e(10)$; approximately 2.302 585 092 994 045
math.Log(*x*)	$\log_e(x)$
math.Log2E	$\frac{1}{\log_e(2)}$; approximately 1.442 695 021 629 333
math.Log10(*x*)	$\log_{10}(x)$
math.Log10E	$\frac{1}{\log_e(10)}$; approximately 0.434 294 492 006 301
math.Log1p(*x*)	$\log_e(1+x)$ but is more accurate than using math.Log() when *x* is near zero
math.Log2(*x*)	$\log_2(x)$
math.Logb(*x*)	The binary exponent of *x*; see also math.Ilogb()
math.Max(*x*, *y*)	The larger of *x* and *y*
math.Min(*x*, *y*)	The smaller of *x* and *y*
math.Mod(*x*, *y*)	The remainder of $\frac{x}{y}$; see also math.Remainder()

Table 2.10 *The Math Package's Constants and Functions #3*

Syntax	Description/result
math.Modf(x)	The whole and fractional parts of x as float64s 69
math.NaN(x)	An IEEE-754 "not a number" value
math.Nextafter(x, y)	The next representable value after x going toward y
math.Pi	The constant π; approximately 3.141 592 653 589 793
math.Phi	The constant φ; approximately 1.618 033 988 749 984
math.Pow(x, y)	x^y
math.Pow10(n)	10^n as a float64; n is of type int
math.Remainder(x, y)	the IEEE-754-compliant remainder of $\frac{x}{y}$; see also math.Mod()
math.Signbit(x)	Returns a bool; true if x is negative (including –0.0)
math.Sin(x)	The sine of x in radians
math.SinCos(x)	The sine and cosine of x in radians
math.Sinh(x)	The hyperbolic sine of x in radians
math.Sqrt(x)	$\sqrt{x}$
math.Sqrt2	$\sqrt{2}$; approximately 1.414 213 562 373 095
math.SqrtE	$\sqrt{e}$; approximately 1.648 721 270 700 128
math.SqrtPi	$\sqrt{\pi}$; approximately 1.772 453 850 905 516
math.SqrtPhi	$\sqrt{\phi}$; approximately 1.272 019 649 514 068
math.Tan(x)	The tangent of x in radians
math.Tanh(x)	The hyperbolic tangent of x in radians
math.Trunc(x)	x with its fractional part set to 0
math.Y0(x)	$Y_0(x)$, the Bessel function of the second kind
math.Y1(x)	$Y_1(x)$, the Bessel function of the second kind
math.Yn(n, x)	$Y_n(x)$, the order-n (where n is of type int) Bessel function of the second kind

All the comparison operations listed in Table 2.3 (57 ◀) can be used with floating-point numbers. Unfortunately, due to the fact that floating-point numbers are held as approximations, comparing them for equality or inequality does not always work intuitively.

```
x, y := 0.0, 0.0
for i := 0; i < 10; i++ {
    x += 0.1
    if i%2 == 0 {
        y += 0.2
    } else {
        fmt.Printf("%-5t %-5t %-5t %-5t", x == y,
            EqualFloat(x, y, -1), EqualFloat(x, y, 0.000000000001),
            EqualFloatPrec(x, y, 6))
        fmt.Println(x, y)
    }
}
```

```
true   true   true   true 0.2 0.2
true   true   true   true 0.4 0.4
false  false  true   true 0.6 0.6000000000000001
false  false  true   true 0.7999999999999999 0.8
false  false  true   true 0.9999999999999999 1
```

Here we start with two float64s with initial values of 0. We add ten 0.1s to the first one and five 0.2s to the second, so at the end both should be 1. However, as the output shown below the code snippet illustrates, perfect accuracy for some floating-point numbers is not possible. In view of this we must be very careful when comparing floating-point numbers for equality or inequality using == and !=. Of course, there are cases where it is sensible to compare floating-point numbers for equality or inequality using the built-in operators—for example, when trying to avoid division by zero, as in, say, if y != 0.0 { return x / y }.

The "%-5t" format prints a bool left-aligned in a field five characters wide— string formatting is covered in the next chapter; §3.5, ➤ 93.

```
func EqualFloat(x, y, limit float64) bool {
    if limit <= 0.0 {
        limit = math.SmallestNonzeroFloat64
    }
    return math.Abs(x-y) <=
        (limit * math.Min(math.Abs(x), math.Abs(y)))
}
```

The EqualFloat() function compares two float64s to the given accuracy—or to the greatest accuracy the machine can achieve if a negative number (e.g., -1) is passed as the limit. It relies on functions (and a constant) from the standard library's math package.

An alternative (and slower) approach is to compare numbers as strings.

```go
func EqualFloatPrec(x, y float64, decimals int) bool {
    a := fmt.Sprintf("%.*f", decimals, x)
    b := fmt.Sprintf("%.*f", decimals, y)
    return len(a) == len(b) && a == b
}
```

For this function the accuracy is specified as the number of digits after the decimal point. The fmt.Sprintf() function's % formatting argument can accept a * placeholder where it expects a number, so here we create two strings based on the two given float64s, formatting each with the specified number of decimal places. If the magnitudes of the numbers differ, then so will the lengths of the a and b strings (e.g., 12.32 vs. 592.85), which gives us a relatively fast short-circuiting equality test. (String formatting is covered in §3.5, ➤ 93.)

In most cases where floating-point numbers are needed the float64 type is the best choice—especially since all the functions in the math package work in terms of float64s. However, Go also provides the float32 type which may be useful when memory is at a premium and we either don't need to use the math package, or are willing to put up with the minor inconvenience of converting to and from float64s when necessary. Since Go's floating-point types are sized it is always safe to read or write them from or to external sources such as files or network connections.

Floating-point numbers can be converted to integers using the standard Go syntax (e.g., int(*float*)), in which case the fractional part is simply discarded. *float → int* Of course, if the floating-point value exceeds the range of the integer type converted to, the resultant integer will have an unpredictable value. We can address this problem using a safe conversion function. For example:

```go
func IntFromFloat64(x float64) int {
    if math.MinInt32 <= x && x <= math.MaxInt32 {
        whole, fraction := math.Modf(x)
        if fraction >= 0.5 {
            whole++
        }
        return int(whole)
    }
    panic(fmt.Sprintf("%g is out of the int32 range", x))
}
```

The Go Specification (golang.org/doc/go_spec.html) states that an int occupies the same number of bits as a uint and that a uint is always 32 or 64 bits. This

implies that an int is at least 32 bits which means that we can safely use the
math.MinInt32 and math.MaxInt32 constants as the int range.

✳ We use the math.Modf() function to separate the whole and fractional parts of the
given number (both as float64s), and rather than simply returning the whole
part (i.e., truncating), we perform a very simple rounding if the fractional part
is ≥ 0.5.

✳ Rather than return an error as we did for our custom Uint8FromInt() function
(58 ◄), we have chosen to treat out-of-range values as important enough to stop
the program, so we have used the built-in panic() function which will cause a
runtime panic and stop the program unless the panic is caught by a recover()
call (§5.5, ➤ 212). This means that if the program runs successfully we know
that no out-of-range conversions were attempted. (Notice also that the function
does not end with a return statement; the Go compiler is smart enough to realize
that a call to panic() means that a normal return cannot occur at that point.)

2.3.2.1. Complex Types

The two complex types supported by Go are shown in Table 2.7 (64 ◄). Complex
numbers can be created using the built-in complex() function or by using
constant literals involving imaginary numbers. Complex numbers' components
can be retrieved using the built-in real() and imag() functions, both of which
return a float64 (or a float32 for complex64s).

Complex numbers support all the arithmetic operations listed in Table 2.4
(59 ◄). The only comparison operators that can be used with complex numbers
are == and != (see Table 2.3, 57 ◄), but these suffer from the same issues as they
do when comparing floating-point numbers. The standard library has a complex
number-specific package, math/cmplx, whose functions are listed in Table 2.11.

Here are some simple examples:

```
f := 3.2e5                     // type: float64
x := -7.3 - 8.9i               // type: complex128 (literal)
y := complex64(-18.3 + 8.9i)   // type: complex64 (conversion)  ❶
z := complex(f, 13.2)          // type: complex128 (construction)  ❷
fmt.Println(x, real(y), imag(z)) // Prints: (-7.3-8.9i) -18.3 13.2
```

Go signifies imaginary numbers using the suffix i as used in pure mathematics.* Here, the numbers x and z are of type complex128, so their real and imaginary parts are of type float64; y is of type complex64 so its components are of
type float32. One subtle point to notice is that using the complex64 type name
(or any other built-in type name for that matter) as a function performs a type
conversion. So here (❶), the complex number -18.3+8.9i (of type complex128—the

---

* By contrast, in engineering and in Python, imaginary numbers are indicated using *j*.

Table 2.11 *The Complex Math Package's Functions*

Import `"math/cmplx"`. *All the functions accept and return* `complex128s` *unless specified otherwise.*

Syntax	Description/result
`cmplx.Abs(x)`	$\lvert x \rvert$, i.e., the absolute value of x as a `float64`
`cmplx.Acos(x)`	The arc cosine of x in radians
`cmplx.Acosh(x)`	The arc hyperbolic cosine of x in radians
`cmplx.Asin(x)`	The arc sine of x in radians
`cmplx.Asinh(x)`	The arc hyperbolic sine of x in radians
`cmplx.Atan(x)`	The arc tangent of x in radians
`cmplx.Atanh(x)`	The arc hyperbolic tangent of x in radians
`cmplx.Conj(x)`	The complex conjugate of x
`cmplx.Cos(x)`	The cosine of x in radians
`cmplx.Cosh(x)`	The hyperbolic cosine of x in radians
`cmplx.Cot(x)`	The cotangent of x in radians
`cmplx.Exp(x)`	e^x
`cmplx.Inf()`	`complex(math.Inf(1), math.Inf(1))`
`cmplx.IsInf(x)`	`true` if `real(x)` or `imag(x)` is $\pm\infty$; otherwise `false`
`cmplx.IsNaN(x)`	`true` if `real(x)` or `imag(x)` is "not a number" and if neither is $\pm\infty$; otherwise `false`
`cmplx.Log(x)`	$\log_e(x)$
`cmplx.Log10(x)`	$\log_{10}(x)$
`cmplx.NaN()`	A complex "not a number" value
`cmplx.Phase(x)`	The phase of x as a `float64` in the range $[-\pi, +\pi]$
`cmplx.Polar(x)`	The absolute value r and phase θ both of type `float64`, satisfying $x = r \times e^{\theta i}$; phase is in the range $[-\pi, +\pi]$
`cmplx.Pow(x, y)`	x^y
`cmplx.Rect(r, θ)`	A `complex128` with polar coordinates r and θ both of type `float64`
`cmplx.Sin(x)`	The sine of x in radians
`cmplx.Sinh(x)`	The hyperbolic sine of x in radians
`cmplx.Sqrt(x)`	$\sqrt{x}$
`cmplx.Tan(x)`	The tangent of x in radians
`cmplx.Tanh(x)`	The hyperbolic tangent of x in radians

inferred complex type for complex literals) is converted to a complex64. However, complex() is a function (there is no type of that name) that takes two floats and returns the corresponding complex128 (70 ◀, ❷).

Another subtle point is that the fmt.Println() function can print complex numbers without formality. (As we will see in Chapter 6 we can make our own types seamlessly cooperate with Go's print functions simply by providing them with a String() method.)

In general the best complex type to use is complex128 since all the functions in the math/cmplx package work in terms of complex128s. However, Go also provides the complex64 type which may be useful when memory is very tight. Since Go's complex types are sized it is always safe to read or write them from or to external sources such as files or network connections.

In this chapter we have looked at Go's Boolean and numeric types and presented tables showing the operators and functions that are available to query and manipulate them. The next chapter covers Go's string type, including thorough coverage of Go's print formatting functionality (§3.5, ➤ 93), which includes, of course, the printing of Booleans and numbers formatted as we want. We will see how to read and write Go data types—including Booleans and numbers—from and to files in Chapter 8. Before closing this chapter, though, we will review a small but complete working example program.

2.4. Example: Statistics

The purpose of this example (and the exercises that follow) is to provide some context for (and practice of) Go programming. Just like in Chapter 1, the example makes use of some Go features that haven't yet been fully covered. This shouldn't cause problems since brief explanations and forward references are provided. The example also introduces some very simple usage of the Go standard library's net/http package—this package makes it incredibly easy to create HTTP servers. As appropriate to the main theme of the chapter, the example and the exercises are numeric in flavor.

The statistics program (in file statistics/statistics.go) is a web application that asks the user to enter a list of numbers and then does some very simple statistical calculations. Figure 2.2 shows the program in action. We will review the program's code in two parts, first the implementation of the mathematical functionality, and then the implementation of the application's web page. We won't show the whole program (e.g., we will skip the imports and most of the constants), since it is available for download, but we will cover enough to make it understandable.

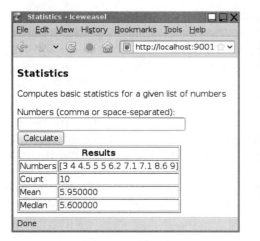
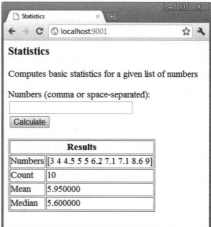

Figure 2.2 *The Statistics program on Linux and Windows*

2.4.1. Implementing Simple Statistics Functions

For convenience we have created an aggregate type that holds the numbers the user entered and the two statistics we plan to calculate.

```
type statistics struct {
    numbers []float64
    mean    float64
    median  float64
}
```

A Go struct is similar to a C struct or to a Java class that has public data fields and no methods—but not like a C++ struct since it isn't a class. As we will see, Go structs provide excellent support for aggregation and embedding (§6.4, ➤ 275), and are also often central to Go's object-oriented functionality (Chapter 6).

```
func getStats(numbers []float64) (stats statistics) {
    stats.numbers = numbers              // should test if slice length is ∅
    sort.Float64s(stats.numbers)
    stats.mean = sum(numbers) / float64(len(numbers))      74
    stats.median = median(numbers)       74
    return stats
}
```

This function accepts a slice of numbers (in this case as obtained by our process-Request() function ➤ 77), and populates its stats result value (of type statistics) with appropriate values. To compute the median we need the numbers to be

sorted into ascending order; this is achieved using the sort package's Float64s()
function which sorts a []float64 in-place. This means that the getStats() function modifies its argument—something that is quite common when slices, references, or pointers are passed to functions. If we wanted to preserve the original
slice of numbers, we could copy it to a temporary slice using the built-in copy()
function (§4.2.3, ➤ 156), and work on the copy.

The *mean* (or *average*) is simply the sum of a sequence of values divided by
the number of values in the sequence. Here we have used a separate helper
function to sum the numbers, and converted the length (count of numbers) to a
float64 to make the types compatible (since sum() returns a float64). This also
ensures that we get floating-point division and avoid the truncation that would
occur if we used integers. The *median* is the middle value; we compute this
separately using the median() function.

We haven't checked for division by zero since our program's logic means that
getStats() is only called when there is at least one number; so if we ever break
the logic the program will terminate with a runtime panic. For a mission-critical
application that should never terminate when problems occur we could use Go's
recover() function to catch panics, restore the application to a sane state, and
continue to run (§5.5, ➤ 212).

```
func sum(numbers []float64) (total float64) {
    for _, x := range numbers {
        total += x
    }
    return total
}
```

This function uses a for ... range loop to iterate over all the numbers (and discarding their index positions) to produce their sum. Thanks to Go always initializing
variables—including named return values—to their zero value, total correctly
starts at zero.

```
func median(numbers []float64) float64 {
    middle := len(numbers) / 2
    result := numbers[middle]
    if len(numbers)%2 == 0 {
        result = (result + numbers[middle-1]) / 2
    }
    return result
}
```

This function must be called with a sorted slice of float64s. It initially takes
the median to be the middle value, but if the number of numbers is even there
are actually two middle values, so in that case we sum those values and divide

by two to get the mean of the two middle values. And at the end we return the result.

In this subsection we have covered the application-specific processing. In the next subsection we will look at the basics of implementing the infrastructure to support a web application that has a single web page. (Readers who aren't interested in web programming might prefer to skip to the exercises or to the next chapter.)

2.4.2. Implementing a Basic HTTP Server

The statistics program provides a single web page on the local host. Here is its main() function.

```
func main() {                    ⌐ path  ⌐ func w. signature : func (http.ResponseWriter, *http.Request)
    http.HandleFunc("/", homePage)          ⌐ default web server
    if err := http.ListenAndServe(":9001", nil); err != nil {
        log.Fatal("failed to start server", err)
    }                                        local host, port 9001
}
```

The http.HandleFunc() function takes two arguments: a path and a reference to a function to call when that path is requested. The function must have the signature func(http.ResponseWriter, *http.Request). We can register as many *path–function* pairs as we like. Here we have registered the / path (i.e., the web application's home page) with a custom homePage() function.

The http.ListenAndServe() function starts up a web server at the given TCP network address; here we have used localhost and port number 9001. The local host is assumed if only the port number is given—we could just as easily have used an address of "localhost:9001" or "127.0.0.1:9001". (The port number we have chosen is arbitrary—simply change the code to use a different one if it conflicts with an existing server.) The second argument is used to specify which kind of server to use—normally we pass nil to indicate that we want to use the default kind.

The program has several string constants but we will only show one of them here.   (constant) string of html 83

```
    form       = `<form action="/" method="POST">
<label for="numbers">Numbers (comma or space-separated):</label><br />
<input type="text" name="numbers" size="30"><br />
<input type="submit" value="Calculate">
</form>`
```

The form string constant contains a *<form>* element which itself contains the *text* and *submit* button *<input>* elements.

```
func homePage(writer http.ResponseWriter, request *http.Request) {
    err := request.ParseForm() // Must be called before writing response
    fmt.Fprint(writer, pageTop, form)
    if err != nil {
        fmt.Fprintf(writer, anError, err)
    } else {
        if numbers, message, ok := processRequest(request); ok {
            stats := getStats(numbers)
            fmt.Fprint(writer, formatStats(stats))
        } else if message != "" {
            fmt.Fprintf(writer, anError, message)
        }
    }
    fmt.Fprint(writer, pageBottom)
}
```

This function is called whenever the statistics web site is visited. The writer argument is where we write our response to (in HTML) and the request argument contains details of the request.

We begin by parsing the form (which will initially have an empty *text <input>* element. We have called the *text <input>* element "numbers" so that we can refer to it when we process the form later on. Also, the form's *action* is set to /, so when the user presses the Calculate button the same page is requested again. This means that the homePage() function is called in all cases, so it must handle the initial case where no numbers have been entered, and subsequent cases where numbers have been entered or where an error has occurred. In fact, all the work is passed on to a custom processRequest() function, so it is in that function that each case is dealt with.

After the parse, we write the pageTop (not shown) and form string constants. If the parse fails for any reason we write an error message; anError is a format string and err is the error value to be formatted. (Format strings are covered later; §3.5, ➤ 93.)

```
anError    = `<p class="error">%s</p>`
```

If the parse succeeds (as it should), we call a custom processRequest() function to retrieve the numbers entered by the user ready for processing. If the numbers are valid we compute the statistics using the getStats() function we saw earlier (73 ◄) and write the formatted results; otherwise we write an error message if we are given one. (When the form is shown for the first time it has no numbers, yet no error has occurred, in which case ok is false and message is empty.) And at the end we print the pageBottom constant string (not shown) which just closes the *<body>* and *<html>* tags.

```go
func processRequest(request *http.Request) ([]float64, string, bool) {
    var numbers []float64
    if slice, found := request.Form["numbers"]; found && len(slice) > 0 {
        text := strings.Replace(slice[0], ",", " ", -1)
        for _, field := range strings.Fields(text) {
            if x, err := strconv.ParseFloat(field, 64); err != nil {
                return numbers, "'" + field + "' is invalid", false
            } else {
                numbers = append(numbers, x)
            }
        }
    }
    if len(numbers) == 0 {
        return numbers, "", false // no data first time form is shown
    }
    return numbers, "", true
}
```

strconv package 113

This function reads the form's data from the request value. If the form is being shown for the first time the "numbers" *text <input>* element is empty. This isn't an error so we return an empty slice of float64s, an empty error message, and false to indicate that there are no statistics to gather—this results in the empty form being shown. If the user has entered some numbers we return either a slice of float64s, an empty error message, and true; or, if one or more numbers is invalid, a possibly empty slice, an error message, and false.

The request value has a Form field of type map[string][]string (§4.3, ➤ 164). This means that the map's keys are strings and its values are slices of strings. So any one key may have any number of strings as its value. For example, if the user has entered the numbers "5 8.2 7 13 6", the Form map will have a "numbers" key with a value of []string{"5 8.2 7 13 6"}, that is, its value will be a slice of strings that actually has only one string. (For comparison, here is an example of a slice of two strings: []string{"1 2 3", "a b c"}.) We check to see if the "numbers" key is present (it ought to be), and if it is—*and* if its value has at least one string—we know that we have numbers to read.

We use the strings.Replace() function to obtain the string of numbers that the user entered but with any commas replaced by spaces. (The third argument is the number of replacements to perform; –1 means do as many as possible.) Having obtained the string of whitespace-separated numbers we then use the strings.Fields() function to split the string (on any amount of whitespace) into a slice of strings which we iterate over straight away using a for ... range loop. (The strings package's functions are covered in §3.6, ➤ 106; the for ... range loop is covered in §5.3, ➤ 203.) For each string ("5", "8.2", etc.) we attempt to convert it to a float64 using the strconv.ParseFloat() function which takes a string to parse and a bit size of 32 or 64 (§3.6, ➤ 106). If the conversion fails we imme-

diately return with whatever float64s we have, a nonempty error message, and
false. If the conversion succeeds we append the float64 to the numbers slice. The
built-in append() function takes a slice and one or more values and returns a slice
that has all the items from the original slice plus the values—the function is
smart enough to reuse the original slice if its capacity is greater than its length,
so it is efficient to use. (We cover append() in §4.2.3, ➤ 156.)

If we haven't already returned due to an error (i.e., an invalid number), we
return the numbers with an empty error message and true, unless there are no
numbers to process (because the form has been shown for the first time) in which
case we return false.　　┌ *takes a statistics struct (73)*
　　　　　　　　　　　　　　　　　┌ *returns a string*　　　　　*420 template*

```
func formatStats(stats statistics) string {
    return fmt.Sprintf(`<table border="1">
<tr><th colspan="2">Results</th></tr>
<tr><td>Numbers</td><td>%v</td></tr>
<tr><td>Count</td><td>%d</td></tr>
<tr><td>Mean</td><td>%f</td></tr>
<tr><td>Median</td><td>%f</td></tr>
</table>`, stats.numbers, len(stats.numbers), stats.mean, stats.median)
}
```

Once the statistics have been computed we must output them to the user,
and since the program is a web application we need to produce HTML. (Go's
standard library has dedicated text/template and html/template packages for
creating data-driven text and HTML, but our needs here are so simple that we
have chosen to do it all by hand. A small text/template-based example is shown
later; §9.4.2, ➤ 419.)

The fmt.Sprintf() function takes a format string and one or more values and returns a string that is a copy of the format string but with the format verbs (e.g.,
%v, %d, %f) replaced with corresponding values. (String formatting is thoroughly
covered in §3.5, ➤ 93.) We had no need to do any HTML escaping since all of our
values are numbers. (If escaping is needed we can use the template.HTMLEscape()
or html.EscapeString() functions.)

As this example illustrates, Go makes it easy to create simple web applications
—providing we know some basic HTML—and provides the html, net/http, html/
template, and text/template packages to make life easier.

2.5. Exercises

There are two exercises for this chapter, both numeric in flavor. The first
involves modifying the statistics program we have just reviewed; the second
involves creating a simple mathematical web application from scratch.

1. Copy the statistics directory to, say, my_statistics and modify my_statistics/statistics.go to produce two more statistical measures: the mode and the standard deviation. When the user clicks the Calculate button it should produce output similar to that shown in Figure 2.3.

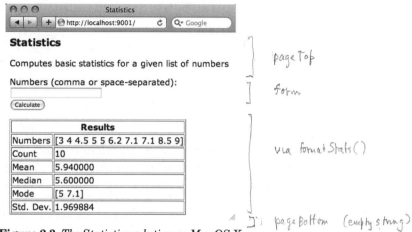

Figure 2.3 *The Statistics solution on Mac OS X*

This involves adding a couple more items to the statistics struct and adding two new functions to perform the calculations. A solution is in the file statistics_ans/statistics.go; this needed about 40 extra lines and made use of the built-in append() function (§4.2.3, ➤ 156) to add numbers to a slice.

The standard deviation function is the easiest to write—it just requires the use of some functions from the math package and can be done in fewer than ten lines. We used the formula $\sigma = \sqrt{\frac{\sum (x - \bar{x})^2}{n-1}}$, where x is each number, $\bar{x}$ is the mean, and n is the number of numbers.

The mode is the most frequently occurring number—or numbers, if two or more are equally the most frequently occurring. However, we return no mode if all of the numbers occur with the same frequency. The mode is trickier than the standard deviation, and needs about 20 lines of code.

2. Create a web application for calculating the solution or solutions to quadratic equations using the standard formula $x = \frac{-b \pm \sqrt{b^2 - 4ac}}{2a}$. Use complex numbers so that it is possible to find solutions even when the discriminant (the $b^2 - 4ac$ part) is negative. Initially, just get the math working, as shown in Figure 2.4's left-hand screenshot (➤ 80). Then, modify your application to produce more intelligent output, as shown in Figure 2.4's right-hand screenshot.

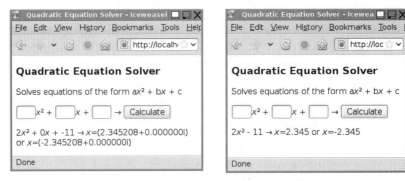

Figure 2.4 *The Quadratic solutions on Linux*

One easy way to get started is to copy the statistics application's main(), homePage(), and processRequest() functions, modifying homePage() to call three new custom functions—formatQuestion(), solve(), and formatSolutions()—and heavily modifying processRequest() to read in three separate floating-point numbers. The file quadratic_ans1/quadratic.go contains an initial application of about 120 lines. This version is smart enough to output just one solution if both solutions are approximately equal by making use of the EqualFloat() function discussed earlier in the chapter (68 ◄).

A second application is in file quadratic_ans2/quadratic.go; this runs to about 160 lines and is much smarter about how it formats the output. For example, it replaces "+ -" with "-" and "1x" with "x", suppresses zero components (e.g., eliminates "0x"), and formats a solution as a floating-point number if the imaginary part is approximately zero. It makes use of some math/cmplx package functions such as cmplx.IsNaN(), and more advanced string formatting (§3.5, ➤ 93).

3

Strings

This chapter covers Go's `string` type and key string-related packages from the standard library. The chapter's sections include coverage of how to write literal strings and use the string operators; how to index and slice (take substrings of) strings; and how to format the output of strings, numbers, and other built-in and custom types.

Go's high-level string-related functionality, such as its `for ... range` loop which iterates over a string character by character, the functions from the `strings` and `strconv` packages, and Go's ability to slice strings, are all that is needed for every-day programming. Nonetheless, this chapter covers Go strings in depth, includ-

Unicode

Prior to Unicode it was not really possible to have plain text files that contained text in different languages—for example, English with some quoted sentences in Japanese and Russian—since separate encodings were used for separate languages and each text file used a single encoding.

Unicode is designed to be able to represent the characters from all of the world's writing systems, so a single text file using a Unicode encoding can contain text in any mixture of languages—as well as math, "dingbats", and other special characters.

Every Unicode character has a unique identifying number called a *code point*. There are more than 100 000 Unicode characters defined, with code points ranging in value from 0x0 to 0x10FFFF (the latter defined in Go as the constant unicode.MaxRune), with some large gaps and various special cases. In Unicode documentation, code points are written using four or more hexadecimal digits in the form U+*hhhh*—for example, U+21D4 for the ⇔ character.

In Go, an individual code point (i.e., a character) is represented by a rune in memory. (The rune type is a synonym for int32; see §2.3.1, 59 ◀.)

Unicode text—whether in files or in memory—must be represented using an encoding. The Unicode standard defines various Unicode Transformation Formats (encodings), such as UTF-8, UTF-16, and UTF-32. Go uses the UTF-8 encoding for strings. UTF-8 is the most widely used encoding; it is also the de facto standard encoding for text files and the default encoding for XML and JSON files.

The UTF-8 encoding uses between one and four bytes to represent each code point. For strings that contain only 7-bit ASCII (US-ASCII) characters, there is a one-to-one relationship between bytes and characters because each 7-bit ASCII character is represented by a single byte (of the same value) in UTF-8. One consequence of this is that UTF-8 stores English text very compactly (one byte per character); another consequence is that a text file encoded using 7-bit ASCII is indistinguishable from a UTF-8-encoded text file.

ing some low-level details such as how strings are represented internally. The low-level aspects are interesting and can be useful to know in some situations.

A Go string is an immutable sequence of arbitrary bytes. In most cases a string's bytes represent Unicode text using the UTF-8 encoding; (see the "Unicode" sidebar above). The use of Unicode means that Go strings can contain text in a mixture of any of the world's languages, without any of the confusions and limitations of code pages.

Go's string type is fundamentally different from the equivalent type in many other languages. Java's *String*, C++'s *std::string*, and Python 3's *str* types are all sequences of *fixed-width* characters (with some caveats), whereas a Go `string` is a sequence of *variable-width* characters where each character is represented by one or more bytes, normally using the UTF-8 encoding.

At first sight it might appear that these other languages' string types are more convenient than Go's since individual characters in their strings can be directly indexed—something only possible in Go if the string exclusively holds 7-bit ASCII characters (since these are all represented by a single UTF-8 byte). In practical terms this is never a problem for Go programmers: first, because direct indexing isn't used much in Go because Go supports character-by-character iteration over strings; second, because the standard library provides a comprehensive range of string searching and manipulation functions; and third, because we can always convert a Go string into a slice of Unicode code points (of type `[]rune`) which can be indexed directly.

Go's use of UTF-8 for its `string` type has several advantages compared with, say, Java or Python, both of which also have Unicode strings. Java represents strings as sequences of code points, each occupying 16 bits; Python versions 2.*x* to 3.2 use the same approach but using 16 or 32 bits depending on how Python is built. For English text this means that Go uses 8 bits per character compared to at least twice that for Java and Python. Another advantage of UTF-8 is that machine endianness doesn't matter, whereas for UTF-16 and UTF-32 it is essential to know the endianness (e.g., UTF-16 little-endian) to be able to decode the text correctly. In addition, since UTF-8 is the world's de facto standard encoding for text files, while other languages must decode and encode such files to convert to and from their internal Unicode representations, Go can read and write such files directly. Furthermore, some major libraries (such as GTK+) use UTF-8 strings natively, so Go can work with them without encoding or decoding.

In practice, Go strings are just as convenient and easy to use as other languages' string types—once we have learned the Go idioms for working with them.

3.1. Literals, Operators, and Escapes

String literals are created using double quotes (") or backticks (`). Double quotes are used to create interpreted string literals—such strings support the escape sequences listed in Table 3.1 (➤ 84) but may not span multiple lines. Backticks are used to create raw string literals—these strings may span multiple lines; they do not support any escape sequences and may contain any character except for a backtick. Interpreted string literals are the most commonly used kind, but raw string literals are useful for writing multiline messages, HTML, and regular expressions. Here are a few examples.

```
text1 := "\"what's that?\", he said" // Interpreted string literal
text2 := `"what's that?", he said`   // Raw string literal
radicals := "√ \u221A \U0000221a"    // radicals == "√ √ √"
```

Table 3.1 *Go's String and Character Escapes*

Escape	Meaning
\\	Backslash (\)
\ooo	Unicode character with the given 3-digit 8-bit octal code point
\'	Single quote ('); only allowed inside character literals
\"	Double quote ("); only allowed inside interpreted string literals
\a	ASCII bell (BEL)
\b	ASCII backspace (BS)
\f	ASCII formfeed (FF)
\n	ASCII linefeed (LF)
\r	ASCII carriage return (CR)
\t	ASCII tab (TAB)
\uhhhh	Unicode character with the given 4-digit 16-bit hex code point
\Uhhhhhhhh	Unicode character with the given 8-digit 32-bit hex code point
\v	ASCII vertical tab (VT)
\xhh	Unicode character with the given 2-digit 8-bit hex code point

The three variables created here are of type string, and text1 and text2 contain exactly the same text. Since .go files use the UTF-8 encoding we can include Unicode characters in them without formality. However, we can still use Unicode escapes as we have done here for the second and third √ symbols. We could not use an octal or hexadecimal escape in this particular case, since their code point range is limited to U+0000 to U+00FF, far too small for the √ symbol's U+221A code point value.

If we want to create a long interpreted string literal without having an equally long line in our code we can create the literal in pieces, joining the pieces using the + concatenation operator. Furthermore, although Go's strings are immutable, they support the += append operator: This replaces the underlying string with its concatenation with the appended string, if the underlying string's capacity isn't large enough to accommodate the appended string. These operators are listed in Table 3.2 (➤ 85). Strings can be compared using the comparison operators (see Table 2.3, 57 ◄). Here is an example that uses some of these operators:

```
book := "The Spirit Level" +                  // String concatenation
        " by Richard Wilkinson"
book += " and Kate Pickett"                    // String append
fmt.Println("Josey" < "José", "Josey" == "José") // String comparisons
```

Table 3.2 *String Operations*

All uses of the [ ] *slice operator are fine for strings containing only 7-bit ASCII characters; but care is needed for strings containing non-ASCII characters (see §3.4, ➤ 90). Strings can be compared using the standard comparison operators:* <, <=, ==, !=, >=, >= *(see Table 2.3, 57* ◄ *and §3.2, ➤ 86.)*

Syntax	Description/result
s += t	Appends string t to the end of string s
s + t	The concatenation of strings s and t
s[n]	The raw byte at index position n (of type uint8) in s
s[n:m]	A string taken from s from index positions n to m - 1
s[n:]	A string taken from s from index positions n to len(s) - 1
s[:m]	A string taken from s from index positions 0 to m - 1
len(s)	The number of bytes in string s
len([]rune(s))	The number of characters in string s—use the faster utf8.RuneCountInString() instead; see Table 3.10 (➤ 118)
[]rune(s)	Converts string s into a slice of Unicode code points
string(chars)	Converts a []rune or []int32 into a string; assumes that the runes or int32s are Unicode code points★
[]byte(s)	Converts string s into a slice of raw bytes without copying; there's no guarantee that the bytes are valid UTF-8
string(bytes)	Converts a []byte or []uint8 into a string without copying; there's no guarantee that the bytes are valid UTF-8
string(i)	Converts i of any integer type into a string; assumes that i is a Unicode code point; e.g., if i is 65, it returns "A"★
strconv. Itoa(i)	The string representation of i of type int and an error; e.g., if i is 65, it returns ("65", nil); see also Tables 3.8 and 3.9 (➤ 114–115)
fmt.Sprint(x)	The string representation of x of any type; e.g., if x is an integer of value 65, it returns "65"; see also Table 3.3 (➤ 94)

This results in book containing the text "The Spirit Level by Richard Wilkinson and Kate Pickett", and "true false" being output to os.Stdout.

★ The conversion always succeeds; invalid integers are converted as the Unicode replacement character U+FFFD which is often depicted as ❷.

3.2. Comparing Strings

As we have noted, Go strings support the usual comparison operators (<, <=, ==, !=, >, >=); these are shown in Table 2.3 (57 ◄). The comparison operators compare strings byte by byte in memory. Comparisons are used directly—for example, to compare two strings for equality, and indirectly—for example, when < is used to compare the strings in a []string that is being sorted. Unfortunately, three problems can arise when performing comparisons—these problems afflict every programming language that uses Unicode strings; none of them is specific to Go.

The first problem is that some Unicode characters can be represented by two or more different byte sequences. For example, the character Å could be the Ångström symbol or simply an *A* with a ring above—the two are often visually indistinguishable. The Ångström symbol's Unicode code point is U+212B, but an *A* with a ring above can be represented by Unicode code point U+00C5 or by the two code points U+0041 (*A*) and U+030A (°; combining ring above). In terms of UTF-8 bytes the Ångström symbol (Å) is represented by the bytes [0xE2, 0x84, 0xAB], the Å character by the bytes [0xC3, 0x85], and an *A* with the ° combining character by the bytes [0x41, 0xCC, 0x81]. Of course, from a user's point of view two Å characters ought to compare and sort as equals no matter what the underlying bytes.

This first problem isn't necessarily as significant as we might imagine since all UTF-8 byte sequences (i.e., strings) in Go are produced using the same code point to bytes mappings. This means, for example, that an *é* character in a Go character or string literal will always be represented by the same bytes. And, of course, if we are only concerned with ASCII characters (i.e., English), the problem doesn't occur at all. And even when we deal with non-ASCII characters, the problem only really arises when we have two different characters that look the same, or when we are reading UTF-8 bytes from outside our program from a source that has used code point to bytes mappings that are legal UTF-8 but which differ from Go's mappings. If this really does turn out to be a problem it is always possible to write a custom normalization function that, for example, ensured that, say, *é* was always represented by the bytes [0xC3, 0xA9] (which Go uses natively) rather than, say, [0x65, 0xCC, 0x81] (i.e., an *e* and an ´ combining character). Normalizing Unicode characters is explained in the Unicode Normalization Forms document (unicode.org/reports/tr15). At the time of this writing, the Go standard library has an *experimental* normalization package (exp/norm).

Since this first problem can only really arise with strings coming from external sources—and then only if they use different code point to bytes mappings than Go—it is probably best handled by isolating the code that accepts external strings. The isolating code could then normalize the strings it receives before providing them to the rest of the program.

The second problem is that there are cases where our users might reasonably expect *different* characters to be considered equal. For example, we might write a program that provides a text search function and a user might type in the word "file". Naturally, they would expect the search to find any occurrences of "file"; but they might also expect the search to match occurrences of "ﬁle" (i.e., an "ﬁ" ligature followed by "le"). Similarly, users might expect a search for "5" to match "5", "₅", "⁵", and maybe even "⑤". As with the first problem, this can be solved by using some form of normalization.

The third problem is that the sorting of some characters is language-specific. One example is that in Swedish *ä* is sorted after *z*, whereas in German phonebooks *ä* is sorted as though it were spelled *ae* and in German dictionaries as though it were spelled *a*. Another example is that although in English we sort *ø* as though it were *o*, in Danish and Norwegian it is sorted after *z*. There are lots of rules along these lines, and they can be complicated by the fact that sometimes the same application is used by people of different nationalities (who therefore expect different sorting orders), and sometimes strings are in a mixture of languages (e.g., some Spanish, others English), and some characters (such as arrows, dingbats, and mathematical symbols) don't really have meaningful sort positions at all.

On the plus side, Go's comparing of strings byte by byte produces an ASCII sort ordering for English. And if we lowercase or uppercase all the strings we want to compare, we can get a more natural English language ordering—as we will see in an example later (§4.2.4, ➤ 160).

3.3. Characters and Strings

In Go, characters are represented in two different (easy-to-interchange) ways. A single character can be represented by a single rune (or int32). From now on we will use the terms "character", "code point", "Unicode character", and "Unicode code point" interchangeably to refer to a rune (or int32) that holds a single character. Go strings represent sequences of zero or more characters—within a string each character is represented by one or more UTF-8 encoded bytes.

We can convert a single character into a one-character string using Go's standard conversion syntax (string(char)). Here is an example.

```
æs := ""
for _, char := range []rune{'æ', 0xE6, 0346, 230, '\xE6', '\u00E6'} {
    fmt.Printf("[0x%X '%c'] ", char, char)
    æs += string(char)
}
```

This will print a line containing the text "[0xE6 'æ']" repeated six times. And at the end the æs string will contain the text ææææææ. (We will see more efficient alternatives to using the string += operator in a loop in a moment.)

An entire string can be converted to a slice of runes (i.e., code points) using the syntax *chars* := []rune(*s*) where *s* is of type string. The *chars* will have type []int32 since rune is a synonym for int32. This can sometimes be useful when we want to parse a string working character by character and at the same time be able to peek at characters before or after the current one. The reverse conversion is equally simple using the syntax *s* := string(*chars*) where *chars* is of type []rune or []int32; *s* will have type string. Neither conversion is free—but both are reasonably fast (O(*n*) where *n* is the number of bytes; see the sidebar "Big-O Notation", ➤ 89). For more string conversions see Table 3.2 (85 ◄); for number↔string conversions see Tables 3.8 and 3.9 (➤ 114–115).

Although convenient, using the string += operator is not the most efficient way to append to a string in a loop. A better approach (and one familiar to Python programmers) is to populate a slice of strings ([]string) one at a time and then concatenate them all in one go using the strings.Join() function. For Go, though, there is an even better way, similar to the way Java's *StringBuilder* works. Here is an example.

```
var buffer bytes.Buffer          // empty bytes.Buffer
for {
    if piece, ok := getNextValidString(); ok {
        buffer.WriteString(piece)
    } else {
        break
    }
}
fmt.Print(buffer.String(), "\n")
```

We begin by creating an empty bytes.Buffer. Then we write each string we want to concatenate into the buffer using its bytes.Buffer.WriteString() method. (We could, of course, write a separator between each string if we wanted to.) At the end, the bytes.Buffer.String() method can be used to retrieve the entire concatenated string. (We will see further uses of the powerful and versatile bytes.Buffer type later, e.g., ➤ 111 and ➤ 201.)

Accumulating strings in a bytes.Buffer is potentially much more memory- and CPU-efficient than using the += operator, especially if the number of strings to concatenate is large.

Go's for ... range loop (§5.3, ➤ 203) can be used to iterate over a string character by character, producing an index position and a code point at each iteration. Here is an example with its output beside it.

Big-O Notation

Big-O notation, O(...), is used in complexity theory to give approximate bounds for processing and for memory use for particular algorithms. Most of the measures are in proportion to *n* which is the number of items to process or the length of the item to process. They could be measures of memory consumption or of processing time.

O(1) means constant time, that is, the fastest possible time no matter what *n*'s size. O(log *n*) means logarithmic time; this is very fast and in proportion to log *n*. O(*n*) means linear time; this is fast and in proportion to *n*. O(n^2) means quadratic time; this is starting to get slow and is in proportion to n^2. O(n^m) means polynomial time which quickly becomes slow as *n* grows, especially if $m \geq 3$. O(*n*!) means factorial time; even for small values of *n* this can become too slow to be practical.

This book uses big-O notation in a few places to give a feel for the costs of processing, for example, the cost of converting from a string to a []rune.

```
phrase := "vått og tørt"
fmt.Printf("string: \"%s\"\n", phrase)
fmt.Println("index rune    char bytes")
for index, char := range phrase {
    fmt.Printf("%-2d    %U  '%c'  % X\n",
        index, char, char,
        []byte(string(char)))
}
```

string: "vått og tørt"			
index	rune	char	bytes
0	U+0076	'v'	76
1	U+00E5	'å'	C3 A5
3	U+0074	't'	74
4	U+0074	't'	74
5	U+0020	' '	20
6	U+006F	'o'	6F
7	U+0067	'g'	67
8	U+0020	' '	20
9	U+0074	't'	74
10	U+00F8	'ø'	C3 B8
12	U+0072	'r'	72
13	U+0074	't'	74

We create the phrase string literal, and then we print it followed by a heading on the next line. Then we iterate over every *character* in the string—Go's for ... range loop decodes UTF-8 bytes into Unicode code points (runes) as it iterates, so we don't have to concern ourselves with the underlying representation. For each character, we print its index position, its code point value (using Unicode notation), the character it represents, and the UTF-8 bytes used to encode the character.

To get the list of bytes we convert the code point (char of type rune) into a string (which will contain a single character consisting of one or more UTF-8-encoded bytes). Then we convert this one-character string into a []byte, that is, a byte slice, so that we can access the actual bytes. The []byte(string) conversion is very fast (O(1)) since under the hood the []byte can simply refer to the string's underlying bytes with no copying required. The same is true of the reverse conversion, string([]byte); again the underlying bytes are not copied, so the conversion is O(1). Table 3.2 (85 ◄) lists Go's string and byte conversions.

The %-2d, %U, %c, and % X format specifiers are explained shortly (§3.5, ➤ 93). As we will see, when the %X format specifier is used for an integer it outputs the integer in hexadecimal, and when it is used for a []byte it outputs a sequence of two-digit hexadecimal numbers, one number per byte. Here we have specified that the bytes should be output space-separated by including a space in the format specifier.

In practical programming using a for ... range loop to iterate over the characters in a string, along with the functions from the strings and fmt packages (and to a lesser extent from the strconv, unicode, and unicode/utf8 packages), provides all the functionality needed for the powerful and convenient processing and manipulation of strings. However, in addition, the string type supports slicing (since under the hood a string is in effect an enhanced []byte), and this can be very useful—providing we are careful not to slice any multibyte characters in half!

3.4. Indexing and Slicing Strings

As Table 3.2 (85 ◄) shows, Go supports string slicing using a subset of the syntax used by Python. This syntax can be used for slices of *any* type, as we will see in Chapter 4.

Since Go strings store their text as UTF-8-encoded bytes we must be careful to only ever slice on character boundaries. This is easy if we have 7-bit ASCII text since every byte represents one character, but for non-ASCII text the situation is more challenging since such characters may be represented by one or more bytes. Usually we don't need to slice strings at all but simply iterate over them character by character using a for ... range loop, but in some situations we really do want to extract substrings using slicing. One way to be sure to use slice indexes that slice on character boundaries is to use functions from Go's strings package, such as strings.Index() or strings.LastIndex(). The strings package's functions are listed in Tables 3.6 and 3.7 (➤ 108–109).

We will begin by looking at the different ways we can perceive a string. Index positions—which are the positions of the string's UTF-8 bytes—begin at 0 and go up to the length of the string minus 1. It is also possible to index back from the end of the slice using indexes of the form len(s) − n where n is the number of bytes counting back from the end. For example, given the assignment s := "naïve", Figure 3.1 shows string s as Unicode characters, code points, and bytes, as well as some valid index positions and a couple of slices.

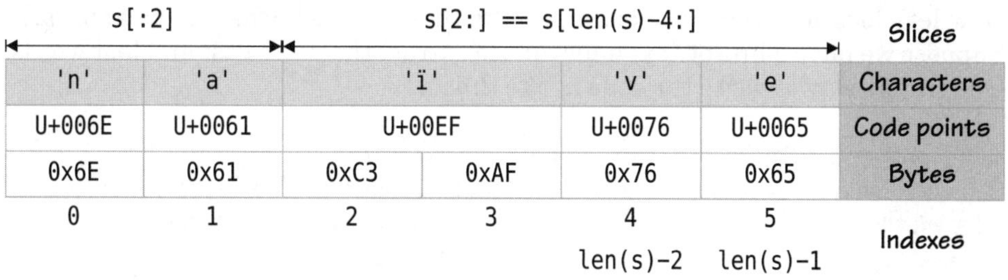

			s[2:] == s[len(s)–4:]			**Slices**
'n'	'a'	'ï'		'v'	'e'	**Characters**
U+006E	U+0061	U+00EF		U+0076	U+0065	**Code points**
0x6E	0x61	0xC3	0xAF	0x76	0x65	**Bytes**
0	1	2	3	4	5	**Indexes**
				len(s)–2	len(s)–1	

Slices row also shows `s[:2]` spanning the first two positions.

Figure 3.1 *Anatomy of a string*

Each index position shown in Figure 3.1 can be used with the [] index operator to return the corresponding ASCII character (as a byte)—for example, s[0] == 'n' and s[len(s) – 1] == 'e'. The index position of the *start* of the ï character is 2, but if we used s[2] we would simply get the first of the UTF-8 bytes used to encode ï (0xC3); such bytes are rarely what we want.

For strings that contain only 7-bit ASCII characters we can extract the first character (as a byte) using the syntax s[0], and the last character using s[len(s) – 1]. However, in general we should use utf8.DecodeRuneInString() to get the first character (as a rune, along with the number of UTF-8 bytes used to represent it), and utf8.DecodeLastRuneInString() to get the last character. (See Table 3.10, ➤ 118.)

If we really need to index individual characters, a couple of options are open to us. For strings that contain only 7-bit ASCII we can simply use the [] index operator which gives us very fast (O(1)) lookups. For non-ASCII strings we can convert the string to a []rune and use the [] index operator. This delivers very fast (O(1)) lookup performance, but at the expense of the one-off conversion which costs both CPU and memory (O(*n*)).

In the case of our example, if we wrote chars := []rune(s), the chars variable would be created as a rune (i.e., int32) slice with the five code points—compared with six bytes—shown in Figure 3.1. Recall that we can easily convert any rune (code point) back to a string—containing one character—using the string(char) syntax.

For arbitrary strings (i.e., those that might contain non-ASCII characters), extracting characters by index is rarely the right approach. Much better is to use string slicing—which also has the convenience of returning a string rather than a byte. To safely slice arbitrary strings, it is best to find the index position where we want to slice up to or from using one of the strings package's functions—see Tables 3.6 and 3.7 (➤ 108–109).

The following equality holds for string slices—and, in fact, for slices of every kind:

```
s == s[:i] + s[i:] // s is a string; i is an int; 0 <= i <= len(s)
```

Now let's look at a real slice example, one that takes a rather naïve approach. Suppose we have a line of text and want to extract the line's first and last words. One simple way to write the code is like this:

```
line := "røde og gule sløjfer"
i := strings.Index(line, " ")      // Get the index of the first space
firstWord := line[:i]              // Slice up to the first space
j := strings.LastIndex(line, " ") // Get the index of the last space
lastWord := line[j+1:]             // Slice from after the last space
fmt.Println(firstWord, lastWord)   // Prints: røde sløjfer
```

The `firstWord` (of type `string`) is assigned the bytes from the `line` from index position 0 (the first byte) to index position `i - 1` (i.e., up to the last byte before the space) since string slices go up to but exclude the end index position. Similarly, the `lastWord` is assigned the bytes from the `line` from index position `j + 1` (the byte after the space), to the end of the `line`'s bytes (i.e., to index position `len(line) - 1`).

Although this example's approach is fine for spaces and would also work for other 7-bit ASCII characters, it isn't suitable for working with arbitrary Unicode whitespace characters such as `U+2028` (Line Separator, LS) or `U+2029` (Paragraph Separator, PS).

Here is how to find the first and last words of a string no matter what whitespace characters are used to separate the words.

```
line := "rå tørt\u2028vær"
i := strings.IndexFunc(line, unicode.IsSpace)      // i == 3
firstWord := line[:i]
j := strings.LastIndexFunc(line, unicode.IsSpace) // j == 9
_, size := utf8.DecodeRuneInString(line[j:])       // size == 3
lastWord := line[j+size:]                          // j + size == 12
fmt.Println(firstWord, lastWord)                   // Prints: rå vær
```

The `line` string is shown as characters, code points, and bytes in Figure 3.2; the figure also shows the byte index positions and the slices used in the code snippet.

The `strings.IndexFunc()` function returns the first index position in the string given as its first argument where the function given as its second argument (with signature `func(rune) bool`) returns `true`. The `strings.LastIndexFunc()` does the same except that it works from the end of the string and returns the last index position for which the function returns `true`. Here we pass the `unicode` package's `IsSpace()` function as the second argument; this function accepts a Unicode code point (of type `rune`) as its sole argument and returns `true` if the code point is of a whitespace character. (See Table 3.11, ➤ 119.) A function's name is a ref-

				line[j:]								

Figure content — *Anatomy of a string with whitespace*:

Slices: line[:i] (indexes 0–2), line[j:] (from index 7), line[j+size:] (from index 12)

Characters	Code points	Bytes	Indexes
'r'	U+0072	0x72	0
'å'	U+00E5	0xC3	1
		0xA5	2
' '	U+0020	0x20	3
't'	U+0074	0x74	4
'ø'	U+00F8	0xC3	5
		0xB8	6
'r'	U+0072	0x72	7
't'	U+0074	0x74	8
'LS'	U+2028	0xE2	9
		0x80	10
		0xA8	11
'v'	U+0076	0x76	12
'æ'	U+00E6	0xC3	13
		0xA6	14
'r'	U+0072	0x72	15

Figure 3.2 *Anatomy of a string with whitespace*

erence to the function, and so can be passed wherever a function parameter is required—so long as the named (i.e., referred to) function's signature matches that specified by the parameter. (See §4.1, ➤ 140.)

Using the strings.IndexFunc() function to find the first whitespace character and slicing the string up to but excluding that character to get the first word is easy. But when searching for the last whitespace character we must be careful because some whitespace characters are encoded as more than a single UTF-8 byte. We solve this problem by using the utf8.DecodeRuneInString() function to give us the number of bytes occupied by the first character in the slice of the string that starts where the last whitespace character begins. We then add this number to the last whitespace character's index position to jump over the last whitespace character—however many bytes are used to represent it—so that we slice only the last word.

3.5. String Formatting with the Fmt Package

Go's standard library's fmt package provides print functions for writing data as strings to the console, to files and other values satisfying the io.Writer interface, and to other strings. These functions are listed in Table 3.3 (➤ 94). Some of the print functions return an error. It is not uncommon to ignore this return value when printing to the console, but the error should always be checked when printing to files, network connections, and so on.★

The fmt package also provides various scan functions (such as fmt.Scan(), fmt.Scanf(), and fmt.Scanln()) for reading data from the console, from files, and from strings. Some of these functions are used in Chapter 8 (§8.1.3.2,

---

★ Go also has two built-in print functions, print() and println(). These should *not* be used; they exist purely for the convenience of Go compiler implementers and may be removed from the language.

➤ 380)—see also, Table 8.2 (➤ 383). An alternative to using the scan functions is to split each string into fields using the `strings.Fields()` function and then convert those that aren't strings to values (e.g., numbers) using functions from the `strconv` package—see Tables 3.8 and 3.9 (➤ 114–115). Recall from Chapter 1 that we can read input typed at the keyboard by creating a `bufio.Reader` to read from `os.Stdin` and use the `bufio.Reader.ReadString()` function to read each line entered (§1.7, 40 ◀).

The easiest way to output values is to use the `fmt.Print()` and `fmt.Println()` functions (to print to `os.Stdout`, i.e., to the console), or the `fmt.Fprint()` and `fmt.Fprintf()` functions to output to a given `io.Writer` (e.g., to a file), or the `fmt.Sprint()` and `fmt.Sprintln()` functions to output to a string.

Table 3.3 *The Fmt Package's Print Functions*

Syntax	Description/result
`fmt.Errorf(format, args...)`	Returns an `error` value containing a string created with the *format* string and the *args*
`fmt.Fprint(writer, args...)`	Writes the *args* to the *writer* each using format %v and space-separating nonstrings; returns the number of bytes written, and an `error` or `nil`
`fmt.Fprintf(writer, format, args...)`	Writes the *args* to the *writer* using the *format* string; returns the number of bytes written, and an `error` or `nil`
`fmt.Fprintln(writer, args...)`	Writes the *args* to the *writer* each using format %v, space-separated and ending with a newline; returns the number of bytes written, and an `error` or `nil`
`fmt.Print(args...)`	Writes the *args* to `os.Stdout` each using format %v and space-separating nonstrings; returns the number of bytes written, and an `error` or `nil`
`fmt.Printf(format, args...)`	Writes the *args* to `os.Stdout` using the *format* string; returns the number of bytes written, and an `error` or `nil`
`fmt.Println(args...)`	Writes the *args* to `os.Stdout` each using format %v, space-separated and ending with a newline; returns the number of bytes written, and an `error` or `nil`
`fmt.Sprint(args...)`	Returns a `string` of the *args*, each formatted using format %v and space-separating nonstrings
`fmt.Sprintf(format, args...)`	Returns a `string` of the *args* formatted using the *format* string
`fmt.Sprintln(args...)`	Returns a `string` of the *args*, each formatted using format %v, space-separated and ending with a newline

Table 3.4 *The Fmt Package's Verbs*

Verbs are mostly used to output single values. If a value is a slice the output is usually a square bracket enclosed sequence of space-separated values, with each value formatted as the verb specifies. If the value is a map only %v or %#v may be used—unless the key and value are of the same type, in which case type-compatible verbs may also be used.

Verb	Description/result
%%	A literal % character
%b	An integer value as a binary (base 2) number, or *(advanced)* a floating-point number in scientific notation with a power of 2 exponent
%c	An integer code point value as a Unicode character
%d	An integer value as a decimal (base 10) number
%e	A floating-point or complex value in scientific notation with e
%E	A floating-point or complex value in scientific notation with E
%f	A floating-point or complex value in standard notation
%g	A floating-point or complex value using %e or %f, whichever produces the most compact output
%G	A floating-point or complex value using %E or %f, whichever produces the most compact output
%o	An integer value as an octal (base 8) number
%p	A value's address as a hexadecimal (base 16) number with a prefix of 0x and using lowercase for the digits a–f *(for debugging)*
%q	The string or []byte as a double-quoted string, or the integer as a single-quoted string, using Go syntax and using escapes where necessary
%s	The string or []byte as raw UTF-8 bytes; this will produce correct Unicode output for a text file or on a UTF-8-savvy console
%t	A bool value as true or false
%T	A value's type using Go syntax
%U	An integer code point value using Unicode notation defaulting to four digits; e.g., fmt.Printf("%U", '¶') outputs U+00B6
%v	A built-in or custom type's value using a default format, or a custom value using its type's String() method if it exists
%x	An integer value as a hexadecimal (base 16) number or a string or []byte value as hexadecimal digits (two per byte), using lowercase for the digits a–f
%X	An integer value as a hexadecimal (base 16) number or a string or []byte value as hexadecimal digits (two per byte), using uppercase for the digits A–F

Table 3.5 *The Fmt Package's Verb Modifiers*

Modifier	Description/result
space	Makes the verb output "-" before negative numbers and a space before positive numbers or to put spaces between the bytes printed when using the %x or %X verbs; e.g., fmt.Printf("% X", "←") outputs E2 86 92
#	Makes the verb use an "alternative" output format: %#o outputs octal with a leading 0 %#p outputs a pointer *without* the leading 0x %#q outputs a string or []byte as a raw string (using backticks) if possible—otherwise outputs a double-quoted string %#v outputs a value as itself using Go syntax %#x outputs hexadecimal with a leading 0x %#X outputs hexadecimal with a leading 0X
+	Makes the verb output + or – for numbers, ASCII characters (with others escaped) for strings, and field names for structs
–	Makes the verb left-justify the value (the default is to right-justify)
0	Makes the verb pad with leading 0s instead of spaces
n.m *n* *.m*	For numbers, makes the verb output a floating-point or complex value using *n* (of type int) characters (or more if necessary to avoid truncation) and with *m* (of type int) digits after the decimal point(s). For strings *n* specifies the minimum field width, and will result in space padding if the string has too few characters, and *.m* specifies the maximum number of the string's characters to use (going from left to right), and will result in the string being truncated if it is too long. Either or both of *m* and *n* can be replaced with * in which case their values are taken from the arguments. Either *n* or *.m* may be omitted.

```
type polar struct{ radius, θ float64 }
p := polar{8.32, .49}
fmt.Print(-18.5, 17, "Elephant", -8+.7i, 0x3C7, '\u03C7', "a", "b", p)
fmt.Println()
fmt.Println(-18.5, 17, "Elephant", -8+.7i, 0x3C7, '\u03C7', "a", "b", p)
```

```
-18.5·17Elephant·(-8+0.7i)·967·967ab{8.32·0.49}
-18.5·17·Elephant·(-8+0.7i)·967·967·a·b·{8.32·0.49}
```

For the sake of clarity, particularly when multiple consecutive spaces are output, we have put a light gray character (·) in the middle of every space shown.

The way that fmt.Print() and fmt.Fprint() handle whitespace is subtly different from the fmt.Println() and fmt.Fprintln() functions. As a rule of thumb the former are most useful for printing a single value or for "converting" a value to a string without error checking (use the strconv packages for proper conversions; ➤ 114–115), since they only output spaces between nonstring values. The latter are better for printing multiple values, since they output a space between each value and add a newline at the end.

Under the hood these functions use the %v (general value) format specifier—and they can print any built-in or custom value without formality. For example, the print functions know nothing about the custom polar type but still manage to print a polar value successfully.

In Chapter 6 we will see how to provide a String() method for custom types; this allows us to output them however we like. If we want to exercise similarly fine control over the printing of built-in types we can use the print functions that accept a format string as their first argument.

The format string used by the fmt.Errorf(), fmt.Printf(), fmt.Fprintf(), and fmt.Sprintf() functions consists of one or more *verbs*—these are format specifiers of the form %ML where M stands for one or more optional verb modifiers and L stands for a particular verb letter. The verbs are listed in Table 3.4 (95 ◀). Some of the verbs can accept one or more modifiers; the modifiers are listed in Table 3.5 (96 ◀).

We will now review some representative examples of format strings so that we can get a clear understanding of how they work. In each case we will show a tiny code snippet and then the output it produces.*

3.5.1. Formatting Booleans

Boolean values are output using the %t (truth value) verb.

```
fmt.Printf("%t %t\n", true, false)
```
```
true·false
```

If we want to output Booleans as integers we must do the conversion ourselves:

```
fmt.Printf("%d %d\n", IntForBool(true), IntForBool(false))
```
```
1·0
```

This makes use of a tiny custom function.

```
func IntForBool(b bool) int {
    if b {
```

---

* C, C++, and Python 2 programmers will find Go's format strings familiar—but with some subtle differences. For example, Go's %d can be used for any integer regardless of its size or signedness.

```
        return 1
    }
    return 0
}
```

We can convert a string back to a Boolean using the `strconv.ParseBool()` function. And, of course, there are similar functions for converting strings to numbers. (See §3.6.2, ➤ 113.)

3.5.2. Formatting Integers

Now we will look at the formatting of integers, starting with binary (base 2) output.

```
fmt.Printf("|%b|%9b|%-9b|%09b|% 9b|\n", 37, 37, 37, 37, 37)
```
```
|100101|···100101|100101···|000100101|···100101|
```

The first format (`%b`) uses the `%b` (binary) verb and outputs an integer as a binary number using as few digits as possible. The second format (`%9b`) specifies a width of 9 characters (which will be exceeded if necessary to avoid truncation), and uses the default right justification. The third format (`%-9b`) uses the – modifier to get left justification. The fourth format (`%09b`) uses 0 padding and the fifth format (`% 9b`) uses space padding.

Octal formatting is similar to binary, but also supports an alternative format. It uses the `%o` (octal) verb.

```
fmt.Printf("|%o|%#o|%# 8o|%#+ 8o|%+08o|\n", 41, 41, 41, 41, -41)
```
```
|51|051|····051|····+051|-0000051|
```

The alternative format is switched on by using the # modifier and causes a leading 0 to be output. The + modifier forces the sign to be output—without it, positive numbers are output without a sign.

Hexadecimal formatting uses the `%x` and `%X` (hexadecimal) verbs, the choice of which specifies whether to use lowercase or uppercase letters for the digits A–F.

```
i := 3931
fmt.Printf("|%x|%X|%8x|%08x|%#04X|0x%04X|\n", i, i, i, i, i, i)
```
```
|f5b|F5B|·····f5b|00000f5b|0X0F5B|0x0F5B|
```

For hexadecimal numbers the alternate format modifier (#) causes a leading 0x or 0X to be output. As with all numbers, if we specify a width that is wider than needed, extra spaces are output to right-justify the number in the given width—and if the width is too small the number is output in its entirety, so there's no risk of digits being truncated.

Decimal integers are output using the %d (decimal) verb. The only characters that can be used for padding are spaces and zeros, but it is easy to pad with other characters using a custom function.

```
i = 569
fmt.Printf("|$%d|$%06d|$%+06d|$%s|\n", i, i, i, Pad(i, 6, '*'))
```

```
|$569|$000569|$+00569|$***569|
```

For the last format we use the %s (string) verb to print a string since that's what our Pad() function returns.

```
func Pad(number, width int, pad rune) string {
    s := fmt.Sprint(number)
    gap := width - utf8.RuneCountInString(s)
    if gap > 0 {
        return strings.Repeat(string(pad), gap) + s
    }
    return s
}
```

The utf8.RuneCountInString() function returns the number of characters in the given string; this is always less than or equal to the number of bytes. The strings.Repeat() function takes a string and a count and returns a new string that contains the given string repeated count times. We chose to pass the padding character as a rune (i.e., as a Unicode code point) to avoid users of the function passing a string which might contain more than one character.

3.5.3. Formatting Characters

Go characters are runes (i.e., int32s), and they can be output as numbers or as Unicode characters.

```
fmt.Printf("%d %#04x %U '%c'\n", 0x3A6, 934, '\u03A6', '\U000003A6')
```

```
934 0x03a6 U+03A6 'Φ'
```

Here we have output the Greek capital letter *Phi* ('Φ') as decimal and hexadecimal integers, as a Unicode code point using the %U (Unicode) verb, and as a Unicode character using the %c (character or code point) verb.

3.5.4. Formatting Floating-Point Numbers

For floating-point numbers we can specify the overall width, the number of digits after the decimal place—and whether to use standard or scientific notation.

```
for _, x := range []float64{-.258, 7194.84, -60897162.0218, 1.500089e-8} {
    fmt.Printf("|%20.5e|%20.5f|%s|\n", x, x, Humanize(x, 20, 5, '*', ','))
}
```

```
|···········-2.58000e-01|···············-0.25800|************-0.25800|
|············7.19484e+03|········· 7194.84000|*********7,194.84000|
|···········-6.08972e+07|·····-60897162.02180|***-60,897,162.02180|
|············1.50009e-08|··············0.00000|*************0.00000|
```

Here we have used a for ... range loop to iterate over the numbers in a slice literal of float64 items.

The custom Humanize() function returns a string representation of the number it is given with grouping separators (for languages that use simple three-digit groups) and padding.

```
func Humanize(amount float64, width, decimals int,
        pad, separator rune) string {
    dollars, cents := math.Modf(amount)
    whole := fmt.Sprintf("%+.0f", dollars)[1:] // Strip "±"
    fraction := ""
    if decimals > 0 {
        fraction = fmt.Sprintf("%+.*f", decimals, cents)[2:] // Strip "±0"
    }
    sep := string(separator)
    for i := len(whole) - 3; i > 0; i -= 3 {
        whole = whole[:i] + sep + whole[i:]
    }
    if amount < 0.0 {
        whole = "-" + whole
    }
    number := whole + fraction
    gap := width - utf8.RuneCountInString(number)
    if gap > 0 {
        return strings.Repeat(string(pad), gap) + number
    }
    return number
}
```

The math.Modf() function returns the whole and fractional parts of a float64 as two float64s. To get the whole part as a string we use the fmt.Sprintf() function with a format that forces the sign to be output and then we immediately slice the string to strip off the sign. We use a similar technique for the fractional part, only this time we use the .m verb modifier specifying the number of decimal digits to use with a * placeholder. (So in this case, if decimals has the value 2 the format effectively becomes %+.2f.) For the fractional part we strip off the leading -0 or +0.

The grouping separators are inserted from right to left in the whole string and then a - sign is added if the number is negative. At the end we concatenate the whole and fractional parts and return the result—padding if required.

The %e, %E, %f, %g, and %G verbs can be used with complex numbers as well as with floating-point numbers. The %e and %E are the scientific format (exponential) verbs, %f is the floating-point verb, and %g and %G are the general floating-point verbs.

One factor to keep in mind, though, is that the modifiers are applied to both the real and imaginary parts of complex numbers individually—for example, a format of %6f will produce a result occupying at least 20 characters if the argument is a complex number.

```
for _, x := range []complex128{2 + 3i, 172.6 - 58.3019i,
        -.827e2 + 9.04831e-3i} {
    fmt.Printf("|%15s|%9.3f|%.2f|%.1e|\n",
        fmt.Sprintf("%6.2f%+.3fi", real(x), imag(x)), x, x, x)
}
```

```
|····2.00+3.000i|(····2.000···+3.000i)|(2.00+3.00i)|(2.0e+00+3.0e+00i)|
|·172.60-58.302i|(··172.600··-58.302i)|(172.60-58.30i)|(1.7e+02-5.8e+01i)|
|···-82.70+0.009i|(···-82.700···+0.009i)|(-82.70+0.01i)|(-8.3e+01+9.0e-03i)|
```

For the first column of complex numbers we wanted the components to have different numbers of digits after the decimal place. To achieve this we formatted the real and imaginary parts individually using fmt.Sprintf(), and then output the result formatted as a string using a format of %15s. For the other columns we used the %f and %e verbs directly—these always put parentheses around complex numbers.

3.5.5. Formatting Strings and Slices

Strings can be output with a minimum field width (which the print functions will pad with spaces if the string is too short), and with a maximum number of characters (which will result in truncation for any string that's too long). Strings can be output as Unicode (i.e., characters), or as a sequence of code points (i.e., runes) or as the UTF-8 bytes that represent them.

```
slogan := "End Óréttlæti♥"
fmt.Printf("%s\n%q\n%+q\n%#q\n", slogan, slogan, slogan, slogan)
```

```
End Óréttlæti♥
"End Óréttlæti♥"
"End \u00d3r\u00e9ttl\u00e6ti\u2665"
`End Óréttlæti♥`
```

The %s verb is used to print strings; we will return to it in a moment. The %q (quoted string) verb is used to print a string as a Go double-quoted string with printable characters printed literally, and with all other characters output using escapes (see Table 3.1, 84 ◄). If the + modifier is used, only ASCII characters (U+0020 to U+007E) are printed literally, with the rest output using escapes. If the # modifier is used the output is a Go raw string where possible, and a double-quoted string otherwise.

Although normally the variable corresponding to a verb is a single value of a compatible type (e.g., an int for the %d verb or for the %x verb), the variable can also be a slice—or a map, providing the map's key and value are both compatible with the verb (e.g., both strings or both numbers).

```
chars := []rune(slogan)
fmt.Printf("%x\n%#x\n%#X\n", chars, chars, chars)
```

```
[45·6e·64·20·d3·72·e9·74·74·6c·e6·74·69·2665]
[0x45·0x6e·0x64·0x20·0xd3·0x72·0xe9·0x74·0x74·0x6c·0xe6·0x74·0x69·0x2665]
[0X45·0X6E·0X64·0X20·0XD3·0X72·0XE9·0X74·0X74·0X6C·0XE6·0X74·0X69·0X2665]
```

Here we print a slice of runes—in this example, a slice of code points—as a sequence of hexadecimal numbers, one per code point, using the %x and %X verbs. If the # modifier is used it forces a leading 0x or 0X to be output for each number.

For most types, slices of the type are output as a square bracket enclosed sequence of space-separated items. An exception is []byte where no brackets or spaces are output unless we use the %v verb.

```
bytes := []byte(slogan)
fmt.Printf("%s\n%x\n%X\n% X\n%v\n", bytes, bytes, bytes, bytes, bytes)
```

```
End·Óréttlæti♥
456e6420c39372c3a974746cc3a67469e299a5
456E6420C39372C3A974746CC3A67469E299A5
45·6E·64·20·C3·93·72·C3·A9·74·74·6C·C3·A6·74·69·E2·99·A5
[69·110·100·32·195·147·114·195·169·116·116·108·195·166·116·105·226·153·165]
```

A slice of bytes—here, the UTF-8 bytes that represent a string—can be printed as a sequence of two-digit hexadecimal numbers, one per byte. If we use the %s verb the bytes are assumed to be UTF-8-encoded Unicode and are printed as a string. There is no alternative hexadecimal format for []bytes, but the numbers can be space-separated as the penultimate output line illustrates. The %v verb outputs []bytes as a square bracket enclosed sequence of space-separated decimal values.

Go right-aligns by default; we can left-align using the - modifier. And, of course, we can specify a minimum field width and the maximum number of characters to output as the next two examples illustrate.

```
s := "Dare to be naïve"
fmt.Printf("|%22s|%-22s|%10s|\n", s, s, s)
```

```
|······Dare·to·be·naïve|Dare·to·be·naïve······|Dare·to·be·naïve|
```

In this snippet, the third format (%10s) specifies a minimum field width of 10 characters, but since the string is longer than this—and the field width is a minimum—the string is printed in full.

```
i := strings.Index(s, "n")
fmt.Printf("|%.10s|%.*s|%-22.10s|%s|\n", s, i, s, s, s)
```

```
|Dare·to·be|Dare·to·be·|Dare·to·be············|Dare·to·be·naïve|
```

Here, the first format (%.10s) specifies that a maximum of 10 characters from the string may be output, so in this case the string is truncated to the specified width. The second format (%.*s) expects to get two arguments—the maximum number of characters to print and a string; here we have used the index position of the string's n character for the maximum which means that all the characters up to but excluding that character are printed. The third format (%-22.10s) specifies both a minimum field width of 22 characters and a maximum number of characters to print of 10 characters—this means that only the string's first 10 characters are printed, but in a field that is 22 characters wide. Since the field width is greater than the number of characters to print, the field is padded with spaces—and left-justified because of the - modifier.

3.5.6. Formatting for Debugging

The %T (type) verb is used to print a built-in or custom value's type, and the %v verb is used to print a built-in value's value. In fact, %v can also print the value of custom types, using a default format for types that do not have a String() method defined, or using the type's String() method if it has one.

```
p := polar{-83.40, 71.60}
fmt.Printf("|%T|%v|%#v|\n", p, p, p)
fmt.Printf("|%T|%v|%t|\n", false, false, false)
fmt.Printf("|%T|%v|%d|\n", 7607, 7607, 7607)
fmt.Printf("|%T|%v|%f|\n", math.E, math.E, math.E)
fmt.Printf("|%T|%v|%f|\n", 5+7i, 5+7i, 5+7i)
s := "Relativity"
fmt.Printf("|%T|\"%v\"|\"%s\"|%q|\n", s, s, s, s)
```

```
|main.polar|{-83.4 71.6}|main.polar{radius:-83.4, θ:71.6}|
|bool|false|false|
|int|7607|7607|
|float64|2.718281828459045|2.718282|
|complex128|(5+7i)|(5.000000+7.000000i)|
|string|"Relativity"|"Relativity"|"Relativity"|
```

This example shows how to output an arbitrary value's type and value using %T and %v. If the %v verb's formatting is satisfactory we can simply use fmt.Print() and similar functions since these use the %v verb's format by default. Using the # alternative format verb modifier with %v affects only struct types and causes them to be output with their type name and field names. For floating-point values, %v formats like the %g verb rather than like the %f verb. The %T format is mostly useful for debugging and includes the package name (in this case main) for custom types. Using the %q verb for strings puts them in quotes which is often convenient when debugging.

Two of Go's types have synonyms: byte for uint8 and rune for int32. Use int32 when handling 32-bit signed integers where int won't do (e.g., reading/writing binary files), and rune for Unicode code points (characters).

```
s := "Alias↔Synonym"
chars := []rune(s)
bytes := []byte(s)
fmt.Printf("%T: %v\n%T: %v\n", chars, chars, bytes, bytes)
```

```
[]int32: [65 108 105 97 115 8596 83 121 110 111 110 121 109]
[]uint8: [65 108 105 97 115 226 134 148 83 121 110 111 110 121 109]
```

As the code snippet illustrates, the %T verb always prints the original type name, not the synonym. Since the string has a non-ASCII character it is clear that we have a slice of runes (code points) and a slice of UTF-8-encoded bytes.

Go can also output any value's address in memory using the %p (pointer) verb.

```
i := 5
f := -48.3124
```

```
s := "Tomás Bretón"
fmt.Printf("|%p → %d|%p → %f|%#p → %s|\n", &i, i, &f, f, &s, s)
```

```
|0xf840000300 → 5|0xf840000308 → -48.312400|f840001990 → Tomás Bretón|
```

The & address of operator is explained in the next chapter (§4.1, ➤ 140). If we use the %p verb with the # modifier, the address's leading 0x is dropped. Outputting memory addresses like this can be useful when debugging.

Go's ability to output slices and maps is also useful for debugging, as is the ability to output channels—that is, the type that can be sent and received through the channel and the channel's memory address.

```
fmt.Println([]float64{math.E, math.Pi, math.Phi})
fmt.Printf("%v\n", []float64{math.E, math.Pi, math.Phi})
fmt.Printf("%#v\n", []float64{math.E, math.Pi, math.Phi})
fmt.Printf("%.5f\n", []float64{math.E, math.Pi, math.Phi})
```

```
[2.718281828459045 3.141592653589793 1.618033988749895]
[2.718281828459045 3.141592653589793 1.618033988749895]
[]float64{2.718281828459045, 3.141592653589793, 1.618033988749895}
[2.71828 3.14159 1.61803]
```

Using the unmodified %v verb, slices are output as square bracket enclosed sequences of space-separated items. Usually we output them using functions like fmt.Print() or fmt.Sprint(), but if we use a formatting output function then the usual verb to use is %v or %#v. However, we can also use a type-compatible verb such as %f for floating-point numbers or %s for strings.

```
fmt.Printf("%q\n", []string{"Software patents", "kill", "innovation"})
fmt.Printf("%v\n", []string{"Software patents", "kill", "innovation"})
fmt.Printf("%#v\n", []string{"Software patents", "kill", "innovation"})
fmt.Printf("%17s\n", []string{"Software patents", "kill", "innovation"})
```

```
["Software patents" "kill" "innovation"]
[Software patents kill innovation]
[]string{"Software patents", "kill", "innovation"}
[ Software patents          kill       innovation]
```

Using the %q verb for outputting slices of strings is particularly useful when the strings contain spaces since it makes each individual string identifiable—something that doesn't happen if we use the %v verb.

The last output might look wrong at first sight since it occupies 53 characters (not including the enclosing square brackets) rather than 51 (three strings of

17 characters, none of which is too big). The apparent discrepancy is due to the space separator that is output between each slice item.

In addition to debugging, the %#v verb may be useful when generating Go code programmatically.

```
fmt.Printf("%v\n", map[int]string{1: "A", 2: "B", 3: "C", 4: "D"})
fmt.Printf("%#v\n", map[int]string{1: "A", 2: "B", 3: "C", 4: "D"})
fmt.Printf("%v\n", map[int]int{1: 1, 2: 2, 3: 4, 4: 8})
fmt.Printf("%#v\n", map[int]int{1: 1, 2: 2, 3: 4, 4: 8})
fmt.Printf("%04b\n", map[int]int{1: 1, 2: 2, 3: 4, 4: 8})
```

```
map[4:D 1:A 2:B 3:C]
map[int] string{4:"D", 1:"A", 2:"B", 3:"C"}
map[4:8 1:1 2:2 3:4]
map[int] int{4:8, 1:1, 2:2, 3:4}
map[0100:1000 0001:0001 0010:0010 0011:0100]
```

Maps are output as the word "map", and then the map's *key–value* pairs (in an arbitrary order since maps are unordered). Just as with slices it is possible to use verbs other than %v—but only if both the key and value are compatible with the verb used, as in the example's last statement. (Maps and slices are covered in detail in Chapter 4.)

The fmt package's print functions are very versatile and can be used to print whatever output we need. The only feature not offered by the package's functions is padding with a particular character (other than zeros or spaces), but as we saw in the custom Pad() (99 ◄) and Humanize() (100 ◄) functions, this is very easy to do.

3.6. Other String-Related Packages

Go's considerable support for strings doesn't stop at indexing and slicing, or with the versatile fmt package's functions. The strings package in particular provides very rich functionality, and the strconv, unicode/utf8, and unicode packages also provide lots of useful functions. Examples that make use of functionality from all these packages are presented in this section. Regular expressions—provided by the powerful regexp package introduced later in this section—are used in several examples throughout the book.

There are other packages in the standard library that provide string-related functionality, and some of them are covered elsewhere in the book either in examples or in exercises.

3.6.1. The Strings Package

A common requirement in string processing is to be able to split a string into a slice of separate strings and then do further processing—for example, convert strings to numbers or trim whitespace.

To get a flavor of how to use some of the `strings` package's functions we will review some tiny examples that show some of the functions in use. All the package's functions are listed in Tables 3.6 and 3.7 (➤ 108–109). Let's start with splitting strings.

```
names := "Niccolò•Noël•Geoffrey•Amélie••Turlough•José"
fmt.Print("|")
for _, name := range strings.Split(names, "•") {
    fmt.Printf("%s|", name)
}
fmt.Println()
```
```
|Niccolò|Noël|Geoffrey|Amélie||Turlough|José|
```

Here we have a bullet-separated list of names (including one blank field) which we split using the `strings.Split()` function. This function takes a string to split and a separator string to split on and does as many splits as possible. (If we want to limit the number of splits we can use the `strings.SplitN()` function instead.) If we used the `strings.SplitAfter()` function the output would look like this:

```
|Niccolò•|Noël•|Geoffrey•|Amélie•|•|Turlough•|José|
```

The `strings.SplitAfter()` function performs the same splits as the `strings.Split()` function but keeps the separator. There is also a `strings.SplitAfterN()` function for when we want to split a specific number of times.

If we need to be able to split on any of two or more different *characters* we can use the `strings.FieldsFunc()` function.

```
for _, record := range []string{"László Lajtha*1892*1963",
    "Édouard Lalo\t1823\t1892", "José Ángel Lamas|1775|1814"} {
    fmt.Println(strings.FieldsFunc(record, func(char rune) bool {
        switch char {
        case '\t', '*', '|':
            return true
        }
        return false
    }))
}
```

Table 3.6 *The Strings Package's Functions #1*

Variables s and t are of type string, *xs is of type* []string, *i is of type* int, *and f is a function with the signature* func(rune) bool. *Index positions are of the first UTF-8 byte of the matching Unicode code point (character) or string, or* –1 *when there isn't a match.*

Syntax	Description/result
strings.Contains(s, t)	true if t occurs in s
strings.Count(s, t)	How many (nonoverlapping) times t occurs in s
strings.EqualFold(s, t)	true if the strings are case-insensitively equal
strings.Fields(s)	The []string that results in splitting s on white-space
strings.FieldsFunc(s, f)	The []string that results in splitting s at every character where f returns true
strings.HasPrefix(s, t)	true if s starts with t
strings.HasSuffix(s, t)	true if s ends with t
strings.Index(s, t)	The index of the first occurrence of t in s
strings.IndexAny(s, t)	The first index in s of any character that is in t
strings.IndexFunc(s, f)	The index of the first character in s for which f returns true
strings.IndexRune(s, char)	The index of the first occurrence of character *char* of type rune in s
strings.Join(xs, t)	A string containing the concatenation of all the strings in *xs*, each separated by t (which can be "")
strings.LastIndex(s, t)	The index of the last occurrence of t in s
strings.LastIndexAny(s, t)	The last index in s of any character that is in t
strings.LastIndexFunc(s, f)	The index of the last character in s for which f returns true
strings.Map(mf, t)	A copy of t with every character replaced or deleted according to the mapping function *mf* with the signature func(rune) rune *(see text)*
strings.NewReader(s)	A pointer to a value that provides Read(), ReadByte(), and ReadRune() methods that operate on s
strings.NewReplacer(...)	A pointer to a value that has methods for replacing each pair of *old, new* strings it is given
strings.Repeat(s, i)	A string consisting of i concatenations of s

Table 3.7 *The Strings Package's Functions #2*

Variable r of type `unicode.SpecialCase` *is used to specify Unicode rules (advanced).*

Syntax	Description/result
`strings.Replace(s, old, new, i)`	A copy of *s* with every nonoverlapping occurrence of `string` *old* replaced by `string` *new* if *i* is –1, or with at most *i* replacements otherwise
`strings.Split(s, t)`	The [ ]`string` that results in splitting *s* on *t* as many times as *t* occurs in *s*
`strings.SplitAfter(s, t)`	Works like `strings.Split()` only the separator is kept in the resultant strings *(see text)*
`strings.SplitAfterN(s, t, i)`	Works like `strings.SplitN()` only the separator is kept in the resultant strings
`strings.SplitN(s, t, i)`	The [ ]`string` that results in splitting *s* on *t*, *i* – 1 times
`strings.Title(s)`	A copy of *s* with the first letter of every word title-cased
`strings.ToLower(s)`	A lowercased copy of *s*
`strings.ToLowerSpecial(r, s)`	A lowercased copy of *s*, prioritizing the rules in *r (advanced)*
`strings.ToTitle(s)`	A title-cased copy of *s*
`strings.ToTitleSpecial(r, s)`	A title-cased copy of *s*, prioritizing the rules in *r (advanced)*
`strings.ToUpper(s)`	An uppercased copy of *s*
`strings.ToUpperSpecial(r, s)`	An uppercased copy of *s*, prioritizing the rules in *r (advanced)*
`strings.Trim(s, t)`	A copy of *s* with the characters in *t* removed from both ends
`strings.TrimFunc(s, f)`	A copy of *s* with the characters for which *f* returns true removed from both ends
`strings.TrimLeft(s, t)`	A copy of *s* with the characters in *t* removed from the start
`strings.TrimLeftFunc(s, f)`	A copy of *s* with the characters for which *f* returns true removed from the start
`strings.TrimRight(s, t)`	A copy of *s* with the characters in *t* removed from the end
`strings.TrimRightFunc(s, f)`	A copy of *s* with the characters for which *f* returns true removed from the end
`strings.TrimSpace(s)`	A copy of *s* with whitespace removed from both ends

```
[László·Lajtha·1892·1963]
[Édouard·Lalo·1823·1892]
[José·Ángel·Lamas·1775·1814]
```

The `strings.FieldsFunc()` function takes a string (the `record` variable in this example) and a reference to a function with the signature `func(rune) bool`. Since the function is so tiny and is used only in one place, we have created it as an anonymous function at the point it is needed. (Functions created this way are closures, although in this particular case we make no use of the enclosed state; see §5.6.3, ➤ 225.) The `strings.FieldsFunc()` function iterates over every character in the string it is given and calls the function it is passed as its second argument with each character. If the called function returns `true` a split is performed. Here we have said that the string should be split on tabs, stars, and vertical bars. (Go's `switch` statement is covered in §5.2.2, ➤ 195.)

We can replace all occurrences of a string within a string using the `strings.Replace()` function. For example:

```
names = " Antônio\tAndré\tFriedrich\t\t\tJean\t\tÉlisabeth\tIsabella \t"
names = strings.Replace(names, "\t", " ", -1)
fmt.Printf("|%s|\n", names)
```

```
| Antônio André· Friedrich· · Jean· Élisabeth Isabella· ·|
```

The `strings.Replace()` function takes a string to work on, a substring to find, a replacement string, and the number of replacements to make (–1 meaning as many as possible), and returns a string with all the (nonoverlapping) replacements performed.

When reading a string that has been entered by a human or that has come from an external source we often want to normalize its whitespace: that is, to get rid of any leading and trailing whitespace and replace each internal sequence of one or more whitespace characters with a single space.

```
fmt.Printf("|%s|\n", SimpleSimplifyWhitespace(names))
```

```
|Antônio·André·Friedrich·Jean·Élisabeth·Isabella|
```

Here is a one-line `SimpleSimplifyWhitespace()` function.

```
func SimpleSimplifyWhitespace(s string) string {
    return strings.Join(strings.Fields(strings.TrimSpace(s)), " ")
}
```

→ return strings. Join (strings . Fields (s))
  not enough ?

The strings.TrimSpace() function returns a copy of the string it is passed with any leading and trailing whitespace stripped off. The strings.Fields() function splits a string on any amount of whitespace and returns a []string. And the strings.Join() function takes a []string and a separator (which could be an empty string, although here we have used a space), and returns a single string with all the []string's strings joined by the separator. By using these three functions in this combination we get whitespace normalization.

Of course, we can more efficiently simplify whitespace doing a single pass using a bytes.Buffer.

```
func SimplifyWhitespace(s string) string {
    var buffer bytes.Buffer
    skip := true
    for _, char := range s {
        if unicode.IsSpace(char) {
            if !skip {
                buffer.WriteRune(' ')
                skip = true
            }
        } else {
            buffer.WriteRune(char)
            skip = false
        }
    }
    s = buffer.String()
    if skip && len(s) > 0 {
        s = s[:len(s)-1]
    }
    return s
}
```

The SimplifyWhitespace() function iterates over the characters in the string it receives, skipping any leading whitespace using the unicode.IsSpace() function (Table 3.11, ➤ 119). Then, it accumulates characters by writing them into a bytes.Buffer and for any sequence of one or more internal whitespaces it writes a single space. At the end any trailing space is stripped off (the algorithm allows at most one), and the resultant string is returned. A much simpler version using regular expressions is shown later (➤ 128).

The strings.Map() function can be used to replace or remove characters from strings. It takes two arguments, the first a mapping function with the signature func(rune) rune and the second a string. The mapping function is called for every character in the string and each character is replaced by the character returned by the function—or deleted if the mapping function returns a negative number.

```
asciiOnly := func(char rune) rune {
    if char > 127 {
        return '?'
    }
    return char
}
fmt.Println(strings.Map(asciiOnly, "Jérôme Österreich"))
```

```
J?r?me·?sterreich
```

Here, instead of creating the mapping function at the call site as we did with the strings.FieldsFunc() example shown earlier (107 ◄), we have created an anonymous mapping function and assigned (a reference to) it to a variable (asciiOnly). We have then used the strings.Map() function, passing it the variable that refers to the mapping function and the string we want to process and printing the result—a string with all non-ASCII characters replaced by "?". We could, of course, have created the mapping function at the call site, but doing it separately as we have done here is more convenient if the function being passed is long, or if we will need to use it more than once.

It is easy to use this approach to delete non-ASCII characters and produce:

```
Jrme·sterreich
```

This is achieved by changing the mapping function to return –1 instead of ? for non-ASCII characters.

We have mentioned previously that it is possible to iterate over every character (Unicode code point) in a string using a for ... range loop (§5.3, ➤ 203). A similar effect can be achieved when reading data from types that implement the ReadRune() function, such as the bufio.Reader.

```
for {
    char, size, err := reader.ReadRune()
    if err != nil { // might occur if the reader is reading a file
        if err == io.EOF { // finished without incident
            break
        }
        panic(err) // a problem occurred
    }
    fmt.Printf("%U '%c' %d: % X\n", char, char, size, []byte(string(char)))
}
```

```
U+0043·'C'·1:·43
U+0061·'a'·1:·61
U+0066·'f'·1:·66
U+00E9·'é'·2:·C3·A9
```

This code snippet reads a string and outputs each character's code point, the character itself, how many UTF-8 bytes the character occupies, and the bytes used to represent the character. In most cases readers operate on files, so here we might imagine that the reader variable was created by calling bufio.New-Reader() on the reader returned by an os.Open() call—something we saw in the first chapter's americanise example (§1.6, 29 ◄). However, in this case the reader was created to operate on a string:

```
reader := strings.NewReader("Café")
```

The *strings.Reader returned by strings.NewReader() offers a subset of the functionality of a bufio.Reader; in particular it provides the strings.Reader.Read(), strings.Reader.ReadByte(), strings.Reader.ReadRune(), strings.Reader.Unread-Byte(), and strings.Reader.UnreadRune() methods. The ability to operate on values that have a particular interface (e.g., provide a ReadRune() method), rather than on values of particular types, is a very powerful and flexible feature of Go, and is covered much more fully in Chapter 6.

3.6.2. The Strconv Package

The strconv package provides many functions for converting strings into other types and other types into strings. The package's functions are listed in Tables 3.8 and 3.9 (► 114–115; see also the fmt package's print and scan functions, §3.5, 93 ◄ and §8.2, ► 383.) Here we will review a few illustrative examples.

One common requirement is to convert a string representation of a truth value into a bool. This can be done using the strconv.ParseBool() function.

```
for _, truth := range []string{"1", "t", "TRUE", "false", "F", "0", "5"} {
    if b, err := strconv.ParseBool(truth); err != nil {
        fmt.Printf("\n{%v}", err)
    } else {
        fmt.Print(b, " ")
    }
}
fmt.Println()
```

```
true·true·true·false·false·false
{strconv.ParseBool:·parsing·"5":·invalid·syntax}
```

Table 3.8 *The Strconv Package's Functions #1*

Parameter bs is a []byte, *base is a number base (2–36), bits is the bit size the result must fit into (8, 16, 32, 64—or 0 for* int's *size for* ints; *32 or 64 for* float64s), *and s is a* string.

Syntax	Description/result
strconv.AppendBool(*bs*, *b*)	*bs* with "true" or "false" appended depending on bool *b*
strconv.AppendFloat(*bs*, *f*, *fmt*, *prec*, *bits*)	*bs* with float64 *f* appended; see strconv.Format-Float() for the other parameters
strconv.AppendInt(*bs*, *i*, *base*)	*bs* with int64 *i* appended using the given *base*
strconv.AppendQuote(*bs*, *s*)	*bs* with *s* appended using strconv.Quote()
strconv.AppendQuote-Rune(*bs*, *char*)	*bs* with rune *char* appended using strconv.QuoteRune()
strconv.AppendQuote-RuneToASCII(*bs*, *char*)	*bs* with rune *char* appended using strconv.QuoteRuneToASCII()
strconv.AppendQuote-ToASCII(*bs*, *s*)	*bs* with *s* appended using strconv.QuoteTo-ASCII()
strconv.AppendUInt(*bs*, *u*, *base*)	*bs* with uint64 *u* appended using the given *base*
strconv.Atoi(*s*) ⤳ *i*	string *s* converted to an int, and an error or nil; see also strconv.ParseInt()
strconv.CanBackquote(*s*)	true if *s* can be represented in Go syntax using backticks
strconv.FormatBool(*tf*)	"true" or "false" depending on bool *tf*
strconv.FormatFloat(*f*, *fmt*, *prec*, *bits*)	float64 *f* as a string. The *fmt* is a byte corresponding to an fmt.Print() verb, 'b' for %b, 'e' for %e, etc. (see Table 3.4, 95 ◀). The *prec* is the number of digits after the decimal point for an *fmt* of 'e', 'E', and 'f'; or the total number of digits for a *fmt* of 'g' and 'G'—use –1 to request the smallest number of digits that can be used while preserving accuracy going the other way (e.g., using strconv.ParseFloat()). The *bits* affects rounding and is usually 64.
strconv.FormatInt(*i*, *base*)	int64 *i* as a string in base *base*
strconv.FormatUInt(*u*, *base*)	uint64 *u* as a string in base *base*
strconv.IsPrint(*c*)	true if rune *c* is a printable character
strconv.Itoa(*i*) ⤳ *s*	int *i* as a string using base 10; see also strconv.FormatInt()

Table 3.9 *The Strconv Package's Functions #2*

Syntax	Description/result
strconv.ParseBool(s)	true and nil if s is "1", "t", "T", "true", "True", or "TRUE"; false and nil if s is "0", "f", "F", "false", "False", or "FALSE"; false and an error otherwise
strconv.ParseFloat(s, bits)	A float64 and nil if s is parseable as a floating-point number, or 0 and an error; bits should be 64; but use 32 if converting to a float32
strconv.ParseInt(s, base, bits)	An int64 and nil if s is parseable as an integer, or 0 and an error; a base of 0 means the base will be deduced from s (a leading "0x" or "0X" means base 16, a leading "0" means base 8; otherwise base 10), or a specific base (2–36) can be given; bits should be 0 if converting to an int or the bit size if converting to a sized integer (e.g., 16 for an int16)
strconv.ParseUint(s, base, bits)	A uint64 and nil or 0 and an error—just the same as strconv.ParseInt() apart from being unsigned
strconv.Quote(s)	A string using Go's double-quoted string syntax to represent string s; see also Table 3.1 (83 ◄)
strconv.QuoteRune(char)	A string using Go's single-quoted string syntax to represent Unicode code point char of type rune
strconv.QuoteRune-ToASCII(char)	A string using Go's single-quoted string syntax to represent Unicode code point char of type rune, using an escape sequence for a non-ASCII character
strconv.QuoteToASCII(s)	A string using Go's double-quoted string syntax to represent string s, using escape sequences for non-ASCII characters
strconv.Unquote(s)	A string that contains the Go syntax single-quoted character or double-quoted or backtick-quoted string in string s and an error
strconv.UnquoteChar(s, b)	A rune (the first character), a bool (whether the first character's UTF-8 representation needs more than one byte), a string (the rest of the string), and an error; if b is set to a single or double quote that quote must be escaped

All the strconv conversion functions return the converted value and an error, with the latter being nil if the conversion succeeded.

```
x, err := strconv.ParseFloat("-99.7", 64)
fmt.Printf("%8T %6v %v\n", x, x, err)
y, err := strconv.ParseInt("71309", 10, 0)
fmt.Printf("%8T %6v %v\n", y, y, err)
z, err := strconv.Atoi("71309")
fmt.Printf("%8T %6v %v\n", z, z, err)
```

```
 float64  -99.7 <nil>
   int64  71309 <nil>
     int  71309 <nil>
```

The strconv.ParseFloat(), strconv.ParseInt(), and strconv.Atoi() ("ASCII to int") functions shown here work much as we would expect. The call strconv.Atoi(s) is almost the same as strconv.ParseInt(s, 10, 0), that is, parse the given string as a base-ten integer and return an integer, only Atoi() returns an int and ParseInt() returns an int64. As we would expect, the strconv.ParseUint() function converts to an unsigned integer type and will fail if there's a leading minus sign in the string it is given. These functions will fail if there is any leading or trailing whitespace, but we can easily eliminate this with the strings.TrimSpace() function or by using the fmt package's scan functions (Table 8.2, ➤ 383). Naturally, the floating-point conversions will accept strings that use standard or exponential notation, such as "984", "424.019", and "3.916e-12".

```
s := strconv.FormatBool(z > 100)
fmt.Println(s)
i, err := strconv.ParseInt("0xDEED", 0, 32)
fmt.Println(i, err)
j, err := strconv.ParseInt("0707", 0, 32)
fmt.Println(j, err)
k, err := strconv.ParseInt("10111010001", 2, 32)
```

```
true
57069 <nil>
455 <nil>
1489 <nil>
```

The strconv.FormatBool() function returns a string representing the Boolean expression it is given as "true" or "false". The strconv.ParseInt() function converts an integer in string form into an int64. The second argument is the base to use, with 0 meaning use the base implied by the string's prefix: "0x" or "0X" for hexadecimal, "0" for octal, and decimal otherwise. In this snippet we have converted a hexadecimal and an octal number using their implied base and a binary number by specifying an explicit base of 2. Valid bases are 2 to 36 inclusive with bases

higher than 10 representing 10 with *A* (or *a*) and so on. The third argument is
the bit size (with 0 signifying the size of an int), so although the function always
returns an int64, the conversion will only succeed if it can be converted perfectly
to an integer of the given bit size.

```
i := 16769023
fmt.Println(strconv.Itoa(i))
fmt.Println(strconv.FormatInt(int64(i), 10))
fmt.Println(strconv.FormatInt(int64(i), 2))
fmt.Println(strconv.FormatInt(int64(i), 16))
```
```
16769023
16769023
111111111101111111111111
ffdfff
```

The strconv.Itoa() ("Integer to ASCII") function returns a string representing
its int argument in base 10. The strconv.FormatInt() function formats an int64
as a string using the given base (which must be specified, and must be between
2 and 36 inclusive).

```
s = "Alle ønsker å være fri."
quoted := strconv.Quote(s)
fmt.Println(quoted)
fmt.Println(strconv.Unquote(quoted))
```
```
"Alle·\u00f8nsker·\u00e5·v\u00e6re·fri."
Alle·ønsker·å·være·fri.·<nil>
```

The strconv.Quote() function returns the string it is given as a Go double-quoted
string and with any nonprintable ASCII characters and any non-ASCII characters represented using escapes. (Go's string escapes are shown in Table 3.1,
84 ◄.) The strconv.Unquote() function takes a string containing a Go double-
quoted string or a raw (backtick-quoted) string or a single-quoted character, and
returns the unquoted string equivalent and an error (or nil).

3.6.3. The Utf8 Package

The unicode/utf8 package provides several useful functions for querying and
manipulating strings and []bytes which hold UTF-8 bytes—many of these are
shown in Table 3.10. Earlier we saw how to use the utf8.DecodeRuneInString()
and utf.DecodeLastRuneInString() functions (91 ◄) to get the first and last
characters in a string.

Table 3.10 *The Utf8 Package's Functions*

Import `"unicode/utf8"`. *Variable b is type* `[]byte`, *s is of type* `string`, *and c is a Unicode code point of type* `rune`.

Syntax	Description/result
`utf8.DecodeLastRune(b)`	The last rune in *b* and the number of bytes it occupies, or U+FFFD (the Unicode replacement character, ❷) and 0, if *b* doesn't end with a valid rune
`utf8.DecodeLast-RuneInString(s)`	The same as `utf8.DecodeLastRune()`, only it takes a string as input
`utf8.DecodeRune(b)`	The first rune in *b* and the number of bytes it occupies, or U+FFFD (the Unicode replacement character, ❷) and 0, if *b* doesn't start with a valid rune
`utf8.DecodeRune-InString(s)`	The same as `utf8.DecodeRune()`, only it takes a string as input
`utf8.EncodeRune(b, c)`	Writes *c* into *b* as UTF-8 bytes and returns the number of bytes written (*b* must have enough space)
`utf8.FullRune(b)`	true if *b* begins with a UTF-8-encoded rune
`utf8.FullRune-InString(b)`	true if *s* begins with a UTF-8-encoded rune
`utf8.RuneCount(b)`	Same as `utf8.RuneCountInString()` but works on a []byte
`utf8.RuneCount-InString(s)`	The number of runes in *s*; this may be less than len(*s*) if *s* contains non-ASCII characters
`utf8.RuneLen(c)`	The number of bytes needed to encode *c*
`utf8.RuneStart(x)`	true if byte *x could* be the first byte of a rune
`utf8.Valid(b)`	true if *b*'s bytes represent valid UTF-8-encoded runes
`utf8.ValidString(s)`	true if *s*'s bytes represent valid UTF-8-encoded runes

3.6.4. The Unicode Package

The `unicode` package provides functions for querying Unicode code points to determine if they meet certain criteria—for example, whether the character they represent is a digit or a lowercase letter. Table 3.11 shows the most commonly used functions. In addition to those functions we would expect, such as `unicode.ToLower()` and `unicode.IsUpper()`, a generic `unicode.Is()` function is provided so that we can check whether a character is in a particular Unicode category.

Table 3.11 *The Unicode Package's Functions*

Variable c is of type rune *and represents a Unicode code point.*

Syntax	Description/result
unicode.Is(table, c)	true if c is in the table *(see text)*
unicode.IsControl(c)	true if c is a control character
unicode.IsDigit(c)	true if c is a decimal digit
unicode.IsGraphic(c)	true if c is a "graphic" character such as a letter, number, punctuation mark, symbol, or space
unicode.IsLetter(c)	true if c is a letter
unicode.IsLower(c)	true if c is a lowercase letter
unicode.IsMark(c)	true if c is a mark character
unicode.IsOneOf(tables, c)	true if c is in one of the tables
unicode.IsPrint(c)	true if c is a printable character
unicode.IsPunct(c)	true if c is a punctuation character
unicode.IsSpace(c)	true if c is a whitespace character
unicode.IsSymbol(c)	true if c is a symbol character
unicode.IsTitle(c)	true if c is a title-case letter
unicode.IsUpper(c)	true if c is an uppercase letter
unicode.SimpleFold(c)	A case-folded copy of the given c
unicode.To(case, c)	The case version of c where case is unicode.LowerCase, unicode.TitleCase, or unicode.UpperCase
unicode.ToLower(c)	The lowercase version of c
unicode.ToTitle(c)	The title-case version of c
unicode.ToUpper(c)	The uppercase version of c

```
fmt.Println(IsHexDigit('8'), IsHexDigit('x'), IsHexDigit('X'),
    IsHexDigit('b'), IsHexDigit('B'))
```

true·false·false·true·true

The unicode package provides the unicode.IsDigit() function to check whether a character is a decimal digit, but there is no similar function to check for hexadecimal digits, so here we have used our own custom IsHexDigit() function.

```
func IsHexDigit(char rune) bool {
    return unicode.Is(unicode.ASCII_Hex_Digit, char)
}
```

This tiny function uses the generic unicode.Is() function in conjunction with the unicode.ASCII_Hex_Digit range to determine whether the given character is a hexadecimal digit. We could easily create similar functions to test for other Unicode characteristics.

3.6.5. The Regexp Package

This subsection presents tables listing the regexp package's functions and the regular expression syntax the package supports, and includes a few illustrative examples. Here and elsewhere in this book, we assume prior knowledge of regular expressions, or "regexeps".*

The regexp package is a Go implementation of Russ Cox's RE2 regular expression engine.° This engine is fast and thread-safe. The RE2 engine doesn't use backtracking, so guarantees linear time execution O(n) where n is the length of the matched string, whereas backtracking engines can easily take exponential time O(2^n) (see the sidebar "Big-O Notation", 89 ◄). The superior performance is gained at the expense of having no support for backreferences in searches. However, it is usually straightforward to work around this constraint by making good use of the regexp API.

Table 3.12 lists the regexp package's functions, including four functions for creating *regexp.Regexp values. These values provide the methods shown in Tables 3.18 and 3.19 (► 124–125). The RE2 engine's syntax supports the escape sequences listed in Table 3.13 (► 121), the character classes listed in Table 3.14 (► 122), the zero-width assertions listed in Table 3.15 (► 122), the quantifiers listed in Table 3.16 (► 123), and the flags listed in Table 3.17 (► 123).

The regexp.Regexp.ReplaceAll() and regexp.Regexp.ReplaceAllString() methods support both numbered and named replacements. Numbered replacements start at $1 for the first capturing parenthesized match. Named replacements refer to named capture groups. Although replacements can be referred to by number or by name (e.g., $2, $filename), it is safest to use braces as delimiters (e.g., ${2}, ${filename}). Use $$ to include a literal $ in a replacement string.

---

* A good textbook that teaches regexeps is *Mastering Regular Expressions;* see Appendix C. The author's book, *Programming in Python 3,* has a chapter that teaches Python regexeps (these support a subset of regexp syntax). This chapter is available as a free download from www.informit.com/title/9780321680563 (click the "Sample Content" link and download Chapter 13).

° Information on RE2, including links to documents covering its rationale, performance, and implementation, is available from code.google.com/p/re2/ .

Table 3.12 *The Regexp Package's Functions*

Variables p and s are of type string, *with p being a regexp pattern.*

Syntax	Description/result
regexp.Match(*p*, *b*)	true and nil if *p* matches *b* of type []byte
regexp.Match-Reader(*p*, *r*)	true and nil if *p* matches the text read by *r* of type io.RuneReader
regexp.Match-String(*p*, *s*)	true and nil if *p* matches *s*
regexp.QuoteMeta(*s*)	A string with all regexp metacharacters safely quoted
regexp.Compile(*p*)	A *regexp.Regexp and nil if *p* compiles successfully; see Tables 3.18 and 3.19 (➤ 124–125)
regexp.Compile-POSIX(*p*)	A *regexp.Regexp and nil if *p* compiles successfully; see Tables 3.18 and 3.19 (➤ 124–125)
regexp.Must-Compile(*p*)	A *regexp.Regexp if *p* compiles successfully, otherwise panics; see Tables 3.18 and 3.19 (➤ 124–125)
regexp.Must-CompilePOSIX(*p*)	A *regexp.Regexp if *p* compiles successfully, otherwise panics; see Tables 3.18 and 3.19 (➤ 124–125)

Table 3.13 *The Regexp Package's Escape Sequences*

Syntax	Description
c	Literal character *c*; e.g., * is a literal * rather than a quantifier
000	Character with the given octal code point
\x*HH*	Character with the given 2-digit hexadecimal code point
\x{*HHHH*}	Character with the given 1–6-digit hexadecimal code point
\a	ASCII bell (BEL) ≡ \007
\f	ASCII formfeed (FF) ≡ \014
\n	ASCII linefeed (LF) ≡ \012
\r	ASCII carriage return (CR) ≡ \015
\t	ASCII tab (TAB) ≡ \011
\v	ASCII vertical tab (VT) ≡ \013
\Q...\E	Matches the ... text literally even if it contains characters like *

Table 3.14 *The Regexp Package's Character Classes*

Syntax	Description
[*chars*]	Any character in *chars*
[^*chars*]	Any character not in *chars*
[:*name*:]	Any ASCII character in the *name* character class: [[:alnum:]] ≡ [0-9A-Za-z] [[:lower:]] ≡ [a-z] [[:alpha:]] ≡ [A-Za-z] [[:print:]] ≡ [-~] [[:ascii:]] ≡ [\x00-\x7F] [[:punct:]] ≡ [!-/:-@[-`{-~] [[:blank:]] ≡ [\t] [[:space:]] ≡ [\t\n\v\f\r] [[:cntrl:]] ≡ [\x00-\x1F\x7F] [[:upper:]] ≡ [A-Z] [[:digit:]] ≡ [0-9] [[:word:]] ≡ [0-9A-Za-z_] [[:graph:]] ≡ [!-~] [[:xdigit:]] ≡ [0-9A-Fa-z]
[:^*name*:]	Any ASCII character not in the *name* character class
.	Any character (including newline if flag s is set)
\d	Any ASCII digit: [0-9]
\D	Any ASCII nondigit: [^0-9]
\s	Any ASCII whitespace: [\t\n\f\r]
\S	Any ASCII nonwhitespace: [^ \t\n\f\r]
\w	Any ASCII "word" character: [0-9A-Za-z_]
\W	Any ASCII non-"word" character: [^0-9A-Za-z_]
\p*N*	Any Unicode character in the *N* one-letter character class; e.g., \pL to match a Unicode letter
\P*N*	Any Unicode character not in the *N* one-letter character class; e.g., \PL to match a Unicode nonletter
\p{*Name*}	Any Unicode character in the *Name* character class; e.g., \p{Ll} matches lowercase letters, \p{Lu} matches uppercase letters, and \p{Greek} matches Greek characters
\P{*Name*}	Any Unicode character not in the *Name* character class

Table 3.15 *The Regexp Package's Zero-Width Assertions*

Syntax	Description/result
^	Start of text (or start of line if flag m is set)
$	End of text (or end of line if flag m is set)
\A	Start of text
\z	End of text
\b	Word boundary (\w followed by \W or \A or \z; or vice versa)
\B	Not a word boundary

Table 3.16 *The Regexp Package's Quantifiers*

Syntax	Description
e? or e{0,1}	Greedily match zero or one occurrence of expression *e*
e+ or e{1,}	Greedily match one or more occurrences of expression *e*
e* or e{0,}	Greedily match zero or more occurrences of expression *e*
e{m,}	Greedily match at least *m* occurrences of expression *e*
e{,n}	Greedily match at most *n* occurrences of expression *e*
e{m,n}	Greedily match at least *m* and at most *n* occurrences of expression *e*
e{m} or e{m}?	Match exactly *m* occurrences of expression *e*
e?? or e{0,1}?	Nongreedily match zero or one occurrence of expression *e*
e+? or e{1,}?	Nongreedily match one or more occurrences of expression *e*
e*? or e{0,}?	Nongreedily match zero or more occurrences of expression *e*
e{m,}?	Nongreedily match at least *m* occurrences of expression *e*
e{,n}?	Nongreedily match at most *n* occurrences of expression *e*
e{m,n}?	Nongreedily match at least *m* and at most *n* occurrences of expression *e*

Table 3.17 *The Regexp Package's Flags and Groups*

Syntax	Description
i	Match case-insensitively (the default is case-sensitive matching)
m	Multiline mode makes ^ and $ match at the start and end of every line (the default is single-line mode)
s	Make . match any character including newlines (the default is for . to match any character except newlines)
U	Make greedy matches nongreedy and vice versa; i.e., swap the meaning of ? after a quantifier (the default is for matches to be greedy unless their quantifier is followed by ? to make them nongreedy)
(?flags)	Apply the given flags from this point on (precede the flag or flags with – to negate)
(?flags:e)	Apply the given flags to expression *e* (precede the flag or flags with – to negate)
(e)	Group and capture the match for expression *e*
(?P<name>e)	Group and capture the match for expression *e* using the capture name *name*
(?:e)	Group but don't capture the match for expression *e*

Table 3.18 *The ∗regexp.Regexp Type's Methods #1*

Variable rx is of type ∗regexp.Regexp; *s is the* string *to match; b is the* [ ]byte *to match; r is the* io.RuneReader *to match; and n is the maximum number of matches (–1 means as many as possible). A* nil *return means no match(es).*

Syntax	Description/result
rx.Expand(...)	Performs the $ replacements done by the Replace-All() method—rarely used directly *(advanced)*
rx.ExpandString(...)	Performs the $ replacements done by the ReplaceAll-String() method—rarely used directly *(advanced)*
rx.Find(b)	A [ ]byte with the leftmost match or nil
rx.FindAll(b, n)	A [ ][ ]byte of all nonoverlapping matches or nil
rx.FindAllIndex(b, n)	An [ ][ ]int (a slice of 2-item slices) each identifying a match or nil; e.g., b[*pos*[0]:*pos*[1]] where *pos* is one of the 2-item slices
rx.FindAllString(s, n)	A [ ]string of all nonoverlapping matches or nil
rx.FindAllString-Index(s, n)	An [ ][ ]int (a slice of 2-item slices) each identifying a match or nil; e.g., s[*pos*[0]:*pos*[1]] where *pos* is one of the 2-item slices
rx.FindAllStringSub-match(s, n)	A [ ][ ]string (a slice of string slices where each string corresponds to a capture) or nil
rx.FindAllStringSub-matchIndex(s, n)	An [ ][ ]int (a slice of 2-item int slices that correspond to captures) or nil
rx.FindAllSub-match(b, n)	A [ ][ ][ ]byte (a slice of slices of [ ]bytes where each [ ]byte corresponds to a capture) or nil
rx.FindAllSubmatch-Index(b, n)	An [ ][ ]int (a slice of 2-item int slices that correspond to captures) or nil
rx.FindIndex(b)	A 2-item [ ]int identifying the leftmost match; e.g., b[*pos*[0]:*pos*[1]] where *pos* is the 2-item slice, or nil
rx.FindReaderIndex(r)	A 2-item [ ]int identifying the leftmost match or nil
rx.FindReaderSub-matchIndex(r)	An [ ]int identifying the leftmost match and captures or nil
rx.FindString(s)	The leftmost match or an empty string
rx.FindString-Index(s)	A 2-item [ ]int identifying the leftmost match or nil
rx.FindStringSub-match(s)	A [ ]string with the leftmost match and captures or nil
rx.FindStringSub-matchIndex(s)	An [ ]int identifying the leftmost match and captures or nil

Table 3.19 *The ∗regexp.Regexp Type's Methods #2*

Variable rx is of type ∗regexp.Regexp; *s is the* string *to match; b is the* []byte *to match.*

Syntax	Description/result
rx.FindSubmatch(*b*)	A [][]byte with the leftmost match and captures or nil
rx.FindSubmatchIndex(*b*)	A [][]byte with the leftmost match and captures or nil
rx.LiteralPrefix()	The possibly empty prefix string that the regexp must begin with and a bool indicating whether the whole regexp is a literal string match
rx.Match(*b*)	true if the regexp matches *b*
rx.MatchReader(*r*)	true if the regexp matches *r* of type io.RuneReader
rx.MatchString(*s*)	true if the regexp matches *s*
rx.NumSubexp()	How many parenthesized groups the regexp has
rx.ReplaceAll(*b*, *br*)	A []byte that is a copy of *b* with every match replaced with *br* of type []byte with $ replacements (*see text*)
rx.ReplaceAllFunc(*b*, *f*)	A []byte that is a copy of *b* with every match replaced with the return value of a call to function *f* of type func([]byte) []byte and whose argument is a match
rx.ReplaceAllLiteral(*b*, *br*)	A []byte that is a copy of *b* with every match replaced with *br* of type []byte
rx.ReplaceAllLiteralString(*s*, *sr*)	A string that is a copy of *s* with every match replaced with *sr* of type string replacements
rx.ReplaceAllString(*s*, *sr*)	A string that is a copy of *s* with every match replaced with *sr* of type string with $ replacements (*see text*)
rx.ReplaceAllStringFunc(*s*, *f*)	A string that is a copy of *s* with every match replaced with the return value of a call to function *f* of type func(string) string and whose argument is a match
rx.String()	A string containing the regexp pattern
rx.SubexpNames()	A []string (which must not be modified), containing the names of all the named subexpressions

An example that typically involves the use of replacements is where we have a list of names of the form *forename1 ... forenameN surname* and want to change the list to have the form *surname, forename1 ... forenameN*. Here is how we can achieve this using the regexp package, and with correct handling of accented and other non-English characters.

```
nameRx := regexp.MustCompile(`(\pL+\.?(?:\s+\pL+\.?)*)\s+(\pL+)`)
for i := 0; i < len(names); i++ {
    names[i] = nameRx.ReplaceAllString(names[i], "${2}, ${1}")
}
```

The names variable is of type []string and initially holds the original names. Once the loop is complete the names variable holds the modified names.

The regexp matches one or more whitespace-separated forenames each consisting of one or more Unicode letters (\pL) optionally followed by a period, followed by whitespace and a surname of one or more Unicode letters.

Using numbered replacements can lead to maintenance problems—for example, if we inserted a new capture group in the middle, at least one of the numbers would be wrong. The solution is to use named replacements since these aren't order-dependent.

```
nameRx := regexp.MustCompile(
    `(?P<forenames>\pL+\.?(?:\s+\pL+\.?)*)\s+(?P<surname>\pL+)`)
for i := 0; i < len(names); i++ {
    names[i] = nameRx.ReplaceAllString(names[i],
        "${surname}, ${forenames}")
}
```

Here we have given the two capture groups meaningful names. This helps make both the regular expression and the replacement string more understandable.

A simple regexp for matching duplicate "words" that relies on backreferences would be written in, say, Python or Perl, as \b(\w+)\s+\1\b. Since the regexp package doesn't support backreferences, to achieve the same effect we must combine a regexp with a few lines of code.

```
wordRx := regexp.MustCompile(`\w+`)
if matches := wordRx.FindAllString(text, -1); matches != nil {
    previous := ""
    for _, match := range matches {
        if match == previous {
            fmt.Println("Duplicate word:", match)
        }
        previous = match
```

```
        }
}
```

The regexp greedily matches one or more "word" characters. The regexp.Regexp.FindAllString() function returns a []string of all nonoverlapping matches. If there was at least one match (i.e., matches is not nil), we iterate over the string slice and print any duplicates by comparing the current matched word with the previous word.

Another common regexp use is to match *key*: *value* lines in configuration files. Here is an example that populates a map based on such lines.

```
valueForKey := make(map[string]string)
keyValueRx := regexp.MustCompile(`\s*([[:alpha:]]\w*)\s*:\s*(.+)`)
if matches := keyValueRx.FindAllStringSubmatch(lines, -1); matches != nil {
    for _, match := range matches {
        valueForKey[match[1]] = strings.TrimRight(match[2], "\t ")
    }
}
```

The regexp says to skip any leading whitespace and match a key which must begin with an English letter followed by zero or more letters, digits, or underscores, followed by optional whitespace, a colon, optional whitespace, and then the value—any characters up to but excluding the newline or end of the string. Incidentally, we could have used the slightly shorter [A-Za-z] instead of [[:alpha:]], or if we wanted to support Unicode keys, (\pL[\pL\p{Nd}_]*), Unicode letter followed by zero or more Unicode letters, decimal digits, or underscores. Since the .+ expression won't match newlines, this regexp will work on a string that contains multiple *key*: *value* lines.

Thanks to the use of greedy matching (which is the default), the regexp will consume any whitespace that precedes the value. But to get rid of whitespace at the end of a value we must use a trim function since the .+ expression's greediness means that following it with \s* would have no effect. Nor could we have used nongreedy matching (e.g., .+?), since that would only match the first word of values that contain two or more space-separated words.

By using the regexp.Regexp.FindAllStringSubmatch() function we will get a slice of slices of strings (or nil); the -1 says to match as many times as possible (without overlaps). In this example, each match will produce a slice of exactly three strings, the first containing the whole match, the second containing the key, and the third containing the value. Both the key and the value will have at least one character because their minimum quantification is one.

Although it is best to parse XML using Go's xml.Decoder, sometimes we may simply have XML-style attributes which have the form *name*="*value*" or *name*='*value*'. For these, a simple regexp is sufficient.

```
attrValueRx := regexp.MustCompile(regexp.QuoteMeta(attrName) +
    `=(?:"([^"]+)"|'([^']+)')`)
if indexes := attrValueRx.FindAllStringSubmatchIndex(attribs, -1);
    indexes != nil {
    for _, positions := range indexes {
        start, end := positions[2], positions[3]
        if start == -1 {
            start, end = positions[4], positions[5]
        }
        fmt.Printf("'%s'\n", attribs[start:end])
    }
}
```

The attrValueRx regexp matches a safely-escaped attribute name followed by an
equals sign and then a double- or single-quoted string. The parentheses used
for the alternation (|) would normally also capture, but in this case we don't
want them to—since we don't want to capture the quotes—so we have made
the parentheses noncapturing ((?:)). Just to show how it is done, instead of
retrieving the actual matching strings we have retrieved index positions. In this
example there will always be three pairs of ([start:end]) indexes, the first pair
for the whole match, the second pair for a double-quoted value, and the third
pair for a single-quoted value. Of course, only one of the values will match, in
which case the other's indexes will both be -1.

Just like the previous examples we have asked to match every nonoverlapping
match in the string, and in this case we get an [][]int of index positions (or
nil). For each positions slice of ints, the whole match is the slice attribs[posi-
tions[0]:positions[1]]. The quoted string is either attribs[positions[2]:posi-
tions[3]] or attribs[positions[4]:positions[5]], depending on the type of quote
used. The code begins with the assumption that double quotes are used, but if
this isn't the case (i.e., start == -1), then it uses the single-quote positions.

Earlier we saw how to write a SimplifyWhitespace() function (111 ◄). Here is
how to achieve the same thing using a regular expression and the strings.Trim-
Space() function.

```
simplifyWhitespaceRx := regexp.MustCompile(`[\s\p{Zl}\p{Zp}]+`)
text = strings.TrimSpace(simplifyWhitespaceRx.ReplaceAllLiteralString(
    text, " "))
```

The regexp does a single pass on the string and the strings.TrimSpace() function
only works on the ends of the string, so the combination of both doesn't do
too much work. The regexp.Regexp.ReplaceAllLiteralString() function takes a
string to work on and a replacement text with which every match is replaced.
(The difference between regexp.Regexp.ReplaceAllString() and regexp.Regexp.
ReplaceAllLiteralString() is that the former does $ replacements and the latter

does not.) So, in this case, every sequence of one or more whitespace characters (ASCII whitespaces and Unicode line and paragraph separators) is replaced with a single space.

For our final regexp example we will see how to do a replacement using a function.

```
unaccentedLatin1Rx := regexp.MustCompile(
    `[ÀÁÂÃÄÅÆÇÈÉÊËÌÍÎÏÐÑÒÓÔÕÖØÙÚÛÜÝàáâãäåæçèéêëìíîïñðòóôõöøùúûüýÿ]+`)
unaccented := unaccentedLatin1Rx.ReplaceAllStringFunc(latin1,
    UnaccentedLatin1)
```

The regexp simply matches one or more accented Latin-1 letters. The regexp.Regexp.ReplaceAllStringFunc() function calls the function passed as its second argument (with signature func(string) string) every time there is a match. The function is given the match's text as its argument and this text is replaced with the text the function returns (which could be an empty string).

```
func UnaccentedLatin1(s string) string {
    chars := make([]rune, 0, len(s))
    for _, char := range s {
        switch char {
        case 'À', 'Á', 'Â', 'Ã', 'Ä', 'Å':
            char = 'A'
        case 'Æ':
            chars = append(chars, 'A')
            char = 'E'
        // ...
        case 'ý', 'ÿ':
            char = 'y'
        }
        chars = append(chars, char)
    }
    return string(chars)
}
```

This simple function replaces every accented Latin-1 character with its unaccented cousin. It also replaces the æ ligature (which is a full character in some languages) with the characters *a* and *e*. Of course, this example is rather artificial since in this case we could just as easily write unaccented := UnaccentedLatin1(latin1) to perform the conversion.

This completes the illustrative regexp examples. Notice that in Tables 3.18 and 3.19, for every "String" regexp function, there is a corresponding function without the "String" that operates on []bytes rather than strings. Also, a few of the book's other examples use the regexp package (e.g., 35 ◀ and ▶ 344).

Now that we have covered Go's `strings` and introduced its string-related packages, we will round off the chapter with an example that makes use of some of Go's string functionality, followed as usual with some exercises.

3.7. Example: M3u2pls

In this section we will briefly review a short but complete program that reads an arbitrary `.m3u` music playlist file given on the command line and outputs an equivalent `.pls` playlist file. The program makes a lot of use of the `strings` package and other material covered in this and previous chapters, as well as introducing a few minor new things.

Here is an extract from an `.m3u` file with an ellipsis (...) used to elide most of the songs.

```
#EXTM3U
#EXTINF:315,David Bowie - Space Oddity
Music/David Bowie/Singles 1/01-Space Oddity.ogg
#EXTINF:-1,David Bowie - Changes
Music/David Bowie/Singles 1/02-Changes.ogg
...
#EXTINF:251,David Bowie - Day In Day Out
Music/David Bowie/Singles 2/18-Day In Day Out.ogg
```

The file begins with the literal string #EXTM3U. Each song is represented by two lines. The first line starts with the literal string #EXTINF: and is followed by the song's duration in seconds, then a comma, and then the song's name. A duration of –1 means that the length is unknown (in both formats). The second line is the path to the file that stores the song—here we are using the open, patent-free Vorbis Audio format in an Ogg container (www.vorbis.com), and Unix-style path separators.

Here is an extract from an equivalent `.pls` file, again with an ellipsis used to elide most of the songs.

```
[playlist]
File1=Music/David Bowie/Singles 1/01-Space Oddity.ogg
Title1=David Bowie - Space Oddity
Length1=315
File2=Music/David Bowie/Singles 1/02-Changes.ogg
Title2=David Bowie - Changes
Length2=-1
...
File33=Music/David Bowie/Singles 2/18-Day In Day Out.ogg
Title33=David Bowie - Day In Day Out
```

```
Length33=251
NumberOfEntries=33
Version=2
```

The .pls file format is slightly more elaborate than the .m3u format. The file
begins with the literal string [playlist]. Each song is represented by three
key–value entries for the filename, title, and duration in seconds. The .pls
format is actually a specialized form of .ini file (Windows initialization format)
where each key (within a square-bracket-titled section) must be unique—hence
the numbering. And the file ends with two lines of metadata.

The m3u2pls program (in file m3u2pls/m3u2pls.go) expects to be run with an .m3u
file specified on the command line and writes an equivalent .pls file to os.Stdout
(i.e., to the console). We can easily use redirection to send the .pls data into an
actual file. Here is an example of the program's usage.

```
$ ./m3u2pls Bowie-Singles.m3u > Bowie-Singles.pls
```

Here we tell the program to read the Bowie-Singles.m3u file and use console
redirection to write the .pls format version to the Bowie-Singles.pls file. (Of
course, it would be nice to be able to convert the other way too—and this is
precisely what the exercise that follows this section involves.)

We will review almost the entire program, skipping only the imports.

```
func main() {
    if len(os.Args) == 1 || !strings.HasSuffix(os.Args[1], ".m3u") {
        fmt.Printf("usage: %s <file.m3u>\n", filepath.Base(os.Args[0]))
        os.Exit(1)
    }

    if rawBytes, err := ioutil.ReadFile(os.Args[1]); err != nil {
        log.Fatal(err)
    } else {
        songs := readM3uPlaylist(string(rawBytes))
        writePlsPlaylist(songs)
    }
}
```

The main() function begins by checking to see if the program has been invoked
with an .m3u file specified on the command line. The strings.HasSuffix() function takes two strings and returns true if the first string ends with the second
string. If no .m3u file has been specified a usage message is output and the program is terminated. The filepath.Base() function returns the basename (i.e.,
the filename) of the given path and the os.Exit() function cleanly terminates the

program—for example, stopping all goroutines and closing any open files—and returns its argument to the operating system.

If an .m3u file has been specified we attempt to read the entire file using the ioutil.ReadFile() function. This function returns all the file's bytes (as a []byte) and an error which will be nil if the file was read without incident. If a problem occurred (e.g., the file doesn't exist or is unreadable), we use the log.Fatal() function to output the error to the console (actually to os.Stderr), and to terminate the program with an exit code of 1.

If the file is successfully read we convert its raw bytes to a string—this assumes that the bytes represent 7-bit ASCII or UTF-8 Unicode—and immediately pass the string to a custom readM3uPlaylist() function for parsing. The function returns a slice of Songs (i.e., a []Song). We then write the song data using a custom writePlsPlaylist() function.

```go
type Song struct {
    Title    string
    Filename string
    Seconds  int
}
```

Here we have defined a custom Song type using a struct (§6.4, ➤ 275) to provide convenient file-format-independent storage for the information about each song.

```go
func readM3uPlaylist(data string) (songs []Song) {
    var song Song              // empty Song to start out
    for _, line := range strings.Split(data, "\n") {
        line = strings.TrimSpace(line)
        if line == "" || strings.HasPrefix(line, "#EXTM3U") {
            continue
        }
        if strings.HasPrefix(line, "#EXTINF:") {
            song.Title, song.Seconds = parseExtinfLine(line)
        } else {
            song.Filename = strings.Map(mapPlatformDirSeparator, line)
        }
        if song.Filename != "" && song.Title != "" && song.Seconds != 0 {
            songs = append(songs, song)
            song = Song{}     // new empty Song
        }
    }
    return songs
}
```

This function accepts the entire contents of an .m3u file as a single string and returns a slice of all the songs it is able to parse from the string. It begins by declaring an empty Song variable called song. Thanks to Go's practice of always initializing things to their zero value, song's initial contents are two empty strings and a Song.Seconds value of 0.

At the heart of the function is a for ... range loop (§5.3, ➤ 203). The strings.Split() function is used to split the single string that holds the entire .m3u file's data into separate lines, and the for loop iterates over each of these lines. If a line is empty or is the first line (i.e., starts with the string literal "#EXTM3U"), the continue statement is reached; this simply passes control back to the for loop to force the next iteration—or the end of the loop if there are no more lines.

If the line begins with the "#EXTINF:" string literal, the line is passed to a custom parseExtinfLine() function for parsing: This function returns a string and an int which are immediately assigned to the current song's Song.Title and Song.Seconds fields. Otherwise, it is assumed that the line holds the filename (including the path) of the current song.

Rather than storing the filename as is, the strings.Map() function is called with a custom mapPlatformDirSeparator() function to convert directory separators into those native for the platform the program is running on, and the resultant string is stored as the current song's Song.Filename. The strings.Map() function is passed a mapping function with signature func(rune) rune and a string. For every character in the string the mapping function is called with the character replaced by the character returned by the passed-in function—which may be the same as the original one, of course. As usual with Go, a character is a rune whose value is the character's Unicode code point.

If the current song's filename and title are both nonempty, and if the song's duration isn't zero, the current song is appended to the songs return value (of type []Song) and the current song is set to its zero value (two empty strings and 0) by assigning an empty Song to it.

```
func parseExtinfLine(line string) (title string, seconds int) {
    if i := strings.IndexAny(line, "-0123456789"); i > -1 {
        const separator = ","
        line = line[i:]
        if j := strings.Index(line, separator); j > -1 {
            title = line[j+len(separator):]
            var err error
            if seconds, err = strconv.Atoi(line[:j]); err != nil {
                log.Printf("failed to read the duration for '%s': %v\n",
                    title, err)
                seconds = -1
            }
        }
```

```
        }
    }
    return title, seconds
}
```

This function is used to parse lines of the form: #EXTINF:*duration,title* and where the *duration* is expected to be an integer, either –1 or greater than zero.

The strings.IndexAny() function is used to find the position of the first digit or the minus sign. An index position of –1 means not found; any other value is the index position of the first occurrence of any of the characters in the string given as the strings.IndexAny() function's second argument, in which case variable i holds the position of the first digit of the duration (or of -).

Once we know where the digits begin we slice the line to start at the digits. This effectively discards the "#EXTINF:" that was at the start of the string, so now the line has the form: *duration,title*.

The second if statement uses the strings.Index() function to get the index position of the first occurrence of the "," string in the line—or –1 if there is no such occurrence.

The title is the text from after the comma to the end of the line. To slice from after the comma we need the comma's starting position (j) and must add to this the number of bytes the comma occupies (len(separator)). Of course, we know that a comma is a 7-bit ASCII character and so has a length of one, but the approach shown here will work with any Unicode character, no matter how many bytes are used to represent it.

The duration is the number whose digits go from the start of the line up to but excluding the j-th byte (where the comma is). We convert the number into an int using the strconv.Atoi() function—and if the conversion fails we simply set the duration to –1 which is an acceptable "unknown duration" value, and log the problem so that the user is aware of it.

```
func mapPlatformDirSeparator(char rune) rune {
    if char == '/' || char == '\\' {
        return filepath.Separator
    }
    return char
}
```

This function is called by the strings.Map() function (inside the readM3uPlaylist() function) for every character in a filename. It replaces any directory separator with the platform-specific directory separator. And any other character is returned unchanged.

Like most cross-platform programming languages and libraries, Go uses Unix-style directory separators internally on all platforms, even on Windows. However, for user-visible output and for human-readable data files, we prefer to use the platform-specific directory separator. To achieve this we can use the filepath.Separator constant which holds the / character on Unix-like systems and the \ character on Windows.

In this example we don't know whether the paths we are reading use forward slashes or backslashes, so we have had to cater for both. However, if we know for sure that a path uses forward slashes we can use the filepath.FromSlash() function on it: This will return the path unchanged on Unix-like systems, but will replace forward slashes with backslashes on Windows.

```go
func writePlsPlaylist(songs []Song) {
    fmt.Println("[playlist]")
    for i, song := range songs {
        i++
        fmt.Printf("File%d=%s\n", i, song.Filename)
        fmt.Printf("Title%d=%s\n", i, song.Title)
        fmt.Printf("Length%d=%d\n", i, song.Seconds)
    }
    fmt.Printf("NumberOfEntries=%d\nVersion=2\n", len(songs))
}
```

This function writes out the songs data in .pls format. It writes the data to os.Stdout (i.e., to the console), so file redirection must be used to get the output into a file.

The function begins by writing the section header ("[playlist]"), and then for every song it writes the song's filename, title, and duration in seconds, each on their own lines. Since each key must be unique a number is appended to each one, starting from 1. And at the end the two items of metadata are written.

3.8. Exercises

There are two exercises for this chapter, the first involving the modification of an existing command-line program, and the second requiring the creation of a web application (optionally) from scratch.

1. The previous section's m3u2pls program does a decent job of converting .m3u playlist files into .pls format. But what would make the program much more useful is if it could also perform the reverse conversion, from .pls format to .m3u format. For this exercise copy the m3u2pls directory to, say, my_playlist and create a new program called playlist that has the required functionality. Its usage message should be usage: playlist <file.[pls|m3u]>.

If the program is called with an .m3u file it should do exactly what the m3u2pls program does: Write the file's data in .pls format to the console. But if the program is called with a .pls file it should write the file's data in .m3u format, again to the console. The new functionality will require about 50 new lines of code. A straightforward solution is provided in the file playlist/playlist.go.

2. Data cleaning, matching, and mining applications that involve people's names can often produce better results by matching names by the way they sound rather than by how they are spelled. Many algorithms for name matching English language names are available, but the oldest and simplest is the Soundex algorithm.

The classic Soundex algorithm produces a soundex value of a capital letter followed by three digits. For example, the names "Robert" and "Rupert" both have the same soundex value of "R163" according to most Soundex algorithms. However, the names "Ashcroft" and "Ashcraft" have a soundex value of "A226" according to some Soundex algorithms (including the one in the exercise solution), but "A261" according to others.

The exercise is to write a web application that supports two web pages. The first page (with path /) should present a simple form through which the user can enter one or more names to see their soundex values—this is illustrated in Figure 3.3's left-hand screenshot. The second page (with path /test) should execute the application's soundex() function on a list of strings and compare each result to what we would expect—this is illustrated in Figure 3.3's right-hand screenshot.

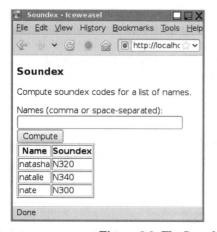 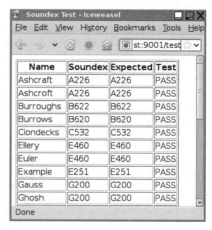

Figure 3.3 *The Soundex application on Linux*

Readers who would like a jump-start could copy one of the other web applications (statistics, statistics_ans, quadratic_ans1, quadratic_ans2) to get the skeleton of the application up and running, and then just focus on the soundex and test page functionality.

A solution is in the file soundex/soundex.go and is about 150 lines; the soundex() function itself is 20 lines although it does rely on an []int that maps capital letters to digits in a slightly subtle way. The solution's algorithm is based on the Python implementation shown on the Rosetta Code web site (rosettacode.org/wiki/Soundex) which produces slightly different results to the Go implementation shown on that site and from the one shown on Wikipedia (en.wikipedia.org/wiki/Soundex). The test data is in the file soundex/soundex-test-data.txt.

Naturally, readers are free to implement whichever version of the algorithm they prefer—or even implement a more advanced algorithm such as one of the Metaphone algorithms—and simply adjust the tests to match.

4 Collection Types

This chapter's first section explains Go's values, pointers, and reference types since an understanding of these is necessary for the rest of the chapter and for subsequent chapters. Go's pointers work just like those in C and C++, both syntactically and semantically—except that Go does not support pointer arithmetic, thus eliminating a whole category of potential bugs that can affect C and C++ programs. Nor does Go need *free()* or *delete* since Go has a garbage collector and manages memory automatically.* Values of Go's reference types are created in a unique and simple way and once created are used rather like Java or Python object references. Go's values work like those in most other mainstream languages.

This chapter's other sections are devoted to Go's built-in collection types. All the built-in collection types are covered—arrays, slices, and maps. These types are

---

* Go's delete() function is used to delete keys from maps as we will see later in this chapter.

so versatile and efficient that between them they comfortably meet almost every need. The standard library provides some additional, more specialized collection types—`container/heap`, `container/list`, and `container/ring`—that might be more efficient for particular use cases. A couple of tiny examples showing a heap and a list are presented in a later chapter (§9.4.3, ➤ 421). And Chapter 6 has an example that shows how to create a balanced binary tree (§6.5.3, ➤ 302).

4.1. Values, Pointers, and Reference Types

In this section we discuss what variables hold (values, pointers, and references —including array values, and slice and map references), whereas in the following sections we explain how to actually use arrays, slices, and maps.

In general, Go variables hold values. That is, we can think of a variable as "being" the value it stores. The exceptions are variables that refer to channels, functions, methods, maps, and slices—these hold references—and variables that hold pointers.

Values that are passed to functions or methods are copied. This is cheap for Booleans and numbers because they only occupy from one to eight bytes each. Passing strings by value is also cheap because Go compilers can safely optimize passing them so that only a small amount of data is actually passed per string, no matter how large the string is, since Go strings are immutable. (The amount per string is 16 bytes on 64-bit machines and 8 bytes on 32-bit machines.★) Of course, if a passed-in string is modified (e.g., using the += operator), behind the scenes Go must do a copy on write which is potentially expensive for large strings—but this is a price that would have to be paid no matter what language was being used.

Unlike C or C++, Go arrays are passed by value—so passing large arrays is expensive. Fortunately, arrays are rarely needed in Go programming since slices are used instead, as we will see in the next section. Passing a slice costs much the same as passing a string (i.e., 16 bytes on 64-bit machines and 12 bytes on 32-bit machines), no matter what the slice's length or capacity.★ Nor is there any copy on write overhead if the slice is modified, because unlike strings, slices are mutable (i.e., if a slice is modified the modification is visible to all the variables—references—that refer to it).

Figure 4.1 illustrates the relationship between variables and the memory they occupy. In the figure, memory addresses are shown in gray since they will vary, and bold is used to indicate changes.

Conceptually, a variable is the name given to a piece of memory that holds a value of a particular type. So if we have the short variable declaration y := 1.5,

---

★ The sizes in bytes were measured on a 64-bit machine and on a 32-bit machine at the time of this writing. The amounts are implementation details that may vary but will never be large.

Statement	Variable	Value	Type	Memory Address
y := 1.5	y	**1.5**	**float64**	0xf8400000f8
y++	y	**2.5**	float64	0xf8400000f8
z := math.Ceil(y)	y	2.5	float64	0xf8400000f8
	x	**2.5**	**float64**	Modifiable *copy* of y in Ceil()
	z	**3.0**	**float64**	0xf84000000c0

Figure 4.1 *Simple values in memory*

Go will set aside enough memory to store a float64 (i.e., 8 bytes) and will put the 1.5 value into this memory. From this point onward—while y remains in scope—Go will treat the variable y as synonymous with the memory that stores the float64 that y is associated with. So if we follow the declaration with the statement y++, Go will increment the value that y is associated with. However, if we pass y to a function or method, Go will pass a *copy* of y; in other words Go will create a new variable that is associated with the called function or method's corresponding parameter name and will copy y's value into the memory set aside for the new variable.

Sometimes we want a function to modify a variable that we pass it. This can be done without formality for reference types as we will see, but value types are copied, so any modifications are applied to the copy and the original value is left unchanged. Also, it can be expensive to pass some values, because they are large (e.g., an array, or a struct with lots of fields). Furthermore, local variables are garbage-collected if they are no longer being used (e.g., when they are not being referred to and they go out of scope), yet in many situations we want to create variables whose lifetime is determined by us rather than by their enclosing scope.

Parameters that are cheap to pass, parameters that are modifiable, and variables whose lifetimes are independent of scope, can all be achieved by using pointers. A *pointer* is a variable that holds another variable's memory address. Pointers are created to point to variables of a particular type—this ensures that Go knows how large (i.e., how many bytes) the pointed-to value occupies. A variable pointed to by a pointer can be modified through the pointer, as we will see shortly. Pointers are cheap to pass (8 bytes on 64-bit machines, 4 bytes on 32-bit machines), regardless of the size of the value they point to. And pointed-to variables persist in memory for as long as there is at least one pointer pointing to them, so their lifetime is independent of the scope in which they were created.*

---

* C and C++ programmers should be aware that although a particular Go compiler may make internal distinctions between stack and heap memory, Go programmers never have to worry about this since Go handles all the memory management itself internally.

In Go the & operator is overloaded. When used as a binary operator it performs a bitwise AND. When used as a unary operator it returns the memory address of its operand—and it is a memory address that a pointer stores. In Figure 4.2's third statement we assign the address of variable x of type int to variable pi which has type *int (pointer to int). The unary & is sometimes called the *address of* operator. The term *pointer* refers to the fact that a variable that holds the memory address of another variable is considered to be "pointing to" the other variable, as illustrated by the arrows in Figure 4.2.

The * operator is also overloaded. It multiplies its operands when used as a binary operator. And when used as a unary operator it provides access to the value pointed to by the variable it is applied to. So, in Figure 4.2, *pi and x can be used interchangeably after the statement pi := &x (but not after pi is assigned to point to a different variable). And since they are both associated with the same int in memory, any changes to one affect the other. The unary * is sometimes called the *contents of* operator or the *indirection* operator or the *dereference* operator.

Figure 4.2 also illustrates that if we change the pointed-to value (say, using x++), the value changes as we would expect, and when we dereference the pointer

Statement	Variable	Value	Type	Memory Address
x := 3	x	3	int	0xf840000148
y := 22	y	22	int	0xf840000150
x == 3 && y == 22				
pi := &x	x	3	int	0xf840000148
	pi	0xf840000148	*int	0xf840000158
*pi == 3 && x == 3 && y == 22				
x++	x	4	int	0xf840000148
	pi	0xf840000148	*int	0xf840000158
*pi == 4 && x == 4 && y == 22				
*pi++	x	5	int	0xf840000148
	pi	0xf840000148	*int	0xf840000158
*pi == 5 && x == 5 && y == 22				
pi := &y	y	y	int	0xf840000150
	pi	0xf840000150	*int	0xf840000158
*pi == 22 && x == 5 && y == 22				
*pi++	y	23	int	0xf840000150
	pi	0xf840000150	*int	0xf840000158
*pi == 23 && x == 5 && y == 23				

Figure 4.2 *Pointers and values*

(*pi), it returns the new value. We can also change the value *through* the pointer. For example, *pi++ means increment the pointed-to value; of course, this will only compile if the value's type supports the ++ operator, as Go's built-in numbers do.

A pointer doesn't have to stay pointing to the same value all the time. For example, toward the bottom of the figure we set the pointer to point to a different value (pi := &y), and then change y through the pointer. We could easily have gone on to change y directly (say, using y++), and then *pi would return y's new value.

It is also possible to have pointers to pointers (and pointers to pointers to pointers, etc.). Using a pointer to refer to a value is called *indirection*. And if we use pointers to pointers we are said to be using multiple levels of indirection. This is quite common in C and C++, but not needed so often in Go because of Go's use of reference types. Here is a very simple example.

```
z := 37    // z is of type int
pi := &z   // pi is of type *int (pointer to int)
ppi := &pi // ppi is of type **int (pointer to pointer to int)
fmt.Println(z, *pi, **ppi)
**ppi++    // Semantically the same as: (*(*ppi))++ and *(*ppi)++
fmt.Println(z, *pi, **ppi)
```

```
37 37 37
38 38 38
```

In this snippet, pi is a pointer of type *int (pointer to int) that is pointing to z of type int, and ppi is a pointer of type **int (pointer to pointer to int) that is pointing to pi. When dereferencing we use one * for each level of indirection, so *ppi dereferences ppi to produce an *int, that is, a memory address, and by applying the * operator a second time (**ppi), we get the pointed-to int.

In addition to being the multiplication and dereferencing operator, the * operator is also overloaded for a third purpose—as a type modifier. When an * is placed on the left of a type name it changes the meaning of the name from specifying a value of the given type to specifying a pointer to a value of the given type. This is shown in Figure 4.2's "Type" column.

Let's look at a tiny example to illustrate some of what we've discussed so far.

```
i := 9
j := 5
product := 0
swapAndProduct1(&i, &j, &product)
fmt.Println(i, j, product)
```

```
5 9 45
```

Here we have created three variables of type int and given them initial values. Then we have called a custom swapAndProduct1() function that takes three int pointers and makes sure that the first two (pointed to) integers are in ascending order and sets the third one's (pointed to) value to the product of the first two. Since the function takes pointers rather than values, we must pass the addresses of the ints, not the ints themselves. Whenever we see the & address of operator being used in a function call, we should assume that the corresponding variable's value might be modified inside the function. Here is the swapAndProduct1() function.

```go
func swapAndProduct1(x, y, product *int) {
    if *x > *y {
        *x, *y = *y, *x
    }
    *product = *x * *y // The compiler would be happy with: *product=*x**y
}
```

The function's parameter declaration's *int uses the * type modifier to specify that the parameters are all pointers to integers. This means, of course, that we can only pass the *addresses* of integer variables (using the & address of operator), not integer variables themselves or literal integer values.

Within the function we are concerned with the values that the pointers point to, so we must use the * dereference operator throughout. In the last executable line we multiply two pointed-to values together and assign the result to another pointer's pointed-to value. Go can distinguish when two consecutive *s mean multiplication and dereference rather than two dereferences, based on the context. Inside the function the pointers are called x, y, and product, but the values they point to are the ints i, j, and product, at the function's call site.

Writing functions in this way is common in C and older C++ code, but is less often necessary in Go. If we have just one or a few values it is more idiomatic in Go to return them, and if we have lots of values it is common to pass them as a slice or map (which can be cheaply passed without using pointers, as we will see shortly), or in a struct passed by pointer if they are all of different types. Here is a simpler alternative function that doesn't use pointers:

```go
i := 9
j := 5
i, j, product := swapAndProduct2(i, j)
fmt.Println(i, j, product)
```
```
5 9 45
```

And here is how we would write the corresponding swapAndProduct2() function.

```
func swapAndProduct2(x, y int) (int, int, int) {
    if x > y {
        x, y = y, x
    }
    return x, y, x * y
}
```

This version of the function is perhaps clearer than the first one; but without using pointers it has the disadvantage that it cannot perform the swap in-place.

In C and C++ it is common to have functions which accept a pointer to a Boolean that is used to indicate success or failure. This can easily be done in Go by including a *bool in a function's signature; but it is much more convenient to return a Boolean success flag (or best of all, an error value), as the last (or only) return value, which is standard practice in Go.

In the code snippets shown so far, we have used the & address of operator to take the address of function parameters or local variables. Thanks to Go's automatic memory management this is always safe, since so long as a pointer refers to a variable, that variable will be kept in memory. This is why it is safe to return pointers to local variables created inside functions in Go (something that is a disastrous error in C and C++ for nonstatic variables).

In situations where we want to pass around modifiable values of nonreference types or to pass values of large types efficiently, we need to use pointers. Go provides two syntaxes for creating variables and at the same time acquiring pointers to them, one using the built-in new() function and the other using the address of operator. We will look at both syntaxes, and at how to create a plain custom struct value, for comparison.

```
type composer struct {
    name      string
    birthYear int
}
```

Given this struct definition we can create composer values or we can create pointers to composer values, that is, variables of type *composer. And in either case we can take advantage of Go's support for struct initialization when we use braces.

```
antónio := composer{"António Teixeira", 1707} // composer value
agnes := new(composer)                         // pointer to composer
agnes.name, agnes.birthYear = "Agnes Zimmermann", 1845
julia := &composer{}                           // pointer to composer
julia.name, julia.birthYear = "Julia Ward Howe", 1819
augusta := &composer{"Augusta Holmès", 1847}  // pointer to composer
```

```
fmt.Println(antónio)
fmt.Println(agnes, augusta, julia)
```

```
{António Teixeira 1707}
&{Agnes Zimmermann 1845} &{Augusta Holmès 1847} &{Julia Ward Howe 1819}
```

When Go prints pointers to structs it prints the dereferenced struct but prefixed with the & address of operator to indicate that it is a pointer. The part of the code snippet where the agnes and julia pointers are created illustrates the following equivalence when the type is one that can be initialized using braces:

$$\text{new}(Type) \equiv \&Type\{\}$$

Both these syntaxes allocate a new zeroed value of the given *Type* and return a pointer to the value. If the *Type* isn't a type that can be initialized using braces then we can use only the built-in new() function. And, of course, we don't have to worry about the value's lifetime or ever delete it, since Go's memory management system takes care of all that for us.

One advantage of using the &*Type*{} syntax for structs is that we can specify initial field values as we did here when creating the augusta pointer. (We can even specify only selected fields and leave the others at their zero values as we will see later; §6.4, ➤ 275.)

In addition to values and pointers, Go has reference types. (Go also has interfaces, but for almost all practical purposes we can consider an interface to be a kind of reference; interfaces are covered later; §6.3, ➤ 265.) A variable of a reference type refers to a hidden value in memory that stores the actual data. Variables holding reference types are cheap to pass (e.g., 16 bytes for a slice and 8 bytes for a map on 64-bit machines), and are used with the same syntax as a value (i.e., we don't need to take a reference type's address or dereference it to access the value it refers to).

Once we reach the stage where we need to return more than four or five values from a function or method, it is best to pass a slice if the values are homogeneous, or to use a pointer to a struct if they are heterogeneous. Passing a slice, or a pointer to a struct, is cheap, and allows us to modify the data in-place. We will look at a couple of small examples to illustrate these points.

```
grades := []int{87, 55, 43, 71, 60, 43, 32, 19, 63}
inflate(grades, 3)
fmt.Println(grades)
```

```
[261 165 129 213 180 129 96 57 189]
```

Here we perform an operation on all the numbers in a slice of ints. Maps and slices are reference types, and any changes made to a map or to a slice's items—

whether directly or inside a function they have been passed to—are visible to all the variables that refer to them.

```go
func inflate(numbers []int, factor int) {
    for i := range numbers {
        numbers[i] *= factor
    }
}
```

The grades slice is passed in as the parameter numbers—but unlike when we pass values, any changes applied to numbers are reflected in grades since they both refer to the same underlying slice.

Since we want to modify the slice's values in-place we have used a loop counter to access each item in turn. We didn't use a for *index, item* … range loop since that gets a copy of each item from the slice it operates on—this would result in the copy being multiplied by the factor each time and then discarded, leaving the original slice unchanged. We could have used a for loop familiar in other languages (e.g., for *i* := 0; *i* < len(numbers); *i*++), but instead we have used the more convenient for *index* := range syntax. (All the for loop syntaxes are covered in the next chapter; §5.3, ➤ 203.)

Let's now imagine that we have a rectangle type that stores a rectangle's position as its top-left and bottom-right *x*, *y* coordinates, and its fill color. We could represent the rectangle's data using a struct.

```go
type rectangle struct {
    x0, y0, x1, y1 int
    fill           color.RGBA
}
```

Now we can create a value of the rectangle type, print it, resize it, and then print it again.

```go
rect := rectangle{4, 8, 20, 10, color.RGBA{0xFF, 0, 0, 0xFF}}
fmt.Println(rect)
resizeRect(&rect, 5, 5)
fmt.Println(rect)
```

```
{4 8 20 10 {255 0 0 255}}
{4 8 25 15 {255 0 0 255}}
```

As we noted in the previous chapter, even though Go knows nothing of our custom rectangle type it is still able to print it in a sensible way. The output shown below the code snippet clearly shows that the custom resizeRect() function correctly did its job. And rather than passing the whole rectangle (at least 16 bytes for the ints alone), we just passed its address (8 bytes on a 64-bit system, no matter how large the struct is).

```
func resizeRect(rect *rectangle, Δwidth, Δheight int) {
    (*rect).x1 += Δwidth // Ugly explicit dereference
    rect.y1 += Δheight   // . automatically dereferences structs
}
```

The function's first statement uses an explicit dereference just to show what is happening under the hood. The (*rect) refers to the actual rectangle value that the pointer points to, and the .x1 refers to the rectangle's x1 field. The second statement shows the idiomatic way to work with struct values—or with pointers to structs—in the latter case relying on Go to do the dereferencing for us. This works because Go's . (dot) selector operator automatically dereferences pointers to structs.*

Certain types in Go are reference types: maps, slices, channels, functions, and methods. Unlike with pointers, there is no special syntax for reference types since they are used just like values. It is also possible to have pointers to the reference types, although this is really only useful—and sometimes essential—for slices. (We will see the use case for using a pointer to a slice in the next chapter; §5.7, ➤ 244.)

If we declare a variable to hold a function, the variable actually gets a reference to the function. Function references know the signature of the function they refer to, so it is not possible to pass a reference to a function that doesn't have the right signature—thus eliminating some really nasty errors and crashes which can occur in languages that allow functions to be passed by pointer but that don't guarantee that such functions have the correct signature. We have already seen a few examples of passing function references—for example, when we passed a mapping function to the strings.Map() function (112 ◄; 132 ◄). We will see many more examples of pointers and reference types throughout the rest of the book.

4.2. Arrays and Slices

A Go array is a fixed-length sequence of items of the same type. Multidimensional arrays can be created simply by using items that are themselves arrays.

Array items are indexed using the [] index operator by their 0-based position, so an array's first item is *array[0]* and its last item is *array[len(array) - 1]*. Arrays are mutable, so we can use the syntax *array[index]* on the left of an assignment

---

* Go doesn't have or need the -> dereferencing operator used in C and C++. Go's . (dot) operator is sufficient for most situations (e.g., to access the fields in a struct or a pointer to a struct), and where it isn't, we can explicitly dereference using as many * operators as there are levels of indirection.

to set the *array*'s item at the given *index* position. We can also use this syntax in an expression on the right of an assignment or in a function call, to access the item.

Arrays are created using the syntaxes:

```
[length]Type
[N]Type{value1, value2, ..., valueN}
[...]Type{value1, value2, ..., valueN}
```

If the ... (ellipsis) operator is used in this context, Go will calculate the array's length for us. (The ellipsis operator is overloaded for other purposes, as we will see later in this chapter and in Chapter 5.) In all cases an array's length is fixed and unchangeable.

Here are some examples that show how to create and index arrays.

```
var buffer [20]byte
var grid1 [3][3]int
grid1[1][0], grid1[1][1], grid1[1][2] = 8, 6, 2
grid2 := [3][3]int{{4, 3}, {8, 6, 2}}
cities := [...]string{"Shanghai", "Mumbai", "Istanbul", "Beijing"}
cities[len(cities)-1] = "Karachi"
fmt.Println("Type     Len Contents")
fmt.Printf("%-8T %2d %v\n", buffer, len(buffer), buffer)
fmt.Printf("%-8T %2d %q\n", cities, len(cities), cities)
fmt.Printf("%-8T %2d %v\n", grid1, len(grid1), grid1)
fmt.Printf("%-8T %2d %v\n", grid2, len(grid2), grid2)
```

```
Type     Len Contents
[20]uint8 20 [0 0 0 0 0 0 0 0 0 0 0 0 0 0 0 0 0 0 0 0]
[4]string  4 ["Shanghai" "Mumbai" "Istanbul" "Karachi"]
[3][3]int  3 [[0 0 0] [8 6 2] [0 0 0]]
[3][3]int  3 [[4 3 0] [8 6 2] [0 0 0]]
```

Go guarantees that all array items are initialized to their zero value if they are not explicitly initialized—or are only partly initialized—when they are created, as the buffer, grid1, and grid2 variables illustrate.

The length of an array is given by the len() function. Since arrays are of fixed size their capacity is always equal to their length, so for arrays the cap() function returns the same number as the len() function. Arrays can be sliced using the same slicing syntax as strings or slices, only the result is a slice and not an array. And just like strings and slices, arrays can be iterated using a for ... range loop (§5.3, ➤ 203).

In general, Go's slices are more flexible, powerful, and convenient than arrays. Arrays are passed by value (i.e., copied)—although the cost of this can be avoided by passing pointers—whereas slices are cheap to pass, regardless of their length or capacity, since they are references. (A slice is passed as a 16-byte value on 64-bit machines and as a 12-byte value on 32-bit machines, no matter how many items it contains.) Arrays are of fixed size whereas slices can be resized. The functions in Go's standard library all use slices rather than arrays in their public APIs.* We recommend always using slices unless there is a very specific need to use an array in a particular case. Both arrays and slices can be sliced using the syntaxes shown in Table 4.1 (➤ 151).

A Go slice is a variable-length fixed-capacity sequence of items of the same type. Despite their fixed capacity, slices can be shrunk by slicing them and can be grown using the efficient built-in append() function, as we will see later in this section. Multidimensional slices can be created quite naturally by using items that are themselves slices—and the lengths of the inner slices in multidimensional slices may vary.

Although arrays and slices store items of the same type there is no limitation in practice. This is because the type used could be an interface. So we could store items of any types provided that they all met the specified interface (i.e., had the method or methods that the interface requires). We can even make an array or slice's type the empty interface, interface{}, which means that we could store any items of any types—although when we accessed an item we would need to use a type assertion or a type switch or introspection to make use of the item. (Interfaces are covered in Chapter 6; reflection is covered in §9.4.9, ➤ 427.)

Slices are created using the syntaxes:

```
make([]Type, length, capacity)
make([]Type, length)
[]Type{}
[]Type{value1, value2, ..., valueN}
```

The built-in make() function is used to create slices, maps, and channels. When used to create a slice it creates a *hidden* zero-value initialized array, and returns a slice reference that refers to the hidden array. The hidden array, like all arrays in Go, is of fixed length, with the length being the slice's *capacity* if the first syntax is used, or the slice's *length* if the second syntax is used, or the number of items in braces if the composite literal (third and fourth) syntax is used.

A slice's capacity is the length of its hidden array, and its length is any amount up to its capacity. In the first syntax the slice's length must be less than or equal to the capacity, although normally this syntax is used when we want the initial length to be less than the capacity. The second, third, and fourth syntaxes are used when we want the length and capacity to be the same. The composite

---

* At the time of this writing, the Go documentation often uses the term *array* when describing parameters that are actually slices.

Table 4.1 *Slice Operations*

Syntax	Description/result
`s[n]`	The item at index position *n* in slice *s*
`s[n:m]`	A slice taken from slice *s* from index positions *n* to *m* - 1
`s[n:]`	A slice taken from slice *s* from index positions *n* to `len(s)` - 1
`s[:m]`	A slice taken from slice *s* from index positions 0 to *m* - 1
`s[:]`	A slice taken from slice *s* from index positions 0 to `len(s)` - 1
`cap(s)`	The capacity of slice *s*; always ≥ `len(s)`
`len(s)`	The number of items in slice *s*; always ≤ `cap(s)`
`s = s[:cap(s)]`	Increase slice *s*'s length to its capacity if they are different

literal (fourth) syntax is very convenient, since it allows us to create a slice with some initial values.

The syntax `[]`*Type*`{}` is equivalent to `make([]`*Type*`, 0)`; both create an empty slice. This isn't useless since we can use the built-in `append()` function to effectively increase a slice's capacity. However, for practical purposes, when we need an initially empty slice it is almost always better to create one using `make()`, giving it a length of zero and a nonzero capacity that is or approximates the number of items we expect the slice to end up with.

Valid index positions for a slice range from 0 to `len(`*slice*`)` - 1. A slice can be resliced to reduce its length, and if a slice's capacity is greater than its length the slice can be resliced to increase its length up to its capacity. We can also increase a slice's capacity using the built-in `append()` function; we will see examples later in this section.

Figure 4.3 (➤ 152) provides a conceptual view of the relationship between slices and their hidden arrays. Here are the slices it shows.

```
s := []string{"A", "B", "C", "D", "E", "F", "G"}
t := s[:5]            // [A B C D E]
u := s[3 : len(s)-1] // [D E F]
fmt.Println(s, t, u)
u[1] = "x"
fmt.Println(s, t, u)

[A B C D E F G] [A B C D E] [D E F]
[A B C D x F G] [A B C D x] [D x F]
```

Since the slices s, t, and u all refer to the same underlying data, a change to one will affect any of the others that refer to the same data.

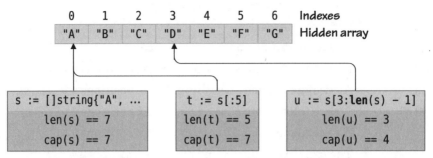

Figure 4.3 *A conceptual view of some slices and their hidden array*

```
s := new([7]string)[:]
s[0], s[1], s[2], s[3], s[4], s[5], s[6] = "A", "B", "C", "D", "E", "F","G"
```

Using the built-in make() function or the composite literal syntax are the best
ways to create slices, but here we show an approach that is not used in practice
but that makes the array–slice relationship obvious. The first statement creates
a pointer to an array using the built-in new() function, and then immediately
takes a slice of the entire array. This will produce a slice with a length and
capacity equal to the array's length, but with every item set to its zero value, in
this case an empty string. The second statement completes the setup of the slice
by setting the individual items to the initial values we want, after which this
slice s is exactly the same as the one created in the previous snippet using the
composite literal syntax.

Here are the slice-based equivalents to the array examples we saw earlier,
except that we have set the buffer's capacity to be greater than its length just to
show how it is done.

```
buffer := make([]byte, 20, 60)
grid1 := make([][]int, 3)
for i := range grid1 {
    grid1[i] = make([]int, 3)
}
grid1[1][0], grid1[1][1], grid1[1][2] = 8, 6, 2
grid2 := [][]int{{4, 3, 0}, {8, 6, 2}, {0, 0, 0}}
cities := []string{"Shanghai", "Mumbai", "Istanbul", "Beijing"}
cities[len(cities)-1] = "Karachi"
fmt.Println("Type    Len Cap Contents")
fmt.Printf("%-8T %2d %3d %v\n", buffer, len(buffer), cap(buffer), buffer)
fmt.Printf("%-8T %2d %3d %q\n", cities, len(cities), cap(cities), cities)
fmt.Printf("%-8T %2d %3d %v\n", grid1, len(grid1), cap(grid1), grid1)
fmt.Printf("%-8T %2d %3d %v\n", grid2, len(grid2), cap(grid2), grid2)
```

```
Type     Len Cap Contents
[]uint8  20  60  [0 0 0 0 0 0 0 0 0 0 0 0 0 0 0 0 0 0 0 0]
[]string 4   4   ["Shanghai" "Mumbai" "Istanbul" "Karachi"]
[][]int  3   3   [[0 0 0] [8 6 2] [0 0 0]]
[][]int  3   3   [[4 3 0] [8 6 2] [0 0 0]]
```

The buffer's contents are only the first len(buffer) items; the other items are inaccessible unless we reslice the buffer—something we will see how to do later on in this section.

We created grid1 as a slice of slices with an initial length of 3 (i.e., it can contain three slices), and a capacity of 3 (since the capacity defaults to the length if it isn't specified). Then we set each of the grid's outermost slices to contain their own 3-item slices. Naturally, we could have made the innermost slices have different lengths if we wanted.

For grid2 we had to specify every value since we created it using the composite literal syntax and Go would have no other way of knowing how many items we wanted. After all, we could have created a slice of different length slices—for example, grid2 := [][]int{{9, 7}, {8}, {4, 2, 6}}, which would make grid2 a slice of length 3 whose slices' lengths are 2, 1, and 3.

4.2.1. Indexing and Slicing Slices

A slice is a reference to a hidden array and slices of slices are also references to the same hidden array. Here is an example to illustrate what this means.

```
s := []string{"A", "B", "C", "D", "E", "F", "G"}
t := s[2:6]
fmt.Println(t, s, "=", s[:4], "+", s[4:])
s[3] = "x"
t[len(t)-1] = "y"
fmt.Println(t, s, "=", s[:4], "+", s[4:])
```
```
[C D E F] [A B C D E F G] = [A B C D] + [E F G]
[C x E y] [A B C x E y G] = [A B C x] + [E y G]
```

When we change the data—whether via the original s slice or from the t slice of the s slice—the same underlying data is changed, so both slices are affected. The code snippet also illustrates that given a slice s and an index position i (0 ≤ i ≤ len(s)), s is equal to the concatenation of s[:i] and s[i:]. We saw a similar equality in the previous chapter in reference to strings:

```
s == s[:i] + s[i:] // s is a string; i is an int; 0 <= i <= len(s)
```

Figure 4.4 shows slice s, including all its valid index positions and the slices used in the code snippet. The first index position in any slice is 0 and the last is always len(s) – 1.

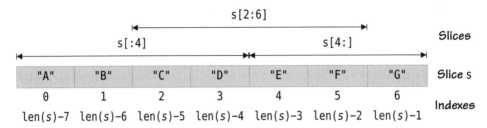

Figure 4.4 *Anatomy of a slice*

Unlike strings, slices don't support the + or += operators. Nonetheless, it is easy to append to slices—and also to insert and remove items, as we will see shortly (§4.2.3, ➤ 156).

4.2.2. Iterating Slices

One frequent requirement is to iterate over all the items in a slice. If we want to access the items without modifying them we can use a for ... range loop; and if we need to modify items we can use a for loop with a loop counter. Here is an example of the former.

```
amounts := []float64{237.81, 261.87, 273.93, 279.99, 281.07, 303.17,
    231.47, 227.33, 209.23, 197.09}
sum := 0.0
for _, amount := range amounts {
    sum += amount
}
fmt.Printf("Σ %.1f → %.1f\n", amounts, sum)
```
```
Σ [237.8 261.9 273.9 280.0 281.1 303.2 231.5 227.3 209.2 197.1] → 2503.0
```

The for ... range loop assigns a 0-based loop counter, which in this case we have discarded using the blank identifier (_), and a *copy* of the corresponding item from the slice. The copy is cheap even for strings (since they are passed by reference). This means that any changes that are applied to the item affect only the copy, not the item in the slice.

Naturally, we can use slicing to iterate over just a portion of the slice. For example, if we just wanted to iterate over the first five items we would write for _, amount := range amounts[:5].

If we want to modify the items in the slice we must use a for loop that just provides valid slice indexes and not copies of the slice's items.

```
for i := range amounts {
    amounts[i] *= 1.05
    sum += amounts[i]
}
fmt.Printf("Σ %.1f → %.1f\n", amounts, sum)
```
```
Σ [249.7 275.0 287.6 294.0 295.1 318.3 243.0 238.7 219.7 206.9] → 2628.1
```

Here we have increased each item in the slice by 5% and accumulated their sum.

Slices can, of course, contain custom items. Here is a custom type with a single custom method.

```
type Product struct {
    name  string
    price float64
}

func (product Product) String() string {
    return fmt.Sprintf("%s (%.2f)", product.name, product.price)
}
```

This defines the Product type as a struct with string and float64 fields. We have also defined a String() method to control how Go prints Product items using the %v verb. (We discussed print verbs earlier; §3.5, 93 ◀. We briefly introduced custom types and methods in §1.5, 21 ◀; much more coverage is provided in Chapter 6.)

```
products := []*Product{{"Spanner", 3.99}, {"Wrench", 2.49},
    {"Screwdriver", 1.99}}
fmt.Println(products)
for _, product := range products {
    product.price += 0.50
}
fmt.Println(products)
```
```
[Spanner (3.99) Wrench (2.49) Screwdriver (1.99)]
[Spanner (4.49) Wrench (2.99) Screwdriver (2.49)]
```

Here we have created a slice of pointers to Products ([]*Product), and immediately initialized the slice with three *Products. This works because Go is smart enough to realize that a []*Product requires pointers to Products. What we have written is really a shorthand for products := []*Product{&Product{"Spanner", 3.99}, &Product{"Wrench", 2.49}, &Product{"Screwdriver", 1.99}}. (Recall from §4.1, 140 ◀, that we can use the &*Type*{} syntax to create a new value of the type and immediately get a pointer to it.)

If we had not defined a `Product.String()` method the `%v` verb (which is used implicitly by `fmt.Println()` and similar functions) would simply print the memory addresses of the `Products` rather than the `Products` themselves. Notice also that the `Product.String()` method takes a `Product` *value*, not a `*Product`—this isn't a problem, though, since Go is smart enough to dereference `*Products` to make them work with custom methods that take `Product` values.*

We noted earlier that the `for ... range` loop cannot be used to modify the items it iterates over. Yet here we have successfully incremented all the prices in the `products` slice. At each iteration the `product` variable is assigned a copy of a `*Product`; this is a pointer that points to the same underlying `Product` as the corresponding one in the `products` slice. Thus, the modification we are applying is to the pointed-to `Product` value, not to the copy of the `*Product` pointer.

4.2.3. Modifying Slices

If we need to append to a slice we can use the built-in `append()` function. This function takes the slice to be appended to and one or more *individual* items to append. If we want to append a slice to a slice we must use the `...` (ellipsis) operator to tell Go to pass the slice to be added as individual values. The values to append must be of the same type as the slice's value type. In the case of a string we can append its individual bytes to a byte slice by using the ellipsis syntax.

```
s := []string{"A", "B", "C", "D", "E", "F", "G"}
t := []string{"K", "L", "M", "N"}
u := []string{"m", "n", "o", "p", "q", "r"}
s = append(s, "h", "i", "j") // Append individual values
s = append(s, t...)          // Append all of a slice's values
s = append(s, u[2:5]...)     // Append a subslice
b := []byte{'U', 'V'}
letters := "wxy"
b = append(b, letters...)    // Append a string's bytes to a byte slice
fmt.Printf("%v\n%s\n", s, b)
```
```
[A B C D E F G h i j K L M N o p q]
UVwxy
```

The built-in `append()` function takes a slice and one or more values and returns a (possibly new) slice which has the original slice's contents, plus the given value or values as its last item or items. If the original slice's capacity is sufficient for the new items (i.e., its length plus the number of new items is within its capac-

---

* One compiler does this as follows. Whenever a method is created that operates on a value, say it is called *Method()*, a wrapper method of the same name and signature is created that has a pointer receiver—in effect, func (*value* `*Type`) Method() { return (*value*).Method() }.

ity), append() puts the new value or values in the empty position or positions at the end and returns the original slice with its length increased by the number of items added. If the original slice doesn't have sufficent capacity, the append() function creates a new slice under the hood and copies the original slice's items into it, plus the new value or values at the end, and returns the new slice—hence the need to assign append()'s return value to the original slice variable.

It sometimes occurs that we want to insert items at the front or in the middle of a slice, not just at the end. Here are some examples that use a custom InsertStringSliceCopy() function that takes a slice to insert into, a slice to insert, and the index position where the insertion should be made.

```
s := []string{"M", "N", "O", "P", "Q", "R"}
x := InsertStringSliceCopy(s, []string{"a", "b", "c"}, 0) // At the front
y := InsertStringSliceCopy(s, []string{"x", "y"}, 3)      // In the middle
z := InsertStringSliceCopy(s, []string{"z"}, len(s))      // At the end
fmt.Printf("%v\n%v\n%v\n%v\n", s, x, y, z)
```

```
[M N O P Q R]
[a b c M N O P Q R]
[M N O x y P Q R]
[M N O P Q R z]
```

The custom InsertStringSliceCopy() function creates a new slice (which is why slice s is unchanged at the end of the snippet), making use of the built-in copy() function to copy the first slice it is given and to insert the second slice.

```
func InsertStringSliceCopy(slice, insertion []string, index int) []string {
    result := make([]string, len(slice)+len(insertion))
    at := copy(result, slice[:index])      //nice
    at += copy(result[at:], insertion)
    copy(result[at:], slice[index:])
    return result
}
```

The built-in copy() function takes two slices (which could be portions of the same slice—even overlapping ones) that contain items of the same type. The function copies the items into the first (destination) slice from the second (source) slice and returns the number of items copied. If the source slice is empty, the copy() function will safely do nothing. If the destination slice's *length* is insufficient to accommodate the source slice's items, the items that don't fit are silently ignored. If the destination slice's capacity is greater than its length, we can increase its length to its capacity with the statement *slice = slice[:cap(slice)]*, before doing the copy.

The slices passed to the built-in copy() function must be of the same type—except that if the first (destination) slice is a []byte the second (source) argument may be a []byte *or* a string. If the source is a string, its bytes are copied into the first argument. (An example of this use is shown in Chapter 6, ➤ 268.)

In the custom InsertStringSliceCopy() function, we begin by creating a new slice (result) that is large enough to hold the items from the two slices passed in. Then we copy a subslice of the first slice (slice[:index]) into the result slice. Next we copy the insertion slice into the result slice starting at the position in the result slice we have reached (at). Then we copy the rest of the first slice (slice[index:]) into the result slice at the next position we have reached (at). For this last copy we ignore the copy() function's return value since we don't need it. And finally, we return the result slice.

If the index position is 0, the slice[:index] in the first copy statement will be slice[:0] (i.e., an empty slice), so no copying is done. Similarly, if the index is greater than or equal to the length of the slice the slice[index:] in the last copy statement will effectively be slice[len(slice):] (i.e., an empty slice), so again, no copying is done.

Here is a function that has almost the same behavior as the InsertStringSlice-Copy() function, but with much shorter and simpler code. The difference is that the InsertStringSlice() function changes the original slice (and possibly the inserted slice), whereas the InsertStringSliceCopy() function does not.

```go
func InsertStringSlice(slice, insertion []string, index int) []string {
    return append(slice[:index], append(insertion, slice[index:]...)...)
}
```

The InsertStringSlice() function appends the end of the original slice from the index position onto the end of the insertion slice, and then appends the resultant slice onto the end of the original slice at the index position. The returned slice is the original slice with the insertion applied. (Recall that append() takes a slice and one or more values, so we must use the ellipsis syntax to transform a slice into its individual values—and in this example, we must do so twice.)

Items can be removed from the beginning and end of slices using Go's standard slice syntax, but removing from the middle can require a little care. We will start by seeing how to remove from the start, end, and middle of a slice, working on the slice in-place. Then we will see how to take a copy of a slice with items removed that leaves the original slice unchanged.

```go
s := []string{"A", "B", "C", "D", "E", "F", "G"}
s = s[2:] // Remove s[:2] from the front
fmt.Println(s)
```

```
[C D E F G]
```

Removing items from the start of a slice is easily achieved by reslicing.

```
s := []string{"A", "B", "C", "D", "E", "F", "G"}
s = s[:4] // Remove s[4:] from the end
fmt.Println(s)

[A B C D]
```

Removing items from the end of a slice is achieved by reslicing, just the same as for removing at the start.

```
s := []string{"A", "B", "C", "D", "E", "F", "G"}
s = append(s[:1], s[5:]...) // Remove s[1:5] from the middle
fmt.Println(s)

[A F G]
```

Retrieving items from the middle of a slice is easy—for example, to get the three middle items of slice s, we would use the expression s[2:5]. But to remove items from the middle of a slice is slightly tricky. Here we have done the removal using the append() function to append the subslice of slice s that follows what we want to delete, to the subslice of slice s that precedes what we want to delete, and assigning the resultant slice back to s.

Clearly, using append() and assigning back to the original slice to remove items, changes the original slice. Here are some examples that use a custom RemoveStringSliceCopy() function that returns a copy of the slice it is given, but with the items from the start and end index positions removed.

```
s := []string{"A", "B", "C", "D", "E", "F", "G"}
x := RemoveStringSliceCopy(s, 0, 2)      // Remove s[:2] from the front
y := RemoveStringSliceCopy(s, 1, 5)      // Remove s[1:5] from the middle
z := RemoveStringSliceCopy(s, 4, len(s)) // Remove s[4:] from the end
fmt.Printf("%v\n%v\n%v\n%v\n", s, x, y, z)

[A B C D E F G]
[C D E F G]
[A F G]
[A B C D]
```

Since the RemoveStringSliceCopy() function copies the items, the original slice is left intact.

```
func RemoveStringSliceCopy(slice []string, start, end int) []string {
    result := make([]string, len(slice)-(end-start))
    at := copy(result, slice[:start])
```

```
    copy(result[at:], slice[end:])
    return result
}
```

In the custom RemoveStringSliceCopy() function, we begin by creating a new slice (result) that is large enough to hold the items it will contain. Then we copy a subslice of the slice up to the start position (slice[:start]) into the result slice. Next we copy the slice from the end position (slice[end:]) into the result slice at the position we have reached (at). And finally, we return the result slice.

It is also possible to create a simpler RemoveStringSlice() function that works on the slice it is given rather than making a copy.

```
func RemoveStringSlice(slice []string, start, end int) []string {
    return append(slice[:start], slice[end:]...)
}
```

This is a generalization of the remove from the middle example that used the built-in append() function shown earlier. The returned slice is the original slice with the items from the start position up to (but excluding) the end position removed.

4.2.4. Sorting and Searching Slices

The standard library's sort package provides functions for sorting slices of ints, float64s, and strings, for checking if such a slice is sorted, and for searching for an item in a sorted slice using the fast binary search algorithm. There are also generic sort.Sort() and sort.Search() functions that can easily be used with custom data. These functions are listed in Table 4.2.

The way that Go sorts numbers holds no surprises, as we saw in an earlier chapter (73 ◀). However, strings are sorted purely in terms of the bytes that represent them, as we discussed in the previous chapter (§3.2, 86 ◀). This means, for example, that string sorting is case-sensitive. Here are a couple of string sorting examples and the results they produce.

```
files := []string{"Test.conf", "util.go", "Makefile", "misc.go", "main.go"}
fmt.Printf("Unsorted:          %q\n", files)
sort.Strings(files)      // Standard library sort function
fmt.Printf("Underlying bytes: %q\n", files)
SortFoldedStrings(files) // Custom sort function
fmt.Printf("Case insensitive: %q\n", files)
```

```
Unsorted:          ["Test.conf" "util.go" "Makefile" "misc.go" "main.go"]
Underlying bytes: ["Makefile" "Test.conf" "main.go" "misc.go" "util.go"]
Case insensitive: ["main.go" "Makefile" "misc.go" "Test.conf" "util.go"]
```

Table 4.2 *The Sort Package's Functions*

Syntax	Description/result
`sort.Float64s(fs)`	Sorts *fs* of type `[]float64` into ascending order
`sort.Float64sAreSorted(fs)`	Returns `true` if *fs* of type `[]float64` is sorted
`sort.Ints(is)`	Sorts *is* of type `[]int` into ascending order
`sort.IntsAreSorted(is)`	Returns `true` if *is* of type `[]int` is sorted
`sort.IsSorted(d)`	Returns `true` if *d* of type `sort.Interface` is sorted
`sort.Search(size, fn)`	Returns the index position in a sorted slice in scope of length *size* where function *fn* with the signature `func(int) bool` returns `true` (*see text*)
`sort.SearchFloat64s(fs, f)`	Returns the index position of *f* of type `float64` in sorted *fs* of type `[]float64`
`sort.SearchInts(is, i)`	Returns the index position of *i* of type `int` in sorted *is* of type `[]int`
`sort.SearchStrings(ss, s)`	Returns the index position of *s* of type `string` in sorted *ss* of type `[]string`
`sort.Sort(d)`	Sorts *d* of type `sort.Interface` (*see text*)
`sort.Strings(ss)`	Sorts *ss* of type `[]string` into ascending order
`sort.StringsAreSorted(ss)`	Returns `true` if *ss* of type `[]string` is sorted

The standard library's `sort.Strings()` function takes a `[]string` and sorts the strings in-place in ascending order in terms of their underlying bytes. If the strings have all been encoded using the same character to bytes mappings (e.g., they were all created in the current program or by other Go programs), this results in code-point ordering. The custom `SortFoldedStrings()` function works in the same way, except that it sorts case-insensitively using the `sort` package's generic `sort.Sort()` function.

The `sort.Sort()` function can sort items of any type that provide the methods in the `sort.Interface`, that is, items of a type that provide the `Len()`, `Less()`, and `Swap()` methods, each with the required signatures. We have created a custom type, `FoldedStrings`, that provides these methods. Here is the complete implementation of the `SortFoldedStrings()` function, the `FoldedStrings` type, and the supporting methods.

```go
func SortFoldedStrings(slice []string) {
    sort.Sort(FoldedStrings(slice))
}
type FoldedStrings []string
func (slice FoldedStrings) Len() int { return len(slice) }
```

```
func (slice FoldedStrings) Less(i, j int) bool {
    return strings.ToLower(slice[i]) < strings.ToLower(slice[j])
}
func (slice FoldedStrings) Swap(i, j int) {
    slice[i], slice[j] = slice[j], slice[i]
}
```

The SortFoldedStrings() function simply calls the standard library's sort.Sort() function to do the work—having (very cheaply) converted the given []string into a FoldedStrings value using Go's standard conversion syntax. In general, whenever we create a custom type that is based on a built-in type we can promote a value of that built-in type to the custom type by doing a conversion in this way. (Custom types are covered in Chapter 6.)

The FoldedStrings type provides the three methods needed to satisfy the sort. Interface interface. All the methods are trivial; case-insensitivity is achieved by using the strings.ToLower() function in the Less() method. (And if we wanted to sort in descending order we could simply change the Less() method's < less than operator to a > greater than operator.)

The SortFoldedStrings() function is perfectly adequate for 7-bit ASCII (i.e., English) strings, but is unlikely to produce a satisfactory ordering for non-English languages as we discussed in the previous chapter (§3.2, 86 ◄). Sorting Unicode strings with correct accounting for non-English languages is not a trivial undertaking. It is explained in detail in the Unicode Collation Algorithm document (unicode.org/reports/tr10).

If we want to search a slice to find the index position of a particular item (if it contains the item), we can easily do so using a for ... range loop.

```
files := []string{"Test.conf", "util.go", "Makefile", "misc.go", "main.go"}
target := "Makefile"
for i, file := range files {
    if file == target {
        fmt.Printf("found \"%s\" at files[%d]\n", file, i)
        break
    }
}
```

```
found "Makefile" at files[2]
```

Using a simple linear search like this is the only option for unsorted data and is fine for small slices (up to hundreds of items). But for larger slices—especially if we are performing searches repeatedly—the linear search is very inefficient, on average requiring half the items to be compared each time.

Go provides a sort.Search() method which uses the binary search algorithm: This requires the comparison of only $\log_2(n)$ items (where n is the number of items) each time. To put this in perspective, a linear search of 1 000 000 items requires 500 000 comparisons on average, with a worst case of 1 000 000 comparisons; a binary search needs at most 20 comparisons, even in the worst case.

```
sort.Strings(files)
fmt.Printf("%q\n", files)          95    dbl quote the string, []byte or int as a string
i := sort.Search(len(files),
    func(i int) bool { return files[i] >= target })
if i < len(files) && files[i] == target {
    fmt.Printf("found \"%s\" at files[%d]\n", files[i], i)
}

["Makefile" "Test.conf" "main.go" "misc.go" "util.go"]
found "Makefile" at files[0]
```

The sort.Search() function takes two arguments: the length of the slice to work on and a function that compares an item in a *sorted* slice with a target item using the >= operator for slices that are sorted in ascending order or the <= operator for slices sorted in descending order. The function must be a closure, that is, it must be created in the scope of the slice it is to work on since it must capture the slice as part of its state. (Closures are covered in §5.6.3, ➤ 225.) The sort.Search() function returns an int; only if this is less than the length of the slice *and* the item at that index position matches the target, can we be sure that we have found the item we are looking for.

Here is a variation that searches a []string that has been sorted case-insensitively and that assumes a lowercase target string.

```
target := "makefile"
SortFoldedStrings(files)
fmt.Printf("%q\n", files)
caseInsensitiveCompare := func(i int) bool {
    return strings.ToLower(files[i]) >= target
}
i := sort.Search(len(files), caseInsensitiveCompare)
if i < len(files) && strings.EqualFold(files[i], target) {     108
    fmt.Printf("found \"%s\" at files[%d]\n", files[i], i)
}

["main.go" "Makefile" "misc.go" "Test.conf" "util.go"]
found "Makefile" at files[1]
```

Here, we have created the comparison function outside of the call to the sort.Search() function. Note, though, that just like in the previous example, the comparison function *must* be a closure created within the scope of the slice it is to work on. We could have done the comparison using the code strings.ToLower(files[i]) == target, but have used the convenient strings.EqualFold() function which compares two strings case-insensitively, instead.

Go's slices are such incredibly convenient, powerful, and versatile data structures that it is difficult to imagine any nontrivial Go program that didn't make significant use of them. We will see them in action later in this chapter (§4.4, ➤ 171).

Although slices can account for most data structure use cases, in some situations we need to be able to store *key–value* pairs with fast lookup by key. This functionality is provided by Go's map type, the subject of the next section.

4.3. Maps

A Go map is an unordered collection of *key–value* pairs whose capacity is limited only by machine memory.* Keys are unique and may only be of a type that sensibly supports the == and != operators—so most of the built-in types can be used as keys (e.g., int, float64, rune, string, comparable arrays and structs, and custom types based on these, as well as pointers). Slices and noncomparable arrays and structs (i.e., those whose items or fields don't support == and !=), or custom types based on them, may not be used as map keys. Pointers, reference types, or values of any built-in or custom type can be used as values—including maps, so it is easy to create data structures of arbitrary complexity. Go's map operations are listed in Table 4.3.

Maps are reference types that are cheap to pass (e.g., 8 bytes on 64-bit machines and 4 bytes on 32-bit machines), no matter how much data they hold. Map lookups are fast—vastly faster than a linear search—although about two orders of magnitude (i.e., 100 times) slower than direct indexing into an array or slice, according to informal experiments.° This is still so fast that it makes sense to use maps wherever they are needed, since performance is very unlikely to be a problem in practice. Figure 4.5 shows a schematic of a map of type map[string]float64.

Since slices cannot be used as map keys it would appear that we cannot use byte slices ([]byte) for keys. However, since the conversions string([]byte) and []byte(string) do not change the bytes, we can safely convert []bytes into strings to use as map keys and then convert them back to []bytes as needed.

A map's keys must all be of the same type, and so must its values—although the key and value types can (and often do) differ. With respect to a map's val-

---

* The Go map data structure is sometimes called a hash map, hash table, unordered map, dictionary, or associative array in other contexts.

° No time complexity data on maps was available at the time of this writing.

Table 4.3 *Map Operations*

Syntax	Description/result
`m[k] = v`	Assigns value *v* to map *m* under key *k*; if *k* is already in the map its previous value is discarded
`delete(m, k)`	Deletes key *k* and its associated value from map *m*, or safely does nothing
`v := m[k]`	Retrieves the value that corresponds to map *m*'s key *k* and assigns it to *v*; or assigns the zero value for the value's type to *v*, if *k* isn't in the map
`v, found := m[k]`	Retrieves the value that corresponds to map *m*'s key *k* and assigns it to *v* and `true` to *found*; or assigns the zero value for the value's type to *v* and `false` to *found*, if *k* isn't in the map
`len(m)`	The number of items (*key–value* pairs) in map *m*

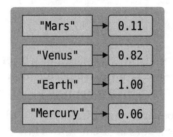

Figure 4.5 *Anatomy of a* map *with* string *keys and* float64 *values*

ues, just as with the items in a slice, there is no limitation in practice. This is because the value type used could be an interface. So we could store values of any types provided that they all met the specified interface (i.e., had the method or methods that the interface requires). We can even make a map's value type the empty interface, interface{}, which means that we could store any values of any types—although when we accessed a value we would need to use a type assertion or a type switch or introspection to make use of it. (Interfaces are covered in Chapter 6; reflection is covered in §9.4.9, ➤ 427.)

Maps are created using the syntaxes:

```
make(map[KeyType]ValueType, initialCapacity)
make(map[KeyType]ValueType)
map[KeyType]ValueType{}
map[KeyType]ValueType{key1: value1, key2: value2, ..., keyN: valueN}
```

The built-in make() function is used to create slices, maps, and channels. When used to create a map it creates an empty map, and if the optional *initialCapacity* is specified, the map is initialized to have enough space for that number of items. If more items are added to the map than the initial capacity allows for, the map will automatically grow to accommodate the new items. The second and third syntaxes are exact equivalents. The last two syntaxes show how to create a map using the composite literal syntax—this is very convenient in practice, either to create a new empty map, or to create a map with some initial values.

4.3.1. Creating and Populating Maps

Here is an example that shows the creation and population of a map with string keys and float64 values.

```
massForPlanet := make(map[string]float64) // Same as: map[string]float64{}
massForPlanet["Mercury"] = 0.06
massForPlanet["Venus"] = 0.82
massForPlanet["Earth"] = 1.00
massForPlanet["Mars"] = 0.11
fmt.Println(massForPlanet)
```

```
map[Venus:0.82 Mars:0.11 Earth:1 Mercury:0.06]
```

For small maps it doesn't really matter whether we specify their initial capacity, but for large maps doing so can improve performance. In general it is best to specify the initial capacity if it is known (even if only approximately).

Maps use the [] index operator just like arrays and slices, only for maps the index inside the square brackets is of the map's key type which might not be an int—here, for example, we have string keys.

To print the map to the console we have used the fmt.Println() function; this uses the %v formatting verb and outputs the map's items space-separated in *key:value* form. Maps are unordered, so on a different machine the order of items printed may be different from that shown here.

As noted earlier, pointers can be used as map keys. We will look at an example whose keys are of type *Point and where Point is defined as follows:

```
type Point struct{ x, y, z int }

func (point Point) String() string {
    return fmt.Sprintf("(%d,%d,%d)", point.x, point.y, point.z)
}
```

The Point type stores three ints. It has a String() method which ensures that when we print a *Point Go will use the String() method rather than simply printing the Point's memory address.

Incidentally, we can always force Go to print a memory address by using the %p format verb; the format verbs were covered earlier (§3.5.6, 103 ◄).

```
triangle := make(map[*Point]string, 3)
triangle[&Point{89, 47, 27}] = "α"
triangle[&Point{86, 65, 86}] = "β"
triangle[&Point{7, 44, 45}] = "γ"
fmt.Println(triangle)
```
```
map[(7,44,45):γ (89,47,27):α (86,65,86):β]
```

Here, we have created a map with an initial capacity and populated it with pointer keys and string values. Each Point is created using the composite literal syntax and using the & operator so that we get a *Point rather than a Point value. (This syntax was introduced earlier in the chapter; 145 ◀.) And thanks to the Point.String() method, when the map is printed we see the *Point values in human-readable form.

Using pointers as map keys means that we can add two Points with the same coordinates, providing that they are created separately (and so have different addresses). But what if we want the map to only store one point for any particular set of coordinates? This can easily be done by storing Point values rather than pointers to Points; after all, Go permits structs to be used as map keys—so long as all their fields' types are comparable with == and !=. Here is an example.

```
nameForPoint := make(map[Point]string) // Same as: map[Point]string{}
nameForPoint[Point{54, 91, 78}] = "x"
nameForPoint[Point{54, 158, 89}] = "y"
fmt.Println(nameForPoint)
```
```
map[(54,91,78):x (54,158,89):y]
```

The nameForPoint map's keys are unique Points whose associated name strings we can change at any time.

```
populationForCity := map[string]int{"Istanbul": 12610000,
    "Karachi": 10620000, "Mumbai": 12690000, "Shanghai": 13680000}
for city, population := range populationForCity {
    fmt.Printf("%-10s %8d\n", city, population)
}
```
```
Shanghai   13680000
Mumbai     12690000
Istanbul   12610000
Karachi    10620000
```

For this subsection's final example we have created an entire map using the composite literal syntax.

When a for ... range loop is applied to a map and there are two variables present, the loop returns a key and a value on each iteration until every *key–value* item has been returned or the loop is broken out of. If just one variable is present only the key is returned on each iteration. Since maps are unordered we cannot know what particular sequence the items will come in. In many situations we just want to iterate over all of a map's items to access or update them, so the iteration order doesn't matter. However, if we want to iterate in, say, key order, it is easy to do as we will see shortly (§4.3.4, ➤ 170).

4.3.2. Map Lookups

Go provides two very similar syntaxes for map lookups, both of which use the [] index operator. Here are a couple of examples of the simplest syntax.

```
population := populationForCity["Mumbai"]
fmt.Println("Mumbai's population is", population)
population = populationForCity["Emerald City"]
fmt.Println("Emerald City's population is", population)
```

```
Mumbai's population is 12690000
Emerald City's population is 0
```

If we look up a key that is present in the map the corresponding value is returned. But if the key is not present then the map's value type's zero value is returned. So, in this example, we cannot tell whether the 0 returned for the "Emerald City" key means that the population of Emerald City really is zero, or that the city isn't in the map. Go's second map lookup syntax provides the solution to this problem.

```
city := "Istanbul"
if population, found := populationForCity[city]; found {
    fmt.Printf("%s's population is %d\n", city, population)
} else {
    fmt.Printf("%s's population data is unavailable\n", city)
}
city = "Emerald City"
_, present := populationForCity[city]
fmt.Printf("%q is in the map == %t\n", city, present)
```

```
Istanbul's population is 12610000
"Emerald City" is in the map == false
```

If we provide *two* variables for the map's [] index operator to return to, the first will get the value that corresponds to the key (or the map's value type's zero value if the key isn't present), and the second will get true (or false if the key isn't present). This allows us to check for a key's existence in the map. And as the example's second lookup illustrates, we can use the blank identifier to stand for the value if all we want to know is whether a particular key is present in the map.

4.3.3. Modifying Maps

Items, that is, *key–value* pairs, can be inserted into maps and deleted from maps. And any given key's value can be changed. Here are a few illustrative examples.

```
fmt.Println(len(populationForCity), populationForCity)
delete(populationForCity, "Shanghai")    // Delete
fmt.Println(len(populationForCity), populationForCity)
populationForCity["Karachi"] = 11620000 // Update
fmt.Println(len(populationForCity), populationForCity)
populationForCity["Beijing"] = 11290000 // Insert
fmt.Println(len(populationForCity), populationForCity)
```

```
4 map[Shanghai:13680000 Mumbai:12690000 Istanbul:12610000 Karachi:10620000]
3 map[Mumbai:12690000 Istanbul:12610000 Karachi:10620000]
3 map[Mumbai:12690000 Istanbul:12610000 Karachi:11620000]
4 map[Mumbai:12690000 Istanbul:12610000 Karachi:11620000 Beijing:11290000]
```

The syntax for inserting and updating map items is identical: If an item with the given key isn't present, a new item with the given key and value will be inserted; and if an item with the given key is present, its value will be set to the given value, and the original value will be discarded. And if we try to delete an item which isn't in the map, Go will safely do nothing.

Keys cannot be changed as such, but the effect of changing a key can be achieved like this:

```
oldKey, newKey := "Beijing", "Tokyo"
value := populationForCity[oldKey]
delete(populationForCity, oldKey)
populationForCity[newKey] = value
fmt.Println(len(populationForCity), populationForCity)
```

```
4 map[Mumbai:12690000 Istanbul:12610000 Karachi:11620000 Tokyo:11290000]
```

We retrieve the old key's value, delete the item which has the old key, and create a new item with the new key and with the old key's value.

4.3.4. Key-Ordered Map Iteration

When producing data for human consumption we often need to present the data in some recognizable order. Here is an example that shows how to output the populationForCity map in alphabetical (strictly speaking, Unicode code point) order of city.

```
cities := make([]string, 0, len(populationForCity))    // OK   Usually do:
for city := range populationForCity {                  // -key, val := range map {...}
    cities = append(cities, city)                      // rather than
}                                                      // key := range map {...}
sort.Strings(cities)
for _, city := range cities {
    fmt.Printf("%-10s %8d\n", city, populationForCity[city])
}
```

```
Beijing    11290000
Istanbul   12610000
Karachi    11620000
Mumbai     12690000
```

We begin by creating a slice of type []string with zero length (i.e., empty), but with enough capacity to hold all of the map's keys. Then we iterate over the map retrieving only the keys (since we have used just one variable, city, rather than the two needed to retrieve each *key–value* pair), and appending each city in turn to the cities slice. Next, we sort the slice, and then we iterate over the slice (ignoring the int index by using the blank identifier), looking up the corresponding city's population at each iteration.

The algorithm shown here—create an empty slice large enough to hold all the map's keys, add all the map's keys to the slice, sort the slice, and iterate over the slice to produce ordered output—can be applied generally for key-ordered map iteration.

An alternative to the approach taken here is to use an ordered data structure in the first place—for example, an ordered map. We will see an example of this in a later chapter (§6.5.3, ➤ 302).

Value ordering is also possible, for example, by doing a map inversion, as we will see in the next subsection.

4.3.5. Map Inversion

We can easily invert a map whose *values* are unique—and whose type is acceptable for use as map keys. Here is an example.

```
cityForPopulation := make(map[int]string, len(populationForCity))
```

```
for city, population := range populationForCity {
    cityForPopulation[population] = city
}
fmt.Println(cityForPopulation)
```
```
map[12610000:Istanbul 11290000:Beijing 12690000:Mumbai 11620000:Karachi]
```

We begin by creating the inverted map—so whereas populationForCity is of type map[string]int, the cityForPopulation map is of type map[int]string. Then we iterate over the original map and insert items into the inverted map using the original map's values as keys and its keys as values.

Of course, map inversion will fail if the values are not all unique—essentially what happens is that the last occurrence of a nonunique value that is encountered is the one who's key is stored (as a value) in the inverted map. This problem can be addressed by creating an inverted map that has multivalued values, so for this example, of type map[int][]string (int keys and []string values). We will see a practical example of this shortly (§4.4.2, ➤ 174).

4.4. Examples

In this section we will review two small examples, the first illustrating one- and two-dimensional slices, and the second illustrating maps, including map inversion where the map's values may not be unique, as well as slices and sorting.

4.4.1. Example: Guess Separator

In some situations we might receive a whole bunch of data files for processing where each file has one record per line, but where different files might use different separators (e.g., tabs or whitespace or "*"s). To be able to process such files in bulk we need to be able to determine the separator used for each file. The guess_separator example shown in this section (in file guess_separator/ guess_separator.go) attempts to identify the separator for the file it is given to work on.

Here is an example of a typical run:

```
$ ./guess_separator information.dat
tab-separated
```

The program reads in the first five lines (or as many lines as the file contains if fewer than five) and uses these to guess the separator that is being used.

As usual, we will review the main() function and the functions it calls (apart from one that's routine), and we will skip the imports.

```go
func main() {
    if len(os.Args) == 1 || os.Args[1] == "-h" || os.Args[1] == "--help" {
        fmt.Printf("usage: %s file\n", filepath.Base(os.Args[0]))
        os.Exit(1)
    }

    separators := []string{"\t", "*", "|", "•"}

    linesRead, lines := readUpToNLines(os.Args[1], 5)
    counts := createCounts(lines, separators, linesRead)
    separator := guessSep(counts, separators, linesRead)
    report(separator)
}
```

The `main()` function begins by checking that a file has been given on the command line, and if one hasn't, the function outputs a usage message and terminates the program.

We create a `[]string` to hold the separators we are interested in; for whitespace-separated files we will adopt the convention that the separator is `""` (the empty string).

The first real processing is to read in the first five lines of the file. The `readUpToN-Lines()` function isn't shown since we have already seen examples of how to read lines from a file (and will see another example in the next subsection). The only thing that is unusual about the `readUpToNLines()` function is that it reads only the number of lines specified—or fewer if the file has fewer lines—and returns the number of lines it actually read as well as the lines themselves.

We will discuss the remaining functions that `main()` calls when we show their source code, starting with the `createCounts()` function.

```go
func createCounts(lines, separators []string, linesRead int) [][]int {
    counts := make([][]int, len(separators))
    for sepIndex := range separators {
        counts[sepIndex] = make([]int, linesRead)
        for lineIndex, line := range lines {
            counts[sepIndex][lineIndex] =
                strings.Count(line, separators[sepIndex])
        }
    }
    return counts
}
```

The purpose of the `createCounts()` function is to populate a matrix that holds the counts of each separator for each line that was read.

The function begins by creating a slice of slices of ints with the same number of slices as there are separators. If there are four separators, this sets counts to the slice [nil nil nil nil]. The outer for loop replaces each nil with an []int that has as many items as the number of lines read. So each nil gets replaced with [0 0 0 0 0], since Go always initializes with a type's zero value.

The inner for loop is used to populate the counts. For each line the number of occurrences of each separator is counted and counts is updated accordingly. The strings.Count() function returns the number of occurrences of its second string argument that occur in its first string argument.

For example, given a tab-separated file which had some bullets, spaces, and stars in some of its fields we might get a counts matrix of [[3 3 3 3 3] [0 0 4 3 0] [0 0 0 0 0] [1 2 2 0 0]]. Each counts item is an []int which contains the counts for the corresponding separator (tab, star, bar, bullet) for each of the five lines. So in this case every line has three tabs, a couple of lines have stars (four in one, three in another), three lines have bullets, and no lines have vertical bars. To us as human readers it is obvious that here the separator is a tab, but of course, the program must discover this for itself, and it does so using the guessSep() function.

```go
func guessSep(counts [][]int, separators []string, linesRead int) string {
    for sepIndex := range separators {
        same := true
        count := counts[sepIndex][0]
        for lineIndex := 1; lineIndex < linesRead; lineIndex++ {
            if counts[sepIndex][lineIndex] != count {
                same = false
                break
            }
        }
        if count > 0 && same {
            return separators[sepIndex]
        }
    }
    return ""
}
```

This function's purpose is to find the first []int in the counts slices whose counts are all the same—and nonzero.

The function iterates over each "row" in counts (one per separator), and initially assumes that all the row's counts are the same. It sets the initial count to the first count, that is, to the number of times the separator occurs in the first line that was read. Then it iterates over the rest, that is, over the separator counts for each of the other lines that was read. If a different count is encountered the inner for loop is broken out of and the next separator tried. If the inner for loop completes without setting same to false, and the count is greater than zero, we have found what we want and immediately return it. If no separator matches we return an empty string—this is our convention to mean that the fields are whitespace-separated, or not separated at all.

```go
func report(separator string) {
    switch separator {
    case "":
        fmt.Println("whitespace-separated or not separated at all")
    case "\t":
        fmt.Println("tab-separated")
    default:
        fmt.Printf("%s-separated\n", separator)
    }
}
```

The report() function is trivial, writing a simple description of the separator used by the file that was read.

This example has shown both one- and two-dimensional slices (separators, lines, and counts) in typical use. In the next example we will look at maps, slices, and sorting.

4.4.2. Example: Word Frequencies

Textual analysis has a variety of uses, from data mining to the study of language itself. In this subsection we will review an example that performs one of the most basic forms of textual analysis: It counts the frequencies of words in the files it is given.

Frequency data can be presented in two different but equally sensible ways—as an alphabetical list of words with their frequencies, and as an ordered list of frequency values and the words that have the corresponding frequencies. The wordfrequency program (in file wordfrequency/wordfrequency.go) produces both kinds of output, as illustrated below.

```
$ ./wordfrequency small-file.txt
Word           Frequency
ability            1
about              1
above              3
...
years              1
you              128
Frequency → Words
```

```
  1 ability, about, absence, absolute, absolutely, abuse, accessible, ...
  2 accept, acquired, after, against, applies, arrange, assumptions, ...
...
128 you
151 or
192 to
221 of
345 the
```

Even for a small file the number of words and the number of different frequencies can be quite large, so here we have elided most of the output.

Producing the first part of the output is straightforward. We can use a map of type map[string]int with word keys and frequency values. But to get the second part of the output we will need to invert the map—and this isn't quite so easy because it is likely that more than one word will have the same frequency. The solution is to invert to a multivalued map of type map[int][]string, that is, a map whose keys are frequencies and whose values are all the words that have the corresponding frequency.

We will begin with the program's main() function and work top-down, and as usual, will omit the imports.

```go
func main() {
    if len(os.Args) == 1 || os.Args[1] == "-h" || os.Args[1] == "--help" {
        fmt.Printf("usage: %s <file1> [<file2> [... <fileN>]]\n",
            filepath.Base(os.Args[0]))
        os.Exit(1)
    }

    frequencyForWord := map[string]int{} // Same as: make(map[string]int)
    for _, filename := range commandLineFiles(os.Args[1:]) {
        updateFrequencies(filename, frequencyForWord)
    }
    reportByWords(frequencyForWord)
    wordsForFrequency := invertStringIntMap(frequencyForWord)
    reportByFrequency(wordsForFrequency)
}
```

The main() function starts by dealing with the command line and then gets down to work.

We begin by creating the simple map that will keep track of the frequency of each unique word in the files read in. We have used the composite literal syntax to create the initially empty map, just to show how it is done. Once we have the map we iterate over each filename given on the command line and for each one attempt to update the frequencyForWord map.

Once the first map is complete we output the first report: an alphabetical list of all the unique words encountered and their corresponding frequencies. Then we create an inverted version of the map and output the second report: a numerically ordered list of frequencies and their associated words.

```go
func commandLineFiles(files []string) []string {
    if runtime.GOOS == "windows" {
        args := make([]string, 0, len(files))
        for _, name := range files {
            if matches, err := filepath.Glob(name); err != nil {
                args = append(args, name) // Invalid pattern
            } else if matches != nil { // At least one match
                args = append(args, matches...)
            }
        }
        return args
    }
    return files
}
```

pass here @

The commandLineFiles() function simply returns the []string it is given on Unix-like platforms such as Linux and Mac OS X, since on these platforms the shell automatically does file globbing (i.e., replaces, say, *.txt with any matching text files, e.g., README.txt, INSTALL.txt, etc.). The Windows shell (cmd.exe) does not do file globbing, so if the user enters, say, *.txt on the command line, that is what the program will receive. To provide reasonable cross-platform uniformity, we do the globbing ourselves when the program is run on Windows. (Another way to handle cross-platform differences is to have platform-specific .go files—this is covered in a later chapter, §9.1.1.1, ➤ 410.)

```go
func updateFrequencies(filename string, frequencyForWord map[string]int) {
    var file *os.File
    var err error
    if file, err = os.Open(filename); err != nil {
        log.Println("failed to open the file: ", err)
        return
    }
    defer file.Close()
    readAndUpdateFrequencies(bufio.NewReader(file), frequencyForWord)
}
```

error here ... @

This function is used purely for the file handling. It opens the given file for reading, defers the closing of the file to when the function returns, and passes on the actual work to the readAndUpdateFrequencies() function. By passing the file reader as a *bufio.Reader (produced by the bufio.NewReader() call), we ensure that the called function can read the file as strings line by line rather than having to read raw bytes.

```go
func readAndUpdateFrequencies(reader *bufio.Reader,
    frequencyForWord map[string]int) {
    for {
        line, err := reader.ReadString('\n')
        for _, word := range SplitOnNonLetters(strings.TrimSpace(line)) {
            if len(word) > utf8.UTFMax ||
                utf8.RuneCountInString(word) > 1 {
                frequencyForWord[strings.ToLower(word)] += 1
            }
        }
        if err != nil {
            if err != io.EOF {
                log.Println("failed to finish reading the file: ", err)
            }
            break
        }
    }
}
```

The first part of this function should be very familiar by now. We create an infinite loop and read the file line by line, breaking out of the loop when we reach the end of the file or if an error occurs (in which case we report the error to the user). We don't terminate the program when we hit an error because there might be many files to read and for this program we prefer to do as much work as possible and report any problems that were encountered rather than stopping at the first error.

The inner for loop is where the interesting processing is done. Any given line might have punctuation, numbers, symbols, and other nonword characters, so we iterate word by word having split the line into words and discarding any non-word characters using a custom SplitOnNonLetters() function. And the string we feed that function in the first place has any whitespace trimmed off both ends.

We only want to include words that contain at least two letters. The easiest way to do this is to use a one-clause if statement, that is, if utf8.RuneCountIn-String(word) > 1, which works fine.

The simple if statement just described is potentially a bit expensive because it will parse the entire word. So in the program we use a two-clause if statement where the first clause takes a much cheaper approach. The first clause checks to see if the number of bytes in the word is greater than utf8.UTFMax (which is a constant of value 4, the maximum number of bytes required to represent a single UTF-8 character). This is a really fast test because Go strings know how many bytes they contain and Go's binary Boolean operators (&& and ||) are short-circuiting (§2.2, 56 ◄). Of course, words consisting of four or fewer bytes (e.g., four 7-bit ASCII characters or a couple of 2-byte UTF-8 characters) will fail this first check, but that isn't a problem because the second check (the rune count) will be fast because it will always have four or fewer characters to count. Is it worth using the two-clause if statement in this situation? It really depends on the input—the more words that need processing and the longer they are, the more potential for savings. The only way to know for certain is to benchmark using real or at least typical data.

```go
func SplitOnNonLetters(s string) []string {
    notALetter := func(char rune) bool { return !unicode.IsLetter(char) }
    return strings.FieldsFunc(s, notALetter)
}
```

This function is used to split a string on nonword characters. First we create an anonymous function that has the signature required by the strings.Fields-Func() function and which returns true for nonletters and false for letters. Then we return the result of calling the strings.FieldsFunc() function with the given string and with the notALetter() function. (We discussed the strings.Fields-Func() function in the previous chapter; 107 ◄.)

```go
func reportByWords(frequencyForWord map[string]int) {
    words := make([]string, 0, len(frequencyForWord))
    wordWidth, frequencyWidth := 0, 0
    for word, frequency := range frequencyForWord {
        words = append(words, word)
        if width := utf8.RuneCountInString(word); width > wordWidth {
            wordWidth = width
        }
        if width := len(fmt.Sprint(frequency)); width > frequencyWidth {
            frequencyWidth = width
        }
    }
    sort.Strings(words)
    gap := wordWidth + frequencyWidth - len("Word") - len("Frequency")
    fmt.Printf("Word %*s%s\n", gap, " ", "Frequency")
    for _, word := range words {
        fmt.Printf("%-*s %*d\n", wordWidth, word, frequencyWidth,
            frequencyForWord[word])
    }
}
```

Once the frequencyForWord map has been populated, the reportByWords() function is called to output its data. We want the output to be in alphabetical (actually, Unicode code point) order, so we begin by creating an empty []string to hold the words that is large enough to hold all the words in the map. We also want to know the width in characters of the longest word and of the highest frequency (i.e., how many digits it has) so that we can produce our output in neat columns: The wordWidth and frequencyWidth variables are used to record these widths.

The first for loop iterates over the items in the map. Each word is appended to the words []string, a very cheap operation because words's capacity is already large enough so all that the append() function has to do is put the given word at the len(words) index position and increment the words slice's length by one.

For each word we count the number of characters it contains and set wordWidth to this amount if it is larger than the existing value. Similarly, we count the number of characters needed to represent the frequency—we can safely use len() for this to count bytes since the fmt.Sprint() function takes a number and returns a string with decimal digits all of which are 7-bit ASCII characters. So at the end of the first for loop we have the widths of the two columns we want to output.

Once the words slice has been populated we sort it. We don't have to worry about case-sensitivity because all the words are lowercase (this was done in the readAndUpdateFrequencies() function; 177 ◄).

After sorting the words we print the two column titles. First we print "Word", then we print spaces so that the *y* of "Frequency" will be right-aligned with the last digit of the frequencies. This is achieved by printing a single space (" ") with a field width of gap characters using the %*s format specifier. An alternative would be to use a format specifier of plain %s and to pass a string of spaces produced by strings.Repeat(" ", gap). (String formatting was covered in the previous chapter; §3.5, 93 ◄.)

And finally, we print the words and their frequencies in two columns with appropriate widths in ascending alphabetical word order.

```go
func invertStringIntMap(intForString map[string]int) map[int][]string {
    stringsForInt := make(map[int][]string, len(intForString))
    for key, value := range intForString {
        stringsForInt[value] = append(stringsForInt[value], key)
    }
    return stringsForInt
}
```

The function begins by creating an empty inverted map. Although we don't know how many items there will be, we have assumed that there will be about the same number as in the original map—after all, there can't be *more*. The processing is straightforward: We simply iterate over the original map and use each value as a key in the inverted map, and add each key to the inverted map's corresponding slice value. Since the new map's values are slices, no data is lost, even if the original map has multiple keys with the same value.

```go
func reportByFrequency(wordsForFrequency map[int][]string) {
    frequencies := make([]int, 0, len(wordsForFrequency))
    for frequency := range wordsForFrequency {
        frequencies = append(frequencies, frequency)
    }
    sort.Ints(frequencies)
    width := len(fmt.Sprint(frequencies[len(frequencies)-1]))
    fmt.Println("Frequency → Words")
    for _, frequency := range frequencies {
        words := wordsForFrequency[frequency]
        sort.Strings(words)
        fmt.Printf("%*d %s\n", width, frequency, strings.Join(words, ", "))
    }
}
```

This function is structurally very similar to the `reportByWords()` function. It begins by creating a slice of frequencies which it then sorts into ascending order. Then it computes the width needed to accommodate the largest frequency and uses that for the first column's width. Next, it outputs the report's title. And finally, it iterates over the frequencies and outputs each one with the words that have that frequency in ascending alphabetical order, comma-separating the words if there is more than one.

We have now reviewed this chapter's two complete examples and gained some insight into using pointers in Go and into the power and convenience of Go's slice and map types. In the next chapter, we will look at how to create custom functions; this will complete the foundations in Go procedural programming. Once functions have been covered we will be ready to tackle object-oriented programming, and after that, concurrent programming.

4.5. Exercises

There are five exercises, each one requiring the creation of a small function, and drawing on the coverage of slices and maps presented in this chapter. We have put all five functions in the same .go file (chap4_ans/chap4_ans.go), and added a main() function that makes use of them all to make testing easier. (Proper unit testing is covered later, in Chapter 9, §9.1.1.3, ➤ 414.)

1. Create a function that accepts an []int and returns an []int which is a copy of the given []int but with duplicates removed. For example, given an argument of []int{9, 1, 9, 5, 4, 4, 2, 1, 5, 4, 8, 8, 4, 3, 6, 9, 5, 7, 5}, the function should return []int{9, 1, 5, 4, 2, 8, 3, 6, 7}. In the chap4_ans.go solution file the function is called UniqueInts(). The function uses composite

literal syntax rather than the built-in make() function and is 11 lines long. It should be quite easy to do.

2. Create a function that accepts an [][]int (i.e., a two-dimensional slice of ints), and returns a single []int that contains all the ints from the two-dimensional slice's first slice, then from its second slice, and so on. For example, if the function is called Flatten():

```
irregularMatrix := [][]int{{1, 2, 3, 4},
    {5, 6, 7, 8},
    {9, 10, 11},
    {12, 13, 14, 15},
    {16, 17, 18, 19, 20}}
slice := Flatten(irregularMatrix)
fmt.Printf("1x%d: %v\n", len(slice), slice)
```
```
1x20: [1 2 3 4 5 6 7 8 9 10 11 12 13 14 15 16 17 18 19 20]
```

The Flatten() function in chap4_ans.go is a mere nine lines. The function is slightly subtle to ensure that it works correctly even when the lengths of the inner slices vary (as they do in the irregularMatrix), but is quite straightforward.

3. Create a function that accepts an []int and a column count (as an int), and that returns an [][]int where each inner slice's length is equal to the given number of columns. For example, if the argument is []int{1, 2, 3, 4, 5, 6, 7, 8, 9, 10, 11, 12, 13, 14, 15, 16, 17, 18, 19, 20}, here are some sample results, each preceded by the number of columns that was passed:

```
3 [[1 2 3] [4 5 6] [7 8 9] [10 11 12] [13 14 15] [16 17 18] [19 20 0]]
4 [[1 2 3 4] [5 6 7 8] [9 10 11 12] [13 14 15 16] [17 18 19 20]]
5 [[1 2 3 4 5] [6 7 8 9 10] [11 12 13 14 15] [16 17 18 19 20]]
6 [[1 2 3 4 5 6] [7 8 9 10 11 12] [13 14 15 16 17 18] [19 20 0 0 0 0]]
```

Notice that since there are 20 ints, neither 3 nor 6 columns are exact multiples, so we have padded the last inner slice with zeros when necessary to keep all column (i.e., inner slice) lengths the same.

The Make2D() function in chap4_ans.go is 12 lines long and makes use of a helper function that's 7 lines long. The Make2D() function and its helper need a little bit of thought to get right, but aren't difficult.

4. Create a function that accepts a []string containing the lines of an .ini-style file and that returns a map[string]map[string]string whose keys are group names and whose values are *key–value* maps of each group's keys and values. Blank lines and lines beginning with ; should be ignored. Each group is indicated by a name in square brackets on its own line, and

each group's keys and values are indicated by one or more lines of the form *key=value*. Here is an example []string that the function could process.

```
iniData := []string{
    "; Cut down copy of Mozilla application.ini file",
    "",
    "[App]",
    "Vendor=Mozilla",
    "Name=Iceweasel",
    "Profile=mozilla/firefox",
    "Version=3.5.16",
    "[Gecko]",
    "MinVersion=1.9.1",
    "MaxVersion=1.9.1.*",
    "[XRE]",
    "EnableProfileMigrator=0",
    "EnableExtensionManager=1",
}
```

Given this data, the function should return the following map which we have "pretty-printed" to make it easier to see its structure.

```
map[Gecko: map[MinVersion: 1.9.1
              MaxVersion: 1.9.1.*]
    XRE: map[EnableProfileMigrator: 0
             EnableExtensionManager: 1]
    App: map[Vendor: Mozilla
             Profile: mozilla/firefox
             Name: Iceweasel
             Version: 3.5.16]]
```

The ParseIni() solution function assumes a group of "General" for any *key–values* that are not within the scope of a group. It is 24 lines long and might take a bit of care to get right.

5. Create a function that accepts a map[string]map[string]string that represents an .ini file's data. The function should print out the data as an .ini file with groups in alphabetical order and keys within groups in alphabetical order, and with a blank line between each group. For example, given the data from the previous exercise the output should be:

```
[App]
Name=Iceweasel
Profile=mozilla/firefox
Vendor=Mozilla
```

```
Version=3.5.16

[Gecko]
MaxVersion=1.9.1.*
MinVersion=1.9.1

[XRE]
EnableExtensionManager=1
EnableProfileMigrator=0
```

The PrintIni() solution function is 21 lines long and should be easier to do than the previous exercise's ParseIni() function.

5 Procedural Programming

The purpose of this chapter is to complete the coverage of Go procedural programming that the earlier chapters began. Go can be used to write purely procedural programs, to write object-oriented programs, or to write programs that combine both paradigms. It is important to learn procedural Go since object-oriented Go builds on the procedural foundations, as does concurrent Go programming.

The previous chapters described and illustrated Go's built-in data types, in the course of which many of Go's statements and control structures were used, and many small custom functions were created. In this chapter we will review Go's statements and control structures in more detail, and also look much more closely at creating and using custom functions. Table 5.1 provides a list of Go's built-in functions, most of which have already been covered.*

Some of this chapter's material has been seen less formally in earlier chapters, and some of the material refers to aspects of Go programming that are covered in subsequent chapters. Forward and backward cross-references are provided where appropriate.

5.1. Statement Basics

Formally, Go's syntax requires the use of semicolons (;) as statement termina-tors in many contexts. However, as we have seen, very few semicolons are need-ed in real Go programs. This is because the compiler will conveniently insert semicolons automatically at the end of nonblank lines that end with an identifi-er, a number literal, a character literal, a string literal, certain keywords (break, continue, fallthrough, return), an increment or decrement operator (++ or --), or a closing parenthesis, bracket, or brace (),], }).

Two common cases where semicolons must be manually inserted are when we want to have two or more statements on the same line and in plain for loops (§5.3, ➤ 203).

An important consequence of the automatic semicolon insertion is that an opening brace cannot occur on its own line.

```
// Correct ✓                        // WRONG! (This won't compile.) ✗
for i := 0; i < 5; i++ {            for i := 0; i < 5; i++
    fmt.Println(i)                  {
}                                           fmt.Println(i)
                                    }
```

The right-hand code snippet won't compile because the compiler will insert a semicolon after the ++. Similarly, if we had an infinite loop (for) with the brace starting on the next line, the compiler would insert a semicolon after the for, and again the code wouldn't compile.

The æsthetics of brace placement usually generate endless arguments—but not in Go. This is partly because the automatic semicolons constrain brace placement and partly because many Go users use the gofmt program which

---

* Table 5.1 does not list the built-in print() and println() functions since they should *not* be used. They exist for the convenience of Go compiler implementers and may be removed from the language. Use functions like fmt.Print() instead (§3.5, 93 ◄).

Table 5.1 *Built-In Functions*

Syntax	Description/result
append(s, ...)	The slice it was given plus the new items at the end if the slice's capacity is sufficient; otherwise a new slice with the original items plus the new items at the end (see §4.2.3, 156 ◄)
cap(x)	The capacity of slice x or the channel buffer capacity of channel x or the length of array (or the array pointed to by) x; see also len() (see §4.2, 148 ◄)
close(ch)	Closes channel ch (but not legal for receive-only channels). No more data can be sent to the channel. Data can continue to be received from the channel (e.g., any sent but not yet received values), and when there are no more values in the channel, receivers will get the channel data type's zero value.
complex(r, i)	A complex128 with the given r (real) and i (imaginary) parts, both of type float64 (see §2.3.2.1, 70 ◄)
copy(dst, src) copy(b, s)	Copies (possibly overlapping) items from the src slice into the dst slice, truncating if there isn't enough room; or copies s of type string's bytes to b of type []byte (see §4.2.3, 156 ◄ and ➤ 268)
delete(m, k)	Deletes the item with key k from map m or safely does nothing if there's no such key (see §4.3, 164 ◄)
imag(cx)	The imaginary part of cx of type complex128 as a float64 (see §2.3.2.1, 70 ◄)
len(x)	The length of slice x or the number of items queued in channel x's buffer or the length of array (or the array pointed to by) x or the number of items in map x or the number of bytes in string x; see also cap() (see §4.2.3, 156 ◄)
make(T) make(T, n) make(T, n, m)	A reference to a slice, map, or channel of type T. If n is given this is a slice's length and capacity, or a hint to a map of how many items to expect, or a channel's buffer size. For slices only, n and m may be given to specify the length and capacity (see 150 ◄ for slices, 165 ◄ for maps, and Chapter 7 for channels).
new(T)	A pointer to a value of type T (see §4.1, 140 ◄)
panic(x)	Raises a catchable runtime exception with value x (see §5.5.1, ➤ 213)
real(cx)	The real part of cx of type complex128 as a float64 (see §2.3.2.1, 70 ◄)
recover()	Catches a runtime exception (see §5.5.1, ➤ 213)

formats Go programs in a standardized way. In fact, all the Go standard library's source code uses gofmt which is why the code has such a consistent layout, even though it is the product of many different programmers' work.*

Go supports the ++ (increment) and -- (decrement) operators listed in Table 2.4 (59 ◄). They are both postfix operators, that is, they must follow the operand they apply to, and they do not return a value. These constraints prevent the operators from being used as expressions, and mean that they cannot be used in semantically ambiguous contexts—for example, we cannot apply one of these operators to an argument in a function call or write $i = i$++ in Go (although we could in C and C++ where the results are undefined).

Assignments are made using the = assignment operator. Variables can be both created and assigned by using = in conjunction with var—for example, var x = 5 creates a new variable x of type int and with value 5. (Exactly the same could be achieved using var x int = 5 or x := 5.) The type of the variable assigned to must be compatible with the value being assigned. If = is used without var the variable on its left-hand side must already exist. Multiple comma-separated variables can be assigned to, and we can use the blank identifier (_), which is compatible with any type, to ignore any of the values being assigned. Multiple assignments make it easy to swap two values without the need for an explicit temporary variable—for example, $a, b = b, a$.

The short variable declaration operator (:=) is used to both declare a new variable and assign to it in a single statement. Multiple comma-separated variables can be used in much the same way as when using the = operator, except that at least one nonblank variable must be new. If there is a variable that already exists it will be assigned to without creating a new variable—unless the := is at the start of a new scope such as in an if or for statement's initializing statement (see §5.2.1, ➤ 192; §5.3, ➤ 203).

```go
a, b, c := 2, 3, 5
for a := 7; a < 8; a++ { // a is unintentionally shadowing the outer a
    b := 11 // b is unintentionally shadowing the outer b
    c = 13  // c is the intended outer c ✓
    fmt.Printf("inner: a→%d b→%d c→%d\n", a, b, c)
}
fmt.Printf("outer: a→%d b→%d  c→%d\n", a, b, c)
```

```
inner: a→7 b→11 c→13
outer: a→2 b→3  c→13
```

---

* At the time of this writing, gofmt did not support line wrapping to a maximum line width, and in some cases gofmt will join two or more wrapped lines to make one long line. The book's source code was automatically extracted from live examples and test programs and inserted into the book's camera-ready PDF file—but this is subject to a hard 75-character-per-line limit. So, for the book's code, gofmt was used, and then long lines were manually wrapped.

This code snippet shows how the := operator can create "shadow" variables. In this snippet, inside the for loop the a and b variables shadow variables from the outer scope, and while legal, this is almost certainly a programming error. On the other hand, there is only one c variable (from the outer scope), so its usage is correct and as intended. Variables that shadow other variables can be very convenient, as we will see shortly, but careless use can cause problems.

As we will discuss later in the chapter, we can write return statements in functions that have one or more *named* return values, without specifying any return values. In such cases, the returned values will be the named return values, which are initialized with their zero values on entry to the function, and which we can change by assigning to them in the body of the function.

```go
func shadow() (err error) { // THIS FUNCTION WILL NOT COMPILE!
    x, err := check1() // x is created; err is assigned to
    if err != nil {
        return // err correctly returned
    }
    if y, err := check2(x); err != nil { // y and inner err are created
        return // inner err shadows outer err so nil is wrongly returned!
    } else {
        fmt.Println(y)
    }
    return // nil returned
}
```

In the shadow() function's first statement the x variable is created and assigned to, but the err variable is simply assigned to since it is already declared as the shadow() function's return value. This works because the := operator must create at least one nonblank variable and that condition is met here. So, if err is not nil, it is correctly returned.

An if statement's simple statement, that is, the optional statement that follows the if and precedes the condition, starts a new scope (§5.2.1, ➤ 192). So, *both* the y and the err variables are created, the latter being a shadow variable. If the err is not nil the err in the outer scope is returned (i.e., the err declared as the shadow() function's return value), which is nil since that was the value assigned to it by the call to check1(), whereas the call to check2() was assigned to the shadowing inner err.

Fortunately, this function's shadow problem is merely a phantom, since the Go compiler will stop with an error message if we use a bare return when any of the return variables has been shadowed. So, this function will not compile as it stands.

One easy solution is to add a line at the start of the function that declares the variables (e.g., var x, y int or x, y := 0, 0), and change := to = for the check1() and check2() calls. (For an example of this approach see the custom americanise() function; 35 ◄.)

Another solution is to use an unnamed return value. This forces us to return an explicit value, so in this case the first two return statements would both become return err (each returning a different but correct err value), and the last one would become return nil.

5.1.1. Type Conversions

Go provides a means of converting between different—compatible—types, and such conversions are useful and safe. For conversions between non-numeric types no loss of accuracy occurs. But for conversions between numeric types, loss of accuracy or other effects may occur. For example, if we have x := uint16(65000) and then use the conversion y := int16(x), since x is outside the int16 range, y's value is set to the unsurprising—but probably undesirable—value of –536.

Here is the conversion syntax:

```
resultOfType := Type(expression)
```

For numbers, essentially we can convert any integer or floating-point number to another integer or floating-point type (with possible loss of accuracy if the target type is smaller than the source type). The same applies to converting between complex128 and complex64 types. We discussed numeric conversions in §2.3 (58 ◄ and 69 ◄).

A string can be converted to a []byte (its underlying UTF-8 bytes) or to a []rune (its Unicode code points), and both a []byte and a []rune can be converted to a string. A single character is a rune (i.e., an int32), and can be converted to a one-character string. String and character conversions were covered in Chapter 3 (87 ◄ and 88 ◄; also Table 3.2, 85 ◄, and Tables 3.8 and 3.9, 114–115 ◄).

Let's look at a tiny illustrative example, starting with a simple custom type.

```
type StringSlice []string
```

This type also has a custom StringSlice.String() function (not shown) that returns a string representation of the string slice in the form used to create a custom StringSlice using composite literal syntax.

```
fancy := StringSlice{"Lithium", "Sodium", "Potassium", "Rubidium"}
fmt.Println(fancy)
plain := []string(fancy)
fmt.Println(plain)
```

```
StringSlice{"Lithium", "Sodium", "Potassium", "Rubidium"}
[Lithium Sodium Potassium Rubidium]
```

The fancy `StringSlice` is printed using its own `StringSlice.String()` function. But once we convert it to a plain `[]string`, it is printed like any other `[]string`. (Creating custom types with their own methods is covered in Chapter 6.)

Conversions for other types will work if the expression and *Type*'s underlying types are the same, or if the expression is an untyped constant that can be represented by type *Type*, or if *Type* is an interface type and the expression implements *Type*'s interface.★

5.1.2. Type Assertions

A type's *method set* is the set of all the methods that can be called on a value of the type—this set is empty for types that have no methods. The Go `interface{}` type is used to represent the empty interface, that is, a value of a type whose method set includes the empty set. Since every type has a method set that includes the empty set (no matter how many methods it has), an `interface{}` can be used to represent a value of *any* Go type. Furthermore, we can convert an `interface{}` to a value of the actual type it holds using a type `switch` (see §5.2.2.2, ➤ 197), or a type assertion, or by doing introspection with Go's `reflect` package (§9.4.9, ➤ 427).°

The use of variables of type `interface{}` (or of custom interface types) can arise when we are handling data received from external sources, when we want to create generic functions, and when doing object-oriented programming. To access the underlying value, one approach is to use a type assertion using one of these syntaxes:

```
resultOfType, boolean := expression.(Type) // Checked
resultOfType := expression.(Type)          // Unchecked; panic() on failure
```

A successful checked type assertion returns the expression as a value of the specified *Type* and `true` to indicate success. If the checked type assertion fails (i.e., the expression's type is not compatible with the specified *Type*), a zero value of the specified *Type* and `false` are returned. Unchecked type assertions either return the expression as a value of the specified *Type* or call the built-in `panic()`

★ Other more obscure conversions are also possible; these are covered in the Go specification (golang. org/doc/go_spec.html).

° Python programmers may find it helpful to think of `interface{}` as being like an instance of *object*, and Java programmers as being like an instance of *Object*, although unlike Java's *Object*, `interface{}` can be used to represent both custom and built-in types. For C and C++ programmers, `interface{}` is rather like a *void*∗ that knows what type it is.

function which will result in program termination if the panic isn't recovered. (Panicking and recovery is covered later; §5.5, ➤ 212.)

Here is a tiny example to illustrate the syntaxes in use.

```
var i interface{} = 99
var s interface{} = []string{"left", "right"}
j := i.(int) // j is of type int (or a panic() has occurred)
fmt.Printf("%T→%d\n", j, j)
if i, ok := i.(int); ok {
    fmt.Printf("%T→%d\n", i, i) // i is a shadow variable of type int
}
if s, ok := s.([]string); ok {
    fmt.Printf("%T→%q\n", s, s) // s is a shadow variable of type []string
}
```

```
int→99
int→99
[]string→["left" "right"]
```

It is quite common when doing type assertions to use the same name for the result variable as for the original variable, that is, to use shadow variables. And, generally, we use checked type assertions only when we expect the expression to be of the specified type. (If the expression could be any one of a number of types, we can use a type switch; §5.2.2.2, ➤ 197.)

Note that if we printed the original i and s variables (both of type interface{}) they would be printed as an int and a []string. This is because when the fmt package's print functions are faced with interface{} types, they are sensible enough to print the actual underlying values.

5.2. Branching

Go provides three branching statements: if, switch, and select—the latter is discussed further on (§5.4.1, ➤ 209). A branching effect can also be achieved using a map whose keys are used to select the "branch" and whose values are corresponding functions to call—something we will see later in the chapter (§5.6.5, ➤ 230).

5.2.1. If Statements

Go's if statement has the following syntax:

```
if optionalStatement1; booleanExpression1 {
    block1
} else if optionalStatement2; booleanExpression2 {
```

```
        block2
    } else {
        block3
    }
```

There may be zero or more else if clauses and zero or one final else clause. Each block consists of zero or more statements.

The braces are mandatory, but a semicolon is needed only if an optional statement is present. The optional statement is a *simple statement* in Go terminology: This means that it may be only an expression, a channel send (using the <- operator), an increment or decrement statement, an assignment, or a short variable declaration. If variables are created in an optional statement (e.g., using the := operator), their scope extends from the point of declaration to the end of the complete if statement—so they exist in the if or else if they are declared in, and in every following branch, and cease to exist at the end of the if statement.

The Boolean expressions must be of type bool. Go will not automatically convert non-bools, so we must always use a comparison operator—for example, if $i == 0$. (The Boolean and comparison operators are listed in Table 2.3, 57 ◄.)

We have already seen numerous examples of if statements in use, and will see many more in the rest of the book. Nonetheless, we will look at two tiny examples, the first to show the value of the optional simple statement, and the second to illustrate a Go if statement idiom.

```
// Canonical ✓                         // Long-winded!
if α := compute(); α < 0 {             {
    fmt.Printf("(%d)\n", -α)               α := compute()
} else {                                   if α < 0 {
    fmt.Println(α)                             fmt.Printf("(%d)\n", -α)
}                                          } else {
                                               fmt.Println(α)
                                           }
                                       }
```

These two code snippets print exactly the same thing. The right-hand snippet must use extra braces to limit the scope of the α variable, whereas the left-hand snippet automatically limits the variable's scope to the if statement.

The second if statement example is the ArchiveFileList() function which is taken from the archive_file_list example (in file archive_file_list/archive_file_list.go). Later on we will use this function's body to compare if and switch statements.

```go
func ArchiveFileList(file string) ([]string, error) {
    if suffix := Suffix(file); suffix == ".gz" {
        return GzipFileList(file)
    } else if suffix == ".tar" || suffix == ".tar.gz" || suffix == ".tgz" {
        return TarFileList(file)
    } else if suffix == ".zip" {
        return ZipFileList(file)
    }
    return nil, errors.New("unrecognized archive")
}
```

The example program reads the files given on the command line, and for those archive files that it can handle (.gz, .tar, .tar.gz, .zip), it prints the name of the archive file and an indented list of the files the archive contains.

Notice that the scope of the suffix variable created in the first if clause extends throughout the entire if … else if … statement, so it is visible in every branch, just like the α variable in the previous example.

The function could have been written using a final else statement, but it is very common in Go to use the structure shown here: an if statement and zero or more else if statements each of which ends with a return statement, with this followed by a return statement rather than a final else statement that ends with a return.

```go
func Suffix(file string) string {
    file = strings.ToLower(filepath.Base(file))
    if i := strings.LastIndex(file, "."); i > -1 {
        if file[i:] == ".bz2" || file[i:] == ".gz" || file[i:] == ".xz" {
            if j := strings.LastIndex(file[:i], ".");
                j > -1 && strings.HasPrefix(file[j:], ".tar") {
                return file[j:]
            }
        }
        return file[i:]
    }
    return file
}
```

The Suffix() function is included for completeness: It takes a filename (which may include a path), and returns the lowercased suffix—also called the extension—that is, the last part of the name that begins with a period. If the filename has no period, it is returned as is (but without any path); if the filename ends in .tar.bz2, .tar.gz, or .tar.xz then this is the suffix that is returned.

5.2.2. Switch Statements

There are two kinds of `switch` statement: expression switches and type switches.
Expression switches will be familiar to C, C++, and Java programmers, whereas
type switches are specific to Go. Both kinds are syntactically very similar, but
unlike C, C++, and Java, Go's switch statements do not fall through (so there
is no need to put a `break` at the end of every `case`); instead we can request
fallthrough explicitly by using the `fallthrough` statement when it is needed.

5.2.2.1. Expression Switches

Go's *expression* `switch` statement has the following syntax:

```
switch optionalStatement; optionalExpression {
case expressionList1: block1
...
case expressionListN: blockN
default: blockD
}
```

The semicolon is required if the optional statement is present, regardless of
whether the optional expression is present. Each block consists of zero or
more statements.

If the `switch` has no optional expression the compiler assumes an expression of
`true`. The optional statement is the same kind of simple statement that can be
used with `if` statements (193 ◄). If variables are created in the optional statement (e.g., using the `:=` operator), their scope extends from the point of declaration to the end of the complete `switch` statement—so they exist in every `case` and
in the `default` case, and cease to exist at the end of the `switch` statement.

The most efficient way to order `cases` is from most likely to least likely, although
this only really matters when there are lots of `cases` and the `switch` is executed
repeatedly. Since cases do *not* automatically fall through, there is no need to
put a `break` at the end of each case's block. If `fallthrough` is wanted we simply
use a `fallthrough` statement. The `default` case is optional and if present may
appear anywhere. If no case's expression matches, the default case is executed
if it is present; otherwise processing continues from the statement following the
`switch` statement.

Each case must have an expression list of one or more comma-separated
expressions whose type matches the `switch` statement's optional expression's
type. If no optional expression is present the compiler sets it to `true`, that is, of
type `bool`, in which case every expression in each `case` clause's expression list
must evaluate to a `bool`.

If a `case` or `default` clause has a `break` statement, the `switch` statement will immediately be broken out of, with control passing to the statement following the

switch statement, or—if the break statement specifies a label—to the innermost enclosing for, switch, or select statement that has the specified label.

Here is a very simple example of a switch statement that has no optional statement and no optional expression.

```go
func BoundedInt(minimum, value, maximum int) int {
    switch {
    case value < minimum:
        return minimum
    case value > maximum:
        return maximum
    }
    return value
}
```

Since there is no optional expression the compiler sets the expression to true; this means that each case clause expression must evaluate to a bool. Here both expressions use Boolean comparison operators.

```go
switch {
case value < minimum:
    return minimum
case value > maximum:
    return maximum
default:
    return value
}
panic("unreachable")
```

Here is an alternative body for the BoundedInt() function. The switch statement now covers every possible case, so control can never reach the end of the function. Nonetheless, Go expects a return at the end—or a panic(), so we have used the latter to better express the function's semantics.

The ArchiveFileList() function shown in the previous subsection (194 ◄) used an if statement to determine which function to call. Here is a naïve switch statement-based version.

```go
switch suffix := Suffix(file); suffix { // Naïve and noncanonical!
case ".gz":
    return GzipFileList(file)
case ".tar":
    fallthrough
case ".tar.gz":
    fallthrough
```

```
    case ".tgz":
        return TarFileList(file)
    case ".zip":
        return ZipFileList(file)
    }
```

This switch statement has both a statement and an expression. In this case the expression is of type string so each case's expression list must contain one or more comma-separated strings to match. We have used the fallthrough statement to ensure that all tar files are processed by the same function.

The suffix variable's scope extends throughout the switch statement to every case (and would extend to the default case if one was present), and ends at the end of the switch statement since at that point the suffix ceases to exist.

```
    switch Suffix(file) { // Canonical ✓
    case ".gz":
        return GzipFileList(file)
    case ".tar", ".tar.gz", ".tgz":
        return TarFileList(file)
    case ".zip":
        return ZipFileList(file)
    }
```

Here is a more compact and canonical version of the preceding switch statement. Instead of a statement and an expression we have simply used an expression: The Suffix() function (that we saw earlier; 194 ◀) returns a string. And instead of using fallthrough statements for tar files, we have used a comma-separated list of all the matching suffixes as that case clause's expression list.

Go's expression switch statements are much more versatile than those provided by C, C++, and Java, and in many cases can be used instead of—and are more compact than—if statements.

5.2.2.2. Type Switches

As we noted when we covered type assertions (§5.1.2, 191 ◀), when we use variables of type interface{} we often want to access the underlying value. If we know the type we can use a type assertion, but if the type may be any one of a number of possible types we can use a type switch statement.

Go's *type* switch statement has the following syntax:

```
    switch optionalStatement; typeSwitchGuard {
    case typeList1: block1
    ...
    case typeListN: blockN
```

```
default: blockD
}
```

The optional statement is the same as in expression switches and if statements.
And the case clauses work the same way as for expression switches except that
they list one or more comma-separated types. The optional default clause and
fallthrough statements are just the same as for expression switches, and as
usual, each block consists of zero or more statements.

The type switch guard is an expression whose result is a type. If the expression
is assigned using the := operator, the variable created has the *value* of the value
in the type switch guard expression, but its *type* depends on the case clauses: In
a case clause with one type in its type list, the variable has that type in that case,
and in case clauses that have two or more types, the variable's type is that of the
type switch guard expression.

The kind of type testing supported by the type switch statement is generally
frowned upon by object-oriented programmers who instead prefer to rely on
polymorphism. Go supports a kind of polymorphism through duck typing (as
we will see in Chapter 6), but nonetheless there are times where explicit type
testing makes sense.

Here is an example of how we might call a simple type classifier function and
the output it produces.

```
classifier(5, -17.9, "ZIP", nil, true, complex(1, 1))
```

```
param #0 is an int
param #1 is a float64
param #2 is a string
param #3 is nil
param #4 is a bool
param #5's type is unknown
```

The classifier() function uses a simple type switch. It is a *variadic* function,
that is, it can accept a variable number of arguments. And since the argument
type is interface{}, the arguments can be of any types. (Functions, including
variadic functions and the ellipsis, are covered later in this chapter; §5.6,
➤ 219.)

```
func classifier(items ...interface{}) {          // variadic 198,221
    for i, x := range items {
        switch x.(type) {          → called the "type switch guard"
        case bool:
            fmt.Printf("param #%d is a bool\n", i)
        case float64:
            fmt.Printf("param #%d is a float64\n", i)
```

```
        case int, int8, int16, int32, int64:
            fmt.Printf("param #%d is an int\n", i)
        case uint, uint8, uint16, uint32, uint64:
            fmt.Printf("param #%d is an unsigned int\n", i)
        case nil:
            fmt.Printf("param #%d is nil\n", i)
        case string:
            fmt.Printf("param #%d is a string\n", i)
        default:
            fmt.Printf("param #%d's type is unknown\n", i)
        }
    }
}
```

The type switch guard used here has the same format as a type assertion, that is, *variable.(Type)*, but using the keyword type instead of an actual type to stand for *any* type.

Sometimes we might want to access an interface{}'s underlying value as well as its type. This can be done by making the type switch guard an assignment (using the := operator), as we will see in a moment.

One common use case for type testing is when we are dealing with data from external sources. For example, if we are parsing data encoded using JSON (JavaScript Object Notation), we must somehow convert the data to the corresponding Go data types. This can be done using Go's json.Unmarshal() function. If we give the function a pointer to a struct with fields that match the JSON data, this function will populate the struct's fields converting each item of JSON data into the data type of its corresponding struct field. But if we do not know the JSON data's structure in advance we cannot give the json.Unmarshal() function a struct. In such cases we can give the function a pointer to an interface{} which the json.Unmarshal() function will set to refer to a map[string]interface{} whose keys are JSON field names and whose values are the corresponding values stored as interface{}s.

Here is an example that shows how we can unmarshal a raw JSON object of unknown structure and how we can create and print a corresponding string representation of the JSON object.

```
MA := []byte(`{"name": "Massachusetts", "area": 27336, "water": 25.7,
               "senators": ["John Kerry", "Scott Brown"]}`)
var object interface{}
if err := json.Unmarshal(MA, &object); err != nil {
    fmt.Println(err)
} else {
    jsonObject := object.(map[string]interface{})    ❶
```

```
        fmt.Println(jsonObjectAsString(jsonObject))
}
```

```
{"senators": ["John Kerry", "Scott Brown"], "name": "Massachusetts",
"water": 25.700000, "area": 27336.000000}
```

If no error occurred when unmarshaling, the object variable of type interface{}
will refer to a variable of type map[string]interface{} whose keys are the JSON
object's field names. The jsonObjectAsString() function accepts a map of this
type and returns a corresponding JSON string. We use an unchecked type
assertion (199 ◄, ❶) to convert the object of type interface{} to the jsonObject
variable of type map[string]interface{}. (Note that the output shown here is
split over two lines to fit the book's page width.)

```
func jsonObjectAsString(jsonObject map[string]interface{}) string {
    var buffer bytes.Buffer
    buffer.WriteString("{")
    comma := ""
    for key, value := range jsonObject {
        buffer.WriteString(comma)
        switch value := value.(type) { // shadow variable    ❶
        case nil:    ❷
            fmt.Fprintf(&buffer, "%q: null", key)
        case bool:
            fmt.Fprintf(&buffer, "%q: %t", key, value)
        case float64:
            fmt.Fprintf(&buffer, "%q: %f", key, value)
        case string:
            fmt.Fprintf(&buffer, "%q: %q", key, value)
        case []interface{}:
            fmt.Fprintf(&buffer, "%q: [", key)
            innerComma := ""
            for _, s := range value {
                if s, ok := s.(string); ok { // shadow variable   ❸
                    fmt.Fprintf(&buffer, "%s%q", innerComma, s)
                    innerComma = ", "
                }
            }
            buffer.WriteString("]")
        }
        comma = ", "
    }
    buffer.WriteString("}")
    return buffer.String()
}
```

This function converts a map representing a JSON object and returns a corresponding string of the object's data in JSON format. JSON arrays inside maps representing JSON objects are themselves represented by the []interface{} type. The function makes one simplifying assumption regarding JSON arrays: It assumes that they have only string items.

To access the data we use a for ... range loop (§5.3, ➤ 203) over the map's keys and values and use a type switch to access and handle each different value type. The switch's type switch guard (200 ◀, ❶) assigns the value (of type interface{}) to a *new* variable called value which has the type of the matching case. This is a situation where it makes sense to shadow a variable (although we are free to create a new variable if we wish). So, if the interface{} value's type is bool, the inner value will be a bool and will match the second case, and similarly for the other cases.

To write the values to the buffer we have used the fmt.Fprintf() function since this is more convenient than writing, say, buffer.WriteString(fmt.Sprintf(...)) (200 ◀, ❷). The fmt.Fprintf() function writes to the io.Writer passed as its first argument. A bytes.Buffer is *not* an io.Writer—but a *bytes.Buffer *is*, which is why we pass the buffer's address. This matter is covered more fully in Chapter 6, but in brief, io.Writer is an interface that can be fulfilled by any value that provides a suitable Write() method. The bytes.Buffer.Write() method takes a pointer receiver (i.e., a *bytes.Buffer, not a bytes.Buffer value), so only a *bytes.Buffer fulfills the interface, which means that we must pass the buffer's address to the fmt.Fprintf() function, not the buffer value itself.

If the JSON object contains JSON arrays, we use an inner for ... range loop to iterate over each of the []interface{}'s items and use a checked type assertion (200 ◀, ❸) which means that we add items to our output only if they really are strings. Again, we use a shadow variable (this time s of type string), since we don't want the interface{}, but rather the value it refers to. (Type assertions were covered earlier; §5.1.2, 191 ◀.)

Of course, if we knew the original JSON object's structure in advance we could simplify the code a great deal. We would need a struct to hold the data and a method for outputting it in string form. Here is the code to unmarshal and print in such cases.

```
var state State
if err := json.Unmarshal(MA, &state); err != nil {
    fmt.Println(err)
}
fmt.Println(state)
```

```
{"name": "Massachusetts", "area": 27336, "water": 25.700000,
"senators": ["John Kerry", "Scott Brown"]}
```

This code looks very similar to the code we had before. However, there is no need for a `jsonObjectAsString()` function; instead we need to define a `State` type and a corresponding `State.String()` method. (Once again, we had to split the output over two lines to fit the book's page width.)

```
type State struct {
    Name      string
    Senators  []string
    Water     float64
    Area      int
}
```

The `struct` is similar to ones we have seen before. Note, though, that each field *must* begin with an uppercase letter to make it exported (public) since the `json.Unmarshal()` function can only populate exported fields. Also, although Go's `encoding/json` package does not distinguish between different numeric types—it treats all JSON numbers as `float64s`—the `json.Unmarshal()` function is smart enough to populate fields of other numeric types as necessary.

```
func (state State) String() string {
    var senators []string
    for _, senator := range state.Senators {
        senators = append(senators, fmt.Sprintf("%q", senator))
    }
    return fmt.Sprintf(
        `{"name": %q, "area": %d, "water": %f, "senators": [%s]}`,
        state.Name, state.Area, state.Water, strings.Join(senators, ", "))
}
```

This method returns a `State` value as a JSON data string.

Most Go programs should not need type assertions and type switches; and even when they are needed, their use should be fairly rare. One use case is where we are passing values that satisfy one interface and want to check if they also satisfy another. (This topic is covered in Chapter 6; e.g., §6.5.2, ➤ 289.) Another use case is when data from external sources must be converted into Go data types. For ease of maintenance, it is almost always best that such code is isolated from the rest of the program. This allows the program to work wholly in terms of Go data types and means that any maintenance needed due to changes to the format or types received from external sources can be localized.

5.3. Looping with For Statements

Go uses two kinds of for statements for looping, plain for statements and for ... range statements. Here are their syntaxes:

```
for { // Infinite loop
    block
}

for booleanExpression { // While loop
    block
}

for optionalPreStatement; booleanExpression; optionalPostStatement { ❶
    block
}

for index, char := range aString { // String per character iteration ❷
    block
}

for index := range aString { // String per character iteration ❸
    block // char, size := utf8.DecodeRuneInString(aString[index:])
}

for index, item := range anArrayOrSlice { // Array or slice iteration ❹
    block
}

for index := range anArrayOrSlice { // Array or slice iteration ❺
    block // item := anArrayOrSlice[index]
}

for key, value := range aMap { // Map iteration ❻
    block
}

for key := range aMap { // Map iteration ❼
    block // value := aMap[key]
}

for item := range aChannel { // Channel iteration
    block
}
```

The braces are mandatory, but a semicolon is only needed if an optional pre- or post-statement is used (❶); both statements must be simple statements. If variables are created in an optional statement or to capture the values produced by a range clause (e.g., using the := operator), their scope extends from the point of declaration to the end of the complete for statement.

The Boolean expression in the plain for loop syntax (203 ◀, ❶) *must* be of type bool since Go will not automatically convert non-bools. (The Boolean and comparison operators are listed in Table 2.3, 57 ◀.)

The second for … range over a string syntax (203 ◀, ❸) gives byte offset indexes. For a 7-bit ASCII string s, of value "XabYcZ", this produces indexes 0, 1, 2, 3, 4, 5. But for a UTF-8 string s, of value "XαβYγZ", the indexes produced are 0, 1, 3, 5, 6, 8. The first for … range over a string syntax (203 ◀, ❷) is almost always more convenient than the second (203 ◀, ❸).

The second for … range over an array or slice syntax (203 ◀, ❺) produces item indexes from 0 to len(slice) - 1 for nonempty slices or arrays. This syntax and the first for … range over an array or slice syntax (203 ◀, ❹) are often useful. These two syntaxes in particular account for why fewer plain for loops (203 ◀, ❶) are needed in Go programs.

The for … range loops over map *key–value* items (203 ◀, ❻) and over map keys (203 ◀, ❼) produce the items or keys in an arbitrary order. If sorted order is required one solution is to use the second syntax (203 ◀, ❼) and populate a slice with the keys and then sort the slice—we saw an example of this in the previous chapter (§4.3.4, 170 ◀). Another solution is to use an ordered data structure in the first place—for example, an ordered map. We will see an example of this in the next chapter (§6.5.3, ➤ 302).

If any of the syntaxes (203 ◀, ❷–❼) are used on an empty string, array, slice, or map, the for loop harmlessly does nothing and the flow of control continues at the following statement.

A for loop can be broken out of at any time with a break statement, with control passing to the statement following the for loop, or—if the break statement specifies a label—to the innermost enclosing for, switch, or select statement that has the specified label. It is also possible to make the flow of control return to the for loop's condition or range clause to force the next iteration (or the end of the loop), by using a continue statement.

We have already seen numerous examples of for statements in use; these include for … range loops (89 ◀, 172 ◀, and 180 ◀), infinite loops (23 ◀ and 45 ◀), and the plain for loop (100 ◀) that is needed less frequently in Go since the other loops are often more convenient. And we will, of course, see many more for loop examples in the rest of the book, including some later in this chapter; so here we will confine ourselves to one small example.

Suppose that we have two-dimensional slices (e.g., of type [][]int), and want to search them to see if they contain a particular value. Here are two ways we can perform the search. Both use the second for … range over an array or slice syntax (203 ◀, ❺).

```
found := false                   found := false
for row := range table {         FOUND:
    for column := range table[row] {   for row := range table {
        if table[row][column] == x {       for column := range table[row] {
            found = true                       if table[row][column] == x {
            break                                  found = true
        }                                          break FOUND
    }                                          }
    if found {                             }
        break                          }
    }
}
```

A label is an identifier followed by a colon. Both code snippets achieve the same thing but the right-hand snippet is shorter and clearer because as soon as the searched-for value (x) is found, it breaks to the outer loop by using a break statement that specifies a label. The advantages of breaking to a label are even greater if we are in a deeply nested series of loops (e.g., iterating over three-dimensional data).

Labels can be applied to for loops, switch statements, and select statements. Both break and continue statements can specify labels and can be used inside for loops. It is also possible to use break statements—either bare or specifying a label—inside switch and select statements.

Labels can also appear as statements in their own right in which case they may be the targets of goto statements (using the syntax goto *label*). If a goto statement jumps past any statement that creates a variable, the Go program's behavior is undefined—if we are lucky it will crash, but probably it will continue to run and produce spurious results. One use case for goto statements is when automatically generating code, since in this circumstance goto can be convenient and the concerns about spaghetti code don't necessarily apply. Although, at the time of this writing, more than 30 of Go's source files use goto statements, none of the book's examples use the goto statement, and we advocate avoiding it.*

5.4. Communication and Concurrency Statements

Go's communication and concurrency features are covered in Chapter 7, but for completeness of our coverage of procedural programming we will describe their basic syntax here.

---

* goto statements have been generally despised since Edsger Dijkstra's famous 1968 letter titled "Go-to statement considered harmful" (www.cs.utexas.edu/users/EWD/ewd02xx/EWD215.PDF).

A *goroutine* is a function or method invocation that executes independently and
concurrently in relation to any other goroutines in a program. Every Go program has at least one goroutine, the main goroutine in which the main package's main() function executes. Goroutines are rather like lightweight threads
or coroutines, in that they can be created in large numbers (whereas even small
numbers of threads can consume a huge amount of machine resources). Goroutines all share the same address space, and Go provides locking primitives
to allow data to be safely shared across goroutines. However, the recommended
approach to concurrent Go programming is to communicate data, rather than to
share it.

A Go *channel* is a bidirectional or unidirectional communication pipe that
can be used to communicate (i.e., send and receive) data between two or more
goroutines.

Between them, goroutines and channels provide a means of lightweight (i.e.,
scalable) concurrency that does not use shared memory and so does not require
locking. Nonetheless, as with all other approaches to concurrency, care must be
exercised when creating concurrent programs and maintenance is usually more
challenging than for nonconcurrent programs. Most operating systems are excellent at running multiple programs at the same time, so exploiting this can
reduce maintenance—for instance, by running multiple programs (or multiple
copies of the same program) each operating on different data. Good programmers write concurrent programs only when the approach has clear advantages
that outweigh the increased maintenance burden.

A goroutine is created using the go statement with the following syntaxes:

```
go function(arguments)
go func(parameters) { block }(arguments)
```

We must either call an existing function or call an anonymous function created
on the spot. The function may have zero or more parameters just like any other
function, and if it has parameters, corresponding arguments must be passed the
same as with any other function call.

Execution of the called function begins immediately—but in a separate
goroutine—and execution of the current goroutine (i.e., the one that has the go
statement) resumes immediately from the next statement. So, after a go statement, there are at least two goroutines running, the original one (initially the
main goroutine), and the newly created one.

In rare cases it is sufficient to start off a bunch of goroutines and wait for them
all to finish, with no communication necessary. In most situations, though,
goroutines need to work cooperatively together, and this can best be achieved by
giving them the ability to communicate. Here are the syntaxes used for sending
and receiving data:

```
channel <- value    // Blocking send        binary op
<-channel           // Receive and discard  unary op
x := <-channel      // Receive and store
x, ok := <-channel // As above & check for channel closed & empty
```

Nonblocking sends are possible using the select statement, and to some extent using buffered channels. 209

Channels are created with the built-in make() function with these syntaxes: ✗

```
make(chan Type)
make(chan Type, capacity)
```

If no buffer capacity is specified the channel is synchronous, so it will block until ✗ the sender is ready to send and the receiver is ready to receive. If a capacity is given the channel is asynchronous and communication will progress without blocking so long as there is unused capacity for sends and there is data in the channel to be received.

Channels are bidirectional by default, but we can make them unidirectional if we want to—for example, to better express our semantics in a way that the compiler can enforce. In Chapter 7 we show how to create unidirectional channels, and from then on use unidirectional channels whenever appropriate.

Let's put all the syntax just discussed in context with a tiny example.★ We will write a createCounter() function which will return a channel that will send an int whenever we ask to receive from it. The first value received will be the start value that we pass to the createCounter() function and each subsequent value will be one more than the one before. Here is how we might create two independent counter channels (each operating in its own goroutine), and the results they produce.

```
counterA := createCounter(2)   // counterA is of type chan int
counterB := createCounter(102) // counterB is of type chan int
for i := 0; i < 5; i++ {
    a := <-counterA
    fmt.Printf("(A→%d, B→%d) ", a, <-counterB)
}
fmt.Println()
```
```
(A→2, B→102) (A→3, B→103) (A→4, B→104) (A→5, B→105) (A→6, B→106)
```

We have shown the receives in two different ways just to show how it is done. The first receive assigns the received value to a variable, and the second passes the received value as an argument to a function.

★ This example was inspired by Andrew Gerrand's blog, nf.id.au/concurrency-patterns-a-source-of -unique-numbe. (There really isn't an "r" on the end.)

The two calls to the createCounter() function are made in the main goroutine, and the two other goroutines, each one created by createCounter(), are both initially blocked. In the main goroutine, as soon as we attempt to receive from one of the channels a send takes place and we receive the value. Then the sending goroutine is blocked again, waiting for a new receive request. The two channels are "infinite", in that they can always send a value. (Of course, if we reach the int limit the next value will wrap.) Once the five values we want have been received from each channel the channels are again blocked and ready for use later on.

How can we get rid of the goroutines that we are using for the counter channels if they are no longer needed? This requires us to get them to break out of their infinite loops, so that they stop sending more data, and then to close the channels they are using. We will see one way to do this in the following subsection—and, of course, Chapter 7 which is devoted to concurrency has much more coverage.

```
func createCounter(start int) chan int {
    next := make(chan int)
    go func(i int) {          // anon. func
        for {
            next <- i
            i++
        }
    }(start)                  // arg to anon. func
    return next
}
```

This function accepts a starting value and creates a channel for sending and receiving ints. It then begins executing an anonymous function in a new goroutine, passing it the start value. The function has an infinite loop that simply sends an int and then increments the int at each iteration. Because the channel was created with zero capacity the send blocks until a receive is requested from the channel. The blocking only affects the anonymous function's goroutine, so the rest of the program's goroutines can continue to run unconcerned. Once the goroutine has been set running (and, of course, at this point it immediately blocks), the function's following statement is immediately executed, and this returns the channel to its caller.

In some situations we may have multiple goroutines executing, each with its own communication channel. We can monitor their communications using a select statement.

5.4.1. Select Statements

Go's select statement has the following syntax:*

```
select {
case sendOrReceive1: block1
...
case sendOrReceiveN: blockN
default: blockD
}
```

handwritten annotations:
`1` `2` `n`

// Set up n channels. At each case,
// have val <- chan; or <- chan; (receive)
// or chan; <- val (send)
// optional: select is "blocking" if this is missing.
timeout in select() 332

In a select statement Go evaluates each send or receive statement in order from
first to last. If any of these statements can proceed (i.e., is not blocked), then
of those that can proceed, an *arbitrary* choice is made as to which one to use. If
none can proceed (i.e., if they are all blocked), there are two possible scenarios.
If a default case is present, the default case is executed and execution resumes
from the statement following the select; but if there is no default case the select
will block until at least one communication can proceed.

A consequence of the select statement's logic is as follows. A select with no
default case is *blocking* and will only complete when one communication case
(receive or send) has occurred. A select with a default case is *nonblocking* and
executes immediately, either because a communication case occurred, or if no
communication channel is ready, by executing the default case.

To get to grips with the syntax we will review two short examples. The first example is rather contrived but does give a good idea of how the select statement
works. The second example shows a more realistic approach to use.

```
channels := make([]chan bool, 6)
for i := range channels {
    channels[i] = make(chan bool)
}
go func() {
    for {
        channels[rand.Intn(6)] <- true
    }
}()
```

handwritten annotations:
// make a slice; each member to be a chan for bool
// make member chan's
rand pkg 426

In this snippet we have created six channels which can send and receive
Booleans. We have then created a single goroutine that has an infinite loop within which one of the channels is chosen at random and sent a true value on every
iteration. The goroutine immediately blocks, of course, since the channels are
unbuffered and we have not yet tried to receive from any of them.

---

* Go's select statement has nothing to do with the POSIX *select()* function used to monitor file
descriptors—for that, use the syscall package's Select() function.

```
for i := 0; i < 36; i++ {
    var x int
    select {
    case <-channels[0]:       // case: receive (bool) from 0th channel
        x = 1
    case <-channels[1]:
        x = 2
    case <-channels[2]:
        x = 3
    case <-channels[3]:
        x = 4
    case <-channels[4]:
        x = 5
    case <-channels[5]:
        x = 6
    }
    fmt.Printf("%d ", x)
}
fmt.Println()
```

```
6 4 6 5 4 1 2 1 2 1 5 5 4 6 2 3 6 5 1 5 4 4 3 2 3 3 3 5 3 6 5 2 2 3 6 2
```

In this snippet we use the six channels to simulate rolls of a fair die (strictly speaking, a pseudo-random die).* The select statement waits for one of the channels to have something to send—the select blocks since we have not provided a default case—and as soon as one or more channels are ready to send one case is chosen pseudo-randomly. Since the select is inside a plain for loop it is executed a fixed number of times.

Now we will look at a more realistic example. Suppose that we want to perform the same expensive computation on two separate data sets and that the computation produces a sequence of results. Here is a skeleton of a function that performs such a computation.

```
func expensiveComputation(data Data, answer chan int, done chan bool) {
    // setup ...
    finished := false
    for !finished {
        // computation ...
        answer <- result
    }
    done <- true
}
```

---

* For proper pseudo-random numbers see the math/rand and crypto/rand packages.

The function is given some data to work on, and two channels. The answer channel is used to send each result to the monitoring code and the done channel is used to notify the monitoring code that the computation has finished.

```
// setup ...
const allDone = 2
doneCount := 0
answerα := make(chan int)
answerβ := make(chan int)
defer func() {
        close(answerα)
        close(answerβ)
    }()
done := make(chan bool)      // channel used by both go routines
defer func() { close(done) }()
go expensiveComputation(data1, answerα, done)
go expensiveComputation(data2, answerβ, done)
for doneCount != allDone {
    var which, result int    // fresh on every iteration
    select {
    case result = <-answerα:
        which = 'α'
    case result = <-answerβ:
        which = 'β'
    case <-done:
        doneCount++
    }
    if which != 0 {
        fmt.Printf("%c→%d ", which, result)
    }
}
fmt.Println()
```

α→3 β→3 α→0 β→9 α→0 β→2 α→9 β→3 α→6 β→1 α→0 β→8 α→8 β→5 α→0 β→0 α→3

Here is the code that sets up the channels, starts the expensive computations, monitors progress, and cleans up at the end—and there isn't a lock in sight.

We begin by creating two channels to accept results, answerα and answerβ, and a channel to keep track of when the computations are finished, done. We create anonymous functions in which the channels are closed and call these in defer statements so that they will be closed when they are no longer needed, that is, when the enclosing function returns. Next, we start off the expensive computations (in their own goroutines), giving each one its own unique data to work on, and for communications, its own unique answer channel, and the done channel that is shared.

We could have given both expensive computations the same answer channels, but if we did that we would not know which one had given which result (which might not matter, of course). If we wanted to use the same channel and wanted to identify the origin of any particular result we could make a single answer channel that operated on a struct—for example, type Answer struct{ id, answer int }.

With the expensive computations started in their goroutines (but blocked, since their channels are unbuffered), we are ready to receive their results. The for loop starts with fresh which and result values on every iteration, and the blocking select statement executes an arbitrary case from those that are ready to proceed. If an answer is ready we set which to indicate its origin and print the origin and the result. If the done channel is ready we increment the doneCount counter—and when this reaches the number of expensive computations we started we know that they are all finished and the for loop ends.

Once outside the for loop we know that both expensive computations' goroutines will no longer send any data on the channels (since they broke out of their own infinite for loops when they were finished; 210 ◀). When the function returns the channels are closed by the defer statements and any resources they use are released. After this the garbage collector is free to get rid of the goroutines themselves since they are no longer executing and the channels they were using are closed.

Go's communication and concurrency features are very flexible and versatile; Chapter 7 is devoted to the subject.

5.5. Defer, Panic, and Recover

The defer statement is used to defer the execution of a function or method (or of an anonymous function created on the spot) until just before the enclosing function or method returns, but after the return values (if any) have been evaluated. This makes it possible to modify a function's *named* return values inside a deferred function (e.g., by assigning to them using the = assignment operator). If more than one defer statement is used in a function or method, they are executed in LIFO (Last In First Out) order.

The most common uses of a defer statement are to ensure that a successfully opened file is closed when we are finished with it, to close channels that are no longer needed, or to catch panics.

```
var file *os.File
var err error
if file, err = os.Open(filename); err != nil {
    log.Println("failed to open the file: ", err)
    return
```

```
        }
        defer file.Close()
```

This is an extract from the wordfrequency program's updateFrequencies() function that was discussed in the previous chapter (176 ◀). It shows a typical pattern for opening a file and deferring closing the file if the open succeeded.

This pattern of creating a value and deferring some kind of close function that cleans up the value (e.g., freeing up any resources the value uses), prior to the value being garbage-collected, is standard in Go.* We can, of course, apply this pattern to our own types by providing them with a Close() or Cleanup() function that can be the subject of a defer statement, although this is rarely needed in practice.

5.5.1. Panic and Recover

Go provides an exception handling mechanism through the use of its built-in panic() and recover() functions. These functions could be used to provide a general-purpose exception handling mechanism, similar to those available in some other languages (e.g., C++, Java, and Python): But to do so is considered to be poor Go style.

Go distinguishes between errors—things that might go wrong and that a program should handle gracefully (e.g., a file that could not be opened)—and exceptions—something that "cannot" happen (e.g., a precondition which should always be true that's actually false).

The idiomatic way to handle errors in Go is to return an error as the last (or only) return value from functions and methods and to always check any returned errors. (The one case where it is common to ignore returned error values is when printing to the console.)

For "cannot happen" situations we can call the built-in panic() function with any value we like (e.g., a string that explains the invariant that has been broken). In other languages we might use an assertion for these situations, but in Go we call panic(). During early development and prior to any releases the simplest and probably the best approach is to call panic() to terminate the program to force problems to be impossible to ignore so that they get fixed. Once we start deploying our application it is best to avoid termination when problems occur if at all possible, and this can be done while still leaving any remaining panic() calls in place by adding deferred recover() calls in our packages. During recovery we can catch and log any panics (so that they remain as visible problems), and return non-nil errors to callers who can then try to restore the program to a sane state from which it can safely continue to run.

★ In C++ destructors are used to clean up values. In Java and Python cleanup is problematic since they cannot guarantee when or even if their *finalizer()/__del__()* method will be called.

When the built-in panic() function is called normal execution of the enclosing function or method stops immediately. Then, any deferred functions or methods are called—just as they would have been had the function returned normally. And, finally, control is returned to the caller—as if the called function or method had called panic(), so the process is then repeated in the caller: Execution stops, deferreds are called, and so on. When main() is reached there is no caller to return to, so at this point the program is terminated with a stack trace dumped to os.Stderr including the value that was given to the original panic() call.

If a panic occurs the process just described is normally what unfolds. However, if one of the deferred functions or methods contains a call to the built-in recover() function (which may be called only inside a deferred function or method), the panic is stopped in its tracks. At this point we can respond to the panic any way we like. One solution is to ignore the panic, in which case control will pass to the caller of the function with the deferred recover() call which will then continue to execute normally. This approach is not recommended, but if used, at the very least the panic should be logged so that the problem isn't completely hidden. Another solution is to do whatever cleanup we like and then call panic() ourselves to continue the propagation of the problem. A more common solution is to create an error value and set that as the (or one of the) return values of the function with the deferred recover() call, thus turning the exception (i.e., a panic()) into an error (i.e., an error).

In almost every case, the Go standard library uses error values rather than panics. For our own custom packages, it is best not to use panic(); or, rather, not to allow panic()s to leave the custom package by using recover() to capture panics and to return errors instead, just like the standard library does.

An illustrative example is Go's basic regular expression package, regexp. This has a few functions for creating regular expressions, including regexp.Compile() and regexp.MustCompile(). The first of these returns a compiled regular expression and nil, or, if the string passed to it isn't a valid regular expression, nil and an error. The second of these returns a compiled regular expression or it panics. The first function is ideal for when the regular expression comes from an external source (e.g., is entered by the user or read from a file). The second function is best when the regular expression is hard-coded into the program since it will ensure that when we run the program, if we made a mistake with a regular expression the program will immediately terminate due to the panic.

When should we allow panics to terminate our programs and when should we stop them with recover()? There are two competing interests that we must consider. As programmers we want our programs to crash as soon as possible if there is a logical error so that we can identify and fix the problem. But we don't want our programs to crash at all once they have been deployed.

For problems that can be caught just by running the program (e.g., invalid regular expressions), we should use panic() (or functions that panic such as regexp.MustCompile()) since we would never deploy an application that crashes as soon as it is run. We must be careful that we do this only in functions we are *certain* will be called simply by running the program—for example, the main package's init() function (if it has one), the main package's main() function, and any init() functions in our custom packages that our program imports—plus, of course, any functions or methods that these functions call. If we use a test suite we can, of course, extend our use of panics to any function or method that the test suite causes to be invoked. Naturally, we must also be sure that such potential panic cases are always exercised no matter what the program's flow of control.

For functions and methods that may or may not be called during any particular run we should use recover() if we call panic() ourselves or if we call functions or methods that panic, and turn panics into errors. Ideally recover()s should be used as close to the panic()s they handle as possible, and where possible and appropriate they should restore the program to a sane state before setting their enclosing function or method's error return value. For the main package's main() function we could put in a top-level "catchall" recover() that logs any caught panics—but unfortunately, the program would then terminate after the deferred recover() had been handled. This can be worked around, as we will see shortly.

We will look at two examples, the first demonstrating how to convert panics into errors, and the second showing how to make programs more robust.

Imagine we have the following function buried deep within a package we are using, but which we cannot change because it is from a third party over whom we have no control.

```
func ConvertInt64ToInt(x int64) int {
    if math.MinInt32 <= x && x <= math.MaxInt32 {
        return int(x)
    }
    panic(fmt.Sprintf("%d is out of the int32 range", x))
}
```

This function safely converts an int64 to an int or panics if the conversion would produce an invalid result.

Why would a function like this use panic() in the first place? We might want to force a crash as soon as something goes wrong so as to flush out programming errors as early as possible. Another use case is where we have a function that calls one or more other functions and so on, but where if anything goes wrong we want to immediately return control to the original function—so we make the called functions panic if they hit a problem, and catch the panic (wherever it came from) using recover(). Normally, we want packages to report problems as errors rather than to panic, so it is fairly common to use panic()s inside a package, and to use recover()s to ensure that the panics don't leak out and are reported as errors. And another use case is to put calls like panic("unreachable") in places that our logic says cannot be reached (e.g., at the end of a function which always returns by using return statements before reaching the end), or calling panic() if a pre- or post-condition is broken. Doing this ensures that if we ever break the logic of such functions we will soon know about it.

If none of the above reasons apply then we ought to avoid panicking and return a non-nil error when problems occur. So, in this example, we want to return an int and nil if a conversion succeeds and int and an error if a conversion fails. Here is a wrapper function that achieves what we want:

```go
func IntFromInt64(x int64) (i int, err error) {
    defer func() {
        if e := recover(); e != nil {
            err = fmt.Errorf("%v", e)
        }
    }()
    i = ConvertInt64ToInt(x)
    return i, nil
}
```

(handwritten annotation: "err")

When this function is called, as usual, Go automatically sets the return values to the zero values for their types, in this case 0 and nil. If the call to the custom ConvertInt64ToInt() function returns normally, we assign its result to the i return value, and return i along with nil to signify that no error occurred. But if the ConvertInt64ToInt() function panics, we catch the panic in the deferred anonymous function and set err to be an error with its text set to the textual representation of the panic it caught.

As the IntFromInt64() function shows, it is straightforward to convert panics into errors.

For our second example we will consider how to make a web server robust in the face of panics. Back in Chapter 2 we reviewed the statistics example (§2.4, 72 ◄). If we made a programming error in that server—for example, if we accidentally passed nil as an image.Image value and called a method on it—we would get a panic that without a call to recover() would terminate the program. This is, of course, a very unsatisfactory situation if the web site is important to us, especially if we want it to run unattended some of the time. What we want is for the server to continue running even if a panic occurs, and to log any panics so that we can track them down and fix them at our leisure.

We have created a modified version of the statistics example (in fact, of the statistics_ans solution), in file statistics_nonstop/statistics.go. One modification that we have made is to add an extra button to the web page, Panic!, that can be clicked to make a panic occur for testing purposes. The most important modification is that we have made the server able to survive panics. And to help us see what is going on, we also log whenever a client is successfully served, when we get a bad request, and if the server was restarted. Here is a tiny sample of a typical log.

```
[127.0.0.1:41373] served OK
[127.0.0.1:41373] served OK
[127.0.0.1:41373] bad request: '6y' is invalid
[127.0.0.1:41373] served OK
[127.0.0.1:41373] caught panic: user clicked panic button!
[127.0.0.1:41373] served OK
```

We have told the log package not to use timestamps simply to make the log output more attractive for the book.

Before looking at the changes we have made, let us briefly remind ourselves of the original code.

```
func main() {
    http.HandleFunc("/", homePage)
    if err := http.ListenAndServe(":9001", nil); err != nil {
        log.Fatal("failed to start server", err)
    }
}

func homePage(writer http.ResponseWriter, request *http.Request) {
    // ...
}
```

This web site has only one page, although the technique we will present can just as easily be applied to sites with multiple pages. If a panic occurs that is not caught by a recover(), that is, if a panic reaches the main() function, the server will terminate, so this is what we must protect against.

```
func homePage(writer http.ResponseWriter, request *http.Request) {
    defer func() { // Needed for every page
        if x := recover(); x != nil {
            log.Printf("[%v] caught panic: %v", request.RemoteAddr, x)
        }
    }()
    // ...
}
```

For a web server to be robust in the face of panics we must make sure that every page handler function has a deferred anonymous function that calls recover().

This will stop any panic from being propagated. However, it cannot stop the page handler from returning (since deferred statements are executed just before a function returns), but that doesn't matter since the http.ListenAndServe() function will call the page handler afresh whenever the page it handles is requested.

Of course, for a large web site with lots of page handlers, adding a deferred function to catch and log panics involves a lot of code duplication and is easy to forget. This can be solved by creating a wrapper function that has the code needed by each page handler. Using the wrapper we can omit the recover code from the page handlers, so long as we change the http.HandleFunc() calls.

```
http.HandleFunc("/", logPanics(homePage))
```

Here we have the original homePage() function (i.e., one that does *not* have a deferred function that calls recover()), relying instead on the logPanics() wrapper function to take care of panics.

```
func logPanics(function func(http.ResponseWriter,
    *http.Request)) func(http.ResponseWriter, *http.Request) {
    return func(writer http.ResponseWriter, request *http.Request) {
        defer func() {
            if x := recover(); x != nil {
                log.Printf("[%v] caught panic: %v", request.RemoteAddr, x)
            }
        }()
        function(writer, request)
    }
}
```

This function takes an HTTP handler function as its sole argument and creates and returns an anonymous function that includes a deferred (also) anonymous function that catches and logs panics, and that calls the passed-in handler function. This has the same effect as adding the deferred panic catcher and logger that we saw in the modified homePage() function, but is much more convenient since we don't have to add the deferred function to any page handler; instead we pass each page handler function to the http.HandleFunc() using the logPanics() wrapper.

A version of the statistics program that uses this technique is in file statistics_nonstop2/statistics.go. Anonymous functions are covered in the next section's subsection on closures (§5.6.3, ➤ 225).

5.6. Custom Functions

Functions are the bedrock of procedural programming and Go provides first-class support for them. Go methods (covered in Chapter 6) are very similar to Go functions, so this section is relevant for both procedural and object-oriented programming.

Here are the fundamental syntaxes for function definitions:

```
func functionName(optionalParameters) optionalReturnType {
    body
}

func functionName(optionalParameters) (optionalReturnValues) {
    body
}
```

A function can take zero or more parameters. If there are no parameters the parentheses are empty. If there is one or more, they are written *params1 type1*, ..., *paramsN typeN*, where *params1* is either a single parameter name or a comma-separated list of two or more parameter names of the given type. Parameters must be passed in the order given: There is no equivalent to Python's named parameters, although a similar effect can be achieved as we will see later (§5.6.1.3, ➤ 222).

The very last parameter's type may be preceded by an ellipsis (...). Such functions are called *variadic*; this means that the function will accept zero or more values of that type as that parameter's value and inside the function that parameter will be of type []*type*.

A function may return zero or more values. If there are none the open brace follows the parameter's closing parenthesis. If there is one unnamed return value it can be written as *type*. If there are two or more unnamed return values, parentheses must be used and they are written as (*type1*, ..., *typeN*). If there are one or more named return values, parentheses must be used and they are written as (*values1 type1*, ..., *valuesN typeN*), where *values1* is either a single return value name or a comma-separated list of two or more return value names of the given type. Function return values may all be unnamed or all be named, but not a mixture of both.

Functions that have one or more return values *must* have at least one `return` statement—or have a call to `panic()` as their final statement. If return values are unnamed, the `return` statement must specify as many values as there are return values, each with a type matching the corresponding return value. If the return values are named the `return` statement can either specify values just like in the unnamed case or be bare (i.e., giving no explicit values to return). Note that although bare `returns` are legal, they are considered poor style—none of the book's examples uses them.

If a function has one or more return values its last executable statement *must* be a return or a panic(). Go compilers are smart enough to realize that a function that ends with a panic won't return normally and so doesn't need a return statement at that point. Unfortunately, current Go compilers don't understand that if a function ends with an if statement that has an unconditional else statement that ends with a return statement, or a switch statement that has a default case that ends with a return statement, no additional return is needed afterward. A common practice in such cases is to either not end with an else or default case and put the return statement after the if or switch, or simply put a panic("unreachable") statement at the end—we saw examples of both approaches earlier (196 ◄).

5.6.1. Function Arguments

We have already seen many examples of custom Go functions that accept a fixed number of arguments of specified types. By using a parameter type of interface{} we can create functions that take arguments of any type. And by using a parameter type that is an interface type—either our own custom interface or one from the standard library—we can create functions that take arguments of any type that has a specific set of methods: We will look at these issues in Chapter 6 (§6.3, ➤ 265).

In this subsection we will look at other possibilities regarding function arguments. In the first subsubsection we will see how to use functions' return values directly as arguments to other functions. In the second subsubsection we will see how to create functions that accept a variable number of arguments. And in the final subsubsection we will discuss a technique that makes it possible to create functions that can accept optional arguments.

5.6.1.1. Function Calls as Function Arguments

If we have a function or method that accepts one or more parameters, we can, of course, call it with corresponding arguments. And in addition, we can call the function with another function or method—providing that the other function returns exactly the number of arguments required (and of the right types).

Here is an example of a function that takes the lengths of the sides of a triangle (as three ints) and outputs the triangle's area using Heron's formula.

```
for i := 1; i <= 4; i++ {
    a, b, c := PythagoreanTriple(i, i+1)
    Δ1 := Heron(a, b, c)
    Δ2 := Heron(PythagoreanTriple(i, i+1))
    fmt.Printf("Δ1 == %10f == Δ2 == %10f\n", Δ1, Δ2)
}
```

```
Δ1 ==     6.000000 == Δ2 ==     6.000000
Δ1 ==    30.000000 == Δ2 ==    30.000000
Δ1 ==    84.000000 == Δ2 ==    84.000000
Δ1 ==   180.000000 == Δ2 ==   180.000000
```

First we obtain the lengths using Euclid's formula for Pythagorean triples, then we apply Heron's formula using the Heron() function which takes exactly three int arguments. Then we repeat the computation, only this time we use the PythagoreanTriple() function directly as the Heron() function's argument, leaving Go to convert the PythagoreanTriple()'s three return values into the Heron() function's three arguments.

```go
func Heron(a, b, c int) float64 {
    α, β, γ := float64(a), float64(b), float64(c)
    s := (α + β + γ) / 2
    return math.Sqrt(s * (s – α) * (s – β) * (s – γ))
}

func PythagoreanTriple(m, n int) (a, b, c int) {
    if m < n {
        m, n = n, m
    }
    return (m * m) – (n * n), (2 * m * n), (m * m) + (n * n)
}
```

The Heron() and PythagoreanTriple() functions are shown for completeness. We have used named return values for the PythagoreanTriple() function purely as a supplement to the function's documentation.

5.6.1.2. Variadic Functions

A *variadic* function is one that can accept zero or more arguments for its last (or only) parameter. Such functions are indicated by placing an ellipsis (...) immediately before the type of the last or only parameter. Inside the function this parameter becomes a slice of the given type. For example, if we had a function with signature Join(xs ...string) string, the xs parameter would be of type []string.

Here is a tiny example that shows the use of a variadic function; in this case one which returns the minimum of the ints it is passed. We will start by looking at how it is called and the output it produces.

```go
fmt.Println(MinimumInt1(5, 3), MinimumInt1(7, 3, -2, 4, 0, -8, -5))
```
```
3 -8
```

The `MinimumInt1()` function can be passed one or more `int`s and returns the smallest of them.

```
func MinimumInt1(first int, rest ...int) int {
    for _, x := range rest {
        if x < first {
            first = x
        }
    }
    return first
}
```

We could easily require a minimum of zero `int`s—for example, `MinimumInt0(ints ...int)`; or require at least two `int`s—for example, `MinimumInt2(first, second int, rest ...int)`.

If we already have a slice of `int`s we can still use the `MinimumInt1()` function to find the minimum.

```
numbers := []int{7, 6, 2, -1, 7, -3, 9}
fmt.Println(MinimumInt1(numbers[0], numbers[1:]...))
```

```
-3
```

The `MinimumInt1()` function requires a single `int` and then zero or more additional `int`s. When calling a variadic function or method we may place an ellipsis after a slice, and this will effectively turn the slice into a sequence of zero or more arguments each corresponding to an item in the slice. (We discussed this earlier when discussing the built-in `append()` function; §4.2.3, 156 ◄.) So, here, we have turned `numbers[1:]...` at the call site into the individual parameters 6, -2, -1, 7, -3, 9 inside the variadic function—and these are all stored in the `rest` slice. If we had the `MinimumInt0()` function just mentioned, we could simplify the call to `MinimumInt0(numbers...)`.

5.6.1.3. Functions with Multiple Optional Arguments

Go does not have any direct support for creating functions with multiple optional arguments of different types. However, it is very easy to achieve this by using a function-specific `struct` and relying on Go's guarantee that all values are initialized to their zero value.

Suppose that we have a function for processing some custom data where the default behavior is simply to process all the data, but where on some occasions we would like to be able to specify the first and last items to be processed, whether to log the function's actions, and to provide an error handling function for invalid items.

One way to do this is to create a function with signature `ProcessItems(items Items, first, last int, audit bool, errorHandler func(item Item))`. In this scheme, a `last` value of 0 is taken to mean the last item whatever its index, and the `errorHandler` function would only be called if present (i.e., if not `nil`). This would mean that for every call where we wanted the default behavior we would have to write `ProcessItems(items, 0, 0, false, nil)`.

A much nicer way of doing things would be to have a signature of `Process-Items(items Items, options Options)`, where the custom `Options` struct type held the other parameter values all of which default to their zero value. This would reduce the most common call to `ProcessItems(items, Options{})`. Then, on those occasions when we needed to specify one or more of the additional parameters, we could do so by specifying their values for particular `Options` fields. (Full coverage of `struct`s is given later; §6.4, ➤ 275.) Let's see what this looks like in code, starting with the `Options` struct.

```
type Options struct {
    First       int  // First item to process
    Last        int  // Last item to process (0 means process all from First)
    Audit       bool // If true all actions are logged
    ErrorHandler func(item Item) // Called for each bad item if not nil
}
```

A `struct` can aggregate or embed one or more fields of any types we like. (The difference between aggregation and embedding is covered in Chapter 6.) Here, the `Options` struct aggregates two `int` fields, a `bool` field, and a function (i.e., function reference) field with the signature `func(Item)` where `Item` is some custom type (in this case the type of one item in the custom `Items` type).

```
ProcessItems(items, Options{})
errorHandler := func(item Item) { log.Println("Invalid:", item) }
ProcessItems(items, Options{Audit: true, ErrorHandler: errorHandler})
```

This snippet shows two calls to the custom `ProcessItems()` function. The first call processes the items using the default options (i.e., processes all items, does not log any actions, and does not call an error handler function for invalid records). In the second call an `Options` value is created that has zero values for `First` and `Last` (and so tells the function to process all the items), and overrides the zero values for the `Audit` and `ErrorHandler` fields so that the function will log its actions and will call the error handler whenever an invalid item is encountered.

This technique of passing a `struct` for optional arguments is used in the standard library—for example, by the `image.jpeg.Encode()` function. We will also see the technique in use later on in Chapter 6 (§6.5.2, ➤ 289).

5.6.2. The init() and main() Functions

Go reserves two function names for special purposes: init() (in all packages) and main() (only in package main). These two functions must always be defined as taking no arguments and returning nothing. A package may have as many init() functions as we like. However, at the time of this writing, at least one Go compiler supports only a single init() function per package, so we recommend using at most one init() function in each package.

Go automatically calls init() functions in packages and the main package's main() function, so these should not be called explicitly. For programs and packages init() functions are optional; but every program must have a single main() function in package main.

The initialization and execution of a Go program always begins with the main package. If there are imports, each imported package is imported in turn. Packages are imported only once even if more than one package has an import statement for the same package. (For example, several packages might import the fmt package, but after it has been imported once it will not be imported again since there is no need.) When a package is imported, if it has its own imports, these are performed first. Then, the package's package-level constants and variables are created. And then the package's init() functions are called (if it has any). Eventually, all the packages imported in the main package (and their imports and so on) are finished, at which point the main package's constants and variables are created and the main package's init() functions are called (if it has any). And finally, the main package's main() function is called and program execution proper begins. This sequence of events is illustrated in Figure 5.1.

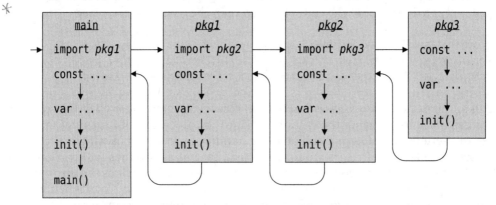

Figure 5.1 *Program startup sequence*

It is possible to put go statements in init() functions, but keep in mind that these run before main.main() is called and so must not depend on anything created in main().

Let's look at an example (taken from Chapter 1's `americanise/americanise.go` file) to see how things work in practice.

```
package main

import (
    "bufio"
    "fmt"
    // ...
    "strings"
)

var britishAmerican = "british-american.txt"

func init() {
    dir, _ := filepath.Split(os.Args[0])
    britishAmerican = filepath.Join(dir, britishAmerican)
}

func main() {
    // ...
}
```

Go begins with the `main` package and since there are imports it does them first, in order, starting with the `bufio` package. The `bufio` package has its own imports, so these are performed next: In each case the imported package's own imports are performed first, then its package-level constants and variables are created and then its `init()` functions are called. Once the `bufio` package has been imported, the `fmt` package is imported—this package imports the `strings` package, so when Go reaches the `main` package's `strings` package import the import is skipped since it has already been done.

When the imports have been completed the package-level `britishAmerican` variable is created. Then the `main` package's `init()` function is called. And finally, the `main` package's `main()` function is called and the program begins executing.

5.6.3. Closures

A *closure* is a function which "captures" any constants and variables that are present in the same scope where it is created, if it refers to them. This means that a closure is able to access such constants and variables when the closure is called, even if it is called far away from the place where it was created. It doesn't matter if any captured constants or variables have gone out of scope—so long as a closure refers to them they are kept alive for the closure to use.

In Go, every anonymous function (or *function literal,* as they are called in the Go specification) is a closure.

A closure is created using almost the same syntax as for a normal function, but with one key difference: The closure has no name (so the keyword func is immediately followed by an opening parenthesis). To make use of a closure we normally assign it to a variable or put it in a data structure (such as a map or slice).

We have already seen several examples of closures—for example, when we use defer or go statements with anonymous functions these functions are closures. We also created closures in other contexts, for example, the makeReplacerFunction() used in the americanise example (§1.6, 29 ◄), and when we passed anonymous functions to the strings.FieldsFunc() and the strings.Map() functions in Chapter 3 (§3.6.1, 107 ◄), and the createCounter() (207 ◄) and logPanics() (218 ◄) functions quoted earlier in this chapter. Nonetheless, we will review a few tiny examples here.

One use of closures is to provide a wrapper function that predefines one or more of the arguments for the wrapped function. For example, suppose we want to add different suffixes to lots of different filenames. Essentially we want to wrap the string + concatenation operator so that one argument varies (i.e., the filename), but the other is fixed (i.e., the suffix).

```
addPng := func(name string) string { return name + ".png" }
addJpg := func(name string) string { return name + ".jpg" }
fmt.Println(addPng("filename"), addJpg("filename"))
```

```
filename.png filename.jpg
```

Both addPng and addJpg are variables that hold references to anonymous functions (i.e., to closures). Such references can be called just like normal named functions as the code snippet illustrates.

In practice, when we want to create many similar functions, rather than making each one individually, we often use a *factory function,* that is, a function that returns a function. Here is a factory function that returns functions that add a suffix to a filename—but only if the suffix isn't already present.

```
func MakeAddSuffix(suffix string) func(string) string {
    return func(name string) string {
        if !strings.HasSuffix(name, suffix) {
            return name + suffix
        }
        return name
    }
}
```

The MakeAddSuffix() factory function returns a closure which has captured the suffix variable at the time the closure was created. The returned closure takes one string argument (e.g., a filename), and returns a string which is the filename with the captured suffix.

```
addZip := MakeAddSuffix(".zip")
addTgz := MakeAddSuffix(".tar.gz")
fmt.Println(addTgz("filename"), addZip("filename"), addZip("gobook.zip"))

filename.tar.gz filename.zip gobook.zip
```

This snippet shows the creation of two closures, addZip() and addTgz(), and some calls to them.

5.6.4. Recursive Functions

A *recursive* function is a function that calls itself, and *mutually recursive* functions are functions that call each other. Go fully supports recursive functions.

Recursive functions generally have the same structure: an "outcase" and a "body". The outcase is usually a conditional statement such as an if statement that is used to stop the recursion based on one of the arguments passed in. The body is where the function does some processing and includes at least one call to itself (or to its mutually recursive partner)—this call must pass an argument that is changed from one it received and that will be checked in the outcase to ensure that the recursion will ultimately finish.

Recursive functions make it easy to work with recursive data structures (such as binary trees), but they can be inefficient for, say, numerical computations.

We will start with a very simple (and inefficient) example, just to show how recursion is done. First we will see a call to a recursive function and its output, then we will see the recursive function itself.

```
for n := 0; n < 20; n++ {
    fmt.Print(Fibonacci(n), " ")
}
fmt.Println()

0 1 1 2 3 5 8 13 21 34 55 89 144 233 377 610 987 1597 2584 4181
```

The Fibonacci() function returns the *n*-th Fibonacci number.

```
func Fibonacci(n int) int {
    if n < 2 {
        return n
    }
    return Fibonacci(n-1) + Fibonacci(n-2)
}
```

The `if` statement serves as the outcase, and it guarantees that the function
will (eventually) stop recursing. This works because whatever n we give to the
function in the first place, each recursive call in the function's body (i.e., in the
`return` statement) works on a value less than n, so n will always be less than 2 at
some point.

For example, if we were to call `Fibonacci(4)` the outcase would not be triggered
and the function would return the sum of the two recursive calls, `Fibonacci(3)`
and `Fibonacci(2)`. The first of these would in turn call `Fibonacci(2)` (which in
turn would call `Fibonacci(1)` and `Fibonacci(0)`) and `Fibonacci(1)`, and the second
would call `Fibonacci(1)` and `Fibonacci(0)`. Once n goes below 2 it is returned. The
sequence of calls is illustrated in Figure 5.2.

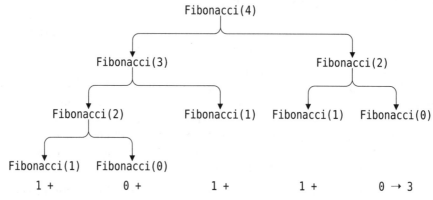

Figure 5.2 *Recursive Fibonacci*

Clearly the `Fibonacci()` function is doing a lot of repeated calculations, even for
a tiny input value like 4. We will see how to avoid this later (§5.6.7.1, ➤ 241).

The Hofstadter Female and Male sequences are integer sequences that are
based on mutually recursive functions. Here is some code that prints the first
20 values in each sequence, followed by the values themselves:

```
females := make([]int, 20)
males := make([]int, len(females))
for n := range females {
    females[n] = HofstadterFemale(n)
    males[n] = HofstadterMale(n)
}
fmt.Println("F", females)
fmt.Println("M", males)

F [1 1 2 2 3 3 4 5 5 6 6 7 8 8 9 9 10 11 11 12]
M [0 0 1 2 2 3 4 4 5 6 6 7 7 8 9 9 10 11 11 12]
```

Here are the two mutually recursive functions that produce the sequences.

```go
func HofstadterFemale(n int) int {
    if n <= 0 {
        return 1
    }
    return n - HofstadterMale(HofstadterFemale(n-1))
}
func HofstadterMale(n int) int {
    if n <= 0 {
        return 0
    }
    return n - HofstadterFemale(HofstadterMale(n-1))
}
```

As usual we begin each function with the outcase to ensure that the recursion will terminate, and in the body where the recursion occurs we always recurse on a reduced value so that eventually the outcase will be satisfied.

Some languages would have a problem with the Hofstadter functions—they would trip up on the fact that the HofstadterFemale() function is defined before the HofstadterMale() function and yet calls the HofstadterMale() function. Such languages would require us to predeclare the HofstadterMale() function. Go has no such limitation since it allows functions to be defined in any order.

Let's look at one last recursion example, a function which determines whether a word is a palindrome (i.e., is the same if its characters are reversed, such as "PULLUP" and "ROTOR").

```go
func IsPalindrome(word string) bool {
    if utf8.RuneCountInString(word) <= 1 {
        return true
    }
    first, sizeOfFirst := utf8.DecodeRuneInString(word)
    last, sizeOfLast := utf8.DecodeLastRuneInString(word)
    if first != last {
        return false
    }
    return IsPalindrome(word[sizeOfFirst : len(word)-sizeOfLast])
}
```

This function starts with the outcase: If the word has zero or one character then it is a palindrome so we return true and are finished. The algorithm we use for the body is to compare the first and last characters: If they are different then the word isn't a palindrome so we can finish immediately by returning false.

But if the first and last characters are the same then we recursively examine a substring of the word that has the first and last characters chopped off.

In the case of "PULLUP", the function compares 'P' and 'P', then calls itself recursively with the string "ULLU" and compares 'U' and 'U', then calls itself with "LL" comparing 'L' and 'L', and finally calls itself with an empty string. For "ROTOR", the function compares 'R' and 'R', then calls itself recursively with "OTO" and compares 'O' and 'O', and then calls itself with "T". So in both of these cases the function returns true. But for "DECIDED", the function compares 'D' and 'D', then calls itself recursively with "ECIDE" and compares 'E' and 'E', then calls itself on "CID" and compares 'C' and 'D', at which point it returns false.

Recall from Chapter 3 (§3.6.3, 117 ◀) that the utf8.DecodeRuneInString() function returns the first character (as a rune) in the string it is given and how many bytes that character occupies. The utf8.DecodeLastRuneInString() works similarly but for the string's last character. We can safely slice string word using the two sizes thus obtained because we know that they will slice the string between characters (i.e., we won't accidentally chop a multibyte character in two).

When a function uses tail recursion, that is, when its last statement is a recursive call, we can usually convert it into a simple loop. Using a loop saves the overhead of repeated function calls; although the additional problem of limited stack space that can affect deeply recursive functions in some languages is much less common in Go programs because of the way Go manages memory. (Incidentally, there is an opportunity to transform the recursive IsPalindrome() function into one that uses a simple loop in the exercises.) Of course, in some situations recursion is the best way to express an algorithm—we will see an example of this in Chapter 6 when we look at the omap.insert() function (▶ 307).

5.6.5. Choosing Functions at Runtime

Since Go functions are first-class values, it is possible to store them (i.e., references to them) in variables—and this makes it possible to choose which function to execute at runtime. Furthermore, Go's ability to create closures means that we can in effect create functions at runtime—so we could have two or more different implementations of the same function (each using a different algorithm), and create just one of them to be used. We will look at both approaches in this subsection.

5.6.5.1. Branching Using Maps and Function References

In two earlier subsections (§5.2.1, 192 ◀ and §5.2.2.1, 195 ◀) we presented extracts from custom ArchiveFileList() functions for calling a particular function based on a filename's suffix. The first version of the function used an if statement that spanned seven lines; the canonical version's switch statement spanned just five lines. But what happens if the number of different file suffixes we want to handle grows? For the if version we would need to add an extra two lines for each additional else if clause; and for the switch version we would need to add one extra line for every new case (or two lines if we format our cases with gofmt). If the function were for a file manager it could easily be required to handle hundreds of suffixes, making the function very long indeed.

```
var FunctionForSuffix = map[string]func(string) ([]string, error){
    ".gz": GzipFileList, ".tar": TarFileList, ".tar.gz": TarFileList,
    ".tgz": TarFileList, ".zip": ZipFileList}

func ArchiveFileListMap(file string) ([]string, error) {
    if function, ok := FunctionForSuffix[Suffix(file)]; ok {
        return function(file)
    }
    return nil, errors.New("unrecognized archive")
}
```

This version of the function makes use of a map whose keys are strings (file suffixes), and whose values are functions with the signature func(string) ([]string, error). (All of the custom functions, GzipFileList(), TarFileList(), and ZipFileList(), are of this type.)

The function uses the [] index operator to retrieve the function that matches the given suffix and to set ok to true; or to return nil and false if the suffix isn't a map key. If there is a matching function the function is called with the filename, and its results returned.

This function is more scalable than using an if or switch statement since no matter how many file *suffix–function* items we add to the FunctionForSuffix map, the function remains unchanged. And unlike a big if or switch statement, map lookup speeds don't really degrade as the number of items increases.* In addition, using a map in this way can make things clearer and also makes it possible to add new items to the map dynamically.

5.6.5.2. Dynamic Function Creation

Another scenario that involves choosing a function at runtime is when we have two or more functions that implement the same functionality using different algorithms and we don't want to commit to any of them when the program is compiled (e.g., to allow us to choose dynamically for benchmarking or regression testing).

For example, if we use strings that contain only 7-bit ASCII characters we can write a much simpler version of the IsPalindrome() function we saw earlier (229 ◄), and at runtime create only the version that our program actually needs.

---

*On a lightly loaded AMD-64 quad-core 3GHz machine we found that using a map was consistently faster than a switch once there were 50 or more cases to consider.

One way to do this is to declare a package-level variable with the function's signature and then to create the appropriate function in an init() function.

```go
var IsPalindrome func(string) bool // Holds a reference to a function

func init() {
    if len(os.Args) > 1 &&
        (os.Args[1] == "-a" || os.Args[1] == "--ascii") {
        os.Args = append(os.Args[:1], os.Args[2:]...) // Strip out arg.
        IsPalindrome = func(s string) bool {  // Simple ASCII-only version
            if len(s) <= 1 {
                return true
            }
            if s[0] != s[len(s)-1] {
                return false
            }
            return IsPalindrome(s[1 : len(s)-1])
        }
    } else {
        IsPalindrome = func(s string) bool { // UTF-8 version
            // ... same as earlier ...
        }
    }
}
```

We have made the choice of IsPalindrome() implementation dependent on a command-line argument. If the argument is given, we strip it out of the os.Args slice (so the rest of the program doesn't have to know or care about it), and create a 7-bit ASCII version of the IsPalindrome() function. The stripping out is slightly subtle since we want os.Args to have its first string and its third and subsequent strings but not its second string (which is "-a" or "--ascii"). We can't use os.Args[0] in the append() call because the first argument must be a slice, so we use os.Args[:1] which is a one-item slice containing os.Args[0] (§4.2.1, 153 ◀). If the ASCII argument isn't present, we create the same version as we saw earlier that works correctly on both 7-bit ASCII and UTF-8 Unicode strings. In the rest of the program the IsPalindrome() function can be called normally, but the actual code that gets executed will vary depending on which version was created. (The source code for this example is in palindrome/palindrome.go.)

5.6.6. Generic Functions

Earlier in the chapter we created a function for finding the smallest of the int arguments it was passed (221 ◀). The algorithm used in that function could also be applied to other numeric types, or even to strings, since it works for any type that supports the < less than operator. In C++, for cases like this, we would create a generic function that is parameterized by type which would result in the compiler creating as many versions of the function as we need (i.e., one per type used). In Go, at the time of this writing, there is no support for type parameterization, so to get the same effect as C++ achieves we must manually create the functions we need (e.g., `MinimumInt()`, `MinimumFloat()`, `MinimumString()`). This way we end up with one function per type used (just like in C++, except that in Go each function must have a unique name).

Go offers various alternative approaches which avoid the need to create functions that are the same except for the types they operate on, at the cost of some runtime efficiency. For small functions that are not used often or which are more than fast enough already, the alternative approaches can be convenient.

Here are some examples that use a generic `Minimum()` function.

```
i := Minimum(4, 3, 8, 2, 9).(int)
fmt.Printf("%T %v\n", i, i)
f := Minimum(9.4, -5.4, 3.8, 17.0, -3.1, 0.0).(float64)
fmt.Printf("%T %v\n", f, f)
s := Minimum("K", "X", "B", "C", "CC", "CA", "D", "M").(string)
fmt.Printf("%T %q\n", s, s)
```

```
int 2
float64 -5.4
string "B"
```

The function returns a value of type `interface{}` which we convert to the built-in type we expect using an unchecked type assertion (§5.1.2, 191 ◄).

```
func Minimum(first interface{}, rest ...interface{}) interface{} {
    minimum := first
    for _, x := range rest {
        switch x := x.(type) {
        case int:
            if x < minimum.(int) {
                minimum = x
            }
        case float64:
            if x < minimum.(float64) {
                minimum = x
            }
        case string:
            if x < minimum.(string) {
                minimum = x
            }
        }
    }
}
```

```
    return minimum
}
```

This function takes at least one value (first) and zero or more other values
(rest). We use the interface{} type since that can be used for any type in Go. We
initially assume that the first value is the smallest and then iterate over the
rest of the values. Whenever we find a value that is smaller than the current
minimum we set the minimum to this value. And at the end we return the
minimum—as an interface{}, hence the need to convert it to a built-in type at the
Minimum() function's call site using an unchecked type assertion.

We still have duplicate code—in each case's if statement's block—but if there
were a lot of duplicate code we could simply set a Boolean in each case (e.g.,
change = true), and then follow the switch with an if change statement that
contained all the common code.

Clearly, using this Minimum() function is less efficient than having type-specific
minimum functions. However, it is worth knowing the technique because it is
useful for cases where the type testing overheads and conversion inconvenience
are outweighed by the advantage of having to define the function only once.

The problem of duplicate code within a generic function isn't so easy to work
around if one or more of the interface{} arguments are actually slices. For
example, here is a function that, given a slice and an item of the same type as
the slice's items, returns the index position of the first occurrence of the item in
the slice—or −1 if the item isn't in the slice.

```
func Index(xs interface{}, x interface{}) int {
    switch slice := xs.(type) {
    case []int:
        for i, y := range slice {
            if y == x.(int) {
                return i
            }
        }
    case []string:
        for i, y := range slice {
            if y == x.(string) {
                return i
            }
        }
    }
    return -1
}
```

We have only bothered to implement the int and string cases—both of which contain essentially the same code.

Here is an example of the Index() function in use and the output it produces. (The code is taken from the contains/contains.go test program.)

```
xs := []int{2, 4, 6, 8}
fmt.Println("5 @", Index(xs, 5), "  6 @", Index(xs, 6))
ys := []string{"C", "B", "K", "A"}
fmt.Println("Z @", Index(ys, "Z"), "  A @", Index(ys, "A"))
```
```
5 @ -1   6 @ 2
Z @ -1   A @ 3
```

What we really need to be able to do is treat the slice generically—that way we could have just one loop and do the type-specific testing inside it. Here is a function that achieves this—and it produces the same output as the above code snippet if we replace calls to Index() with calls to IndexReflectX().

```
func IndexReflectX(xs interface{}, x interface{}) int { // Long-winded way
    if slice := reflect.ValueOf(xs); slice.Kind() == reflect.Slice {
        for i := 0; i < slice.Len(); i++ {
            switch y := slice.Index(i).Interface().(type) {
            case int:
                if y == x.(int) {
                    return i
                }
            case string:
                if y == x.(string) {
                    return i
                }
            }
        }
    }
    return -1
}
```

The function begins by using Go's reflection support (provided by the reflect package; §9.4.9, ➤ 427), to convert the xs interface{} into a slice-typed reflect.Value. Such values provide the methods we need to traverse the slice's items and to extract any items we are interested in. Here, we access each item in turn and use the reflect.Value.Interface() function to pull out the value as an interface{} which we immediately assign to y inside a type switch. This ensures that y has the item's actual type (e.g., int or string) which can be directly compared with the unchecked type-asserted x value.

In fact, the `reflect` package can take on far more of the work, so we can simplify this function considerably.

```go
func IndexReflect(xs interface{}, x interface{}) int {
    if slice := reflect.ValueOf(xs); slice.Kind() == reflect.Slice {
        for i := 0; i < slice.Len(); i++ {
            if reflect.DeepEqual(x, slice.Index(i)) {
                return i
            }
        }
    }
    return -1
}
```

Here we rely on the `reflect.DeepEqual()` function to do the comparison for us. This versatile reflection function can also be used to compare arrays, slices, and structs.

Here is a type-specific function for finding the index of an item in a slice.

```go
func IntSliceIndex(xs []int, x int) int {
    for i, y := range xs {
        if x == y {
            return i
        }
    }
    return -1
}
```

This is much nicer and simpler than the generic versions but requires us to create one function like this per type we want to work on—with the only changes being their names and the types specified in the functions' signatures.

We can combine the benefits of a generic approach—implementing one algorithm—with the simplicity and efficiency of type-specific functions by using custom types, a topic that is covered more thoroughly in the next chapter.

Here is a type-specific function for finding the index position of an item in an `[]int` and the generic function it uses to do the actual work.

```go
func IntIndexSlicer(ints []int, x int) int {
    return IndexSlicer(IntSlice(ints), x)
}

func IndexSlicer(slice Slicer, x interface{}) int {
    for i := 0; i < slice.Len(); i++ {
        if slice.EqualTo(i, x) {
```

```
            return i
        }
    }
    return -1
}
```

The `IntIndexSlicer()` function takes an `[]int` to search and an `int` to find and passes these on to the generic `IndexSlicer()` function. The `IndexSlicer()` function operates in terms of a `Slicer` value—the `Slicer` type is a custom interface that is met by any value that provides the `Slicer` methods (`Slicer.EqualTo()` and `Slicer.Len()`).

```
type Slicer interface {
    EqualTo(i int, x interface{}) bool
    Len() int
}

type IntSlice []int

func (slice IntSlice) EqualTo(i int, x interface{}) bool {
    return slice[i] == x.(int)
}
func (slice IntSlice) Len() int { return len(slice) }
```

The `Slicer` interface specifies the two methods we need to implement the generic `IndexSlicer()` function.

The `IntSlice` type is based on an `[]int` (which is why the `IntIndexSlicer()` function can convert the `[]int` it is passed into an `IntSlice` without formality), and implements the two methods required to fulfill the `Slicer` interface. The `IntSlice.EqualTo()` method takes a slice index position and a value and returns `true` if the item at the given index is equal to the value. The `Slicer` interface specifies the value as a generic `interface{}` rather than an `int` so that the `Slicer` interface can be implemented by other slice types (e.g., `FloatSlice` and `StringSlice`), so we must convert the value to the actual type. In this case we can safely use an unchecked type assertion because we know that the value ultimately comes from a call to the `IntIndexSlicer()` function which has a corresponding `int` argument.

We can implement other custom slice types that satisfy the `Slicer` interface and can then be used with the generic `IndexSlicer()` function.

```
type StringSlice []string

func (slice StringSlice) EqualTo(i int, x interface{}) bool {
    return slice[i] == x.(string)
}
```

```
func (slice StringSlice) Len() int { return len(slice) }
```

The only difference between the StringSlice and the IntSlice is the underlying
slice's type ([]string rather than []int) and the unchecked type assertion's type
(string vs. int). The same applies to the FloatSlice (which uses []float64 and
float64).

This last example uses techniques that we saw earlier when we discussed
custom sorting (§4.2.4, 160 ◄), and are used to implement the standard library's
sort package's sort functions. Full coverage of custom interfaces and custom
types is provided in Chapter 6.

When working with slices (or maps) it is often possible to create generic functions that don't need to do type testing or type assertions, and that don't need to
use custom interfaces. Instead, we can make our generic functions higher order
functions that abstract away all the type-specific aspects, as we will see in the
next subsection.

5.6.7. Higher Order Functions

A *higher order function* is a function that takes one or more other functions as
arguments and uses them in its own body.

Let's look at a very short and simple higher order function—but one whose
functionality may not be immediately apparent.

```
func SliceIndex(limit int, predicate func(i int) bool) int {
    for i := 0; i < limit; i++ {
        if predicate(i) {
            return i
        }
    }
    return −1
}
```

This is a generic function that returns the index position of an item in a slice for
which the predicate() function returns true. So, this function can do exactly the
same job as the Index(), IndexReflect(), IntSliceIndex(), and IntIndexSlicer()
functions discussed in the previous subsection—but with no code duplication
and no type switching or type assertions.

The SliceIndex() function doesn't know or care about the slice's or the item's
types—indeed, the function knows nothing of the slice or the item it (indirectly) operates on. The function expects its first argument to be the length of the
slice and the second argument to be a function that returns a Boolean for any
given index position in the slice indicating whether the desired item is at that
position.

Here are four example calls and their results.

```
xs := []int{2, 4, 6, 8}
ys := []string{"C", "B", "K", "A"}
fmt.Println(
    SliceIndex(len(xs), func(i int) bool { return xs[i] == 5 }),
    SliceIndex(len(xs), func(i int) bool { return xs[i] == 6 }),
    SliceIndex(len(ys), func(i int) bool { return ys[i] == "Z" }),
    SliceIndex(len(ys), func(i int) bool { return ys[i] == "A" }))
```
```
-1 2 -1 3
```

The anonymous functions passed as second arguments to the SliceIndex() function are, of course, closures—so the slices they refer to (xs and ys) *must* be in scope when these functions are created. (The technique used here is the same as Go's standard library uses for the sort.Search() function.)

In fact, the SliceIndex() function is a general-purpose function that need not have anything to do with slices.

```
i := SliceIndex(math.MaxInt32,
    func(i int) bool { return i > 0 && i%27 == 0 && i%51 == 0 })
fmt.Println(i)
```
```
459
```

In this snippet we have used the SliceIndex() function to find the least natural number that is divisible by both 27 and 51. The way this works is slightly subtle. The SliceIndex() function iterates from 0 to the given limit (in this case math.MaxInt32), and at each iteration it calls the anonymous function (the predicate). As soon as the predicate returns true, the SliceIndex() function returns, passing back the index position that was reached. In this case the "index position" is actually the natural number we were looking for.

In addition to searching unsorted slices it is often useful to filter them to discard items that are no longer of interest. Here is a simple higher order filtering function in action. The function filters an []int using the function it is passed to determine which ints are kept and which are dropped.

```
readings := []int{4, -3, 2, -7, 8, 19, -11, 7, 18, -6}
even := IntFilter(readings, func(i int) bool { return i%2 == 0 })
fmt.Println(even)
```
```
[4 2 8 18 -6]
```

Here, we have filtered out odd numbers from the readings slice.

```
func IntFilter(slice []int, predicate func(int) bool) []int {
    filtered := make([]int, 0, len(slice))
    for i := 0; i < len(slice); i++ {
        if predicate(slice[i]) {
            filtered = append(filtered, slice[i])
        }
    }
    return filtered
}
```

The IntFilter() function takes an []int and a predicate filter function that is used to decide which items are kept and which are dropped. The IntFilter() function returns a new slice that contains those ints from the given slice for which the predicate() function returns true.

Filtering a slice is quite a common requirement so it is a pity that the IntFilter() function can only operate on []ints. Fortunately, it is perfectly possible to create a generic filter function using the same techniques as we used for the SliceIndex() function.

```
func Filter(limit int, predicate func(int) bool, appender func(int)) {
    for i := 0; i < limit; i++ {
        if predicate(i) {
            appender(i)
        }
    }
}
```

Just like the SliceIndex() function, the Filter() function knows nothing about what it operates on beyond the given limit. The Filter() function relies on the predicate() and appender() functions it is passed to do the filtering and appending.

```
readings := []int{4, -3, 2, -7, 8, 19, -11, 7, 18, -6}
even := make([]int, 0, len(readings))
Filter(len(readings), func(i int) bool { return readings[i]%2 == 0 },
    func(i int) { even = append(even, readings[i]) })
fmt.Println(even)
```
```
[4 2 8 18 -6]
```

This code does exactly the same processing as the earlier snippet, only here we must create the new even slice outside the Filter() function. The first anonymous function we pass to Filter() is the filter function—it takes an index position in the slice and returns true if the item at that position is even. The second anonymous function appends the item at the given index position in the original slice to the new slice. Both slices must be in scope when the anonymous functions (closures) passed to the Filter() function are created, since the slices must be captured by the anonymous functions so as to be accessible.

```
parts := []string{"X15", "T14", "X23", "A41", "L19", "X57", "A63"}
var Xparts []string
Filter(len(parts), func(i int) bool { return parts[i][0] == 'X' },
    func(i int) { Xparts = append(Xparts, parts[i]) })
fmt.Println(Xparts)
```
```
[X15 X23 X57]
```

This second example of use is purely to emphasize the type genericity of the Filter() function—here working on strings rather than ints.

```
var product int64 = 1
Filter(26, func(i int) bool { return i%2 != 0 },
    func(i int) { product *= int64(i) })
fmt.Println(product)
```
```
7905853580625
```

This final filter snippet illustrates that just like the SliceIndex() function, the Filter() function doesn't have to be used on slices at all. Here we have used the Filter() function to compute the product of the odd natural numbers in the range [1, 25].

5.6.7.1. Memoizing Pure Functions

A *pure function* is a function which always produces the same result for a given argument or arguments—and that has no side effects. If a pure function is expensive to compute and frequently used with the same arguments, we can use memoization to reduce the processing overhead—at the price of using more memory. The *memoization* technique is where we store the results of a computation so that when the same computation is next requested we are able to return the stored results rather than perform the computation all over again.

The recursive Fibonacci algorithm is expensive and involves repeatedly computing the same things as we saw earlier in Figure 5.2 (228 ◄). In this case the easiest solution is to use a nonrecursive algorithm, but just to show how we can use memoization, we will create a recursive memoized Fibonacci function.

```
type memoizeFunction func(int, ...int) interface{}

var Fibonacci memoizeFunction

func init() {
```

```
        Fibonacci = Memoize(func(x int, xs ...int) interface{} {
            if x < 2 {
                return x
            }
            return Fibonacci(x-1).(int) + Fibonacci(x-2).(int)
        })
}
```

The Memoize() function which we will review in a moment memoizes any function that takes at least one int and that returns an interface{}. For convenience we have created the memoizeFunction type which specifies such functions, and then declared Fibonacci to be a variable that stores a function of this type. Then, in the program's init() function, we have created an anonymous function to perform the Fibonacci calculation—and immediately passed this function to the Memoize() function. In turn, the Memoize() function returns a function of type memoizeFunction which we assign to the package's Fibonacci variable.

In this particular example we only need to pass a single argument to the Fibonacci function, so we ignore any extra ints (i.e., we ignore xs—which should be an empty slice in this case). Also, when we sum the results of the recursive calls we must be sure to use unchecked type assertions to convert the returned interface{}s to their underlying ints.

Now we can use Fibonacci() like any other function, and thanks to the memoization it will not repeat any calculations.

```
fmt.Println("Fibonacci(45) =", Fibonacci(45).(int))
```
```
Fibonacci(45) = 1134903170
```

Here is an example of the recursive memoized Fibonacci() function in use, and the output it produces. We have used an unchecked type assertion on its return value to convert the returned interface{} to an int. (Strictly speaking there is no need to do the conversion here since the fmt package's print functions are smart enough to do this themselves, but this way we can see a realistic use.)

```
func Memoize(function memoizeFunction) memoizeFunction {
    cache := make(map[string]interface{})
    return func(x int, xs ...int) interface{} {
        key := fmt.Sprint(x)
        for _, i := range xs {
            key += fmt.Sprintf(",%d", i)
        }
        if value, found := cache[key]; found {
            return value
        }
```

```
        value := function(x, xs...)
        cache[key] = value
        return value
    }
}
```

The Memoize() function we have used here is very basic. It takes a memoizeFunction function as argument (with the signature func(int, ...int) interface{}) and returns a function with the same signature.

We use a map to cache precomputed results with string keys and interface{} values. The map is captured by the anonymous function (closure) that the Memoize() function returns. The key is made up of all the integer arguments joined together in a single comma-separated string. (Go maps require keys that have fully defined == and != operators—strings meet this requirement, but slices do not; §4.3, 164 ◀.) Once the key has been computed we see if there is a corresponding *key–value* pair in the map—if there is we don't need to recompute anything and can simply return the cached value. Otherwise we perform the computation by calling the function that we were given to memoize with the integer argument or arguments. We then cache the result in the map so that we will never need to recompute for these particular arguments, and finally, we return the computed value.

Memoization is useful for relatively expensive pure functions (whether or not they are recursive) that are called lots of times with the same arguments. For example, if we were converting large numbers of integers into roman numerals and lots of the numbers were repeated it might make sense to use the Memoize() function to avoid repeated computations. Naturally, it is best to time expensive operations (e.g., by using the time package or a profiler) to see if memoization (or any other potential optimization) is worthwhile.

```
var RomanForDecimal memoizeFunction
func init() {
    decimals := []int{1000, 900, 500, 400, 100, 90, 50, 40, 10, 9, 5, 4, 1}
    romans := []string{"M", "CM", "D", "CD", "C", "XC", "L", "XL", "X",
        "IX", "V", "IV", "I"}
    RomanForDecimal = Memoize(func(x int, xs ...int) interface{} {
        if x < 0 || x > 3999 {
            panic("RomanForDecimal() only handles integers [0, 3999]")
        }
        var buffer bytes.Buffer
        for i, decimal := range decimals {
            remainder := x / decimal
            x %= decimal
            if remainder > 0 {
```

```
                buffer.WriteString(strings.Repeat(romans[i], remainder))
            }
        }
        return buffer.String()
    })
}
```

The `RomanForDecimal()` function is declared globally (well, inside its package; see Chapter 9) as a `memoizeFunction` and created in the `init()` function. The `decimals` and `romans` slices are local to the `init()` function, but are kept alive so long as the `RomanForDecimal()` function is used since it is a closure that has captured them.

Go functions (and methods) are incredibly flexible and powerful, and offer several different ways to achieve genericity when that is required.

5.7. Example: Indent Sort

In this section we will review a custom function that sorts a slice of strings. What makes this function special (and why the standard library's `sort.Strings()` function is insufficient on its own) is that the strings are sorted hierarchically, that is, within their level of indentation. (The function is in the book's source code in the file `indent_sort/indent_sort.go`.)

Note that the algorithm used for the `SortedIndentedStrings()` function makes a critical simplifying assumption: A string's indentation is measured by the number of leading spaces or tabs it has, so we are able to work in terms of single bytes rather than having to concern ourselves with multibyte whitespace characters. (If we really want to handle multibyte whitespace characters, one easy solution is to replace each such character with a single space or tab in the strings before feeding them to the `SortedIndentedStrings()` function, for example, using the `strings.Map()` function.)

Let's begin with a program that calls the function and outputs some unsorted indented strings and the sorted strings, side by side for comparison (➤ 245).

Between them, the `SortedIndentedStrings()` function and its helper functions and types use recursive functions, function references, and pointers to slices. So, although what the function does is easy to see, the implementation of the solution requires some thought. The solution uses some important Go function features that were introduced in this chapter, as well as some ideas and techniques that were covered in Chapter 4 and which are explained more fully in Chapter 6.

The keys to our solution are the custom `Entry` and `Entries` types. For each string in the original slice we will create an `Entry` whose key field will be used for sorting, whose value field is the original string, and whose children field is a slice

```
func main() {
    fmt.Println("|     Original     |      Sorted      |")
    fmt.Println("|------------------|------------------|")
    sorted := SortedIndentedStrings(original) // original is a []string
    for i := range original {                 // set in a global var
        fmt.Printf("|%-19s|%-19s|\n", original[i], sorted[i])
    }
}
```

```
|     Original      |      Sorted       |
|-------------------|-------------------|
|Nonmetals          |Alkali Metals      |
|   Hydrogen        |   Lithium         |
|   Carbon          |   Potassium       |
|   Nitrogen        |   Sodium          |
|   Oxygen          |Inner Transitionals|
|Inner Transitionals|   Actinides       |
|   Lanthanides     |      Curium       |
|      Europium     |      Plutonium    |
|      Cerium       |      Uranium      |
|   Actinides       |   Lanthanides     |
|      Uranium      |      Cerium       |
|      Plutonium    |      Europium     |
|      Curium       |Nonmetals          |
|Alkali Metals      |   Carbon          |
|   Lithium         |   Hydrogen        |
|   Sodium          |   Nitrogen        |
|   Potassium       |   Oxygen          |
```

of the string's child Entrys (which could be empty, but if not, whose own Entrys could have children, and so on, recursively).

```
type Entry struct {
    key      string
    value    string
    children Entries
}
type Entries []Entry

func (entries Entries) Len() int { return len(entries) }

func (entries Entries) Less(i, j int) bool {
    return entries[i].key < entries[j].key
}
```

```
func (entries Entries) Swap(i, j int) {
    entries[i], entries[j] = entries[j], entries[i]
}
```

The sort.Interface interface defined in the sort package specifies three methods, Len(), Less(), and Swap(), with the same signatures as the Entries methods of the same names. This means that we can trivially sort an Entries value using the standard library's sort.Sort() function.

```
func SortedIndentedStrings(slice []string) []string {
    entries := populateEntries(slice)
    return sortedEntries(entries)
}
```

This is the exported (public) function that does the work, although we have refactored it to pass on everything to helper functions. The populateEntries() function takes a []string and returns a corresponding Entries (of underlying type []Entry). The sortedEntries() function takes the Entries and returns a corresponding []string hierarchically (by indentation) sorted.

```
func populateEntries(slice []string) Entries {
    indent, indentSize := computeIndent(slice)
    entries := make(Entries, 0)
    for _, item := range slice {
        i, level := 0, 0
        for strings.HasPrefix(item[i:], indent) {
            i += indentSize
            level++
        }
        key := strings.ToLower(strings.TrimSpace(item))
        addEntry(level, key, item, &entries)
    }
    return entries
}
```

The populateEntries() function begins by obtaining what signifies one level of indent in the given slice as a string (e.g., a string of four spaces) and the indent's size (the number of bytes one level of indent occupies). It then creates an empty Entries value and iterates over every string in the slice. For each string it determines the string's level of indentation, and then creates a sort key. Next, the function calls the custom addEntry() function, passing it the string's level, the key, the string itself (item), and the address of the entries so that the addEntry() function can create a new Entry and add it to the entries in the right way. And at the end the entries are returned.

```go
func computeIndent(slice []string) (string, int) {
    for _, item := range slice {
        if len(item) > 0 && (item[0] == ' ' || item[0] == '\t') {
            whitespace := rune(item[0])
            for i, char := range item[1:] {
                if char != whitespace {
                    return strings.Repeat(string(whitespace), i), i
                }
            }
        }
    }
    return "", 0
}
```

This function is used to determine what character (space or tab) is used for indentation, and how many of these characters are used to signify one level of indent.

The function must potentially iterate over all the strings, because top-level strings have no indentation. But as soon as it finds one string with a leading tab or space it returns a string representing one level of indent and a count of how many characters are used for one level of indent.

```go
func addEntry(level int, key, value string, entries *Entries) {
    if level == 0 {
        *entries = append(*entries, Entry{key, value, make(Entries, 0)})
    } else {
        addEntry(level-1, key, value,
            &((*entries)[entries.Len()-1].children))
    }
}
```

This is a recursive function that creates each new Entry and adds it to the entries either directly or as the child of another Entry if the value string is indented.

We must parameterize the function with an *Entries rather than pass the entries by reference (which is the default for slices), since we want to append to the entries and appending to a reference would produce a useless local copy leaving the original data untouched.

If level is 0 then we have a top-level entry that must be added directly to the *entries. In fact, the situation is subtler—the level is relative to the given *entries, which is initially the top-level Entries, but if this function is called recursively, could be another Entry's child Entries. The new Entry is added using the built-in append() function, and using the * contents of operator to access the underlying entries value that is being pointed to. This ensures that any changes are visible to the caller. The new Entry that is added has the given key and value, and its own empty children Entries. This is the function's recursive outcase.

If the level is greater than 0 we have an indented entry that must be added as a child of the first preceding entry that has one less level of indentation. The code to do this is a single recursive call to the addEntry() function and the last argument is probably the most complicated expression we have seen so far.

The subexpression entries.Len() - 1 produces an int that is the index position of the last item in the Entries value that *entries points to. (The Entries.Len() method takes an Entries value rather than an *Entries, but Go is smart enough to automatically dereference the entries pointer and call the method on the pointed-to Entries value.) The complete expression (apart from the outer &(...) part) accesses the last Entry in the Entries' children field (which itself is of type Entries). So, if we consider the expression as a whole we are taking the address of the last Entry in the Entries children field—this is of type *Entries which is exactly what's needed for the recursive call.

To help clarify what is happening, here is some less compact code that does exactly the same thing as the addEntry() function's recursive call to itself in the else block.

```
theEntries := *entries
lastEntry := &theEntries[theEntries.Len()-1]
addEntry(level-1, key, value, &lastEntry.children)
```

First, we create the theEntries variable to hold the value pointed to by the *entries pointer—this is cheap since no actual copying is done; in effect, theEntries is set as an alias to the pointed-to Entries value. Next we take the *address* of (i.e., a pointer to) the last entry. If we didn't take the address we would get a new entry that is a copy of the last entry—and a copy is of no use here. Finally, we do the recursive addEntry() call, passing the address of the last entry's children field.

```
func sortedEntries(entries Entries) []string {
    var indentedSlice []string
    sort.Sort(entries)
    for _, entry := range entries {
        populateIndentedStrings(entry, &indentedSlice)
    }
    return indentedSlice
}
```

When this sortedEntries() function is called, the structure of the Entries reflects that of the "Original" strings that the program outputs, with indented strings being children of their parent (as children of type Entries fields), and so on (245 ◄).

Once the Entries value has been populated, the SortedIndentedStrings() function calls this function to create a corresponding sorted []string. The function begins by creating an empty []string which it will use to hold the results. It then sorts the entries—thanks to the Entries' support of the sort.Interface methods the sort.Sort() function can be used without formality and the sorting is by each Entry's key field since that is how the Entries.Less() method is implemented (245 ◀). The sort applies only to the top-level Entrys, of course, and has no effect on their unsorted children.

To sort the children, and their children, recursively, the function iterates over the top-level entries and for each one calls the populateIndentedStrings() function. The call is made with the Entry and with a pointer to the []string we want to populate.

Slices can be passed to functions to be updated (e.g., to have items replaced), but here we need to append to the slice. The built-in append() function sometimes returns a reference to a new slice (if the original's capacity is insufficient). The way we handle this here is to pass a pointer to a slice and set the contents that the pointer points to, to the slice returned by append(). (If we didn't use a pointer we would simply get a local slice which would not be visible to the caller.) An alternative approach is to pass in the slice value, and return the appended slice which must then be assigned to the original slice (e.g., *slice = function(slice)*); however, this can be tricky to get right with recursive functions.

```
func populateIndentedStrings(entry Entry, indentedSlice *[]string) {
    *indentedSlice = append(*indentedSlice, entry.value)
    sort.Sort(entry.children)
    for _, child := range entry.children {
        populateIndentedStrings(child, indentedSlice)
    }
}
```

This function appends the given entry value to the slice that is being built up, sorts the entry's children, and then calls itself recursively for every child. This has the effect of sorting every entry's children, and their children, and so on, so that the entire indented slice of strings is sorted.

We have now completed our coverage of Go's built-in data types and procedural programming support. In the next chapter we will build on all this to present Go's object-oriented programming facilities, and in the chapter after that we will study Go's support for concurrent programming.

5.8. Exercises

There are four exercises for this chapter. The first involves changing one of the examples, some of whose code was shown in the chapter, and the others require the creation of new functions. All the exercises are very short—the first is easy, the second is straightforward, but the third and fourth are quite challenging!

1. Copy the `archive_file_list` directory to, say, `my_archive_file_list`. Then modify the `archive_file_list/archive_file_list.go` file: Remove all the code for supporting different `ArchiveFileList()` functions except for `Archive-FileListMap()` which should be renamed `ArchiveFileList()`. Then add the capability of handling `.tar.bz2` (tarballs compressed with bzip2) files. This involves deleting about 11 lines from `main()`, deleting four functions, importing an additional package, adding one entry to the `FunctionForSuffix` map, and adding a few lines to the `TarFileList()` function. A solution is given in `archive_file_list_ans/archive_file_list.go`.

2. Create nonrecursive versions of the recursive `IsPalindrome()` functions shown earlier in the chapter (229 ◀ and 232 ◀). In the `palindrome_ans/palindrome.go` solution file the nonrecursive ASCII-only function is 10 lines long and is radically different in structure to the recursive version. On the other hand, the nonrecursive UTF-8 function is 14 lines long and is very similar to the recursive version—although it does require some care.

3. Create a `CommonPrefix()` function that takes a `[]string` argument and returns a `string` with the common prefix (which might be an empty string) of all the strings passed in. A solution is given in `common_prefix/common_prefix.go`; the solution is 22 lines long and uses a `[][]rune` to hold the strings to ensure that when iterating we work in terms of whole characters even if the strings have non-ASCII characters. The solution builds up the result in a `bytes.Buffer`. Despite being very short, this function is by no means easy! (Some examples follow the next exercise.)

4. Create a `CommonPathPrefix()` function that takes a `[]string` of paths and returns a `string` with the common prefix (which might be an empty string) of all the paths passed in—the prefix must consist of zero or more complete path components. A solution is given in `common_prefix/common_prefix.go`; the solution is 27 lines long and uses a `[][]string` to hold the paths and the `filepath.Separator` to identify the platform-specific path separator. The solution builds up the result in a `[]string` and joins them together as a single path at the end using the `filepath.Join()` function. Despite being really short, this function is challenging! (Some examples follow.)

Here is the output of the `common_prefix` program that exercises the functions referred to in Exercises 3 and 4. The first of each pair of lines is a slice of strings and the second line has the common prefix produced by the `CommonPrefix()` and `CommonPathPrefix()` functions with an indication of whether the common prefixes are the same.

```
$ ./common_prefix
["/home/user/goeg" "/home/user/goeg/prefix" "/home/user/goeg/prefix/extra"]
char × path prefix: "/home/user/goeg" == "/home/user/goeg"

["/home/user/goeg" "/home/user/goeg/prefix" "/home/user/prefix/extra"]
char × path prefix: "/home/user/" != "/home/user"

["/pecan/π/goeg" "/pecan/π/goeg/prefix" "/pecan/π/prefix/extra"]
char × path prefix: "/pecan/π/" != "/pecan/π"

["/pecan/π/circle" "/pecan/π/circle/prefix" "/pecan/π/circle/prefix/extra"]
char × path prefix: "/pecan/π/circle" == "/pecan/π/circle"

["/home/user/goeg" "/home/users/goeg" "/home/userspace/goeg"]
char × path prefix: "/home/user" != "/home"

["/home/user/goeg" "/tmp/user" "/var/log"]
char × path prefix: "/" == "/"

["/home/mark/goeg" "/home/user/goeg"]
char × path prefix: "/home/" != "/home"

["home/user/goeg" "/tmp/user" "/var/log"]
char × path prefix: "" == ""
```

6 Object-Oriented Programming

The aim of this chapter is to show how to do object-oriented programming the Go way. Programmers coming from a procedural background (e.g., C) should find everything in this chapter builds nicely on what they already know and what the earlier chapters covered. But programmers coming from an inheritance-based object-oriented background (e.g., C++, Java, Python) will need to put aside many of the concepts and idioms they are used to—in particular, those relating to inheritance—since Go takes a radically different approach to object-oriented programming.

Go's standard library mostly provides packages of functions, although where appropriate it also provides custom types that have methods. In earlier chapters we created values of some custom types (e.g., `regexp.Regexp` and `os.File`) and called methods on them. Furthermore, we even created our own simple custom types and corresponding methods—for example, to support printing and sorting—so the basic use of Go types and calling their methods is already familiar.

The chapter's very short first section introduces some key concepts in Go object-oriented programming. The second section covers the creation of methodless custom types, with subsections on adding methods to custom types and on cre-

253

ating construction functions and validating field data to provide all the fundamentals needed to create fully fledged custom types. The third section covers
interfaces—these are fundamental to Go's approach to type-safe duck typing.
The fourth section covers `structs`, introducing many new details that have not
been seen earlier.

The chapter's long final section presents three complete examples of custom
types that draw on most of the material covered in the chapter's earlier sections
and a fair amount of material from earlier chapters. The first of these examples
is a simple custom single-valued data type, the second is a small family of data
types, and the third is a generic collection type.

6.1. Key Concepts

What makes Go object orientation so different from, say, C++, Java, and (to a
lesser extent) Python, is that it does not support inheritance. When object-oriented programming first became popular inheritance was touted as one of its
biggest advantages. But now, after a few decades of experience, it has turned
out that this feature has some significant drawbacks, especially when it comes to
maintaining large systems. Instead of using both aggregation and inheritance
like most other object-oriented languages, Go supports aggregation (also called
composition) and *embedding* exclusively. To see the difference between aggregation and embedding let's look at a tiny code snippet.

```
type ColoredPoint struct {
    color.Color     // Anonymous field (embedding)
    x, y        int // Named fields (aggregation)
}        └ fields
```

Here, `color.Color` is a type from the `image/color` package and `x` and `y` are `int`s. In
Go terminology, `color.Color`, `x`, and `y` are all *fields* in the `ColoredPoint` `struct`. The
`color.Color` field is anonymous (since it has no variable name) and is therefore
an embedded field. The `x` and `y` fields are named aggregated fields. If we created
a `ColoredPoint` value (e.g., `point := ColoredPoint{}`), the fields would be accessed
as `point.Color`, `point.x`, and `point.y`. Notice also that when accessing a field of
a type from another package we only use the last component of the name, that
is, `Color` and not `color.Color`. (We will discuss these matters in more detail in
§6.2.1.1, ➤ 261, §6.3, ➤ 265, and §6.4, ➤ 275.)

The terms "class", "object", and "instance" are so well established in conventional inheritance-hierarchy-style object orientation, that in Go we avoid them altogether. Instead, we talk about "types" and "values", where values of custom
types may have methods.

Without inheritance there are no virtual functions. Go's answer to this is to
support type-safe duck typing. In Go, parameters can be specified as concrete

types (e.g., int, string, *os.File, *MyType*), or as interfaces—that is, values that provide the methods that fulfill the interface. For a parameter specified as an interface we can pass *any* value—so long as it has the methods that the interface requires. For example, if we have a value that provides a method with the signature Write([]byte) (int, error) we can pass that value as an io.Writer (i.e., as a value that satisfies the io.Writer interface) to any function that has an io.Writer parameter, no matter what the value's actual type is. This is incredibly flexible and powerful, especially when combined with Go's clever support for accessing the methods of embedded values.

One advantage of inheritance is that some methods need only be implemented once in a base class for all the subclasses to benefit. Go provides two solutions for this. One solution is to use embedding. If we embed a type, the method need be created only once for the embedded type and is available to all those types that include the embedded type.* Another solution is to provide separate versions of the method for all the types we want to have it—but to make these thin wrappers (typically one-liners) that simply pass on the work to a single function that all the methods make use of.

Another unusual aspect of Go object-oriented programming is that interfaces, values, and methods are kept separate. Interfaces are used to specify method signatures, structs are used to specify aggregated and embedded values, and methods are used to specify operations on custom types (which are often structs). There is no explicit connection between a custom type's methods and any particular interface—but if the type's methods fulfill one or more interfaces, values of the type can be used wherever values of those interfaces are expected. Of course, every type fulfills the empty interface (interface{}), so any value can be used where the empty interface is specified.

One way of thinking about the Go approach is to consider that *is-a* relationships are defined by interfaces, that is, purely in terms of method signatures. So, a value that satisfies the io.Reader interface (i.e., that has a method with the signature Read([]byte) (int, error)) isn't a reader because of what it *is* (a file, a buffer, or some custom type), but because of what methods it provides, in this case Read(). This is illustrated in Figure 6.1 (➤ 256). The *has-a* relationship is expressed by using structs in which we aggregate or embed values of the particular types we need as the constituents of a custom type.

Although it isn't possible to add methods to built-in types, it is very easy to create custom types based on built-in types and to add any methods we like to them. Values of such types can call the methods we have provided, and can also be used with any functions, methods, or operators that their underlying type provides. For example, if we have type Integer int, we can add values of this type using the int + operator without formality. And once we have a custom type, we

---

*In some other languages, what in Go terminology is called *embedding*, is known as *delegation*.

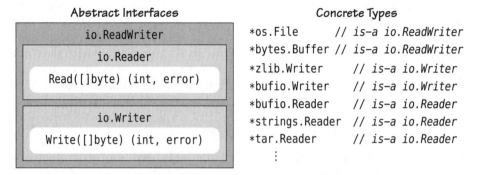

Figure 6.1 *Interfaces and types for reading and writing byte slices*

can also add custom methods—for example, func (i Integer) Double() Integer { return i * 2 }, as we will see shortly (§6.2.1, ➤ 258).

Not only are custom types based on built-in types easy to create, they are also very efficient to use. Converting to or from a built-in type has no runtime cost since the conversion is effectively done at compile time. In view of this it is entirely practical to "promote" values of built-in types to a custom type to use the custom type's methods, and to "demote" such values to the underlying built-in type when we want to pass them to functions whose parameters are of built-in types. We saw an example of promotion earlier when we converted a []string to a FoldedStrings (162 ◄), and we will see an example of demotion when we first look at the Count type later in this chapter (➤ 259).

6.2. Custom Types

Custom types are created using Go's type statement with the following syntax:

```
type typeName typeSpecification
```

The *typeName* can be any valid Go identifier that is unique to the enclosing package or function. The *typeSpecification* can be any built-in type (such as a string, int, slice, map, or channel), an interface (see §6.3, ➤ 265), a struct (seen in earlier chapters, with more coverage later in this one, §6.4, ➤ 275), or a function signature.

In some situations creating a custom type is sufficient, while in others we need to add methods to the custom type to make it really useful. Here are some examples of methodless custom types.

```
type Count int
type StringMap map[string]string
type FloatChan chan float64
```

None of these custom types look particularly useful on their own, although using types like this can improve a program's readability and can also make it possible to change the underlying type later on, so they serve as a basic abstraction mechanism.

```
var i Count = 7
i++
fmt.Println(i)
sm := make(StringMap)
sm["key1"] = "value1"
sm["key2"] = "value2"
fmt.Println(sm)
fc := make(FloatChan, 1)
fc <- 2.29558714939
fmt.Println(<-fc)
```
```
8
map[key2:value2 key1:value1]
2.29558714939
```

Types like Count, StringMap, and FloatChan that are based directly on a built-in type can be used in the same way as the built-in type—for example, we can use the built-in append() function on a custom type StringSlice []string type—but we must convert them (at no cost because it is done at compile time) to the underlying built-in type if we need to pass them to a function that expects their underlying type. And sometimes we need to do the reverse and promote the value of a built-in type to a custom type to benefit from the custom type's methods. We saw an example of this when we converted a []string to a FoldedStrings value in the SortFoldedStrings() function (162 ◀).

func signature

```
type RuneForRuneFunc func(rune) rune
```

When working with higher order functions (§5.6.7, 238 ◀) it is often convenient to define custom types that specify the signatures of the functions we want to pass. Here we have specified the signature of a function that takes and returns a single rune.

```
var removePunctuation RuneForRuneFunc
```

The removePunctuation variable is created to refer to a function of type RuneForRuneFunc (i.e., with the signature func(rune) rune). Like all Go variables it is automatically initialized to its zero value, so in this case to nil.

```
phrases := []string{"Day; dusk, and night.", "All day long"}
removePunctuation = func(char rune) rune {
```

this matches RuneForRune

```
    if unicode.Is(unicode.Terminal_Punctuation, char) {
        return -1
    }
    return char
}
processPhrases(phrases, removePunctuation)
```

Here we have created an anonymous function that matches the RuneForRuneFunc
signature and passed it to the custom processPhrases() function.

```
func processPhrases(phrases []string, function RuneForRuneFunc) {
    for _, phrase := range phrases {
        fmt.Println(strings.Map(function, phrase))    // func is the keyword
    }                                                 // "function" is variable
}                                                     //       name

Day dusk and night
All day long
```

Using RuneForRuneFunc as a type rather than the underlying func(rune) rune is
more meaningful for human readers; it also provides some abstraction. (The
strings.Map() function was covered in Chapter 3, 111 ◀.)

Creating custom types based on built-in types or function signatures can be
useful, but doesn't get us very far. What we need are custom methods, the
subject of the next subsection.

6.2.1. Adding Methods

A method is a special kind of function that is called on a value of a custom type
and that is (usually) passed the value it is called on. The value is passed as a
pointer or value depending on how the method is defined. The syntax for defining methods is almost identical to that for defining functions, except that between the func keyword and the method's name we must write the *receiver*—this
is written in parentheses, either as the type of value that the method belongs
to or as a variable name and the type. When the method is called, the receiver's
variable (if present) is automatically set to the value or pointer that the method
was called on.

We can add one or more methods to any custom type. A method's receiver is
always a value of the type or a pointer to a value of the type. However, every method name must be unique for any given type. One consequence of the
unique name requirement is that we cannot have two methods of the same
name where one takes a pointer and the other a value. Another consequence is
that there is no support for overloaded methods, that is, methods with the same
name but different signatures. One way to provide the equivalent of overloaded

methods is to use variadic methods (i.e., methods that take a variable number of arguments; see §5.6, 219 ◄ and §5.6.1.2, 221 ◄); however, the Go way is to use uniquely named functions. For example, the `strings.Reader` type provides three different read methods: `strings.Reader.Read()`, `strings.Reader.ReadByte()`, and `strings.Reader.ReadRune()`.

@ 261

```go
type Count int

func (count *Count) Increment()  { *count++ }
func (count *Count) Decrement()  { *count-- }
func (count Count) IsZero() bool { return count == 0 }
```

This simple `int`-based custom type supports three methods, of which the first two are declared to accept pointer receivers since both modify the value they are called on.*

```go
var count Count
i := int(count)
count.Increment()
j := int(count)
count.Decrement()
k := int(count)
fmt.Println(count, i, j, k, count.IsZero())
```
```
0 0 1 0 true
```

This snippet shows the `Count` type in action. It doesn't look like much, but we will use it in this chapter's fourth section (➤ 278).

Let's look at a slightly more elaborate custom type, this time based on a `struct`. (We will return to this example in §6.3.1, ➤ 270.)

ⓑ 261

```go
type Part struct {
    Id   int    // Named field (aggregation)
    Name string // Named field (aggregation)
}

func (part *Part) LowerCase() {
    part.Name = strings.ToLower(part.Name)
}

func (part *Part) UpperCase() {
    part.Name = strings.ToUpper(part.Name)
}
```

---

* In C++ and Java receivers are always called *this* and in Python *self*; in Go the practice is to give them more meaningful type-specific names.

```
func (part Part) String() string {
    return fmt.Sprintf("«%d %q»", part.Id, part.Name)
}

func (part Part) HasPrefix(prefix string) bool {
    return strings.HasPrefix(part.Name, prefix)
}
```

We have made the String() and HasPrefix() methods accept a value receiver purely to show how it is done. Of course, methods that accept values rather than pointers cannot modify the value they are called on.

```
part := Part{5, "wrench"}
part.UpperCase()
part.Id += 11
fmt.Println(part, part.HasPrefix("w"))
```

```
«16 "WRENCH"» false
```

 ⚹ When custom types are based on structs we can create values of them using the type name and a brace-enclosed list of initializing values. (And as we will see in the next subsection, Go also has a syntax whereby we can provide just those values we want to, and rely on Go to zero-initialize the rest.)

 ⚹ Once the part value is created we can call methods on it (e.g., Part.UpperCase()), access its exported (public) fields (e.g., Part.Id), and print it, safe in the knowledge that Go's print functions are intelligent enough to use the custom type's String() method if it has one.

 ⚹ A type's *method set* is the set of all the methods that can be called on a value of the type.

 ⚹ If we have a pointer to a value of a custom type, its method set consists of all the methods defined for the type—whether they accept a value or a pointer. If we call a method that takes a value, on a pointer, Go is smart enough to dereference the pointer and pass the underlying value as the method's receiver.

 ⚹ If we have a value of a custom type, its method set consists of all those methods defined for the type that accept a value receiver—but *not* those methods that accept a pointer receiver. This isn't as limiting as it sounds, since if we have a value we can still call a method that has a pointer receiver and rely on Go to pass the value's address—providing the value is addressable (i.e., it is a variable, a dereferenced pointer, an array or slice item, or an addressable field in a struct). So, given the call *value*.*Method*() where *Method*() requires a pointer and *value* is an addressable value, Go will treat the code as if we had written (&*value*).*Method*().

The *Count type's method set consists of the three methods, Increment(), Decre- @ 259
ment(), and IsZero(); whereas the Count type's method set is the single method,
IsZero(). All these methods can be called on a *Count—and also on a Count value,
providing that it is addressable, as we saw in the snippet shown earlier (259 ◄).
The *Part type's method set consists of the four methods, LowerCase(), Upper- ⓑ 259
Case(), String(), and HasPrefix(); while the Part type's method set consists of just
the String() and HasPrefix() methods. However, the LowerCase() and UpperCase()
methods can also be used on addressable Part values, as the earlier code snippet
illustrates (260 ◄).   ⓒ 260

Defining methods that accept value receivers works well for types that are
small, such as numbers. Such methods cannot modify the value they are called
on since they get a copy of the value as their receiver. If we have values of large
types or values we want to modify we need to use methods that accept pointer
receivers. This makes method calls as cheap as possible (since the receiver is
passed as a 32- or 64-bit pointer, no matter how large the value the method is
called on is).

6.2.1.1. Overriding Methods

As we will see later in this chapter, it is possible to create struct types that
include one or more types (including interface types) as *embedded* fields (§6.4.1,
► 275). A particular convenience of this approach is that any methods on the
embedded type can be called on the custom struct as if they were the struct's
own methods, and they will be passed the embedded field as their receiver.

```
type Item struct {
    id        string  // Named field (aggregation)
    price     float64 // Named field (aggregation)
    quantity  int     // Named field (aggregation)
}

func (item *Item) Cost() float64 {
    return item.price * float64(item.quantity)
}

type SpecialItem struct {
    Item            // Anonymous field (embedding)
    catalogId int   // Named field (aggregation)
}
```

Here, the SpecialItem embeds an Item type. This means that we can call the
Item's Cost() method on a SpecialItem.

```
special := SpecialItem{Item{"Green", 3, 5}, 207}
fmt.Println(special.id, special.price, special.quantity, special.catalogId)
fmt.Println(special.Cost())
```

```
Green 3 5 207
15
```

When we call `special.Cost()`, since the `SpecialItem` type does not have its own `Cost()` method, Go uses the `Item.Cost()` method—and passes it the embedded `Item` value, *not* the entire `SpecialItem` that the method was originally called on.

As we will see later, if any of the embedded `Item`'s fields has the same name as one of the `SpecialItem`'s fields, we can still access the embedded `Item`'s fields by using the type as part of the name—for example, `special.Item.price`.

It is possible to override the methods of an embedded field simply by creating a new method for the embedding `struct` that has the same name as one of the embedded fields' methods. For example, suppose we have a new item type:

```
type LuxuryItem struct {
    Item            // Anonymous field (embedding)
    markup float64 // Named field (aggregation)
}
```

As it stands, if we call the `Cost()` method on a `LuxuryItem`, the embedded `Item.Cost()` method will be used, just like it is for `SpecialItems`. Here are three different implementations that override the embedded method (only one of which may be used, of course!).

```
/*
func (item *LuxuryItem) Cost() float64 { // Needlessly verbose!
    return item.Item.price * float64(item.Item.quantity) * item.markup
}

func (item *LuxuryItem) Cost() float64 { // Needless duplication!
    return item.price * float64(item.quantity) * item.markup
}
*/

func (item *LuxuryItem) Cost() float64 { // Ideal ✓
    return item.Item.Cost() * item.markup
}
```

The last implementation takes advantage of the embedded `Cost()` method. Of course, there is no requirement that overriding methods make any use of the embedded methods they override if we don't want them to. (Embedding fields in `struct`s is covered later; §6.4.1, ➤ 275.)

6.2.1.2. Method Expressions

Just as we can assign and pass functions, we can also assign and pass *method expressions*. A method expression is a function that must be passed a value of the method's type as its first argument. (The term *unbound method* is often used in other languages for this concept.)

```
asStringV := Part.String    // Effective signature: func(Part) string
sv := asStringV(part)
hasPrefix := Part.HasPrefix // Effective signature: func(Part, string) bool
asStringP := (*Part).String // Effective signature: func(*Part) string
sp := asStringP(&part)
lower := (*Part).LowerCase  // Effective signature: func(*Part)
lower(&part)
fmt.Println(sv, sp, hasPrefix(part, "w"), part)
```

```
«16 ."WRENCH"» «16 "WRENCH"» true «16 "wrench"»
```

Here we have created four method expressions: asStringV() which takes a Part value as its sole argument, hasPrefix() which takes a Part as its first argument and a string as its second argument, and asStringP() and lower() which both take a *Part as their sole argument.

Method expressions are an advanced feature which can be very useful on the uncommon occasions when they are needed.

All the custom types we have created so far potentially suffer from a critical flaw. None of them provide any means of ensuring that the data they are initialized with is valid (or is forced to be valid), nor any means of ensuring that the type's data (or fields in the case of struct types) cannot be given invalid data. For example, the Part.Id and Part.Name fields can be set to any values we like. But what if we wanted to apply constraints—for example, only allow IDs to be positive integers greater than zero, or only allow names that had a specific format? We will address these issues in the next subsection where we will create a small but complete custom type with validated fields.

6.2.2. Validated Types

For many simple custom types, no validation is necessary. For example, we might have type Point { X, Y int }, for which any values of X and Y are valid. Furthermore, since Go guarantees to initialize all variables (including struct fields) to their zero values, the need for explicit constructors is reduced.

For those situations where the default zero-value initialization isn't sufficient, we can create a construction function. Go doesn't support constructors, so we must call construction functions explicitly. To support this we must document the type as having an invalid zero value and provide one or more construction functions that can be used to create valid values.

We can use a similar approach when it comes to fields that must be validated. We can make such fields unexported and provide exported accessor methods in which we can put the necessary validation.*

Let's look at a small but complete custom type that illustrates these points.

```
type Place struct {
    latitude, longitude float64
    Name                string
}

func New(latitude, longitude float64, name string) *Place {
    return &Place{saneAngle(0, latitude), saneAngle(0, longitude), name}
}
```
not necessary here... read value. But OK and good consistency
```
func (place *Place) Latitude() float64 { return place.latitude }

func (place *Place) SetLatitude(latitude float64) {
    place.latitude = saneAngle(place.latitude, latitude)
}

func (place *Place) Longitude() float64 { return place.longitude }

func (place *Place) SetLongitude(longitude float64) {
    place.longitude = saneAngle(place.longitude, longitude)
}

func (place *Place) String() string {     // Fulfills fmt.Stringer i/f
    return fmt.Sprintf("(%.3f°, %.3f°) %q", place.latitude,
        place.longitude, place.Name)      // %s string, dbl-quoted
}                                         // [] byte

func (original *Place) Copy() *Place {
    return &Place{original.latitude, original.longitude, original.Name}
}
```

The Place type is exported (from the place package), but its latitude and longitude fields are unexported because they require validation. We have provided a construction function, New(), to ensure that we always create valid *place.Places. It is a Go convention to call construction functions New(), or if there is more than one, for their names to begin with "New". (We haven't shown the saneAngle() function since it is beside the point—it takes the old angle and the new angle and returns the new if the new is in range; otherwise it returns the old.) And

---

* Recall that in Go, identifiers are unexported (i.e., only visible within the package in which they are defined) if they start with a lowercase letter, and identifiers are exported (i.e., visible in any package that imports the package in which they are defined) if they start with an uppercase letter.

by providing getters and setters for the unexported fields, we have ensured that only valid values can be set.

The String() method means that *Place values fulfill the fmt.Stringer interface, so *Places will print the way we want rather than using Go's default formatting. We have also provided a Copy() method—and not used any validation for it since we know that the original is already valid.

```
newYork := place.New(40.716667, -74, "New York") // newYork is a *Place
fmt.Println(newYork)
baltimore := newYork.Copy() // baltimore is a *Place
baltimore.SetLatitude(newYork.Latitude() - 1.43333)
baltimore.SetLongitude(newYork.Longitude() - 2.61667)
baltimore.Name = "Baltimore"
fmt.Println(baltimore)
```

```
(40.717°, -74.000°) "New York"
(39.283°, -76.617°) "Baltimore"
```

We put the Place type in the place package and call place.New() to create *Places. Once we have a *Place we can call its methods in the same way as we do for any of the standard library's custom types.

6.3. Interfaces

In Go an *interface* is a custom type that specifies a set of one or more method signatures. Interfaces are wholly abstract, so it is not possible to instantiate an interface. However, it is possible to create a variable whose type is that of an interface—and which can then be assigned a value of any concrete type that has the methods the interface requires.

The interface{} type is the interface that specifies the empty set of methods. Every value satisfies the interface{} type whether the value has methods or not—after all, if a value does have methods, its set of methods includes the empty set of methods as well as the methods it actually has. This is why the interface{} type can be used for *any* value. We cannot call methods directly on a value passed as an interface{} (even if it has some), since the interface it is fulfilling has no methods. So, in general, it is better to pass values either as their actual type or as an interface that has the methods that we want to use. Of course, if we do use the interface{} type for values with methods, we can access those methods by using a type assertion (§5.1.2, 191 ◄) or a type switch (§5.2.2.2, 197 ◄), or even by using introspection (§9.4.9, ➤ 427).

Here is a very simple interface.

```
type Exchanger interface {
    Exchange()    .
}
```

The Exchanger interface specifies a single method, Exchange(), which takes no arguments and returns nothing. We have followed the Go convention for interface names, which is that they should end with *er*. It is quite common to have interfaces with only one method—for example, the standard library's io.Reader and io.Writer interfaces each specify a single method. Notice that an interface is really specifying an API (Application Programming Interface), that is, zero or more methods—although it says nothing about what those methods actually do.

A nonempty interface on its own is not usually of any use; to make it useful we must create some custom types that have the methods the interface requires.* Here are two such types.

```
type StringPair struct{ first, second string }

func (pair *StringPair) Exchange() {
    pair.first, pair.second = pair.second, pair.first
}

type Point [2]int

func (point *Point) Exchange() { point[0], point[1] = point[1], point[0] }
```

The custom StringPair and Point types are completely different, but since both provide an Exchange() method, both satisfy the Exchanger interface. This means that we can create StringPair and Point values and pass them to functions that accept Exchangers.

Notice that although both the StringPair and Point types fulfill the Exchanger interface, nowhere have we said this explicitly—there are no "implements" or "inherits" statements. The mere fact that the StringPair and Point types provide the methods (in this case just one method) that the interface specifies, is sufficient for Go to know that they satisfy the interface.

The methods' receivers are specified as pointers to their types so that we can change the (pointed to) values the methods are called on.

Although Go is smart enough to print custom types in a sensible way, we usually prefer to take control over their string representation. This can easily be done by adding a method that fulfills the fmt.Stringer interface, that is, a method with the signature String() string.

---

* If we were creating a framework we might create interfaces but no types that implement them, and require users of the framework to create such types for use with the framework.

```
func (pair StringPair) String() string {
    return fmt.Sprintf("%q+%q", pair.first, pair.second)
}
```

This method returns a string that consists of each of the strings in double quotes with a "+" sign between them. With this method defined, Go's fmt package's print methods will use it to print StringPair values—and also *StringPairs, since Go will dereference such pointers to get the pointed-to value.

Here is a code snippet that shows the creation of some custom Exchanger values, some calls to the Exchange() method, and a call to a custom exchangeThese() function that accepts Exchanger values.

```
jekyll := StringPair{"Henry", "Jekyll"}
hyde := StringPair{"Edward", "Hyde"}
point := Point{5, -3}
fmt.Println("Before: ", jekyll, hyde, point)
jekyll.Exchange() // Treated as: (&jekyll).Exchange()
hyde.Exchange()   // Treated as: (&hyde).Exchange()
point.Exchange()  // Treated as: (&point).Exchange()
fmt.Println("After #1:", jekyll, hyde, point)
exchangeThese(&jekyll, &hyde, &point)          ≥8
fmt.Println("After #2:", jekyll, hyde, point)
```

```
Before:   "Henry"+"Jekyll" "Edward"+"Hyde" [5 -3]
After #1: "Jekyll"+"Henry" "Hyde"+"Edward" [-3 5]
After #2: "Henry"+"Jekyll" "Edward"+"Hyde" [5 -3]
```

All the variables are created as values, yet the Exchange() methods require pointer receivers. This isn't a problem since, as we noted earlier, Go is smart enough to pass a value's address when we call a method on it that requires a pointer—providing the value is addressable. So, in the snippet, jekyll.Exchange() is automatically treated as if it were written (&jekyll).Exchange(), and the same for the others.

In the call to the exchangeThese() function, we must pass the values' addresses explicitly. If, for instance, we passed the hyde value of type StringPair, the Go compiler would notice that StringPairs do not fulfill the Exchanger interface—since there is no Exchange() method with a StringPair receiver—and would stop compiling and report the problem. However, if we pass a *StringPair (e.g., &hyde), the compilation will complete successfully. This works because there is an Exchange() method which takes a *StringPair receiver which means that *StringPairs fulfill the Exchanger interface.

Here is the exchangeThese() function.

```
func exchangeThese(exchangers ...Exchanger) {
    for _, exchanger := range exchangers {
        exchanger.Exchange()
    }
}
```

This function doesn't know or care that we passed it two *StringPairs and one
*Point; all that it requires is that the parameters it is passed are Exchangers—and
this requirement is enforced by the compiler, hence the duck typing used here
is type-safe.

In addition to satisfying our own custom interfaces, we can satisfy those in the
standard library or any others we want, as we saw when we defined the String-
Pair.String() method to fulfill the fmt.Stringer interface. Another example
is the io.Reader interface which specifies a single method with the signature
Read([]byte) (int, error) that when called writes the data of the value it is
called on to the given []byte. The writing is destructive, that is, each byte written
is removed from the called-on value.

```
func (pair *StringPair) Read(data []byte) (n int, err error) {
    if pair.first == "" && pair.second == "" {
        return 0, io.EOF
    }
    if pair.first != "" {
        n = copy(data, pair.first)     // string copied to []byte
        pair.first = pair.first[n:]    // remove bytes that were written
    }
    if n < len(data) && pair.second != "" {
        m := copy(data[n:], pair.second)
        pair.second = pair.second[m:]  // remove bytes that were written
        n += m
    }
    return n, nil
}
```

By implementing this method we have made the StringPair type fulfill the
io.Reader interface. So now StringPairs (or, strictly speaking, *StringPairs since
some of the methods require pointer receivers) are Exchangers *and* fmt.Stringers
and io.Readers—with no need to say that *StringPair "implements" Exchanger or
any of the other interfaces. And we could, of course, add further methods and
fulfill additional interfaces if we wished.

The method uses the built-in copy() function (§4.2.3, 156 ◀). This function can
be used to copy into a slice from another slice of the same type—but here we
have used it in its other form to copy into a []byte the bytes in a string. The
copy() function never copies more bytes than the destination []byte has room for,

and returns the number of bytes copied. The custom StringPair.Read() method writes bytes from its first string (and removes any that are written), and then does the same for its second string. If both strings are empty the method returns a byte count of zero and io.EOF. Incidentally, the method would work perfectly well if the second if statement's statements were executed unconditionally and if the third if statement's condition's second clause was deleted—but at some (perhaps insignificant) cost in efficiency.

Here it was necessary to use a pointer receiver since the Read() method modifies the value it is called on. And in general, we prefer to use pointer receivers except for small values, since pointers are cheaper to pass than all but the smallest values.

With the Read() method in place we can make use of it.

```
const size = 16
robert := &StringPair{"Robert L.", "Stevenson"}
david := StringPair{"David", "Balfour"}
for _, reader := range []io.Reader{robert, &david} {
    raw, err := ToBytes(reader, size)
    if err != nil {
        fmt.Println(err)
    }
    fmt.Printf("%q\n", raw)
}
```
```
"Robert L.Stevens"
"DavidBalfour"
```

This snippet creates two io.Readers. Since we implemented the StringPair. Read() method to take a pointer receiver, only *StringPairs satisfy the io.Reader() interface, not StringPair values. For the first StringPair we have created the value and set the robert variable to be a pointer to it, and for the second StringPair we set the david variable to be a StringPair value—and so must use its address in the []io.Reader slice.

Once the variables are set up, we iterate over them, and for each one we use a custom ToBytes() function to copy their data into a []byte and then we print the raw bytes as a double-quoted string.

The ToBytes() function takes an io.Reader (i.e., *any* value that has a method with the signature Read([]byte) (int, error), such as an *os.File), and a size limit, and returns a []byte that contains the reader's data and also an error.

```
func ToBytes(reader io.Reader, size int) ([]byte, error) {
    data := make([]byte, size)
    n, err := reader.Read(data)
```

```
    if err != nil {
        return data, err
    }
    return data[:n], nil // Slice off any unused bytes
}
```

Just like the exchangeThese() function we saw earlier, this function does not
know or care what specific type of value it is passed—so long as it is an io.Reader
of some kind.

If the read is successful, the data slice is resliced to reduce its length to the
number of bytes actually read. If we didn't do this and the size was too large
we would have the data read followed by bytes (each of value 0x00). For example,
without the slicing, david would be output as "DavidBalfour\x00\x00\x00\x00".

Notice that there is no explicit connection between an interface and any types
that satisfy it—we don't have to say that a custom type "inherits" or "extends"
or "implements" an interface; simply giving a type the requisite methods is
sufficient. This makes Go incredibly flexible—we can easily add new interfaces,
types, and methods at any time, with no inheritance tree to disrupt.

6.3.1. Interface Embedding

Go interfaces (and structs, as we will see in the next section) have excellent support for embedding. Interfaces can embed other interfaces and the effect is almost the same as if we had written the embedded interface's method signatures
in the interface that embeds it. Let's illustrate this with a simple example.

```
type LowerCaser interface {
    LowerCase()
}

type UpperCaser interface {
    UpperCase()
}

type LowerUpperCaser interface {
    LowerCaser // As if we had written LowerCase()
    UpperCaser // As if we had written UpperCase()
}
```

The LowerCaser interface specifies a single method, LowerCase(), that takes
no arguments and returns nothing. The UpperCaser interface is similar. The
LowerUpperCaser interface embeds the two other interfaces. This means that for
a concrete type to satisfy the LowerUpperCaser interface, it must have LowerCase()
and UpperCase() methods.

In this tiny example the embedding doesn't look like much of a win. However, if we added extra methods to the first two interfaces (say, `LowerCaseSpecial()` and `UpperCaseSpecial()`), the `LowerUpperCaser` interface would automatically include them without us having to touch its code.

```
type FixCaser interface {
    FixCase()
}

type ChangeCaser interface {
    LowerUpperCaser // As if we had written LowerCase(); UpperCase()
    FixCaser        // As if we had written FixCase()
}
```

We have now added two more interfaces, so we now have a kind of hierarchy of embedded interfaces, as Figure 6.2 illustrates.

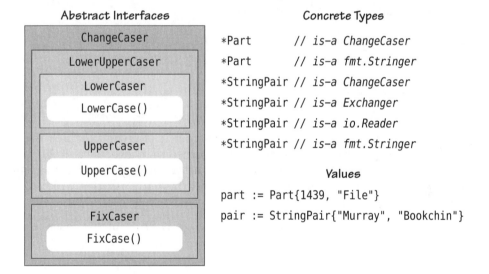

Figure 6.2 *Caser interfaces, types, and example values*

The interfaces are, of course, of no use on their own; we need concrete types that implement them for them to be useful.

```
func (part *Part) FixCase() {
    part.Name = fixCase(part.Name)
}
```

We saw the custom `Part` type earlier (260 ◄). Here we have added a single additional method, `FixCase()`, which works on the `Part`'s `Name` field, just like the `LowerCase()` and `UpperCase()` methods we saw earlier. All the case-changing methods take pointer receivers since they modify the value they are called on. The LowerCase() and UpperCase() methods are implemented by using standard library functions, and the FixCase() method relies on the custom fixCase() function—this pattern of tiny methods that rely on functions to do the work is very common in Go.

The Part.String() method (260 ◀) fulfills the standard library's fmt.Stringer interface and means that any Part (or *Part) will be printed using the string returned by this method.

```go
func fixCase(s string) string {
    var chars []rune
    upper := true
    for _, char := range s {
        if upper {
            char = unicode.ToUpper(char)
        } else {
            char = unicode.ToLower(char)
        }
        chars = append(chars, char)
        upper = unicode.IsSpace(char) || unicode.Is(unicode.Hyphen, char)
    }
    return string(chars)
}
```

This simple function returns a copy of the string it is given in which every character has been lowercased, except for the very first character and the first character after each whitespace or hyphen character, which are uppercased. For example, given the string "lobelia sackville-baggins", the function will return "Lobelia Sackville-Baggins".

Naturally, we can make any custom type satisfy any or all of the caser interfaces.

```go
func (pair *StringPair) UpperCase() {
    pair.first = strings.ToUpper(pair.first)
    pair.second = strings.ToUpper(pair.second)
}
func (pair *StringPair) FixCase() {
    pair.first = fixCase(pair.first)
    pair.second = fixCase(pair.second)
}
```

Here we have added methods to the StringPair type we created earlier (266 ◀) to make it satisfy the LowerCaser, UpperCaser, and FixCaser interfaces—although we have not shown the `StringPair.LowerCase()` method since it is structurally identical to the `StringPair.UpperCase()` method.

Both the `*Part` and `*StringPair` types satisfy all the caser interfaces, including the `ChangeCaser` interface since that embeds interfaces that the types fulfill. They also both satisfy the standard library's `fmt.Stringer` interface. And the `*StringPair` type also satisfies our `Exchanger` interface and the standard library's `io.Reader` interface.

We are not obliged to fulfill every interface—for example, if we chose not to implement the `StringPair.FixCase()` method the `*StringPair` type would satisfy only the `LowerCaser`, `UpperCaser`, `LowerUpperCaser`, `Exchanger`, `fmt.Stringer`, and `io.Reader` interfaces.

Let's create a couple of these values and see some of the methods in use.

```
toastRack := Part{8427, "TOAST RACK"}
toastRack.LowerCase()
lobelia := StringPair{"LOBELIA", "SACKVILLE-BAGGINS"}
lobelia.FixCase()
fmt.Println(toastRack, lobelia)
```
```
«8427 "toast rack"» "Lobelia"+"Sackville-Baggins"
```

The methods are called and behave as we would expect. But what happens if we have a bunch of such values and want to call a method on them? Here is a bad way to do it.

```
for _, x := range []interface{}{&toastRack, &lobelia} { // UNSAFE!
    x.(LowerUpperCaser).UpperCase() // Unchecked type assertion
}
```

We must use pointers to the values since all the caser methods modify the value they are called on and so require pointer receivers.

The approach used in this snippet has two deficiencies. The minor deficiency is that the unchecked type assertion is to the `LowerUpperCaser` interface which is more general than the interface we actually need. We could have done worse, though, and used the `ChangeCaser` interface since that is even more general. But we could not use the `FixCaser` interface since that provides only the Fix-Case() method. What we should do is use the most specific interface that is sufficient—in this case the `UpperCaser` interface. This approach's major deficiency is that we use an unchecked type assertion at all since this could result in a panic!

```
for _, x := range []interface{}{&toastRack, &lobelia} {
    if x, ok := x.(LowerCaser); ok { // shadow variable
```

```
        x.LowerCase()
    }
```

This code snippet uses a safer approach and sensibly uses the most specific interface for the job—but it is rather unwieldy. The problem is that we are using a slice of generic interface{} values rather than values of a particular type, or that satisfy a particular interface. Of course, if all we are given is an []interface{}, then this is the best we can do.

```
for _, x := range []FixCaser{&toastRack, &lobelia} { // Ideal ✓
    x.FixCase()
}
```

This snippet illustrates the best approach: Instead of type checking raw generic interface{} values we specify the slice as FixCasers—the most specific interface type that is sufficient for our needs—and leave all the type checking to the compiler.

Another aspect of the flexibility of interfaces is that they can be created after the fact. For example, suppose we create some custom types, some of which have an IsValid() bool method. If, later on, we discover that we have a function that receives a value of one of our custom types and that we want to call the IsValid() method if the value supports it, this can easily be done.

```
type IsValider interface {
    IsValid() bool
}
```

First, we create an interface that specifies the methods we want to check for.

```
if thing, ok := x.(IsValider); ok {
    if !thing.IsValid() {
        reportInvalid(thing)
    } else {
        // ... process valid thing ...
    }
}
```

With the interface in place we can now check any custom value to see if it provides an IsValid() bool method, and if it does, we can call that method.

Interfaces provide a powerful abstraction mechanism that allows us to specify sets of methods such that we can use interface parameters for functions or methods that are concerned only with what a value can do, rather than caring about what the value's type is. We will see further uses of them later in this chapter (§6.5.2, ➤ 289).

6.4. Structs

The simplest custom types in Go are based on Go's built-in types—for example, type Integer int creates a custom Integer type to which we could add our own methods. Custom types can also be based on structs which are used to aggregate and embed values together. This is particularly useful when the values—called *fields* in the context of structs—are of different types, and so cannot be stored in a slice (unless we use an []interface{}). Go's structs are much closer to C's structs than C++'s (e.g., they are not classes), and they are more convenient to use because of their excellent support for embedding.

We have already seen numerous examples of structs in earlier chapters and in this chapter, and we will see many more throughout the rest of the book. Nonetheless, there are some struct features that we have not yet seen, so we will begin with some illustrative examples to show them.

```
points := [][2]int{{4, 6}, {}, {-7, 11}, {15, 17}, {14, -8}}
for _, point := range points {
    fmt.Printf("(%d, %d) ", point[0], point[1])
}
```

The snippet's points variable is a slice of arrays of type [2]int, so we must use the [] index operator to get each coordinate. (Incidentally, the {} item is the same as {0, 0} thanks to Go's automatic zero-value initialization.) For small amounts of simple data this works fine, but there is a nicer way to do this using an anonymous struct.

```
points := []struct{ x, y int }{{4, 6}, {}, {-7, 11}, {15, 17}, {14, -8}}
for _, point := range points {
    fmt.Printf("(%d, %d) ", point.x, point.y)
}
```

Here, the snippet's points variable is a slice of struct{ x, y int}s. Although the struct itself is unnamed, we can access its data via its named fields which is easier and safer than using array indexes.

6.4.1. Struct Aggregation and Embedding

We can embed structs in the same way as we can embed interfaces or other types, that is, by including the type name of a struct as an anonymous field inside another struct. (Of course, if we gave the inner struct a variable name it would be an aggregated named field rather than an embedded anonymous field.)

Usually an embedded field's fields can be accessed directly using the . (dot) selector operator without mentioning the type name, but if the containing struct has a named field whose name is the same as one of the embedded struct's fields, then we must use the embedded struct's type name to disambiguate.

Every field name in a struct must be unique. For embedded (i.e., anonymous) fields the uniqueness requirement is sufficiently strict to avoid ambiguity. For example, if we have an embedded field of type Integer, we can have other fields called, say, Integer2 or BigInteger, since they are distinctly different, but we cannot have fields called, say, Matrix.Integer or *Integer since the last component of these names is exactly the same as the Integer embedded field, and the uniqueness of field names is based on their last component.

6.4.1.1. Embedding Values

Let's start by looking at a simple example involving two structs.

```
type Person struct {
    Title     string   // Named field (aggregation)
    Forenames []string // Named field (aggregation)
    Surname   string   // Named field (aggregation)
}

type Author1 struct {
    Names    Person   // Named field (aggregation)
    Title    []string // Named field (aggregation)
    YearBorn int      // Named field (aggregation)
}
```

We have seen many similar examples in earlier chapters. Here, the Author1 struct's fields are all named. This is how we can use these structs and the output that's produced (using a custom Author1.String() method, not shown).

```
author1 := Author1{Person{"Mr", []string{"Robert", "Louis", "Balfour"},
    "Stevenson"}, []string{"Kidnapped", "Treasure Island"}, 1850}
fmt.Println(author1)
author1.Names.Title = ""
author1.Names.Forenames = []string{"Oscar", "Fingal", "O'Flahertie",
    "Wills"}
author1.Names.Surname = "Wilde"
author1.Title = []string{"The Picture of Dorian Gray"}
author1.YearBorn += 4
fmt.Println(author1)
```

```
Stevenson, Robert Louis Balfour, Mr (1850) "Kidnapped" "Treasure Island"
Wilde, Oscar Fingal O'Flahertie Wills (1854) "The Picture of Dorian Gray"
```

We begin by creating an Author1 value, populating all of its fields in order, and printing it. Then we change the value's fields and print it again.

```
type Author2 struct {
    Person              // Anonymous field (embedding)
    Title    []string   // Named field (aggregation)
    YearBorn int        // Named field (aggregation)
}
```

To embed an anonymous field we use the name of the type (or interface, as we will see later) that we want to embed, without specifying a variable name for it. We can access such a field's own fields directly (i.e., without specifying the type or interface's name), or using the type or interface's name if we need to disambiguate from another name in the containing `struct`.

The `Author2` struct shown here embeds a `Person` struct as an anonymous field. This means that we can access the `Person` fields directly (except when we need to disambiguate).

```
author2 := Author2{Person{"Mr", []string{"Robert", "Louis", "Balfour"},
    "Stevenson"}, []string{"Kidnapped", "Treasure Island"}, 1850}
fmt.Println(author2)
author2.Title = []string{"The Picture of Dorian Gray"}
author2.Person.Title = "" // Must use the type name to disambiguate
author2.Forenames = []string{"Oscar", "Fingal", "O'Flahertie", "Wills"}
author2.Surname = "Wilde" // Same as: author2.Person.Surname = "Wilde"
author2.YearBorn += 4
fmt.Println(author2)
```

The code snippet showing the use of the `Author1` struct is repeated here using the `Author2` struct—it produces identical output (assuming we have created an `Author2.String()` method that does the same as the `Author1.String()` method).

By embedding `Person` as an anonymous field, we get almost the same effect as if we had added the `Person` struct's fields directly—but not quite, since if we added the fields themselves we would end up with two `Title` fields which wouldn't compile.

The creation of the `Author2` value is identical to when we created the `Author1` value, but now we can refer directly to the `Person` fields (e.g., author2.Forenames)—except when we need to disambiguate (author2.Person.Title vs. author2.Title).

6.4.1.2. Embedding Anonymous Values That Have Methods

If an embedded field has methods we can call them on the containing `struct`, and only the embedded field will be passed as the methods' receiver.

```
type Tasks struct {
    slice []string // Named field (aggregation)
    Count           // Anonymous field (embedding)
}

func (tasks *Tasks) Add(task string) {
    tasks.slice = append(tasks.slice, task)
    tasks.Increment() // As if we had written: tasks.Count.Increment()
}

func (tasks *Tasks) Tally() int {
    return int(tasks.Count)
}
```

We saw the custom Count type earlier (259 ◀). The Tasks struct has two fields: an aggregated slice of strings and an embedded Count value. As the implementation of the Tasks.Add() method illustrates, we can access the anonymous Count value's methods directly.

```
tasks := Tasks{}
fmt.Println(tasks.IsZero(), tasks.Tally(), tasks)
tasks.Add("One")
tasks.Add("Two")
fmt.Println(tasks.IsZero(), tasks.Tally(), tasks)
```
```
true 0 {[] 0}
false 2 {[One Two] 2}
```

Here we have created a Tasks value, and called the Tasks.Add(), Tasks.Tally(), and Tasks.Count.IsZero() (as Tasks.IsZero()) methods on it. Even though we have not defined a Tasks.String() method, Go still produces sensible output when asked to print the Tasks. (Note that we could not call the Tally() method Count() since that would have caused a name collision with the embedded Tasks.Count value and would not have compiled.)

It is important to remember that when an embedded field's method is called on a value that contains that field, it is only the embedded field that gets passed as the method's receiver. So when Tasks.IsZero(), Tasks.Increment(), or any other Count method is called on a Tasks value, these methods receive a Count (or *Count value), not the Tasks value.

In this example the Tasks type has its own methods (Add() and Tally()), and also the embedded Count type's methods (Increment(), Decrement(), and IsZero()). It is, of course, possible for the Tasks type to override any or all of the Count type's methods simply by implementing its own methods of the same names. (We saw an example of this earlier; §6.2.1.1, 261 ◀.)

6.4.1.3. Embedding Interfaces

In addition to aggregating and embedding concrete types in structs, it is also possible to aggregate and embed interfaces. (Naturally, the converse—aggregating or embedding a struct in an interface—isn't possible, because an interface is a wholly abstract type, so such aggregating or embedding would not make sense.) When a struct includes an aggregated (named) or embedded (anonymous) field of an interface type, it means that the struct can store in that field *any* value that satisfies the interface's specification.

We will round off our coverage of structs by looking at a simple example that shows how we might support "option" values that have short and long names (e.g., "-o" and "--outfile"), a value of a particular type (int, float64, string), and some common methods. (This example is designed to be illustrative rather than elegant. For a fully functional option parser see the standard library's flag package, or one of the third-party option parsers from godashboard.appspot .com/project.)

```go
type Optioner interface {
    Name() string
    IsValid() bool
}

type OptionCommon struct {
    ShortName string "short option name"
    LongName  string "long option name"
}
```

The Optioner interface specifies the generic methods that all our option types must provide. The OptionCommon struct has the two fields that are common to every option. Go allows us to annotate struct fields with strings (called *tags* in Go terminology). These tags have no functional purpose, but—unlike comments—they are accessible using Go's reflection support (§9.4.9, ➤ 427). Some programmers use the tags to specify field validation—for example, with tags like "check:len(2,30)" for a string, or "check:range(0,500)" for a number, and with whatever semantics the programmer creates.

```go
type IntOption struct {
    OptionCommon         // Anonymous field (embedding)
    Value, Min, Max int  // Named fields (aggregation)
}

func (option IntOption) Name() string {
    return name(option.ShortName, option.LongName)
}

func (option IntOption) IsValid() bool {
```

```
        return option.Min <= option.Value && option.Value <= option.Max
}

func name(shortName, longName string) string {
    if longName == "" {
        return shortName
    }
    return longName
}
```

This is the complete implementation of the custom IntOption type plus the supporting unexported name() function. Since the OptionCommon struct is embedded we can access its fields directly—as we do in the IntOption.Name() method. The IntOption satisfies the Optioner interface (since it provides the Name() and IsValid() methods with the correct signatures).

Although the processing done by the name() function is very simple we have chosen to use a separate function rather than implement it in the IntOption.Name() method. This makes the IntOption.Name() method very short and means that we can reuse the functionality in other custom options. So, for example, the GenericOption.Name() and StringOption.Name() methods' bodies are identical to the IntOption.Name() method's single statement body, with all three relying on the name() function to do the actual work. This is a common pattern in Go, and we will see it again in the chapter's last section.

The StringOption's implementation is very similar to the IntOption so we have not shown it. (The differences are that its Value field is of type string and its IsValid() method returns true if the Value is nonempty.) For the FloatOption we have used interface embedding, just to show how it is done.

```
type FloatOption struct {
    Optioner // Anonymous field (interface embedding: needs concrete type)
    Value float64 // Named field (aggregation)
}
```

This is the complete implementation of the FloatOption. The embedded Optioner field means that when we create FloatOption values we must assign to the embedded field *any* value that satisfies the Optioner interface.

```
type GenericOption struct {
    OptionCommon // Anonymous field (embedding)
}

func (option GenericOption) Name() string {
    return name(option.ShortName, option.LongName)
}
```

```go
func (option GenericOption) IsValid() bool {
    return true
}
```

This is the complete implementation of the GenericOption, a type that fulfills the Optioner interface.

The FloatOption type has an embedded field of type Optioner, so FloatOption values require a concrete type that fulfills the Optioner interface for this field. This need can be met by assigning a GenericOption value to a FloatOption value's Optioner field.

Now that we have all the pieces in place (the IntOption, the FloatOption, etc.), let's see how to create and use them.

```go
fileOption := StringOption{OptionCommon{"f", "file"}, "index.html"}
topOption := IntOption{
    OptionCommon: OptionCommon{"t", "top"},
    Max: 100,
}
sizeOption := FloatOption{
    GenericOption{OptionCommon{"s", "size"}}, 19.5}
for _, option := range []Optioner{topOption, fileOption, sizeOption} {
    fmt.Print("name=", option.Name(), " • valid=", option.IsValid())
    fmt.Print(" • value=")
    switch option := option.(type) { // shadow variable
    case IntOption:
        fmt.Print(option.Value, " • min=", option.Min,
            " • max=", option.Max, "\n")
    case StringOption:
        fmt.Println(option.Value)
    case FloatOption:
        fmt.Println(option.Value)
    }
}
```

```
name=top • valid=true • value=0 • min=0 • max=100
name=file • valid=true • value=index.html
name=size • valid=true • value=19.5
```

The fileOption StringOption is created conventionally, with every field being assigned a suitable value in order. But for the topOption IntOption we only need to assign to the OptionCommon and Max fields since the zero value is fine for the others (i.e., for the Value and Min fields). Go allows us to create structs and initialize only those fields we want to by using the syntax *fieldName: fieldValue*. When this syntax is used, any fields that are not explicitly assigned to are automatically set to their zero value.

The sizeOption FloatOption's first field is an Optioner interface, so we must supply a concrete type that satisfies this interface. Here we have created a GenericOption value for this purpose.

With three different options created we can iterate over them using an []Optioner, that is, a slice of values that satisfy the Optioner interface. Within the loop the option variable holds each option (of type Optioner) in turn. We can call any method specified by the Optioner interface on the option variable, and do so here by calling the Option.Name() and Option.IsValid() methods.

Each option type has a Value field, but they are of different types—for example, IntOption.Value is an int whereas StringOption.Value is a string. So, to be able to access the type-specific Value fields (and similarly, any other type-specific fields or methods), we must convert the given option to the correct type. This is easily achieved using a type switch (§5.2.2.2, 197 ◀). In the snippet's type switch we have used a shadow variable (option) which always has the correct type for the case that is executed (e.g., in the IntOption case, option is of type IntOption, etc.), and so we are able to access any type-specific fields or methods within each case.

6.5. Examples

Now that we know how to create custom types we are ready to look at some more realistic and complete examples. The first example shows how to create a simple custom value type. The second example shows how to create a set of related interfaces and structs using embedding, and how to provide not only type-construction functions, but also a factory function that can create values of all the package's exported types. The third example shows how to implement a complete custom generic collection type.

6.5.1. Example: FuzzyBool—A Single-Valued Custom Type

In this section we will see how to create a single-valued custom type and its supporting methods. This example is in file fuzzy/fuzzybool/fuzzybool.go and is based on a struct.

The built-in bool type is two-valued (true and false), but in some areas of artificial intelligence, fuzzy Booleans are used. These have values corresponding to "true" and "false", and also to intermediates between them. In our implementation we will use floating-point values, with 0.0 denoting false and 1.0 denoting true. In this system, 0.5 means 50% true (50% false), and 0.25 means 25% true (75% false), and so on. Here are some usage examples and the results they produce.

```
func main() {
    a, _ := fuzzybool.New(0)    // Safe to ignore err value when using
    b, _ := fuzzybool.New(.25) // known valid values; must check if using
    c, _ := fuzzybool.New(.75) // variables though.
    d := c.Copy()
    if err := d.Set(1); err != nil {
        fmt.Println(err)
    }
    process(a, b, c, d)
    s := []*fuzzybool.FuzzyBool{a, b, c, d}
    fmt.Println(s)
}

func process(a, b, c, d *fuzzybool.FuzzyBool) {
    fmt.Println("Original:", a, b, c, d)
    fmt.Println("Not:     ", a.Not(), b.Not(), c.Not(), d.Not())
    fmt.Println("Not Not: ", a.Not().Not(), b.Not().Not(), c.Not().Not(),
        d.Not().Not())
    fmt.Print("0.And(.25)→", a.And(b), "• .25.And(.75)→", b.And(c),
        "• .75.And(1)→", c.And(d), " • .25.And(.75,1)→", b.And(c, d), "\n")
    fmt.Print("0.Or(.25)→", a.Or(b), "• .25.Or(.75)→", b.Or(c),
        "• .75.Or(1)→", c.Or(d), " • .25.Or(.75,1)→", b.Or(c, d), "\n")
    fmt.Println("a < c, a == c, a > c:", a.Less(c), a.Equal(c), c.Less(a))
    fmt.Println("Bool:    ", a.Bool(), b.Bool(), c.Bool(), d.Bool())
    fmt.Println("Float:   ", a.Float(), b.Float(), c.Float(), d.Float())
}
```

```
Original: 0% 25% 75% 100%
Not:      100% 75% 25% 0%
Not Not: 0% 25% 75% 100%
0.And(.25)→0%  .25.And(.75)→25%  .75.And(1)→75%  0.And(.25,.75,1)→0%
0.Or(.25)→25%  .25.Or(.75)→75%  .75.Or(1)→100%  0.Or(.25,.75,1)→100%
a < c, a == c, a > c: true false false
Bool:     false false true true
Float:    0 0.25 0.75 1
[0% 25% 75% 100%]
```

The custom type is called FuzzyBool. We will start by looking at the type definition, and then the construction function. And we will finish up by looking at the methods.

```
type FuzzyBool struct{ value float32 }
```

The FuzzyBool type is based on a struct that contains a single float32. The value is unexported so anyone who imports the fuzzybool package must use the construction function (which we have called New(), in accordance with Go convention), to create fuzzy Booleans. This means, of course, that we can ensure that only valid fuzzy Booleans are created.

Since the FuzzyBool type is based on a struct that contains a value whose type is unique inside the struct, we could simplify the type to type FuzzyBool struct { float32 }. This would mean changing the code that accesses the value—and which we will see in some of the following methods—from *fuzzy*.value to *fuzzy*.float32. We preferred to use a named variable partly because we found it more æsthetically pleasing, and partly because if we wanted to change the underlying type (to, say, float64), we would have far fewer changes to make.

Further variations are also possible since the struct contains only a single value. For example, we could change the type to type FuzzyBool float32 to make it based directly on a float32. Doing this works perfectly well, but requires slightly more code and is a bit trickier to implement than the struct-based approach used here. However, if we constrain ourselves to creating immutable fuzzy Booleans (where the only difference is that instead of setting a new value with the Set() method we would have to assign a new fuzzy Boolean), we can greatly simplify the code by basing the type directly on a float32.

```
func New(value interface{}) (*FuzzyBool, error) {
    amount, err := float32ForValue(value)
    return &FuzzyBool{amount}, err
}
```

For the convenience of fuzzy Boolean users, rather than accept only a float32 as the initializing value we also accept float64s (Go's default floating-point type), ints (the default integer type), and bools. This flexibility is achieved by using a custom float32ForValue() function which returns a float32 and nil for the given value—or which returns 0.0 and an error if the value is not of a type it can handle.

If we passed a value of an invalid type we have made a programming error and want to know about it straight away. But we don't want the application to crash on our users. So, instead of just returning a *FuzzyBool, we also return an error. If we pass a known valid literal to New() (as in the earlier snippet; 283 ◀), we can safely ignore the error; but if we pass a variable, we should check the error that is returned in case it isn't nil.

The New() function returns a pointer to a FuzzyBool rather than a value because we have chosen to make the fuzzy Booleans in this implementation mutable. This means that those methods which modify a fuzzy Boolean (in this example, just one, Set()) must take a pointer receiver, not a value.[*]

---

[*] In fact, we could return a FuzzyBool value and still have a mutable type, as the book's source code's fuzzy_value example illustrates.

A reasonable rule of thumb is to create methods that take receiver values for immutable types, and methods that take pointers for mutable types. (For mutable types, having some methods take values and others take pointers is perfectly possible—but can be inconvenient in practice.) It is also best to use pointers for large struct types (e.g., those with two or more fields), to keep the cost of passing them to a single pointer.

```go
func float32ForValue(value interface{}) (fuzzy float32, err error) {
    switch value := value.(type) { // shadow variable
    case float32:
        fuzzy = value
    case float64:
        fuzzy = float32(value)
    case int:
        fuzzy = float32(value)
    case bool:
        fuzzy = 0
        if value {
            fuzzy = 1
        }
    default:
        return 0, fmt.Errorf("float32ForValue(): %v is not a "+
            "number or Boolean", value)
    }
    if fuzzy < 0 {
        fuzzy = 0
    } else if fuzzy > 1 {
        fuzzy = 1
    }
    return fuzzy, nil
}
```

This unexported helper function is used by the New() and Set() methods to convert a value into a float32 in the range [0.0, 1.0]. Handling the different types is easily accomplished by using a type switch (§5.2.2.2, 197 ◄).

If the function is called with a value of an invalid type we return a non-nil error. This gives the caller responsibility for checking the return value and responding appropriately if an error has occurred. The caller could panic on error and cause the application to crash with a traceback, or it could handle the problem itself. It is often better for low-level functions like this to return an error when they hit a problem because they don't know enough about the program's logic to know how or whether to handle it, and to push the problem up to the caller which should be in a better position to know what to do.

While we consider passing in a value of an invalid type to be a programming error and therefore worthy of returning a non-nil error, we have chosen to treat out-of-range values much more leniently, and simply clamp them to the nearest valid value.

```go
func (fuzzy *FuzzyBool) String() string {
    return fmt.Sprintf("%.0f%%", 100*fuzzy.value)
}
```

This method satisfies the fmt.Stringer interface. This means that fuzzy Booleans will be printed as we have specified, and that a fuzzy Boolean can be passed wherever an fmt.Stringer value is expected.

We have chosen the string representation of fuzzy Booleans to be whole number percentages. (Recall that the "%.0f" string format specifies a floating-point number with no decimal point or decimal digits and the "%%" format specifies a literal % character. String formatting was covered earlier; §3.5, 93 ◄.)

```go
func (fuzzy *FuzzyBool) Set(value interface{}) (err error) {
    fuzzy.value, err = float32ForValue(value)
    return err
}
```

The presence of this method is what makes our fuzzy Booleans mutable. The method is very similar to the New() function, only here we work on an existing *FuzzyBool rather than creating a new one. If the returned error is not nil then the fuzzy Boolean's value will be invalid, so we expect our callers to check the return value.

```go
func (fuzzy *FuzzyBool) Copy() *FuzzyBool {
    return &FuzzyBool{fuzzy.value}
}
```

For custom types that are passed around as pointers, it is often convenient to provide a Copy() method. Here, we simply create a new FuzzyBool, with the same value as that of the receiver, and return a pointer to it. There is no need to do any validation since we know that the receiver's value is valid. This assumes, of course, that the original value had a nil error when it was created with New(), and similarly for any subsequent calls to the Set() method.

```go
func (fuzzy *FuzzyBool) Not() *FuzzyBool {
    return &FuzzyBool{1 - fuzzy.value}
}
```

This is the first of the logical operator methods, and like all the methods, it works on a *FuzzyBool receiver.

There are three sensible ways we could have designed this method. One way would be to have it change the value it is called on and return nothing. Another way is to change the value and also return the value—this is the approach taken by many of the big.Int and big.Rat types' methods in the standard library. This approach means that operations can be chained (e.g., b.Not().Not()). It can also save memory (since values are reused rather than created), but can easily catch us off guard when we forget that the returned value is the same as the one the method is called on—and that it has been changed. The other way is to do what we have done here: Leave the value untouched and return a new fuzzy Boolean whose value is the result of the logical operation. This is easy to understand and use, and supports chaining—but at the price of creating more values. We have taken this last approach with all the fuzzy Boolean logical operator methods.

Incidentally, the fuzzy NOT logic is simple, returning 1.0 for 0.0 and 0.0 for 1.0, 0.75 for 0.25 and 0.25 for 0.75, 0.5 for 0.5, and so on.

```go
func (fuzzy *FuzzyBool) And(first *FuzzyBool,
    rest ...*FuzzyBool) *FuzzyBool {
    minimum := fuzzy.value
    rest = append(rest, first)
    for _, other := range rest {
        if minimum > other.value {
            minimum = other.value
        }
    }
    return &FuzzyBool{minimum}
}
```

The logic for fuzzy AND is to return the minimum of the given fuzzy values. The method's signature guarantees that when the method is called it will be given at least one other *FuzzyBool to work with (first), and will accept zero or more additional ones (rest). The method simply appends the first onto the (possibly empty) rest slice, and then iterates over the slice setting the minimum if its value is bigger than the iteration's current other value. And just like the Not() method, we return a new *FuzzyBool, and leave the fuzzy Boolean the method was called on unchanged.

The logic for fuzzy OR is to return the maximum of the given fuzzy values. We have not shown the Or() method since it is structurally identical to the And() method. The only differences are that the Or() method uses a maximum variable instead of a minimum variable and compares using the < less than operator instead of the > greater than operator.

```go
func (fuzzy *FuzzyBool) Less(other *FuzzyBool) bool {
    return fuzzy.value < other.value
}
```

```
func (fuzzy *FuzzyBool) Equal(other *FuzzyBool) bool {
    return fuzzy.value == other.value
}
```

These two methods allow us to compare fuzzy Booleans in terms of the float32s
they contain; both methods produce bool results.

```
func (fuzzy *FuzzyBool) Bool() bool {
    return fuzzy.value >= .5
}

func (fuzzy *FuzzyBool) Float() float64 {
    return float64(fuzzy.value)
}
```

The fuzzybool.New() construction function can be seen as a conversion function
since given a float32, float64, int, or bool, it produces a *FuzzyBool. These two
methods perform similar conversions going the other way.

The FuzzyBool type provides a complete fuzzy Boolean data type that can be
used like any other custom data type. So, *FuzzyBools may be stored in slices,
and in maps as keys or values or both. Of course, if we use *FuzzyBools as map
keys we will be able to store multiple fuzzy Booleans even if they have the same
value because they will each have a unique address. One solution is to use a
value-based fuzzy Boolean (such as the fuzzy_value example in the book's source
code). Alternatively, we could use a custom collection type that stored pointers
but which uses their values for comparisons: The custom omap.Map type can do
this, providing we supply a suitable less than function (§6.5.3, ➤ 302).

In addition to the fuzzy Boolean type shown in this subsection, the book's examples also include three alternative fuzzy Boolean implementations for comparison: These are not shown in the book or discussed beyond this paragraph. The
first two alternatives are in the files fuzzy_value/fuzzybool/fuzzybool.go and
fuzzy_mutable/fuzzybool/fuzzybool.go—these have exactly the same functionality as the version described in this subsection (in file fuzzy/fuzzybool/fuzzy-
bool.go). The fuzzy_value version works in terms of FuzzyBool values rather than
*FuzzyBools, and the fuzzy_mutable version is based directly on a float32 rather
than on a struct. The fuzzy_mutable's code is slightly longer and trickier than
the struct-based version shown here. The third alternative provides slightly
less functionality because it provides an immutable fuzzy Boolean type. Again,
it is directly based on a float32; this version is in file fuzzy_immutable/fuzzy-
bool/fuzzybool.go. It is the simplest of the three implementations.

6.5.2. Example: Shapes—A Family of Custom Types

When we have a set of related classes—such as shapes—upon which we might want to apply some generic operations (e.g., asking a shape to draw itself), there are two broad approaches we can take to implementing them. The one most likely to be familiar to C++, Java, and Python programmers is to use a hierarchy—in Go's case, of embedded interfaces. However, it is often more convenient and versatile to create independent interfaces that can be freely composed. In this subsection we will show both approaches, the first in file shaper1/ shapes/shapes.go and the second in file shaper2/shapes/shapes.go. (Note that when the packages' types, functions, and methods are the same—which most of them are—we will simply refer to the "shapes package". Naturally, we will distinguish them as the "shaper1 shapes package" or the "shaper2 shapes package" when discussing code that is specific to one of them.)

Figure 6.3 shows an example of what the shapes package can do—in this case it is used to create a white rectangle and to draw on it a circle and some polygons with different numbers of sides and using various colors.

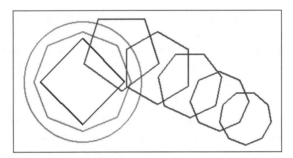

Figure 6.3 *The shaper example's shapes.png file*

The shapes package provides three exported functions for working with images and three types for creating shapes values—two of which are exported. The hierarchical shapes1 shapes package provides three exported interfaces and the compositional shapes2 shapes package provides five exported interfaces. We will begin with the image-related code—the convenience functions—then we will look at the interfaces (in two separate subsubsections), and finally, we will review the concrete shape-related code.

6.5.2.1. Package-Level Convenience Functions

The standard library's image package provides the image.Image interface. This interface specifies three methods: image.Image.ColorModel() to return the image's color model (as a color.Model), image.Image.Bounds() to return the image's bounding box (as an image.Rectangle), and image.Image.At(x, y) which returns the color.Color value for the given pixel. Notice that there is no image.Image method for setting a pixel—even though several image types provide a Set(x, y int, fill color.Color) method. However, the image/draw package provides the draw.Image interface which embeds the image.Image interface and also has a Set() method. The draw.Image interface is fulfilled by the standard library's image.Gray and image.RGBA types, among others.

```
func FilledImage(width, height int, fill color.Color) draw.Image {
    if fill == nil { // We silently treat a nil color as black
        fill = color.Black
    }
    width = saneLength(width)
    height = saneLength(height)
    img := image.NewRGBA(image.Rect(0, 0, width, height))
    draw.Draw(img, img.Bounds(), &image.Uniform{fill}, image.ZP, draw.Src)
    return img
}
```

This is an exported convenience function that creates an image of the given size uniformly filled with the given color.

We begin by silently replacing a nil color with black, and ensuring that both dimensions are sensible. Then we create an image.RGBA value (an image that defines its colors using red, green, blue, and alpha—transparency—values), and return it as a draw.Image, since we are only concerned with what we can do with it, not with what its actual type happens to be.

The draw.Draw() function takes a destination image (of type draw.Image), a rectangle that specifies where the drawing should be done (in this case the entire destination image), a source image to copy from (in this case an infinite-sized image filled with the given color), the point where the destination rectangle to be drawn in should go (image.ZP is the zero point, i.e., point (0, 0)), and how the drawing should be done. Here we have specified draw.Src so the function will simply copy from the source onto the destination. So, the effect we achieve here is to copy the given color to every pixel in the target image. (The draw package also has a draw.DrawMask() function that supports some of the Porter-Duff compositing operations.)

```
var saneLength, saneRadius, saneSides func(int) int

func init() {
    saneLength = makeBoundedIntFunc(1, 4096)
    saneRadius = makeBoundedIntFunc(1, 1024)
    saneSides = makeBoundedIntFunc(3, 60)
}
```

We have defined three unexported variables to hold helper functions all of which take an int and return an int. And we have given the package an init() function in which the variables are assigned suitable anonymous functions.

```go
func makeBoundedIntFunc(minimum, maximum int) func(int) int {
    return func(x int) int {
        valid := x
        switch {
        case x < minimum:
            valid = minimum
        case x > maximum:
            valid = maximum
        }
        if valid != x {
            log.Printf("%s(): replaced %d with %d\n", caller(1), x, valid)
        }
        return valid
    }
}
```

This function returns a function that given a value x, returns x if it is between the minimum and maximum (inclusive), or returns the closest bounding value.

If x is out of range, in addition to returning a valid alternative, we also log the problem. However, we don't want to report the problem as existing in the function created here (i.e., in saneLength(), saneRadius(), or saneSides()), because the problem belongs to their caller. So, instead of logging the name of the function created here, we log the name of the function's caller using a custom caller() function.

```go
func caller(steps int) string {
    name := "?"
    if pc, _, _, ok := runtime.Caller(steps + 1); ok {
        name = filepath.Base(runtime.FuncForPC(pc).Name())
    }
    return name
}
```

The runtime.Caller() function returns information about the functions that have been called and not yet returned in the current goroutine. The int argument says how far (i.e., how many functions) back we want to look. An argument of 0 looks at the current function (i.e., this function, shapes.caller()), and an argument of 1 looks at this function's caller, and so on. We add the 1 so as to start from this function's caller.

We are given four pieces of information by the runtime.Caller() function: the program counter (which we have stored in variable pc), the filename and line number at which the call took place (both of which we have ignored by using blank identifiers), and a Boolean flag (which we have stored in the ok variable) that reports on whether the information could be retrieved.

If we successfully retrieve the program counter we then call the runtime.Func-
ForPC() function which returns a *runtime.Func value and on which we call the
runtime.Func.Name() method to retrieve the name of the called function. The
name is returned like a file path, for example, /home/mark/goeg/src/shaper1/
shapes.FilledRectangle for a function, or /home/mark/goeg/src/shaper1/shapes.
*shape•SetFill for a method. The path is unnecessary for a small project, so
we have stripped it off using the filepath.Base() function. We then return
the name.

For example, if we called the shapes.FilledImage() function and passed it an
out-of-range width or height such as 5 000, the problem will be corrected in
the saneLength() function. In addition, since a problem occurred, a log output
will be produced, in this case saying "shapes.FilledRectangle(): replaced 5000
with 4096". This works because the saneLength() function calls caller() with
an argument of 1, to which caller() adds 1 to produce 2, so caller() goes three
functions up—itself (0), saneLength() (1), and FilledImage() (2).

```
func DrawShapes(img draw.Image, x, y int, shapes ...Shaper) error {
    for _, shape := range shapes {
        if err := shape.Draw(img, x, y); err != nil {
            return err
        }
    }
    return nil
}
```

This is another exported convenience function, and the only one to differ between the two shapes package implementations. The one shown here is from
the hierarchical shapes1 shapes package. The compositional shapes2 shapes package differs only in the function's signature where it accepts Drawers, that is, values which satisfy the Drawer interface (i.e., have a Draw() method), rather than
Shapers which must have Draw(), Fill(), and SetFill() methods. So, in this case,
the compositional approach means that we use a more specific and less demanding argument type (Drawer) than the hierarchical approach requires (Shaper). We
will review these interfaces in the next two subsubsections.

The body and behavior of the function is the same in both cases. The function
takes a draw.Image to draw on, a position (as an x, y coordinate), and zero or more
Shaper (or Drawer) values. Inside the loop each shape is told to draw itself on the
image at the given position. The x, y coordinates are checked in the lower-level
shape-specific Draw() methods and if they are invalid we will get a non-nil error
which we immediately return to the caller.

For Figure 6.3 (289 ◀), we used a modified version of this function that draws
each shape three times, once at the given x, y position, once offset by one pixel
to the right, and once offset one pixel down. This was done to make the lines
thicker for the screenshot.

```go
func SaveImage(img image.Image, filename string) error {
    file, err := os.Create(filename)
    if err != nil {
        return err
    }
    defer file.Close()
    switch strings.ToLower(filepath.Ext(filename)) {
    case ".jpg", ".jpeg":
        return jpeg.Encode(file, img, nil)
    case ".png":
        return png.Encode(file, img)
    }
    return fmt.Errorf("shapes.SaveImage(): '%s' has an unrecognized "+
        "suffix", filename)
}
```

This is the last of the exported convenience functions. Given an image that fulfills the image.Image interface—which includes any that fulfill the draw.Image interface since that embeds an image.Image—the function attempts to save the image to a file with the given name. If the os.Create() call fails (e.g., due to an empty filename or an I/O error), or if the filename has an unrecognized suffix, or if the image encoding fails, the function will return a non-nil error.

At the time of this writing, Go's standard library had support for reading and writing two image file formats: .png (Portable Network Graphics) and .jpg (Joint Photographic Experts Group). Packages that support additional image formats are available from godashboard.appspot.com/project. The jpeg.Encode() function has an extra parameter which can be used to fine-tune how the image is saved—we have passed nil which means that the default settings will be used.

These encoders can panic—for example, if passed a nil image.Image—so if we want to protect the program against our own mistakes we would need to put a deferred function with a call to recover(), either in this function or farther up the call chain (see §5.5.1, 213 ◄). We have opted *not* to add such protection since the test suite (not shown) has sufficient calls of the function for there to be confidence that such a programming error would immediately be triggered and lead to a termination—and therefore would be almost impossible to miss.

Given the draw.Image interface we can specify image values whose individual pixels can be set to colors of our choice. And with the DrawShapes() function we can draw shapes (that fulfill the Shaper—or Drawer—interface) on such an image. We can save images to disk using the SaveImage() function. With these convenience functions in place, what we need is to create the interfaces (e.g., Shaper or Drawer, etc.), and the concrete types and their methods to satisfy the interfaces.

6.5.2.2. A Hierarchy of Embedded Interfaces

Programmers with a conventional inheritance-based object-oriented background are likely to use Go's ability to embed interfaces to create a hierarchy of interfaces. The recommended way is to use the compositional approach which we will cover in the next subsubsection. Here are the interfaces used in the hierarchical shapes1 shapes package.

```go
type Shaper interface {
    Fill() color.Color
    SetFill(fill color.Color)
    Draw(img draw.Image, x, y int) error
}

type CircularShaper interface {
    Shaper // Fill(); SetFill(); Draw()
    Radius() int
    SetRadius(radius int)
}

type RegularPolygonalShaper interface {
    CircularShaper // Fill(); SetFill(); Draw(); Radius(); SetRadius()
    Sides() int
    SetSides(sides int)
}
```

We have created a hierarchy—by embedding, not inheritance—of three interfaces to specify the methods we want our shape values to have.

The Shaper interface defines methods to get and set a fill color of type color. Color and a method for drawing itself onto a draw.Image at a given position. The CircularShaper interface embeds an anonymous Shaper and adds a getter and setter for a radius of type int. Similarly, the RegularPolygonalShaper interface embeds an anonymous CircularShaper (and therefore also a Shaper) and adds a getter and setter for a number of sides of type int.

Although creating hierarchies like this may be familiar—and works—it is probably not the best way to do things in Go. This is because it locks us into a hierarchy when we don't need a hierarchy at all: What we really need is to just say that this particular shape supports some relevant interfaces. This gives us much more flexibility, as we will see in the next subsubsection.

6.5.2.3. Freely Composable Independent Interfaces

For the shapes we mostly want to say what specific things they can do (draw, get/set a fill color, get/set a radius, etc.), with a little bit of genericity. Here are the interfaces in the compositional shapes2 shapes package.

```
type Shaper interface {
    Drawer // Draw()
    Filler // Fill(); SetFill()
}

type Drawer interface {
    Draw(img draw.Image, x, y int) error
}

type Filler interface {
    Fill() color.Color
    SetFill(fill color.Color)
}

type Radiuser interface {
    Radius() int
    SetRadius(radius int)
}

type Sideser interface {
    Sides() int
    SetSides(sides int)
}
```

This package's Shaper interface is a convenient way of specifying shapes generically, that is, shapes which can be drawn and which can get/set a fill color. Each of the other interfaces specifies one very specific behavior (counting getting and setting as one).

Having many independent interfaces is much more flexible than using a hierarchy. For example, we were able to be much more specific about the shapes passed to the DrawShapes() function than was possible using a hierarchy (292 ◀). Also, with no hierarchy to preserve we can add other interfaces much more freely, and, of course, with these more fine-grained interfaces we can compose with them much more readily—as we did to create the Shaper interface.

The two different versions of the shapes package have completely different interfaces (although both have a Shaper interface, its body differs between them). Nonetheless, since interfaces and concrete types are completely separate and independent, these differences have no effect whatsoever on the concrete implementations that fulfill them.

6.5.2.4. Concrete Types and Methods

This is the last subsubsection covering the shapes package; it is here that we will review the concrete implementations that satisfy the interfaces described in the previous two subsubsections.

```
type shape struct{ fill color.Color }

func newShape(fill color.Color) shape {
    if fill == nil { // We silently treat a nil color as black
        fill = color.Black
    }
    return shape{fill}
}

func (shape shape) Fill() color.Color { return shape.fill }

func (shape *shape) SetFill(fill color.Color) {
    if fill == nil { // We silently treat a nil color as black
        fill = color.Black
    }
    shape.fill = fill
}
```

This simple type is unexported so it is only accessible inside the shapes package.
This means that no shape value can be created outside the package.

In the hierarchical shaper1 shapes package this type does not fulfill any of the
interfaces because it does not have a Draw() method. But in the compositional
shaper2 shapes package it fulfills the Filler interface.

In the code as it stands, only the Circle type (which we will cover in a moment)
directly embeds a shape. So, in theory, we could have incorporated the color.Color
value into the Circle type and made the color getter and setter take *Circles
instead of shapes, and eliminated the shape type altogether. However, we prefer
to keep the shape type because it gives us the flexibility to add additional shape
interfaces and types that might be based directly on the shape type (i.e., to have
a color), rather than on the Circle type (e.g., because they don't have a notion of
radius). This flexibility will come in handy in one of the exercises.

```
type Circle struct {
    shape
    radius int
}

func NewCircle(fill color.Color, radius int) *Circle {
    return &Circle{newShape(fill), saneRadius(radius)}
}

func (circle *Circle) Radius() int {
    return circle.radius
}

func (circle *Circle) SetRadius(radius int) {
    circle.radius = saneRadius(radius)
```

```
}
func (circle *Circle) Draw(img draw.Image, x, y int) error {
    // ... ~30 lines elided ...
}
func (circle *Circle) String() string {
    return fmt.Sprintf("circle(fill=%v, radius=%d)", circle.fill,
        circle.radius)
}
```

This is the complete implementation of the Circle type. Although we can create concrete *Circle values, we can pass them around as interfaces, which gives us a lot of flexibility. For example, the DrawShapes() function (292 ◀) accepts Shapers (or Drawers), no matter what their underlying concrete type is.

In the hierarchical shaper1 shapes package this type satisfies the CircularShaper and Shaper interfaces. In the compositional shaper2 shapes package it satisfies the Filler, Radiuser, Drawer, and Shaper interfaces. And in both cases the type also satisfies the fmt.Stringer interface.

Since Go doesn't have constructors and we have unexported fields, we must provide construction functions which must be called explicitly. The Circle's construction function is NewCircle(); later on we will see that the package also has a New() function that can create a value of any of the package's shapes. The saneRadius() helper function returns the given int if it is in a specified range or a sensible value otherwise; we saw it created earlier (290 ◀).

The code for the Draw() method has been elided (although it is in the book's source code), since our concern in this chapter is with creating custom interfaces and types rather than with graphics.

```
type RegularPolygon struct {
    *Circle
    sides int
}
func NewRegularPolygon(fill color.Color, radius,
    sides int) *RegularPolygon {
    return &RegularPolygon{NewCircle(fill, radius), saneSides(sides)}
}
func (polygon *RegularPolygon) Sides() int {
    return polygon.sides
}
func (polygon *RegularPolygon) SetSides(sides int) {
    polygon.sides = saneSides(sides)
}
```

```
func (polygon *RegularPolygon) Draw(img draw.Image, x, y int) error {
    // ... ~55 lines including two helper functions elided ...
}

func (polygon *RegularPolygon) String() string {
    return fmt.Sprintf("polygon(fill=%v, radius=%d, sides=%d)",
        polygon.Fill(), polygon.Radius(), polygon.sides)
}
```

Here is the complete implementation of the RegularPolygon type used to provide regular polygon shapes. This type is very similar to the Circle type, only it has a more complicated Draw() method (whose body has been elided). Since the RegularPolygon embeds a *Circle we have populated that field using the NewCircle() function (which handles the validation). The saneSides() helper function is just like the saneRadius() and saneLength() functions (290 ◄).

In the hierarchical shaper1 shapes package this type satisfies the RegularPolygonalShaper, CircularShaper, Shaper, and fmt.Stringer interfaces. In the compositional shaper2 shapes package it satisfies the Filler, Radiuser, Sideser, Drawer, Shaper, and fmt.Stringer interfaces.

The NewCircle() and NewRegularPolygon() functions allow us to create *Circle and *RegularPolygon values, and since their types fulfill the Shaper and other interfaces, we can pass them around as Shapers or as values of any of the other interfaces that they fulfill. We can call any Shaper method on such values (i.e., Fill(), SetFill(), and Draw()). And if we want to call a non-Shaper method on a Shaper value, we can do so using a type assertion or type switch to access the value as a value of the interface whose method we want to call. We will see an example when we look at the showShapeDetails() functions (➤ 300).

It is easy to imagine that we could create many other shape types, some building on shape, others on Circle or RegularPolygon. Furthermore, there may be situations when we would like to create shapes whose shape was determined at runtime, for example, by using a shape name. For this purpose we can create a factory function, that is, a function which returns shape type values where the specific type of the value returned depends upon an argument.

```
type Option struct {
    Fill   color.Color
    Radius int
}

func New(shape string, option Option) (Shaper, error) {
    sidesForShape := map[string]int{"triangle": 3, "square": 4,
        "pentagon": 5, "hexagon": 6, "heptagon": 7, "octagon": 8,
        "enneagon": 9, "nonagon": 9, "decagon": 10}
    if sides, found := sidesForShape[shape]; found {
```

```
        return NewRegularPolygon(option.Fill, option.Radius, sides), nil
    }
    if shape != "circle" {
        return nil, fmt.Errorf("shapes.New(): invalid shape '%s'", shape)
    }
    return NewCircle(option.Fill, option.Radius), nil
}
```

This factory function requires two arguments: the name of the shape to be created and a custom Option value in which optional shape-specific parameters can be specified. (The use of structs to make functions capable of handling multiple optional arguments was covered in Chapter 5; §5.6.1.3, 222 ◀.) The function returns a shape that fulfills the Shaper interface and nil, or if an invalid shape name is given, nil and an error. (Recall that the Shaper interface differs between the two shapes packages' implementations; §6.5.2.2, 294 ◀ and §6.5.2.3, 294 ◀.) The particular shape created depends on the shape string that is passed. There is no need to validate the color or radius since that is handled by the shapes.shape.SetFill() method and the shapes.saneRadius() function that are ultimately called by the NewRegularPolygon() and NewCircle() methods—and similarly for the sides.

```
polygon := shapes.NewRegularPolygon(color.RGBA{0, 0x7F, 0, 0xFF}, 65, 4)
showShapeDetails(polygon)  ❶
y = 30
for i, radius := range []int{60, 55, 50, 45, 40} {
    polygon.SetRadius(radius)
    polygon.SetSides(i + 5)
    x += radius
    y += height / 8
    if err := shapes.DrawShapes(img, x, y, polygon); err != nil {
        fmt.Println(err)
    }
}
```

This little snippet shows how some of the polygons shown in Figure 6.3 (289 ◀) were created using the DrawShapes() function (292 ◀). The showShapeDetails() function (above, ❶; ➤ 300) is used to print the details of *any* kind of shape. This is possible because the function accepts any value that satisfies the Shaper interface (i.e., any of our shapes), rather than a specific concrete shape type (such as a *Circle or *RegularPolygon).

Since the Shaper interface differs between the two shapes packages there are two different showShapeDetails() implementations. Here is the one for the hierarchical shaper1 version.

Embedding Is Not Inheritance

In this subsection, the shaper example illustrates how to use struct embedding to achieve an inheritance-like effect. This technique may appeal to those porting C++ or Java code to Go (or to those learning Go from a C++ or Java background). However, although this approach works:
The Go way is not to simulate inheritance, but to avoid it altogether.

In the context of the example this would mean having independent structs:

```
type Circle struct {          type RegularPolygon struct {
    color.Color                   color.Color
    Radius int                    Radius int
}                                 Sides int
                              }
```

This still allows us to pass generic shape values—after all, if both shapes have Draw() methods that satisfy a Drawer interface, then both Circles and RegularPolygons can be passed as Drawer values.

Another point to note is that here we have made all the fields exported, with no validation at all. This means that we must validate the fields when they are used, rather than when they are set. Both approaches to validation are sensible: Which is best depends on the circumstances.

The book's shaper3 example uses the structs shown above and has the same functionality as the shaper1 and shaper2 examples shown in this section. However, shaper3 is written in a more Go-like style, with no embedding and doing its validation at the point of use.

```
func showShapeDetails(shape shapes.Shaper) {
    fmt.Print("fill=", shape.Fill(), " ") // All shapes have a fill color
    if shape, ok := shape.(shapes.CircularShaper); ok { // shadow variable
        fmt.Print("radius=", shape.Radius(), " ")
        if shape, ok := shape.(shapes.RegularPolygonalShaper); ok {//shadow
            fmt.Print("sides=", shape.Sides(), " ")
        }
    }
    fmt.Println()
}
```

In the shaper1 shapes package's interface hierarchy, the Shaper interface specifies Fill() and SetFill() methods, so these can be used immediately. But for other methods we must use checked type assertions to see if the shape passed in satisfies the interfaces that have the methods we want to call. Here, for example, we only access the Radius() method if the shape fulfills the CircularShaper interface, and similarly for the `RegularPolygonalShaper`'s `Sides()` method. (Recall that `RegularPolygonalShaper` embeds a `CircularShaper`.)

The `shaper2` version of the `showShapeDetails()` function is similar to the `shaper1` version.

```go
func showShapeDetails(shape shapes.Shaper) {
    fmt.Print("fill=", shape.Fill(), " ") // All shapes have a fill color
    if shape, ok := shape.(shapes.Radiuser); ok { // shadow variable
        fmt.Print("radius=", shape.Radius(), " ")
    }
    if shape, ok := shape.(shapes.Sideser); ok { // shadow variable
        fmt.Print("sides=", shape.Sides(), " ")
    }
    fmt.Println()
}
```

The compositional `shaper2` shapes package has a convenient `Shaper` interface that embeds the `Drawer` and `Filler` interfaces, so we know that the passed-in shape has a `Fill()` method. And unlike `shaper1`'s hierarchical `interface`s, here we are able to use very specific type assertions to access the `Radius()` and `Sides()` methods for shapes that support them.

If new methods or fields are added to `shape`, `Circle`, or `RegularPolygon`, our code will continue to work unchanged. But if we add new methods to any of the `interface`s, then we would have to update the affected shape types to provide the methods or our code would break. A better alternative is to create new `interface`s with the additional methods and embed the existing `interface`s inside them. This won't break any existing code and gives us the option to add or not add the new methods to the existing types, depending on whether we want them to fulfill the new `interface`s as well as the ones they already fulfill.

We recommend using the compositional approach to `interface`s rather than a hierarchical approach. And as for `struct` embedding, we recommend doing things the Go way, that is, having independent `struct`s and not trying to simulate inheritance. Of course, once sufficient Go experience has been gained, such choices can be made on the basis of technical merit rather than to ease translation or out of habit.

In addition to the `shaper1` and `shaper2` examples shown in this subsection, the book's examples include `shaper3` which shows a "purer" Go approach. The `shaper3` version has just one `interface`, `Drawer`, and independent `Circle` and `RegularPolygon` `struct`s (as shown in the sidebar "Embedding Is Not Inheritance", 300 ◄). Also, `shaper3` uses shape values rather than pointers, and does its validation at the point of use. It is worth looking at the `shaper2/shapes/shapes.go` and `shaper3/shapes/shapes.go` files, to compare and contrast the two approaches.

6.5.3. Example: Ordered Map—A Generic Collection Type

This chapter's final example is of a generic ordered map type that stores *key–value* pairs like Go's built-in map type, only with all the pairs stored in key order. The ordered map uses a left-leaning red-black tree so it is very fast, with a lookup time complexity of $O(\log_2 n)$.* By comparison, an unbalanced binary tree's performance can degrade to that of a linked list ($O(n)$) if items are added in order. Balanced trees do not suffer from this defect because they maintain the tree's balance as items are added and removed and thereby preserve their excellent performance characteristics.

Programmers with a background in inheritance-based object orientation (e.g., C++, Java, Python) are likely to want to make the ordered map's keys support the < less than operator or a Less(*other*) bool method. This can easily be done by defining a Lesser interface that requires such a method, and providing tiny wrapper types for int, string, *MyType*, and so on, that implement the method. However, the right way to do this in Go is somewhat different.

For our Go ordered map we will impose no direct constraint on the key type. Instead, we give each map a "less than" function to use for comparing its keys. This means that it doesn't matter whether our keys support the < operator or not—so long as we can provide a suitable less than comparison function for them.

Before looking at the implementation, let's look at some examples of use, starting with the creation and population of an ordered map.

```
words := []string{"Puttering", "About", "in", "a", "Small", "Land"}
wordForWord := omap.NewCaseFoldedKeyed()
for _, word := range words {
    wordForWord.Insert(word, strings.ToUpper(word))
}
```

Our ordered map is in package omap and is of type Map. To create a Map we must use the omap.New() function, or one of the other Map construction functions, such as the omap.NewCaseFoldedKeyed() function we have used here, since the Map's zero value is not usable. This particular construction function creates an empty Map with a predefined less than function that compares string keys case-insensitively, and returns a pointer to it (i.e., a *Map).

---

* Our ordered map implementation is based on the left-leaning red-black trees described by Robert Sedgewick in www.cs.princeton.edu/~rs/talks/LLRB/LLRB.pdf and www.cs.princeton.edu/~rs/talks/LLRB/RedBlack.pdf. At the time of this writing, the Java implementations presented in these papers were incomplete and had some errors, so we used ideas from Lee Stanza's C++ code at www.teach-solaisgames.com/articles/balanced_left_leaning.html to complete our implementation.

Every *key–value* pair is added using the omap.Map.Insert() method which accepts two interface{} values, that is, a key and a value of any types. (However, the key must be of a type that is compatible with the less than function, so in this example keys must be strings.) The Insert() method returns true if a new item was inserted, and false if an item with the given key already existed (in which case that item's value is replaced by the new given value—this is the same behavior as the built-in map type).

```
wordForWord.Do(func(key, value interface{}) {
    fmt.Printf("%v→%v\n", key, value)
})
```

```
a→A
About→ABOUT
in→IN
Land→LAND
Puttering→PUTTERING
Small→SMALL
```

The omap.Map.Do() method takes a function with the signature func(interface{}, interface{}) as argument and calls this function on every item in the ordered map—in key order—and passing in the key and value as the arguments for each call. Here we have used the Do() method to print all of the wordForWord's keys and values.

In addition to inserting items and calling a method on all the map's items, we can also query how many items are in the map, search for items, and delete items.

```
fmt.Println("length before deleting:", wordForWord.Len())
_, containsSmall := wordForWord.Find("small")
fmt.Println("contains small:", containsSmall)
for _, key := range []string{"big", "medium", "small"} {
    fmt.Printf("%t ", wordForWord.Delete(key))
}
_, containsSmall = wordForWord.Find("small")
fmt.Println("\nlength after deleting: ", wordForWord.Len())
fmt.Println("contains small:", containsSmall)
```

```
length before deleting: 6
contains small: true
false false true
length after deleting:  5
contains small: false
```

The omap.Map.Len() method returns the number of items in the ordered map.

The `omap.Map.Find()` method returns the value of the item with the given key
as an `interface{}` and `true`, or `nil` and `false` if there is no such item. The `omap.`
`Map.Delete()` method deletes the item with the given key and returns `true`—or
safely does nothing if there is no such item, and returns `false`.

If we want to store keys of a custom type we can do so by creating the `Map` with
the `omap.New()` function and supplying it with a suitable less than method.

For example, here is an implementation of a very simple custom type.

```go
type Point struct{ X, Y int }

func (point Point) String() string {
    return fmt.Sprintf("(%d, %d)", point.X, point.Y)
}
```

Now we will see how to create an ordered map that stores *Points as keys and
their distance from the origin as values.

In the following snippet we have created an empty `Map` and given it a less than
function for comparing *Point keys. Then we have created a slice of *Points and
populated the map from the points. And finally, we have used the `omap.Map.Do()`
method to print the map's keys and values in key order.

```go
distanceForPoint := omap.New(func(a, b interface{}) bool {
    α, β := a.(*Point), b.(*Point)
    if α.X != β.X {
        return α.X < β.X
    }
    return α.Y < β.Y
})
points := []*Point{{3, 1}, {1, 2}, {2, 3}, {1, 3}, {3, 2}, {2, 1}, {2, 2}}
for _, point := range points {
    distance := math.Hypot(float64(point.X), float64(point.Y))
    distanceForPoint.Insert(point, distance)
}
distanceForPoint.Do(func(key, value interface{}) {
    fmt.Printf("%v → %.2v\n", key, value)
})
```

```
(1, 2) → 2.2
(1, 3) → 3.2
(2, 1) → 2.2
(2, 2) → 2.8
(2, 3) → 3.6
(3, 1) → 3.2
(3, 2) → 3.6
```

Recall from Chapter 4 (155 ◀) that Go is smart enough to allow us to drop inner type names and ampersands when creating slice literals, so here the creation of the points slice is really a shorthand for points := []*Point{&Point{3, 1}, &Point{1, 2}, ... }.

Although not shown, we can use the ordered map Delete(), Find(), and Len() methods on the distanceForPoint map in exactly the same way as we did for the wordForWord map, but using *Point keys for the first two (since the less than function works in terms of *Points, not Points).

Now that we have seen the ordered map in use we will review its implementation. We won't cover the Delete() method's helper method and functions, because some of them are rather tricky and covering them won't really add to our knowledge of Go programming. (All these functions are in the book's source code, of course, in the file qtrac.eu/omap/omap.go.) We will start by looking at the two types used to implement the ordered map (Map and node), and then the construction functions. Then we will look at the Map's methods and some of their helper functions. As is common in Go programming, most methods are quite short with more complicated processing passed on to helper functions.

```
type Map struct {
    root    *node
    less    func(interface{}, interface{}) bool
    length int
}

type node struct {
    key, value  interface{}
    red          bool
    left, right *node
}
```

The ordered map is implemented in terms of two custom struct types. The first struct type is the Map struct which holds the root of the left-leaning red-black tree, a less than function that is used to compare keys, and a length which holds the number of items in the map. This type's fields are all unexported and the less function's zero value is nil, so creating a Map variable will produce an invalid Map. The Map type's documentation explains this and directs users to use one of the omap package's construction functions to create valid Maps.

The second struct type is the node struct which represents a single *key–value* item. In addition to its key and value fields, the node struct has three additional fields needed to implement the tree. The red field of type bool is used to identify whether a node is "red" (true) or "black" (false)—this is used when portions of the tree are rotated to maintain its balance. The left and right fields of type *node hold pointers to a node's left and right subtrees (which can be nil).

The omap package provides several construction functions; here, we will look at the generic omap.New() function and a couple of others.

```
func New(less func(interface{}, interface{}) bool) *Map {
    return &Map{less: less}
}
```

This is the package's generic function for creating an ordered map for any built-in or custom type for which we can provide a suitable less than function.

```
func NewCaseFoldedKeyed() *Map {
    return &Map{less: func(a, b interface{}) bool {
        return strings.ToLower(a.(string)) < strings.ToLower(b.(string))
    }}
}
```

This construction function creates an empty ordered map that has string keys which are compared case-insensitively.

```
func NewIntKeyed() *Map {
    return &Map{less: func(a, b interface{}) bool {
        return a.(int) < b.(int)
    }}
}
```

This construction function creates an empty ordered map that has int keys.

The omap package also has an omap.NewStringKeyed() function for creating an ordered map with case-sensitive string keys (the implementation is almost identical to omap.NewCaseFoldedKeyed() but without the strings.ToLower() calls), and an omap.NewFloat64Keyed() function which is just like the omap.NewIntKeyed() function except that it uses float64s instead of ints.

```
func (m *Map) Insert(key, value interface{}) (inserted bool) {
    m.root, inserted = m.insert(m.root, key, value)
    m.root.red = false
    if inserted {
        m.length++
    }
    return inserted
}
```

This method is structurally typical of many Go methods in that it passes most of its work on to a helper, in this case the unexported insert() method. The tree's root might change as the result of an insertion, either because the tree was empty and now contains a single node which must become the root, or because the insertion resulted in rotations to keep the tree balanced and which involved the root.

The insert() method returns the tree's root whether it changed or not, and also a Boolean. The Boolean is true if a new item was inserted, and in this case we increment the map's length. If the Boolean is false it means that an item with the given key was already in the map, so all that was done was to replace the item's current value with the given value, and the map's length is left unchanged. (We won't explain why nodes are made red or black or why they are rotated. These matters are fully explained in Robert Sedgewick's papers—see the footnote; 302 ◀.)

```go
func (m *Map) insert(root *node, key, value interface{}) (*node, bool) {
    inserted := false
    if root == nil { // If the key was in the tree it would belong here
        return &node{key: key, value: value, red: true}, true
    }
    if isRed(root.left) && isRed(root.right) {
        colorFlip(root)
    }
    if m.less(key, root.key) {
        root.left, inserted = m.insert(root.left, key, value)
    } else if m.less(root.key, key) {
        root.right, inserted = m.insert(root.right, key, value)
    } else { // The key is already in the tree so just replace its value
        root.value = value
    }
    if isRed(root.right) && !isRed(root.left) {
        root = rotateLeft(root)
    }
    if isRed(root.left) && isRed(root.left.left) {
        root = rotateRight(root)
    }
    return root, inserted
}
```

This is a recursive function that traverses the tree to find the place where the given key belongs, and rotates subtrees as necessary to maintain the tree's balance. When the Insert() method calls this method the root that is passed in is the root of the entire tree (or nil if the tree is empty), but on subsequent recursive calls the root is the root of a subtree (which could be nil).

If the new key isn't the same as any existing key the traversal will reach the right place to insert the new key—and this will be a nil leaf. At this point we create and return a new *node to be the leaf and with its own leaves both nil.

We don't have to explicitly initialize the new node's left and right fields (i.e., its leaves) since Go will automatically set them to their zero values (i.e., nil), so we use the struct's *key: value* syntax to initialize just those fields that have nonzero values.

If the new key is the same as an existing key we reuse the existing key's node, and simply replace its value with the new value. (This is the same behavior as the built-in map type.) A consequence of this is that every item in an ordered map has a unique key.

```
func isRed(root *node) bool { return root != nil && root.red }
```

This tiny helper function returns whether the given node is red; it treats nil nodes as black.

```
func colorFlip(root *node) {
    root.red = !root.red
    if root.left != nil {
        root.left.red = !root.left.red
    }
    if root.right != nil {
        root.right.red = !root.right.red
    }
}
```

This helper function flips the colors of the given node and of its non-nil leaves.

```
func rotateLeft(root *node) *node {       func rotateRight(root *node) *node {
    x := root.right                           x := root.left
    root.right = x.left                       root.left = x.right
    x.left = root                             x.right = root
    x.red = root.red                          x.red = root.red
    root.red = true                           root.red = true
    return x                                  return x
}                                         }
```

These functions rotate the root's subtree to maintain the subtree's balance.

```
func (m *Map) Find(key interface{}) (value interface{}, found bool) {
    root := m.root
    for root != nil {
        if m.less(key, root.key) {
            root = root.left
        } else if m.less(root.key, key) {
            root = root.right
        } else {
```

```
            return root.value, true
        }
    }
    return nil, false
}
```

Since this method's implementation is straightforward and uses iteration rather than recursion there is no need to create a helper function.

The Find() method identifies the item to find by comparing for equality the current root's key (as the method traverses the tree), with the given key, using the less() function. This is done by using the logical equivalence $x = y \iff \neg (x < y \lor y < x)$. This is valid for ints, float64s, strings, the custom Point type, and many other types, but is not true for all types. It would be easy to extend the omap.Map type to accept a separate equals function if it were needed.

Notice that we have used named return values although we never explicitly assign to them. Of course, they are assigned to implicitly in the return statements. Naming return values like this can be a useful supplement to a function or method's documentation. Here, for instance, it is obvious from the signature Find(key interface{}) (value interface{}, found bool) what is being returned—it would not be quite so obvious if the signature was Find(key interface{}) (interface{}, bool).

```
func (m *Map) Delete(key interface{}) (deleted bool) {
    if m.root != nil {
        if m.root, deleted = m.remove(m.root, key); m.root != nil {
            m.root.red = false
        }
    }
    if deleted {
        m.length--
    }
    return deleted
}
```

Deleting an item from a left-leaning red-black tree is tricky, so we have passed the work on to an unexported remove() method plus that method's helper functions, none of which are shown. If the ordered map is empty—or if no item in the map has the given key—then Delete() safely does nothing and returns false. If the tree has a single item, and that is the one deleted, then the *omap.Map receiver's root will be set to nil (and the tree will be empty). If a deletion takes place we return true and decrement the map's length.

Incidentally, the remove() method identifies the item to be deleted using the same equality equivalence as the Find() method uses.

```
func (m *Map) Do(function func(interface{}, interface{})) {
    do(m.root, function)
}

func do(root *node, function func(interface{}, interface{})) {
    if root != nil {
        do(root.left, function)
        function(root.key, root.value)
        do(root.right, function)
    }
}
```

The Do() method and its do() helper function are used to traverse all the items in the ordered map—in key order—and call the given function for each item, passing in the item's key and value each time.

```
func (m *Map) Len() int {
    return m.length
}
```

This method simply returns the map's length. The length is incremented and decremented in the omap.Map.Insert() and omap.Map.Delete() methods we have already seen.

This completes our review of the ordered map custom collection type, and brings us to the end of our coverage of object-oriented Go programming.

When it comes to custom types for which any value is valid we can simply create the type (e.g., using a struct) and make the type and its fields exported (starting with uppercase letters), and that is sufficient. (For examples, see the standard library's image.Point and image.Rectangle types.)

For custom types that require validation (e.g., those that are based on structs with one or more fields and which require at least one of the fields to be validated), Go has a particular programming idiom. The fields that must be validated are made unexported (start with a lowercase letter) and we provide getter and setter accessor methods for them.

In the case of types whose zero values are invalid, we make the relevant fields unexported and provide accessor methods. We also document the fact that the zero value is invalid, and provide an exported construction function (typically called New()). The construction function normally returns a pointer to a value of the type with all the fields set to valid values.

We can pass values and pointers to values with exported—and unexported— fields, and in the case of types which satisfy one or more interfaces, we can, of course, pass them as interfaces when this is useful, that is, when we care only about how they behave, not what they are.

Clearly those programmers coming from a more inheritance-based object-oriented background (such as C++, Java, or Python) will need to adapt their thinking. However, the power and convenience of Go's duck typing and `interfaces`, and the lack of painful-to-maintain inheritance hierarchies, make the investment in learning well worthwhile. Go's approach to object-oriented programming works extremely well, providing it is done in the spirit of the Go way.

6.6. Exercises

There are three exercises for this chapter. The first involves the creation of a small but complete custom type whose fields must be validated. The second involves adding new functionality to one of the custom types we discussed in this chapter. The third requires the creation of a small custom collection type. The first two exercises are not difficult; however, the third exercise is quite challenging.

1. Create a new package called `font` (e.g., in `my_font/font.go`). The purpose of the package is to provide values that represent font properties (e.g., a font's family and size). There should be a `New()` function that takes a family and size (both of which must be validated) and returns a `*Font` (with valid unexported fields). Also provide getters and validating setters. For validation, don't allow empty family names and only allow font sizes between 5 and 144 points inclusive: If invalid values are given set valid values (or the previous values for setters), and log the problem. Be sure to provide a method that satisfies the `fmt.Stringer` interface.

   Here is an example of how to create, manipulate, and print a font using the package.

   ```
   titleFont := font.New("serif", 11)
   titleFont.SetFamily("Helvetica")
   titleFont.SetSize(20)
   fmt.Println(titleFont)
   ```
   ```
   {font-family: "Helvetica"; font-size: 20pt;}
   ```

   Once the package is ready, copy the example's `font/font_test.go` file into the `my_font` directory and run `go test` to do some very basic testing.

   A solution is given in `font/font.go`. The entire package is around 50 lines of code. Incidentally, we chose to make the `String()` method return the font's details in CSS (Cascading Style Sheet) style. It would be straightforward, if a little tedious, to extend this package to handle all the CSS font attributes, such as weight, style, and variant.

2. Copy an entire `shaper` example (the hierarchical `shaper1`, the compositional `shaper2`, or the Go-style `shaper3`, whichever you prefer—although we recom-

mend shaper2 or shaper3—including its subdirectory) into a new directory, say, my_shaper. Edit the my_shaper/shaper[123].go file: Delete the imports except for image and shapes, and delete all the statements inside the main() function. Edit the my_shaper/shapes/shapes.go file to add support for a new shape called Rectangle. This shape should have a point of origin and a width and height (all of which the image.Rectangle type provides), a fill color, and a Boolean indicating whether the shape should be filled. Add the Rectangle in the same style as the other shapes, that is, with unexported fields and with an interface (e.g., a hierarchical RectangularShaper or a compositional Rectangler and Filleder), or with no interface and exported fields (in Go style), to specify the type's API. The Draw() method isn't difficult, especially if you use the unexported drawLine() function that is inside the shapes package, and the draw.Draw() function. Remember also to update the New() function so that it can create rectangles—and extend the Option type accordingly.

Once the rectangle has been added, fill in the my_shaper/shaper[123].go file's main() function to create and save an image like that shown in Figure 6.4.

Figure 6.4 *An image created using the* Rectangle *type*

Three solutions are given; a hierarchical one in the shaper_ans1 directory, a compositional one in the shaper_ans2 directory, and a Go-style one in the shaper_ans3 directory. Here is the RectangularShaper interface used in the shaper_ans1 solution:

```
type RectangularShaper interface {
    Shaper // Fill(); SetFill(); Draw()
    Rect() image.Rectangle
    SetRect(image.Rectangle)
    Filled() bool
    SetFilled(bool)
}
```

For the shaper_ans2 solution we have the Rectangler and Filleder interfaces:

```
type Rectangler interface {
    Rect() image.Rectangle
    SetRect(image.Rectangle)
}

type Filleder interface {
    Filled() bool
    SetFilled(bool)
}
```

No new `interface` is needed for the Go-style version.

The code for the concrete `Rectangle` type itself is the same for the hierarchical and compositional approaches and features unexported fields with getters and setters. But for the Go-style version, use exported fields and only validate at the point of use.

```
type Rectangle struct {
    color.Color
    image.Rectangle
    Filled bool
}
```

In `shaper_ans1/shapes/shapes.go`, the `Rectangle` type and its supporting methods are less than 50 lines. The `Option` type needs a couple more lines and the `New()` function five more lines. In `shaper_ans1/shaper1.go`, the new `main()` function is less than 20 lines. It is very similar for the `shaper_ans2` solution's Go files. The `shaper_ans3` solution requires the least extra code.

More ambitious readers might like to take the example further by providing separate fill and outline colors with a `nil` color signifying that the fill or outline should not be drawn, and a non-`nil` color being the color to fill or outline with.

3. Create a custom collection type in package `my_oslice` called `Slice`. This type must implement an ordered slice. Provide several construction functions, for example, `New(func(interface{}, interface{}) bool)`, which accepts a less than function, and some others with predefined less than functions such as `NewStringSlice()` and `NewIntSlice()`. The `*oslice.Slice` type should provide a `Clear()` method to empty the slice, an `Add(interface{})` method for inserting an item into the correct place in the slice, a `Remove(interface{})` bool method for removing the first occurrence of the specified item and which reports if the item was removed, an `Index(interface{})` int method to return the index position of the first occurrence of the specified item (or –1), an `At(int)` `interface{}` method to return the item at the given index position (and which panics if the index is out of range), and a `Len()` int method which reports how many items are in the slice.

```go
func bisectLeft(slice []interface{},
    less func(interface{}, interface{}) bool, x interface{}) int {
    left, right := 0, len(slice)
    for left < right {
        middle := int((left + right) / 2)
        if less(slice[middle], x) {
            left = middle + 1
        } else {
            right = middle
        }
    }
    return left
}
```

The bisectLeft() function is used in the solution and might prove useful. If it returns len(slice), the item isn't in the slice and belongs at the end. Any other value means either that the item is in the slice at the returned position, or that it isn't in the slice but belongs at the returned position.

Some readers might like to copy the oslice/oslice_test.go file to the my_oslice directory to test their solution. A solution is given in oslice/ oslice.go and is less than 100 lines. The Add() method is quite tricky, but the code from Chapter 4's InsertStringSlice() function (158 ◄) should prove helpful.

7 Concurrent Programming

Concurrent programming allows developers to implement parallel algorithms and to write programs that take advantage of multiple processors and multiple cores. The downside is that in most mainstream programming languages (such as C, C++, and Java) it is much harder to write, maintain, and debug concurrent programs than single-threaded programs. Furthermore, it isn't always possible to split up processing to make using multiple threads worthwhile. And in any case, the hoped-for performance benefits are not always achieved due to the overhead of threading itself, or simply because it is much easier to make mistakes in threaded programs.

One solution is to avoid threading altogether. For example, we can pass the burdens on to the operating system by using multiprocessing. However, this has the disadvantages that it leaves us responsible for handling all the inter-process communication ourselves, and usually has more overhead than shared-memory concurrency.

The Go solution is threefold. First, Go provides high-level support for concurrent programming that makes it much easier to do correctly; second, concurrent processing is done in goroutines that are much more lightweight than threads; and third, automatic garbage collection relieves programmers of the sometimes fiendishly complex memory management required by concurrent programs.

Go's built-in high-level API for writing concurrent programs is based on CSP (Communicating Sequential Processes). This means that explicit locking—and all the care required to lock and unlock at the right times—can be avoided, with synchronization achieved by sending and receiving data via thread-safe channels. This greatly simplifies the writing of concurrent programs. And whereas

315

dozens or scores of threads could overburden a typical desktop computer, the same machine could happily cope with hundreds, thousands, or even tens of thousands of goroutines. Go's approach makes it easier for programmers to reason about their concurrent programs in terms of what they want the programs to achieve rather than in terms of locking and other low-level details.

While most other languages have support for very low-level concurrent operations (atomic adds and compare and swaps), and some low-level facilities such as mutexes, no other mainstream language has the kind of built-in high-level concurrency support that Go offers (except, perhaps, as add-on libraries that are not an integral part of the language).

In addition to the high-level concurrency support that is the subject of this chapter, Go also provides the same low-level functionality as other languages provide. At the lowest level the standard library's sync/atomic package provides functions for performing atomic additions and compare and swap operations. These advanced functions are designed to support the implementation of thread-safe synchronization algorithms and data structures—they are not intended for use by application programmers. Go's sync package provides the conventional low-level concurrency primitives: wait conditions and mutexes. These are as high-level as it gets in most other languages, so application programmers are often forced to use them.

Go application programmers are expected to use Go's high-level facilities—channels and goroutines—for concurrent programming. In addition, the sync. Once type can be used to call a function once only, no matter how many times the call is made, and the sync.WaitGroup type provides a high-level synchronization mechanism, as we will see later.

We have already covered the basic syntax and usage of channels and goroutines in Chapter 5 (§5.4, 205 ◄). None of that material is repeated here, although knowledge of it is assumed, so it might be helpful to reread or at least skim that section before continuing.

This chapter begins with an overview of some key concepts in Go concurrent programming. Then the chapter presents five complete working programs that illustrate Go concurrent programming and which between them show some standard patterns of use. The first example shows how to create a pipeline where each section of the pipe executes in its own goroutine to maximize throughput. The second example shows how to split work over a fixed number of goroutines that output their results independently of each other. The third example shows how to create a thread-safe data structure—without a lock or low-level primitive in sight. The fourth example shows how to perform independent pieces of work in a fixed number of goroutines and whose results must be merged together, with three different approaches shown. The fifth example shows how to create a processing-dependent number of goroutines and how to merge the work from these goroutines into a single set of results.

7.1. Key Concepts

In concurrent programming we typically want to split up the processing that needs doing over one or more goroutines (in addition to the main orchestrating goroutine), and either output results as soon as they are computed or gather the results for outputting at the end.

Even with Go's high-level approach to concurrency there are pitfalls that we must avoid. One such pitfall is when the program finishes almost immediately but produces no results. Go programs automatically terminate when the main goroutine terminates—even if other goroutines are processing at the time—so we must be careful to keep the main goroutine alive long enough for all the work to be done.

Another pitfall we must avoid is deadlock. One form of this problem is essentially the opposite of the first pitfall: The main goroutine and all the processing goroutines are alive even though all the work has been done. This is typically due to a failure to report the completion of processing. Another cause of deadlock is when two different goroutines (or threads) are using locks to protect resources and try to acquire the same locks at the same time, as illustrated in Figure 7.1. This kind of deadlock can only occur when locking is used, so is a common risk in other languages but quite rare in Go, since Go applications can avoid the use of locks by using channels.

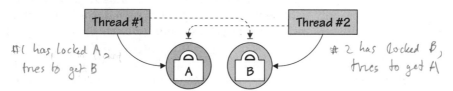

Figure 7.1 *Deadlock: two or more blocked threads trying to acquire each other's locks*

The most common way to avoid premature termination and nontermination is to make the main goroutine wait for a "done" channel to report that the work is finished (as we will see in a moment, and also in §7.2.2, ➤ 326 and §7.2.4, ➤ 341). (It is also possible to use a sentinel value sent as the last "result", but this is rather clumsy compared to the other approaches.)

Another way to avoid the pitfalls is to wait for all the processing goroutines to report that they are finished using a sync.WaitGroup. However, using a sync.WaitGroup itself can cause a deadlock, particularly if the sync.WaitGroup.Wait() call occurs in the main goroutine when all the processing goroutines are blocked (e.g., waiting to receive on a channel). We will see how to use a sync.WaitGroup later (§7.2.5, ➤ 349).

It is still possible to get deadlocks in Go, even if we use only channels, and don't use locks. For example, suppose we have a set of goroutines that can ask each

other to execute functions (e.g., by sending requests to each other). Now if one of
the requested functions does a send to the goroutine in which it is executing—for
example, to pass it some data—we will get a deadlock. This is illustrated in
Figure 7.2. (Later on we will see an example where this kind of deadlock is
possible; ➤ 337 and ➤ 340.)

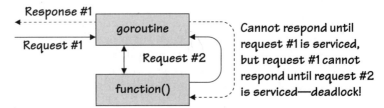

Figure 7.2 *Deadlock: a goroutine that tries to service a request with a request to itself*

Channels provide a lock-free means of communication between concurrently
running goroutines. (Under the hood locks may be used, but these are an implementation detail that we don't have to concern ourselves with.) When a channel
communication takes place, at the moment of communication the sending and
receiving channels (and their respective goroutines) are synchronized.

By default channels are bidirectional, that is, we can send values into them and
we can receive values from them. However, it is quite common for a channel that
is a field in a struct or a channel that is passed as a parameter to be used unidirectionally, that is, only to be sent to, or only to be received from. In such cases
we can express the semantics (and force the compiler to check for us) by specifying the channel's direction. For example, the type chan<- *Type* is a send-only
channel and the type <-chan *Type* is a receive-only channel. We have not used this
syntax in earlier chapters, because it is never required—we can always use chan
Type instead—and there was plenty of other material to learn. But from now on
we will use unidirectional channels wherever they are appropriate, since they
provide additional compile-time checking and are best practice.

Sending values such as bools, ints, and float64s through channels is intrinsically
safe since these are copied, so there is no risk of inadvertent concurrent access
to the same value. Similarly, sending strings is safe since they are immutable.

Sending pointers or references (e.g., slices or maps) through channels is not intrinsically safe since the pointed-to or referred-to value could be changed by
the sending goroutine and by the receiving goroutine at the same time—with
unpredictable results. So, when it comes to pointers and references, we must
make sure that they can only ever be accessed by one goroutine at any one time,
that is, accesses must be serialized. The exception is where the documentation
specifically says it is safe to pass a pointer—for example, the same *regexp.Reg-
exp can safely be used in as many goroutines as we like, because none of the
methods called on the pointed-to value change the value's state.

One way to serialize accesses is to use mutexes. Another way is to apply a policy that a pointer or reference is only ever sent once, and once sent the sender never accesses it again. This leaves the receiver free to access the pointed-to or referred-to value—and to send on the pointer or reference providing both sender and receiver follow the same policy. (We will see an example of using this policy-based approach later; §7.2.4.3, ➤ 347.) A downside of policy-based approaches is that they require discipline. A third way to work safely with pointers or references is to provide them with exported methods that cannot change the pointed-to or referred-to value and unexported methods that can perform changes. Such pointers or references could then be passed around and accessed concurrently through their exported methods, with only one goroutine allowed to use their unexported methods (e.g., inside their own package; packages are covered in Chapter 9).

It is also possible to send interface values—that is, values that meet a particular interface—through channels. Values of read-only interfaces can safely be used in any number of goroutines (unless the documentation says otherwise), but values of interfaces that include methods for changing a value's state must be treated in the same way as pointers, with accesses to them serialized.

For instance, if we create a new image using the `image.NewRGBA()` function we will get an `*image.RGBA`. This type fulfills both the `image.Image` interface (which has only getter methods, and so is read-only) and the `draw.Image` interface (which has all the `image.Image` methods plus a `Set()` method). So, it is safe to pass the same `*image.RGBA` value to as many goroutines as we like—providing we pass it to functions that accept an `image.Image`. (Unfortunately, the safety could be subverted by the receiving method using a type assertion to, say, a `draw.Image` interface, so it is wise to have a policy that disallows such things.) And if we want to use the same `*image.RGBA` value in multiple goroutines that might change it, we should either send it as an `*image.RGBA` or as a `draw.Image`, and in either case we must ensure that all accesses to it are serialized.

One of the simplest ways to use concurrency is to use one goroutine to prepare jobs to do and another goroutine to do the jobs, leaving the main goroutine and some channels to orchestrate everything. For example, here is how we might create a "jobs" channel and a "done" channel in the main goroutine.

```
jobs := make(chan Job)
done := make(chan bool, len(jobList))
```

Here we have created an unbuffered `jobs` channel to pass values of some custom `Job` type. We have also created a buffered `done` channel whose buffer size corresponds to the number of jobs to be done based on the jobs available in variable `jobList` of type `[]Job` (whose initialization isn't shown).

With the channels and job list set up, we can begin.

jobs := make (chan Job)
done := make (chan bool, len (jobList))

```
go func() {                      // fixed slice
    for _, job := range jobList {
        jobs <- job // Blocks waiting for a receive
    }
    close(jobs)    // Sender closes channel
}()
```

This snippet creates the first additional goroutine. It iterates over the jobList slice and sends each job to the jobs channel. Because the channel is unbuffered the goroutine is immediately blocked and will remain blocked until another goroutine tries to receive from the jobs channel. Once all the jobs have been sent to the jobs channel the channel is closed so that receivers will know when there are no more jobs to do.

will ran

The semantics of this snippet are not entirely obvious! The for loop ~~runs~~ to completion and then closes the jobs channel—but this takes place concurrently with any other goroutines in the program. Furthermore, the go statement will return immediately, leaving the code to be executed in its own goroutine—and, of course, with no one trying to receive jobs at this time, the goroutine blocks. So, right after this go statement, the program has two goroutines, the main goroutine which continues to the next statement, and this newly created goroutine that is blocked waiting for another goroutine to do a receive on the jobs channel. Hence, it will take some time before the for loop completes and the channel is closed.

```
go func() {                      // channel
    for job := range jobs { // Blocks waiting for a send ... does job <- chan
        fmt.Println(job) // Do one job
        done <- true
    }
}()
```

This snippet creates the second additional goroutine. This goroutine iterates over the jobs channel, and for each job it receives, it processes the job (here, just prints it), and sends true on the done channel for every job that it completes. (We could just as well send false, since we only care about how many sends are performed on the done channel, not about the actual values sent.)

Just like the first go statement, this statement returns immediately, and the for statement blocks waiting for a send. So, at this point, three concurrent goroutines are executing—the main goroutine and the two additional goroutines, as Figure 7.3 illustrates.

Since we have already got a send waiting (in goroutine #1), that job is received straight away (by goroutine #2) and processed. Meanwhile goroutine #1 is again blocked, this time waiting to send its second job. Once goroutine #2 has finished

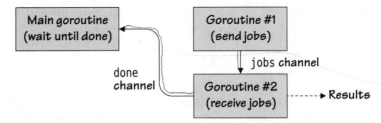

Figure 7.3 *Concurrent independent preparation and processing*

processing it sends to the done channel—this channel is buffered and so doesn't block sends. Control then returns to goroutine #2's for loop and the next job is sent from goroutine #1 and received by goroutine #2, and so on, until all the jobs are done.

```
                    n
for i := 0; i < len(jobList); i++ {          // in main()
    <-done // Blocks waiting for a receive   // terminates when n bools have
}                                            // been received
terminate after this...
```

This final snippet begins execution immediately after the two additional goroutines have been created and begun executing. This code is in the main goroutine and its purpose is to ensure that the main goroutine does not terminate until all the jobs are done.

The for loop iterates as many times as there are jobs, but at each iteration, a receive is done on the done channel (with the result thrown away) to ensure that each iteration is synchronized with the completion of a job. If there is nothing to receive (i.e., because a job is being done but hasn't finished), the receive will block. Once all the jobs are finished the number of sends to and receives from the done channel will equal the number of iterations and the for loop will finally complete. At this point the main goroutine can finish, thus terminating the program, and we can be sure that all the processing has been completed.

Two rules of thumb should normally be applied to channels. First, we need only close a channel if we will be checking that it is closed later on (e.g., using a for ... range loop, a select, or a checked receive using the <- operator). Second, a channel should be closed by the sending goroutine, not by a receiving goroutine. It is perfectly sensible not to close channels that are never checked for being closed—channels are very lightweight, so they don't tie up resources in the same way as, say, an open file.

In this example, the jobs channel is iterated over using a for ... range loop, so we close it—and do this inside the sending goroutine—in accordance with our rules of thumb. On the other hand, we did not bother to close the done channel, since no statement depends on it being closed later on.

This example illustrates a common pattern in Go concurrent programming, although in this particular case using concurrency isn't really a win. Some of the examples that follow in the next section use patterns similar to the one shown here—and also make good use of concurrency.

7.2. Examples

Although Go uses relatively little syntax to provide goroutines and channels (<-, chan, go, select), this is sufficient to implement concurrency in a rich variety of ways. In fact, so many different approaches are possible that is not practical to set forth every possible variation in this chapter. So, instead, we will look at three patterns that are commonly used for concurrent programs—a pipeline, multiple independent concurrent jobs (with and without synchronized results), and multiple inter-dependent concurrent jobs—and see particular ways that these can be realized using Go's concurrency support.

Between them, the examples shown here and the exercises at the end should provide sufficient insight into and practice of concurrent Go programming, that both these and other approaches can be used confidently in new programs.

7.2.1. Example: Filter

This first example is designed to show a particular concurrent programming pattern. The program could easily be adapted to do other work that would benefit from the program's approach to concurrency.

Those with a Unix background may have noticed that Go's channels are reminiscent of Unix pipes (except that channels are bidirectional whereas pipes are unidirectional). Such pipes can be used to create pipelines where one program's output is fed to another program as input, whose output in turn is fed to a third program, and so on. For example, we can get a list of all the Go files in Go's source tree (excluding test files) using the Unix pipeline command find $GOROOT/src -name "*.go" | grep -v test.go. One of the beauties of this approach is that it is easy to extend. For example, we could add | xargs wc -l to get each file listed with a count of the number of lines it contains (plus a total at the end), and add | sort -n to get the files listed in line count order (fewest to most).

Real Unix-style pipelines can be created using the standard library's io.Pipe() function. For example, the Go standard library uses this function to compare images (see file go/src/pkg/image/png/reader_test.go).

In addition to using io.Pipe() to create Unix-style pipelines it is also possible to create pipelines using channels, and it is this latter technique that we will review here.

The filter example program (in file filter/filter.go), accepts some command-line arguments (e.g., to specify minimum and maximum file sizes and acceptable file suffixes) and a list of files, and outputs those files from the list which match

the command-line-given criteria. Here is the body of the program's two-line
main() function.

slice

```
minSize, maxSize, suffixes, files := handleCommandLine()          @
sink(filterSize(minSize, maxSize, filterSuffixes(suffixes, source(files))))
```

325 :last   last-1   last-2   last-3

The handleCommandLine() function (not shown) uses the standard library's flag
package to process command-line arguments. The pipeline works from the
innermost function call (source(files)) to the outermost (sink()). Here is the
same pipeline laid out in an easy-to-understand way.

layout of structure... not actual code

```
channel1 := source(files)
channel2 := filterSuffixes(suffixes, channel1)
channel3 := filterSize(minSize, maxSize, channel2)
sink(channel3)
```

receive-only

The source() function takes a slice of filenames and returns a channel of type   @
chan string that is assigned to the channel1 variable. The source() function sends
each filename in turn to the channel. The two filter functions each take filter
criteria and a chan string, and each return their own chan string. In this example,
the first filter's returned channel is assigned to channel2 and the second to
channel3. The filters iterate over the items in the channel they receive and send
each item that matches their criteria to the channel they have returned. The
sink() function takes a channel and iterates over its items, printing each one.

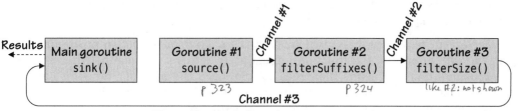

Figure 7.4 *A pipeline of concurrent goroutines*

Figure 7.4 provides a schematic illustration of what is happening. In the case of
the filter program the sink() function executes in the main goroutine and each
pipeline function (e.g., source(), filterSuffixes(), and filterSize()) executes
in its own goroutine. This means that each call to a pipeline function returns
straight away and execution quickly reaches the sink() function. At this point
all the goroutines are executing concurrently, either waiting to send or waiting
to receive until all the files have been processed.

receive only

```
func source(files []string) <-chan string {           @
    out := make(chan string, 1000)     // buffered channel, bidirectional
    go func() {
        for _, filename := range files {    // iterate over slice
```

```
                out <- filename
        }
        close(out)
    }()
    return out
}
```

This function creates a channel for passing filenames. It uses a buffered channel since in tests this improved throughput. (As is often the case we have traded memory for speed.)

Once the output channel has been created we create a goroutine which iterates over the files and sends each one to the channel. When all the files have been sent we close the channel. As usual, the go statement returns immediately, so there may be quite a long gap in time between sending the first item and sending the last item and closing the channel. The send to the channel does not block (at least, not for the first 1000 files—or for however many files there are if fewer than a 1000)—but does block if there are more to send, at least until one or more are received from the channel.

✳ As we noted earlier, by default channels are bidirectional, but we can constrain a channel to be unidirectional. Recall from the previous section that the type chan<- *Type* is a send-only channel and the type <-chan *Type* is a receive-only channel. At the end of the function the bidirectional out channel is returned as a unidirectional receive-only channel so that filenames can be received from it. We could, of course, have returned it as a bidirectional channel, but this way we have better expressed our intentions.

✳ After executing the go statement to start the anonymous function processing in its own goroutine, the function immediately returns the channel that the goroutine's function sends filenames to. So, once the source() function has been called, there are two goroutines executing—the main goroutine and the additional one created in the function.

filter criteria · *channel parm* · *receive-only return*

returns receive only channel

```
func filterSuffixes(suffixes []string, in <-chan string) <-chan string {
    out := make(chan string, cap(in)) // bidirectional initially
    go func() {                        // ← // 1000; out has same capacity as in
        for filename := range in {     // iterate over filenames arriving via in channel
            if len(suffixes) == 0 {
                out <- filename
                continue
            }
            ext := strings.ToLower(filepath.Ext(filename))   // import File/filepath
            for _, suffix := range suffixes {
                if ext == suffix {
                    out <- filename
```

```
                            break
                    }
                }
            }
            close(out)          // When in is closed by sender, arrive here and close out
        }()
        return out
}
```

This is the first of the two filter functions and the only one shown since the filterSize() function is structurally almost the same.

The in channel parameter can be a receive-only channel or a bidirectional channel, but in either case, within the filterSuffixes() function the type declaration ensures that it may only be received from. (And as we know from the source() function's return value, the in channel is, in fact, a receive only channel.) Correspondingly, we have returned the bidirectional out channel as a receive-only channel, just as we did for the source() function. In both cases, we could leave out the <-s and the function would work just the same. However, by including directions we have precisely expressed the semantics we want the function to have—and ensured that the compiler enforces them.

The filterSuffixes() function begins by creating an output channel with a buffer size that is the same size as the incoming channel, so as to maximize throughput. The function then creates a goroutine to do its processing. Inside the goroutine the in channel is iterated over (i.e., each filename is received in turn). If no suffixes have been specified then any suffix is acceptable in which case each filename received is simply sent to the output channel. If there are acceptable suffixes and the filename's lowercased suffix matches any of them, it is sent to the output channel; otherwise it is discarded. (The filepath.Ext() function returns a filename's extension—that is, its suffix—including the leading period; or an empty string for names that have no extension.)

Just like the source() function, once all the processing is finished the output channel is closed—although it may take some time to reach this point. And after the goroutine has been created the output channel is returned so that the next function in the pipeline can receive filenames from it.

At this point three goroutines are running; the main goroutine, the source() function's goroutine, and this function's goroutine. And after the call to filterSize() there will be a fourth goroutine, with all of them working concurrently.

```
                                      , receive-only channel
func sink(in <-chan string) {
    for filename := range in {
        fmt.Println(filename)     // loops when string is received else
    }                             // blocks until the in channel is closed
}                                 // by sender
```

The source() function and the two filter functions do their processing in their own concurrent goroutines, communicating via channels. The sink() function operates in the main goroutine on the last channel that is returned by the other functions, iterating over the filenames that have successfully passed through the filters (if any) and outputting them.

The sink() function's range statement iterates over the receive-only in channel, printing filenames or being blocked until the channel is closed, thus ensuring that the main goroutine does not terminate until all the processing in the other goroutines is done.

Naturally, we could add additional functions to the pipeline, either to filter out filenames or to process the files that had got through the filtering so far, so long as each new function accepted an input channel (the previous function's output channel) and returned its own output channel. And, of course, we could base the channels on a struct rather than a simple string, if we wanted to pass more sophisticated values through the pipeline.

While the pipeline shown in this subsection is a good illustration of a pipeline framework, the particular processing done at each stage is really too little to benefit from the pipeline approach. The kind of pipeline that would benefit from concurrency is one where each stage of the pipeline potentially had a lot of work to do, perhaps with the amount depending on the item being processed, so that as much of the time as possible, every goroutine was busy.

7.2.2. Example: Concurrent Grep

One common concurrent programming pattern is where we have multiple jobs to do, each of which can run to completion independently of the others. For example, the Go standard library's net/http package's HTTP server follows this pattern, with each request being served concurrently in its own goroutine and with no communication between the goroutines. In this subsection we will illustrate one approach to implementing this pattern using variants of a cgrep "concurrent grep" program as an example.

Unlike the standard library's HTTP server, the cgrep examples spread their processing over a fixed number of goroutines, rather than creating them ad hoc. (We will see an example that creates a variable number of goroutines later; §7.2.5, ➤ 349.)

The cgrep programs take a regular expression and a list of files on the command line and output the filename, line number, and every line in every file where the regular expression matches. If there are no matches, there is no output at all.

The cgrep1 program (in file cgrep1/cgrep.go) uses three channels, two of which are used for sending and receiving structs.

```
type Job struct {
    filename string        // name of file to be searched for match
    results  chan<- Result // channel where result (if any) is to be sent   Send-only
}            send-only channel                                              channel
```

This `struct` is used to specify each job: the name of the file to be processed and the channel where any result is to be sent. We could have defined the results field as `results chan Result`, but since we only want Job values to send Results into the channel and never receive from it, we have specified that the channel is a unidirectional send-only channel.

```
type Result struct {
    filename string
    lino     int
    line     string
}
```

Each result is encapsulated by a value of this `struct`'s type, and contains the filename, the line number (`lino`), and the matching line.

```
func main() {
    runtime.GOMAXPROCS(runtime.NumCPU()) // Use all the machine's cores    *
    if len(os.Args) < 3 || os.Args[1] == "-h" || os.Args[1] == "--help" {
        fmt.Printf("usage: %s <regexp> <files>\n",
            filepath.Base(os.Args[0]))
        os.Exit(1)
    }                                           re to compile
    if lineRx, err := regexp.Compile(os.Args[1]); err != nil {
        log.Fatalf("invalid regexp: %s\n", err)
    } else {
        grep(lineRx, commandLineFiles(os.Args[2:]))        176
    }           compiled re    files to search
}           328: orchestrate the work
```

The program's `main()` function's first statement tells the Go runtime system to use as many processors (cores) as the system has available. Calling `runtime.GO-` ✳ `MAXPROCS(0)` returns the number of processors and changes nothing; calling it with a positive number sets the number of processors the Go runtime should use. The `runtime.NumCPU()` function returns how many logical processors/cores the machine has.* We put this line at the start of most concurrent Go programs, but eventually it will be redundant because Go's runtime system will become smart enough to automatically adapt to the machine it is running on.

---

*Some processors claim to have more cores than they really have; see en.wikipedia.org/wiki/Hyper-threading.

The main() function handles the command-line arguments (a regular expression and a list of files) and calls the grep() function to do—or rather, to orchestrate—the work. (We saw the custom commandLineFiles() function in an earlier chapter; 176 ◀.)

The lineRx (of type *regexp.Regexp; §3.6.5, 120 ◀) that is created here is passed to the grep() function and will eventually be shared by all the worker goroutines. This should be a cause of concern since, in general, we must assume that any shared pointed-to value is not thread-safe. In such cases we must provide the safety ourselves, for example, by using a mutex. Alternatively, we could sacrifice a little bit of memory and provide one value (e.g., one regexp) per worker goroutine rather than share a single value. Fortunately, in the specific case of *regexp.Regexp, Go's documentation says that the pointed-to value is thread-safe. This means that it is safe to share a *regexp.Regexp with as many goroutines as need to use it.

```
var workers = runtime.NumCPU()

func grep(lineRx *regexp.Regexp, filenames []string) {
    jobs := make(chan Job, workers)    // workers is a count of CPU's
    results := make(chan Result, minimum(1000, len(filenames)))
    done := make(chan struct{}, workers)

    go addJobs(jobs, filenames, results) // Executes in its own goroutine
    for i := 0; i < workers; i++ {
        go doJobs(done, lineRx, jobs) // Each executes in its own goroutine
    }
    go awaitCompletion(done, results) // Executes in its own goroutine
    processResults(results)           // Blocks until the work is done
}
```

This function creates the three bidirectional channels needed by the program. The jobs are spread over as many worker goroutines as the number of processors the machine has, so we make the jobs and done channels' buffer sizes this number to minimize needless blocking. (Of course, it would be easy to add a command-line option to let the user specify how many worker goroutines to use, regardless of the number of processors.) For the results channel we use a much larger buffer, just as we did for the previous subsection's filter example, and using a custom minimum() function (not shown; see §5.6.1.2, 221 ◀ for possible implementations, or the cgrep.go source code for the one used here).

Instead of making the done channel's type chan bool and not caring whether true or false is sent, since all that matters is *whether* something is sent, we have made the channel's type chan struct{} (i.e., an empty struct) to more clearly express our semantics. The only thing we can send on a channel of this type is an empty struct value (struct{}{}), which is just what we need to signify a send where the value doesn't matter.

arrows show channels, not invocations

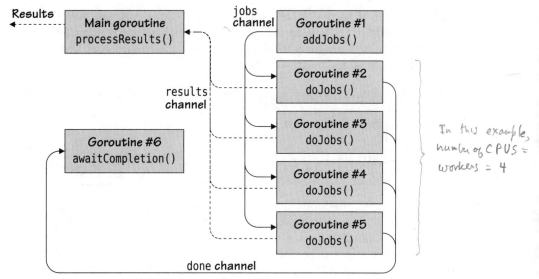

In this example, number of CPUs = workers = 4

Figure 7.5 *Multiple independent concurrent jobs*

With the channels in place we call the addJobs() function to start adding jobs to
the jobs channel—this function does its work in a goroutine. Next we call the
doJobs() function to perform the actual work: In fact, we call the function four
times, so we get four separate executions, each doing their work in their own
goroutine. Then we call the awaitCompletion() function which waits—in its own
goroutine—for all the work to be done and then closes the results channel. Finally, we call the processResults() function which executes in the main goroutine. This function processes results received from the results channel, blocking
when no results are available, and finishing only when all the results have been
received. Figure 7.5 shows a schematic view of the program's concurrency pattern.

```
                send-only                              send-only
func addJobs(jobs chan<- Job, filenames []string, results chan<- Result) {
    for _, filename := range filenames {
        jobs <- Job{filename, results}   // put Job struct on channel.
    }                                    // Initially, 4 jobs are put immediately
    close(jobs)
}
```

This function sends every filename to the jobs channel (one by one) as a Job
value. The jobs channel has a buffer size of four (to match the number of worker
goroutines), so the first four jobs are added immediately and then the goroutine
in which this function is executed is blocked waiting for a job to be received to
free up room in the jobs channel to send another job. Once all the jobs have been
sent—which will depend on how many filenames are to be processed and how
long the processing takes—the jobs channel is finally closed.

Although both of the actual channels passed into the function are bidirectional, we have specified them both to be unidirectional send-only channels since that is how the jobs channel is used inside the function and how the Job.results channel is defined in the Job struct.

send-only   *recv-only*

```
func doJobs(done chan<- struct{}, lineRx *regexp.Regexp, jobs <-chan Job) {
    for job := range jobs {
        job.Do(lineRx)
    }
    done <- struct{}{}    // When this go routine (one of 4) has no more word
}                         // write an empty struct to the done channel
```

333

each in 1 of 4 separate goroutines

This function is called four times ~~in four separate goroutines~~, so there are four invocations to share the work. Each invocation iterates over the same shared jobs channel (declared as a receive-only channel), and each is blocked (i.e., blocks the goroutine it is executing in) until a job becomes available for it to receive. For each job that an invocation gets to do, the function calls the job's Job.Do() method (which we will review further on). When an invocation runs out of jobs it signifies that it has finished by sending an empty struct to the done channel (which is declared as a send-only channel).

Incidentally, it is a Go convention that functions that have channel parameters have the destination channels first, followed by the source channels.

```
func awaitCompletion(done <-chan struct{}, results chan Result) {
    for i := 0; i < workers; i++ {
        <-done
    }
    close(results)
}
```

This function (along with the processResults() function) ensures that the main goroutine waits until all the processing is done before terminating, thus avoiding the pitfalls mentioned in the previous section (§7.1, 317 ◄). It is executed in its own goroutine and waits for as many receives on the done channel as there are workers—blocking its goroutine while it waits. Once the loop terminates the results channel is closed so that the receiver will know when it has received the last result. Note that we cannot pass the results channel as a receive-only channel (<-chan Result), since Go disallows closing such channels. We don't bother closing the done channel since we never use it in a context where it is checked for being closed.

```
func processResults(results <-chan Result) {
    for result := range results {
        fmt.Printf("%s:%d:%s\n", result.filename, result.lino, result.line)
```

```
        }
}
```

This function executes in the main goroutine, iterating over the results channel —or blocking waiting for results. Once all the results have been received and processed (i.e., printed), the loop will finish, the function will return, and the program will terminate.

Go's concurrency support is so flexible that the approach used here for waiting for the jobs to be done, closing the channels, and outputting the results can be done in various other ways. For example, the cgrep2 program (in file cgrep2/cgrep.go) is a variation on the cgrep1 program discussed in this subsection which has no awaitCompletion() or processResults() functions, but instead has a single waitAndProcessResults() function.

in cgrep2

```go
func waitAndProcessResults(done <-chan struct{}, results <-chan Result) {
    for working := workers; working > 0; {
        select { // Blocking
        case result := <-results:
            fmt.Printf("%s:%d:%s\n", result.filename, result.lino,
                result.line)
        case <-done:
            working--
        }
    }
DONE:
    for {
        select { // Nonblocking
        case result := <-results:
            fmt.Printf("%s:%d:%s\n", result.filename, result.lino,
                result.line)
        default:
            break DONE
        }
    }
}
```

The function begins with a for loop that will execute so long as there are active worker goroutines. Each time the for loop's select is executed, it blocks waiting to receive a result or a done value. (If we had used a nonblocking select, i.e., one with a default case, we would have effectively created a CPU-wasting spin-lock.) The for loop ends when there are no more active worker goroutines, that is, after all the workers have sent a value to the done channel.

Once all the workers have finished, we start a second for loop. Inside this loop we use a nonblocking select. If the results channel has any unprocessed results left, the first case matches, a result is output, and then the for loop executes the select statement again. This repeats until all the unprocessed results have been output. But as soon as there is no result to receive (which could be straight away if the results channel is empty when the for loop is entered), we break to the DONE label. (A bare break is not sufficient since that would only break out of the select statement.) This second for loop isn't CPU-wasting because at each iteration either there is a result to output or we are finished, so there is no needless waiting.

For this particular example the waitAndProcessResults() function is longer and more complicated than the original code's awaitCompletion() and processResults() functions. However, using select statements can be beneficial when there are several different channels to handle. For example, we could stop processing after a specified amount of time has passed even if the results are incomplete at that point, by using a select statement.

Here is our third and final variation, cgrep3 (in file cgrep3/cgrep.go).

```go
func waitAndProcessResults(timeout int64, done <-chan struct{},
    results <-chan Result) {
    finish := time.After(time.Duration(timeout))
    for working := workers; working > 0; {
        select { // Blocking
        case result := <-results:
            fmt.Printf("%s:%d:%s\n", result.filename, result.lino,
                result.line)
        case <-finish:
            fmt.Println("timed out")
            return // Time's up so finish with what results there were
        case <-done:
            working--
        }
    }
    for {
        select { // Nonblocking
        case result := <-results:
            fmt.Printf("%s:%d:%s\n", result.filename, result.lino,
                result.line)
        case <-finish:
            fmt.Println("timed out")
            return // Time's up so finish with what results there were
        default:
            return
        }
    }
}
```

This is a variation of cgrep2, the difference being that we pass in a timeout value. The time.After() function takes a time.Duration value (essentially a number of nanoseconds), and returns a channel on which it returns the current time after *at least* time.Duration nanoseconds have passed. Here, we have assigned the returned channel to the finish variable and include a receive case for it in both for loops' select statements. If we get a timeout (i.e., if the finish channel sends a value), we return from the function and the program finishes, even if work is still being done.

If all the results are gathered before the timeout occurs (i.e., all the workers are done), the first for loop is terminated and the second for loop is started the same as for the cgrep2 example. The only differences here are that instead of breaking out of the second for loop, we have simply done a return from the second select's default case; and we have included a timeout case.

Now that we have seen how the concurrency is handled, we will finish our coverage of the cgrep examples by reviewing how each job is processed.

```go
func (job Job) Do(lineRx *regexp.Regexp) {
    file, err := os.Open(job.filename)
    if err != nil {
        log.Printf("error: %s\n", err)
        return
    }
    defer file.Close()
    reader := bufio.NewReader(file)
    for lino := 1; ; lino++ {
        line, err := reader.ReadBytes('\n')
        line = bytes.TrimRight(line, "\n\r")
        if lineRx.Match(line) {
            job.results <- Result{job.filename, lino, string(line)}
        }
        if err != nil {
            if err != io.EOF {
                log.Printf("error:%d: %s\n", lino, err)
            }
            break
        }
    }
}
```

string from bytes

struct

This method is used to process each file. It is passed a *regexp.Regexp, a pointer which—unusually for a pointer—is thread-safe, so it doesn't matter how many different goroutines make use of it. Practically all of the function should be familiar by now: We open the file for reading, handle any error, and if there is no error we defer closing the file. Then we create a buffered reader to make it easy to iterate over the file's contents line by line. Whenever we get a matching line we send a `Result` value to the `results` channel: The send will block if the `results` channel's buffer is full. Any file that is processed could produce any number of results, including zero if none of the file's lines match the regexp.

As is common when processing a text file in Go, if an error occurs when reading a line we handle it *after* working on the line. If the `bufio.Reader.ReadBytes()` method encounters an error (including end of file), it returns any bytes read prior to the error along with the error. Sometimes the very last line of a text file doesn't end with a newline, so to make sure that we process the very last line (whether or not it ends in a newline), we handle the error after processing the line. The disadvantage of handling the error afterward is that if the regexp can match an empty string and we get a non-`nil` not-`io.EOF` error, we will get a spurious match. (This can be worked around, of course.)

The `bufio.Reader.ReadBytes()` method returns the bytes up to and including the specified byte (or up to the end of the file if the specified byte isn't present). We don't want the newline, so we remove it using the `bytes.TrimRight()` method which removes from the right of the given line, the given character or characters. (This is just like the `strings.TrimRight()` function; 109 ◄.) To make our program work cross-platform we trim both newline and carriage return characters.

Another small detail to note is that we read the lines as byte slices and do the matching using the `regexp.Regexp.Match()` method rather than `regexp.Regexp.MatchString()`. So we only do the (very cheap) conversion from []byte to `string` for matching lines. Also, we count line numbers from one rather than zero since that is conventional.

A particularly nice aspect of the `cgrep` programs' design is that their concurrency frameworks are both simple and separate from the actual processing (which is done by the `Job.Do()` method), with the only connection between these two aspects being the `results` channel. This separation of concerns is common in concurrent Go programs and compares very favorably with the use of lower-level concurrency constructs (such as mutexes) where the locking and unlocking code is often needed throughout the program and can obscure and complicate the program's logic.

7.2.3. Example: Thread-Safe Map

Go's `sync` and `sync/atomic` packages provide the low-level operations needed to create concurrent algorithms and data structures. However, it is also possible to take an existing data structure—such as a map or slice (or an `omap.Map`; §6.5.3, 302 ◄)—and make it thread-safe by ensuring that all accesses are serialized using Go's high-level channels.

In this subsection we will develop a thread-safe map that has `string` keys and `interface{}` values (i.e., *any* values) and that can safely be shared by as many goroutines as we like—and without a lock in sight. (Of course, if we store and retrieve pointer or reference values, they must be treated as read-only or accesses to them must be serialized.) The thread-safe map is in file safemap/safemap.go and consists of an exported SafeMap interface that specifies the methods that the safe map supports, and an unexported safeMap concrete type that fulfills the interface. We will see the safe map in action in the next subsection (§7.2.4, ➤ 341).

The safe map is implemented by executing an unexported method that captures a map inside a goroutine. The only way to access the map is via channels, and this in itself is sufficient to ensure that all map accesses are serialized. The method runs an infinite loop on an incoming channel that blocks waiting for commands (i.e., "insert this", "delete that", etc.).

We will begin by looking at the SafeMap interface, then at the safeMap type's exported methods, then at the safemap package's New() function, and finally at the unexported safeMap.run() method.

```go
type SafeMap interface {
    Insert(string, interface{})
    Delete(string)
    Find(string) (interface{}, bool)
    Len() int
    Update(string, UpdateFunc)
    Close() map[string]interface{}
}

type UpdateFunc func(interface{}, bool) interface{}
```

All these methods are provided by the safeMap type. (We discussed the pattern of having an exported interface and an unexported concrete type in the previous chapter.)

The UpdateFunc type makes it convenient to specify the signature of an update function: We will discuss this when we cover the Update() method further on.

```go
type safeMap chan commandData

type commandData struct {
    action  commandAction
    key     string
    value   interface{}
    result  chan<- interface{}
    data    chan<- map[string]interface{}
    updater UpdateFunc
}

type commandAction int
```

```
const (
    remove commandAction = iota
    end
    find
    insert
    length
    update
)
```

The `safeMap` type is based on a channel that can send and receive values of the custom `commandData` type. Each `commandData` value specifies the `action` that is to be taken and also the data necessary to perform the action—for example, most of the methods require a `key` to identify which item to work on. We will see all of the fields in use as we review the `safeMap`'s methods.

Notice that both the `result` and `data` channels are declared as unidirectional send-only channels; in other words, the safe map itself can send values to them, but cannot receive from them. As we will see, the methods that create these channels create them as bidirectional channels and so these channels are able to receive whatever the safe map sends to them.

```
func (sm safeMap) Insert(key string, value interface{}) {
    sm <- commandData{action: insert, key: key, value: value}
}
```

This method is the safe map equivalent of *m[key] = value* where *m* is a map[string] interface{}. It creates a `commandData` value with the `insert` action and with the given `key` and `value` and sends the command to the safe map—which as we have just seen is a type based on a `chan commandData`. (We covered creating `struct`s with some values initialized and the others set to their zero values by Go earlier; §6.4, 275 ◄.)

When we review the `safemap` package's `New()` function we will see that the `safeMap` returned by the `New()` function (as a `SafeMap`) is associated with a goroutine. The `safeMap.run()` method is executed in the goroutine, and is a closure which has captured the `safeMap` channel. The method also contains the underlying `map` that is used to store the safe map's items, and has a `for` loop which iterates over the `safeMap` channel and that performs each command it receives from the channel on the underlying `map`.

```
func (sm safeMap) Delete(key string) {
    sm <- commandData{action: remove, key: key}
}
```

This method tells the safe map to delete the item with the given key—or to safely do nothing.

```
type findResult struct {
    value interface{}
    found bool
}

func (sm safeMap) Find(key string) (value interface{}, found bool) {
    reply := make(chan interface{})
    sm <- commandData{action: find, key: key, result: reply}
    result := (<-reply).(findResult)
    return result.value, result.found
}
```

The safeMap.Find() method creates its own reply channel so that it can receive
a response from the safe map—which may only send to the reply channel—and
then sends a find command with the given key and with its own reply channel to
the safe map. Since none of the channels are buffered, when we send a command
the send is blocked until no other goroutines are sending to the safe map. Once
the command has been sent we immediately receive back the reply (which for
a find command comes packaged up as a findResult struct), whose constituents
we return to the caller. Incidentally, the use of names for the return values is
purely to make their purpose obvious.

```
func (sm safeMap) Len() int {
    reply := make(chan interface{})
    sm <- commandData{action: length, result: reply}
    return (<-reply).(int)
}
```

This method has a similar structure to the Find() method in that it creates and
sends its own reply channel and passes on the received reply to its caller.

```
func (sm safeMap) Update(key string, updater UpdateFunc) {
    sm <- commandData{action: update, key: key, updater: updater}
}
```

This method seems somewhat incongruous with its unusual signature whose
second argument is of type func(interface{}, bool) interface{} (335 ◄). The
method sends an update command with the given key and with an updater
function to the safe map. Once the command is received the updater function
is called with the value of the item with the given key (or nil if there is no such
item) and a bool indicating whether the item exists. The item's value is set to
the updater function's return value (with a new item with the given key and the
returned value being created if necessary).

It is important to note that if the updater function calls a safeMap method, then we will get a deadlock! We will explain why when we cover the safemap.safe-Map.run() method further on.

But why do we need this strange method, and how do we use it?

When it comes to inserting, deleting, or finding items from the safe map, we can use the Insert(), Delete(), and Find() methods perfectly well. But what happens when we want to update an existing item? For example, what if we are using the map to keep the prices of various parts and want to increase the price of a part by 5%? With a normal map we can simply write m[key] *= 1.05, knowing that thanks to Go's automatic zero-value setting, if an item with the given *key* exists its value will be incremented by 5%, and otherwise a new item with the *key* will be created with a value of zero. Here is how we might try to achieve the same thing using a safe map that holds float64 values.

```go
if price, found := priceMap.Find(part); found { // WRONG!
    priceMap.Insert(part, price.(float64)*1.05)
}
```

The problem with the code shown here is that it is possible that one or more other goroutines sharing the same priceMap could change the map in between the Find() and Insert() calls shown here, so there is no guarantee that at the time of the Insert() the price we are inserting really is exactly 5% more than the original price.

What we need to do is an *atomic* update, that is, to retrieve and update the value as a single uninterruptible operation. This is what the Update() method allows us to do.

```go
priceMap.Update(part, func(price interface{}, found bool) interface{} {
    if found {
        return price.(float64) * 1.05
    }
    return 0.0
})
```

This code snippet shows how to do an atomic update. If there is no item with the given key a new item with a value of 0.0 will be created; otherwise the existing item's value will be incremented by 5%. Since this update takes place in the safe map's goroutine in response to an update command, no other command (e.g., from another goroutine) can be executed in the middle.

```go
func (sm safeMap) Close() map[string]interface{} {
    reply := make(chan map[string]interface{})
    sm <- commandData{action: end, data: reply}
```

```
      return <-reply
}
```

The Close() method works in a similar way to the Find() and Len() methods, only it serves two different purposes. First, it closes the safeMap channel (inside the safeMap.run() method), so that no further updates can take place. This will cause the for ... range loop in the safeMap.run() method to terminate and will therefore free up the goroutine in which it is executing for garbage collection. Second, it returns the underlying map[string]interface{} which the caller can keep or ignore. The Close() method can only ever be called once per safe map, no matter how many goroutines are accessing the safe map, and once called no other method can be called. This means that if we keep the returned map we can safely access it just like a normal map (i.e., in a single goroutine).

We have now completed our review of the safeMap's exported methods. The last things we need to look at are the safemap package's New() function in which a safeMap is created and returned as a SafeMap for use outside the package, and the safeMap.run() method which captures the channel, provides the map[string] interface{} to store the data, and handles all the communications.

```
func New() SafeMap {
    sm := make(safeMap) // type safeMap chan commandData
    go sm.run()
    return sm
}
```

The safeMap is of type chan commandData, so we must use the built-in make() function to create the channel and return a reference to it. Once we have the safe map we call its unexported run() method to create the map used for storage and to receive commands. The run() method is executed in its own goroutine, and as usual the go statement returns immediately. At the end, the function returns the safeMap as a SafeMap interface to the New() function's caller.

```
func (sm safeMap) run() {
    store := make(map[string]interface{})
    for command := range sm {
        switch command.action {
        case insert:
            store[command.key] = command.value
        case remove:
            delete(store, command.key)
        case find:
            value, found := store[command.key]
            command.result <- findResult{value, found}
        case length:
```

```
              command.result <- len(store)
        case update:
              value, found := store[command.key]
              store[command.key] = command.updater(value, found)
        case end:
              close(sm)
              command.data <- store
        }
    }
}
```

Once the storage map is created, the run() method starts an effectively infinite loop that iterates over the safe map channel, blocking if there is no command to receive.

Since the store is no more than an ordinary map, all the actions that correspond to each command that is received are straightforward to understand. One slightly tricky case is update where the item's value is set to the return value of the command.updater() function (as we saw earlier; 337 ◄). The end case corresponds to a Close() call; this first closes the safe map channel to prevent any further commands being received, and then sends the storage map back to the caller.

Note that if the command.updater() function were to call a safeMap method we will get a deadlock. This is because the update case cannot finish until the command.updater() function returns, but if the function has called a safeMap method, that call will be blocked waiting to be processed until the update case has finished, so neither will be able to finish. This kind of deadlock was illustrated earlier in Figure 7.2 (318 ◄).

Clearly, there is a certain amount of overhead using a safe map compared with an ordinary map. Each command requires the creation of a commandData struct and for this to be sent through a channel, with sends from however many goroutines we create to access the safe map being automatically serialized under the hood by Go. One alternative is to use an ordinary map but protect accesses to it with a sync.Mutex or a sync.RWMutex. Another alternative is to create a custom thread-safe data structure such as those described in the literature (e.g., see *The Art of Multiprocessor Programming* in Appendix C, ➤ 441). Another alternative is to keep goroutine-specific maps so that no synchronization is needed at all—and then to just merge the maps at the end. Nonetheless, the safe map described here is easy to use and may prove sufficient for many purposes. We will see the safe map in action in the next subsection, along with a couple of the alternative approaches for comparison.

7.2.4. Example: Apache Report

A frequent requirement in concurrent programs is for the concurrent processing
to update a shared data structure. One common solution is to use a mutex to
serialize accesses to the data structure. In Go, we can either use a mutex or use
channels to serialize accesses. In this subsection we will begin by showing an
approach that uses channels and the generic safe map developed in the previous
subsection. Then we will look at how to achieve the same thing using a shared
map protected by a mutex. And finally, we will review how to use local maps that
are independent and therefore don't need serialized accesses so as to maximize
throughput, with channels used to serialize the updating of a common map at
the end.

The apachereport programs all do the same thing: They read an Apache web
server's access.log file specified on the command line and output the number
of accesses to each unique HTML page that the log has recorded. These log
files can easily grow huge, so we have used one separate goroutine to read lines
from the file and three additional goroutines to share the processing of the lines.
Each HTML page must be added to a map with a count of 1 the first time it is
seen, and this count must be incremented each time the page is seen again. So,
although multiple goroutines are independently processing lines from the log
file, they must all update the same map. Each version of the program handles
the updating of the map in a different way.

7.2.4.1. Synchronizing with a Shared Thread-Safe Map

In this subsubsection we will review the apachereport1 program (in file apachere-
port1/apachereport.go). This program uses the safe map developed in the previous section to provide a shared thread-safe map. The program's concurrency
structure is illustrated in Figure 7.6 (➤ 342).

In the figure, goroutine #2 is used to populate the work channel with lines from
the log file and goroutines #3 to #5 process each line and update the shared
safeMap. The operations on the safeMap itself take place in yet another goroutine,
so the program uses six goroutines in total.

```
var workers = runtime.NumCPU()

func main() {
    runtime.GOMAXPROCS(runtime.NumCPU()) // Use all the machine's cores
    if len(os.Args) != 2 || os.Args[1] == "-h" || os.Args[1] == "--help" {
        fmt.Printf("usage: %s <file.log>\n", filepath.Base(os.Args[0]))
        os.Exit(1)
    }
    lines := make(chan string, workers*4)
    done := make(chan struct{}, workers)
```

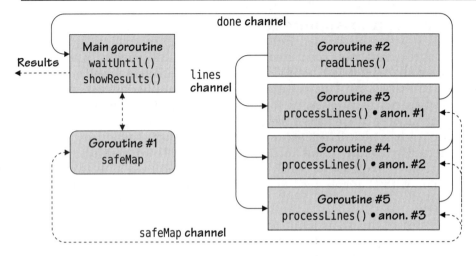

Figure 7.6 *Multiple inter-dependent concurrent jobs with synchronized results*

```
    pageMap := safemap.New()
    go readLines(os.Args[1], lines)
    processLines(done, pageMap, lines)
    waitUntil(done)
    showResults(pageMap)
}
```

The main() function begins by making sure that the Go runtime system will use all of the machine's processors. Then it creates the two channels needed to organize the processing. The lines channel will be sent each line from the log file and the worker goroutines will each receive lines from this channel. We have given the lines channel a small buffer to reduce the likelihood of the worker goroutines being blocked waiting for lines. The done channel is used to keep track of when all the work is done, and since we only care about the occurrence of sends and receives rather than their values, we use empty structs. The done channel is buffered so that it doesn't block when a goroutine wants to announce that it has finished its work.

With the channels in place we create a new unexported safeMap which is returned by the safemap.New() function as an exported SafeMap interface that can freely be passed around. We then start off the goroutine for reading lines from the files and then the goroutines for processing the lines. Then we wait for all the worker goroutines to be finished, after which we can output the results.

```
func readLines(filename string, lines chan<- string) {
    file, err := os.Open(filename)
    if err != nil {
        log.Fatal("failed to open the file:", err)
```

```
        }
        defer file.Close()
        reader := bufio.NewReader(file)
        for {
            line, err := reader.ReadString('\n')
            if line != "" {
                lines <- line
            }
            if err != nil {
                if err != io.EOF {
                    log.Println("failed to finish reading the file:", err)
                }
                break
            }
        }
        close(lines)
}
```

This function should be very familiar since it is so similar to ones we have seen before. The first key aspect is that each line is sent to the lines send-only channel—this will block if the channel's buffer becomes full, until another goroutine receives from the channel. Naturally, even if there is blocking, it only affects this goroutine; all the others will continue unaffected. The second key aspect is that once all the lines have been sent we close the lines channel; this tells prospective receivers that there is no more data to receive. Keep in mind, though, that this goroutine executes concurrently with the program's other goroutines—in particular, the line processing worker goroutines—so the close() statement isn't reached until most of the work has been done.

```
func processLines(done chan<- struct{}, pageMap safemap.SafeMap,
    lines <-chan string) {
    getRx := regexp.MustCompile(`GET[ \t]+([^ \t\n]+[.]html?)`)
    incrementer := func(value interface{}, found bool) interface{} {
        if found {
            return value.(int) + 1
        }
        return 1
    }
    for i := 0; i < workers; i++ {
        go func() {
            for line := range lines {
                if matches := getRx.FindStringSubmatch(line);
                    matches != nil {
                    pageMap.Update(matches[1], incrementer)
                }
```

```
            }
         done <- struct{}{}
      }()
   }
}
```

This function follows the Go parameter ordering convention of having destination channels first (in this case the done channel), followed by the source channels (in this case the lines channel).

The function creates the goroutines (three in this example) that do the work. Each goroutine shares the same *regexp.Regexp (since, unusually for pointed-to values, this is documented to be thread-safe), and the same incrementer() function (since it has no side effects and doesn't access any shared data). They also share the same pageMap (of type SafeMap interface), since even the methods that modify a SafeMap are thread-safe.

The regexp.Regexp.FindStringSubmatch() function returns nil if there is no match, or a []string where the first item is the entire matching text and each subsequent item corresponds to the text that matches a parenthesized subexpression in the regular expression. In this case we have one such subexpression, so if we get a match at all, the []string will have exactly two items in it, the entire matching text and the text matched by the parenthesized subexpression, in this case the filename of an HTML page.

Each worker goroutine receives different lines that are read by the goroutine created in the readLines() function from the lines receive-only channel. If a line matches the regular expression that identifies GET requests on HTML files, the safeMap.Update() method is called with the page filename (matches[1]) and with the incrementer() function. The incrementer() function is executed inside the safe map's goroutine and returns an incremented value for existing pages and a value of 1 for pages that are new to the map. (Recall from the previous subsection that if the function passed to the safeMap.Update() method calls any other SafeMap method we will get a deadlock.) When there are no more pages to process, each worker goroutine sends an empty struct to the done send-only channel to signify that it has finished its work.

```
func waitUntil(done <-chan struct{}) {
    for i := 0; i < workers; i++ {
        <-done
    }
}
```

This function executes in the main goroutine and blocks waiting on the done receive-only channel. When every worker goroutine has sent an empty struct to the done channel, the for loop finishes. As usual, we don't bother to close the done channel since we never use it in a context where it is checked for being closed. By blocking, this function ensures that the processing gets done before the main goroutine terminates.

```
func showResults(pageMap safemap.SafeMap) {
    pages := pageMap.Close()
    for page, count := range pages {
        fmt.Printf("%8d %s\n", count, page)
    }
}
```

Once all the lines have been read and all the matches added to the safe map, this function is called to output the results. It begins by calling the safemap. safeMap.Close() method which closes the safe map's channel, terminates the safeMap.run() method executing in a goroutine, and returns the underlying map[string]interface{} to the caller. The returned map can no longer be accessed using the safe map's channel and so can safely be used in a single goroutine (or multiple goroutines if we serialize accesses using a mutex). From this point, we only access the map in the main goroutine, so no serialization is necessary. We simply iterate over the map's *key–value* pairs and print them to the console.

Using a value of type SafeMap interface provides thread safety and simple syntax with no need to concern ourselves with locks. One disadvantage of this approach is that the safe map's values are generic interface{} values rather than of a specific type, hence the need to use a type assertion in the incrementer() function. (We will discuss another disadvantage further on; §7.2.4.3, ➤ 347.)

7.2.4.2. Synchronizing with a Mutex-Protected Map

We will now compare and contrast the clean channel-based approach to the traditional mutex-based approach. To do this we will briefly discuss the apachereport2 program (in file apachereport2/apachereport.go). This is a variation of the apachereport1 program that uses a custom data type which encapsulates a map and a mutex instead of using a SafeMap. The two programs do the same job but are different in that the apachereport2 program stores int values in its map rather than the interface{}s used by the generic SafeMap, and also only provides the minimal and specific functionality required to do the job—an Increment() method—compared to the safe map's complete set of methods.

```
type pageMap struct {
    countForPage map[string]int
    mutex        *sync.RWMutex
}
```

One advantage of using a specific custom type is that we can use the exact data types that we need rather than having to use the generic interface{} type.

```
func NewPageMap() *pageMap {
    return &pageMap{make(map[string]int), new(sync.RWMutex)}
}
```

This function returns a ready-to-use *pageMap. (Incidentally, we could have created the read-write mutex pointer using the syntax &sync.RWMutex{} instead of new(sync.RWMutex); we discussed this equivalence in §4.1, 140 ◄.)

```
func (pm *pageMap) Increment(page string) {
    pm.mutex.Lock()
    defer pm.mutex.Unlock()
    pm.countForPage[page]++
}
```

Every method that modifies the countForPage map must serialize its accesses to the map using the mutex. The pattern used here is canonical: Lock the mutex; defer unlocking the mutex so that whenever we return, the unlocking is guaranteed (even in the face of a panic); and perform the access—ideally for as short a time as possible.

Thanks to Go's automatic zero initialization, the first time a page is accessed in the countForPage map (i.e., when it isn't in the map), it is added to the map with a value of 0, which is then immediately incremented. Correspondingly, on subsequent accesses to a page that is already in the map, its existing value will be incremented.

Every method that accesses the countForPage map must serialize that access using a mutex. For updates to the map, the sync.RWMutex.Lock() and sync.RWMutex. Unlock() methods shown here must be used, but for read-only accesses, we can use different read-only methods.

```
func (pm *pageMap) Len() int {
    pm.mutex.RLock()
    defer pm.mutex.RUnlock()
    return len(pm.countForPage)
}
```

This method is included purely to show how to use a read lock. The pattern of use is the same as for a normal lock, but read locks are potentially more efficient (since we are promising to read but not update the protected resource). For example, if we have multiple goroutines all reading the same countForPage map, they can all safely execute concurrently using a read lock. But if even one of them acquires a normal (read-write) lock—and hence the ability to change the map—then no other lock can be granted.

```
pageMap.Increment(matches[1])
```

With the pageMap type in place the worker goroutines can update the shared map using the statement shown here.

7.2.4.3. Synchronizing by Merging Local Maps via Channels

Whether we use a safe map or a plain map protected by a mutex, we might reasonably expect that by increasing the number of worker goroutines we would increase the overall speed of the program. However, since accesses to the safe map or to the plain map are serialized (behind the scenes in the case of the safe map), as we add goroutines, contention will increase.

As is often the case, we can trade some memory in exchange for increased speed. So, for example, we could let every worker goroutine have its own plain map. This would maximize throughput since there would be no contention at all during processing, but at the price of using extra memory (since most likely every map would have some or even all pages in common). At the end, of course, we would have to merge these maps—and that could be a bottleneck since, while one map was being merged, any others that were ready to merge would have to wait.

The apachereport3 program (in file apachereport3/apachereport.go) uses local goroutine-specific plain maps and merges them into a single overall map at the end. The code is almost identical to the apachereport1 and apachereport2 programs, so we will very briefly review the key differences. The program's concurrency structure is illustrated by Figure 7.7.

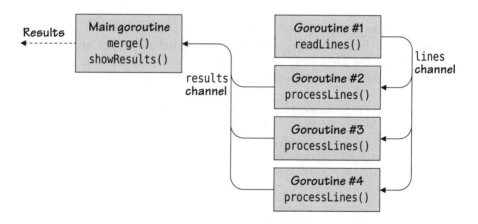

Figure 7.7 *Multiple inter-dependent concurrent jobs with synchronized results*

```
// ...
lines := make(chan string, workers*4)
results := make(chan map[string]int, workers)
```

```
go readLines(os.Args[1], lines)
getRx := regexp.MustCompile(`GET[ \t]+([^ \t\n]+[.]html?)`)
for i := 0; i < workers; i++ {
    go processLines(results, getRx, lines)
}
totalForPage := make(map[string]int)
merge(results, totalForPage)
showResults(totalForPage)
// ...
```

This is an extract from apachereport3's main() function. Instead of having a done channel we have a results channel through which the local goroutine-specific maps are sent once they have been fully populated. We also create an overall map (totalForPage) into which all the results will be merged.

```
func processLines(results chan<- map[string]int, getRx *regexp.Regexp,
    lines <-chan string) {
    countForPage := make(map[string]int)
    for line := range lines {
        if matches := getRx.FindStringSubmatch(line); matches != nil {
            countForPage[matches[1]]++
        }
    }
    results <- countForPage
}
```

This function is almost the same as the version shown before. The key differences are first that we have created a local map to hold page counts, and second that we return the local map to the results channel (rather than sending, say, a struct{}{} to a done channel), once the function has finished processing lines.

```
func merge(results <-chan map[string]int, totalForPage map[string]int) {
    for i := 0; i < workers; i++ {
        countForPage := <-results
        for page, count := range countForPage {
            totalForPage[page] += count
        }
    }
}
```

This function is structurally the same as the waitUntil() function we saw earlier, only this time we make use of the received value, using it to update the overall totalForPage map. Note that the maps received here are never accessed by their sending goroutines after they have been sent, so no locking is necessary.

The showResults() function is almost the same as before (so isn't shown), only it accepts the totalForPage map as its argument and iterates over this map printing counts and pages.

The apachereport3 program's code is simpler and cleaner than that needed by apachereport1 and apachereport2, and the concurrency model it uses—each goroutine populating its own uncontended data structure and merging results at the end—should prove useful in many different contexts.

Of course, it is only natural for programmers used to the locking paradigm to be tempted to use mutexes to serialize accesses in Go programs. However, the Go documentation strongly recommends the use of goroutines and channels with its mantra of *"don't communicate by sharing memory, instead, share memory by communicating",* and Go compilers are being optimized above all to support this concurrency model.

7.2.5. Example: Find Duplicates

This chapter's final concurrency example is a program that attempts to find duplicate files using file sizes and SHA-1 values rather than filenames.★

The program we will review is called findduplicates (in file findduplicates/find-duplicates.go). The program uses the standard library's filepath.Walk() function to iterate over all the files and directories in a given path, including subdirectories, and subsubdirectories, and so on. The program uses a variable number of goroutines depending on the work it does. For each "big" file, a new goroutine is created on the fly to compute that file's SHA-1, while each "small" file's SHA-1 is computed in the current goroutine. This means that we don't know in advance how many goroutines any particular run of the program will use, although we can—and do—set an upper limit.

One way of handling a variable number of goroutines is to use a "done" channel just like in earlier examples, only this time keeping a running count of how many goroutines are created. An easier way is to use a sync.WaitGroup which achieves the same thing but passes on the counting to Go.

```
const maxGoroutines = 100

func main() {
    runtime.GOMAXPROCS(runtime.NumCPU()) // Use all the machine's cores
    if len(os.Args) == 1 || os.Args[1] == "-h" || os.Args[1] == "--help" {
        fmt.Printf("usage: %s <path>\n", filepath.Base(os.Args[0]))
        os.Exit(1)
    }
```

★ The SHA-1 secure hash algorithm produces a 20-byte value for any given chunk of data—such as a file. Identical files will have the same SHA-1 values and different files will almost always have different SHA-1 values.

```
    infoChan := make(chan fileInfo, maxGoroutines*2)
    go findDuplicates(infoChan, os.Args[1])
    pathData := mergeResults(infoChan)
    outputResults(pathData)
}
```

The main() function accepts a directory to start the processing from and orchestrates all the work. It begins by creating a channel for passing fileInfo values (which we will look at shortly). We have buffered the channel because experiments showed that this consistently improved performance.

Next, the function executes the findDuplicates() function in a goroutine, and then calls the mergeResults() function that reads the infoChan channel until it is closed. Once the merged data is returned, the results are output.

The program's goroutines and flow of communications are illustrated in Figure 7.8. The figure's results channel is for values of type fileInfo; these values are sent to the infoChan channel by a "walker" function (of type filepath.Walk-Func) that we pass to the filepath.Walk() function. The filepath.Walk() function is itself called in the findDuplicates() function. The results are received by the mergeResults() function. The goroutines in the figure are created by the findDuplicates() function and by the walker function. In addition, the standard library's filepath.Walk() function might create its own goroutines (e.g., one to process each directory), although how it actually works is an implementation detail.

```
type fileInfo struct {
    sha1 []byte
    size int64
    path string
}
```

This type is used to summarize the data for each file. If two files' SHA-1s and sizes are the same they are considered to be duplicates—no matter what their paths or filenames are.

```
func findDuplicates(infoChan chan fileInfo, dirname string) {
    waiter := &sync.WaitGroup{}
    filepath.Walk(dirname, makeWalkFunc(infoChan, waiter))
    waiter.Wait() // Blocks until all the work is done
    close(infoChan)
}
```

This function calls the filepath.Walk() function to walk the directory's tree (starting at dirname), and for every file and directory it calls the filepath.Walk-Func function it is passed as its second argument.

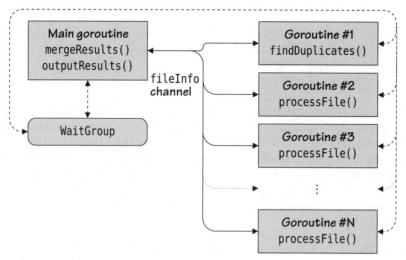

Figure 7.8 *Multiple independent concurrent jobs with synchronized results*

Our walker function will create an arbitrary number of goroutines, so we need to make sure that we wait until they have all finished before the findDuplicates() function returns. We have done this by creating a sync.WaitGroup. Each time we create a new goroutine we call sync.WaitGroup.Add(), and each time a goroutine completes its work we call sync.WaitGroup.Done(). Once all the goroutines have been set running we then wait for them all to finish by calling sync.WaitGroup.Wait()—which blocks until the number of done announcements equals the number added.

Once all the worker goroutines are finished there will be no more fileInfo values sent to the infoChan, so we close the channel. Naturally, the mergeResults() function will still be able to read the channel, until it has read all the channel's items.

```
const maxSizeOfSmallFile = 1024 * 32

func makeWalkFunc(infoChan chan fileInfo,
    waiter *sync.WaitGroup) func(string, os.FileInfo, error) error {
    return func(path string, info os.FileInfo, err error) error {
        if err == nil && info.Size() > 0 &&
            (info.Mode()&os.ModeType == 0) {
            if info.Size() < maxSizeOfSmallFile ||
                runtime.NumGoroutine() > maxGoroutines {
                processFile(path, info, infoChan, nil)
            } else {
                waiter.Add(1)
                go processFile(path, info, infoChan,
                    func() { waiter.Done() })
```

```
            }
        }
        return nil // We ignore all errors
    }
}
```

This function creates and returns an anonymous function of type filepath.Walk-Func (i.e., that has signature func(string, os.FileInfo, error) error). This function will be called for every file and directory that the filepath.Walk() function encounters. The path is the file or directory name, the info has the results of a *stat* call on the path, and the err either is nil or has the details of any problem that was encountered regarding the path. We can skip directories by returning an error value of filepath.SkipDir, and we can stop the walk by returning any other non-nil error.

We have chosen to process only regular files of nonzero size. (Of course, all files of size 0 bytes are the same, but we ignore such files.) The os.ModeType is a bitmask that has bits set for directories, symbolic links, named pipes, sockets, and devices—so if none of these are set we have a regular file.

If the file is "small" (in this case of up to 32KiB), we compute its SHA-1 immediately using a custom processFile() function. But for all other files we create a new goroutine in which the processFile() function is executed asynchronously. This means that small files will block (until we've computed their SHA-1), but big files will not since their computation is done in a separate goroutine. Either way, when the computation is complete the resultant fileInfo value is sent to the infoChan channel.

We need only call the sync.WaitGroup.Add() method when we create a new goroutine, but whenever we do so we must be sure to call the corresponding sync.WaitGroup.Done() method once the goroutine has finished its work. We do this by taking advantage of Go's support for closures (§5.6.3, 225 ◀). If we call the processFile() function in a new goroutine we pass an anonymous function as the last argument—when this anonymous function is called it will call the sync.WaitGroup.Done() method. The processFile() function is expected to do a deferred call on this anonymous function to ensure that Done() gets called when the goroutine finishes. If we call the processFile() method in the current goroutine, we pass nil instead of an anonymous function.

Why didn't we simply process *every* file in a new goroutine? Go would have no problem with that since we can create hundreds or thousands of goroutines without hitting any problems. Unfortunately, most operating systems impose a limit as to how many files may be open at the same time. For Windows the default limit could be as small as 512 although this can be increased to 2 048. Mac OS X systems may have a default limit as low as 256 files, and Linux systems a default limit of 1 024—however, Unix-like systems like these can usually have their limit set to tens or hundreds of thousands or more. Clearly, if we created one goroutine per file we could easily exceed the limit on some platforms.

We have avoided the "too many open files" problem by combining two tactics. First, we process small files in one goroutine (or perhaps in just a few goroutines if the filepath.Walk() function happens to spread its work over multiple goroutines and calls the walker function in them concurrently). This ensures that if we hit a directory with thousands of tiny files we don't have too many open at once because only one or a few goroutines can process them at the same time.

We should be able to afford to process big files in their own goroutines since the very fact that they are large means that we are unlikely to be able to be fast enough to open too many of them at the same time. But if we do end up processing too many big files, that is, if we start to have too many goroutines, the second tactic will kick in. (The runtime.NumGoroutine() function tells us how many goroutines exist at the time the function is called.)

If we have too many goroutines we stop creating new goroutines for processing big files, and instead process every file—no matter what size it is—in the current goroutine. This forces the program to use the same goroutine (or same few goroutines) to process each subsequent file, and thus keeps a lid on the number of goroutines, and as a consequence also limits the number of files that we have open at the same time. Meanwhile, as each of the goroutines already processing big files finish and are removed by Go's runtime system, the number of goroutines in use will decrease. So, at some point, there will be fewer goroutines than our limit, and we will once again start creating new goroutines to process big files.

```go
func processFile(filename string, info os.FileInfo,
    infoChan chan fileInfo, done func()) {
    if done != nil {
        defer done()
    }
    file, err := os.Open(filename)
    if err != nil {
        log.Println("error:", err)
        return
    }
    defer file.Close()
    hash := sha1.New()
    if size, err := io.Copy(hash, file);
        size != info.Size() || err != nil {
        if err != nil {
            log.Println("error:", err)
        } else {
            log.Println("error: failed to read the whole file:", filename)
```

```
        }
        return
    }
    infoChan <- fileInfo{hash.Sum(nil), info.Size(), filename}
}
```

This function is called from the current goroutine or in a newly created additional goroutine to compute the given file's SHA-1 and to send the file's details to the infoChan channel.

If the done variable is not nil, this function has been called in a new goroutine, so we defer a call to the done() function (which simply contains a call to the sync.WaitGroup.Done() method; 352 ◄). This is to ensure that for every sync.WaitGroup.Add() call, there is a corresponding Done() call, since this is essential to the correct operation of the sync.WaitGroup.Wait() function. If the variable is nil we safely ignore it.

Next, we open the given file for reading, and defer closing it, in the usual way. The standard library's crypto/sha1 package provides the sha1.New() function which returns a value that satisfies the hash.Hash interface. This interface provides a Sum() method that returns the hash value (i.e., the 20-byte SHA-1 hash in this case), and also fulfills the io.Writer interface. (We pass in nil to make the Sum() method give us a new []byte; alternatively, we could pass it an existing []byte to which it will append the hash sum.)

We could have read in the entire contents of the file and then called the sha1.Write() method to write the file into the hash, but we have opted to take a much more efficient approach and used the io.Copy() function instead. This function takes a writer to write to (in this case the hash), and a reader to read from (here, the open file), and copies from the latter to the former. When the copy has finished, io.Copy() returns the number of bytes copied and either nil or an error if a problem occurred. Since the SHA-1 hash can work on chunks of data at a time, the maximum amount of memory used by the io.Copy() call will be the size of the buffer used by the SHA-1 plus some fixed overhead. If we had read the entire file into memory first, we would have used the same amount of buffer and overhead memory—plus enough memory to store the whole file. So, especially for larger files, using io.Copy() achieves real savings.

Once the computation is done we send a fileInfo value to the infoChan channel with the SHA-1 value, the file's size (available from the os.FileInfo passed to the processFile() function from the walker function), and the filename (including the full path).

```
type pathsInfo struct {
    size  int64
    paths []string
}
```

This struct type is used to store the details of each duplicate file, that is, its size, and all the file's paths and filenames. It is used by the mergeResults() and outputResults() functions.

```
func mergeResults(infoChan <-chan fileInfo) map[string]*pathsInfo {
    pathData := make(map[string]*pathsInfo)
    format := fmt.Sprintf("%%016X:%%%dX", sha1.Size*2) // == "%016X:%40X"
    for info := range infoChan {
        key := fmt.Sprintf(format, info.size, info.sha1)
        value, found := pathData[key]
        if !found {
            value = &pathsInfo{size: info.size}
            pathData[key] = value
        }
        value.paths = append(value.paths, info.path)
    }
    return pathData
}
```

This function begins by creating a map to store duplicate files. The keys are strings composed of the file's size, a colon, and the file's SHA-1, and the values are *pathsInfos.

To produce the keys we have created a format string which has 16 zero-padded hexadecimal digits to represent the file's size and enough hexadecimal digits to represent the file's SHA-1. We have used leading zeros for the file size part of the key so that we can sort the keys by size later on. The sha1.Size constant holds the number of bytes occupied by an SHA-1 (i.e., 20). Since one byte represented in hexadecimal has two digits, we must use twice as many characters as there are bytes for the SHA-1 in the format string. (Incidentally, we could have created the format string with format = "%016X:" + fmt.Sprintf("%dX", sha1.Size*2).)

Although multiple goroutines send to the infoChan channel, this function (in the main goroutine) is the only one that receives from the channel. The for loop receives fileInfo values—or blocks waiting. The loop ends when all the values have been received and the infoChan channel is closed. For each fileInfo value received, a map key string is computed. If the map doesn't have an item with the key, we create a suitable value with the given file size, and with an empty slice of paths, and add it to the map under the new key. Then, with the new or existing item in the map, we append to the item's paths the path of the file in the fileInfo value.

And at the end, this will result in duplicate files having path slices with more than one path, and nonduplicates having path slices with exactly one path. Once all the fileInfo values have been processed and the map populated, the function returns the map ready for further processing.

```go
func outputResults(pathData map[string]*pathsInfo) {
    keys := make([]string, 0, len(pathData))
    for key := range pathData {
        keys = append(keys, key)
    }
    sort.Strings(keys)
    for _, key := range keys {
        value := pathData[key]
        if len(value.paths) > 1 {
            fmt.Printf("%d duplicate files (%s bytes):\n",
                len(value.paths), commas(value.size))
            sort.Strings(value.paths)
            for _, name := range value.paths {
                fmt.Printf("\t%s\n", name)
            }
        }
    }
}
```

The pathData map's keys are strings that begin with each file's size in 16 hexadecimal digits padded with leading zeros. (16 digits was chosen since this is large
enough to represent an int64.) This means that by retrieving and sorting the
keys we can get the files in size order from smallest to biggest. So, the function
begins by creating a keys slice to which each of the map's keys are appended,
after which the keys are sorted. Then, the function iterates over the size-sorted
slice of keys, retrieving the corresponding pathsInfo value. For those that have
more than one path the files' size is output followed by an indented list of the
duplicate files in path-sorted order, as shown below.

```
$ ./findduplicates $GOROOT
2 duplicate files (67 bytes):
        /home/mark/opt/go/test/fixedbugs/bug248.dir/bug0.go
        /home/mark/opt/go/test/fixedbugs/bug248.dir/bug1.go
...
4 duplicate files (785 bytes):
        /home/mark/opt/go/doc/gopher/gophercolor16x16.png
        /home/mark/opt/go/favicon.ico
        /home/mark/opt/go/misc/dashboard/godashboard/static/favicon.ico
        /home/mark/opt/go/src/pkg/archive/zip/testdata/gophercolor16x16.png
...
2 duplicate files (1,371,249 bytes):
        /home/mark/opt/go/bin/ebnflint
        /home/mark/opt/go/src/cmd/ebnflint/ebnflint
```

We have, of course, elided many lines as the ellipses indicate.

```go
func commas(x int64) string {
    value := fmt.Sprint(x)
    for i := len(value) - 3; i > 0; i -= 3 {
        value = value[:i] + "," + value[i:]
    }
    return value
}
```

Most humans find it difficult to parse long numbers (e.g., 1371249), so we have used this simple commas() function to insert grouping commas to make the sizes easier to read. The function accepts a single int64 value, so if we have a plain int or an integer of some other size, we must convert it—for example, commas(int64(*i*)).*

This completes our review of the findduplicates program and of Go concurrent programming generally. Go's support for concurrency (<-, chan, go, select) is very flexible and there are many more variations on how to do things than we have had the space to show here. Nonetheless, the examples—and the exercises that follow—should be sufficient to provide a good understanding of how to do concurrent programming in Go, and offer a useful starting point for creating new concurrent programs.

Of course, it is not possible to state definitively which of the approaches we have covered (or the other possible approaches) is the best to use, since each one may prove best in different circumstances. The performance profile of each approach is affected by the particular machine, the number of goroutines, and whether the processing is purely in-memory or involves external data (such as accessing files or network communications). A reliable means of finding out which is the best approach for a particular program is to time (or profile) the program using real (or realistic) data using different approaches and different numbers of goroutines.

7.3. Exercises

This chapter has three exercises. The first involves creating a thread-safe data structure. The second and third require the creation of small but complete concurrent programs, with the third exercise being fairly challenging.

1. Create a thread-safe slice type called safeSlice and the following exported SafeSlice interface:

---

* At the time of this writing, Go has no locale support.

```
type SafeSlice interface {
    Append(interface{})      // Append the given item to the slice
    At(int) interface{}      // Return the item at the given index position
    Close() []interface{}    // Close the channel and return the slice
    Delete(int)              // Delete the item at the given index position
    Len() int                // Return the number of items in the slice
    Update(int, UpdateFunc)  // Update the item at the given index position
}
```

It will also be necessary to create a safeSlice.run() method in which the underlying slice (of type []interface{}) is created, and which runs an "infinite" loop iterating over the communications channel, and a New() function in which the safe slice is created and the safeSlice.run() method executed in a goroutine.

The safe slice implementation can easily be modeled on the safe map covered earlier (§7.2.3, 334 ◄), and has the same deadlock risk in the safeSlice.Update() method. A solution is given in the safeslice/safeslice.go file and is under 100 lines. (The apachereport4 program can be used for testing since it uses the safeslice package.)

2. Create a program that accepts one or more image filenames on the command line, and for each one prints a line on the console as an HTML tag of the form <img src="*filename*" width="*width*" height="*height*" />. The program should process the images concurrently using a fixed number of worker goroutines, and the order of output doesn't matter (so long as each line is output complete!). The filenames should be output without paths. Allow any files to be given on the command line, but ignore those that aren't regular files or that aren't images, and ignore all errors.

   The standard library's image.DecodeConfig() function can retrieve an image's width and height from an io.Reader (as returned by os.Open()), without having to read the entire image. For this function to be able to recognize various image formats, (.jpg, .png, etc.), it is necessary to import the corresponding packages. However, we don't need to access these packages directly, so to avoid the Go compiler giving us "imported and not used" errors, we must import the packages to the blank identifier (e.g., _ "image/jpeg"; _ "image/png", etc.). We discuss these kinds of import in the next chapter.

   The book's examples include two implementations, imagetag1 which is single-threaded (no additional goroutines, no channels), and imagetag2 which is concurrent in a similar way to this chapter's cgrep2 example. If you just want to focus on the concurrency aspects you might like to copy the imagetag1/imagetag1.go file to, say, the my_imagetag directory and convert it from being single-threaded to concurrent. This will involve modifying the main() and process() functions, and the addition of around 40 lines of code. Windows users might like to use the commandLineFiles() function (176 ◄) to handle file globbing; both implementations already include this. The more confident reader might prefer to try writing the program entirely from scratch. The solution in imagetag2/imagetag2.go takes one of many different possible approaches and is around 100 lines.

3. Create a concurrent program that uses a fixed number of worker goroutines and that accepts one or more HTML files on the command line. The program should read each HTML file and every time it finds an <img> tag it should check to see if the tag has width and height attributes, and if not, it should ascertain the image's width and height and add the missing attribute or attributes. The concurrency structure could be done in a similar way to one of the apachereport examples (but not the mutex-using apachereport2 version), except that there is no need for a results channel.

Since Go 1 doesn't have an HTML parser, for this exercise we use the regexp and strings packages.* We searched for image tags using the regular expression string `<[iI][mM][gG][^>]+>`, and we identified image filenames within image tags using the regular expression `src=["']([^"']+)["']`. (These regexeps are not very sophisticated since we want to focus on concurrency, not regular expressions, for which see §3.6.5, 120 ◄.) Use the image.DecodeConfig() function discussed in the previous exercise (along with all the imports) to get each image's size. As usual, Windows users might like to use the commandLineFiles() function (176 ◄) to handle file globbing.

The concurrency aspects of this program are quite straightforward, but the processing is quite tricky. This is a welcome change from concurrent programming in some other languages where the concurrency aspects overwhelm the actual processing that needs to be done.

Two solutions are provided. The first solution, sizeimages1 (in file sizeimages1/sizeimages1.go), does everything it should, but has one disadvantage: It can only find the image files if it is run in the same directory as the HTML files. This limitation is due to the fact that we replace each <img> tag with an updated tag using the regexp.Regexp.ReplaceAllStringFunc() method. This method expects to be passed a replacer function with signature func(string) string with the string passed in being the matched text and the returned string being the replacement. A typical string passed in might be `<img src="splash.png"/>`. The replacer function has no idea what the path to the splash.png file is, and so must assume the current directory, and hence the limitation that sizeimages1 must be run in the same directory as the HTML files.

It might be tempting to try to solve the problem by using a global *directory* string and assigning the current HTML file's path to it before using the replacer function—but this won't work in all situations. Why? The

---

* An HTML parser is in development and may be available by the time you read this.

second solution, sizeimages2 (in file sizeimages2/sizeimages2.go), solves the problem by creating a fresh replacer function as a closure that captures the HTML file's directory each time it is needed. Then, the replacer function uses the captured directory as the image's path for image files that have relative paths.

This is probably the most challenging exercise in the book so far, and will require looking up functions in the image, regexp, and strings packages. The sizeimages1.go file is around 160 lines, with sizeimages2.go under 170 lines.

8

File Handling

In earlier chapters we saw several examples of reading, creating, and writing text files. In this chapter we will look in more detail at Go's file handling facilities and in particular how to read and write files in standard formats (such as XML and JSON), as well as custom plain text and binary formats.

Since we have now covered all of Go's language features (apart from creating programs with our own custom packages and with third-party packages—which is covered in the next chapter), we are free to use all the facilities that Go provides. We will take advantage of this freedom and make use of closures (§5.6.3, 225 ◀) to avoid repetitive code, and in some cases make more advanced use of Go's support for object orientation, in particular adding methods to functions.

This chapter's focus is on files rather than directories or the file system generally. For directories, the previous chapter's findduplicates example (§7.2.5, 349 ◀) shows how to iterate over the files and subdirectories of a directory using the filepath.Walk() function. In addition, the standard library's os package's os.File type provides methods for reading the names in a directory (os.File.Readdirnames()), and for retrieving os.FileInfo values for each item in a directory (os.File.Readdir()).

This chapter's first section shows how to write and read files using standard and custom file formats. The second section covers Go's support for handling archive files and compression.

8.1. Custom Data Files

It is quite common for programs to maintain internal data structures and to provide import/export functionality to support data interchange, and also to facilitate the processing of their data by external tools. Since our concern here is with file handling, we will focus purely on how to write and read data to and from standard and custom formats from and into a program's internal data structures.

For this section we will use the same data for all the examples so that we can get a direct comparison between the various file formats. All the code is taken from the invoicedata program (in the invoicedata directory in the files invoicedata.go, gob.go, inv.go, jsn.go, txt.go, and xml.go). The program takes two filenames as command-line arguments, one to read and one to write (and which must be different). The program then reads the data from the first file (in whatever format its suffix indicates) and writes the same data to the second file (again, using whatever format its suffix indicates).

The files created by invoicedata work cross-platform, that is, a file created on, say, Windows, is readable on Mac OS X and Linux, and vice versa, no matter which format it is. Gzip-compressed files (e.g., invoices.gob.gz) can be read and written seamlessly; compression is covered in the second section (§8.2, ➤ 397).

The data consists of an []*Invoice, that is, a slice of pointers to Invoice values. Each invoice is held in an Invoice value, and each invoice holds zero or more items in its Items field of type []*Item (slice of pointers to Item).

```
type Invoice struct {              type Item struct {
    Id         int                     Id       string
    CustomerId int                     Price    float64
    Raised     time.Time               Quantity int
    Due        time.Time               Note     string
    Paid       bool                }
    Note       string
    Items      []*Item
}
```

These two structs are used to hold the data. Table 8.1 shows some informal comparisons of how long it took to read and write the same 50 000 random invoices, and the size of the file occupied by those invoices in each format. The timings are in seconds rounded up to the nearest tenth of a second—they should be taken as unitless since they will undoubtedly vary on different hardware under different

Table 8.1 *Format Speed and Size Comparisons*

Suffix	Read	Write	Size (KiB)	Read/Write LOC	Format
.gob	0.3	0.2	7 948	21 + 11 = 32	Go Binary
.gob.gz	0.5	1.5	2 589		
.jsn	4.5	2.2	16 283	32 + 17 = 49	JSON
.jsn.gz	4.5	3.4	2 678		
.xml	6.7	1.2	18 917	45 + 30 = 75	XML
.xml.gz	6.9	2.7	2 730		
.txt	1.9	1.0	12 375	86 + 53 = 139	Plain text (UTF-8)
.txt.gz	2.2	2.2	2 514		
.inv	1.7	3.5	7 250	128 + 87 = 215	Custom binary
.inv.gz	1.6	2.6	2 400		

loads. The size column shows the sizes in kibibytes—these should be very consistent across machines. For this data set, the compressed sizes are surprisingly similar, even though the uncompressed sizes vary considerably. The lines of code exclude code that is common to all formats (e.g., the code for decompressing and compressing and the structs).

The timings and file sizes are what we would reasonably expect—apart from the extremely fast reading and writing of the plain text format. This is thanks to the fmt package's excellent print and scan functions in conjunction with a custom text format that we designed to be easy to parse. For the JSON and XML formats, instead of using the default storage for time.Time values (an ISO-8601 date/time string), we have simply stored the date part—this has slightly reduced the file size at the expense of some processing speed and some additional code. For example, the JSON code would run faster, and be about the same number of lines as the Go binary code, if we allowed it to handle time.Time values itself.

For binary data, the Go binary format is the most convenient to use—it is very fast, is extremely compact, requires very little code, and is relatively easy to adapt to data changes. However, if we use custom types that are not initially gob-encodable and have to make them satisfy the gob.Encoder and gob.Decoder interfaces, this can considerably slow down writing and reading in gob format, and also bloat out the file size.

For human-readable data, XML is probably the best format to use—particularly since it is so useful as a data interchange format. More lines are required to handle XML format than JSON format. This is because Go 1 doesn't have an xml.Marshaler interface (a lack that is expected to be made good in a later Go 1.*x* release), and also because we have used parallel data types (XMLInvoice and XMLItem) to help map between the XML data and the invoice data (Invoice and Item). Applications that use XML as their external storage format would not need the parallel data types or the conversions that the invoicedata program needs, so are likely to be faster and require less code than the invoicedata example suggests.

In addition to reading and writing speed, file size, and lines of code, there is one other issue that we should consider: format robustness. For example, if we add one field to the Invoice struct and one field to the Item struct, then we will need to change our file formats. How easy is it to adapt our code to write and read the new format—and also be able to continue reading the old format? Providing we take care to version our file formats such changes are pretty straightforward to cater to (as one of the chapter's exercises will demonstrate)—with the exception of JSON format for which adapting the code to be able to read both the old and new formats is slightly tricky.

In addition to the Invoice and Item structs, all the file formats share some constants:

```
const (
    fileType       = "INVOICES"  // Used by text formats
    magicNumber    = 0x125D      // Used by binary formats
    fileVersion    = 100         // Used by all formats
    dateFormat     = "2006-01-02" // This date must always be used
)                                              format
```

The magicNumber is used to uniquely identify invoice files.* The fileVersion indicates the invoice file version—using this makes it easier to change the program later on to accommodate changes to the data. The dateFormat shows how we want dates formatted in human-readable formats and is discussed later on (➤ 368).

We have also created a couple of interfaces.

```
type InvoicesMarshaler interface {
    MarshalInvoices(writer io.Writer, invoices []*Invoice) error
}

type InvoicesUnmarshaler interface {
    UnmarshalInvoices(reader io.Reader) ([]*Invoice, error)
}
```

The purpose of these is to make it easy to use a reader or writer for a specific format in a generic way. For example, here is the function the invoicedata program uses to read invoices from an open file.

---

* There is no universal repository of magic numbers, so we cannot be certain that any particular magic number hasn't been used before.

```
func readInvoices(reader io.Reader, suffix string) ([]*Invoice, error) {
    var unmarshaler InvoicesUnmarshaler
    switch suffix {
    case ".gob":
        unmarshaler = GobMarshaler{}
    case ".inv":
        unmarshaler = InvMarshaler{}
    case ".jsn", ".json":
        unmarshaler = JSONMarshaler{}
    case ".txt":
        unmarshaler = TxtMarshaler{}
    case ".xml":
        unmarshaler = XMLMarshaler{}
    }
    if unmarshaler != nil {
        return unmarshaler.UnmarshalInvoices(reader)
    }
    return nil, fmt.Errorf("unrecognized input suffix: %s", suffix)
}
```

The reader is any value that satisfies the io.Reader interface, such as an open
file (of type *os.File), or a gzip decompressor (of type *gzip.Reader), or a
string.Reader. The suffix string is the file's suffix (after any .gz suffix has been
stripped off). The GobMarshaler, InvMarshaler, and so on, are custom types which
provide the MarshalInvoices() and UnmarshalInvoices() methods (and therefore
satisfy the InvoicesMarshaler and InvoicesUnmarshaler interfaces), as we will see
in the following subsections.

8.1.1. Handling JSON Files

According to www.json.org, JSON (JavaScript Object Notation) is a lightweight
data interchange format that is easy for humans to read and write, and easy
for machines to parse and generate. JSON is a plain text format using the
UTF-8 encoding. JSON has become increasingly popular—particularly for
transferring data over network connections—because it is more convenient to
write, is (usually) much more compact, and requires much less processing power
to parse than XML.

Here is the data for a single invoice in JSON format, but with most of the
invoice's second item's fields elided.

```
{
    "Id": 4461,
    "CustomerId": 917,
    "Raised": "2012-07-22",
```

```
        "Due": "2012-08-21",
        "Paid": true,
        "Note": "Use trade entrance",
        "Items": [
            {
                "Id": "AM2574",
                "Price": 415.8,
                "Quantity": 5,
                "Note": ""
            },
            {
                "Id": "MI7296",
                ...
            }
        ]
}
```

Normally, the encoding/json package writes JSON data without any unnecessary whitespace, but we have shown it here with indentation and spaces to
make it easier to see the data's structure. Although the encoding/json package
supports time.Times, we have chosen to implement our own custom MarshalJSON()
and UnmarshalJSON() Invoice methods to handle the raised and due dates ourselves. This allows us to store shorter date strings (since for our data the time
elements are always zero), such as "2012-09-06", rather than full date/times such
as "2012-09-06T00:00:00Z".

8.1.1.1. Writing JSON Files

We have created a type based on an empty struct to give us something with
which to associate the JSON-specific MarshalInvoices() and UnmarshalInvoices()
methods.

```
type JSONMarshaler struct{}
```

This type fulfills the generic InvoicesMarshaler and InvoicesUnmarshaler interfaces that we saw earlier (365 ◄).

Here is a method for writing an entire data set of []*Invoice items to an
io.Writer in JSON format using the encoding/json package's standard Go to
JSON marshaling conversions. The writer could be an *os.File returned by
the os.Create() function, or a *gzip.Writer returned by the gzip.NewWriter()
function—or anything else that fulfills the io.Writer interface.

```
func (JSONMarshaler) MarshalInvoices(writer io.Writer,
    invoices []*Invoice) error {
```

```
    encoder := json.NewEncoder(writer)
    if err := encoder.Encode(fileType); err != nil {
        return err
    }
    if err := encoder.Encode(fileVersion); err != nil {
        return err
    }
    return encoder.Encode(invoices)
}
```

The `JSONMarshaler` type has no data so we don't need to assign its value to a receiver variable.

We begin by creating a JSON encoder that wraps the `io.Writer` and provides an encoder to which we can write our JSON-encodable data.

We write the data using the `json.Encoder.Encode()` method. This method copes perfectly with our slice of invoices each of which contains its own slice of items. The method returns an `error` or `nil`; if we get an error we immediately return it to the caller.

Writing a file type and a file version isn't strictly necessary, but as one of the exercises will illustrate, doing so makes it much easier to change the file format later on (e.g., to accommodate additional fields in the `Invoice` and `Item` structs), and be able to read both this format and the new format.

Notice that the method isn't really concerned with the types of the data it encodes, so it is trivial to create similar functions for writing other JSON-encodable data. Furthermore, the `JSONMarshaler.MarshalInvoices()` method will not require any changes to write a new format providing that all the new fields are exported and JSON-encodable.

If the code shown here was all of the program's JSON-related code, then it would work perfectly well as it is. However, since we want to exercise finer control over the JSON output—in particular the formatting of `time.Time` values—we have provided the `Invoice` type with a `MarshalJSON()` method that satisfies the `json.Marshaler` interface. The `json.Encode()` function is smart enough to check whether a value it is asked to encode is a `json.Marshaler`, and if it is, the function uses the value's own `MarshalJSON()` method rather than using its own built-in encoding code.

```
type JSONInvoice struct {
    Id         int
    CustomerId int
    Raised     string // time.Time in Invoice struct
    Due        string // time.Time in Invoice struct
    Paid       bool
```

```
    Note        string
    Items       []*Item
}

func (invoice Invoice) MarshalJSON() ([]byte, error) {
    jsonInvoice := JSONInvoice{
        invoice.Id,
        invoice.CustomerId,
        invoice.Raised.Format(dateFormat),
        invoice.Due.Format(dateFormat),
        invoice.Paid,
        invoice.Note,
        invoice.Items,
    }
    return json.Marshal(jsonInvoice)
}
```

The custom Invoice.MarshalJSON() method takes an existing Invoice and returns
a JSON-encoded version of it. The function's first statement simply copies the
invoice's fields into a custom JSONInvoice struct, converting the two time.Time
values into strings. Since the JSONInvoice struct's fields are all Booleans,
numbers, or strings, the struct can be JSON-encoded using the json.Marshal()
function, so we use this function to do almost all of the work.

To write date/times (i.e., time.Time values) as strings, we must use the time.Time.
Format() method. This method takes a format string which indicates how
the date/time must be written. The format string is rather unusual in that
it must be a string representation of Unix time 1136243045, that is, the precise date/time 2006-01-02T15:04:05Z07:00, or, as here, some subset of that
date/time. The choice of this particular date/time is arbitrary, but fixed—no other value will do for specifying date, time, and date/time formats.

If we want to create our own date/time formats they must always be written
in terms of the Go date/time. For example, if we wanted to write a date in the
form weekday, month, day, year, we must use a format such as "Mon, Jan 02, 2006",
or "Mon, Jan _2, 2006" if we want to suppress leading zeros. The time package's
documentation has full details—and also lists some predefined format strings.

8.1.1.2. Reading JSON Files

Reading JSON data is just as easy as writing it—especially if we read it
back into top-level variables of the same types as the ones written. The JSON-
Marshaler.UnmarshalInvoices() method takes an io.Reader which could be an
*os.File returned by the os.Open() function, or a *gzip.Reader returned by the
gzip.NewReader() function—or anything else that fulfills the io.Reader interface.

```go
func (JSONMarshaler) UnmarshalInvoices(reader io.Reader) ([]*Invoice,
    error) {
    decoder := json.NewDecoder(reader)
    var kind string
    if err := decoder.Decode(&kind); err != nil {
        return nil, err
    }
    if kind != fileType {
        return nil, errors.New("cannot read non-invoices json file")
    }
    var version int
    if err := decoder.Decode(&version); err != nil {
        return nil, err
    }
    if version > fileVersion {
        return nil, fmt.Errorf("version %d is too new to read", version)
    }
    var invoices []*Invoice
    err := decoder.Decode(&invoices)
    return invoices, err
}
```

We have three items of data to read in: the file type, the file version, and the entire invoices data. The json.Decoder.Decode() method takes a pointer to the value it must populate with the JSON data it decodes, and returns an error or nil. We use the first two variables (kind and version) to check that we have a JSON invoices file and that the file version is one we can handle. Then we read the invoices, in the process of which the json.Decoder.Decode() method will increase the size of the invoices slice to accommodate the invoices it reads and will populate the slice with pointers to Invoices (and their Items) that the function creates on the fly as necessary. At the end, the method returns the invoices and nil—or it returns nil and an error if a problem occurred.

If we had relied purely on the json package's built-in functionality and left the raised and due dates to be marshaled in the default way, the code shown here would be sufficient on its own to unmarshal a JSON-format invoices file. However, since we have chosen to marshal the invoice data's raised and due time.Times in a custom way (i.e., storing only the date parts), we must provide our own custom unmarshaling method that understands our custom marshaling.

```go
func (invoice *Invoice) UnmarshalJSON(data []byte) (err error) {
    var jsonInvoice JSONInvoice
    if err = json.Unmarshal(data, &jsonInvoice); err != nil {
        return err
    }
```

```
    var raised, due time.Time
    if raised, err = time.Parse(dateFormat, jsonInvoice.Raised);
        err != nil {
        return err
    }
    if due, err = time.Parse(dateFormat, jsonInvoice.Due); err != nil {
        return err
    }
    *invoice = Invoice{
        jsonInvoice.Id,
        jsonInvoice.CustomerId,
        raised,
        due,
        jsonInvoice.Paid,
        jsonInvoice.Note,
        jsonInvoice.Items,
    }
    return nil
}
```

This method uses the same JSONInvoice struct as before, and relies on the standard json.Unmarshal() function to populate it with an invoice's data. We then create and assign an Invoice with the unmarshaled data and with the dates converted into time.Time values.

Naturally, the json.Decoder.Decode() method is smart enough to check if a value it is being asked to decode into satisfies the json.Unmarshaler interface, and if it does, it uses the value's own UnmarshalJSON() method.

If the invoices data is changed by the addition of exported fields, this method will continue to work as is—but only if we make our Invoice.UnmarshalJSON() method version-sensitive. Furthermore, if the new fields' zero values are not acceptable, then when reading files in the original format we must post-process the data to give the new fields sensible values. (One of the exercises involves the addition of new fields and just this kind of post-processing.)

JSON is an easy format to work with, especially if we create suitable structs with exported fields, although it can be tricky to support two or more versions of a JSON file format. Also, the json.Encoder.Encode() and json.Decoder.Decode() functions (and the json.Marshal() and json.Unmarshal() functions) are *not* perfect inverses of each other—this means, for example, that it is possible to marshal data that cannot then be unmarshaled back into the same form as the original data. So, we must take care to check that they work correctly for our particular data.

Incidentally, there is a JSON-like format called BSON (Binary JSON) which is much more compact than JSON and much faster to write and read. A Go package that provides BSON support (gobson) is available from the godash-board.appspot.com/project web page. (Installing and using third-party packages is covered in Chapter 9.)

8.1.2. Handling XML Files

The XML (eXtensible Markup Language) format is widely used both as a data interchange format and as a file format in its own right. XML is a much more complex and sophisticated format than JSON, but is generally more verbose and tedious to write by hand.

The encoding/xml package can encode and decode structs to and from XML format in a similar way to the encoding/json package. However, the XML encoding and decoding functionality is much more demanding than for the encoding/json package. This is partly because the encoding/xml package requires struct fields to have suitably formatted tags (whereas they are not always needed for JSON). Also, Go 1's encoding/xml package does not have an xml.Marshaler interface, so we must write more code to handle XML than for the JSON and Go binary formats. (This is expected to be resolved in a later Go 1.x release.)

Here is a single example invoice in XML format with newlines and extra whitespace included to make it fit the page and be easier to read.

```
<INVOICE Id="2640" CustomerId="968" Raised="2012-08-27" Due="2012-09-26"
    Paid="false"><NOTE>See special Terms &amp; Conditions</NOTE>
    <ITEM Id="MI2419" Price="342.80" Quantity="1"><NOTE></NOTE></ITEM>
    <ITEM Id="OU5941" Price="448.99" Quantity="3"><NOTE>
        &quot;Blue&quot; ordered but will accept &quot;Navy&quot;</NOTE>
    </ITEM>
    <ITEM Id="IF9284" Price="475.01" Quantity="1"><NOTE></NOTE></ITEM>
    <ITEM Id="TI4394" Price="417.79" Quantity="2"><NOTE></NOTE></ITEM>
    <ITEM Id="VG4325" Price="80.67" Quantity="5"><NOTE></NOTE></ITEM>
</INVOICE>
```

Having raw character data in tags (e.g., for the invoices' and items' Note fields) is rather tricky to handle when using the xml package's encoder and decoder, so the invoicedata example uses explicit <NOTE> tags.

8.1.2.1. Writing XML Files

The encoding/xml package requires us to use structs whose fields have encoding/xml package-specific tags. In view of this, we cannot use the Invoice and Item structs directly for XML. So we have created the XML-specific XMLInvoices, XMLInvoice, and XMLItem structs to solve this. And since the invoicedata program requires us to have parallel sets of structs, we must also provide a means of converting between them. Of course, applications that use XML as their primary storage format would need only one `struct` (or one set of `structs`) and would add the necessary `encoding/xml` package tags directly to those `structs`' fields.

Here is the `XMLInvoices` struct that will be used to hold the entire data set.

```
type XMLInvoices struct {
    XMLName xml.Name        `xml:"INVOICES"`
    Version int             `xml:"version,attr"`
    Invoice []*XMLInvoice `xml:"INVOICE"`
}
```

No `struct` tag has any intrinsic semantics in Go—they are just strings accessible using Go's reflection interface (§9.4.9, ➤ 427). However, the `encoding/xml` package requires us to use such tags to provide it with information about how we want it to map our `structs`' fields to or from XML. An `xml.Name` field is used to name the tag that will contain the `struct` that the field is in. Fields tagged with `xml:",attr"` will become attributes of the tag using the field name as the attribute name. We can force another name to be used if we wish, by preceding the comma with the name we want to use. We have done so here to make the `Version` field become an attribute called `version`, rather than accepting the default name of `Version`. If the tag just contains a name, this name is used to indicate nested tags, `<INVOICE>` in this example. One important subtlety to note is that instead of calling the `XMLInvoices`'s invoices field `Invoices`, we have called it `Invoice` to (case-insensitively) match the tag name.

Here is the original `Invoice` struct and the parallel XML-equivalent `XMLInvoice`.

```
                                      type XMLInvoice struct {
type Invoice struct {                     XMLName    xml.Name  `xml:"INVOICE"`
    Id         int                        Id         int       `xml:",attr"`
    CustomerId int                        CustomerId int       `xml:",attr"`
    Raised     time.Time                  Raised     string    `xml:",attr"`
    Due        time.Time                  Due        string    `xml:",attr"`
    Paid       bool                       Paid       bool      `xml:",attr"`
    Note       string                     Note       string    `xml:"NOTE"`
    Items      []*Item                    Item       []*XMLItem `xml:"ITEM"`
}                                     }
```

We have used the default names for the attributes here—for example, field `Cus-tomerId` will become an attribute with exactly the same name. There are two nested tags, `<NOTE>` and `<ITEM>`, and just as for the `XMLInvoices` struct, instead of calling the XML invoice's items field `Items`, we have called it `Item` to (case-insensitively) match the tag name.

We have made the `XMLInvoice`'s `Raised` and `Due` fields `strings` since we want to handle their values ourselves (just storing dates), rather than allow the `encoding/xml` package to store full date/time strings.

Here is the original Item struct and the parallel XML-equivalent XMLItem.

```
                                    type XMLItem struct {
type Item struct {                      XMLName  xml.Name `xml:"ITEM"`
    Id       string                     Id       string   `xml:",attr"`
    Price    float64                    Price    float64  `xml:",attr"`
    Quantity int                        Quantity int      `xml:",attr"`
    Note     string                     Note     string   `xml:"NOTE"`
}                                   }
```

The XMLItem's fields are tagged to make them attributes, except for the Note field which will become a nested <NOTE> tag, and the XMLName field which holds the item's own XML tag name.

Just as we did for the JSON format, for XML we have created an empty struct to give us something with which to associate the XML-specific MarshalInvoices() and UnmarshalInvoices() methods.

```
type XMLMarshaler struct{}
```

This type fulfills the generic InvoicesMarshaler and InvoicesUnmarshaler interfaces that we saw earlier (365 ◄).

```
func (XMLMarshaler) MarshalInvoices(writer io.Writer,
    invoices []*Invoice) error {
    if _, err := writer.Write([]byte(xml.Header)); err != nil {
        return err
    }
    xmlInvoices := XMLInvoicesForInvoices(invoices)
    encoder := xml.NewEncoder(writer)
    return encoder.Encode(xmlInvoices)
}
```

This method takes an io.Writer (i.e., anything that satisfies the io.Writer interface such as an open file or open compressed file), into which it can write XML. The method begins by writing the standard XML header, <?xml version="1.0" encoding="UTF-8"?> (the xml.Header constant also includes a trailing newline). Then it converts all the invoices and their items into the equivalent XML structs. Although this looks like it will use as much memory again as the original data, because Go's strings are immutable, under the hood only references to the original strings will be copied into the XML structs, so the overhead will not be as great as it appears. And for applications that use structs with XML tags directly, no conversion is necessary.

Once we have populated the xmlInvoices (of type XMLInvoices), we create a new xml.Encoder, passing it the io.Writer we want it to write to. Then we encode all

the data as XML and return the encoder's return value—which will be either an
error or nil.

```go
func XMLInvoicesForInvoices(invoices []*Invoice) *XMLInvoices {
    xmlInvoices := &XMLInvoices{
        Version: fileVersion,
        Invoice: make([]*XMLInvoice, 0, len(invoices)),
    }
    for _, invoice := range invoices {
        xmlInvoices.Invoice = append(xmlInvoices.Invoice,
            XMLInvoiceForInvoice(invoice))
    }
    return xmlInvoices
}
```

This function takes an []*Invoice and returns an *XMLInvoices that has all the
data converted to *XMLInvoices (and containing *XMLItems rather than *Items),
relying on the XmlInvoiceForInvoice() function to do all the work.

We never have to populate an xml.Name field ourselves (unless we want to use
namespaces), so here when we create the *XMLInvoices we need only populate the
Version field to ensure that our <INVOICES> tag has a version attribute—for example, <INVOICES version="100">. We have also set the Invoice field to be an empty
slice with sufficient capacity for all the invoices. This isn't strictly necessary, but
is potentially more efficient than leaving the field's initial value as nil, since it
means the built-in append() function will never have to allocate memory and copy
data to grow the slice behind the scenes.

```go
func XMLInvoiceForInvoice(invoice *Invoice) *XMLInvoice {
    xmlInvoice := &XMLInvoice{
        Id:         invoice.Id,
        CustomerId: invoice.CustomerId,
        Raised:     invoice.Raised.Format(dateFormat),
        Due:        invoice.Due.Format(dateFormat),
        Paid:       invoice.Paid,
        Note:       invoice.Note,
        Item:       make([]*XMLItem, 0, len(invoice.Items)),
    }
    for _, item := range invoice.Items {
        xmlItem := &XMLItem{
            Id:       item.Id,
            Price:    item.Price,
            Quantity: item.Quantity,
            Note:     item.Note,
        }
```

```
          xmlInvoice.Item = append(xmlInvoice.Item, xmlItem)
    }
    return xmlInvoice
}
```

This function takes an Invoice and returns the equivalent XMLInvoice. The conversion is straightforward: We simply copy most of the Invoice field values to the corresponding XMLInvoice fields. Since we have chosen to handle the raised and due dates ourselves (so that we store only dates and not full date/times), we convert them to strings. And for the Invoice.Items field we append each item as an XMLItem to the XMLInvoice.Item slice. We used the same potential optimization as before, creating the Item slice to have sufficient capacity to avoid append() ever having to allocate memory and copy data. We discussed the writing of time.Time values when covering the JSON format earlier (368 ◀).

One final point to note is that nowhere in our code do we do any XML-escaping—this is taken care of automatically by the xml.Encoder.Encode() method.

8.1.2.2. Reading XML Files

Reading XML files is slightly more involved than writing, especially if we have to parse some fields ourselves (such as dates); but it isn't difficult if we use suitable XML-tagged structs.

```
func (XMLMarshaler) UnmarshalInvoices(reader io.Reader) ([]*Invoice,
    error) {
    xmlInvoices := &XMLInvoices{}
    decoder := xml.NewDecoder(reader)
    if err := decoder.Decode(xmlInvoices); err != nil {
        return nil, err
    }
    if xmlInvoices.Version > fileVersion {
        return nil, fmt.Errorf("version %d is too new to read",
            xmlInvoices.Version)
    }
    return xmlInvoices.Invoices()
}
```

This method takes an io.Reader (i.e., anything that satisfies the io.Reader interface such as an open file or open compressed file), from which to read XML. The method begins by creating a pointer to an empty XMLInvoices struct and an xml.Decoder for reading the io.Reader. The entire XML file is then parsed by the xml.Decoder.Decode() method, and if the parse is successful the *XMLInvoices struct is populated with the XML file's data. If the parse failed (e.g., if there was an XML syntax error or if the file isn't an invoices file), the decoder will return an error which we immediately pass to the caller. If the parse is successful we check the version, and if it is one we can handle we convert all the XML structs back to the structs used internally in our program. Naturally, this conversion step would be unnecessary if we used only XML-tagged structs.

```
func (xmlInvoices *XMLInvoices) Invoices() (invoices []*Invoice,
    err error) {
    invoices = make([]*Invoice, 0, len(xmlInvoices.Invoice))
    for _, xmlInvoice := range xmlInvoices.Invoice {
        invoice, err := xmlInvoice.Invoice()
        if err != nil {
            return nil, err
        }
        invoices = append(invoices, invoice)
    }
    return invoices, nil
}
```

The XMLInvoices.Invoices() method converts an *XMLInvoices into an []*Invoice. It is the inverse of the XmlInvoicesForInvoices() function (374 ◄), and passes all the conversion work onto the XMLInvoice.Invoice() method.

```
func (xmlInvoice *XMLInvoice) Invoice() (invoice *Invoice, err error) {
    invoice = &Invoice{
        Id:         xmlInvoice.Id,
        CustomerId: xmlInvoice.CustomerId,
        Paid:       xmlInvoice.Paid,
        Note:       strings.TrimSpace(xmlInvoice.Note),
        Items:      make([]*Item, 0, len(xmlInvoice.Item)),
    }
    if invoice.Raised, err = time.Parse(dateFormat, xmlInvoice.Raised);
        err != nil {
        return nil, err
    }
    if invoice.Due, err = time.Parse(dateFormat, xmlInvoice.Due);
        err != nil {
        return nil, err
    }
    for _, xmlItem := range xmlInvoice.Item {
        item := &Item{
            Id:       xmlItem.Id,
            Price:    xmlItem.Price,
            Quantity: xmlItem.Quantity,
            Note:     strings.TrimSpace(xmlItem.Note),
        }
        invoice.Items = append(invoice.Items, item)
```

```
    }
    return invoice, nil
}
```

This XMLInvoice.Invoice() method is used to return the *Invoice that's equivalent to the *XMLInvoice it is called on.

The method begins by creating an Invoice with most of the fields populated from the XMLInvoice, and with the Items field set to an empty slice with sufficient capacity for the items.

Then the two date/time valued fields are populated manually, since we opted to handle these ourselves. The time.Parse() function takes a date/time format string (which, as noted earlier, must be based on the precise date/time 2006-01-02T15:04:05Z07:00), and a string to parse, and returns the equivalent time.Time and nil—or nil and an error.

Next, the invoice's Items field is populated by iterating over the *XMLItems in the XMLInvoice's Item field and creating equivalent *Items. And at the end, the *Invoice is returned.

Just as when writing XML, we don't have to concern ourselves with unescaping any XML we read—the xml.Decoder.Decode() function takes care of this automatically.

The xml package supports much more sophisticated tags than we have needed here, including nesting. For example, the tag name `xml:"Books>Author"` would result in the XML <Books><Author>content</Author></Books>. Also, in addition to `xml:",attr"`, the package supports `xml:",chardata"` to write the field as character data, `xml:",innerxml"` to write the field verbatim, and `xml:",comment"` to write the field as an XML comment. So, by using tagged structs we are able to take full advantage of the convenient encoding and decoding functions, and at the same time exercise considerable control over how the XML is written and read.

8.1.3. Handling Plain Text Files

For plain text files we must create our own custom format, ideally one that is easy to parse and extend.

Here is the data for a single invoice in a custom plain text format.

```
INVOICE ID=5441 CUSTOMER=960 RAISED=2012-09-06 DUE=2012-10-06 PAID=true
ITEM ID=BE9066 PRICE=400.89 QUANTITY=7: Keep out of <direct> sunlight
ITEM ID=AM7240 PRICE=183.69 QUANTITY=2
ITEM ID=PT9110 PRICE=105.40 QUANTITY=3: Flammable
```

The format for each invoice is an INVOICE line, then one or more ITEM lines, and finally a form-feed character. Each line (whether for invoices or their items) has the same essential structure: a word identifying the type of line, a sequence of space-separated *key=values*, and optionally, a colon-space followed by note text.

8.1.3.1. Writing Plain Text Files

Writing plain text is straightforward thanks to Go's powerful and flexible fmt package's print functions. (These were covered earlier; §3.5, 93 ◄.)

```
type TxtMarshaler struct{}

func (TxtMarshaler) MarshalInvoices(writer io.Writer,
    invoices []*Invoice) error {
    bufferedWriter := bufio.NewWriter(writer)
    defer bufferedWriter.Flush()
    var write writerFunc = func(format string,
        args ...interface{}) error {
        _, err := fmt.Fprintf(bufferedWriter, format, args...)
        return err
    }
    if err := write("%s %d\n", fileType, fileVersion); err != nil {
        return err
    }
    for _, invoice := range invoices {
        if err := write.writeInvoice(invoice); err != nil {
            return err
        }
    }
    return nil
}
```

This method begins by creating a buffered reader to operate on the file it is passed. It is essential that we defer the flushing of the buffer to guarantee that everything we write really does get written to the file (unless an error occurs).

Rather than checking every write with code of the form if _, err := fmt.Fprintf(bufferedWriter, ...); err != nil { return err } we have created a function literal that provides two simplifications. First, the write() function ignores the number of bytes written that the fmt.Fprintf() function reports. Second, the function captures the bufferedWriter so we don't have to mention it explicitly in our code.

We could have simply passed our write() function to helper functions, for example, *writeInvoice*(write, invoice). But instead we have gone a step further and have added methods to the writerFunc type. This is done simply by declaring methods (i.e., funcs) that take a writerFunc as their receiver, just as we would do for any other type. This is what allows us to make calls like `write.writeInvoice(invoice)`, that is, to be able to call methods on the `write()` function itself; and since such methods receive the `write()` function as their receiver, they can make use of it.

Notice that we had to explicitly specify the `write()` function's type (`writerFunc`)—had we not done so, Go would consider its type to be `func(string, ...interface{})` `error` (which it is, of course) and would not have allowed us to call `writerFunc` methods on it (unless we used a type conversion to type `writerFunc`).

With the convenient `write()` function (and its methods) now available, we begin by writing the file type and file version (the latter to make it easier to adapt to changing data). Then, we iterate over every invoice, and for each one we call the `write()` function's `writeInvoice()` method.

```go
const noteSep = ":"

type writerFunc func(string, ...interface{}) error

func (write writerFunc) writeInvoice(invoice *Invoice) error {
    note := ""
    if invoice.Note != "" {
        note = noteSep + " " + invoice.Note
    }
    if err := write("INVOICE ID=%d CUSTOMER=%d RAISED=%s DUE=%s "+
        "PAID=%t%s\n", invoice.Id, invoice.CustomerId,
        invoice.Raised.Format(dateFormat),
        invoice.Due.Format(dateFormat), invoice.Paid, note); err != nil {
        return err
    }
    if err := write.writeItems(invoice.Items); err != nil {
        return err
    }
    return write("\f\n")
}
```

This method is used to write each invoice. It accepts the invoice to write and writes using the `write()` function it is called on.

The invoice line is written in one go. If a note is present we write it preceded by colon-space; otherwise we write nothing at all for it. For the date/times (i.e., `time.Time` values), we use the `time.Time.Format()` method, the same as we did when writing the data in JSON and XML format (368 ◄). And for the Boolean we use the `%t` format verb (§3.5.1, 97 ◄); alternatively we could have used the `%v` verb or the `strconv.FormatBool()` function (116 ◄).

Once the invoice line has been written, we write the items, and at the end, we write a form-feed and a newline to indicate the end of the invoice's data.

```go
func (write writerFunc) writeItems(items []*Item) error {
    for _, item := range items {
        note := ""
        if item.Note != "" {
            note = noteSep + " " + item.Note
        }
        if err := write("ITEM ID=%s PRICE=%.2f QUANTITY=%d%s\n", item.Id,
            item.Price, item.Quantity, note); err != nil {
            return err
        }
    }
    return nil
}
```

The writeItems() method accepts the invoice's items and writes using the write()
function it is called on. It iterates over all the items, writing each one in turn,
and just as for invoices, writes only nonempty notes.

8.1.3.2. Reading Plain Text Files

It is almost as easy to open and read in plain text as it is to write it—but
parsing the text to reconstruct the original data can be tricky depending on the
complexity of the format.

There are four approaches that can be used. The first three approaches involve
splitting lines up and then using conversion functions such as strconv.Atoi()
and time.Parse() for nonstring fields. These approaches are, first, manual parsing (e.g., character by character or word by word)—this can be tedious to implement, fragile, and slow; second, using the fmt.Fields() or fmt.Split() functions
to split up each line; and third, using regular expressions. For the invoicedata
program we have used the fourth approach: This does not require us to split up
lines or to use conversion functions since almost everything we need can be handled by the fmt package's scan functions.

```go
func (TxtMarshaler) UnmarshalInvoices(reader io.Reader) ([]*Invoice,
    error) {
    bufferedReader := bufio.NewReader(reader)
    if err := checkTxtVersion(bufferedReader); err != nil {
        return nil, err
    }
    var invoices []*Invoice
    eof := false
    for lino := 2; !eof; lino++ {
        line, err := bufferedReader.ReadString('\n')
        if err == io.EOF {
```

```
                err = nil        // io.EOF isn't really an error
                eof = true       // this will end the loop at the next iteration
            } else if err != nil {
                return nil, err // finish immediately for real errors
            }
            if invoices, err = parseTxtLine(lino, line, invoices); err != nil {
                return nil, err
            }
        }
    }
    return invoices, nil
}
```

This method creates a buffered reader for the io.Reader it is passed, and passes each line in turn to a parser function. As usual for text files, we handle io. EOF specially, so that the last line is always read whether or not it ends with a newline. (Of course, this is rather liberal for this particular format.)

The file is read line by line using 1-based line numbering, as is conventional. The first line is checked to see that it has a valid file type and version, hence the line number (lino) begins at 2 when processing the actual invoice data.

Since we are working line by line and each invoice is represented by two or more lines (an INVOICE line and one or more ITEM lines), we need to keep track of the current invoice so that we can add to it as each line is read. This is easily done because invoices are appended to the invoices slice, so the current invoice is always the one at position invoices[len(invoices)-1].

When the parseTxtLine() function parses an INVOICE line it creates a new Invoice value and appends a pointer to this value to the invoices slice.

There are two techniques we can use if we want to append to a slice inside a function. The first technique is to pass a pointer to the slice and operate on the pointed-to slice. The second technique is to pass in the slice value and return the (possibly modified) slice back for the caller to assign to the original slice. The parseTxtLine() function uses the second technique. (We saw an example of the first technique earlier; §5.7, 244 ◀.)

```
func parseTxtLine(lino int, line string, invoices []*Invoice) ([]*Invoice,
    error) {
    var err error
    if strings.HasPrefix(line, "INVOICE") {
        var invoice *Invoice
        invoice, err = parseTxtInvoice(lino, line)
        invoices = append(invoices, invoice)
    } else if strings.HasPrefix(line, "ITEM") {
        if len(invoices) == 0 {
            err = fmt.Errorf("item outside of an invoice line %d", lino)
```

```
        } else {
            var item *Item
            item, err = parseTxtItem(lino, line)
            items := &invoices[len(invoices)-1].Items  ❶
            *items = append(*items, item)
        }
    }
    return invoices, err
}
```

This function takes a line number (lino; used for error reporting), the line to parse, and the slice of invoices that we want to populate.

If the line begins with the text "INVOICE", we call the parseTxtInvoice() function to parse the line and create an Invoice value—and to return a pointer to it. We then append this *Invoice to the invoices slice, and at the end return the invoices and nil or an error. Note that at this point the invoice is incomplete—we only have its ID, customer ID, raised and due dates, whether it has been paid, and any note—but we have none of its items.

If the line begins with the text "ITEM", we first check to see that there is a current invoice, (i.e., that the invoices slice isn't empty). If there is, we call the parseTxtItem() function to parse the line and create an Item value—and to return a pointer to the item. We must then add the item to the current invoice's items. This is done by taking a pointer to the current invoice's items (❶) and setting this pointer's value (i.e., the []*Item it points to) to the result of appending the new *Item to it. Of course, we could have added the *Item directly, using the code invoices[len(invoices)-1].Items = append(invoices[len(invoices)-1].Items, item).

Any other lines (e.g., empty and form-feed lines) are ignored. Incidentally, in theory this function would be faster if we made the "ITEM" case the first one since there are usually far more items than invoices or empty lines.

```
func parseTxtInvoice(lino int, line string) (invoice *Invoice,
    err error) {
    invoice = &Invoice{}
    var raised, due string
    if _, err = fmt.Sscanf(line, "INVOICE ID=%d CUSTOMER=%d "+
        "RAISED=%s DUE=%s PAID=%t", &invoice.Id, &invoice.CustomerId,
        &raised, &due, &invoice.Paid); err != nil {
        return nil, fmt.Errorf("invalid invoice %v line %d", err, lino)
    }
    if invoice.Raised, err = time.Parse(dateFormat, raised); err != nil {
        return nil, fmt.Errorf("invalid raised %v line %d", err, lino)
    }
```

```
    if invoice.Due, err = time.Parse(dateFormat, due); err != nil {
        return nil, fmt.Errorf("invalid due %v line %d", err, lino)
    }
    if i := strings.Index(line, noteSep); i > -1 {
        invoice.Note = strings.TrimSpace(line[i+len(noteSep):])
    }
    return invoice, nil
}
```

We begin by creating a zero-valued Invoice value and assigning a pointer to it
to the invoice variable (of type *Invoice). The scan functions can handle strings,
numbers, and Booleans, but not time.Time values, so we handle the raised and
due dates by scanning them in as strings and then parsing these separately. The
scan functions are listed in Table 8.2.

Table 8.2 *The Fmt Package's Scan Functions*

Parameter r is an io.Reader *to read from; s is a string to read from; fs is a format string as
used by the* fmt *package's print functions (see Table 3.4, 95 ◀); args stands for one or more
pointers (i.e., addresses) of values to populate. All the scan functions return the number
of items successfully parsed (i.e., populated) and either* nil *or an* error.

Syntax	Description
fmt.Fscan(r, args)	Reads r for successive space- or newline-separated values to populate *args*
fmt.Fscanf(r, fs, args)	Reads r for successive space-separated values as specified by the *fs* format to populate *args*
fmt.Fscanln(r, args)	Reads r for successive space-separated values to populate *args* and expects a newline or io.EOF at the end
fmt.Scan(args)	Reads os.Stdin for successive space-separated values to populate *args*
fmt.Scanf(fs, args)	Reads os.Stdin for successive space-separated values as specified by the *fs* format to populate *args*
fmt.Scanln(args)	Reads os.Stdin for successive space-separated values to populate *args* and expects a newline or io.EOF at the end
fmt.Sscan(s, args)	Reads s for successive space- or newline-separated values to populate *args*
fmt.Sscanf(s, fs, args)	Reads s for successive space-separated values as specified by the *fs* format to populate *args*
fmt.Sscanln(s, args)	Reads s for successive space-separated values to populate *args* and expects a newline or io.EOF at the end

If the `fmt.Sscanf()` function wasn't able to read in as many items as we provided values for, or if some other error occurred (e.g., a read error), it will return a non-nil error.

The dates are parsed using the `time.Parse()` function that was discussed in an earlier subsubsection (§8.1.2.2, 375 ◄). If the invoice line has a colon it means that there is a note at the end, so we retrieve this with any whitespace trimmed off. We could have used the expression `line[i+1:]` rather than `line[i+len(noteSep):]` since we know that the `noteSep`'s colon character occupies a single UTF-8 byte, but we prefer to be defensive and use an approach that will work for any character, no matter how many bytes it occupies.

```
func parseTxtItem(lino int, line string) (item *Item, err error) {
    item = &Item{}
    if _, err = fmt.Sscanf(line, "ITEM ID=%s PRICE=%f QUANTITY=%d",
        &item.Id, &item.Price, &item.Quantity); err != nil {
        return nil, fmt.Errorf("invalid item %v line %d", err, lino)
    }
    if i := strings.Index(line, noteSep); i > -1 {
        item.Note = strings.TrimSpace(line[i+len(noteSep):])
    }
    return item, nil
}
```

This function works just like the `parseTxtInvoice()` function we have just seen, except that all the item values, apart from the note, can be scanned directly.

```
func checkTxtVersion(bufferedReader *bufio.Reader) error {
    var version int
    if _, err := fmt.Fscanf(bufferedReader, "INVOICES %d\n", &version);
        err != nil {
        return errors.New("cannot read non-invoices text file")
    } else if version > fileVersion {
        return fmt.Errorf("version %d is too new to read", version)
    }
    return nil
}
```

This function is used to read the very first line of the invoices text file. It uses the `fmt.Fscanf()` function to read the `bufio.Reader` directly. If the file isn't an invoices file or if the version is too recent for the program to handle, it reports an error; otherwise it returns nil.

Writing text files is easy using the `fmt` package's print functions. Parsing text files is fairly challenging but we are well provided for with Go's `regexp` package, its `strings.Fields()` and `strings.Split()` functions, and the `fmt` package's scan functions.

8.1.4. Handling Go Binary Files

The Go binary ("gob") format is a self-describing sequence of binary values. Internally, the Go binary format consists of a sequence of zero or more chunks, each of which has a byte count, a sequence of zero or more *typeId–typeSpecification* pairs, and a *typeId–value* pair. The *typeId–typeSpecification* pairs may be omitted if the value pair's *typeId* is predefined (e.g., `bool`, `int`, `string`, etc.); otherwise each of the type pairs is used to describe a custom type (e.g., a custom `struct`). Type pair *typeId*s are negated to distinguish between type pairs and value pairs. As we will see, we don't need to know any of the internals to make use of gob format, since the `encoding/gob` package takes care of all the low-level details for us, behind the scenes.*

The `encoding/gob` package provides encoder and decoder functionality in much the same way as the `encoding/json` package does, and is just as easy to use. In general, gob format is the most convenient Go format to use for data files or for transmitting data over network connections, providing that human readability is not a requirement.

8.1.4.1. Writing Go Binary Files

Here is a method for writing an entire data set of `[]*Invoice` items to an open file (or anything else that fulfills the `io.Writer` interface) in gob format.

```
type GobMarshaler struct{}

func (GobMarshaler) MarshalInvoices(writer io.Writer,
    invoices []*Invoice) error {
    encoder := gob.NewEncoder(writer)
    if err := encoder.Encode(magicNumber); err != nil {
        return err
    }
    if err := encoder.Encode(fileVersion); err != nil {
        return err
    }
    return encoder.Encode(invoices)
}
```

We begin by creating a gob encoder that wraps the `io.Writer` and provides a writer to which we can write our data.

---

*A more detailed description of the format is given in the documentation, golang.org/pkg/encoding/gob/. And Rob Pike has written an interesting blog post on gob format, blog.golang.org/2011/03/gobs-of-data.html .

We write the data using the gob.Encoder.Encode() method. This method copes perfectly with our slice of invoices each of which contains its own slice of items. The method returns an error or nil; if we get an error we immediately return it to the caller.

Writing a magic number and a file version isn't necessary, of course, but as one of the exercises will show, doing this makes it easier to change the file format later on.

Notice that the method isn't really concerned with the types of the data it encodes, so it is trivial to create similar functions for writing gob data. Furthermore, the GobMarshaler.MarshalInvoices() method will not require any changes to write in a new format.

Since our Invoice struct's fields are all Booleans, numbers, strings, time.Times, or structs (i.e., Items) which themselves only contain Booleans, numbers, strings, time.Times, or structs, the code shown here works as is.

If our structs contained fields that are not gob-encodable we would have to make our structs satisfy the gob.GobEncoder and gob.GobDecoder interfaces. The gob encoder is smart enough to check whether a value it is asked to encode is a gob.GobEncoder, and if it is, the encoder uses the value's own GobEncode() method rather than using its own built-in encoding code. The same thing applies to decoding with the check being made for a GobDecode() method that satisfies the gob.GobDecoder interface. (The invoicedata example's source code's gob.go file includes the—unnecessary, and commented out—code to make an Invoice a gob encoder and decoder, just to show an easy way to do it.) Making a struct satisfy these interfaces can significantly slow down gob writing and reading, as well as producing larger files.

8.1.4.2. Reading Go Binary Files

Reading gob data is just as easy as writing it—providing we read it back into top-level variables of the same types as the ones written. The GobMarshaler.UnmarshalInvoices() method takes an io.Reader (e.g., a file opened for reading) from which to read the gob data.

```go
func (GobMarshaler) UnmarshalInvoices(reader io.Reader) ([]*Invoice,
    error) {
    decoder := gob.NewDecoder(reader)
    var magic int
    if err := decoder.Decode(&magic); err != nil {
        return nil, err
    }
    if magic != magicNumber {
        return nil, errors.New("cannot read non-invoices gob file")
    }
```

```
    var version int
    if err := decoder.Decode(&version); err != nil {
        return nil, err
    }
    if version > fileVersion {
        return nil, fmt.Errorf("version %d is too new to read", version)
    }
    var invoices []*Invoice
    err := decoder.Decode(&invoices)
    return invoices, err
}
```

We have three items of data to read in: the magic number, the file version, and all the invoices data. The gob.Decoder.Decode() method takes a pointer to the value it must populate with the gob data it decodes, and returns an error or nil. We use the first two variables (magic and version) to check that we have a gob invoices file and that the file version is one we can handle. Then we read the invoices, in the process of which the gob.Decoder.Decode() method will increase the size of the invoices slice to accommodate the invoices it reads and will populate the slice with pointers to Invoices (and their Items) that the function creates on the fly as necessary. At the end, the method returns the invoices and nil or an error if a problem occurred.

If the invoices data is changed by the addition of exported fields, this method will continue to work as is for Booleans, numbers, strings, time.Times, and structs containing these types. Of course, for data that contains other types, we must update the methods that satisfy the gob.GobEncoder and gob.GobDecoder interfaces.

When dealing with struct types, the gob format is very flexible, coping seamlessly with some differences. For example, if a struct that has a value is written in gob format, the value can be read back into the same struct—or into many similar struct types, perhaps one which has a pointer to the value, or where the type of the value is different but compatible (int vs. uint or similar). And as the invoicedata example shows, gob format has no problem handling nested data (although, at the time of this writing, it cannot handle recursive values). The gob documentation discusses what differences the format can cope with and explains the format's internals, none of which need concern us providing we use the same types for writing and for reading—just as we have done in this example.

8.1.5. Handling Custom Binary Files

Although Go's encoding/gob package is very easy to use and requires very little code, we might still need to create our own custom binary formats. A custom binary format is likely to achieve the most compact data representation possible and can be very fast to write and read. In practice, we have found that writing and reading in Go Binary format is dramatically faster than using a custom binary format—and creates files that are not much bigger. However, some of this advantage is lost if we must handle data that isn't gob-encodable by satisfying the gob.GobEncoder and gob.GobDecoder interfaces. Of course, in some situations we may need to interoperate with other software that uses its own custom binary format that we must be able to write and read, so knowing how to work with binary files can be very useful.

Figure 8.1 provides a schematic view of how the .inv custom binary format represents a single invoice. Integer values are represented by integers of specific sizes and signedness. Booleans are represented by an int8 with value 1 for true and 0 for false. Strings are represented by a byte count (of type int32) followed by a []byte of their UTF-8-encoded bytes. For dates we have taken a slightly unusual approach by representing them as int32s based on treating an ISO-8601 format date (without the hyphens) as a number. For example, we represent the date 2006-01-02 as the integer 20 060 102. Each invoice's items are represented by a count of how many items there are followed by the items themselves. (Recall that unlike invoice IDs, item IDs are strings and not ints; 362 ◄.)

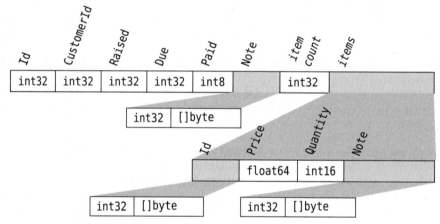

Figure 8.1 *The .inv custom binary format*

8.1.5.1. Writing Custom Binary Files

Writing data in binary format is straightforward thanks to the encoding/binary package's binary.Write() function.

```go
type InvMarshaler struct{}

var byteOrder = binary.LittleEndian

func (InvMarshaler) MarshalInvoices(writer io.Writer,
    invoices []*Invoice) error {
```

```
    var write invWriterFunc = func(x interface{}) error {
        return binary.Write(writer, byteOrder, x)
    }
    if err := write(uint32(magicNumber)); err != nil {
        return err
    }
    if err := write(uint16(fileVersion)); err != nil {
        return err
    }
    if err := write(int32(len(invoices))); err != nil {
        return err
    }
    for _, invoice := range invoices {
        if err := write.writeInvoice(invoice); err != nil {
            return err
        }
    }
    return nil
}
```

This method writes all the invoices to the given io.Writer. It begins by creating a convenience write() function which captures both the io.Writer and the byte order we want to use. Just as we did for .txt format, we have set the write() function to be of a specific type (invWriterFunc), and have created some methods for the write() function (e.g., invWriterFunc.writeInvoices()), to make it more convenient to use later on.

Note that it is *essential* that we use the same byte order for writing and reading binary data. (We can't make our byteOrder a constant, because binary.Little-Endian—or binary.BigEndian for that matter—isn't a simple value like a string or number.)

Writing the data is very similar to what we have seen before for other formats. One important difference is that once we have written the magic number and file version, we write a count of how many invoices are going to be written. (It would also have been possible to skip the count and simply write out the invoices; then, when reading back, we would have to keep reading one invoice at a time until we reached io.EOF.)

```
type invWriterFunc func(interface{}) error

func (write invWriterFunc) writeInvoice(invoice *Invoice) error {
    for _, i := range []int{invoice.Id, invoice.CustomerId} {
        if err := write(int32(i)); err != nil {
            return err
        }
```

```
    }
    for _, date := range []time.Time{invoice.Raised, invoice.Due} {
        if err := write.writeDate(date); err != nil {
            return err
        }
    }
    if err := write.writeBool(invoice.Paid); err != nil {
        return err
    }
    if err := write.writeString(invoice.Note); err != nil {
        return err
    }
    if err := write(int32(len(invoice.Items))); err != nil {
        return err
    }
    for _, item := range invoice.Items {
        if err := write.writeItem(item); err != nil {
            return err
        }
    }
    return nil
}
```

The writeInvoice() method is called for each invoice. It accepts a pointer to the invoice to write and writes using the write() function it is called on.

The method begins by writing the invoice's ID and customer ID as int32s. It is legal to write plain ints, but this is nonportable since the size of an int may vary depending on the underlying machine and the version of Go being used, so it is very important to always write specifically signed and sized integers such as uint32, int32, and so on. Next, we write the raised and due dates using a custom writeDate() method, and then the paid Boolean and the note string, again using custom methods. Finally, we write a count of how many items the invoice has, followed by the items themselves, each written by the custom writeItem() method.

```
const invDateFormat = "20060102" // This date must always be used.

func (write invWriterFunc) writeDate(date time.Time) error {
    i, err := strconv.Atoi(date.Format(invDateFormat))
    if err != nil {
        return err
    }
    return write(int32(i))
}
```

We discussed the time.Time.Format() function—and why we must use the specific date 2006-01-02 in format strings—earlier (368 ◄). Here we have used an ISO-8601-like format, but with no hyphens so that we get a string of exactly eight digits with leading zeros for single-digit month and day numbers. We then convert this string into an integer—for example, if we have the date 2012-08-05, we convert it to an equivalent number, that is, 20 120 805, and then write this number as an int32.

Incidentally, if we wanted to store date/times rather than just dates, or just wanted a faster computation, we could replace calls to this method with write(int64(*date*.Unix()))) and store the seconds since the Unix epoch. The corresponding reader would be something like var *d* int64; if err := binary.Read(*reader*, *byteOrder*, &*d*); err != nil { return err }; *date* := time.Unix(*d*, 0).

```
func (write invWriterFunc) writeBool(b bool) error {
    var v int8
    if b {
        v = 1
    }
    return write(v)
}
```

At the time of this writing, the encoding/binary package has no support for writing or reading bools so we have created this simple method to handle them. Incidentally, we didn't need to use a conversion (e.g., int8(v)), because variable v is already a signed and sized type.

```
func (write invWriterFunc) writeString(s string) error {
    if err := write(int32(len(s))); err != nil {
        return err
    }
    return write([]byte(s))
}
```

Strings must be written out as their underlying UTF-8-encoded bytes. Here, we first write a count of how many bytes we will write and then the bytes themselves. (If we had fixed-width data we wouldn't need the count, of course, providing that when it came to reading, we created an empty []byte of the same size as was written.)

```
func (write invWriterFunc) writeItem(item *Item) error {
    if err := write.writeString(item.Id); err != nil {
        return err
    }
    if err := write(item.Price); err != nil {
        return err
```

```
    }
    if err := write(int16(item.Quantity)); err != nil {
        return err
    }
    return write.writeString(item.Note)
}
```

This method is called to write every item for every invoice. For the string ID and
for the note we use the invWriterFunc.writeString() method, and for the quantity
we use an integer of a particular size and signedness. For the price, though, we
write it as is since it is already a sized type (float64).

There's nothing difficult about writing binary data, providing we are careful
to write counts before variable-width data so that we know how many items to
read back in. Using gob format is much more convenient, of course, but using a
custom binary format should produce smaller files.

8.1.5.2. Reading Custom Binary Files

Reading custom binary data is almost as straightforward as writing it. We don't
have to parse the data as such; we just read each datum, using the same byte
ordering as was used for writing, into a value of the same type as was written.

```
func (InvMarshaler) UnmarshalInvoices(reader io.Reader) ([]*Invoice,
    error) {
    if err := checkInvVersion(reader); err != nil {
        return nil, err
    }
    count, err := readIntFromInt32(reader)
    if err != nil {
        return nil, err
    }
    invoices := make([]*Invoice, 0, count)
    for i := 0; i < count; i++ {
        invoice, err := readInvInvoice(reader)
        if err != nil {
            return nil, err
        }
        invoices = append(invoices, invoice)
    }
    return invoices, nil
}
```

This method begins by checking that we have an invoices file of a version that
we can handle. Then it reads in the number of invoices in the file using a custom
readIntFromInt32() function. We set the invoices slice to have zero length (i.e.,

no invoices), but with the exact capacity that we need. Then we read in each invoice in turn and append it to the invoices slice.

An alternative approach would have been to replace the make() call with make([]*invoice, count) and the append() line with invoices[i] = invoice. However, we prefer to create slices with the capacity they need, since this is potentially faster than growing a slice on the fly. After all, if we append to a slice whose length is equal to its capacity, a new slice will be created under the hood and the original slice's data will be copied into it—whereas if the capacity is sufficient in the first place, no copying is required.

```go
func checkInvVersion(reader io.Reader) error {
    var magic uint32
    if err := binary.Read(reader, byteOrder, &magic); err != nil {
        return err
    }
    if magic != magicNumber {
        return errors.New("cannot read non-invoices inv file")
    }
    var version uint16
    if err := binary.Read(reader, byteOrder, &version); err != nil {
        return err
    }
    if version > fileVersion {
        return fmt.Errorf("version %d is too new to read", version)
    }
    return nil
}
```

This function tries to read in the file's magic number and version. It returns nil if the file is acceptable and an error otherwise.

The binary.Read() function is the complement of the binary.Write() function—it takes an io.Reader to read from, the byte order to use, and a pointer to an item of the exact type for it to populate.

```go
func readIntFromInt32(reader io.Reader) (int, error) {
    var i32 int32
    err := binary.Read(reader, byteOrder, &i32)
    return int(i32), err
}
```

This custom helper function is used to read an int32 from a binary file and return it as a plain int.

```
func readInvInvoice(reader io.Reader) (invoice *Invoice, err error) {
    invoice = &Invoice{}
    for _, pId := range []*int{&invoice.Id, &invoice.CustomerId} {
        if *pId, err = readIntFromInt32(reader); err != nil {
            return nil, err
        }
    }
    for _, pDate := range []*time.Time{&invoice.Raised, &invoice.Due} {
        if *pDate, err = readInvDate(reader); err != nil {
            return nil, err
        }
    }
    if invoice.Paid, err = readBoolFromInt8(reader); err != nil {
        return nil, err
    }
    if invoice.Note, err = readInvString(reader); err != nil {
        return nil, err
    }
    var count int
    if count, err = readIntFromInt32(reader); err != nil {
        return nil, err
    }
    invoice.Items, err = readInvItems(reader, count)
    return invoice, err
}
```

This function is called to read each invoice in turn. It begins by creating a new zero-valued invoice and storing a pointer to it in the `invoice` variable.

The invoice ID and customer ID are read using the custom `readIntFromInt32()` function. The code is slightly subtle in that we iterate over pointers to the invoice ID and customer ID and assign the `int` returned by the function to the value that the pointer (`pId`) points to.

An alternative would be to handle each ID separately—for example, `if invoice.Id, err = readIntFromInt32(reader); err != nil { return err }`, and so on.

Reading the raised and due dates follows exactly the same pattern as reading the IDs, only this time we use a custom `readInvDate()` function.

Just as for the IDs, we could have handled each date separately and more simply—for example, `if invoice.Due, err = readInvDate(reader); err != nil { return err }`, and so on.

The paid Boolean and the note string are read in using helper functions that we will review in a moment. After the invoice's data has been read we read how many items it has and then read them all in using the readInvItems() function, passing it the io.Reader to read from and the number of items to read.

```
func readInvDate(reader io.Reader) (time.Time, error) {
    var n int32
    if err := binary.Read(reader, byteOrder, &n); err != nil {
        return time.Time{}, err
    }
    return time.Parse(invDateFormat, fmt.Sprint(n))
}
```

This function reads an int32 that represents a date (e.g., 20 130 501), and then parses the string representation of the number as a date and returns the corresponding time.Time (e.g., 2013-05-01).

```
func readBoolFromInt8(reader io.Reader) (bool, error) {
    var i8 int8
    err := binary.Read(reader, byteOrder, &i8)
    return i8 == 1, err
}
```

This simple helper returns true if the int8 it reads is 1; and false otherwise.

```
func readInvString(reader io.Reader) (string, error) {
    var length int32
    if err := binary.Read(reader, byteOrder, &length); err != nil {
        return "", nil
    }
    raw := make([]byte, length)
    if err := binary.Read(reader, byteOrder, &raw); err != nil {
        return "", err
    }
    return string(raw), nil
}
```

This function reads in a []byte, but the principle it uses applies to slices of any type that have been written preceded by a count of how many items they contain.

First, the number of items is read into the length variable. Then a slice of this exact length is created. When the binary.Read() function is passed a pointer to a slice it reads as many items of the slice's type as there are items in the slice (or fails and returns a non-nil error). Notice that it is the slice's *length* that matters, not its capacity (which may equal or exceed the length).

In this case the []byte holds UTF-8-encoded bytes that we return converted to a string.

```go
func readInvItems(reader io.Reader, count int) ([]*Item, error) {
    items := make([]*Item, 0, count)
    for i := 0; i < count; i++ {
        item, err := readInvItem(reader)
        if err != nil {
            return nil, err
        }
        items = append(items, item)
    }
    return items, nil
}
```

This function reads in all of an invoice's items. It knows how many items to read because it is passed the count.

```go
func readInvItem(reader io.Reader) (item *Item, err error) {
    item = &Item{}
    if item.Id, err = readInvString(reader); err != nil {
        return nil, err
    }
    if err = binary.Read(reader, byteOrder, &item.Price); err != nil {
        return nil, err
    }
    if item.Quantity, err = readIntFromInt16(reader); err != nil {
        return nil, err
    }
    item.Note, err = readInvString(reader)
    return item, nil
}
```

This function reads each individual item. Structurally, it is very similar to the readInvInvoice() function in that it creates a zero-valued Item and stores a pointer to it in the item variable, and then populates the item's fields. The price can be read directly since that was written as a float64—that is, as a sized type—and the Item.Price field has the same type. (We have omitted the readIntFromInt16() function since it is almost identical to the readIntFromInt32() function we saw earlier; 393 ◄.)

This completes our review of writing and reading custom binary data. Working with binary data isn't difficult, so long as we are careful to use specifically signed and sized integers and to precede variable-length values (e.g., slices) with their length.

Go's support for binary files includes random access. In such cases we must open the file using the os.OpenFile() function (rather than os.Open()), and pass suitable permission flags and mode (e.g., os.O_RDWR "read–write") arguments.* We can then use the os.File.Seek() method to position ourselves in the file for reading or writing, or the os.File.ReadAt() and os.File.WriteAt() methods for reading or writing from or to the file at specific byte offsets. Other useful methods are also provided, including os.File.Stat() which returns an os.FileInfo that provides details of the file's size, permissions, and date/times.

8.2. Archive Files

Go's standard library provides support for several compression formats. This includes gzip, so it is easy to make Go programs able to seamlessly write and read files with gzip compression if they end with a .gz suffix and without compression otherwise. In addition, the library has packages which allow us to write and read .zip files and tarballs (.tar and .tar.gz), and to read .bz2 files (typically, .tar.bz2 files).

In this section we will review extracts from two programs. The first, pack (in file pack/pack.go), accepts the name of an archive and a list of files to store in the archive on the command line. It determines which file format to use based on the archive filename's suffix. The second, unpack (in file unpack/unpack.go), also accepts the name of an archive on the command line, and attempts to extract all the archive's files, recreating the directory structure as it goes if necessary.

8.2.1. Creating Zip Archives

To use the zip package for zipping we must first open a file to write to and then create a *zip.Writer to write into it. Then, for each file we want to put in the .zip archive, we must read the file and write its contents into an io.Writer obtained from the *zip.Writer. The pack program uses two functions, createZip() and writeFileToZip(), to create a .zip file using this approach.

```
func createZip(filename string, files []string) error {
    file, err := os.Create(filename)
    if err != nil {
        return err
    }
    defer file.Close()
    zipper := zip.NewWriter(file)
```

---

* File permission flags are traditionally written using octal numbers, as indicated by a leading 0. A value of 0666 makes the file readable and writable by everyone—however, a *umask* of 0022 (a common setting) modifies this to 0644, thus making a file readable and writable by its creator and readable but not writable by everyone else.

```
    defer zipper.Close()
    for _, name := range files {
        if err := writeFileToZip(zipper, name); err != nil {
            return err
        }
    }
    return nil
}
```

This function creates an empty .zip file, then creates a *zip.Writer (zipper) to write to the file, and then iterates over all of the files, writing each one in turn to the .zip file.

The createZip() and writeFileToZip() functions are both very short and so it might be tempting to incorporate them into a single function. This would be unwise since it would mean that in the for loop we would open file after file (i.e., all those in the files slice), and might exceed the operating system's capacity for open files—something we discussed briefly in the previous chapter (352 ◄). Of course, instead of deferring the os.File.Close() calls we could do them at each iteration; but this would take some care to ensure that the file is closed whether or not an error occurs. So, the simplest and cleanest solution it to always create a separate function for handling each individual file as we have done here.

```
func writeFileToZip(zipper *zip.Writer, filename string) error {
    file, err := os.Open(filename)
    if err != nil {
        return err
    }
    defer file.Close()
    info, err := file.Stat()
    if err != nil {
        return err
    }
    header, err := zip.FileInfoHeader(info)
    if err != nil {
        return err
    }
    header.Name = sanitizedName(filename)
    writer, err := zipper.CreateHeader(header)
    if err != nil {
        return err
    }
    _, err = io.Copy(writer, file)
    return err
}
```

We begin by opening the file to be zipped ready for reading, and defer closing it, in the familiar way.

Next, we call the os.File.Stat() method to retrieve the file's timestamp and permission values as an os.FileInfo value. We then feed this value into the zip.FileInfoHeader() function which returns a zip.FileHeader value that is populated with the timestamp, permissions, and filename. We are not obliged to use the same filename in the archive as the original filename, and here we have chosen to overwrite the filename (in the zip.FileHeader.Name field) with a sanitized version.

With the header set up we call the zip.CreateHeader() function, passing it the header as argument. This creates an entry in the .zip archive with the header's timestamp, permissions, and filename, and returns an io.Writer that we can use to write the contents of the file to be archived. For this purpose, we have used the io.Copy() function—this returns the number of bytes copied (which we have discarded), and either nil or an error.

If an error occurs at any point we return it immediately for the caller to handle. And if there is no error, at the end, the .zip archive contains the given file.

```
func sanitizedName(filename string) string {
    if len(filename) > 1 && filename[1] == ':' &&
        runtime.GOOS == "windows" {
        filename = filename[2:]
    }
    filename = filepath.ToSlash(filename)
    filename = strings.TrimLeft(filename, "/.")
    return strings.Replace(filename, "../", "", -1)
}
```

If an archive contains files with absolute paths or paths that include .. path components, when we unpack the archive we could end up overwriting important files by accident. To reduce this risk we sanitize the name of every file we store in the archive.

The sanitizedName() function gets rid of a leading drive letter and colon (if present), then strips away any leading directory separators and periods, and any .. path components. It also forces file separators to be slashes.

8.2.2. Creating Optionally Compressed Tarballs

Creating tarballs is fairly similar to creating .zip archives, with the key differences being that we write all the data to the same writer, and that we must write a full header before each file's data, not just a filename. Our implementation for the pack program uses the createTar() and writeFileToTar() functions.

```go
func createTar(filename string, files []string) error {
    file, err := os.Create(filename)
    if err != nil {
        return err
    }
    defer file.Close()
    var fileWriter io.WriteCloser = file
    if strings.HasSuffix(filename, ".gz") {
        fileWriter = gzip.NewWriter(file)
        defer fileWriter.Close()
    }
    writer := tar.NewWriter(fileWriter)
    defer writer.Close()
    for _, name := range files {
        if err := writeFileToTar(writer, name); err != nil {
            return err
        }
    }
    return nil
}
```

This function creates the given tarball file and adds gzip filtering if the filename's suffix indicates that the tarball should be compressed. The gzip. NewWriter() function returns a *gzip.Writer which fulfills the io.WriteCloser interface (just as the opened *os.File does).

Once the file is ready for writing to, we create a *tar.Writer to write to it. Then we iterate over all the files and attempt to write each one in turn.

```go
func writeFileToTar(writer *tar.Writer, filename string) error {
    file, err := os.Open(filename)
    if err != nil {
        return err
    }
    defer file.Close()
    stat, err := file.Stat()
    if err != nil {
        return err
    }
    header := &tar.Header{
        Name:   sanitizedName(filename),
        Mode:   int64(stat.Mode()),
        Uid:    os.Getuid(),
        Gid:    os.Getgid(),
        Size:   stat.Size(),
```

```
        ModTime: stat.ModTime(),
    }
    if err = writer.WriteHeader(header); err != nil {
        return err
    }
    _, err = io.Copy(writer, file)
    return err
}
```

This function begins by opening the given file for reading and deferring closing the file. It then does a *stat* call on the file to retrieve the file's mode, size, and modification date/time—this data is used to populate the *tar.Header that must be created for each file that is written to the tarball. (In addition we set the header's user and group IDs; these are used on Unix-like systems.) We should always at the very least set the header's filename (the Name field), and we *must* set its Size field to the size of the file, or the tarball will be invalid.

Once the *.tar.Header has been created and populated, we write the header into the tarball. Then, finally, we copy the file's contents into the tarball.

8.2.3. Unpacking Zip Archives

Unzipping a .zip file is just as straightforward as zipping one, only we must re-create the directory structure if the archive contains filenames that include paths.

```
func unpackZip(filename string) error {
    reader, err := zip.OpenReader(filename)
    if err != nil {
        return err
    }
    defer reader.Close()
    for _, zipFile := range reader.Reader.File {
        name := sanitizedName(zipFile.Name)
        mode := zipFile.Mode()
        if mode.IsDir() {
            if err = os.MkdirAll(name, 0755); err != nil {
                return err
            }
        } else {
            if err = unpackZippedFile(name, zipFile); err != nil {
                return err
            }
        }
    }
}
```

```
        return nil
}
```

This function opens the given .zip file for reading. Instead of us having to call os.Open() to open the file and then calling zip.NewReader(), the zip package provides the zip.OpenReader() function which conveniently does both and returns a *zip.ReadCloser for us to work with. The most important aspect of the zip.ReadCloser is that it contains an exported zip.Reader struct field that contains a []*zip.File—a slice of pointers to zip.File structs, each one representing a file inside the .zip file.

We iterate over each of the reader's zip.File structs and create a sanitized file or directory name (using the same sanitizedName() function as we used in the pack program; 399 ◄), to reduce the risk of overwriting important files.

If we have a directory (as reported by the *zip.File's os.FileMode's IsDir() method), we try to create the directory. The os.MkdirAll() function has the useful properties that it will create any intermediate directories that are necessary to create the specified directory, and that it safely does nothing and returns nil if the directory already exists.* If we have a file, we pass on the work of unzipping it to a custom unpackZippedFile() function.

```
func unpackZippedFile(filename string, zipFile *zip.File) error {
    writer, err := os.Create(filename)
    if err != nil {
        return err
    }
    defer writer.Close()
    reader, err := zipFile.Open()
    if err != nil {
        return err
    }
    defer reader.Close()
    if _, err = io.Copy(writer, reader); err != nil {
        return err
    }
    if filename == zipFile.Name {
        fmt.Println(filename)
    } else {
        fmt.Printf("%s [%s]\n", filename, zipFile.Name)
    }
    return nil
}
```

---

*As noted earlier, file permission flags are traditionally written using octal numbers, with 0666 being a sensible choice for files. For directories, a sensible choice is 0755.

This function extracts a single file from the .zip archive file and writes it to the file system. It begins in the usual way by creating the file to be written. Then it opens the given .zip file's file using the zip.File.Open() function and writes the archived file's data to the newly created file.

At the end, providing no error has occurred, the function prints the name of the file it created to the console, with the original filename in brackets if the sanitized filename is different.

Incidentally, the *zip.File type has other useful methods, such as zip.File. Mode() (used earlier in the unpackZip() function), zip.File.ModTime() (which returns the file's modification time as a time.Time), and zip.FileInfo() which returns the file's os.FileInfo value.

8.2.4. Unpacking Optionally Compressed Tarballs

Unpacking tar files is slightly easier than packing them. However, just as when we unzip a .zip file, we must re-create the directory structure if the archive contains filenames that include paths.

```go
func unpackTar(filename string) error {
    file, err := os.Open(filename)
    if err != nil {
        return err
    }
    defer file.Close()
    var fileReader io.ReadCloser = file
    if strings.HasSuffix(filename, ".gz") {
        if fileReader, err = gzip.NewReader(file); err != nil {
            return err
        }
        defer fileReader.Close()
    }
    reader := tar.NewReader(fileReader)
    return unpackTarFiles(reader)
}
```

This function opens the tarball in Go's conventional way and defers closing the file. If the file is gzip-compressed we create a gzip decompression filter and defer closing it. The gzip.NewReader() function returns a *gzip.Reader which fulfills the io.ReadCloser interface, just as the file (of type *os.File) does.

With the file reader set up, we create a *tar.Reader to read from it and pass on the rest of the work to a helper function.

```
func unpackTarFiles(reader *tar.Reader) error {
    for {
        header, err := reader.Next()
        if err != nil {
            if err == io.EOF {
                return nil // OK
            }
            return err
        }
        filename := sanitizedName(header.Name)
        switch header.Typeflag {
        case tar.TypeDir:
            if err = os.MkdirAll(filename, 0755); err != nil {
                return err
            }
        case tar.TypeReg:
            if err = unpackTarFile(filename, header.Name, reader);
                err != nil {
                return err
            }
        }
    }
    return nil
}
```

This function has an infinite loop that iterates over each tarball entry until
io.EOF is reached (or until an error occurs). The tar.Next() method returns the
first—or next—tarball entry's *tar.Header struct, or reports an error. If the error
is io.EOF it just means that we have finished so we return a nil error value.

If a *tar.Header is successfully obtained we create a sanitized filename based on
the header's Name field. Then we switch depending on the entry's type flag. For
this simple example program we only consider directories and regular files, but
in fact, tarballs can contain various other entries (e.g., symbolic links).

If the entry is for a directory we create the directory just the same as we did for
directories in .zip files (402 ◄). And if the entry is for a file we pass on the work
to a helper function.

```
func unpackTarFile(filename, tarFilename string,
    reader *tar.Reader) error {
    writer, err := os.Create(filename)
    if err != nil {
        return err
    }
    defer writer.Close()
```

```
    if _, err = io.Copy(writer, reader); err != nil {
        return err
    }
    if filename == tarFilename {
        fmt.Println(filename)
    } else {
        fmt.Printf("%s [%s]\n", filename, tarFilename)
    }
    return nil
}
```

This function creates a new file for the tarball's next entry, and defers closing it. Then it copies the tarball's next entry's data to the file. And just like we did for the unpackZippedFile() function, we print name of the file that was created to the console, with the original filename in brackets if the sanitized filename is different.

This concludes our coverage of compressed and archive files, and of file handling in general. Go's approach to file handling using the io.Reader, io.ReadCloser, io.Writer, and io.WriteCloser interfaces makes it easy to read and write files or other streams (such as network connections or even strings) using the same consistent coding patterns.

8.3. Exercises

There are three exercises for this chapter. The first one involves a small but slightly subtle modification to one of the programs presented in this chapter. The second requires the writing of a short—but tricky—new program from scratch. The third involves substantial changes to another of this chapter's examples.

1. Copy the unpack directory to, say, my_unpack, and modify the unpack.go program so that it can additionally unpack .tar.bz2 (bzip2-compressed) files. This requires small changes to a couple of functions, and the addition of about ten lines to the unpackTar() function. The change is a tiny bit tricky because the bzip2.NewReader() function doesn't return an io.ReadCloser. A solution is provided in the file unpack_ans/unpack.go which is about ten lines longer than the original example.

2. Windows text files (.txt) often use the UTF-16-LE (UTF-16 little-endian) encoding. UTF-16-encoded files must always begin with a byte order mark, [0xFF, 0xFE] for little-endian or [0xFE, 0xFF] for big-endian. Write a program that reads a UTF-16-encoded file named on the command line, and writes out the same text using the UTF-8 encoding either to os.Stdout or to a file named on the command line. Be sure to read both little- and big-endian UTF-16 encodings correctly. The book's examples come with a couple of

tiny test files: utf16-to-utf8/utf-16-be.txt and utf16-to-utf8/utf-16-le.txt. The binary package's Read() function can read uint16 values (which is what UTF-16 characters are) using a specified endianness. And the unicode/utf16 package's Decode() function can convert a slice of uint16 values to a slice of code points (i.e., to a []rune); so wrapping the result of a utf16.Decode() call in string() is sufficient to produce a UTF-8-encoded string. A solution is in the file utf16-to-utf8/utf16-to-utf8.go, and is around 50 lines excluding imports.

3. Copy the invoicedata directory to, say, my_invoicedata, and modify the invoicedata program in a few distinct ways. First, change the Invoice and Item structs to those shown below.

```
type Invoice struct { // fileVersion        type Item struct { // fileVersion
    Id          int       // 100                Id       string  // 100
    CustomerId  int       // 100                Price    float64 // 100
    DepartmentId string   // 101                Quantity int     // 100
    Raised      time.Time // 100                TaxBand  int     // 101
    Due         time.Time // 100                Note     string  // 100
    Paid        bool      // 100            }
    Note        string    // 100
    Items       []*Item   // 100
}
```

Now modify the program so that it always writes invoices in the new format (i.e., one that handles the new structs), and can read in invoices in the original format or in the new format.

When the program reads in data in the original format, the zero values for the extra fields are not acceptable, so populate these fields with values according to these rules: Set an invoice's department ID to "GEN" if the invoice ID is less than 3000, to "MKT" if the ID is less than 4000, to "COM" if the ID is less than 5000, to "EXP" if the ID is less than 6000, to "INP" if the ID is less than 7000, to "TZZ" if the ID is less than 8000, to "V20" if the ID is less than 9000, and to "X15" otherwise. Set each item's tax band to the integer value of the item ID's third character. For example, if the ID is "JU4661", the tax band should be 4.

A solution is provided in the invoicedata_ans directory. The solution adds three functions to invoicedata.go: one to update all the invoices in an []*Invoice (i.e., to provide acceptable values for the new fields), one to update an individual invoice, and one to update an individual item. The solution needed changes to all the .go files, with the jsn.go, xml.go, and txt.go files most affected. In all, the changes amount to around 150 lines of additional code.

9 Packages

The Go standard library has a large number of packages, which provide a wide range of functionality out of the box. In addition, many third-party packages are available from the Go Dashboard at `godashboard.appspot.com/project`.

Go also allows us to create our own custom packages. These packages can be installed into our copy of Go's standard library, or kept in our own Go tree (i.e., in the, or one of the, `GOPATH` paths).

In this chapter we will look at how to create and import packages, including our own custom packages and third-party packages. Then we will very briefly review some of the commands (programs) supplied with the *gc* compiler. And finally, we will briefly review Go's standard library so that we can avoid reinventing the wheel.

9.1. Custom Packages

Up to now, almost all of the examples we have reviewed have been in a single package: main. For any given package, Go allows us to split the package's code over as many files as we like, providing only that they are all in the same directory. For example, Chapter 8's invoicedata example uses a single package (main), even though it consists of six separate files (invoicedata.go, gob.go, inv.go, jsn.go, txt.go, and xml.go). This is achieved simply by making the first statement in each file (excluding comments), package main.

For larger applications we might want to create application-specific packages to help partition an application's functionality into logical units. Also, we might want to create packages containing functionality that we want a family of applications to be able to use. Go doesn't make any distinction between a package intended for use by a single application and a package to be shared across our applications; however, we can create an implied distinction by putting our application-specific packages in subdirectories of our application and shared packages in subdirectories directly under a GOPATH *source directory*. A GOPATH source directory is a directory called src; every directory in the GOPATH should contain an src directory, since this is what Go's tools (commands) expect. The source code for our programs and packages should be kept in subdirectories under the (or a, if there is more than one) GOPATH src directory.

It is also possible to install our own packages directly into the Go tree (i.e., under GOROOT), but there is no advantage to doing this and it could be inconvenient on systems where Go is installed using a package management system or an installer or even if it is built by hand.

9.1.1. Creating Custom Packages

It is best to create custom packages in the GOPATH src directory (or one of the GOPATH src directories). Application-specific packages can be created within the application directory, but packages we want to share ought to be created directly under a GOPATH src directory, ideally under a unique directory to avoid name conflicts.

By convention, the source code for a package is put in a directory with the same name as the package. The source code may be split across as many files as we like and the files can have arbitrary names (so long as they end with .go). In this book we have adopted the convention of giving the .go file (or one of them, if there is more than one) the same name as the package.

The stacker example from Chapter 1 (§1.5, 21 ◀) consists of a program (in file stacker.go) and an application-specific package (stack in file stack.go), and uses the following directory layout:

    aGoPath/src/stacker/stacker.go

aGoPath/src/stacker/stack/stack.go

Here, *aGoPath* is the GOPATH directory (if there is just one), or one of the colon-(semicolon on Windows) separated paths in the GOPATH environment variable.

If we are in the stacker directory and execute the command go build, we will get an executable called stacker (stacker.exe on Windows). However, if we want the executable to be in a GOPATH bin directory, or if we want other programs to be able to use the stacker/stack package, we must use go install.

When go install builds the stacker program it creates two directories (if they don't exist): *aGoPath*/bin containing the stacker executable, and *aGoPath*/pkg/linux_amd64/stacker, which contains the static stack package's binary library file. (Naturally, the operating system/architecture directory will match those of the machine being used, e.g., windows_386 for 32-bit Windows.)

The stack package can be imported by the stacker program with the statement import "stacker/stack", that is, giving its full (Unix-style) path, but excluding the *aGoPath*/src part. In fact, *any* program or package in the GOPATH can use exactly this import since Go doesn't distinguish between application-specific and shared packages.

The ordered map from Chapter 6 (§6.5.3, 302 ◄; in file omap.go) is in package omap. It is intended to be used by multiple applications. To avoid name conflicts, we have created a directory for packages we want to share under our GOPATH directory (or one of our GOPATH directories), and given it what should be a unique name (in this case a domain name). Here is the directory structure:

aGoPath/src/qtrac.eu/omap/omap.go

Any of our programs (so long as they are in a GOPATH path) can access the ordered map package using import "qtrac.eu/omap". If we had other shared packages we would put them under *aGoPath*/src/qtrac.eu, alongside the ordered map package.

When go install builds the omap package it creates the *aGoPath*/pkg/linux_amd64/qtrac.eu directory (if it doesn't exist) containing the omap package's binary library file, with the operating system/architecture subdirectory varying depending on the machine.

If we want to create packages inside other packages, we can do so without formality. First we create a package directory, say, *aGoPath*/src/my_package. And then we create one subdirectory per package underneath that, for example, *aGoPath*/src/my_package/pkg1 and *aGoPath*/src/my_package/pkg2, along with their corresponding files *aGoPath*/src/my_package/pkg1/pkg1.go and *aGoPath*/src/my_package/pkg2/pkg2.go. Then, to import, say, pkg2, we would write import "my_package/pkg2". The Go source code's archive package is an example of this approach. It is also possible to have code in the package itself (in this example, by creating the file *aGoPath*/src/my_package/my_package.go). See the source code's image package for an example of this.

Go packages are imported from under GOROOT (specifically, $GOROOT/pkg/${GOOS}_ ${GOARCH}, e.g., /opt/go/pkg/linux_amd64), and from under the directory or directories in the GOPATH environment variable. This means that name conflicts are possible. The easiest way to avoid name conflicts is to ensure that GOPATH paths have a unique directory, such as a domain name as we used for the omap package.

The go program works seamlessly with packages from the standard library and from GOPATH paths, as well as understanding the platform-specific source files discussed in the following subsubsection.

9.1.1.1. Platform-Specific Code

In some situations we need to have code that differs between platforms. For example, on Unix-like systems the shell does wildcard expansion (called *globbing*), so *.txt on the command line might be received by the program as, say, ["README.txt", "INSTALL.txt"] in the os.Args[1:] slice. But on Windows the program would just get ["*.txt"]. We can get the program to do such globbing using the filepath.Glob() function, but of course, we need only do this on Windows.

One solution is to decide whether to use filepath.Glob() at runtime by using the test if runtime.GOOS == "windows" { ... }, and this is what most of the book's examples do (e.g., cgrep1/cgrep.go). Another solution is to put platform-specific code into its own .go file or files. For example, the cgrep3 program consists of three files, cgrep.go, util_linux.go, and util_windows.go. Inside util_linux.go there is a single function defined.

```go
func commandLineFiles(files []string) []string { return files }
```

Clearly, this function doesn't do any file globbing since there is no need to on Linux. The util_windows.go file defines a different function that has the *same* name.

```go
func commandLineFiles(files []string) []string {
    args := make([]string, 0, len(files))
    for _, name := range files {
        if matches, err := filepath.Glob(name); err != nil {
            args = append(args, name) // Invalid pattern
        } else if matches != nil { // At least one match
            args = append(args, matches...)
        }
    }
    return args
}
```

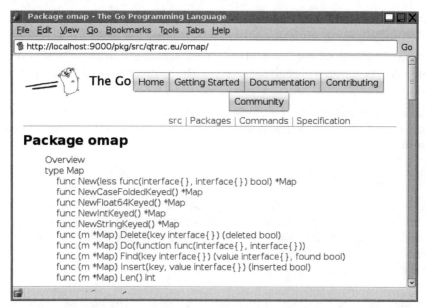

Figure 9.1 *The omap package's documentation*

When we build `cgrep3` using `go build`, on Linux machines the `util_linux.go` file will be compiled and the `util_windows.go` file will be ignored—and vice versa on Windows machines. This ensures that only one of the `commandLineFiles()` functions is compiled for any particular build.

On Mac OS X and FreeBSD systems neither `util_linux.go` nor `util_windows.go` will be compiled, so the build will fail. Since the shells on both these plat-forms do globbing, we can either soft (symbolic) link or copy `util_linux.go` to `util_darwin.go` and to `util_freebsd.go` (and similarly for any other platforms that Go supports and that are required). With these links or copies in place, the program will build on Mac OS X and FreeBSD platforms.

9.1.1.2. Documenting Packages

Ie, on Mac OSX say :
ln -s util-linux.go util-darwin.go

Packages, particularly those that are intended to be shared, need decent docu-mentation. Go provides a documentation tool, godoc, that can be used to show the documentation for packages and functions on the console, or can be used as a web server to serve the documentation as web pages, as illustrated in Fig-ure 9.1.* If the package is in a GOPATH, godoc will automatically find it and provide a link to it at the left of the "Packages" link. If the package is not in a GOPATH, run godoc with the –path option (in addition to the –http option), giving it the path to

---

* The documentation screenshots show godoc's HTML rendering at the time of this writing; it may have changed since.

the package, and again godoc will provide a link next to the "Packages" link. (We discussed godoc in the sidebar "The Go Documentation", 8 ◀.)

What constitutes good documentation is a contentious matter, so in this subsubsection we will concern ourselves purely with the mechanics of documenting Go packages.

By default only exported types, ~~classes~~, constants, and variables are shown by godoc, so all of these should be documented. Documentation is written directly in source code files.

```
// Package omap implements an efficient key-ordered map.
//
// Keys and values may be of any type, but all keys must be comparable
// using the less than function that is passed in to the omap.New()
// function, or the less than function provided by the omap.New*()
// construction functions.
package omap
```

For a package, the comment immediately preceding the package statement is used as the package's description, with the first line (up to the first period if there is one, or to the newline) serving as a one-line summary. This is an example taken from the omap package (in file qtrac.eu/omap/omap.go—this package was covered in Chapter 6, §6.5.3, 302 ◀).

```
// Map is a key-ordered map.
// The zero value is an invalid map! Use one of the construction functions
// (e.g., New()), to create a map for a specific key type.
type Map struct {
```

The documentation for an exported type must be written immediately before the type statement and should always indicate whether the type's zero value is valid.

```
// New returns an empty Map that uses the given less than function to
// compare keys. For example:
//     type Point { X, Y int }
//     pointMap := omap.New(func(a, b interface{}) bool {
//         α, β := a.(Point), b.(Point)
//         if α.X != β.X {
//             return α.X < β.X
//         }
//         return α.Y < β.Y
//     })
func New(less func(interface{}, interface{}) bool) *Map {
```

New takes as its single arg a function.
This function takes two args each of which can be anything,
and returns a bool

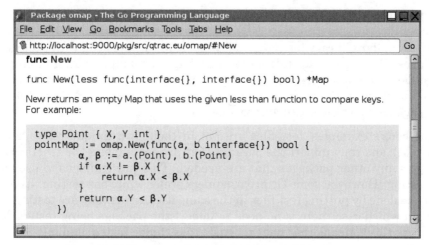

Figure 9.2 *The* omap *package's* New() *function's documentation*

The documentation for functions and methods must immediately precede their first line. This is the documentation for the omap package's generic New() construction function.

Figure 9.2 shows what the function's documentation looks like when godoc is used to serve it as a web page. This figure also illustrates that indented text in the documentation is rendered as "code" in HTML. However, at the time of this writing, godoc has no support for any kind of markup (e.g., bold, italic, links, etc.).

```
// NewCaseFoldedKeyed returns an empty Map that accepts case-insensitive
// string keys.
func NewCaseFoldedKeyed() *Map {
```

The above snippet shows the documentation for one of the convenience construction functions that provides a predefined less than function.

```
// Insert inserts a new key-value into the Map and returns true; or
// replaces an existing key-value pair's value if the keys are equal and
// returns false. For example:
//      inserted := myMap.Insert(key, value).
func (m *Map) Insert(key, value interface{}) (inserted bool) {
```

And here is the documentation for the Insert() method. Notice that it is conventional in Go to start a function or method's documentation with the function or method's name, and (unconventionally) not to use parentheses when referring to functions or methods.

9.1.1.3. Unit Testing and Benchmarking Packages

go test

The Go standard library includes good support for unit testing with the testing packages. Setting up unit testing for a package is a simple matter of creating a test file in the same directory as the package we want to test. This file's name should begin with the package name and end with _test.go. For example, the omap package's test file is called omap_test.go.

In the book's examples, test files are put in their own unique package (e.g., omap_test), and they import the package they are testing and the testing package, plus any other packages that are needed. This constrains us to use black box testing. However, some Go programmers prefer white box testing. This can easily be done by putting test files in the same package as they are testing (e.g., omap), in which case there is no need to import the package being tested. This latter approach means that nonexported types can be tested, and methods can be added to nonexported types specifically to support testing.

The test file is unusual in that it has no main() function. Instead, it has one or more exported functions whose name begins with Test and which take a single argument of type *testing.T and that return nothing. We can add any supporting functions we need, of course, providing their names don't start with Test.

```go
func TestStringKeyOMapInsertion(t *testing.T) {
    wordForWord := omap.NewCaseFoldedKeyed()
    for _, word := range []string{"one", "Two", "THREE", "four", "Five"} {
        wordForWord.Insert(word, word)
    }
    var words []string
    wordForWord.Do(func(_, value interface{}) {
        words = append(words, value.(string))
    })
    actual, expected := strings.Join(words, ""), "FivefouroneTHREETwo"
    if actual != expected {
        t.Errorf("%q != %q", actual, expected)
    }
}
```

Here is one of the tests in the omap_test.go file. It begins by creating an empty omap.Map, then it inserts some string keys (which are treated case-insensitively), and string values. We then iterate over all the *key–value* pairs in the map using the Map.Do() method, and append each value to a slice of strings. Finally, we join the strings into a single string and see if this matches what we expect. If the match fails we call the testing.T.Errorf() method to report the failure and provide some explanation. If no error or failure function is called then the test is assumed to have passed.

Here is an example test run where the tests pass.

```
$ go test
ok          qtrac.eu/omap
PASS
```

And here is the same test run, but this time with verbose output switched on
using the –test.v option.

```
$ go test –test.v
ok          qtrac.eu/omap
=== RUN TestStringKeyOMapInsertion-4
--- PASS: TestStringKeyOMapInsertion-4 (0.00 seconds)
=== RUN TestIntKeyOMapFind-4
--- PASS: TestIntKeyOMapFind-4 (0.00 seconds)
=== RUN TestIntKeyOMapDelete-4
--- PASS: TestIntKeyOMapDelete-4 (0.00 seconds)
=== RUN TestPassing-4
--- PASS: TestPassing-4 (0.00 seconds)
PASS
```

If we change the constant string to force the test to fail and run the tests again
(in the default nonverbose mode), here is the output we will get.

```
$ go test
FAIL          qtrac.eu/omap
--- FAIL: TestStringKeyOMapInsertion-4 (0.01 seconds)
      omap_test.go:35: "FivefouroneTHREETwo" != "FivefouroneTHREEToo"
FAIL
```

In addition to the Errorf() method used in the example, the testing package's
*testing.T type has various other methods such as testing.T.Fail(), testing.
T.Fatal(), and so on. All these methods provide us with a good level of control
over how we respond to test failures.

In addition, the testing package has support for benchmarking. Benchmark
functions can be added to *package*_test.go files in the same way as test functions,
only in this case the functions' names must begin with Benchmark and they
receive a single *testing.B argument and return nothing.

```
func BenchmarkOMapFindSuccess(b *testing.B) {
    b.StopTimer() // Don't time creation and population
    intMap := omap.NewIntKeyed()
    for i := 0; i < 1e6; i++ {          // 1e6 == 1 000 000
        intMap.Insert(i, i)
```

```
    }
    b.StartTimer() // Time the Find() method succeeding
    for i := 0; i < b.N; i++ {        // no. of iterations
        intMap.Find(i % 1e6)
    }
}
```

This function begins by stopping the timer since we don't want to time the creation and population of the omap.Map. Then we create an empty omap.Map and populate it with a million *key–value* pairs.

By default go test does not run any benchmarks, so if we want them to be run we must explicitly say so by using the -test.bench option and providing it with a regular expression that matches the names of the benchmarks we want to run. A regexp of .* matches anything, that is, all the benchmark functions in the test file, but plain . also works.

```
$ go test -test.bench=.        // run all benchmarks
PASS        qtrac.eu/omap
PASS                                ?          ┌─ no. of iterations      ┌─ avg time
BenchmarkOMapFindSuccess-4        1000000                 1380 ns/op
BenchmarkOMapFindFailure-4        1000000                 1350 ns/op
```

This output shows that two benchmarks were run with 1 000 000 loop iterations each, and with the given numbers of nanoseconds per operation. The number of iterations (i.e., the value of b.N) is chosen by go test, but we can use the -test.benchtime option to set the approximate number of seconds we want each benchmark to run if we prefer.

In addition to the omap package, a few of the book's other examples have *package_test.go* files.

9.1.2. Importing Packages

import alias "pkg"
// refer to alias.name, etc

Go allows us to alias package names. This feature can be convenient and useful—for example, making it easy to switch between two implementations of a package. For instance, we could import a package like this: import bio "bio_v1", so that in our code the bio_v1 package is accessed as bio instead of bio_v1. Later, when a more mature implementation is available, we could switch to it by changing the import to import bio "bio_v2". This will work if both bio_v1 and bio_v2 provide the same APIs (or if bio_v2's API is a superset of bio_v1's), and means that the rest of the code can be left unchanged. On the other hand, aliasing standard library package names is probably best avoided, since it could cause confusion or irritation to maintainers later on.

As we mentioned in Chapter 5 (§5.6.2, 224 ◄), when a package is imported its init() functions are executed (if it has any). In some situations we don't want to make explicit use of a package, but do want its init() functions to be executed.

For example, if we are processing images we might want to register all the image formats that Go supports, but not actually use any functions from the packages that provide the formats. Here is the import statement for the imagetag1 program's imagetag1.go file (from Chapter 7's exercises).

```
import (
    "fmt"
    "image"
    "os"
    "path/filepath"
    "runtime"

    _ "image/gif"       // alias the package to the blank identifier
    _ "image/jpeg"
    _ "image/png"
)
```

Here we import the image/gif, image/jpeg, and image/png packages purely to execute their init() functions (which registers their image format with the image package). Each of these packages is aliased to the blank identifier, so Go will not complain about us not making explicit use of any of them in our code.

9.2. Third-Party Packages

The go tool that we have used throughout the book to build programs and packages (e.g., the omap package) can also be used to download, build, and install third-party packages. (Of course, this assumes that our computer is connected to the Internet.) A list of third-party packages is maintained at godashboard.appspot.com/project. (An alternative approach is to download the source code—often obtained as a copy directly from a distributed version control system—and build the package ourselves locally.)

To install one of the Go Dashboard's packages, first click its link to go to the package's home page. Somewhere on the package's web site there should be a go get command that shows how to download and install the package.

For example, if we were to click the Go Dashboard's freetype-go.googlecode.com/hg/freetype link, it would take us to the code.google.com/p/freetype-go/ page which shows the installation command up front (at the time of this writing): go get freetype-go.googlecode.com/hg/freetype.

When it comes to third-party packages, go get must, of course, install them somewhere. By default it will use the first path listed in the GOPATH environment variable if that is set, and failing that it will put the package under the GOROOT directory. If we want to force go get to use the GOROOT directory, we can simply unset the GOPATH environment variable before running go get.

If we execute the go get command it will silently download, build, and install the package. We can view the newly installed package's documentation by running godoc as a web server (e.g., godoc -http=:8000), and navigating to the package.

To avoid name conflicts, third-party packages usually use domain names to ensure uniqueness. For example, to use the FreeType package we would use an import statement of import "freetype-go.googlecode.com/hg/freetype". Of course, when it comes to using functions from the package, as always we only need to use the last component of the name—for example, font, err := freetype.ParseFont(fontdata). And in the unlikely event of a name collision in the last component, we can always use aliasing, for instance, import ftype "freetype-go.googlecode.com/hg/freetype", and then in our code font, err := ftype.ParseFont(fontdata).

Third party packages are normally available for Go 1, but some might require a later Go version, or have multiple downloads available—for example, ones that work with the cutting edge development versions of Go. In general, it is best to always use a stable version of Go (e.g., Go 1), and to use packages that are compatible with it.

9.3. A Brief Survey of Go's Commands

A Go installation for the *gc* compiler naturally includes compilers and linkers (6g, 6l, etc.), but also a number of other tools. The most useful of these is go, which can be used as a build tool for our own programs and packages, as a tool for downloading and installing third-party programs and packages, and as a tool for executing unit tests and for benchmarking, as we saw earlier (§9.1.1.3, 414 ◀). Execute go help for a full list of the commands available and go help *command* for help on the specified *command*. There is also the godoc tool for showing documentation ("The Go Documentation", 8 ◀).

[margin note: go help]

In addition to the tools we have used in the book, there are several other tools and go tool commands, a few of which we will mention here. One is go vet which does some simple error checking on Go programs, specifically on the fmt package's print functions.

[margin note: go fix]

Another command is go fix. Sometimes a new Go release incorporates changes to the language—or more often, to library APIs—that invalidate existing code. By running go fix over our code base, all of our code can be automatically updated. We *strongly* recommend that .go files are registered with a version control system, and that they are all checked in, or are at least backed up, before running go fix. This will allow us to easily see what changes were applied and be able to roll back any or all of them if the fixes break the code. We can also use go fix's -diff option in the first place, since this shows the changes go fix would apply without actually applying them.

The last command we will mention is gofmt. This command formats Go code in a standardized way and its use is highly recommended by the Go developers. The advantages of gofmt are that it eliminates arguments over the best way to lay out code, and that it ensures that all Go code has a uniform look. All the book's code was formatted using gofmt (but lines longer than 75 characters were then manually wrapped to fit on the book's pages).

gofmt

9.4. A Brief Survey of the Go Standard Library

The Go standard library includes a large number of packages that between them provide a wide range of functionality. The overview provided here is highly selective and very brief. This is because the contents of the library are likely to continue to grow after this book is published, so it is best to look at the library APIs online (golang.org/pkg/) or locally using godoc, both to see the most up-to-date information and to get a comprehensive overview of what is available in each package.

The exp "experimental" package is where packages that might *potentially* be added to the standard library begin life, so these packages should not be used unless we specifically want to participate in their development (e.g., testing, commenting, or submitting patches). The exp package is normally available when pulling Go from Google's Go source tree, and but it may not be included in prebuilt packages. All the other packages are okay to use, although at the time of this writing, some were incomplete.

9.4.1. Archive and Compression Packages

Go can read and write tarballs and .zip files. The relevant packages are archive/tar and archive/zip, and for compressed tarballs, compress/gzip and compress/bzip2. The book's pack and unpack examples illustrate the use of these (§8.2, 397 ◄).

Other compression formats are also supported; for example, Lempel-Ziv-Welch (compress/lzw) which is used for .tiff images and .pdf files.

9.4.2. Bytes and String-Related Packages

The bytes and strings packages have many functions in common, only the former operates on []byte values and the latter on string values. For strings, the strings package provides all the most useful utilities to find substrings, replace substrings, split strings, trim strings, and change case (see §3.6.1, 107 ◄). The strconv package provides conversions from numbers and Booleans to strings and vice versa (see §3.6.2, 113 ◄).

The fmt package provides a variety of extremely useful print and scan functions. The print functions were covered in Chapter 3 (§3.5, 93 ◄) with examples of use shown throughout the book, and the scan functions are shown in Table 8.2 (383 ◄), with some examples of use nearby (§8.1.3.2, 380 ◄).

The unicode package provides functions for determining character properties, such as whether a character is a printable character, or whether it is a digit (see §3.6.4, 118 ◄). The unicode/utf8 and unicode/utf16 packages provide functions for decoding and encoding runes (i.e., Unicode code points/characters). For the unicode/utf8 package, see §3.6.3, 117 ◄. Some use of the unicode/utf16 package is shown in Chapter 8's utf16-to-utf8 exercise solution.

✳   The text/template and html/template packages can be used to create templates which can then be used to generate textual output (e.g., HTML), based on data that is fed into them. Here is a tiny and very simple example of the text/template package in use.

```
type GiniIndex struct {
    Country string
    Index   float64
}
gini := []GiniIndex{{"Japan", 54.7}, {"China", 55.0}, {"U.S.A.", 80.1}}
giniTable := template.New("giniTable")
giniTable.Parse(                         ⌐ template name
    `<TABLE>` +
    `{{range .}}` +
    `{{printf "<TR><TD>%s</TD><TD>%.1f%%</TD></TR>" .Country .Index}}` +
    `{{end}}` +
    `</TABLE>`)
err := giniTable.Execute(os.Stdout, gini)
```

```
<TABLE>
<TR><TD>Japan</TD><TD>54.7%</TD></TR>
<TR><TD>China</TD><TD>55.0%</TD></TR>
<TR><TD>U.S.A.</TD><TD>80.1%</TD></TR>
</TABLE>
```

The template.New() function creates a new *template.Template with the given name. Template names are useful to identify templates that are in effect nested inside other templates. The template.Template.Parse() function parses a template (typically from an .html file), ready for use. The template.Template.Execute() function executes the template sending the resultant output to the given io.Writer, and reading the data that should be used to populate the template from its second argument. In this example, we have output to os.Stdout and passed the gini slice of GiniIndex structs as the data. (We have split the output over several lines to make it clearer.)

Inside a template, actions are enclosed in double braces ({{ and }}). The
{{range}} … {{end}} action can be used to iterate over every item in a slice; here
we have set each GiniIndex in the slice to the dot (.), that is, to be the current
item. We can access a struct's exported fields using their names, preceded, of
course, with the dot to signify the current item. The {{printf}} action works just
like the fmt.Printf() function, but with spaces replacing the parentheses and
argument-separating commas.

The text/template and html/template packages support a sophisticated templat-
ing language in their own right, with many actions, including iteration and conditional branching, support for variables and method calls, and much else be-
sides. In addition, the html/template package is safe against code injection.

9.4.3. Collection Packages

Slices are the most efficient collection type provided by Go, but sometimes
it is useful or necessary to use a more specialized collection type. For many
situations the built-in map type is sufficient, but the Go standard library also
provides the container package which contains various collection packages.

The container/heap package provides functions for manipulating a heap, where
the heap must be a value of a custom type that satisfies the heap.Interface
defined in the heap package. A heap (strictly speaking, a *min-heap*) maintains
its values in an order such that the first element is always the smallest (or
largest for a *max-heap*)—this is known as the heap property. The heap.Interface
embeds the sort.Interface and adds Push() and Pop() methods. (We discussed
the sort.Interface in §4.2.4, 160 ◄ and §5.7, 244 ◄.)

It is easy to create a simple custom heap type that satisfies the heap.Interface.
Here is an example of such a heap in use.

```
ints := &IntHeap{5, 1, 6, 7, 9, 8, 2, 4}
heap.Init(ints) // Heapify
ints.Push(9)    // IntHeap.Push() doesn't preserve the heap property
ints.Push(7)
ints.Push(3)
heap.Init(ints) // Must reheapify after heap-breaking changes
for ints.Len() > 0 {
    fmt.Printf("%v ", heap.Pop(ints))
}
fmt.Println() // prints: 1 2 3 4 5 6 7 7 8 9 9
```

Here is the complete custom heap implementation.

```
type IntHeap []int

func (ints *IntHeap) Less(i, j int) bool {
```

```
    return (*ints)[i] < (*ints)[j]
}
func (ints *IntHeap) Swap(i, j int) {
    (*ints)[i], (*ints)[j] = (*ints)[j], (*ints)[i]
}
func (ints *IntHeap) Len() int {
    return len(*ints)
}
func (ints *IntHeap) Pop() interface{} {
    x := (*ints)[ints.Len()-1]
    *ints = (*ints)[:ints.Len()-1]
    return x
}
func (ints *IntHeap) Push(x interface{}) {
    *ints = append(*ints, x.(int))
}
```

This implementation is sufficient for many situations. We could make the code slightly nicer to read by specifying the type as type IntHeap struct { ints []int }, since then we could refer to ints.ints rather than *ints inside the methods.

The container/list package provides a doubly linked list. Items added to the list are added as interface{} values. Items retrieved from the list have type list.Element, with the original value accessible as list.Element.Value.

```
items := list.New()
for _, x := range strings.Split("ABCDEFGH", "") {
    items.PushFront(x)
}
items.PushBack(9)
for element := items.Front(); element != nil; element = element.Next() {
    switch value := element.Value.(type) {
    case string:
        fmt.Printf("%s ", value)
    case int:
        fmt.Printf("%d ", value)
    }
}
fmt.Println() // prints: H G F E D B A 9
```

In this example we push eight single-letter strings onto the front of a new list and then push an int onto the end. Then we iterate over the list's elements and print each element's value. We didn't really need the type switch since we could have printed using `fmt.Printf("%v ", element.Value)`, but if we weren't merely printing we would need the type `switch` if the list contained elements of different types. Of course, if all the elements had the same type we could use a type assertion—for example, `element.Value.(string)` for `string` elements. (Type switches were covered in §5.2.2.2, 197 ◄ and type assertions in §5.1.2, 191 ◄.)

In addition to the methods shown in the snippet above, the `list.List` type provides many other methods, including `Back()`, `Init()` (to clear the list), `InsertAfter()`, `InsertBefore()`, `Len()`, `MoveToBack()`, `MoveToFront()`, `PushBackList()` (to push one list onto the end of another), and `Remove()`.

The standard library also provides the `container/ring` package which implements a circular list.*

While all the collection types hold their data in memory, Go also has a `database/sql` package that provides a generic interface for SQL databases. To work with actual databases, separate database-specific driver packages must be installed. These, along with many other collection packages, are available from the Go Dashboard (`godashboard.appspot.com/project`). And as we saw earlier, the book's source code includes the ordered map `omap.Map` type which is based on a left-leaning red-black tree (§6.5.3, 302 ◄).

9.4.4. File, Operating System, and Related Packages

The standard library provides many packages to support file and directory handling and interaction with the operating system. In many cases these packages provide operating-system-neutral abstractions that make it straightforward to create cross-platform Go applications.

The `os` ("operating system") package provides functions for operating-system interactions, such as changing the current working directory, changing file mode and ownership, getting and setting environment variables, and creating and removing files and directories. In addition, this package provides functions for creating and opening files (`os.Create()` and `os.Open()`), and for retrieving file attributes (e.g., via the `os.FileInfo` type), all of which we have seen used in earlier chapters. (See, for example, §7.2.5, 349 ◄, and Chapter 8.)

Once a file is opened, especially in the case of text files, it is very common to want to access it via a buffer (e.g., to read lines as strings rather than as byte slices). The functionality we need is provided by the `bufio` package, and again, we have seen many examples of its use in earlier chapters. In addition to using `bufio.Readers` and `bufio.Writers` for reading and writing strings, we can also read (and unread) runes, read (and unread) single bytes, read multiple bytes, as well as write runes and single or multiple bytes.

---

* Older versions of Go may have the `container/vector` package. This package is deprecated—use slices and the built-in `append()` function instead (§4.2, 148 ◄).

The io ("input/output") package provides a large number of functions for working with io.Readers and io.Writers. (Both of these interfaces are satisfied by *os.File values.) For example, we have used the io.Copy() function to copy data from a reader to a writer (§8.2.1, 397 ◀). This package also contains functions for creating synchronous in-memory pipes.

The io/ioutil package provides a few high-level convenience functions. Among others, the package provides the ioutil.ReadAll() function that reads all of an io.Reader's data and returns it as a []byte; the ioutil.ReadFile() function that does the same but accepts a string argument (the filename) rather than an io.Reader; the ioutil.TempFile() function which returns a temporary file (an *os.File); and the ioutil.WriteFile() function which writes a []byte to a file whose name it is given.

The path package has functions for manipulating Unix-style paths such as Linux and Mac OS X paths, URL paths, git "references", FTP files, and so on. The path/filepath package provides the same functions as path—and many others—and is designed to provide platform-neutral path handling. This package also provides the filepath.Walk() function for recursively iterating over all the files and directories in a given path, as we saw in an earlier chapter (§7.2.5, 349 ◀).

The runtime package contains many functions and types that give access to Go's runtime system. Most of these are advanced and should not be needed when creating standard maintainable Go programs. However, a couple of the package's constants can be useful—for example, runtime.GOOS which holds a string (e.g., "darwin", "freebsd", "linux", or "windows"), and runtime.GOARCH which also holds a string (e.g., "386", "amd64", or "arm"). The runtime.GOROOT() function returns the GOROOT environment variable's value (or the Go build's root if the environment variable isn't set), and the runtime.Version() function returns the Go version (as a string). We saw how to use the runtime.GOMAXPROCS() and runtime.NumCPU() functions to ensure that Go uses all the machine's processors, in Chapter 7 (327 ◀).

9.4.4.1. File Format-Related Packages

Go's excellent support for file handling applies both to text files (using the 7-bit ASCII encoding or the UTF-8 and UTF-16 Unicode encodings), and to binary files. Go provides specific packages for handling JSON and XML files, as well as its own very fast, compact, and convenient Go binary format. (All of these formats, plus custom binary formats, were covered in Chapter 8.)

In addition, Go has a csv package for reading .csv ("comma-separated values") files. This package treats such files as records (one per line) each of which consists of (comma-separated) fields. The package is quite versatile—for example, it is possible to change the delimiter (e.g., from a comma to a tab or other character), as well as other aspects of how it reads and writes records and fields.

The encoding package contains several packages, one of which, encoding/binary, we have already used for reading and writing binary data (§8.1.5, 387 ◀). The other packages provide encoding and decoding for various other formats—for example, the encoding/base64 package can be used to encode and decode URLs which often use this format.

9.4.5. Graphics-Related Packages

Go's image package provides some high-level functions and types for creating and holding image data. It also has a number of packages that provide encoders and decoders for various standard graphics file formats, such as image/jpeg and image/png. We discussed some of these earlier in this chapter (§9.1.2, 416 ◀), and in one of Chapter 7's exercises.

The image/draw package provides some basic drawing functionality as we saw in Chapter 6 (§6.5.2, 289 ◀). The third-party freetype package adds more functions for drawing. The freetype package itself can draw text using any specified TrueType font, and the freetype/raster package can draw lines and cubic and quadratic curves. (We discussed obtaining and installing the freetype package earlier; §9.2, 417 ◀.)

9.4.6. Mathematics Packages

The math/big package provides unlimited (except by memory) size integers (big.Int) and rationals (big.Rat); these were discussed earlier (§2.3, 57 ◀). The pi_by_digits example shows the use of big.Ints (§2.3.1.1, 61 ◀). The math/big package also provides a big.ProbablyPrime() function.

The math package provides all the standard mathematical functions (based on float64s) and several standard constants. See Tables 2.8, 2.9, and 2.10 (65–67 ◀).

The math/cmplx package provides some standard functions for complex numbers (based on complex128s). See Table 2.11 (71 ◀).

9.4.7. Miscellaneous Packages

In addition to the packages that can be roughly grouped together, the standard library contains a number of packages that stand more or less alone.

The crypto package can provide hashes using the MD5, SHA-1, SHA-224, SHA-256, SHA-384, and SHA-512 algorithms. (Support for each algorithm is supplied by a package, e.g., crypto/sha512.) In addition, the crypto package has packages that provide encryption and decryption using a variety of algorithms, such as AES, DES, and so on, each in packages with corresponding names (e.g., crypto/aes, crypto/des).

The exec package is used to run external programs. This can also be done using the os.StartProcess() function, but the exec.Cmd type is much more convenient to use.

The flag package provides a command-line parser. It accepts X11-style options (e.g., -width, not GNU-style -w and --width). The package produces a very basic usage message and does not provide any validation beyond a value's type. (So, the package can be used to specify an int option, but not what values are acceptable.) Several alternatives are available from the Go Dashboard (godashboard.appspot.com/project).

The log package provides functions for logging information (by default to os.Stdout), and for terminating the program or panicking with a log message. The log package's output destination can be changed to any io.Writer using the log.SetOutput() function. Log messages are output in the form of a timestamp and then the message; the timestamp can be eliminated by calling log.SetFlags(0) before the first log function call. It is also possible to create custom loggers using the log.New() function.

The math/rand package provides many useful pseudo-random number generating functions including rand.Int() which returns a random int and rand.Intn(n) which returns a random int in the range $[0, n)$. The crypto/rand package has a function for producing cryptographically strong pseudo-random numbers.

The regexp package provides a very fast and powerful regular expression engine that supports the RE2 engine's syntax. We have used this package in several of the book's examples, although we have deliberately used simple regexeps and not used the package's full power so as not to stray off-topic. The package was introduced earlier (§3.6.5, 120 ◀).

The sort package provides convenience functions for sorting slices of ints, float64s, and strings, and for performing fast (binary chop) searches on such sorted slices. It also provides generic sort.Sort() and sort.Search() functions that can be used for custom data. (See, for example, §4.2.4, 160 ◀; Table 4.2, 161 ◀; and §5.6.7, 238 ◀.)

The time package has functions for measuring time and for parsing and formating date, date/time, and time values. The time.After() function can be used to send the current time on the channel it returns after a specified number of nanoseconds have passed, as we saw in an earlier example (332 ◀). The time.Tick() and time.NewTicker() functions can be used to provide a channel to which a "tick" is sent repeatedly at a specified interval. The time.Time struct has methods for providing the current time, for formatting a date/time as a string, and for parsing date/times. (We saw time.Time examples in Chapter 8, e.g., 375 ◀).

9.4.8. Networking Packages

The Go standard library has many packages that support networking and related programming. The net package provides functions and types for communicating using Unix domain and network sockets, TCP/IP, and UDP. The package also provides functions for domain name resolution.

The net/http package makes use of the net package and has functionality for parsing HTTP requests and replies, and provides a basic HTTP client. The net/http package also includes an easy-to-extend HTTP server, as we saw in Chapter 2 (§2.4, 72 ◄) and Chapter 3's exercises. The net/url package provides URL parsing and query escaping.

Some other high-level networking packages are included in the standard library. One is the net/rpc ("Remote Procedure Call") package which allows a server to provide objects whose exported methods can be called by clients. Another is the net/smtp ("Simple Mail Transport Protocol") package which can be used to send email.

9.4.9. The Reflect Package

The reflect package provides runtime reflection (also called *introspection*), that is, the ability to access and interact with values of arbitrary types at runtime.

The package also provides some useful utility functions such as reflect.Deep-Equal() which can compare any two values—for example, slices, which aren't comparable using the == and != operators.

Every value in Go has two attributes: its actual value and its type. The reflect.TypeOf() function can tell us the type of any value.

```
x := 8.6
y := float32(2.5)
fmt.Printf("var x %v = %v\n", reflect.TypeOf(x), x)
fmt.Printf("var y %v = %v\n", reflect.TypeOf(y), y)

var x float64 = 8.6
var y float32 = 2.5
```

Here we have output two floating-point variables and their types as Go var declarations using reflection.

When the reflect.ValueOf() function is called on a value it returns a reflect.Value which holds the value but isn't the value itself. If we want to access the held value we must use one of the reflect.Value methods.

```
word := "Chameleon"
value := reflect.ValueOf(word)
```

```
text := value.String()
fmt.Println(text)
```
```
Chameleon
```

The reflect.Value type has many methods for extracting the underlying type including reflect.Value.Bool(), reflect.Value.Complex(), reflect.Value.Float(), reflect.Value.Int(), and reflect.Value.String().

The reflect package can also work with collection types such as slices and maps, as well as with structs; it can even access structs' tag text. (This ability is used by the json and xml encoders and decoders, as we saw in Chapter 8.)

```go
type Contact struct {
    Name string "check:len(3,40)"
    Id   int    "check:range(1,999999)"
}
person := Contact{"Bjork", 0xDEEDED}
personType := reflect.TypeOf(person)
if nameField, ok := personType.FieldByName("Name"); ok {
    fmt.Printf("%q %q %q\n", nameField.Type, nameField.Name, nameField.Tag)
}
```
```
"string" "Name" "check:len(3,40)"
```

The underlying value held by a reflect.Value can be changed *if* it is "settable". The setability can be checked by calling reflect.Value.CanSet(), which returns a bool.

```go
presidents := []string{"Obama", "Bushy", "Clinton"}
sliceValue := reflect.ValueOf(presidents)
value = sliceValue.Index(1)
value.SetString("Bush")
fmt.Println(presidents)
```
```
[Obama Bush Clinton]
```

Although Go strings are immutable, any given item in a []string can be replaced by another string, and this is what we have done here. (Naturally, in this particular example, the easiest way to perform the change would be to write presidents[1] = "Bush", and not use introspection at all.)

It is not possible to change immutable values themselves, but we can replace an immutable value with another value if we have the original value's address.

```go
count := 1
if value = reflect.ValueOf(count); value.CanSet() {
```

```
    value.SetInt(2) // Would panic! Can't set an int.
}
fmt.Print(count, " ")
value = reflect.ValueOf(&count)
// Can't call SetInt() on value since value is a *int not an int
pointee := value.Elem()
pointee.SetInt(3) // OK. Can replace a pointed-to value.
fmt.Println(count)
```

```
1 3
```

This snippet's output shows that the if condition's conditional evaluates to false, so its body isn't executed. Although we cannot set immutable values such as ints, float64s, or strings, we can use the reflect.Value.Elem() method to retrieve a reflect.Value through which we can set a pointed-to value, and this is what we do at the end of the snippet.

It is also possible to use reflection to call arbitrary functions and methods. Here is an example that calls a custom TitleCase() function (not shown) twice, once conventionally and once using reflection.

```
caption := "greg egan's dark integers"
title := TitleCase(caption)
fmt.Println(title)

titleFuncValue := reflect.ValueOf(TitleCase)
values := titleFuncValue.Call([]reflect.Value{reflect.ValueOf(caption)})
title = values[0].String()
fmt.Println(title)
```

```
Greg Egan's Dark Integers
Greg Egan's Dark Integers
```

The reflect.Value.Call() method takes and returns a slice of type []reflect. Value. In this case we pass in a single value (i.e., as a slice of length 1), and retrieve a single result value.

We can call methods similarly—and in fact, we can even query to see if a method exists and call it only if it does.

```
a := list.New()                          // a.Len() == 0
b := list.New()
b.PushFront(1)                           // b.Len() == 1
c := stack.Stack{}
c.Push(0.5)
c.Push(1.5)                              // c.Len() == 2
d := map[string]int{"A": 1, "B": 2, "C": 3} // len(d) == 3
```

```
e := "Four"                              // len(e) == 4
f := []int{5, 0, 4, 1, 3}                // len(f) == 5
fmt.Println(Len(a), Len(b), Len(c), Len(d), Len(e), Len(f))
```

```
0 1 2 3 4 5
```

Here we create two lists (using the container/list package), one of which we add an item to. We also create a stack (using the custom stacker/stack package we created in Chapter 1; §1.5, 21 ◄), and add two items to it. And we create a map, a string, and a slice of ints, all of different lengths. We then use a generic custom Len() function to get their lengths.

```
func Len(x interface{}) int {
    value := reflect.ValueOf(x)
    switch reflect.TypeOf(x).Kind() {
    case reflect.Array, reflect.Chan, reflect.Map, reflect.Slice,
        reflect.String:
        return value.Len()
    default:
        if method := value.MethodByName("Len"); method.IsValid() {
            values := method.Call(nil)
            return int(values[0].Int())
        }
    }
    panic(fmt.Sprintf("'%v' does not have a length", x))
}
```

This function returns the length of the value it is passed or panics if the value's type isn't one that supports the notion of length.

We begin by getting the value as a reflect.Value since we will need this further on. Then we switch depending on the value's reflect.Kind. If the value's kind is one of the built-in types that supports the built-in len() function, we can call the reflect.Value.Len() function directly on the value. Otherwise, we have either a type that doesn't support the notion of length, or a type that has a Len() method. We use the reflect.Value.MethodByName() method to retrieve the method—or to retrieve an invalid reflect.Value. If the method is valid we call it. There are no arguments to pass in this case because conventional Len() methods take no arguments.

When we retrieve a method using the reflect.Value.MethodByName() method, the returned reflect.Value holds both the method *and* the value. So, when we call reflect.Value.Call(), the value is passed as the receiver.

The reflect.Value.Int() method returns an int64; we have converted this to a plain int to match the generic Len() function's return value's type.

If a value is passed in that doesn't support the built-in `len()` function and doesn't have a `Len()` method, the generic `Len()` function panics. We could have handled this error case in other ways—for example, by returning –1 to signify "no length available", or by returning an `int` and an `error`.

Go's `reflect` package is incredibly flexible and allows us to do things at runtime that depend on the program's dynamic state. However, to quote Rob Pike, reflection is *"a powerful tool that should be used with care and avoided unless strictly necessary"*.*

9.5. Exercises

This chapter has three inter-related exercises. The first exercise involves the creation of a small custom package. The second exercise involves the creation of a test for the package. And the third exercise is to write a program that makes use of the package. The exercises increase in difficulty with the third one being rather challenging.

1. Create a package, called, say, `my_linkutil` (in file `my_linkutil/my_linkutil.go`). The package should provide two functions. The first function is `LinksFromURL(string) ([]string, error)` which given a URL string (e.g., `"http://www.qtrac.eu/index.html"`), returns a slice of all the web page's *unique* anchor links (i.e., `<a>` tags' `href` attribute values), and `nil` (or `nil` and an error). The second function is `LinksFromReader(io.Reader) ([]string, error)` which does the same thing only it reads from an io.Reader (e.g., an open file or an `http.Response.Body`). The `LinksFromURL()` function should use the `LinksFromReader()` function internally.

   A solution is given in `linkcheck/linkutil/linkutil.go`. The solution's first function is about 11 lines and makes use of the `net/http` package's `http.Get()` function. The second function is around 16 lines and makes use of the `regexp.Regexp.FindAllSubmatch()` function.

2. Go's standard library provides support for HTTP testing (e.g., the `net/http/httptest` package), but for this exercise we will be content with testing the `my_linkutil.LinksFromReader()` function developed in the previous exercise. To this end, create a test file (e.g., `my_linkutil/my_linkutil_test.go`) containing a single test, `TestLinksFromReader(*testing.T)`. The test should read in an HTML file from the file system and a links file which lists the file's unique anchor links, and it should then compare the links found in the HTML file by the `my_linkutil.LinksFromReader()` function with the links in the links file.

---

* Rob Pike has written an interesting and useful blog entry on Go reflection, `blog.golang.org/2011/09/laws-of-reflection.html`.

It may be convenient to copy the linkcheck/linkutil/index.html and link-check/linkutil/index.links files into the my_linkutil directory for use by the test program.

A solution is given in the file linkcheck/linkutil/linkutil_test.go. The solution's test function is around 40 lines and makes use of the sort.Strings() function to order the found and expected links and the reflect.DeepEqual() function to do the comparison. To help testers the test function lists the first nonmatching links if the test fails.

3. Write a program called, say, my_linkcheck which accepts a single URL on the command line (with or without the http:// prefix), and that checks that every link is valid. The program should work recursively, checking every linked-to page—but excluding non-HTTP links, non-HTML files, and links to external sites. Every page that is checked should be checked in a separate goroutine—this will result in many concurrent network accesses, which will be much faster than doing each access sequentially. Naturally, some of the same links will be present on different pages and such links should only be checked once. The program should, of course, use the my_linkutil package developed in the first exercise.

A solution is given in linkcheck/linkcheck.go and is around 150 lines. To avoid checking duplicate links the solution keeps a map of the URLs it has seen. The map is kept inside a separate goroutine and three channels are used to communicate with it—one to add a URL, one to query whether a URL has been seen, and one to respond to the query. (An alternative would be to use the safemap from Chapter 7.) An extract from the solution's output for the command line linkcheck www.qtrac.eu is shown below (with many lines elided either completely or partially).

```
+ read http://www.qtrac.eu
...
+ read http://www.qtrac.eu/gobook.html
+ read http://www.qtrac.eu/gobook-errata.html
...
+ read http://www.qtrac.eu/comparepdf.html
+ read http://www.qtrac.eu/index.html
...
+ links on http://www.qtrac.eu/index.html
    + checked http://ptgmedia.pearsoncmg.com/.../python/python2python3.pdf
    + checked http://www.froglogic.com
    - can't check non-http link: mailto:someone@somewhere.com
    + checked http://savannah.nongnu.org/projects/lout/
+ read http://www.qtrac.eu/py3book-errata.html
+ links on http://www.qtrac.eu
    + checked http://endsoftpatents.org/innovating-without-patents
```

```
+ links on http://www.qtrac.eu/gobook.html
  + checked http://golang.org
  + checked http://www.qtrac.eu/gobook.html#eg
  + checked http://www.informit.com/store/product.aspx?isbn=0321680561
  + checked http://safari.informit.com/9780321680563
  + checked http://www.qtrac.eu/gobook.tar.gz
  + checked http://www.qtrac.eu/gobook.zip
  - can't check non-http link: ftp://ftp.cs.usyd.edu.au/jeff/lout/
  + checked http://safari.informit.com/9780132764100
  + checked http://www.qtrac.eu/gobook.html#toc
  + checked http://www.informit.com/store/product.aspx?isbn=0321774637
...
```

A Epilogue

The Go developers took a long hard look at some of the most widely used programming languages and tried to discern which features were really useful and productive to have, and which were redundant or even counterproductive. They also drew on the many decades of programming experience that they collectively have had. As a result they produced the Go programming language.

In the tradition of Objective-C and C++, Go is an object-oriented "better C". Like Java, Go has its own syntax, so it doesn't have to maintain C compatibility in the way that Objective-C and C++ do. But unlike Java, Go compiles to native code and isn't limited to the speed of a virtual machine.

In addition to Go's novel approach to object orientation with its emphasis on abstract interfaces and concrete types with smart embedding and aggregation, Go also supports advanced features such as function literals and closures. And Go's built-in map and slice types between them serve almost every data structure need. Go's Unicode-based string type uses the world's de facto standard encoding (UTF-8), and the standard library provides excellent support at both the byte and character level.

Go's support for concurrency is outstanding. Its lightweight goroutines and its type-safe and high-level channels make it much easier to create concurrent programs compared with many other languages (e.g., C, C++, or Java). And Go's lightning-fast compilation times are a breath of fresh air, especially to anyone used to building large C++ programs and libraries.

Go is already being used by a variety of commercial and noncommercial organizations. And Go is used internally by Google, as well as being available alongside Java and Python, as a language for developing web applications with the Google App Engine (`code.google.com/appengine/docs/go/overview.html`).

The language is still evolving quite quickly, yet thanks to the go fix tool, it is easy to update code to work with the latest release. Furthermore, the Go developers intend to keep all Go 1.x versions backward compatible with Go 1 to ensure that Go users have a language that is both stable and being improved at the same time.

Go's standard library is very wide ranging, but even in those cases where it doesn't have the functionality we need, we can always see if what we want is available from the Go Dashboard (`godashboard.appspot.com/project`), or in some

435

cases we can use external libraries written in other languages. The best place to go for the latest information on Go is golang.org; this web site has the current release's documentation, the (very readable) language specification, the Go Dashboard, blogs, videos, and numerous other supporting documents.

Most people learning Go will have knowledge of some other programming language (e.g., C++, Java, Python), and will come to Go with experience of inheritance-based object orientation. Go deliberately doesn't support inheritance, so while it is relatively easy to convert code between, say, C++ and Java, when it comes to Go it is best to go back to the fundamentals of what the code is designed to do—rather than how it does it—and rewrite from scratch in Go. Perhaps the most important distinction is that inheritance-based languages allow code and data to be mixed, whereas Go forces them to be kept separate. This separation gives great flexibility, and also makes it much easier to create concurrent programs, but it can take time and practice for programmers used to inheritance-based languages to adapt to the Go approach. Russ Cox, one of Go's core developers, says:

> *"It's unfortunate that every time someone asks for inheritance the answer is 'well, there's embedding'. Embedding is useful and a kind of inheritance, but when people come looking for inheritance, embedding is not the answer. The answer is: you're thinking in C++, or in Python or Java or Eiffel or whatever. Don't do that. Think in Go."*

Go is a fascinating language to learn and use, as well as being a pleasure to program with. Go programmers may well find it worth their while to join the Go mailing list—this has many excellent posters and is an ideal place for discussion and for questions (groups.google.com/group/golang-nuts). And since Go is developed in the open, it is possible to become a Go developer to help maintain, improve, and extend the language itself (golang.org/doc/contribute.html).

B The Dangers of Software Patents

Patents are a curious anomaly in capitalist economies, since they are the grant of a private monopoly by the State. Adam Smith roundly condemns monopolies in *The Wealth of Nations*.

In modern times patents enjoy widespread support from a broad range of businesses—from small vacuum cleaner manufacturers to giant pharmaceutical companies. But when it comes to *software* patents, it is difficult to find anyone who positively supports them except for patent trolls (companies that buy and lease out patent rights but which create nothing themselves), and their lawyers. Back in 1991 Bill Gates said, "If people had understood how patents would be granted when most of today's ideas were invented, and had taken out patents, the industry would be at a complete standstill today." Of course, his view appears to be somewhat more nuanced today.

Software patents affect every business that produces software—whether for sale or for in-house use. Even nonsoftware giants such as Kraft Foods and Ford Motor Co. are having to spend large sums of money defending against software patent lawsuits. But every programmer is exposed to risk. For example, linked lists have been patented—but not by their inventors Allen Newell, Cliff Shaw, and Herbert Simon when they came up with the idea back in 1955–6, but by someone else, 50 years later (www.google.com/patents/about?id=26aJAAAAEBAJ&dq=linked+list). The same thing has happened with skip lists, invented by William Pugh in 1990 and patented over a decade later by someone else. Sadly, there are tens of thousands of other software patents that could be cited as examples, although we will mention just one more, "A system and method causes a computer to detect and perform actions on structures identified in computer data" granted to Apple in 1999 and which covers all software that manipulates data structures (www.google.com/patents?id=aFEWAAAAEBAJ&dq=5,946,647).

It is easy to imagine that overly broad, obvious, or otherwise meritless patents would be easy to invalidate, but in practice, even giants like Google have found themselves paying out millions of dollars in legal fees to defend themselves. How then can startups and small and medium-sized enterprises (SMEs) hope to bring innovative software to market without being shaken down—again and again—by patent troll "businesses" which feed like parasites on the work of others?

Here is how the system works in the U.S.—and anywhere else that has similar patent systems. First of all, keep in mind that patents are enforceable even if the "violator" doesn't know about the patent. Also, fines for patent violation can be huge. Now imagine that a software developer working on some closed-source software completely independently develops a smart algorithm for performing some operation. A patent troll hears on the grapevine that the developer's company has a new innovation that might make some money. So the troll takes out an injunction against the developer claiming a violation of one of their really general patents (such as the Apple one mentioned above). Now the source code must be submitted for independent analysis. Naturally, the analysis will cover not just the cited patent, but all of the patents held by the troll. The troll now gets to see the developer's smart algorithm and might even try to patent it—after all they have deep pockets for legal fees and SMEs usually don't. Of course, trolls don't want to go to court since their "business model" is based on extortion: They want the developer to sell their products and to pay license fees for the general patents that the troll says have been violated. Of course, most if not all of the patents are unenforceable, in that they have no merit—but fighting in the courts would bankrupt most SMEs, so they end up paying license fees. And once they are paying this gives added legitimacy to the troll who can then cite their list of licensees to their next victim.

Big companies can afford to acquire patents and defend themselves from patent trolls, and don't necessarily have much sympathy for SMEs which might be, or grow to be, potential rivals—so most of them don't seem to be concerned. Some companies, including open source company Red Hat, are filing software patents as a defense that can be used to do cross-licensing deals and minimize legal costs. How effective such action will be when giants like Apple, Google, and Microsoft have built up or acquired patent portfolios at a cost of *billions* of dollars, remains to be seen. Companies that have made such huge investments are unlikely to want to end the patent regime—however destructive it is—as this would incur massive write-offs that would be hard to justify to shareholders or to CEOs whose compensation depends on their company's share price.

SMEs and individual innovators usually don't have the financial muscle to defend themselves from patent troll shakedowns. A very few might try their luck by moving overseas, but most will end up paying serious money for defense (or going out of business in the process), or paying license fees on meritless patents. Software patents are already having a chilling effect on individual and SME software innovation in the U.S., making it harder and more expensive for these businesses—and thereby reducing their capacity to expand and create more jobs for programmers. Of course, many lawyers do benefit from software patents—to the tune of US$11.2 billion in 2008 alone*—while even prosoftware patent economists don't seem to be able to count a single cent in economic benefits deriving from software patents.

---

* See esp.wikidot.com/local--files/2008-state-of-softpatents/feb_08-summary_report.pdf.

Nor do software developers outside the U.S. have cause for joy either; some have already had to withdraw their software from the U.S. market to avoid the patent troll protection racket. This means that some innovative software is no longer available in the U.S., potentially giving a competitive advantage to non-U.S. businesses. Furthermore, the Anti-Counterfeiting Trade Agreement (ACTA) specifically covers patents of all kinds, and is being adopted by many countries throughout the world—including the European Union—but not, at the time of this writing, Brazil, China, or Russia. And in addition, the European so called "unitary patent" (www.unitary-patent.eu) is likely to bring U.S.-style patents to the entire EU.

Software is a form of intellectual property that is perfectly well protected by copyright. (For example, Bill Gates was, for a time, the world's richest person—purely on the basis of software copyright, and prior to the pernicious idea of patenting software.) Despite the success of applying copyright to software, the U.S. and many other countries have chosen—or been forced by international trade agreements—to incorporate software into their patent regimes. Let us imagine for a moment that all the meritless patents (e.g., those that are overly broad, obvious, or for which there is prior art) were somehow to disappear. This would greatly reduce the shakedowns and would be a boon for innovation. But it still leaves open the key question: Should software be patentable at all?

In most countries—including the U.S.—it is not possible to patent mathematical formulas, no matter how new or original they are. Yet mathematical formulas are ideas (which is what patents are designed to "protect"). And we know from the Church-Turing thesis that the logic of any software can be reduced to a mathematical formula, so really, software is mathematics written in a very particular form. This is exactly the argument Donald Knuth makes against the patenting of software. (See Professor Knuth's short and fascinating letter on this topic: www.progfree.org/Patents/knuth-to-pto.txt.)

The problem is solvable—but will require legislation to outlaw software patents (or to designate software as mathematics, which is what it is), and to reign in patent offices (whose income is often proportional to the number of patents they grant, irrespective of merit). This is difficult because gaining the attention of politicians is expensive, and, of course, those who can afford to acquire patents can certainly afford to lobby. Also, the subject is so dry and industry-specific that it will hardly make any politician's career. But there are people lobbying for change, and doing so in a bipartisan manner. Probably the best starting point to learn more about why software patents are so disastrous and how to combat them is endsoftpatents.org (and in Europe, www.nosoftwarepatents.com).

& www.eff.org/patent

C Selected Bibliography

Advanced Programming in the UNIX® Environment, Second Edition

W. Richard Stevens and Stephen A. Rago (Addison-Wesley, 2005, ISBN-13: 978-0-201-43307-4)

A thorough in-depth introduction to Unix programming using the Unix system call APIs and the standard C library. (The book's examples are in C.)

The Art of Multiprocessor Programming

Maurice Herlihy and Nir Shavit (Morgan Kaufmann, 2008, ISBN-13: 978-0-12-370591-4)

This book provides a thorough introduction to mostly low-level multithreaded programming, including small but complete working examples (in Java) that demonstrate all the key techniques.

Clean Code: A Handbook of Agile Software Craftsmanship

Robert C. Martin (Prentice Hall, 2009, ISBN-13: 978-0-13-235088-4)

This book addresses many of the "tactical" issues in programming: good naming, function design, refactoring, and similar. The book has many interesting and useful ideas that should help any programmer improve their coding style and make their programs more maintainable. (The book's examples are in Java.)

Code Complete: A Practical Handbook of Software Construction, Second Edition

Steve McConnell (Microsoft Press, 2004, ISBN-13: 978-0-7356-1967-8)

This book shows how to build solid software, going beyond the language specifics into the realms of ideas, principles, and practices. The book is packed with ideas that will make any programmer think more deeply about their programming.

Design Patterns: Elements of Reusable Object-Oriented Software

Erich Gamma, Richard Helm, Ralph Johnson, and John Vlissides (Addison-Wesley, 1995, ISBN-13: 978-0-201-63361-0)

One of the most influential programming books of modern times, even if it isn't always easy to read. The design patterns are fascinating and of great practical use in everyday programming.

Domain-Driven Design: Tackling Complexity in the Heart of Software

Eric Evans (Addison-Wesley, 2004, ISBN-13: 978-0-321-12521-7)

A very interesting book on software design, particularly useful for large multiperson projects. At heart it is about creating and refining domain models that represent what the system is designed to do, and about creating a ubiquitous language through which all those involved with the system—not just software engineers—can communicate their ideas.

Don't Make Me Think!: A Common Sense Approach to Web Usability, Second Edition

Steve Krug (New Riders, 2006, ISBN-13: 978-0-321-34475-5)

A short, interesting, and very practical book on web usability backed up by considerable research and experience. Applying the easy-to-understand ideas in this book will improve any web site of any size.

Linux Programming by Example: The Fundamentals

Arnold Robbins (Prentice Hall, 2004, ISBN-13: 978-0-13-142964-2)

A useful and accessible introduction to Linux programming using the Linux system call APIs. (The book's examples are in C.)

Mastering Regular Expressions, Third Edition

Jeffrey E.F. Friedl (O'Reilly, 2006, ISBN-13: 978-0-596-52812-6)

This is the standard text on regular expressions—a very interesting and useful book.

Index

Mark Summerfield

Mark is a computer science graduate with many years of experience working in the software industry, primarily as a programmer. He has also spent many years writing and editing technical documentation. Mark owns Qtrac Ltd. (www.qtrac.eu), where he works as an independent programmer, author, editor, and trainer, specializing in the C++, Go, and Python languages, and the Qt, PyQt, and PySide libraries.

Other books by Mark Summerfield:

- *Advanced Qt Programming* (2011, ISBN-13: 978-0-321-63590-7)
- *Programming in Python 3* (First Edition, 2009, ISBN-13: 978-0-13-712929-4; Second Edition, 2010, ISBN-13: 978-0-321-68056-3)
- *Rapid GUI Programming with Python and Qt* (2008, ISBN-13: 978-0-13-235418-9)

Other books by Jasmin Blanchette and Mark Summerfield:

- *C++ GUI Programming with Qt 4* (First Edition, 2006, ISBN-13: 978-0-13-187249-3; Second Edition, 2008, ISBN-13: 978-0-13-235416-5)
- *C++ GUI Programming with Qt 3* (2004, ISBN-13:!978-0-13-124072-8)

Production

The text was written using *gvim*. The typesetting—including all the diagrams—was done using the *lout* typesetting language. All of the code snippets were automatically extracted directly from the example programs and from test programs using a custom tool written in Go. The index was compiled by the author. The text and source code was version-controlled using *Mercurial*. The monospaced code font was derived from a condensed version of DejaVu Mono and modified using *FontForge*. The book was previewed using *evince* and *gv*, and converted to PDF by *Ghostscript*. The cover was provided by the publisher. Note that only *printed* editions are definitive: *eBook* versions are not under the author's control and are often retypeset, which can introduce errors.

All the editing and processing was done on Debian and Ubuntu systems. All the example programs have been tested using the official *gc* Go compiler on Linux, Mac OS X, and Windows using Go 1 and should work with all subsequent Go 1.*x* versions.